Social Media and Online Consumer Decision Making in the Fashion Industry

Theodore Tarnanidis
International Hellenic University, Greece

Eyridiki Papachristou
International Hellenic University, Greece

Michail Karypidis
International Hellenic University, Greece

Vasileios Ismyrlis
Hellenic Open University, Greece & Hellenic Statistical Authority, Greece

A volume in the Advances in Marketing, Customer Relationship Management, and E-Services (AMCRMES) Book Series

IGI Global
PUBLISHER of TIMELY KNOWLEDGE

Published in the United States of America by
IGI Global
Business Science Reference (an imprint of IGI Global)
701 E. Chocolate Avenue
Hershey PA, USA 17033
Tel: 717-533-8845
Fax: 717-533-8661
E-mail: cust@igi-global.com
Web site: http://www.igi-global.com

Library of Congress Cataloging-in-Publication Data

Names: Tarnanidis, Theodore, 1977- editor. | Papachristou, Eyridiki, 1975- editor. | Karypidis, Michail, 1975- editor. | Ismyrlis, Vasileios, 1971- editor.
Title: Social media and online consumer decision making in the fashion industry / edited by Theodore Tarnanidis, Eyridiki Papachristou, Michail Karypidis, and Vasileios Ismyrlis.
Description: Hershey, PA : Business Science Reference, [2023] | Includes bibliographical references and index. | Summary: "The main objective of the proposed book is to force relevant businesses in the current sector to take advantage of the use of social media communication technologies for improving their marketing strategies. Web-based social media tools are pertinent for businesses to energize their core competencies and capabilities. Thus, this book will aim to discuss how the fashion businesses can benefit from the social media innovation approaches in digital environment"-- Provided by publisher.
Identifiers: LCCN 2023017923 (print) | LCCN 2023017924 (ebook) | ISBN 9781668487532 (hardcover) | ISBN 9781668487549 (paperback) | ISBN 9781668487556 (ebook)
Subjects: LCSH: Fashion merchandising, | Clothing trade--Marketing. | Social media.
Classification: LCC HD9940.A2 S623 2023 (print) | LCC HD9940.A2 (ebook) | DDC 746.9/20688--dc23/eng/20230710
LC record available at https://lccn.loc.gov/2023017923
LC ebook record available at https://lccn.loc.gov/2023017924

This book is published in the IGI Global book series Advances in Marketing, Customer Relationship Management, and E-Services (AMCRMES) (ISSN: 2327-5502; eISSN: 2327-5529)

British Cataloguing in Publication Data
A Cataloguing in Publication record for this book is available from the British Library.

Advances in Marketing, Customer Relationship Management, and E-Services (AMCRMES) Book Series

Eldon Y. Li
National Chengchi University, Taiwan & California Polytechnic State University, USA

ISSN:2327-5502
EISSN:2327-5529

Mission

Business processes, services, and communications are important factors in the management of good customer relationship, which is the foundation of any well organized business. Technology continues to play a vital role in the organization and automation of business processes for marketing, sales, and customer service. These features aid in the attraction of new clients and maintaining existing relationships.

The Advances in Marketing, Customer Relationship Management, and E-Services (AMCRMES) Book Series addresses success factors for customer relationship management, marketing, and electronic services and its performance outcomes. This collection of reference source covers aspects of consumer behavior and marketing business strategies aiming towards researchers, scholars, and practitioners in the fields of marketing management.

Coverage

- Social Networking and Marketing
- Web Mining and Marketing
- Relationship Marketing
- Customer Retention
- Electronic Services
- Cases on CRM Implementation
- E-Service Innovation
- Customer Relationship Management
- CRM and customer trust
- Text Mining and Marketing

IGI Global is currently accepting manuscripts for publication within this series. To submit a proposal for a volume in this series, please contact our Acquisition Editors at Acquisitions@igi-global.com or visit: http://www.igi-global.com/publish/.

The Advances in Marketing, Customer Relationship Management, and E-Services (AMCRMES) Book Series (ISSN 2327-5502) is published by IGI Global, 701 E. Chocolate Avenue, Hershey, PA 17033-1240, USA, www.igi-global.com. This series is composed of titles available for purchase individually; each title is edited to be contextually exclusive from any other title within the series. For pricing and ordering information please visit http://www.igi-global.com/book-series/advances-marketing-customer-relationship-management/37150. Postmaster: Send all address changes to above address.

Titles in this Series

For a list of additional titles in this series, please visit: www.igi-global.com/book-series

Global Developments in Nation Branding and Promotion Theoretical and Practical Approaches
Andreas Masouras (Neapolis University, Cyprus) Sofia Daskou (Neapolis University, Cyprus) Victoria Pistikou (Democritus University of Thrace, Greece) Dimitrios Dimitriou (Democritus University of Thrace, Greece) and Tim Friesner (University of Wincheste, UK)
Information Science Reference • © 2023 • 324pp • H/C (ISBN: 9781668459027) • US $240.00

Achieving Economic Growth and Welfare Through Green Consumerism
Punitha Sinnappan (Sunway Business School, Sunway University, Malysia)
Business Science Reference • © 2023 • 302pp • H/C (ISBN: 9781668481400) • US $250.00

Confronting Security and Privacy Challenges in Digital Marketing
Paulo Botelho Pires (Centre for Organizational and Social Studies, Polytechnic of Porto, Portugal) José Duarte Santos (Accounting and Business School, Polytechnic of Porto, Portugal) Inês Veiga Pereira (Accounting and Business School, Polytechnic of Porto, Portugal) and Ana Isabel Torres (University of Aveiro, Portugal)
Business Science Reference • © 2023 • 393pp • H/C (ISBN: 9781668489581) • US $250.00

The Rise of Blockchain Applications in Customer Experience
Mohammed Majeed (Tamale Technical University, Ghana) Kwame Simpe Ofori (International University of Grand Bassam, Cote D'Ivoire) George Kofi Amoako (Ghana Communication Technology University, Ghana) Abdul-Raheed Alolo (Tamale Technical University (TaTu), Ghana) and Gideon Awini (University of Ghana Business School, Ghana)
Business Science Reference • © 2023 • 300pp • H/C (ISBN: 9781668476499) • US $250.00

Contemporary Approaches of Digital Marketing and the Role of Machine Intelligence
Afzal Sayed Munna (University of Sunderland in London, UK) Md Sadeque Imam Shaikh (University of Wales Trinity Saint David, UK) and Baha Uddin Kazi (Ryerson University, Canada)
Business Science Reference • © 2023 • 310pp • H/C (ISBN: 9781668477359) • US $250.00

The Role of Brands in an Era of Over-Information
Ricardo Fontes Correia (Polytechnic Institute of Bragança, Portugal) Dominyka Venciūtė (ISM - University of Management and Economics, Lithuania) and Bruno Miguel Sousa (Polytechnic Institute of Cávado and Ave, Portugal)
Business Science Reference • © 2023 • 330pp • H/C (ISBN: 9781668483510) • US $250.00

IGI Global
PUBLISHER of TIMELY KNOWLEDGE

701 East Chocolate Avenue, Hershey, PA 17033, USA
Tel: 717-533-8845 x100 • Fax: 717-533-8661
E-Mail: cust@igi-global.com • www.igi-global.com

Editorial Advisory Board

Table of Contents

Detailed Table of Contents

for secondhand fashion on the Depop platform. To identify best practices, comments associated with Instagram posts that mentioned Depop were analysed to assess attitudes towards second-hand fashion. Ten influencers who promoted Depop in their Instagram content were identified, and their visual and textual content were analysed. This chapter provides several recommendations on how secondhand clothing platforms can best use social media influencers to market to consumers' interests. It can also contribute to research within the wider field of marketing in the circular economy.

Social networks affect positively the consumers' brand loyalty. They represent a key tool to efficiently maintain existing consumers and/or to attract new ones. An increasingly more used strategy by several fashion brands is to engage influencers for mentions on social network platforms, also in view of brand strategies to reach certain types of consumers. In this chapter, the author proposes in a conceptual framework a novel approach to efficiently reveal the influencers' language adopted on social networks for sponsored with respect to not sponsored contents, and by also taking care of aspects related to the consumers' engagement. The core component of the approach is the structural topic model, which is a substantial improvement of the latent Dirichlet allocation method. The structural topic model can provide promising results which can be successfully employed by interested practitioners and brand managers to efficiently define marketing strategies, or to strengthen existing ones.

This study positions itself within the place-as-living-entity view and within the growing body of literature on the relational views of place. This study considers how consumption acts and activities provide a relational view of place. It also acknowledges that while all kinds of consumption may involve a relationship with place at some level or the other, a relational view is distinguishable in terms of ties or kinship with place that individuals perceive as of value and valuable in their lives. More essentially, a relational view involves a contribution or participation in the construction or shaping of the nature and meaning of place and its boundaries. As Coffin and Chatzidakis observe, place-making is not confined to the simple creation and manipulation of meanings; rather, it is and must be understood in terms of claiming an area in territorial acts (as those of consumption).

About 1,000 million users are active on Instagram monthly, and the number of daily users is 500 million. Fifty percent of Instagrammers follow at least one business account, and 130 million Instagrammers tap on a shopping post to learn about products offered in the app every month. Moreover, more than 200 million Instagrammers visit at least one business profile every day. The objective of the study is to

Social media influencers (SMIs) in the fashion industry become professional individuals who have a large following on social media platforms such as Instagram, Facebook, TikTok, and YouTube. Many SMIs in the fashion industry have become successful in their own right and have gained significant influence in the fashion world projecting their branded personas. Fashion industry SMIs can face several challenges including the need to constantly create new and rich content; develop engaged narratives; pressure to maintain a certain image, the rivalry from other influencers. However, there are also many opportunities for SMIs in the fashion industry. Some say it is fertile ground. They can also collaborate directly with brands and use their influence to promote products and services. Having said that, more research is needed to grant reliable data to empower SMIs with accurate knowledge. Based on a systematic bibliometric literature review at Scopus, this research aims to appraise challenges and opportunities in building a SMI landscape in fashion.

South Asia's large size and economic diversification make it a diverse market. This diversity becomes crucial for marketers to reach consumers and share social media information about their products. Social media positively impacts branding and helps in fostering positive customer relationships. The chapter focuses on the South Asian market with detail on the social media marketing applications followed by the fashion brands in this region. The chapter sees the details from a theoretical lens and tries to comprehend the benefits and applications of social media marketing for fashion brands in South Asia. The chapter proposes an approach to designing a social media strategy and provides guidelines on how fashion brands can effectively use social media marketing. The chapter concludes by considering some obstacles the industry could face in the South Asian region and suggesting ways to overcome them by strategically using social media marketing.

The use of social media to promote clothing and textile businesses has revealed several changes in consumer behavior during the post-COVID-19 era. In this study, the social media tools which provide useful information in regards to consumer preferences and their decision-making processes in the fashion industry are presented. Moreover, the marketing strategy used and the strong presence of social media influencers in the fashion industry both during and after the COVID-19 pandemic period are also examined. A mixed research methodology is applied through the conduction of interviews with 20 owners of small fashion businesses and a questionnaire survey of 200 consumers who use social media for their

Preface

Today, several fashion brands use these strategies to increase awareness about their brand and accordingly to manipulate consumers' decision-making patterns. Further, consumers use social media platforms in order to find relevant and reliable information for structuring their preferences and making evaluations. The changes in the digital age through the use of web 2.0 tools, provide to consumers a plethora of interactive and user control information that help them to acquire and share valuable contents of the most famous sites, like the Facebook, Twitter, Linkedin, Instagram, Pinterest YouTube, etc., which in turn drive and monitor their purchase decision preferences. Therefore, the bulk of information produced by the social media tools mirrors to marketing decision-makers the consumers' wants, beliefs, commitment habits and purchasing intentions as it provides useful insights in the development of marketing strategies. Specifically, this book focuses on the effort of clothing/fashion entrepreneurs to best evaluate the effects of social media on the consumer decision-making process with the use of different techniques and tools.

The book consists of 17 chapters representing all issues the use of social media in the current sector, while demonstrating the wide-ranging of different interests of our target audience. Chapter 1 ('A Systematic Review of the Features and Functionalities of Mobile Applications (Apps) in the Fashion Industry: Their Impact on Consumer-Brand Relationships and Purchase Intention – Implications for the Metaverse') provides an in-depth analysis of the features, functionalities, and impact of fashion mobile Apps on consumer behaviour in the fashion industry. By examining a wide range of scholarly articles and research studies, this review identifies key themes and explores future implications for the industry. The findings reveal that fashion mobile Apps have the potential to significantly influence consumer brand relationships and purchase intention. The review highlights the evolution of fashion mobile Apps, from basic browsing and shopping functionalities to more advanced features such as virtual try-on, personalized recommendations, and social integration. The study also underscores the impact of fashion mobile Apps on consumer brand relationships, as they foster increased engagement, loyalty, and emotional connection with brands. The study further discusses the implications of fashion mobile Apps for the emerging metaverse. As virtual and augmented reality technologies gain prominence, fashion mobile Apps can act as gateways to immersive experiences, allowing consumers to virtually try on clothing, explore virtual fashion shows, and interact with virtual brand environments. This integration with the metaverse holds significant potential for the future of the fashion industry. Therefore, this systematic review provides valuable insights into the features, functionalities, and impact of fashion mobile Apps on consumer behaviours.

Chapter 2 ('An Empirical Investigation on Influence of Social Networks on Purchase Decision Making: An Indian Perspective') examines the factors which influence the intention to use facebook among Generation Y consumers and its influence on purchase decision making. A quantitative research methodology was used and the data was collected from 404 respondents in Bangalore city. Partial Least Square Structural Equation Model using R software was used to analyse data collected. The findings showed that perceived usefulness, perceived enjoyment, perceived credibility and subjective norm have a significant influence on intention to use Face book while perceived ease of use does not have a significant influence on intention to use Face book. Perceived enjoyment has the highest influence on intention to use Face book followed by subjective norm, perceived credibility and perceived usefulness. The results of this study also indicated that intention to use facebook has a significant positive effect on consumers' The findings of this study contribute to an understanding of the importance of the selected factors in affecting the intention to use facebook.

Chapter 3 ('Analyzing Big Data Using Recent Machine Learning Techniques to Assist Consumers in Online Purchase Decision') examines applies machine learning (ML) algorithms classify sentiments and assist customers in their purchase decision. Many organizations are predicting the possible correlation between growth of the business and customer satisfaction. On different social media platforms customers gives 'ratings' to a specific product or service. ML helps in knowing the reasons and assists the businesses to improvise in the weaker sections. Natural language processing integrates data & applies "tokenization" to extract the tokens (words) from the datasets (feedbacks). A set of positive, negative and neutral words and sentences can be compared to find the relevance. Naïve Bayes classifier, KNN classifier etc. helps knowing the trend & processes the large volume of data in minimal time. This approach helps increasing the predictive power of the model and tests remaining data. Bayesian factor robustness helps analyzing different attribute specifications from the large volume.

Chapter 4 ('Consumer Decision-Making Processes in Clothing, Textile, and Fashion') reveals how social media shapes consumer decision-making processes when purchasing textile and ready-made clothing products and to what extent it affects these processes positively or negatively. Accordingly, in this section, first of all, information about the consumer purchasing process and how this process works in the clothing, fashion and textile sectors and to what extent it affects these processes positively or negatively.

Chapter 5 ('Effects of Instagram Influencers on the Adoption of Secondhand Fashion Consumption: Case Studies of Instagram Influencers in Depop') provides an overview of the best practices that social media influencers on Instagram could use to persuade their followers to shop for secondhand fashion on the Depop platform. To identify best practices, comments associated with Instagram posts that mentioned Depop were analysed to assess attitudes towards second-hand fashion. Ten influencers who promoted Depop in their Instagram content were identified, and their visual and textual content were analysed. This chapter has several recommendations on how secondhand clothing platforms can best use social media influencers to market to consumers' interests. It can also contribute to research within the wider field of marketing in the circular economy.

Chapter 6 ('Fashion Brands and Social Networks: Influencers' Narratives, Sponsorship, and Consumers' Engagement') proposes in a conceptual framework a novel approach to efficiently reveal the influencers' language adopted on social networks for sponsored with respect to not sponsored contents, and by also taking care of aspects related to the consumers' engagement. The core component of the approach is the Structural Topic Model, which is a substantial improvement of the Latent Dirichlet Allocation method. The Structural Topic Model can provide promising results which can be successfully employed by interested practitioners and brand managers to efficiently define marketing strategies, or to strengthen existing ones.

Chapter 7 ('How Consumption Provides a Relational Understanding of Place') considers how consumption acts and activities provide a relational view of place. It also acknowledges that while all kinds of consumption may involve a relationship with place at some level or the other, a relational view is distinguishable in terms of ties or kinship with place that individuals perceive as of value and valuable in their lives. More essentially, a relational view involves a contribution or participation in the construction or shaping of the nature and meaning of place and its boundaries. As Coffin and Chatzidakis observe place-making is not confined to the simple creation and manipulation of meanings, rather is and must be understood in terms of claiming an area in territorial acts (as those of consumption).

Chapter 8 ('Instagram's Marketing Strategy of the Main Fast Fashion Brands: Best Practices to Improve Customer Engagement') assesses the Instagram strategy of four of the main fast fashion brands: Zara, H&M, Mango and Forever 21. Results show videos achieve 3.88 times more engagement than pictures. The effect of the shopping bag tool, which has been recently introduced, is very promising: the pictures with the shopping bag tool achieved a 121.03% higher average. The authors also found spontaneity increases engagement, while Zara, H&M and Mango posts experienced an increase in the average likes in the pictures that had faces in them.

Chapter 9 ('Instagramma in Fashion: The Impact of Social Media on Purchase Decisions') provides an analysis of the social media usage of everyday, senior females in the fashion context. Data were collected via a series of 38 interviews with women aged 50 and older. Findings showed that the majority of the senior females interviewed were following influencers online and these activities were impacting their purchase behaviors. Furthermore, the senior females in the sample had developed their own sense of style from information they gathered online and projected themselves on their social media accounts as if they too were influencers. Theoretical and managerial implications of the study are also discussed.

Chapter 10 ('Intentions to Purchase Sustainable Fashion: Influencer and Worth-of-Mouth Determinants') investigates the determinants that influence the sustainable fashion purchase intention. More specifically the chapter examines the constructs influencer credibility, influencer expertise, influencer similarity, influencer's parasocial relationship, E-WOM homophily, E-WOM expertise, trust in the influencer, trust in social media, performance expectation, consumer knowledge, environmental beliefs, brand awareness and willingness to pay more and their effect on purchase intention. The research methodology consisted of consumer interviews that were conducted using an online platform, and structural equation modeling was used to test the research hypotheses. The results obtained indicate that consumer knowledge and willingness to pay more are the only constructs that positively affect the purchase intention of sustainable fashion.

Chapter 11 ('Role of Information and Communication Technologies in Sustainable Clothing and Textile Industry') presents the ability of ICTs to open up parts of the supply chain (other than basic manufacturing and processing) in clothing and textile industry as well. ICT technology is used at various stages of the design process. Presently, it is rapidly changing the textile industry. From employee attendance (clocking in) to shipment dispatching is dependent on information technology. Garment industry are fully depended on IT or ERP. This chapter presents latest trends of companies that have successfully used ICTs to move, for example, into higher-value activities such as design and logistics, or to access niche markets. The study aims to investigate the uses of information and communication technology in Clothing and textile industry and examine the recent trends of ICT usage in companies within Textile industry and identify the factors to be considered by companies in textile industry before investing in ICT.

Chapter 12 ('Role of Social Media Influencers in Fashion and Clothing') provides an overview of the influence of social media influencers in the fashion and clothing industry. With the increasing presence of social media in people's lives, individuals are easily influenced by what they see online, leading to the adoption of trends promoted by influencers. Influencers, who have established their personal brand and gained a substantial following, play a key role in shaping consumer preferences and driving sales. Social media platforms allow fashion brands to connect with their audience, democratizing fashion shows and enabling direct interaction. The rise of fast fashion and the influence of fashion influencers have contributed to the growth of the clothing industry. Businesses are now utilizing AI-powered analytics and dedicated platforms to enhance their influencer marketing strategies. In summary, social media influencers have a significant impact on consumer behavior, driving sales and shaping trends in the fashion and clothing industry.

Chapter 13 ('Role of Social Media to Enhance Brand Engagement and Brand Perception of the Textile, Apparel, and Fashion Industries') presents the growth of the apparel industry in India is taking place at a brisk pace and significant growth in private consumption is expected to create strong domestic demand for textiles and apparel. While textile and apparel exports from India are expected to increase rapidly, it is the manmade garments that remain the most significant contributor to the total revenue generated by this sector. The era of social media has moved fashion into the hands of the mass consumer base, which has access to large volumes of information through smartphones, mobile apps, and social networking sites. Apparel and fashion brands are using social networking sites to propagate what they term their DNA. Using social networking platforms tools like Instagram, Facebook and Twitter to drive influencer marketing, display and document outfits, help consumers compare brands, build brand-consumer loyalty and commitment and generate trust and credibility for the brand. These platforms enable TAF brands to monitor their social media presence through social media metrics.

Chapter 14 ('Social Media Influencers in Fashion: Challenges and Opportunities') provides an overview of the influence of social media influencers in the fashion and clothing industry. With the increasing presence of social media in people's lives, individuals are easily influenced by what they see online, leading to the adoption of trends promoted by influencers. Influencers, who have established their personal brand and gained a substantial following, play a key role in shaping consumer preferences and driving sales. Social media platforms allow fashion brands to connect with their audience, democratizing fashion shows and enabling direct interaction. The rise of fast fashion and the influence of fashion influencers have contributed to the growth of the clothing industry. Businesses are now utilizing AI-powered analytics and dedicated platforms to enhance their influencer marketing strategies. In summary, social media influencers have a significant impact on consumer behavior, driving sales and shaping trends in the fashion and clothing industry.

Chapter 15 ('Social Media Marketing Applications and Fashion Brands: A South-Asian Perspective') focuses on the South Asian market with detail on the social media marketing applications followed by the fashion brands in this region. The chapter sees the details from a theoretical lens and tries to comprehend the benefits and applications of social media marketing for fashion brands in South Asia. The chapter proposes an approach to designing a social media strategy and provides guidelines on how fashion brands can effectively use social media marketing. The chapter concludes by considering some obstacles the industry could face in the South Asian region and suggesting ways to overcome them by strategically using social media marketing.

Chapter 16 ('The Use of Social Media in the Fashion Industry During the Post-COVID-19 Period: Evidence From Central Greece') analyses the marketing strategy used and the strong presence of social media influencers in the fashion industry both during and after the Covid-19 pandemic period are also examined. A mixed research methodology is applied through the conduction of interviews with 20 owners of small fashion businesses and a questionnaire survey of 200 consumers who use social media for their purchases from the region of Thessaly in Central Greece. Furthermore, the results are analyzed and the research findings are discussed in detail. Finally, suggestions for further research are also included.

Chapter 17 ('How Social Media Affects Consumer Behavior in the Fashion Industry') examines the fashion industry and its presence on social media. To what extent does social media influence consumer purchasing behavior? Which social media is used the most? To what extent do so-called influencers influence purchasing decisions? How powerful and decisive is electronic word of mouth (eWOM) in influencing a consumer either positively or negatively.

The main objective of the proposed book is to force relevant businesses in the current sector to take advantage of the use of social media communication technologies for improving their marketing strategies. Web-based social media tools are pertinent for businesses to energize their core competencies and capabilities. Thus, this book discusses how the fashion businesses can benefit from the social media innovation approaches in digital environment in the clothing and fashion industry. In particular topics discussed in the publication include (but are not limited to) the following: Web based social media platforms models in clothing, textile and fashion, mobile apps in the clothing, textile and fashion, the future of social media communications in fashion and clothing,, innovative electronic & mobile models in clothing, textile and fashion. We believe, the book will bring together scholars of different research backgrounds. And also, we hope readers will find this book essential for upgrading their existing work and education. Finally, we like to express our special appreciation to all contributors of the accepted chapters.

Finally, the development of the book owes much to many people. We wish to thank the authors for submitting their chapters to our book. We are grateful that they responded to our invitation. Thanks are also given to the editorial board for supporting it so wholeheartedly, and particularly those who contributed with research work and reviewing of submitted papers. We hope the published book ('Social Media and Online Consumer Decision Making in the Fashion Industry') to be a major catalyst within representing ideas and research work in the specific field.

Theodore Tarnanidis
International Hellenic University, Greece

Eyridiki Papachristou
International Hellenic University, Greece

Michail Karypidis
International Hellenic University, Greece

Vasileios Ismyrlis
Hellenic Open University, Greece & Hellenic Statistical Authority, Greece

Chapter 1
A Systematic Review of the Features and Functionalities of Mobile Applications (Apps) in the Fashion Industry:
Their Impact on Consumer-Brand Relationships and Purchase Intention – Implications for the Metaverse

Abdullah Suhluli
University of Manchester, UK

Gianpaolo Vignali
University of Manchester, UK

Daniella Ryding
University of Manchester, UK

ABSTRACT

The rapid growth and widespread use of mobile technology has had a significant impact on many industries, including the clothing, textile, and fashion industries. In recent years, the use of mobile applications (apps) has become increasingly popular in these sectors, providing a convenient and accessible platform for consumers to engage with brands and make purchases. In the past decade, much research has focused on the evolution of the use of this technology; however, limited research exists on understanding how consumers interact with apps and the extent to which they impact on purchase intention. This chapter will review current mobile applications providing an overview of their features and functionalities. Furthermore, this chapter will provide a gap in the literature that outlines the current state of play in the fashion industry amongst the major fashion retailers.

DOI: 10.4018/978-1-6684-8753-2.ch001

INTRODUCTION

The fashion industry has witnessed a significant transformation in recent years with the rise of mobile applications that cater to the needs and preferences of fashion-conscious consumers. These apps offer a range of features that allow users to engage with fashion brands, explore new styles, make purchases, and connect with other fashion enthusiasts. With the emergence of the metaverse, a virtual space where users can interact and engage with digital content, the fashion industry is experiencing new opportunities and challenges in the realm of mobile apps (Wang et al., 2022). This systematic review aims to critically analyse the features and functionalities of mobile apps in the fashion industry and their impact on consumer brand relationships and purchase intention, with implications for the metaverse.

Evolution of Mobile Applications in the Fashion Industry

This part provides an overview of the rapid evolution of mobile apps in the fashion industry, highlighting their emergence as a popular platform for fashion-related activities and transactions. It discusses the types of fashion apps available in the market and their increasing significance. According to the researcher Kang, Mobile applications have become a significant part of the fashion industry, transforming the way consumers engage with fashion brands, discover new styles, and make purchases. The evolution of mobile apps has reshaped the landscape of the fashion industry, impacting consumer behaviour, brand interactions, and purchase decisions (Kang, 2019). In recent years, the authors Chetioui and others have studied that the proliferation of smartphones and the widespread use of mobile internet have created new opportunities for fashion brands to connect with consumers. Fashion apps have gained popularity due to their convenience, accessibility, and ability to offer personalized experiences to users. Fashion apps are now available in various forms, including those from fashion retailers, and fashion marketplaces (Chetioui et al., 2020). These apps offer a wide range of features and functionalities, making them an integral part of the fashion ecosystem (Gazzola et al., 2020).

One of the key drivers of the evolution of fashion apps is changing the consumers behaviour. Consumers are increasingly relying on mobile devices for fashion-related activities (Biørn-Hansen et al., 2020). Likewise, the authors Moisander and others discussed that mobile apps provide a convenient way for consumers to engage with fashion brands, allowing them to browse through product catalogues, receive personalized recommendations, and make purchases. This shift in consumer behaviour has led to the rapid adoption of fashion apps by both established fashion brands and emerging fashion startups (Moisander et al., 2020). Another factor contributing to the evolution of fashion apps is the advancement of mobile technologies. With the advent of augmented reality (AR) and virtual reality (VR) technologies, fashion apps now offer immersive and interactive experiences to users (Kim et al., 2023). Users can virtually try on clothes, experiment with different styles, and visualize how fashion items would look on them through their smartphones. This has revolutionized the way consumers interact with fashion brands, allowing for a more engaging and personalized experience (Kang, 2019).

Social media integration has also played a significant role in the evolution of fashion apps. Many fashion apps now allow users to share their fashion preferences, get fashion inspiration, and receive feedback (Zhao et al., 2019). This social component of fashion apps has not only enhanced user engagement but also fostered a sense of community among fashion enthusiasts, creating a social ecosystem within the apps.

Furthermore, gamification elements have also been incorporated into fashion apps, adding a fun and interactive element to the user experience (Vahdat et al., 2021). The evolution of fashion apps has also been influenced by the changing landscape of the retail industry and has been studied by Silva et al., With the rise of e-commerce, fashion brands are constantly looking for ways to enhance their online presence and offer seamless shopping experiences. Fashion apps have emerged as a powerful tool for fashion brands to drive online sales, as they provide a convenient shopping experience (Silva et al., 2020). Many fashion apps offer features such as virtual wardrobe management, personalized product recommendations, and easy checkout options, making the online shopping smoother and enjoyable.

Moreover, the COVID-19 pandemic has further accelerated the evolution of fashion apps. Consumers have turned to mobile apps for their fashion needs more than ever before in the lockdown period. Fashion apps have provided a safe and convenient way to shop and stay connected with the fashion world. Therefore, the evolution of mobile applications in the fashion industry has been remarkable, reshaping the way consumers engage with fashion brands and influencing their purchase decisions.

Features and Functionalities of Fashion Mobile Apps

This section critically examines the various features and functionalities offered by fashion mobile apps, including virtual wardrobe management, personalized recommendations, augmented reality (AR) and virtual reality (VR) experiences, social media integration, and gamification elements. According to the authors Hendijani Fard & Marvi, one of the key features of fashion mobile apps in the metaverse is the ability to virtually try on clothing and accessories. Through augmented reality (AR) or virtual reality (VR) technologies, users can visualize how virtual fashion items would look on them in real-time (Hendijani Fard & Marvi, 2019). Virtual product try-on allows users to virtually dress up their digital representations. This feature provides a novel and immersive way for users to explore and interact with virtual fashion items, enhancing the overall user experience and engagement. Fashion mobile apps in the metaverse also facilitate social interaction and community building among users (Soni et al., 2019).

As studied by the authors Soni et al., fashion mobile apps in the metaverse often offer customizable features, allowing users to create their unique virtual fashion items. Users can customize virtual fashion items and create their virtual fashion avatars. The user interface and navigation of fashion mobile apps in the metaverse are critical for ensuring a seamless and intuitive user experience (Tahirah Abdullah et al., 2020). These apps often feature user-friendly interfaces with clear navigation menus, intuitive icons, and easy-to-use controls. Understanding the features of fashion mobile apps in the metaverse is crucial for fashion brands and marketers to develop effective strategies to engage with consumers, enhance brand relationships, and drive purchase intention (Soni et al., 2019). By providing a comprehensive overview of these features, this systematic review aims to shed light on the key aspects of fashion mobile apps in the metaverse and their impact on consumers behaviour.

Impact of Fashion Mobile Apps on Consumer-Brand Relationships

This section reviews the existing literature on the impact of fashion mobile apps on consumer-brand relationships. The impact of fashion mobile apps on consumer brand relationships is a crucial aspect of understanding the effectiveness of these apps in the fashion industry. In today's digital age, mobile apps have become a powerful tool for fashion brands to connect with consumers and establish long-term relationships. The researchers Lissitsa and Kol, fashion mobile apps offer various features and functionalities that can influence consumer-brand interactions. These include personalized product recommendations, virtual try-on experiences, social media integration, gamification elements, and virtual wardrobe management, among others. These features provide opportunities to engage with the brand and interact with the app (Lissitsa & Kol, 2021). Fashion apps can collect data on consumer preferences and it can be used to offer personalized product recommendations (Rausch & Kopplin, 2021). Fashion mobile apps that encourage high levels of engagement and interaction can have a positive impact on consumer-brand relationships. Social media integration allows users to share their fashion choices, seek feedbacks, and engage in conversations around the brand (Shi et al., 2020). A well-designed app that offers personalized experiences, customization options, and engaging features can create a positive impression and emotional connection with the brand. This emotional connection can lead to increased brand loyalty, where consumers are more likely to repurchase, recommend the brand to others, and brand advocacy on social media platforms (Sumarliah et al., 2022). Henceforth, the impact of fashion mobile app is multifaceted. Fashion mobile apps that offer meaningful interactions can foster stronger brand relationships and leading to increased brand loyalty.

Influence of Fashion Mobile Apps on Purchase Intention

This section explores the relationship between fashion mobile apps and consumers' purchase intention. It discusses how the features and functionalities of these apps affect consumers' decision-making processes. It also examines the role of trust, convenience, and user experience in driving purchase intention through fashion mobile apps. The influence of fashion mobile apps on purchase intention is a critical factor in understanding the impact of these apps on consumer behaviour and their potential to drive sales in the fashion industry.

As mobile apps become increasingly popular among fashion brands and consumers, understanding how these apps influence consumers' purchase intention is crucial for brands seeking to leverage mobile technology to drive sales (Djafarova & Bowes, 2021). The authors Akram et al. studied that mobile apps offer convenience to consumers by providing a user-friendly shopping experience. With just a few taps on their smartphones, consumers can browse through a wide range of products, access personalized recommendations, view virtual try-on experiences, make purchases, and track their orders (Akram et al., 2020). The convenience offered by fashion mobile apps can significantly impact consumers' purchase intention, as it simplifies the shopping process. Consumers are more likely to make purchases from brands with mobile apps that offer convenient and frictionless shopping experiences, leading to increased purchase intention (Shi et al., 2020). Trust is a crucial factor in consumers' purchase intention, and fashion mobile apps can influence consumers' trust in multiple ways. As stated by the authors Lynch & Barnes, a well-designed app offers a secure and reliable platform and provides transparent information about products. Social influence plays a significant role in consumers' purchase intention, and fashion mobile apps can leverage social elements to impact consumer behaviour (Umair Manzoor et al., 2020). Fashion apps that integrate social media features can influence consumers' purchase intention through social influence. Consumers are more likely to make purchases from fashion brands that are popular among their social circles, as social approval and recommendations are strong motivators for purchase decisions (Lynch & Barnes, 2020). In summary, fashion mobile apps can significantly influence consumers' purchase intention through various factors such as convenience, trust, social influence, and perceived value. It is significant for fashion brands to understand the influence of their mobile apps on consumers' purchase intentions and design their apps to provide a trustworthy shopping experience.

Metaverse in Fashion Mobile Apps

This section discusses the potential implications of fashion mobile apps for the metaverse, a virtual space where users can interact with digital content. It explores how the features and functionalities of fashion apps can be integrated into the metaverse to create novel and engaging fashion experiences for consumers. It also highlights the challenges and opportunities of incorporating fashion apps into the metaverse from both theoretical and practical perspectives.

The emergence of the metaverse as a virtual space where users interact with digital representations of themselves and their surroundings has significant implications for various industries, including the fashion industry. Fashion mobile apps, with their features and functionalities, can play a crucial role in shaping and influencing the metaverse and the way consumers engage with fashion in this virtual space (Liang et al., 2020). In this section, we will explore the implications of fashion mobile apps for the metaverse. Fashion mobile apps can enable virtual fashion experiences within the metaverse, allowing users to try on virtual outfits, customize avatars, and create unique virtual fashion identities (Idrees et al., 2023). This can be a valuable feature for consumers who want to express their fashion sense in the metaverse (Joy et al., 2022). In a recent study, Jang and Kim have also mentioned that fashion mobile apps can also facilitate brand engagement in the metaverse by providing immersive and interactive brand experiences. Brands can create virtual showrooms, fashion events, and brand spaces within the metaverse (Dai & Zhao, 2022). These virtual brand spaces can allow users to explore the brand's history, philosophy, and collections, engage with brand ambassadors or influencers, and participate in virtual events. This can influence purchase behaviour in the metaverse by providing seamless purchasing options(Jang & Kim, 2023).

Users can browse and select virtual fashion items within the metaverse through their mobile apps and make purchases using digital payments. Fashion mobile apps can also enable virtual fashion items to be linked with physical fashion items, allowing users to seamlessly transition. Also, the mobile app can offer unique opportunities for innovation and personalization in the fashion industry (Joy et al., 2022). Fashion mobile apps can also enable personalized virtual fashion experiences, where users can create avatars that reflect their personal style and preferences and interact with virtual fashion items that are tailored to their tastes. This level of innovation and personalization can create novel and engaging experiences for users in the metaverse, leading to increased brand loyalty (Weiss, 2022).

Privacy and security of user data, intellectual property rights, virtual item ownership, and interoperability among different metaverse platforms are some of the key challenges that fashion brands and app developers need to navigate (P. Vamsi Krishna, 2023). Ensuring user trust and data protection should be a top priority for fashion app developers in the metaverse. Additionally, the rapidly evolving landscape of the metaverse, with different platforms, technologies, and user behaviours, may require continuous adaptation and updates to fashion mobile apps to remain relevant and effective in the virtual space (Jeon & Kim, 2022). Therefore, fashion mobile apps have the potential to greatly impact the metaverse and consumer behaviours. Virtual fashion experiences, brand engagement, purchase behaviour, innovation, and personalization are some of the key implications of fashion mobile apps for the metaverse. However, challenges and considerations related to user privacy, data protection, interoperability, authenticity, and intellectual property rights need to be carefully addressed. Fashion brands and app developers need to adapt and evolve their mobile apps to meet the changing needs and expectations of users in the metaverse, and leverage the opportunities offered by this virtual space to create immersive and engaging fashion experiences.

Problem Statement

The metaverse is a virtual space that offers unique opportunities for fashion brands and marketers to engage with consumers and create immersive fashion experiences. Mobile applications play a significant role in this space, providing users with various features. However, there is a lack of comprehensive understanding of these features and functionalities, their impact on consumer brand relationships, and purchase intention in the metaverse. Fashion brands and marketers need to understand the evolving landscape of mobile applications in the fashion industry to effectively leverage the potential of the metaverse for consumer engagement and purchase intention. Without a clear understanding of the impact of these Apps on consumer behaviour in the metaverse, fashion brands may struggle to design and implement effective strategies to engage with consumers. Therefore, the problem statement of this systematic review is to address the knowledge gap regarding the features and functionalities of mobile applications in the fashion industry and their impact on consumer brand relationships and purchase intention in the metaverse.

Aim and Objective

The aim of this systematic review is to comprehensively examine the features and functionalities of mobile applications in the fashion industry within the metaverse and their impact on consumer brand relationships and purchase intention.

The objectives of this chapter are,

- To critically evaluate the existing research on the influence of fashion mobile apps on consumer brand relationships, including brand engagement, loyalty, and trust.
- To assess the impact of fashion mobile apps on consumer purchase intention, including factors such as virtual product try-on, virtual fashion experiences, and virtual fashion shows.
- To identify the benefits of fashion mobile apps in metaverse for virtual fashion experience.
- To provide insights and recommendations for future research and practice in the field of fashion mobile apps in the metaverse based on the findings of the systematic review.

RESEARCH METHODOLOGY

The current study design will be a systematic review, and the Preferred Reporting Items for Systematic Reviews and Meta-Analyses (PRISMA) guidelines will be used for conducting this review (Liberati et al., 2009).

Keywords

A comprehensive search was conducted across multiple databases to identify relevant studies on the topic. The search strategy involved the use of appropriate keywords to conduct a manual search in tandem with cross-referencing strategy in place. Cross-referencing here would mean scouring the bibliography section of identified articles to find additional pertinent articles from those papers. The keywords that will be used for this study are listed below.

Table 1. Sample keywords

Mobile Applications	Metaverse	Fashion Retail	Virtual Try-On	Shopping Behaviour
Fashion industry	Virtual reality	Consumer engagement	Digital marketing	User experience
Consumer behaviour	Augmented reality	Social media	Customization	Fashion trends
Brand relationships	Digital technology	E-commerce	Consumer trust	User interface
Purchase intention	User interface	Mobile user experience	Fashion marketing	Fashion technology
Fashion apps	Fashion consumption	Mobile shopping	Digital innovation	Fashion user interface
Fashion user experience design	Database search	Systematic review	Meta-analysis	Online shopping
Consumer psychology	Retail technology	Virtual fashion experiences	Digital experiences	Mobile app functionalities
Virtual shopping	Fashion consumption behaviours	Digital transformation	Virtual fitting	Fashion e-commerce
Consumer decision-making	Mobile app features	Fashion consumer behaviour	Mobile commerce	Fashion branding

Boolean operators (e.g., AND, OR) and truncation were utilized to refine the search and retrieve the most relevant articles. The search was executed over leading databases and limited to studies published in English and the publication date between the periods of 2014 to 2023 to ensure recent and relevant literature was included. A total of nine studies were initially identified from the search process. After removing duplicates, the remaining studies were screened based on their titles and abstracts to determine their relevance to the research question. The article screening process and eligibility assessment process were carried out by the author. The articles were initially screened based on their title, followed by the abstract of the article. Studies that were not directly related to mobile applications in the fashion industry, consumer brand relationships, purchase intention, or the metaverse were excluded from the secondary screening.

Inclusion and Exclusion Criteria

The Inclusion Criteria to be included in this systematic review are studies published between the periods of 2014-2023 that should be considered. Further, the studies published in leading peer-reviewed journals, and which are in English languages are to be reviewed. The Exclusion Criteria to be considered to exclude a study from this review are the studies published prior to the period 2014, studies that are not directly related to the topic of mobile applications in the fashion industry or their impact on consumer brand relationships and purchase intention in the metaverse may be excluded. Studies published in mediocre journals or those that were found in grey literature or unpublished studies and that are not in the English Language are to be excluded from the systematic review.

Data Extraction

The data extraction process in this systematic review involved carefully reviewing the selected studies in full-text format and extracting relevant information. This included extracting data such as study title, author(s), publication year, research design, sample size, data collection methods, and key findings related to the features and functionalities of fashion mobile apps, their impact on consumer brand relationships, and purchase intention in the metaverse. The data extraction process was carried out meticulously to ensure accurate and reliable data was collected from each study. The extracted data were then organized and synthesized to identify common themes, patterns, and trends related to the research question.

This process allowed for a comprehensive overview of the findings from the selected studies and helped to identify key insights related to the impact of fashion mobile apps on consumer brand relationships and purchase intention in the metaverse.

Figure 1. PRISMA chart

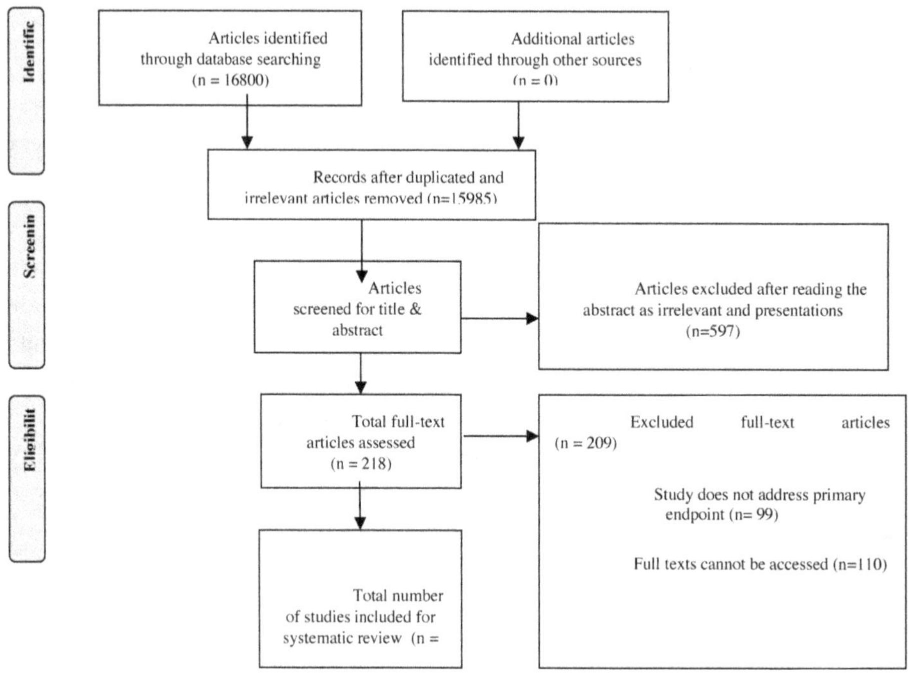

Quality Appraisal

The quality appraisal process involves assessing the rigor, validity, and reliability of the research methods used in the included studies.

Study design: Assess the appropriateness of the study design for the research question. Randomized controlled trials (RCTs) or well-conducted observational studies are generally considered to be of higher quality compared to cross-sectional or retrospective studies.

Sample size and representativeness: Evaluate the sample size and whether the sample is representative of the target population. Studies with larger sample sizes and diverse samples that are representative of the population of interest are generally considered to be of higher quality. Data collection methods: Assess the validity and reliability of the data collection methods used in the studies. Studies that use validated and reliable measures, appropriate data collection instruments, and systematic data collection procedures are generally considered to be of higher quality. Data analysis and statistical methods: Evaluate the appropriateness and rigor of the data analysis and statistical methods used in the studies. Studies that use appropriate statistical tests, control for confounding variables, and report effect sizes or confidence intervals are generally considered to be of higher quality. Reporting and publication bias: Assess the completeness and transparency of reporting in the studies. Studies that provide detailed information on the study design, methodology, results, and limitations, and minimize potential publication bias through comprehensive search and inclusion/exclusion criteria, are generally considered to be of higher quality. Research ethics: Evaluate whether the studies adhere to ethical standards, such as obtaining informed consent, protecting participant confidentiality, and complying with relevant research ethics guidelines. It's important to use a standardized quality appraisal tool or checklist, if available, to ensure consistency and reliability in the appraisal process. The quality appraisal should be conducted independently.

Ethical Statement

All analyses will be carried out based on previously published studies, and therefore, no ethical approval and individual consent will be required. Additionally, to prevent ethical issues with regards to plagiarism and copyrights, the findings from the selected articles will be duly paraphrased along with acknowledging the work of the authors via the addition of references. Further the inclusion and exclusion criteria were applied rigorously, and nine were selected for full-text review.

RESULT AND DISCUSSION

The results of the systematic review shed light on the key findings related to the features and functionalities of fashion mobile apps, their impact on consumer-brand relationships and purchase intention, and their implications for the metaverse. These findings also have important implications for the future of consumer behaviours and the evolving digital landscape. The extracted data were synthesized to identify common themes, patterns, and trends related to the features and functionalities of fashion mobile apps, their impact on consumer brand relationships, and purchase intention in the metaverse. The findings were meticulously analysed and organized in a descriptive manner to provide a comprehensive overview of the current state of knowledge in the field. Table 1 shows the overview of the reviewed papers.

Table 3 and 4 depicts the distribution of publications for each year and the number of papers published in key journals, respectively. From Table 3, in the years 2018,2021 and 2023, two papers were selected, whereas in the years 2014, 2015 and 2020, one paper was selected. In Table 4, in each journal, one paper was published in the selected reviewed papers. Figure 2 shows the distribution of papers in each country in the selected papers, and it can be observed that USA leads high with three papers and whereas for the other countries (Korea, US, UK, Hong Kong, both USA and UK combined and Hungary) one paper was selected. Figure 3 depicts the distribution of research methodologies, in which online survey methodology is high with five papers.

Features and Functionalities of Fashion Mobile Apps

The results of the systematic review revealed that fashion mobile apps offer a diverse array of features and functionalities that enhance the consumer experience. These include virtual try-on capabilities, personalized recommendations, social sharing options, mobile shopping features, fashion trend analysis, and

Table 2. Overview of the selected papers

Author, Year	Journal	Country and Location	Objective	Methodology	Dependent and Independent Variables	Sample Size and Gender	Study Intervention
(Pop et al., 2023)	Technological Forecasting and Social Change	Hungary	Explore the direct and indirect impact of utilitarian, hedonic, & social attributes on consumer attitude & purchase intention	Online Survey	utilitarian, hedonic, & social attributes (IV) consumer attitude & purchase intention (DV), attitude (MEDV), Channel switching behaviour (MODV)		
Scholz & Duffy et al., 2018(Scholz & Duffy, 2018)	Journal of retailing & Consumer Services	USA & UK	1. What are consumers' activities and experiences with an AR shopping app that they use within their domestic space? 2. what consumer-brand relationships can be facilitated through augmented reality	Ethnographic study (Qualitative study)	NA	n=9	At Home
(Lau & Ki, 2021)	Journal of Fashion and Textiles	Hong Kong	1.Do the gamification-, customization-, and engagement-elements of VR fashion apps satisfy consumers' intrinsic needs for competence, autonomy, and relatedness, respectively? 2. If so, does this fulfil intrinsic needs (i.e., competence, autonomy and relatedness) and shape consumers' positive behavioural intention (i.e., the intentions to continuously use the VR app and make in-app purchases)?	Online Survey Questionnaire	Challenge, achievement, avatar customization, avatar identification, social presence, social support (IV), competence need fulfilment, autonomy need fulfilment, related need fulfilment, intention to continuously, intention to make in-app purchases (DV)	n=251 & Male=105, Female=146.	Chinese consumers
(Baek et al., 2018)	International Journal of Advertising	USA	This study examines how augmented reality technology affects consumers' brand perceptions and purchase intentions.	Survey Questionnaire	Study 1: Study 2: AR viewing (IV), Self-brand connections (Med. variable), Purchase intention (DV)	Study 1: n=174, undergraduates from a North eastern University in the United States. Study 2:n=209, undergraduates from a North eastern University.	
(Park & Kim, 2023)	Clothing and Textiles Research Journal	USA	Study 1: We tested whether virtual try-on leads to greater cognitive elaboration (H1a) and greater purchase intentions (H1b) than 3D virtual stores and static pictures. A one-factor (technologies: virtual try-on, a 3D virtual store, and static pictures) between-subjects design was used. Study 2: First, we tested H1 in a more controlled lab environment to minimize potential confounding factors related to an online experiment and increase internal validity	Study 1: Survey questionnaire, Study 2: Survey questionnaire	Study 1: Cognitive elaboration (IV), Purchase intention (DV) Study 2: Website technologies (IV), Shopping goals (Mod. variable), Cognitive elaboration (Med. variable), Purchase intention (DV)	Study 1: n=404, U.S Consumer. Study 2: n=196, female students	

continued on following page

Table 2. Continued

Author, Year	Journal	Country and Location	Objective	Methodology	Dependent and Independent Variables	Sample Size and Gender	Study Intervention
(Baytar et al., 2020)	Journal of Fashion Marketing and Management	USA	The present study examined whether AR conveys reliable apparel product information in terms of fit, size, and product performance; and how AR affects attitudes toward apparel and purchase intentions when shopping online	Survey Questionnaire (SOR Model)	Product information in terms of fit, size, and product performance, attitudes toward apparel (IV), purchase intention (DV)	n=87, Female college students aged 18 and above	
(Watson et al., 2018)	International Journal of Retail & Distribution Management	UK	To examine the effects of augmented reality (AR) (specifically augmentation) on consumers' affective and behavioural responses and to assess whether consumers' hedonic motivation for shopping moderates this relationship.	Online experiment	Augmentation, Modality, Interactivity (IV), Consumer traits, Demographics, Situational context (Mod. Variables), Purchase intention (DV), Positive effective response (Med. Variables)	n=162, female aged (18-35)	
(Yaoyuneyong et al., 2014)	Journal of Global Fashion Marketing	US	To propose that use of VDR will reduce consumers' perceived risks regarding buying apparel online and have a positive effect on consumer self-confidence, customer – brand relationships and consumers' online e-shopping behaviour	NA	Factors governing the adoption of VDR Technology: Economic motivation to shop online, Entertainment value, Informativeness, web irritation, Consumer Innovativeness (IV), Use of VDR (DV), consumer behaviour, Consumer self-confidence, Customer-Brand Relationship, Perceived Risk of purchasing Apparel Online, Online shopping (DV)	NA	
(Rhee & Lee, 2021)	Sustainability	Korea	This study examined the relationship between virtual fitting (VF) experience satisfaction, brand advocacy, mobile purchase intention, and offline purchase intention from an omnichannel perspective to understand how VF based on augmented reality (AR) impacts the customer purchase journey. The study also investigated the moderating effect of a customer's product involvement, which is a personal characteristic.	Mobile survey through Questionnaire	VF experience satisfaction (IV), Brand advocacy (Med.Variable), Mobile purchase intention, and Offline purchase intention (DV).	n=100, South Korean male and female customers in their 20s and 30s who had purchased sneakers in the past year.	

virtual styling tools. These findings have important implications for the future of fashion retail as mobile apps continue to evolve and offer increasingly immersive and interactive experiences for consumers.

In the paper (Scholz & Duffy, 2018), the author discussed the consumers' activities and experiences with an AR shopping app that they use within their domestic space. This study was conducted in USA & UK as a qualitative study. Further, another study (Lau & Ki, 2021) has discussed the gamification, customization, and engagement-elements of VR fashion apps which satisfy the consumers' intrinsic

Table 3. Distribution of publications per year

Year	Number of Papers
2014	1
2015	1
2018	2
2020	1
2021	2
2023	2

Table 4. Number of papers published in key journals

Journal Name	No of Papers
Technological Forecasting and Social Change	1
Journal of Retailing and Consumer Services	1
Journal of Fashion and Textiles	1
International Journal of Advertising	1
Clothing and Textiles Research Journal	1
Journal of Fashion Marketing and Management	1
International Journal of Retail & Distribution Management	1
Journal of Global Fashion Marketing	1
Sustainability	1

Figure 2. Distribution of papers per countries

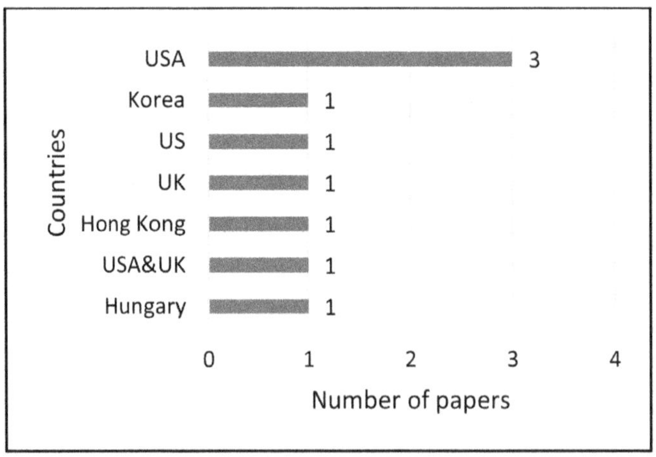

needs for competence, autonomy, and relatedness, which was conducted in Hong Kong. Also, the authors of the study identified the intentions of consumers for continuously using the VR app and making in-app purchases. Henceforth, the proposed study can identify the advancement of technologies such

Figure 3. Distribution of research methodologies

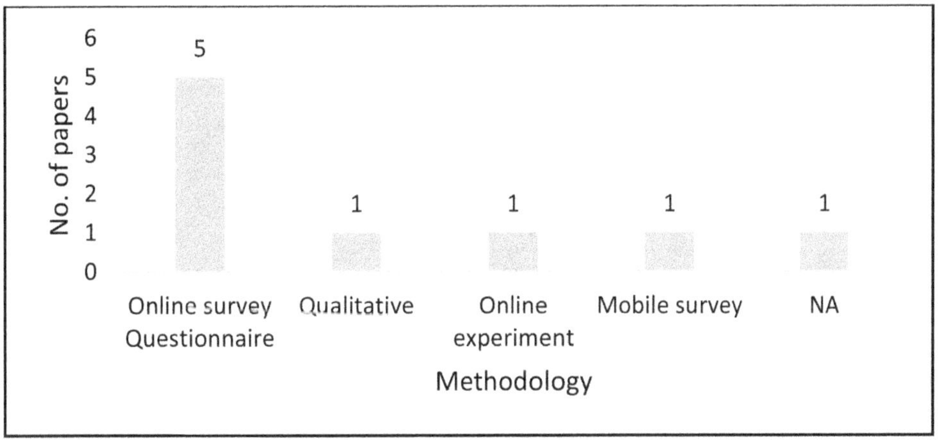

as augmented reality (AR) and virtual reality (VR), fashion mobile apps have the potential to transform the way consumers shop for fashion items, try on virtual clothes, and engage with fashion brands in a virtual environment. The future impact of these features and functionalities can revolutionize the way fashion brands interact with consumers and influence their purchase decisions. Table 2 helps to understand better about the mobile application in fashion industry for the studies reviewed and the table helps in understanding the performance of the mobile application in fashion industry and Table 3 outlines the mobile application used in Fashion Industry.

Impact of Fashion Mobile Apps on Consumer-Brand Relationships

The results indicated that fashion mobile apps have a significant impact on consumer-brand relationships. These apps facilitate brand engagement, loyalty, and emotional connection by providing consumers with opportunities to interact with brands, access exclusive content, and participate in brand-related activities. An ethnographic study was conducted by the researchers (Scholz & Duffy, 2018) on whether consumer-brand relationships can be facilitated through augmented reality. The other authors Baek et al.(2018), conducted a survey questionnaire in the USA to examine how augmented reality technology affects the brand perceptions and purchase intentions of consumers. Likewise, the authors (Yaoyuneyong et al., 2014) proposed the use of VDR, which helps to reduce consumers' perceived risks in regard to buying apparel online and also has a positive effect on consumer self-confidence, customer – brand relationships and consumers' online e-shopping behaviour (Watson et al., 2018).

Therefore, the findings from the proposed work suggest that fashion mobile apps can play a pivotal role in building and maintaining strong brand-consumer relationships. As technology continues to advance, fashion brands can leverage mobile apps to further deepen their relationships with consumers by offering personalized and tailored experiences. The future impact of these consumer-brand relationships fostered by mobile apps can lead to increased customer retention and brand loyalty.

Table 5. Performance of the mobile application utilized for the studies reviewed

Author, Year	Mobile Application Name	Core Technology	Description	User Ranking	Number of Downloads	Author	Year
(Pop et al., 2023)	Fast fashion mobile app	Version Varies with device, Requires Android Varies with device, Content rating Rated for 3+, Released on May 7, 2014	Download the Myntra update for a fashion app. Shop online for fashionable clothing for women, men, girls & kids clothes - everyone can enjoy trendy fashion. From clothes, fashionable shoes, branded makeup, lipsticks, skincare, accessories to hair care & home products, Myntra is your one-stop lifestyle online shop.	4.3	100,000,000+		Updated on Apr 25, 2023
(Scholz & Duffy, 2018)	Sephora's Mobile AR shopping app	Version 23.6.1 Requires Android 7.0 and up Content rating Rated for 3+, Interactive elements Users Interact,	Skincare, makeup, and beauty products from top brands with the best shopping experience. Have another question? Live chat with one of our beauty associates to get an unbiased opinion and recommendation for you. Easily order or reserve products online to pick up in-store.	4.8	5,000,000+	Sephora USA, Inc.	Updated on Apr 5,2023
(Lau & Ki, 2021)	Taobao Life, a 3D avatar-based and game-featured virtual world on the Taobao app	Version 10.22.10.20 Requires Android 4.0 and up Content rating Everyone Interactive elements Users Interact, Shares Location	Mobile Taobao is an online shopping platform and mobile shopping app that brings high-quality online shopping experience to more than hundreds of millions of users. Every day, consumers from all over the world come to Taobao for "shopping": to discover good things, find fun, and share experiences... Taobao can satisfy people's life in searching and browsing products, adding to shopping carts, placing orders for payment, logistics inquiries, customer service exchanges, and posting shopping. Comment, share high-quality products, etc., and help you find more local life discount information. Open the APP is a shopping mall, go shopping without going out. Visit anytime you want! Intimate to meet your needs! Mobile Taobao provides a variety of payment methods for online shopping, such as (in some regions) international credit cards, local banks, Alipay and other local cross-border payment methods, payment is faster and smoother! Simple and easy-to-understand trading interface, buying things is so safe, fast and convenient.	2.3	10,000,000+	Taobao	Sep 15, 2010
(Baek et al., 2018)	Ray-Ban Virtual Mirror	Version 5.4.1+30703 Requires Android 9 and up Content rating Rated for 3+	Augment is an ARCore-based* mobile app to visualize 3D models in Augmented Reality, integrated in real time in their actual size and environment. Augment is the perfect Augmented Reality app to boost your sales, engage your customers or simply bring your ideas to life. Add your own 3D models at http://augment.com or browse our public gallery. *ARCore compatible device is needed to run the application.	3.5	1,000,000+	Augment	Apr 29, 2011

continued on following page

Table 5. Continued

Author, Year	Mobile Application Name	Core Technology	Description	User Ranking	Number of Downloads	Author	Year
(Park & Kim, 2023)	virtual try-on" technology (AR) and the "3D virtual store" (VR)	Version 1.0.1 Requires Android 5.0 and up Content rating Rated for 3+	"virtual" technology, including augmented reality (AR) and virtual reality (VR) will be the key in the retail industry because it can provide highly interactive, personalized experiences in a virtual environment (Taylor, 2020) and place "... consumers in quasi-physical store conditions."	3.2	100+	Unthinkable Solutions LLP	Nov 29, 2022
(Baytar et al., 2020)	Augment - 3D Augmented Reality	Version 5.4.1+30703 Requires Android 9 and up Content rating Rated for 3+	Augment is an AR Core-based* mobile app to visualize 3D models in Augmented Reality, integrated in real-time in their actual size and environment. Augment is the perfect Augmented Reality app to boost your sales, engage your customers or simply bring your ideas to life. Add your own 3D models at http://augment.com or browse our public gallery. *ARCore compatible device is needed to run the application. With Augment, - View 3D models in augmented reality thanks to ARCore. - Compare multiple 3D models side by side. - Easily view 3D models in different colours and textures. - Capture, save, and share 'Place' on-site to refer back to this background for other 3D models.	3.5	1,000,000+	Augment	Apr 29, 2011
(Watson et al., 2018)	AR makeup retail app	Version 5.4.1+30703 Requires Android 9 and up Content rating Everyone	Augment is an ARCore-based* mobile app to visualize 3D models in Augmented Reality, integrated in real-time in their actual size and environment. Augment is the perfect Augmented Reality app to boost your sales, engage your customers or simply bring your ideas to life. Add your own 3D models at http://augment.com or browse our public gallery. *ARCore compatible device is needed to run the application. With Augment, - View 3D models in augmented reality thanks to ARCore. - Compare multiple 3D models side by side. - Easily view 3D models in different colours and textures. - Capture, save, and share 'Place' on-site to refer back to this background for other 3D models.	3.7	1,000,000+	Augment	Apr 29, 2011

continued on following page

Table 5. Continued

Author, Year	Mobile Application Name	Core Technology	Description	User Ranking	Number of Downloads	Author	Year
(Yaoyuneyong et al., 2014)		Version 5.4.1+30703 Requires Android 9 and up Content rating Rated for 3+	Augment is an ARCore-based* mobile app to visualize 3D models in Augmented Reality, integrated in real time in their actual size and environment. Augment is the perfect Augmented Reality app to boost your sales, engage your customers or simply bring your ideas to life. Add your own 3D models at http://augment.com or browse our public gallery. *ARCore compatible device is needed to run the application.	3.5	1,000,000+	Augment	Apr 29, 2011
(Rhee & Lee, 2021)	A shop	Version 1.5.0 Requires Android 4.4 and up Content rating Everyone			1,000+	Vatfree.com	09-Dec-2019

Influence of Fashion Mobile Apps on Purchase Intention

The results of the systematic review revealed that fashion mobile apps have a positive influence on consumers' purchase intention. These apps provide convenient and seamless shopping experiences, personalized product recommendations, and easy checkout options. From this point of view, in the study (Rhee & Lee, 2021), the researchers examined the relationship between VF experience satisfaction, brand advocacy, mobile purchase intention, and offline purchase intention from an omnichannel perspective. Through the study can understand how VF-based AR impacts the customer purchase journey. The study also investigates the moderating effect of a customer's product involvement, which is a personal characteristic. Further, the researchers' Park & Kim (2023) studied whether virtual try-on leads to greater cognitive elaboration (H1a) and greater purchase intentions (H1b) than do 3D virtual stores and static pictures. This may also be helpful to understand the benefit of metaverse by utilizing a virtual try-on. Also, the authors have tested H1 in a more controlled lab environment to minimize potential confounding factors related to an online experiment and increase internal validity. Likewise, the authors (2020) examined whether AR conveys reliable apparel product information in terms of fit, size, and product performance; and how AR affects attitudes toward apparel and purchase intentions when shopping online.As a conclusion, findings suggest that fashion mobile apps can serve as an effective sales channel, driving higher purchase intention among consumers. As mobile apps continue to evolve and offer enhanced shopping experiences, the future impact of fashion mobile apps on purchase intention is expected to increase. Fashion brands can capitalize on these findings by continuously improving and innovating their mobile apps to provide compelling shopping experiences that drive higher purchase intention among consumers.

Benefits of Metaverse in Fashion Mobile Apps

The results highlighted the potential implications of fashion mobile apps for the metaverse, a virtual reality space where users interact with digital environments. As the metaverse continues to gain traction and becomes an increasingly prominent aspect of the digital landscape, fashion mobile apps can play a

Table 6. Mobile application used in fashion industry

Author, Year	Theory / Model	Application / Functionality	Variables	User Experience (UX) Design	Features
Pop et al., 2023	S-O-R	fast fashion mobile apps	consumers' shopping experience	NA	NA
Scholz & Duffy et al., 2018	Practice theory	Augmented reality (AR)		Dissatisfactory	Core features of the media text (i.e., how AR content is merged with consumers' bodies) as well as other aspects of the media object through which consumer's access AR content (i.e., the touch ID function of the smartphone device) contribute to the dissolving of boundaries between consumers, social others, objects, and the brand
Lau and Ki (2021)	Self-determination theory	Virtual reality (VR)	The context of Taobao Life, a 3D avatar-based and game-featured virtual world on the Taobao app	Sense of self-efficacy (i.e., the belief that s/he has the ability to accomplish a task) or a sense of mastery, it helps fulfil his/her need for competence	face, skin colour, hairstyle, clothes, and accessories, resemble those of the game player, s/he tends to identify those avatars as an extension of him/herself
Baek et al., (2015)	Self-attention theory/ TAM	Augmented reality (AR)	purchase sunglasses from a variety of styles and designs, a computer camera to try on sunglasses, a virtual mirror on a computer screen and overlays or surrounds a shopper's image with computer-generated product images	presence and interactivity	virtual mirror
Park et al., (2023)	Transactional theory	Augmented reality (AR)/ Virtual reality (VR)/3D-Virtual store		The first website offers virtual try-on technology and participants could virtually try on the apparel products by overlaying the product's image on their own reflection using a webcam. The second website offers users the opportunities to walk through the 3D version of Elatic's physical store while navigating on different hot spots to move around the space and observing apparel products	Features including product images and descriptions, layouts, and product options remained consistent across the three experimental conditions. The major differences among the websites were the visual form and website technologies over the shopping experience
Baytar & Shih (2020)	S-O-R stimulus-organism-response	Augmented reality (AR) apparel	Online apparel shopping, apparel product information in terms of fit, size, and product performance	AR can make users feel significantly more "locally present" as compared to seeing pictures or 360-spin formats of the products, suggesting that retailers who sell products that consumers need to try on before buying can use AR technologies.	Image interactive technologies (IIT) are website features designed to simulate actual product experiences by enabling online shoppers to (1) view products from different angles; (2) change design features; and (3) see how apparel products look on their bodies/avatars to understand garment fit and appearance.
Watson, Alexander, Salavati (2018)	S-O-R stimulus-organism-response	Augmented reality (AR)		The app overlays the user's face via the front-facing camera with the previously scanned makeup looks. This means that, after scanning the face of a real-life friend or a model in a print campaign, the user sees the scanned makeup look applied to their own face.	(interactivity, hypertexuality, modality, connectivity, location-specificity, mobility, virtuality

continued on following page

Table 6. Continued

Author, Year	Theory / Model	Application / Functionality	Variables	User Experience (UX) Design	Features
Yaoyuneyong et al., 2014	Uses and Gratifications (U&G)	Augmented reality (AR)/ Virtual reality (VR)		Entertainment refers to the extent to which a media format is fun for users, Users demand accuracy, timeliness and usefulness in online content, and websites which fulfil informational needs create favourable attitudes.	Webcam VDR's social-sharing features open opportunities for retailers to expand the boundaries of company-customer relationships through social merchandising
Rhee and Lee (2021)	NA	Virtual Fitting (VF) based on augmented reality (AR)	The fashion industry, online channels, mobile channels, and social media shopping	Users freely utilize multiple channels depending on the advantages each one offers	NA

pivotal role in shaping the consumer experience. The future impact of fashion mobile apps on the metaverse can be significant, with fashion brands leveraging these apps to create virtual showrooms, virtual fashion events, and personalized fashion. Additionally, the integration of fashion mobile apps with the metaverse has the potential to revolutionize the way consumers interact with fashion brands and make purchase decisions. Virtual fashion experiences enabled by these apps can create a unique and immersive shopping journey for consumers. This can lead to increased consumer engagement and higher purchase intention. Furthermore, the implications of fashion mobile apps for the metaverse extend beyond the immediate impact on consumer behaviour. These apps can also create new business opportunities for fashion brands in the virtual world. Virtual fashion events, collaborations, and sponsorships can also be facilitated through fashion mobile apps. The findings of this systematic review have significant implications for the future of fashion retail and the evolving digital landscape. Fashion brands need to recognize the increasing importance of mobile apps in shaping consumer behaviours and the potential of the metaverse as a new frontier for fashion experiences. By leveraging the features and functionalities of fashion mobile apps, brands can enhance their consumer-brand relationships, influence purchase intention, and create unique and immersive virtual fashion experiences. This can lead to increased customer loyalty, brand advocacy, and business growth in the digital era. Table 4 explains the consumer brand relationship findings, purchase intention findings, and limitations of each study reviewed.

According to the above table, majority of the reviewed study has their limitation in feature and purchase intention perspective hence this proposed systematic review overcomes those limitation by revealing ang highlighting the variations in the effectiveness of different features and functionalities across different mobile apps and consumer segments.In conclusion, the results of this systematic review highlight the significant impact of fashion mobile apps on consumer behaviours. The future implications of these findings are vast, with fashion brands having the opportunity to leverage mobile apps to create innovative and immersive shopping experiences, strengthen brand-consumer relationships, and tap into the potential of the metaverse as a new frontier for fashion retail. This study provides valuable insights for fashion brands, marketers, and researchers to understand the key features and functionalities of fashion mobile apps and their implications for the ever-evolving digital landscape of the metaverse.

Discussion

The review revealed that fashion mobile apps offer diverse features and functionalities that cater to the needs and preferences of modern consumers. These features include virtual try-ons (Park & Kim, 2023),

Table 7. Findings and limitation

Author, Year	Consumer-Brand Relationship Findings	Purchase Intention Findings	Limitations of the Study
Pop et al., 2023			
Scholz & Duffy et al., 2018	The brand maintains a special place in customers' lives that goes beyond a task-oriented engagement with retail in their private daily rhythm and "me-time."	The study discovered that while pleasure and play are valued components of the user experience, the final purchase decision is less significant in customers' activities with a branded app.	'Shopping on the move' is highly emphasised as the primary strategy for mobile marketing in managerial practise and academic publications. Future studies might take use of this widened perspective on AR and look at the meanings and connections that develop in non-domestic settings. Future studies might take use of this widened perspective on AR and look at the meanings and connections that develop in non-domestic settings. The interior context of AR encounters might be further illuminated by future research that examines the immediate and long-term effects of AR on customers' self.
Lau and Ki (2021)	VR fashion app usage, the fulfil of consumers' needs for competence and autonomy has positive effect on their app usage behaviour; but not the fulfil of their need for relatedness.	in-app purchase intention, competence need fulfilment (H8a: β=–0.29, p > 0.05) and relatedness need fulfilment (H8c: β=–0.02, p > 0.05) had no significant effect on in-app purchase intention	VR apps indeed can have a positive marketing effect by fulfilling consumers' inherent needs for competence and autonomy by employing their apps' gamified (i.e., challenge and achievement) and personalized features (i.e., avatar customization and identification)
Baek et al., (2015)	The authors discovered no discernible difference in SBCs between the self-viewing condition and the other-viewing condition (M = 2.47) (=.05, t =.39, p =.70). H3(a) for SBCs was subsequently supported. In addition, the link between augmentation and the pleasant emotional response is moderated by hedonic purchasing motive.	Researchers discovered no discernible change in purchase intentions between the self-watching condition (M D 2.91) and the other viewing condition (M D 3.09) (b D.09, t D.63, p D.53). H3(b) for purchasing intents was therefore supported.	First off, the scope of the study is limited to web-based AR virtual mirrors; however, future studies may broaden the applicability of our findings to other AR situations. The results' generalizability is constrained by the sampling of college students. It is necessary to do further research with non-student samples. It would also be intriguing to repeat the results with different product categories, including household furnishings (like the IKEA AR catalogue) or cosmetics (like the Shisedio AR beauty mirror).
Park et al., (2023)	The number of participants who thought their purchase intentions were related to searching for and finding specific information was higher in the searching condition than in the browsing condition (M searching = 3.93, M browsing = 4.80, t =3.83, p =.00). Therefore, it was successful to manipulate shoppers' goals.	It was shown that the primary effects of shopping goals and website features on purchase intentions were both independently significant (F(1, 189) = 4.89, p =.028, and F (1, 189) = 12.99, p =.00, correspondingly). Virtual try-on and static photos worked better than 3D virtual stores when clients only intended to browse the internet.	Although the results demonstrated the interaction between a website's technological advances and a shopping objective, future research may examine mediating effects in the searching group by utilising various clothing types (such as functional clothing) that require greater cognitive evaluation or by using a larger sample. Future research in this field would also be interesting if it contrasted established, well-known clothing manufacturers with new, unheard-of enterprises.
Baytar & Shih (2020)	Between the physically tried-on dress sizes (M = 2.65; SD = 1.23) and the virtually tried-on AR dress sizes (M = 2.69; SD = 1.16) there was no statistically significant difference (t(86) = -1.75; p = 0.41). Nine of the 10 variables that looked at how participants' perceptions of their AR dress performance and actual dress performance differed were determined to be statistically significant. Results from the MANOVA revealed that the high telepresence group tended to have more positive attitudes towards the apparel product when using AR (M Low Telepresence = 5.04 (SD = 0.14), M High Telepresence = 5.50 (SD 5 0.16)) and greater purchase intentions towards the apparel product (M Low Telepresence = 3.88 (SD = 0.24), M High Telepresence = 4.77 (SD = 0.27)) than the low telepresence group [F (1, 83) = 3.15; p < 0.05, partial η2 = 0.071].	Participants indicated greater purchase intentions during physical try-on (M =4.74, SD = 1.71) as compared to AR try-on (M = 4.27, SD = 1.70) (ΔM = 0.47, SD = 1.94, t(85) = 2.32, p < 0.05)	Future research should examine the effects of various AR try-on situations on telepresence utilising more theoretical models, other providers, and advanced AR features. The experimental design was chosen with the possibility of a carry-over effect. It is possible that the participants' learning of the product, which may have been reinforced by experiencing the same product twice—first virtually and then physically—led to attitudes and purchase intentions being higher in the physical try-on condition.

continued on following page

Table 7. Continued

Author, Year	Consumer-Brand Relationship Findings	Purchase Intention Findings	Limitations of the Study
Watson, Alexander, Salavati (2018)	H1 proposed a positive relationship between augmentation and positive affective response. In order to test this hypothesis a t-test was executed. Those respondents who IJRDM Downloaded by New Mexico State University At 01:38 03 July 2018 (PT) had experienced the augmentation had an average positive affect score of 4.87, compared with those who had not of 3.78 (p ¼ 0.00), supporting H1.	positive affective response mediated the relationship between augmentation and purchase intention, supporting H2 (F-change statistic ¼ 35.01, p ¼ 0.00). The total indirect effect was 0.616 (SE 0.1381, z ¼ 4.4606).	The results may not be generalizable to other types of augmentation due to the chosen study methodology. Therefore, it is urged for researchers to test the suggested model with other AR stimuli. Furthermore, expanding the study's generalizability by doing it again with other demographics
Yaoyuneyong et al., 2014	use of VDR will reduce consumers' perceived risks regarding buying apparel online and have a positive effect on consumer self-confidence, customer – brand relationships and consumers' online e-shopping behaviour.	VDRs to 'try on' apparel products, they are gratified by and satisfied with VDRs' functionality regarding their entertainment and informative values, resulting in increasing intention to buy	The effectiveness of the model suggested in this study should be the subject of further study.
Rhee and Lee (2021)	The results were confirmed to have a high explanatory power of ~0.79. f2 indicated a value of 0.07–1.22 except between the customer satisfaction and offline purchase intention variables (f 2 = 0.00), confirming that it had a medium or higher effect size, and a Q2 value greater than 0 for all potential variables, indicating a predictive fit.	Satisfaction with the VF experience was found to have a positive effect on brand advocacy ($\beta = 0.74$, $p < 0.001$) and mobile purchase intention ($\beta = 0.65$, $p < 0.001$). Brand advocacy was found to have a positive effect on both mobile purchase intention ($\beta = 0.22$, $p < 0.01$) and offline purchase intention ($\beta = 0.37$, $p < 0.01$); thus, H4 and H5 were both supported	Future studies should also look into whether prior VF experiences, especially AR encounters, might impact enjoyment. Additionally, the sample was restricted to those in their 20s and 30s who are experienced with using digital devices; yet, due to social distance norms, mobile purchasing has grown among adults in their 40s and 50s as well. Finally, this study looked at how users of AR technology-based services for the fashion sector responded to VF contents. Future research should compare the proposed

personalized recommendations, social media integration, mobile commerce capabilities, AR and VR experiences, and interactive technologies. The findings indicate that these features have a significant impact on consumer brand relationships Watson et al (2018) by enhancing engagement, trust, loyalty, and emotional connections with fashion brands. Consumers tend to develop stronger relationships with fashion brands that offer unique and immersive experiences through their mobile apps, leading to increased brand loyalty and advocacy (Yaoyuneyong et al., 2014)Furthermore, the review found that fashion mobile apps also have a positive influence on consumer purchase intention which have been failed in the previous papers (Park & Kim, 2023) (Pop et al., 2023). By providing convenience, ease of use, and seamless shopping experiences, these apps facilitate the purchase decision-making process. The convenience of browsing and shopping on mobile apps can lead to higher purchase intention among consumers (Rhee & Lee, 2021) (Park & Kim, 2023).

CONCLUSION AND FUTURE SCOPE

The fashion industry has witnessed a significant transformation with the advent of mobile applications that have revolutionized the way consumers interact with fashion brands and make purchase decisions. This systematic review aimed to synthesize the existing literature on the features and functionalities of fashion mobile Apps and their impact on consumer brand relationships and purchase intention, with implications for the metaverse. The review findings highlight that fashion mobile Apps offer a wide range of features and functionalities that enhance the consumer-brand relationship. Moreover, fashion mobile Apps also influence consumers' purchase intention by providing convenient shopping experiences and reducing perceived riskThe review also underscores the potential implications of fashion mobile Apps for the metaverse. As the metaverse continues to gain momentum as a virtual world where consumers interact with digital representations of brands, products, and services, fashion mobile Apps can serve as a key enablers. With features such as AR and VR experiences, consumers can virtually try on clothing and accessories, customize avatars with fashion items, and engage in immersive shopping experiences within the metaverse. This has significant implications for the future of fashion retail.

The findings of this systematic review have several theoretical and practical implications. From a theoretical standpoint, the review contributes to the literature on consumer behaviour, branding, and retailing by shedding light on the impact of fashion mobile Apps on consumer-brand relationships and purchase intention. The review provides insights into the underlying mechanisms and factors that influence consumers' interactions with fashion mobile Apps. From a practical standpoint, the review offers valuable implications for fashion retailers, marketers, and developers of fashion mobile Apps. The findings suggest that fashion retailers should invest in developing and enhancing the features and functionalities of their mobile Apps to provide consumers with a seamless shopping experience. By leveraging AR, VR, and other innovative technologies, fashion brands can create unique and immersive experiences that drive consumer engagement, brand loyalty, and purchase intention. Moreover, fashion retailers should also explore the potential of the metaverse as a virtual retail space and consider incorporating fashion mobile Apps as a key component of their metaverse strategies.

The review also focused on specific features and functionalities of fashion mobile Apps. Further, the review included studies from a variety of research designs, and the quality and rigour of these studies may vary. In conclusion, this systematic review provides a comprehensive overview of the features and functionalities of mobile applications in the fashion industry and their impact on consumer brand relationships and purchase intention, with implications for the metaverse. The findings highlight the significant role of fashion mobile Apps in shaping consumer behaviour, brand perception, and purchase intention and their potential for driving immersive and personalized experiences within the metaverse. The theoretical and practical implications of this review can inform future research and strategies for fashion retailers, marketers, and developers of fashion mobile Apps in the dynamic and evolving landscape of the fashion industry.

Future Scope

Based on the findings of this systematic review, there are several potential areas for future research and implications for the fashion industry in the context of mobile applications and the metaverse.

User Experience (UX) Design: The design of fashion mobile Apps is critical for enhancing consumer engagement and satisfaction. Future research can focus on UX design principles and best practices for fashion mobile Apps, including usability, aesthetics, navigation, and responsiveness. Studies can investigate how different design elements and features impact user experience and how UX design can be optimized to create seamless, enjoyable, and memorable interactions with fashion mobile Apps.

Privacy and Security: Privacy and security concerns are important considerations in the use of mobile Apps, including fashion Apps. Future research can explore consumer perceptions and behaviours related to privacy and security in the context of fashion mobile Apps.

Long-Term Effects on Consumer Behaviour: The long-term effects of fashion mobile Apps on consumer behaviour, brand loyalty, and purchase intention remain an interesting area for future research. Studies can investigate the long-term effects of fashion mobile Apps on consumer behaviour, such as repeat purchase behaviour, brand loyalty, and post-purchase satisfaction. Longitudinal studies can track consumer behaviours over an extended period of time to understand how the use of fashion mobile Apps may impact consumer attitudes. This can provide valuable insights into the sustained impact of fashion mobile Apps on consumer behaviour and their effectiveness as a marketing tool for fashion brands and retailers.

Sustainable Fashion: Future research on sustainable fashion can explore how fashion mobile Apps can be leveraged to promote sustainable fashion practices. Studies can investigate consumer perceptions and behaviours related to sustainable fashion within the context of fashion mobile Apps and how these Apps can contribute to promoting sustainability in the fashion industry

Impact on Small and Medium-Sized Enterprises (SMEs): Future research on SMEs can investigate the impact of fashion mobile Apps on SMEs, including their adoption, challenges, and opportunities. Studies can explore how fashion mobile Apps can support SMEs in reaching consumers, enhancing their competitiveness, and improving their business performance. Future research can explore how fashion mobile Apps can be integrated with offline retail.

In conclusion, this systematic review provides valuable insights into the current state of research on mobile Apps in the fashion industry. However, there are several avenues for future research and implications for the fashion industry in the context of mobile Apps and the metaverse. Further research can explore the evolving landscape of fashion mobile Apps, consumer engagement in the metaverse, the effectiveness of AR and VR experiences, cross-cultural perspectives, social media integration, UX design principles, privacy and security concerns, business models and monetization strategies, long-term effects on consumer behaviour, sustainable fashion, consumer empowerment, social and ethical issues, impact on SMEs, and integration with offline retail. These areas of research can contribute to a deeper understanding of the role of fashion mobile Apps in shaping consumer behaviour, improving consumer experiences, and driving innovation in the fashion industry. Fashion brands, retailers, and researchers can leverage these insights to develop strategies, policies, and interventions that align with consumer preferences, needs, and aspirations in the era of fashion mobile Apps and the metaverse.

REFERENCES

Abdullah, T., Siti, N. S. D., Zainuddin, S. A., Azmi, N. F., & Siti, A. S. (2020). Impact Of Social Media Influencer On Instagram User Purchase Intention Towards The Fashion Products: The Perspectives Of Students. *European Journal of Molecular & Clinical Medicine, 7*(8), 1–10. https://www.ejmcm.com/article_4700_1df3f69fec2f7e3402c757af9e91f3ae.pdf

Akram, U., Ansari, A. R., Fu, G., & Junaid, M. (2020). Feeling hungry? let's order through mobile! examining the fast food mobile commerce in China. *Journal of Retailing and Consumer Services*, *56*, 102142. doi:10.1016/j.jretconser.2020.102142

Baek, T. H., Yoo, C. Y., & Yoon, S. (2018). Augment yourself through virtual mirror: The impact of self-viewing and narcissism on consumer responses. *International Journal of Advertising*, *37*(3), 421–439. doi:10.1080/02650487.2016.1244887

Baytar, F., Chung, T., & Shin, E. (2020). Evaluating garments in augmented reality when shopping online. *Journal of Fashion Marketing and Management*, *24*(4), 667–683. doi:10.1108/JFMM-05-2018-0077

Biørn-Hansen, A., Rieger, C., Grønli, T.-M., Majchrzak, T. A., & Ghinea, G. (2020). An empirical investigation of performance overhead in cross-platform mobile development frameworks. *Empirical Software Engineering*, *25*(4), 2997–3040. doi:10.100710664-020-09827-6

Chetioui, Y., Benlafqih, H., & Lebdaoui, H. (2020). How fashion influencers contribute to consumers' purchase intention. *Journal of Fashion Marketing and Management*, *24*(3), 361–380. doi:10.1108/JFMM-08-2019-0157

Dai, J.-Y., & Zhao, L. (2022). Happiness and Fashion Culture of Smart Kidswear from the perspective of Metaverse. *2022 10th International Conference on Orange Technology (ICOT)*, 1–4. 10.1109/ICOT56925.2022.10008154

Djafarova, E., & Bowes, T. (2021). 'Instagram made Me buy it': Generation Z impulse purchases in fashion industry. *Journal of Retailing and Consumer Services*, *59*, 102345. doi:10.1016/j.jretconser.2020.102345

Gazzola, P., Pavione, E., Pezzetti, R., & Grechi, D. (2020). Trends in the Fashion Industry. The Perception of Sustainability and Circular Economy: A Gender/Generation Quantitative Approach. *Sustainability (Basel)*, *12*(7), 2809. doi:10.3390u12072809

Hendijani Fard, M., & Marvi, R. (2019). Viral marketing and purchase intentions of mobile applications users. *International Journal of Emerging Markets*, *15*(2), 287–301. doi:10.1108/IJOEM-06-2018-0291

Idrees, S., Vignali, G., & Gill, S. (2023). Interactive Marketing with Virtual Commerce Tools: Purchasing Right Size and Fitted Garment in Fashion Metaverse. In The Palgrave Handbook of Interactive Marketing (pp. 329–351). Springer International Publishing. doi:10.1007/978-3-031-14961-0_15

Jang, J., & Kim, J. (2023). Exploring the Impact of Avatar Customization in Metaverse: The Role of the Class Mode on Task Engagement and Expectancy-Value Beliefs for Fashion Education. *Mobile Information Systems*, *2023*, 1–13. doi:10.1155/2023/2967579

Jeon, H.-J., & Kim, G.-D. (2022). Suggestion of Metaverse based Online Fashion Shopping Mall Application Service : Focused on the Virtual Fitting Service. *Journal of Digital Contents Society*, *23*(4), 589–601. doi:10.9728/dcs.2022.23.4.589

Joy, A., Zhu, Y., Peña, C., & Brouard, M. (2022). Digital future of luxury brands: Metaverse, digital fashion, and non-fungible tokens. *Strategic Change*, *31*(3), 337–343. doi:10.1002/jsc.2502

Kang, J.-Y. M. (2019). What drives omnichannel shopping behaviours? *Journal of Fashion Marketing and Management*, *23*(2), 224–238. doi:10.1108/JFMM-07-2018-0088

Kim, J.-H., Kim, M., Park, M., & Yoo, J. (2023). Immersive interactive technologies and virtual shopping experiences: Differences in consumer perceptions between augmented reality (AR) and virtual reality (VR). *Telematics and Informatics*, *77*, 101936. doi:10.1016/j.tele.2022.101936

Lau, O., & Ki, C.-W. (2021). Can consumers' gamified, personalized, and engaging experiences with VR fashion apps increase in-app purchase intention by fulfilling needs? *Fashion and Textiles*, *8*(1), 36. doi:10.118640691-021-00270-9

Liang, Y., Lee, S.-H., & Workman, J. E. (2020). Implementation of Artificial Intelligence in Fashion: Are Consumers Ready? *Clothing & Textiles Research Journal*, *38*(1), 3–18. doi:10.1177/0887302X19873437

Liberati, A., Altman, D. G., Tetzlaff, J., Mulrow, C., Gøtzsche, P. C., Ioannidis, J. P. A., Clarke, M., Devereaux, P. J., Kleijnen, J., & Moher, D. (2009). The PRISMA Statement for Reporting Systematic Reviews and Meta-Analyses of Studies That Evaluate Health Care Interventions: Explanation and Elaboration. *PLoS Medicine*, *6*(7), e1000100. doi:10.1371/journal.pmed.1000100 PMID:19621070

Lissitsa, S., & Kol, O. (2021). Four generational cohorts and hedonic m-shopping: Association between personality traits and purchase intention. *Electronic Commerce Research*, *21*(2), 545–570. doi:10.100710660-019-09381-4

Lynch, S., & Barnes, L. (2020). Omnichannel fashion retailing: Examining the customer decision-making journey. *Journal of Fashion Marketing and Management*, *24*(3), 471–493. doi:10.1108/JFMM-09-2019-0192

Manzoor, U., Baig, S. A., Hashim, M., & Sami, A. (2020). Impact of Social Media Marketing on Consumer's Purchase Intentions: The Mediating role of Customer Trust. *International Journal of Entrepreneurial Research*, *3*(2), 41–48. doi:10.31580/ijer.v3i2.1386

Moisander, J., Närvänen, E., & Valtonen, A. (2020). Interpretive marketing research. In *Marketing Management* (pp. 237–253). Routledge. doi:10.4324/9780203710807-19

Park, H., & Kim, S. (2023). Do Augmented and Virtual Reality Technologies Increase Consumers' Purchase Intentions? The Role of Cognitive Elaboration and Shopping Goals. *Clothing & Textiles Research Journal*, *41*(2), 91–106. doi:10.1177/0887302X21994287

Pop, R.-A., Hlédik, E., & Dabija, D.-C. (2023). Predicting consumers' purchase intention through fast fashion mobile apps: The mediating role of attitude and the moderating role of COVID-19. *Technological Forecasting and Social Change*, *186*, 122111. doi:10.1016/j.techfore.2022.122111

Rausch, T. M., & Kopplin, C. S. (2021). Bridge the gap: Consumers' purchase intention and behaviour regarding sustainable clothing. *Journal of Cleaner Production*, *278*, 123882. doi:10.1016/j.jclepro.2020.123882

Rhee, H.-L., & Lee, K.-H. (2021). Enhancing the Sneakers Shopping Experience through Virtual Fitting Using Augmented Reality. *Sustainability (Basel)*, *13*(11), 6336. doi:10.3390u13116336

Scholz, J., & Duffy, K. (2018). We ARe at home: How augmented reality reshapes mobile marketing and consumer-brand relationships. *Journal of Retailing and Consumer Services*, *44*, 11–23. doi:10.1016/j.jretconser.2018.05.004

Shi, S., Wang, Y., Chen, X., & Zhang, Q. (2020). Conceptualization of omnichannel customer experience and its impact on shopping intention: A mixed-method approach. *International Journal of Information Management*, *50*, 325–336. doi:10.1016/j.ijinfomgt.2019.09.001

Silva, S. C., Duarte, P., & Sundetova, A. (2020). Multichannel versus omnichannel: A price-segmented comparison from the fashion industry. *International Journal of Retail & Distribution Management*, *48*(4), 417–430. doi:10.1108/IJRDM-07-2019-0232

Soni, M., Jain, K., & Kumar, B. (2019). Factors affecting the adoption of fashion mobile shopping applications. *Journal of Global Fashion Marketing*, *10*(4), 358–376. doi:10.1080/20932685.2019.1649165

Sumarliah, E., Usmanova, K., Mousa, K., & Indriya, I. (2022). E-commerce in the fashion business: The roles of the COVID-19 situational factors, hedonic and utilitarian motives on consumers' intention to purchase online. *International Journal of Fashion Design. Technology and Education*, *15*(2), 167–177. doi:10.1080/17543266.2021.1958926

Vahdat, A., Alizadeh, A., Quach, S., & Hamelin, N. (2021). Would you like to shop via mobile app technology? The technology acceptance model, social factors and purchase intention. *Australasian Marketing Journal*, *29*(2), 187–197. doi:10.1016/j.ausmj.2020.01.002

Vamsi Krishna, P. (2023). Investigating the effects of the metaverse on business models. *Journal of Advances in Management, Engineering and Science*, *1*(1), 1–13. https://brpublications.com/wp-content/uploads/2023/03/paper6.pdf

Wang, Y., Ko, E., & Wang, H. (2022). Augmented reality (AR) app use in the beauty product industry and consumer purchase intention. *Asia Pacific Journal of Marketing and Logistics*, *34*(1), 110–131. doi:10.1108/APJML-11-2019-0684

Watson, A., Alexander, B., & Salavati, L. (2018). The impact of experiential augmented reality applications on fashion purchase intention. *International Journal of Retail & Distribution Management*, *48*(5), 433–451. doi:10.1108/IJRDM-06-2017-0117

Weiss, C. (2022). Fashion retailing in the metaverse. *Fashion, Style & Popular Culture*, *9*(4), 523–538. doi:10.1386/fspc_00159_1

Yaoyuneyong, G., Foster, J. K., & Flynn, L. R. (2014). Factors impacting the efficacy of augmented reality virtual dressing room technology as a tool for online visual merchandising. *Journal of Global Fashion Marketing*, *5*(4), 283–296. doi:10.1080/20932685.2014.926129

Zhao, L., Lee, S. H., & Copeland, L. R. (2019). Social media and Chinese consumers' environmentally sustainable apparel purchase intentions. *Asia Pacific Journal of Marketing and Logistics*, *31*(4), 855–874. doi:10.1108/APJML-08-2017-0183

Chapter 2
An Empirical Investigation on the Influence of Social Networks on Purchase Decision Making: An Indian Perspective

K. S. Kalavathy
CMS Business School, Jain University, India

H. R. Swapna
Jain University, India

Anitha Nallasivam
CMS Business School, Jain University, India

Digvijay Pandey
IET Lucknow, India

Darshan A. Mahajan
National Institute of Construction Management and Research, Pune, India

Pankaj Dadheech
Swami Keshvanand Institute of Technology, Management, and Gramothan, India

ABSTRACT

The purpose of this chapter is to examine the factors which influence the intention to use Facebook among Generation Y consumers and its influence on purchase decision making. A quantitative research methodology was used, and the data was collected from 404 respondents in Bangalore city. Partial least square structural equation model using R software was used to analyse data collected. The findings showed that perceived usefulness, perceived enjoyment, perceived credibility, and subjective norm have a significant influence on intention to use Facebook while perceived ease of use does not have a significant influence on intention to use Facebook. Perceived enjoyment has the highest influence on

DOI: 10.4018/978-1-6684-8753-2.ch002

intention to use Facebook followed by subjective norm, perceived credibility, and perceived usefulness. The results of this study also indicated that intention to use Facebook has a significant positive effect on consumers. The findings of this study contribute to an understanding of the importance of the selected factors in affecting the intention to use Facebook.

INTRODUCTION

Web 2.0 has become an integral part of today's individual. Several formats of social interactions taking place daily have been successful in creating a social movement. Hillman and Trier (2013) state that social influence "provides a wide array of inputs to understand how actions of people are influenced by other individuals as an outcome of interaction. "This indicates that social influence is a spontaneous process, which can be utilized by both companies and individuals to transform a persons' attitude or behavior.

The immeasurable potential of interacting with other users have led to the creation of online communities developed around special interests or demographics (Birdsall, 2007).

Godes and Mayzlin (2004) established that social media platforms are very economical and simple option to connect and collect consumer to consumer interaction. Research on consumer-to-consumer communication establishes that these interactions initiate significant results for firms. This online environment supports a distinct outlook for the contemporary social influence theories (Snijders and Helms, 2014). Social networking has gained high acceptance, particularly among younger generations. The efficacy of these groups as platforms for communication has been recognized by business men and politicians alike.

Social media sites such as YouTube, Twitter and Facebook are a result of the emergence of Web 2.0 technologies. These networks have provided a platform which is enabling users to create and share brand related information online in their social circuits consisting of family, classmates, friends and other people known (Hennig-Thurau, 2003). Previous research has demonstrated that such communications have influenced the purchase decisions of consumers (Muntinga et. al 2011), built brand attitudes and influenced marketing decisions.

Social networking sites are user generated, user centered and emerged as media platforms which are highly influential (Zhang and Daugherty, 2010).Though social networks have gained popularity among different age groups, they have particularly gained immense acceptance and usage among young social groups (Lin and Lu, 2011).Among the existing social networking sites Facebook is the most visited, largest and most popular site. It is one of the online social platforms that was developed and designed to promote active social engagements real time (Alomoush, Yaseen and Alma'aitah,2012).

In the information technology literature behavioral Intention is a very important variable which influences the adoption of any new technology. Hence it is very crucial to identify the factors which influence the intention to use Facebook and how this influences purchase decision making.The next section presents the theoretical framework of the study followed by research methodology, analysis of results, discussion, implications and conclusion.

Theoretical Framework of the Study

The initial TAM is built from extrinsic variables, perceived ease of use (PEOU) and perceived usefulness (PU), attitude towards using, Behavioral Intention and actual usage. The basic idea of the framework is that PEOU and PU directly influence the intention of users to use Information Technology. The behaviour of an individual is a result of his or her behavioural intention and both these factors are together controlled by subjective norms and individual attitudes (Fishbein and Ajzen,1975). The effect of the degree of evaluation that an individual relates with using a particular system determines attitude towards the same (Davis, 1993). In Theory of planned behavior(TPB) perceived behavioral control was included as a factor which determines behavior (Shih, 2004). Constructs namely Attitude, Belief, Intention and Behavioural relationship are generally used to predict behaviour of individuals in both TRA and TPB Models. Building upon TRA, Davis, Bagozzi & Warshaw (1989) put forward 'The Technology Acceptance Model' (TAM). The model assumes that the belief of the user about a new information system influence the user acceptance and subsequent adoption of the system. Many studies have focused on the extension of this model to understand the antecedents of adoption of social networks.

Lim and Coleman (2012) examined the perception of US University business students towards perceived usefulness and ease of use towards using social networking sites .The results revealed that perceived ease of use was an important determinant of perceived usefulness and perceived usefulness was an important determinant of usage. The findings of the empirical investigation revealed that PEOU and PU did not have any impact on user attitudes or intentions, drama had a significant negative effect on intention to use social networks while perceived enjoyment was the most significant determinant of attitude.

The study carried out by Taghaviezhad et al (2015) in Iran to understand the determinants of usage of social networks revealed that, PEOU, PU, external variables, attitudes and intention to use have a significant influence on social networks usage.

Teo (2016) included emotional attachment to the TAM model. The outcome indicated that PU, emotional attachment and attitudes have a direct influence on Facebook usage while PEOU indirectly affected Facebook usage of students.

TAM Model has been effectively applied in a wide array of studies connected to many computer mediated technologies. The extended TAM for this research work is developed based on extensive literature reviews. Empirical and theoretical research has supported TAM in the context of various Information systems like Internet Banking (Zandhersami & Parisa Geranmaych, 2014), Facebook banking (Cuong, Linh & Ha,2015), Online shopping (Aldhmour, Fairouz & Isra, 2016), Problem based learning (Yang and Lin,2011),Collaborative learning (Rahimi,Othman and Musa, 2013), e-learning (Haitham,2014) . Though previous research have considered TAM in different contexts, very limited research has been done in the area of intention to use facebook and purchase decision making. Thus this paper aims to examine the antecedents of intention to use Facebook and its influence on purchase decision making.

To examine the factors influencing the intention to use Facebook, the constructs (Perceived usefulness and perceived ease of use) have been adopted from Technology Acceptance model developed by Davis et. al (1989). This research has considered an extension of TAM as a theoretical framework to investigate the factors which influence the intention to use Facebook. Hence in addition to perceived usefulness and perceived ease of use, the constructs Perceived enjoyment, Perceived Credibility and subjective norms are used for this study.

- **Perceived Usefulness**

According to TAM model (Davis, 1989) and other connected earlier studies of Theory of Planned Behavior and Theory of Reasoned Action (Ajzen and Fishbein, 1980) the principal element for prospective users to consider, during decision making in the context of adopting new technology is Perceived

Figure 1. Proposed model used to identify the factors that influence adoption of Facebook and its influence on purchase decision making
Source: Technology Acceptance Model by Davis et al. (1989)

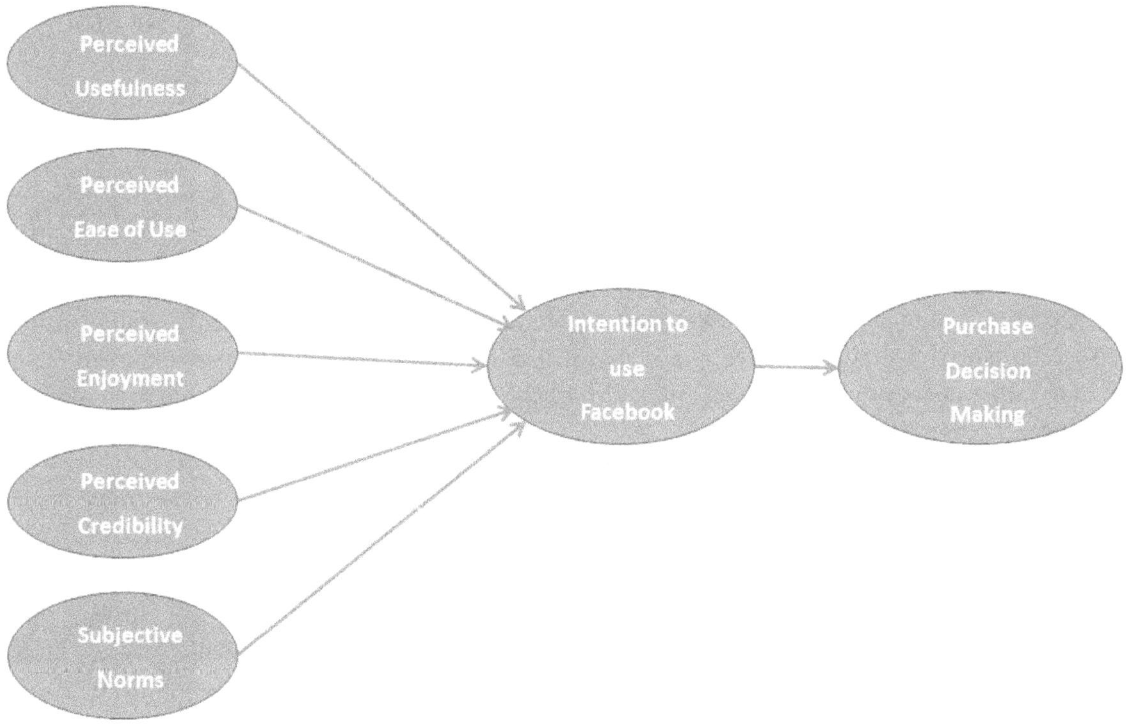

usefulness. Perceived usefulness is the "extent to which an individual accepts that using a specific system is likely to enhance his or her job related performance". Customers in the 21st century are more probable to adopt technologies which are innovative and useful (Pikkarainen, Pikkarainen, Karjaluoto, H. and Pahnila, 2004). This leads us to the first hypothesis presented below:

H1: Perceived usefulness has a significant influence on intention to use Facebook.

- **Perceived Ease of Use**

Perceived Ease of use, another important component of TAM (Davis, 1989) corresponds to the extent to which new technology users perceive that using the product/service is easy. If the customers perceive the use of a particular application as easy, the acceptance of the product is likely to be high (Cheng, Lam and Yeung, 2006).The main reason for this is that the customers are more certain of the outcomes by using same routes in similar contexts without additional cost (Gefen and Straub, 1997).In this regard Facebook has to create applications which are easy to use. Perceived Ease of use is a crucial factor in the process of adoption of new technology(Mann and Sahni, 2012).Based on the above discussion the second hypothesis is presented.

H2: Perceived ease of use has a significant influence on intention to use Facebook.

- **Perceived Enjoyment**

Perceived Enjoyment refers to the enjoyment the user derives while using the technology, along with other performance outcomes resulting from technology use (Venkatesh 2000). Enjoyment is defined as the innate benefit obtained through the use of technology (Davis, Bagozzi and Warshaw, 1992). It is considered as a major driver for adopting new technology and a source of intrinsic motivation. This leads us to the third hypothesis proposed below.

H3: Perceived enjoyment has a significant influence on intention to use Facebook.

- **Subjective Norm**

The fourth construct subjective norm is selected from the Theory of Reasoned Action (TRA) Model proposed by Ajzen and Fishbein (1980). Subjective norm is defined as the persons' understanding about the expectations of other individuals who matter to an individual whether he ought to or not engage in the specific behavior in focus (Ajzen and Fishbein, 1980). It is the societal pressure anindividualperceives to either engage or not to engage in specific behavior.Based on the above discussion the fourth hypothesis is presented

H4: Subjective norms have a significant influence on intention to use Facebook.

- **Perceived Credibility**

Perceived Credibility is perceived as trustworthiness and expertise (Wathen and Burkell, 2002). Credibility is "the degree to which consumers perceive the companies as trustworthy. Sources high on credibility are relatively more persuasive in comparison to those that are low on credibility (Walker and Kent, 2012). Social media platform users not only review content but also create content. Credibility of information is a crucial factor as we encounter loads of information in everyday life.It is quite usual to come across false information which is flooded on social media. Hence perceived credibility is considered as one of the critical components that affect the intention of using Facebook. Based on the above discussion the fourth hypothesis is presented

H5: Perceived credibility has a significant influence on intention to use Facebook

- **Behavioral Intention**

Intentions are specific actions which individuals consider on the basis of cognitive thinking. Behavior Intention is shaped by attitude, both negative and positive. Hence the researcher has considered that users'attitude toward Facebookwould have an influence on their behavioral intention. The questions formulated in the research instrument focus on whether the respondents are currently using, planning to use or will continue to use Facebook.

H6: Intention to use Facebook has significant influence on using Facebook for purchase decision making.

Research Methodology

Information technology has influenced the life and work of millennials to a great extent as they are the first generation to have grown up and experienced life in the digital terrain (Bennett, Maton and Kervin, 2008). They depend very heavily on technology to interact with others, seek entertainment and regulate their emotions too (Park and Gursoy, 2012).Generation Y relentlessly searches for consumes shares and contributes to content along with work and play on social platforms. The behavior of generation Y has been discussed frequently, but not thoroughly researched. The Generation Y's active usage of social media has evoked a great interest in the marketers and researchers as they give a clear view on how the behavior will be futuristically(Bolton et al, 2013). Hence the selection of Generation Y is highly pertinent to the topic being studied. There has been no comprehensive acceptance on the beginning and end points for Generation Y. The researcher has followed the classification of Generation Y members i.e., people born between 1981 and 1999 (Bolton.et.al, 2013).

Generation Y consumers include individuals who belong to the age group between 18-32 years of age. The population considered for this study is Gen Y consumers using Facebook and residing in the city of Bangalore. The researcher has used Slovins' formula $n = N/1 + Ne^2$ where N = total population, e = margin of error.

According to 2011 census of Bangalore district, the total population in the age group of 18-32 years is 33,02,470 (www.indiastat.com). This population includes both rural and urban Bangalore. Hence an assumption is made that the population cannot be more than 33, 02,470. Using Slovins' formula with a margin of error as .05,we arrive at a sample size of 400.A sample size of 404 has been considered for this study.The sample has been selected through convenience sampling method. Convenience sampling method has been used to select the desired sample.

Based on the theoretical framework and the objectives a questionnaire has been developed. The data for this study was collected using a survey method. A survey technique uses the question and answer format to collect large amounts of data. Typically, self-administered research instruments have become the most frequently used data collection technique in survey research. According to Hair *et al.* (2008:165), surveys are the ideal option when a researcher is interested in studying motives and attitudes. Furthermore, they note that one of the main advantages of surveys is that a researcher can focus on a particular target population they wish to study. Both primary and secondary data was collected for the purpose of the study. A structured questionnaire comprising of pre-determined and logically related closed ended questions was used to collect primary data.

The research instrument was designed through extensive literature review. The questionnaire designed for the study uses a 5 point Likert scale ranging from "strongly agree" to "Strongly disagree". Likert scale is a rating scale which is extensively used and necessitates the respondents to denote the level of agreement or disagreement with the statements included in the questionnaire (Malhotra et.al, 2010). Each item in the scale has five response categories ranging from "strongly agree" to "strongly disagree." Likert scale is selected for this study as it is easy to construct, administer and easy for the respondents to understand (Malhotra et.al, 2010).The items for the constructs namely perceived usefulness and perceived ease of use was adopted from Davis (1993),Perceived enjoyment from Liao, Tsou and Shu (2008), Perceived credibility from Li and Suh (2015), Subjective norm from Peslak, Ceccucci and Sendall (2011), Intention to use Facebook from Liao, Tsou and Shu (2008) and items for using Facebook for purchase decision was framed by Researcher.

A pilot study conducted with 50 respondents gave clarity to the instruments for research. Cronbach α values for all the items in the questionnaire was more than 0.7 and hence considered reliable for research (Field, 2009).

Analysis of Results

'R' software has been used for analysis of data using Partial Least Square Structural Equation Model (PLSSEM). PLSSEM has the ability to simultaneously consider both measurement and structural model useful for theory building (Vinzi et al., 2010).

The Cronbach alpha values (Table 1) ranging between 0.695 and 0.808are above the threshold value of 0.7 (Nunnally, 1978). The composite reliability values (Table 1) between 0.832 and 0.904 are above 0.70 indicating that there are no issues regarding internal consistency. The AVE value for the first order constructs ranging between 0.623 and 0.759are above the cut-off value of 0.5 (Hair et al, 2011) indicating that there are no convergent validity issues. For each of the construct in Table.no.2 square root of AVE is found to be higher than the correlation values assuring the absence of discriminant validity.

The regression results for endogenous constructs have been considered in addition to the inspection of path coefficient. Table no.4 represents the T-value, significant value and R^2which is the amount of variance explained by the exogenous latent variable on the endogenous latent variable.

Table no.4 relating to intention to use Facebook shows that, except the path from Perceived Ease of Use, all other paths seem to be significant at 5% level. In case of FB Purchase Decision, the path from Intention to use FB on FB Purchase Decision seems to be significant at 5% level. The average prediction of the entire model accounts for 45% (0.454).

Table no. 5 represents the bootstrap validation of the path between independent variable and dependent variable. From the table it is noted that, except the path from Perceived Ease of Use to Intention to use

Figure 2. Model depicting the influence of various factors on intention to use Facebook and its influence on purchase decision making

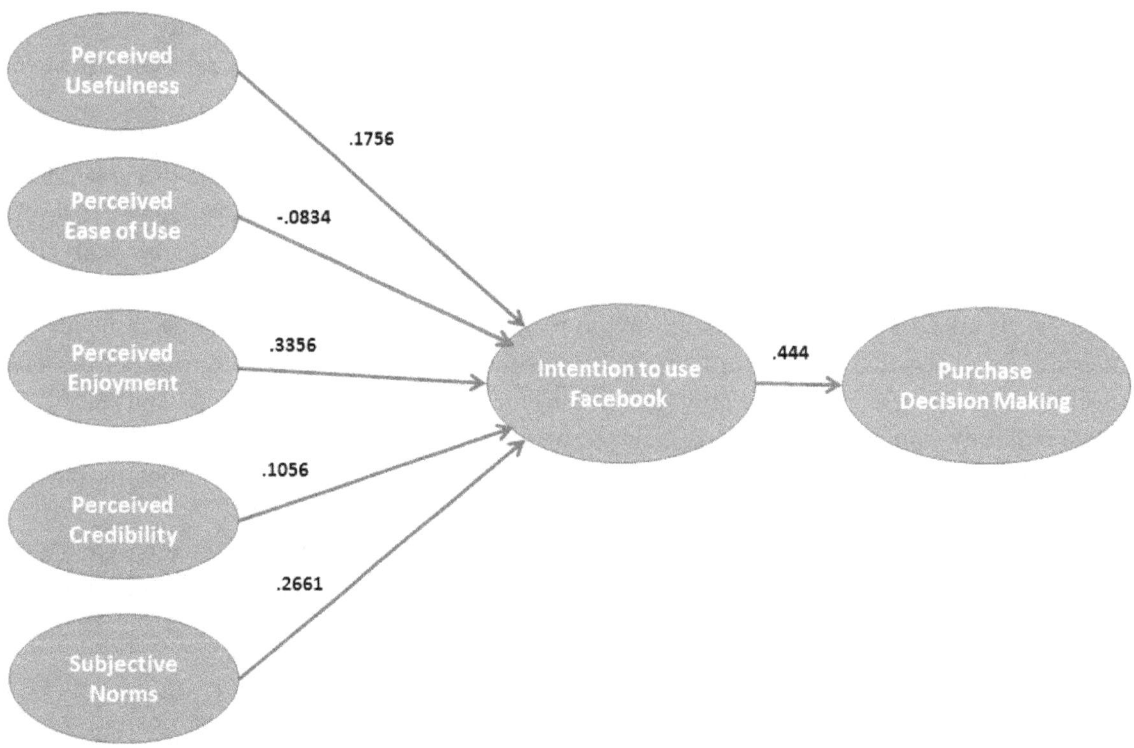

Facebook (-0.08) all other paths are significant at 5% level of significance which can be seen from the bootstrap intervals as it does not have zero within the percentile .025 and percentile .0975. On the basis of the above results we accept the hypotheses H1,H3, H4,H5 and H6. Perceived usefulness, perceived enjoyment, perceived credibility and subjective norm have a significant influence on intention to use Face book and intention to use Facebook has a significant influence on purchase decision making. Perceived ease of use does not have a significant influence on intention to use Facebook. Hence we reject Hypothesis H2.

The path between Perceived Enjoyment to Intention to use Facebook (0.34) has the highest value followed by subjective norm, perceived credibility and perceived usefulness. In case of path from Intention to use Facebook towards using Facebook for Purchase decision (0.44) the path is significant at 5% level.

Literally, these coefficients signify that every one unit of increment in Perceived Enjoyment strengthens its influence on intention to use Facebook by .34 times, while every one unit of increment in Subjective norm strengthens its influence on intention to use Facebook by .27 times, every one unit of increment in Perceived usefulness strengthens its influence on intention to use Facebook by .17 times and every one unit of increment in Perceived credibility strengthens its influence on intention to use Facebook by .11 times. Perceived ease of use does not have any significant influence on intention to use Facebook. Further one unit of increment in intention to use Facebook increases Facebook usage for purchase decisions by .44 times. The results also reveal that users' intention to use Facebook significantly increases their Facebook usage intention for purchase decisions.

Discussion

The results regarding Perceived usefulness are in conformance with many research studies.[(Davis et.al(1989), Keil, Beranek and Konsynksi (1995), James and Ron (2011), Leng, Lada and Muhammad (2011), Nasir et.al (2015)].Facebook is a very useful platform for users to not only stay connected with their friends but also make new friendships beyond cultural and geographical boundaries. It enables them to create a social identity for themselves online. It also helps them to get information about products and services. Facebook accords users the opportunity for self-expression and endows them with the feeling of being loved and liked by people who matter to them. Facebook provides users job leads and many applications which they can enjoy. Facebook has been adopted by generation Y users due to these reasons and has become a part of their daily lives.

The results related to perceived ease of use is in congruence with the studies of Keil.et.al (1995), Hu.et, al (1999), Chau and Hu (2001) and Curran.et.al (2011). The studies by Hu.et.al (1999) and Chau and Hu (2001) advocated that ease of use has no significant influence on perceived usefulness and attitude. They were of the opinion that this might express the constraints in the applicability of TAM model to technologies, users or both. The study by Keil.et.al (1995) conforms that is of use is a less important factor than perceived usefulness in deciding system use. They further added that low usefulness cannot be compensated by any amount of ease of use. It has become extremely important to understand that user interface refinement can overcome the impediments of low acceptance and use. Chau and Hu (2001) observed that "the increase in the competency of the user might specifically weaken the explanatory power of TAM. One possible justification is that "internet is considered easy to use in recent times and the benefits from learning through internet are already well known to students" (James and Sammy, 1983). Since this study involves Generation Y users, who are technologically savvy, ease of use of Facebook does not emerge as a significant factor.

The results with respect to perceived enjoyment are similar to the results of Davis et.al (1989) and Curran.et.al, (2011). Davis et.al, (1989) opined that perceived enjoyment an intrinsic motivation factor was significantly related to perceived ease of use and extended the TAM to include this factor (Lee. et.al.,2003). Curran.et.al, (2011) in their study found intention to use facebook is strongly influenced by attitude of the user. This reiterates the fact that social network users get a lot of enjoyment from using social networking. Users will be disappointed if the experience is less than enjoyable.

The results provide support for subjective norm as a factor influencing intention to use Facebook. This outcome is in line with the observation that individuals who are matter to generation Y users, mainly their friends and family can influence their behavior, i.e., using Facebook. The perceived social pressure has positively influenced Gen Y users to adopt Facebook and also use it in the context of purchase decisions. The results are in conformance with the studies of Foltz et.al, (2016) in the context of social networking security settings.

Perceived information credibility is considered very significant for the existence of any new media (Mackay.J.B, and Lowrey.W, 2011). Gaziano.C (1988) posits that "readers will pay very little attention to information that they consider believable". It very strongly predicts the readers' future actions with respect to recommendation or accepting the views of the information received. Facebook would not have achieved the penetration that it has achieved today if users had not perceived it credible. Hence Perceived credibility has a considerable impact on adoption of Facebook.

The study also posits the positive influence that users 'adoption of Facebook has on their intention to use it for purchase decisions. This is in agreement with multitudinous studies [Boyd and Ellison(2008), Hutter.et.al, (2013), Turri.et.al, (2013), Martinka (2012), Durban&WeiLei (2012), Desai.et.al. (2012)]. Although Facebook started as a platform for people to interact with each other, it has also provided organisations possibilities to create fan pages for the products or the firm. This has become an important tool to communicate with the stake holder. The knowledge the consumers gain through social media is considered extremely valuable due to features like variety of viewpoints covered, accessibility, exclusivity and being real time.

Implications

The examination of the factors influencing the adoption of Facebook has provided useful results. Perceived enjoyment followed by subjective norms, perceived usefulness and perceived credibility significantly influence the adoption of Facebook.

Since users of social networks derive a lot of enjoyment using social networks, they will be disappointed if the experience is less enjoyable. Since the main benefit of using Facebook is to connect to friends, enjoyment is expected to influence adoption of Facebook. Connecting to friends provides enjoyment, inducing interest and pleasure. As users have already experienced it as a medium of enjoyment, they consider enjoyment as a significant factor. Social network sites vendors should assimilate elements which include fun into their sites by giving special impetus to functions which are rich in entertainment like creative contents, games, video sharing, and so on to keep Generation Y consumers happy and entertained.

Subjective Norm is the "Social pressure perceived to engage or not engage in a particular behavior"(Tarkiainen and Sundquist, 2005).Social circle incentive has augmented the usage of social networks. The need to belong to this communication circle puts pressure on users to have more social participations. This can expand through wider usage of social networks across the population.

Subjective Norm is the understanding of an individual with respect to the importance they accord to meet others' beliefs. While contemplating whether to perform an action or not the opinions of one's family members and friends matter. If an individual feels that their family, relatives and friends favor an idea, the behavior intention would be amplified. On the contrary if an individual think that their family, relatives and friends are not in favor of an idea, the behavior intention will reduce. The number of friends on any particular social site is an important predictor of motives (Tarkiainen et.al, 2005). People in India are motivated to use Information technology in various fields in order to stay in tune with the social change that has occurred as a result of IT. Another reason could be the emotional fear (Lelisho et.al, 2023)of being left behind their friends who use Facebook.

In the context of technology adoption in a market the subjective norm construct can be strengthened through positive word of mouth. A positive 'buzz' can be highly beneficial. Since Generation Y users are more technology savvy and responsive to changes, they are considerably influenced by features of technology and views of peers than older students. Since computer usage has become very common, managers should acknowledge that utility, usability and social features are now less prominent in forming attitude, intentions and behavior (Schepers et al., 2006). The peer influence grows stronger compared to family influence among the youngsters. Hence peers are becoming an important socialization factor for this group (Lerner & Steinberg, 2009).

Though it is impossible to erase online rumors, information that is credible on online social networks can play a crucial role for the sustenance of social networks. Vendors should take due cognizance of various elements of medium credibility if they want to make sure that users view the User Generated Content on their networks as credible and beneficia (Pandey et.al, 2020,2021 and 2022)l. Managers of social network platforms must ensure high level of transparency and interaction (Perceived willingness of individuals to share information frankly and freely with others) on their platform to be certain of high information credibility levels. They should also be cognizant of the factors which impact credibility of information, especially when the necessity for reliable sources and truth is high. Information users should pay more attention to augment strength (extent of completeness and logic of a message) of a message (Ruhonan et al., 2015).

On the basis of this investigation, future studies should continue to identify the determinants which influence frequent use of social networking sites to further our present comprehension of this new and burgeoning phenomenon of communication and to assist in the advancement of pertinent policies and strategies.

CONCLUSION

This research corroborates the robustness of TAM, and predominantly extends support for the application of the model in the context of predicting Facebook adoption among Generation Y consumers. The current research extends support for integrating perceived usefulness, subjective norm, perceived enjoyment and perceived credibility into the basic model as the results have indicated that they have a significant influence on intention to use Facebook. The marketers should attempt to extensively utilize social networks to foster better electronic word of mouth communications and thereby solicit the interest of Generation Y users. On the one hand, the results extend the scientific debate on Generation Y's behavior intentions. On the other hand, they provide valuable evidence to embolden managers to integrate social networks like Facebook into their marketing strategies. The features of Facebook should be exploited by organizations for building and augmenting competitive advantage.

REFERENCES

Ajzen, I., & Fishbein, M. (1980). *Understanding Attitudes and predicting social Behavior*. Prentice- Hall.

Aldhmour, F., & Sarayrah, I. (2016). An investigation of factors influencing consumers? Intention to use online shopping: An empirical study in south of Jordan. *Journal of Internet Banking and Commerce*, 21.

Alomoush, K. S., Yaseen, S. G., & Alma'aitah, M. A. (2012). The Impact of Arab Cultural Values on Online Social Networking: The Case of Facebook. *World Academy of Science, Engineering and Technology*, 67.

Alshibly, H. (2014). An Empirical Investigation into Factors Influencing the Intention to Use E-learning System: An Extended Technology Acceptance Model. *British Journal of Applied Science and Technology, 4*. Advance online publication. doi:10.9734/BJAST/2014/10033

Bailey, James, & Pearson, W., Sammy. (1983). Development of a Tool for Measuring and Analyzing Computer User Satisfaction. *Management Science*, *29*, 530–545. doi:10.1287/mnsc.29.5.530

Bennett, S., Maton, K., & Kervin, L. (2008). The digital natives' debate: A critical review of the evidence. *British Journal of Educational Technology*, *39*(5), 775–786.

Birdsall, W. F. (2007). Web 2.0 as a social movement. *Webology, 4*(2). http://www.webology.ir/2007/v4n2/a40.html

Boyd, D. M., & Ellison, N. B. (2008). Social network sites: Definition, history and scholarship. *Journal of Computer-Mediated Communication*, *13*(1), 210–230.

Chau, P. Y. K., & Hu, P. J. H. (2001). Information technology acceptance by individual professionals: A model comparison approach. *Decision Sciences*, *32*(4), 699–719.

Cheng, T., Lam, D., & Yeung, C. (2006). Adoption of internet banking: An empirical study in Hong Kong. *Decision Support Systems*, *42*, 1158–1572.

Cuong, Linh, & Ha. (2015). Factors affecting Intention to use Facebook – Banking of Generation Y in Vietnam. *International Journal of Financial Research, 6*(4).

Curran, J. (2011). Academy of Marketing Studies Journal. *Suppl. Special*, *15*(1), 21–38.

Darban, A. (2012). *The impact of online social networks on consumers purchase decision-The study of food retailers* [Master's Thesis]. Jonkoping International Business School, Jonkoping University.

Davis, F. (1993). Users' acceptance of information technology: System characteristics, users' perception and behavioural impacts. *International Journal of Man-Machine Studies*, *38*(3), 475–487.

Davis, F., Bagozzi, R. P., & Warshaw, P. R. (1989). User acceptance of computer technology: A comparison of two theoretical models. *Management Science*, *35*(8), 982–1002.

Davis, F. D. (1989). Perceived usefulness, perceived ease of use, and user acceptance of information technology. *Management Information Systems Quarterly*, *13*(3), 319–340.

Davis, F. D., Bagozzi, R. P., & Warshaw, P. R. (1992). Extrinsic and Intrinsic Motivation to Use Computers in the Workplace. *Journal of Applied Social Psychology*, *22*(14), 1111–1132.

Desai, Shukla, & Thakkar. (2012). Effect of facebook on purchasing behavior of youth. *International Journal of Research in Computer Application and Management, 2*(11).

Field, A. (2009). *Discovering Statistics using SPSS*. Sage.

Fishbein, M., & Ajzen, I. (1975). *Belief, attitude, intention and behavior: An introduction to theory and research*. Addison-Wesley.

Foltz, C., Newkirk, H., & Schwager, P. (2016). An Empirical Investigation of Factors that Influence Individual Behavior toward Changing Social Networking Security Settings. *Journal of Theoretical and Applied Electronic Commerce Research*, *11*, 2–2. doi:10.4067/S0718-18762016000200002

Fornell, C., & Larcker, D. F. (1981). Evaluating Structural Equation Models with Unobservable Variables and Measurement Error. *JMR, Journal of Marketing Research*, *18*, 39–50.

Gaziano, C. (1988). How credible is the credibility crisis? *The Journalism Quarterly*, *65*, 267–278, 375.

Gefen, D., & Straub, D. W. (1997). Gender differences in the perception and use of e-mail:an extension of the technology acceptance model. *Management Information Systems Quarterly*, *21*(4), 389–399.

Godes, D., & Mayzlin, D. (2004). Using online conversations to study word-of-mouth communication. *Marketing Science*, *23*(4), 545 560.

Hair, J. F., Hult, G. T. M., Ringle, C. M., & Sarstedt, M. (2014). *A primer on partial least squares structural equation modeling (PLS-SEM)*. Sage.

Hair, J. F., Ringle, C. M., & Sarstedt, M. (2011). PLS-SEM: Indeed a silver bullet. *Journal of Marketing Theory and Practice*, *19*(2), 139–151.

Hu, Chau, & Sheng, & Kar. (1999). Examining the technology acceptance model using physician acceptance of telemedicine technology. *Journal of Management Information Systems*, *16*(2), 91–112.

Hutter, K., Hautz, J., Dennhardt, S., & Fuller, J. (2013). The impact of user interactions in social media on brand awareness and purchase intention, the case of MINI on facebook. *Journal of Product and Brand Management*, *22*(5/6), 342–345.

Keil, M. (1995). Usefulness and Ease of use: Field study evidence regarding task consideration. *Decision Support Systems*, *13*, 75–91.

Lee, J., Cho, H., Gay, G., Davison, B., & Ingraffea, T. (2003). Technology acceptance and social networking in distance learning. *Journal of Educational Technology & Society*, *6*(2), 50–61.

Lelisho, M. E., Pandey, D., Alemu, B. D., Pandey, B. K., & Tareke, S. A. (2023). The negative impact of social media during COVID-19 pandemic. *Trends in Psychology*, *31*(1), 123–142.

Leng, G. S., Lada, S., & Muhammad, M. Z. (2011, August). An Exploration of Social Networking Sites (SNS) Adoption in Malaysia using Technology Acceptance Model (TAM), Theory of Planned Behavior (TPB) and Intrusive Motivation. *Journal of Internet Banking and Commerce*, *16*(2).

Lerner, R. M., & Steinberg, L. (2009). *Individual Bases Adolescent Development*. Handbook of Adolescent Psychology. John Wiley and Sons.

Li, R., & Suh, A. (2015). Factors influencing information credibility on social media platforms: Evidence form Facebook pages. *Procedia Computer Science*, *72*, 314–328.

Lin, K., & Lu, H. (2011). Intention to Continue Using Facebook Fan Pages from the Perspective of Social Capital Theory. *Cyberpsychology, Behavior, and Social Networking*, *14*.

Mackay, J. B., & Lowrey, W. (2011). The credibility divide: Reader trust of online newspapers and blogs. *Journal of Media Sociology*, *3*(1-4), 39–57.

Mann, B.J.S., & Sahni, S.K. (2012). Profiling Adopter Categories of Internet Banking in India: An Empirical Study. *Vision: The Journal of Business Perspective, 16*(4), 283-295.

Martinka, L. (2012). *How social media communities impact consumer behavior* [Dissertation]. Gonzaga University.

Muntinga, D. G., Moorman, M., & Smit, E. G. (2011). Introducing COBRAs; exploring motivations for brand-related social media use. *International Journal of Advertising*, *30*, 13–46. doi:10.2501/IJA-30-1-013-046

Naresh & Dash. (2013). *Marketing Research: An applied orientation*. Pearson.

Nasir, M. A., Yago, M., & Wu, J. (2015). Influence of psychographics and risk perception of internet banking adoption: Current State of affairs in Britain. *Marketing Intelligence and Planning*. Accessed at https://www.researchgate.net/publication/281752024

Nunnally, J. C. (1978). *Psychometric theory* (2nd ed.). Mc Graw Hill.

Pandey, D., Aswari, A., Taufiqurakman, M., Khalim, A., & Azahrah, F. F. (2021). System Of Education Changes Due to Covid-19 Pandemic. *Asian Journal of Advances in Research*, 10-15.

Pandey, B. K., Mane, D., Nassa, V. K. K., Pandey, D., Dutta, S., Ventayen, R. J. M., & Rastogi, R. (2021). Secure text extraction from complex degraded images by applying steganography and deep learning. In *Multidisciplinary approach to modern digital steganography* (pp. 146–163). IGI Global.

Pandey, B. K., Pandey, D., Wairya, S., & Agarwal, G. (2021). An advanced morphological component analysis, steganography, and deep learning-based system to transmit secure textual data. *International Journal of Distributed Artificial Intelligence*, *13*(2), 40–62.

Pandey, B. K., Pandey, D., Wairya, S., Agarwal, G., Dadeech, P., Dogiwal, S. R., & Pramanik, S. (2022). Application of integrated steganography and image compressing techniques for confidential information transmission. *Cyber Security and Network Security*, 169-191.

Pandey, B. K., Pandey, D., Wariya, S., & Agarwal, G. (2021). A deep neural network-based approach for extracting textual images from deteriorate images. *EAI Endorsed Transactions on Industrial Networks and Intelligent Systems*, *8*(28), e3–e3.

Pandey, B. K., Pandey, D., Wariya, S., Aggarwal, G., & Rastogi, R. (2021). Deep learning and particle swarm optimisation-based techniques for visually impaired humans' text recognition and identification. *Augmented Human Research*, *6*, 1–14.

Pandey, D., Wairya, S., & Pradhan, B. (2022). Understanding COVID-19 response by twitter users: A text analysis approach. *Heliyon*, *8*(8), e09994.

Park, J., & Gursoy, D. (2012). Generation effects on work engagement among U.S. hotel employees. *International Journal of Hospitality Management*, *31*(4), 1195–1202.

Peslak, A., Cecucci, W., & Sendall, P. (2011). *An Empirical Study of Social Networking Behavior using theory of Reasoned action*. Conference for Information Systems Applied Research.

Pikkarainen, T., Pikkarainen, K., Karjaluoto, H., & Pahnila, S. (2004). Consumer acceptance of online banking: An extension of the technology acceptance model. *Internet Research*, *14*, 224–235.

Remco & Helms. (2014). *Analyzing social influence through social media*. IADIS International Conference on Information Systems, Madrid, Spain.

Ruth, Parasuraman, Hoefnagels, Migchels, Kabadayi, Gruber, Komarova, & Solnet. (2013). Understanding Generation Y and their use of social media: A review and research agenda. *Journal of Service Management, 24*(3), 245-267.

Sarah, Kearns, Bennett, & Kawalek. (2011). Consumer Behavior in Social Networking Sites: Implications for marketers. *Irish Journal of Management*, *30*(2), 47.

Shih, H.-P. (2004). An empirical study on predicting user acceptance of e-shopping on the web. *Information & Management*, *41*(6), 351–368.

Thorsten, Gwinner, Walsh, & Gremler. (2003). Electronic word of mouth via consumer opinion platform: What motivates consumers to articulate themselves on the internet? *Journal of Interactive Marketing*, *18*(1), 38–52.

Turri, A. M., Sumith, K. H., & Kemp, E. (2013). Developing affective brand commitment through social media. *Journal of Electronic Commerce Research*, 201–214.

Venkatesh, V., & Davis, F. D. (2000). A theoretical extension of the technology acceptance model: Four longitudinal field studies. *Management Science*, *46*, 186–204. doi:10.1287/mnsc.46.2.186.11926

Walker, M., & Kent, A. (2012). The Roles of Credibility and Social Consciousness in the Corporate Philanthropy-Consumer Behavior Relationship. *Journal of Business Ethics, 116*(2), 341-353.

Wathen, C. N., & Burkell, J. (2002). Believe it or not: Factors influencing credibility on the Web. *Journal of the American Society for Information Science and Technology*, *53*(2), 134–144.

Yang & Lin. (2011). Factors affecting intention to use Facebook to support problem-based learning among employees in a Taiwanese manufacturing company. *African Journal of Business Management, 5*, 9014-9022.

Zandhersami, H., & Geranmaych, P. (2014). Determinants of user acceptance of internet banking: An empirical study. *Management Science Letters*, *4*, 1369–1374.

Zhang, J., & Daugherty, T. (2009). Third-Person Effect and Social Networking: Implications for Online Marketing and Word-Of-Mouth Communication. *American Journal of Business*, *24*(2), 53–69.

ANNEXURE

Table 1. Internal consistency and convergent validity

First Order Constructs	Items	Outer Loadings	Cronbach Alpha	Composite Reliability	AVE
Perceived Usefulness	v12.1	0.812	0.783	0.874	0.697
	v12.2	0.858			
	v12.3	0.835			
Perceived Ease of use	v12.4	0.874	0.762	0.863	0.677
	v12.5	0.849			
	v12.6	0.74			
Perceived Enjoyment	v12.7	0.857	0.747	0.856	0.666
	v12.8	0.851			
	v12.9	0.735			
Perceived Credibility	v12.11	0.865	0.841	0.904	0.759
	v12.12	0.893			
	v12.13	0.855			
Subjective Norms	v12.14	0.863	0.695	0.832	0.623
	v12.15	0.848			
	v12.16	0.636			
Intention to use Facebook	v12.17	0.837	0.808	0.886	0.722
	v12.18	0.876			
	v12.19	0.836			
Facebook Purchase Decision	v12.20	0.849	0.739	0.852	0.654
	v12.21	0.803			
	v12.22	0.773			

Table 2. Correlation matrix and square root of AVE

	1	2	3	4	5	6	7
Perceived Usefulness	0.83						
Perceived Ease of use	0.686	0.82					
Perceived Enjoyment	0.527	0.501	0.82				
Perceived Credibility	0.457	0.435	0.422	0.87			
Subjective Norms	0.399	0.396	0.446	0.34	0.79		
Intention to use FB	0.45	0.357	0.549	0.382	0.488	0.85	
FB Purchase Decision	0.649	0.631	0.48	0.509	0.391	0.444	0.81

Note: Square root of AVE are represented as bold in the diagonal

Table 3. Factor loadings and cross-loadings

	Items	1	2	3	4	5	6	7
1.Perceived Usefulness	v12.1	0.812	0.545	0.471	0.362	0.355	0.369	0.561
	v12.2	0.858	0.579	0.44	0.373	0.311	0.348	0.541
	v12.3	0.835	0.59	0.411	0.406	0.33	0.405	0.525
2.Perceived Ease of use	v12.4	0.556	0.874	0.426	0.372	0.337	0.336	0.514
	v12.5	0.604	0.849	0.447	0.359	0.348	0.295	0.579
	v12.6	0.541	0.74	0.362	0.347	0.293	0.24	0.465
3.Perceived Enjoyment	v12.7	0.41	0.371	0.857	0.362	0.357	0.498	0.383
	v12.8	0.359	0.346	0.851	0.312	0.394	0.44	0.33
	v12.9	0.537	0.531	0.735	0.362	0.342	0.4	0.476
4.Perceived Credibility	v12.11	0.401	0.387	0.386	0.865	0.331	0.348	0.41
	v12.12	0.398	0.352	0.326	0.893	0.24	0.323	0.449
	v12.13	0.395	0.398	0.389	0.855	0.315	0.325	0.472
	v12.14	0.338	0.306	0.425	0.243	0.863	0.419	0.328
5.Subjective Norms	v12.15	0.293	0.321	0.344	0.264	0.848	0.442	0.273
	v12.16	0.335	0.332	0.275	0.335	0.636	0.27	0.359
6.Intention to use Facebook	v12.17	0.36	0.281	0.493	0.29	0.368	0.837	0.342
	v12.18	0.375	0.296	0.486	0.338	0.411	0.876	0.361
	v12.19	0.409	0.33	0.425	0.342	0.461	0.836	0.424
7.FB Purchase Decision	v12.20	0.617	0.557	0.39	0.434	0.32	0.366	0.849
	v12.21	0.455	0.477	0.417	0.439	0.349	0.404	0.803
	v12.22	0.512	0.502	0.351	0.348	0.269	0.291	0.773

Table 4. Structural model assessment

Intention to Use Facebook						**GoF**
	Estimate	**Std. Error**	**T Value**	**P Value**	**R2**	**0.454**
Intercept	0	0.04	0	1	0.4	
Perceived Usefulness	0.18	0.06	3	0		
Perceived Ease of use	-0.08	0.06	-1.46	0.15		
Perceived Enjoyment	0.34	0.05	6.6	0		
Perceived Credibility	0.11	0.05	2.25	0.03		
Subjective Norms	0.27	0.05	5.74	0		
FB Purchase Decision						
	Estimate	Std. Error	T value	P value	R2	
Intercept	0	0.05	0	1	0.2	
Intention to use FB	0.44	0.05	9.64	0		

Table 5. Bootstrap validation

Paths			Original	Mean. Boot	St. Error	perc.025	perc.975
Perceived Usefulness	→	Intention to use FB	0.18	0.18	0.06	0.05	0.29
Perceived Ease of use	→	Intention to use FB	-0.08	-0.08	0.06	-0.2	0.04
Perceived Enjoyment	→	Intention to use FB	0.34	0.34	0.05	0.25	0.42
Perceived Credibility	→	Intention to use FB	0.11	0.1	0.05	0.01	0.2
Subjective Norms	→	Intention to use FB	0.27	0.27	0.06	0.16	0.38
Intention to use FB	→	FB Purchase Decision	0.44	0.45	0.04	0.36	0.53

Chapter 3
Analyzing Big Data Using Recent Machine Learning Techniques to Assist Consumers in Online Purchase Decision

Santosh Ramkrishna Durugkar
Independent Researcher, India

ABSTRACT

Sentiments can be expressed in a variety of ways like angry, happy, sad, surprised, etc. Recent machine learning (ML) algorithms classify sentiments and assist customers in their purchase decision. Many organizations are predicting the possible correlation between growth of the business and customer satisfaction. On different social media platforms, customers give 'ratings' to a specific product or service. ML helps in knowing the reasons and assists the businesses to improvise in the weaker sections. Natural language processing integrates data and applies "tokenization" to extract the tokens (words) from the datasets (feedbacks). A set of positive, negative, and neutral words and sentences can be compared to find the relevance. Naïve Bayes classifier, KNN classifier, etc. help knowing the trend and processes the large volume of data in minimal time. This approach helps increasing the predictive power of the model and tests remaining data. Bayesian factor robustness helps analyzing different attribute specifications from the large volume.

INTRODUCTION

Sentiment analysis has similar names like opinion mining, opinion extraction, sentiment mining, and subjective analysis. Analyzing the sentiments is the 'key trend' in many business applications as it directly affects the business growth. It tries to process the given data and retrieve desired sentiments based on mood, emotion, different interpersonal stances, and attitudes. Using a bag of words, annotated lexicons,

DOI: 10.4018/978-1-6684-8753-2.ch003

syntactic patterns, and paragraphs one can interpret the features of sentiments. There are many applications that can be used in various industries like hotel, education, medical, etc. Ultimate objective is to improve the quality of services and the products. Continuous 'feedbacks' and 'improvising accordingly' helps businesses grow rapidly. Machine learning (ML) tools and techniques helps identifying different patterns from the feedbacks received from 'n' customers. One can apply classification methods such as Naïve Bayes to classify the given data used for prediction. Other techniques can be used such as linear regression, deep learning methods, support vector machine (SVM) etc. The model can be designed to help the developers to extract the polarity of words/sentences under the following scale:

a. Positive
b. Very positive
c. Neutral / can't say
d. Negative

It is possible to apply the "scaling" like 10- best and 01- worst ratings. Many businesses are applying such techniques to get the feedbacks from the customers. In many countries a CCI – consumer confidence index based on sentiment analysis is prepared to analyze the business growth. Study suggests this index gives brief idea how people think about government policies or a specific business.

Sentiment analysis model can consist of following steps:

a. Extracting feedbacks from different platforms and applying "tokenization"
b. Vectorization
c. Training & Testing the selected data
d. Testing the remaining data
e. Evaluating the results
f. Predicting the future data and assisting the customers in purchase decisions

Types of sentiment analysis: -

Based on Grading

- *Positive*
- *Very positive*
- *Negative*
- *Neutral*

Emotion detection

- *Happiness*
- *Sadness*

Table 1. Different categories of the sentiments

Happy	Surprised	Not happy
Angry	Neutral	Disappointed
Excited	Scared	Kind

- *Anger*
- *Disgust*
- *Neutral*

Aspect based sentiment analysis

- *Focuses on specific 'product' or 'service'*

Intent based sentiment analysis

- *Getting 'intent' of the customers & finding the 'reasons' behind such intents.*

Aspect-Based Sentiment Analysis

"The voice quality of cellphone is very good". In this example of aspect based sentiment analysis, aspect is '*voice quality*'. Customer evaluated the performance of cellphone on the basis of 'voice quality'. Feedbacks received from customers based on this approach helps improving business strategies by focusing on the products or services offered by the organization.

Intent-Based Sentiment Analysis

It is based on the 'intents' of the customers and analyzes the intentions behind the given ratings, feedbacks, etc. Users/customers posts messages, social media posts, opinions/feedbacks on different products or services and intent based sentiment analysis analyzes all those intentions.

Intent classification is based on machine learning and natural language processing (NLP) which processes different 'words', 'texts', or 'messages' with a specific intent. E.g. if a user post a message 'tried to purchase 'xyz' product using the website but unable to add it into the cart' – meaning is user wish to purchase that product and categorizes it under the 'interested' intent.

Examples of Sentiment Analysis

1. Monitoring social media

There is an incredible growth of active social media users, posts and messages. Every day there is an increase in the large volume of 'web data'. To process such large volume of data and retrieve meaningful information one can use 'sentiment analysis' tools.

2. Customer support

In today's competitive world, every business has its own '*customer support*' team to assist their valuable customers. It is necessary to treat their 'complaints', 'service related queries' on high priority and provide better solutions within stipulated time. If the queries are solved within time with better solution, it helps maintaining the customer base.

- 'Customer support representative hold me for 20 minutes and yet my queries are not solved'.
- After reading the above statement it is cleared that, customer is not happy with the support team and it is expected not to hold any customer for long time.

3. Feedback analysis

There are many techniques, third party agencies available to note a 'feedback' from the customers. Customers can give different ratings, scores to the products and services offered. If the 'feedback' is negative, then there is a room to improvise the products and services.

4. Research in marketing

As discussed earlier for any business there could be many competitors in the market. Research in marketing helps distinguishing features, services, and products offered by different companies. Market research takes feedback from customers about 'new' as well as 'existing' products.

- AI (artificial intelligence) and ML (machine learning) based sentiment analysis tool for banking, healthcare, call centers etc.

5. Product analysis

Sentiment analysis helps acquiring feedback from customers. It analyzes the product, price and service on the basis of all the feedbacks received and focus on the weakness. Product analysis using sentiment analysis tools improves the quality and stand in a competition.

- If someone takes a feedback from the customers and asks about a 'XYZ' brand. Customer's feedback must be noted for analysis purpose.
- During the feedback if customers are giving 'positive or negative' ratings for the products and services offered by the brand 'XYZ' then it helps improve the business.

Challenges in Sentiment Analysis

There are some challenges in the sentiment analysis process as listed below:

- **Tone:** It is hard to identify the tone of the sentences and therefore more sophisticated tools are required to identify the correct meaning.
- **Polarity:** It is easier to handle the 'good', 'bad' feedbacks. If the customer gives feedback such as "*not so good*" which quite challenging.
- **Comparison:** If the customer gives feedback such as "*product A is bigger than B*" then the system should not mishandle it i.e. correct and all the necessary specifications must be considered.
- **Handling sentiment analysis in multilingual environment:** A statement/word used in expressing interest or feedback can lose its whole meaning if translated into another language.
- **Audio / visual feedback:** Model must be capable enough to handle the audio / visual data by interpreting the correct meaning.

LITERATURE REVIEW

Authors (Jiang & Leung, 2014) have suggested that large volume of data is collected from heterogeneous sources. Handling such data became a difficult task. This paper focused on identifying the interesting patterns from this big data which reduces the computational efforts as the data size gets reduced. Authors have suggested using frequent pattern mining could be a useful solution implemented with MapReduce tool. Authors have surveyed big data analytics and tools involved in this process, quantitative processes involved used to mine required data from large volume. Few techniques are already surveyed by the authors are as follows:

1. Cloud computing
2. Data analytics
3. Machine learning
4. Data analytics

Authors (Kanagasabai et al., 2016) have proposed a hybrid approach which is based on classification methods. Classification, it is based on the identified features / feature set. Hence, one thing is clear that records / values or the Datasets itself must be processed in the initial phase. Then sampling can be performed where one can select the representative data and using this representative data it is possible to find the desired, accurate results. Hybrid approach – it is based on classifying the web pages. Web page classification based on the contents, link structure etc. However, if the collection is large in size then it cannot be a feasible task. Hence, authors have suggested classifying based on URLs. All URLs - incoming and outgoing needs to be analyzed. One paper referred by the authors suggested that, processing URLs can be based on tokenization. Authors have termed this accuracy as recall. Interesting method is discussed by the authors is a n-gram which works based on words and forming the feature sets could be a better approach. To implement this system authors suggested developing a URL classifier by embedding n-gram method. Comparing and retrieving the accurate relevant results SVM support vector machine model can be used.

The paper (Nikolov et al., 2017) has discussed data cleaning with its importance in effective and efficient retrieval. This paper describes the data anomalies with different steps to handle these anomalies. Authors have considered these anomalies for improving the quality of software products. Dealing with large volume of data require to process it in the earlier phases as maximum time and efforts are required in executing the data cleaning. In data driven applications, it is necessary to process the large volume of data which many be in unstructured and structured format or at most in semi-structured format. Once users identify and process this type of data then can perform the classification, clustering, etc. steps suggested in the data mining. In this process it seems easier to process the structured and semi-structured data. However, it becomes quite difficult to process the unstructured data. This unstructured data may be documents, may be audio and video files etc. In this paper authors have discussed data wrangling, ETL (extraction, transform & load). Authors have focused on cost effective way for the execution of this data wrangling process. ETL plays an important role in data wrangling. Nowadays, applications are dealing with big data where the data is large in size, its nature is heterogeneous. Big data processing requires time and efforts to reduce the same there is need to develop a cost effective model. This cost effective model deals with the variety and veracity of the big data. In the paper authors have focused on automating the wrangling process. In this automation, context data reference and main data will be considered.

The process of capturing the contextual data plays an important role which helps in better data retrieval (Abel et al., 2017; Boyapati et al., 20202). Authors have noted big data can be processed to capture required important information can be aggregated to visualize. Once this aggregated information is collected and trained, using the same pattern other emerging patterns could be investigated to find the *abnormal patterns*.

In this way, authors have suggested one can develop a visualization framework. Authors have suggested developing Uniform Architecture to handle the heterogeneous data, avoiding complexity in processing such data. This framework can avoid the data redundancy and unbalanced data structures (Ajayan et al., 2018). Data steam is nothing but a sequence of stream to detect the anomaly patterns. It is obvious that if the size of data stream is large then it requires sufficient available memory else it cannot be saved in the memory. This paper is based on detecting the anomaly patterns which can be implemented using outlier detection methods. Author has proposed a drift detection approach for handling streaming data. Drift detection detects the new emerging patterns in the data stream (Park, C. H. 2018).

Authors (Agrawal et al., 2018) have focused on churn analysis – it is an approach to find why customers closes / ceases their relationships with an organization. This approach is very useful and creates a scope for organizations for improving their strategies. Strategies are nothing but the way of working, day-to-day operations etc. Analyzing the customer's behavior and finding the root cause behind broken relationship between the organization and customers. Authors have proposed a system based on neural network and deep learning methods.

To develop this system initial step is to classify the features. Features must be identified, i.e. Usage patterns (features), customer features, other supporting features, etc. Authors (Abd El-Jawad et al., 2018) have discussed the tremendous increase in volume of data. This increase is due to 'n' users of social media and their messages on the web. Users are giving their opinions about any topic, subject, etc. These messages are collected, process to find the sentiments. Authors have proposed a hybrid system i.e. combination of text mining, neural networks and deep learning algorithms. With the sentiment analysis viewpoints can be generated. These are nothing but classifying the positive and negative conclusions about a certain subject. In this proposed system authors have used dataset of the TWITTER users.

A paper referred by the authors (Bao et al., 2019) suggests applying the sample rebalancing, feature learning, discriminative learning, etc. *K*-means clustering algorithm could be a best algorithm where K centers are predefined and acts as latent points. These latent points can be known as landmark points and are capable to define the data distribution under their respective classes. Authors have combined CNN and RNN using ensemble learning, in the previous papers ensemble learning technique is already discussed. Authors (Goularas & Kamis, 2019; Onan, A. 2021) have used Twitter data for sentiment analysis. In recent years due to increase in 'n' users of the social media there is a notable increase in the volume of data. Authors have discussed this social media data can be used for sentiment analysis. However, this data is heterogeneous in nature which must be processed, represented in an unified way. Semantic analysis plays an important role in this case to extract the sentiments. This approach helps the end users in customer analysis, product analysis and purchasing habits.

Authors (Ahmad et al., 2019; Kahani & Mighan, 2021) have focused on use of recent deep learning methods in speech recognition, classifying the images, language processing, etc. To process the big data efficient and effective algorithms are required, new techniques such as machine learning, deep learning etc. can be applied to process this large volume of data. A predictive model is proposed by the authors (Cao et al., 2019; Smart, P. S., 2021) is based on deep learning methods. Authors have used stack auto-encoder network to extract the features from datasets. In the next phase of this model logistic regression is used to classify the customers. A backpropagation algorithm is used to tune the parameters applied and training the logistic regression. Customer churn analysis is the backbone for any business as every business wants to maintain their customer segment. If there is observable churn or drift in customers, then it will affect the business.

In the paper (Annareddy & Tammina, 2020) authors have proposed a deep learning technique convolutional neural network to grab the sentiments for evaluation purpose. In the introductory section of this paper authors have mentioned a tremendous increase in the social data on the platforms such as Twitter, Facebook and Instagram. 'n' people are using social media platforms and giving their comments on a particular topic, item or on the news. These comments, opinions can be extracted to find the similar patterns which could be useful for the organization. Authors have discussed long short-term memory LSTM, Gated recurrent unit, bidirectional long short-term memory, and convolutional neural network (CNN), deep learning methods etc. Authors (Aydin & Salur, 2020) have experimented word embedding, extracting the features, classifying the features and forming the sentiments on datasets. Authors have at last compared and presented a study after applying the basic models on datasets. In the introductory part of the paper authors have mentioned the tremendous increase in the users on the social media platform and their reviews, opinions, feedbacks. Authors (Kang et al., 2020; Caraka et al., 2020) have presented a comparative study of different deep learning classification models. Extensive study has been conducted by the authors using 08 deep learning models, 03 CNN models, 05 recurrent neural network models. This comparative study is executed on 13 datasets. Rapid growth of e-commerce websites, applications, and users are increased and their messages, reviews, feedbacks, opinions, etc. about a certain topic / subject too. It is impossible for someone to process and analyze these reviews and feedbacks manually and hence machine learning methods, algorithms can be applied. Algorithms can process it in a less time and produce appropriate results.

RESEARCH METHODS

Sentiment Analysis

Proposed system works on the following principles:

- Preparation of sets of positive, negative and neutral words.
- Setting the threshold value
- Extracting the meaningful and relevant patterns from the given dataset.
    - The model should consider lists of positive, negative and neutral words. Evaluating the derived patterns against these sets and calculating the overall percentage (effectiveness in expressing the sentiment) of sentence in terms of positive, negative and neutral.

Part of speech tagging (POS) is the example of sentiment analysis, which identifies given document for verbs, nouns, adverbs and adjectives. A model needs to be developed to test the remaining data. Using the methods specified under deep learning results can be obtained quickly. Low-level tokenization and syntax analysis can be a part of the sentiment analysis process. Given 'sentences', 'texts', 'posts' or messages can be divided into tokens and 'tagging' helps to classify these tokens into 'segments'. Tagging is known as 'labeling' i.e. assigning 'labels' to classify the generated tokens. Part of speech tagging consist of following – nouns, singular noun, plural noun, adverb, interjection, verbs, comma, colon, semi-colon, left and right bracket, etc. Based on these factors parts of speech tagging are known as assigning it to the words from the sentences. POS is very useful in information retrieval where the ultimate goal is to retrieve meaningful, relevant information from the large volume of data.

Data Wrangling

Data wrangling is mainly used in accessing and analyzing data. This process can reduce the time required to analyze and present the required data and helps in decision-making skills. It helps in finding outliers and unnecessary data from the given dataset. It removes the errors and enables complex data easier to access. Data wrangling integrates data from multiple sources and analyzes it to identify the gaps. It tries to remove the 'outlier's for better analysis. Data wrangling general steps are - discovery, structuring, cleaning, enriching, verifying, and representing the results. There are many tools available to use data wrangling technique as follows:

- Python
- Pandas
- Plotly
- Excel spreadsheets
- Tabula
- OpenRefine
- CSVKit

Its advantages are as follows:

1. It enhances the usability of 'raw' data.
2. Integrates data from a variety of sources to store it in a single centralized place.
3. Helps keeping watch on 'data flow'
4. Removes errors, noise and missed elements.
5. Helps in better decision making.
6. Represents data in standardized form.

Algorithmic Details

Algorithm for the business applications may consist of following steps:

1. Collecting the data from different sources
2. Integrating it in a repository
3. Data preprocessing
4. Finding different anomalies, if any
5. Data wrangling
6. Tuning the dataset using deep learning techniques
7. Applying classification techniques such as naïve bayes
8. Evaluating the patterns

Table 2. Sample dataset used for data wrangling

Country	Age	Salary	Quantity Purchased	ID
India	45	35000	30	A12
China	35	50000	35	A13
US	30	45000	20	B12
UK	28	30000	55	B13
Iraq	23		45	J45
AUS	32	25000	50	C12
Brazil	22	20000	33	C13
Russia	28	30000	30	D11
Srilanka	30	50000	60	D12
India	35	25000	40	E12
US	60	40000	10	E21
UK	50	18000	15	F23
Norway	59	9000		G45
Iran	34	3000		H55

grouped = details.groupby('age') .... (q1)
print (grouped.get_group (30))... (q2)

Table 3. Output of data wrangling

	Country	Age	Salary	Quantity Purchased	ID
2	US	30	45000.0	20.0	B12
8	Srilanka	30	50000.0	60.0	D12

Naive Bayes Classification

If the given data is properly classified then it helps identify 'stored' historical patterns to predict the sentiments. It is used in finding the probabilities and a set of features are classified independently of each other. It is a probabilistic classifier which works on probabilities like 'prior' and 'posterior' probabilities. It is used in many applications such as 'spam filtration', 'sentiment analysis', 'classifying the objects', 'real-time estimation', 'calculating the credit score' etc. It is based on 'Bayes' theorem as shown below. Many applications use *Gaussian* Naïve *Bayes* classification method. Naïve byes can be used in real-time data prediction, classifying data among different classes, sentiment analysis, email systems and systems used for recommendation purposes.

$P (A|B) = P (B|A) P (A) / P (B)$

Above formulae calculates 'posterior' probability i.e. probability of 'A' when 'B' occurs. P(A) is prior/initial probability, P(B) is probability of evidences. Naïve Bayes considers 'words' are independent of other words. Hence, in this case approach context is not important. If there are sentences like 'I like this movie' and 'this movie I like' will be treated as 'same' by the Naïve Bayes classifier.

This classifier consists of steps as shown below:

1. Preprocessing the input data
2. Dividing the data into 'training' and 'testing' data.
3. Applying the Naïve Bayes classifier
4. Calculating the accuracy of classifier
5. Visualize the obtained results

However, there are few limitations to the Naïve Bayes classification like it considers all the 'features' are independent. In real-case scenario it is not possible to have independent features only. Classification may give ambiguous results if the specific category not available to assign any feature. Therefore, it is suggested to apply 'smoothing' technique to solve such issues. Training and use of sentiment classification approach consists of following steps –

- Loading pre-trained words
- Loading lexicons with positive and negative words
- Train the classifier these words
- Calculate the 'mean' scores

Using Naïve Bayes classification one can model the probabilistic relationships among the attributes and the class variable. This method uses a theory of probability. E.g. if there are 'n' classes and 'm' students then probability can be defined as follows:

P (A) = m/n

- **Bayesian Correlation Matrix Plot**

It helps the end-user to correlate different variables available in the given dataset. In the Bayesian correlation matrix plot, one can easily identify the correlation between *rating and the sentiment* given by the different users. One can easily understand as the rating increases, it increases the positive sentiment. Such plots can be used in advanced analytics and help in summarizing the dataset. This correlation matrix plots help in diagnosis purposes.

- **Bayesian Correlation Pairwise Plots**

Bayesian correlation plot helps in identifying highly correlated attributes. Once a model successfully identifies correlated attributes, predicting power of the model gets better. Bayes factor robustness check helps quickly examining the attribute's specifications. Even though there is large volume of distributions available in the dataset, it is possible for the users to analyze them.

Maximum Entropy classification

It is a machine learning technique to find the probabilities from the given data and known as probabilistic classifier. It is widely used in many applications such as classification, sentiment analysis, detecting language and retrieving meaningful information from the same. It is used to solve multi-class problem to find relevance of the words, sentences, and different posts by the users. It works on getting the maximum uniformity (uniform distribution) from the given input data. It is assumed that, higher the entropy there could be higher uniformity. 'Entropy' in maximum entropy classification is nothing but the measurement of improper or disordered data.

Collaborative Filtering

Once the model train and tests the remaining the sample data, one can use collaborative filtering method to filter out the similarity. Collaborative filtering finds 'common interests' of different users. It works on calculating the 'similarity measures' to identify the similarity between 'n' users. In our sample dataset, system can filter out the similar ratings given by the users. Similar sentiments, ratings can be grouped in one cluster for future analysis. Collaborative filtering can play a vital role in recommendation systems. It can be classified in 02 categories – user-based and item based. User-based collaborative filtering identifies similarity between 'users' and 'item-based' collaborative filtering on 'items'. Estimating the users choice for the specific products or services could be possible using 'collaborative filtering' method. One can say with the help of collaborative filtering it is possible to suggest the products user may like. User based collaborative filtering deals with 'n' users/customers and their 'ratings' or 'feedbacks'. In the collaborative filtering approach 'positive' and 'negative' ratings are separated to identify the similarity between these ratings. All the ratings and feedbacks in the collaborative filtering give 'suggestions' which can be used in 'recommender' systems.

FINDINGS

It can be applied on the sentence level, document level and attribute level. Social media platform consists of messages, posts, reviews etc. One can process this heterogeneous data to get maximum relevance. As discussed sentiment analysis can have polarities e.g. positive or negative. Few papers referred by the authors suggest one can develop a classifier based on naïve Bayes, SVM approaches. Feature extraction and processing those features are the necessary steps to be considered in the initial phase of the classifiers.

Today's data-driven applications process data from variety of sources. Data retrieved from these heterogeneous sources represented in an aggregate and unique format. Hence to process such large volume of data next-generation big-data processing systems needs to be developed. There are many applications based on contextual data useful for identifying the traffic intensity, changing users per application, weather conditions etc., and serve as next- generation business-specific systems. In such systems data abstraction and representation are the important tasks. Granularity can be applied in the data processing step. Granularity will process the data from low granularity to high granularity. Sampling plays an important role in the data processing. "Sampling" plays an important role in sentiment analysis. If one observes the trend of digitization, can conclude with the increase in 'n' users large volume of data increased rapidly. However, this large volume of data is heterogeneous integrated from different sources.

Transformation of this data is necessary. There are many sampling methods exists like random sampling partition (RSP). 'Sampling' improves the performance and retrieves better results. However, sampling, scaling and speeding up requires strong algorithms to process large volume of data. A common strategy divide-and-conquer can be used to create 'segments' or 'classes'. Big data analytics helps the users fulfilling their daily business needs, identifying the customer segment and forecast the business strategies. Traditional learning do not supports in depth learning whereas recent machine learning (ML), deep learning (DL) methods such as supervised and unsupervised classification, clustering etc. can be applied to get the better results. Suppose the set of positive, negative and neutral words are as shown below -

positive_vocab = ['excellent', 'good', 'enjoyed', 'nice', 'outstanding', 'awesome', 'very good', 'great']
negative_vocab = ['bad','poor','disappointed']
neutral_vocab = ['average', 'reasonable']
Sentence = "*movie is good. However the action scenes are average and music is bad*". As per the sentiment analysis and the datasets of positive, negative and neutral vocabularies listed above the results are as follows-
Positive: 0.6923076923076923
Negative: 0.07692307692307693
Neutral: 0.23076923076923078

Similarly, if the following sample dataset is used for sentiment analysis model gives accuracy of 88.88% and the results are as follows –

Confusion matrix for the above sample dataset is as follows:

Table 4. Sample dataset used for sentiment analysis

Name	Review	Rating	Sentiment	Sent_ID
santosh	a big, big, big, round of applause;	11	5	1
bhushan	direction is not acuarate not sure	8	3	2
santosh	action scenes are best	15	4	3
ameer	very little bit, of comedy	7	3	4
sumeet	best actor in the film is;	9	5	5
amit	producer is the best;	12	5	6
neha	music is average,	10	4	7
sneha	best film	15	5	8
kunal	average music	8	3	9
arun	best film	14	5	10
sachin	best film@	11	4	11
ayush	great movie	13	4	12
prakash	average photography,	8	3	13
aman	best action;	14	5	14
atul	disappointed!!	7	2	15

Table 5. Confusion matrix

0	1	0	0
0	2	0	0
0	0	3	0
0	0	0	3

Table 6. X-test

-1.08347	-1.29987	-1.29987
-0.361158	-0.185695	-0.185695
-1.08347	-1.29987	-1.29987
1.08347	0.928477	0.928477
-1.44463	-2.41404	-2.41404
-0.722315	0.928477	0.928477
1.44463	-0.185695	-0.185695
1.08347	0.928477	0.928477
0	-0.185695	-0.185695

Table 7. X-train

1.44463	0.928477	0.928477
0.722315	-0.185695	-0.185695
-1.44463	-1.29987	-1.29987
0	0.928477	0.928477
0.361158	0.928477	0.928477
-1.08347	-1.29987	-1.29987

Table 8. Y-predicted

Ypredicted	Ytest	Y*train*
3	3	5
4	4	4
3	3	3
5	5	5
3	2	5
5	5	3
4	4	
5	5	
4	4	

Figure 1. Prior and posterior

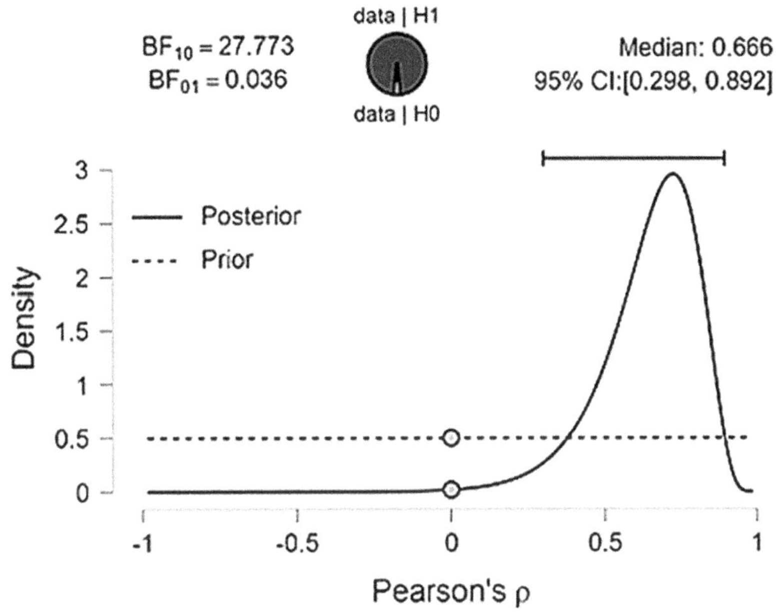

Prior and posterior helps presenting the evidences obtained as shown in above Figure 1. Prior as its name suggests 'initially' works on originality before getting new evidences whereas 'posterior' works on new (processed) information.

Bayes Factor Robustness Check

Figure 2. Bayes factor robustness check

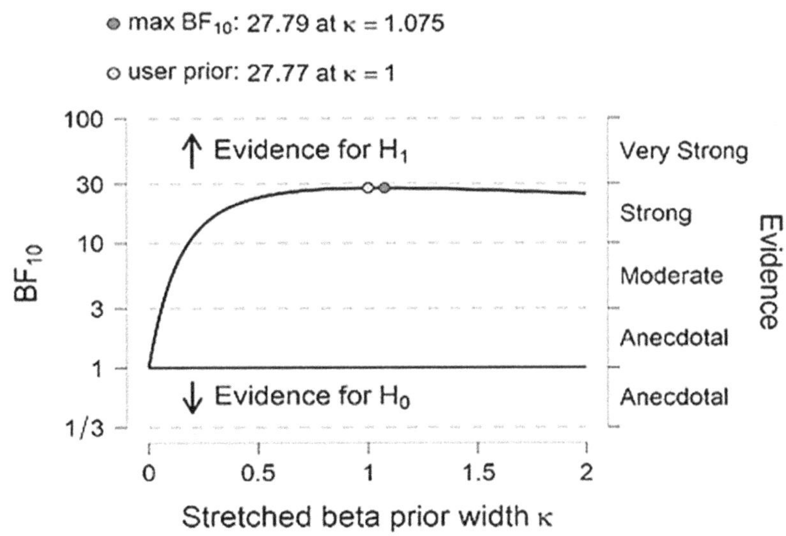

DISCUSSION

There are many methods which can be applied to enhance the performance of sentiment analysis systems. One can go from identifying the term frequencies and inverse document frequencies, i.e (TF*IDF) and removing the stop words or those occurring frequently. As discussed in the earlier sections applying Naïve Bayes classification, collaborative filtering, etc. are the few methods which give significant results. Data wrangling is the basic step that can be applied to the given dataset for effective retrieval of the desired results. Once the results are retrieved one can validate the same like Bayesian factor robustness check as shown in the Figure 1 and Figure 2.

The important point in sentiment analysis is to correlate the variables, i.e. variables or factors affecting others. Such systems must help the analyst to evaluate the data based on primary variables and get the rid of problem by proposing feasible solutions. It is recommended that, sentiment analysis systems (models) should be capable enough to provide real time solutions or remedial actions immediately. Classification plays an important role in the sentiment analysis to categorize the data. Therefore, with the help of basic application (software) of the business if the "sentiment analysis" layer is added then it will surely help in the growth of the businesses. Sentiment analysis can be termed as 'opinion mining' helps predicting the 'future trend' through text, messages, social media posts, etc. It gives directions to the businesses to grow rapidly and increase revenue. However, the main aim is to 'retain' the customer base and positive efforts to increase the same.

NEW CHALLENGES

There could be many challenges as follows –

- A strong system to handle large volume of customers and employees
    - Integrating 'n' feedbacks from 'm' people
- Classifying the feedbacks in different categories
- Applying robust techniques and algorithms
- Representing the results in an understandable manner
- **Tone**
    - It relates to the 'style' of verbal communication and 'writing style'. If it is more difficult to detect then the accuracy of the proposed model gets decreased.
- **Handling polarity**
    - Polarity refers to handling the ambiguity, e.g. treating the words 'good', 'not so bad' and 'average' etc.
- **Sarcasm**
    - Getting the true context from the all positive as well as negative feedbacks.
- Fake feedbacks, opinions, posts, messages contribute in wrong results.

PRACTICAL AND MANAGERIAL IMPLICATIONS

It helps managers to apply necessary steps to improve the quality of the services and products. It helps retaining the staff of the business by giving them required environment in the organization. Such model helps to grow the businesses rapidly and maximizes the revenue.

FUTURE RESEARCH

This approach focuses on improving the businesses by collecting the feedbacks from users. Those users could be employees or customers and gives different ratings about the products / services offered by the business. In future research one can have a model integrated with the business application to handle such process internally. Meaning is that, there should be no need to handle the data (datasets / feedbacks) differently on different platform and know the patterns. Business applications (software) should have such analytic module to know the trend and suggest remedial steps immediately. One can say a type of automated intelligent system can be implemented which handles the feedbacks in real-time manner. It is possible to develop 'highly personalized' systems to get better results. Future research can be conducted on 'multimodality' i.e. integration of different messages, posts, comments, feedbacks etc. It helps deriving meaningful information (sentiment). Such type of multimodal sentiment analysis can be processed using 'fusion' approach at different levels like – feature level, decision level and hybrid fusion. It is also possible to work on datasets from different languages i.e. multilingual sentiment analysis approach. Many researchers and scientists are working on the application of 'sentiment analysis' on big-data which retrieves meaningful information within minimum time. Social media consists of texts, messages, pictures, videos, and audios. Therefore, robust sentiment analysis tool can be developed to get perfect 'sentiment'. Facial expression recognition (FER) predicts the emotion behind given input images can be used to get the 'sentiment'. There are different emotions like anger, happiness, sadness, disgust, fear, etc. There are other factors like gestures, muscle movements which contribute in getting the perfect emotion. These all factors can be used to get the 'sentiment' of the user. A model combining different expressions, EEG & ECG signals can be developed to get the emotion. This integrated approach is treated as "multi-modal fusion emotion recognition" where fusion takes place in expressions and 'n' EEG physiological signals. These signals are related to the brain and any change in the brain state can be represented using the same. Many emotion recognitions can be based on speech signals, different facial expressions, EEG and ECG signals with which sentiment can be identified. A method can be proposed based on supervised learning approach to train the data i.e. facial expressions and EEG or ECG signals. With the help of sentiment analysis one can measure the 'feelings', 'stress', 'frustration levels' of the users and also keep watching the 'tone' (speech). Sentiment analysis can recognize the 'sentiments', 'stress level' etc. with their changes if any. To a new user/customer complete insight can be given about a product or service. It also increases ROI (return on investment) and increases the revenue of the business. There are various sentiment analysis tools available like Monkeylearn, Gramex, IBM Watson, Lexalytics, Amazon comprehend, Google Cloud, NLP, etc. Many researchers are working on 'spam' detection and sentiments behind those spams. Researchers are also developing a fully automatic sentiment analysis tool. Developing a sentiment analysis tool to evaluate the services offered by government could help improve in weak areas. Based on the processing of multimodal data a 'depression' detection and prevention sentiment analysis tool can be developed. An 'ensemble classifier' integrating all the classifiers can be developed to get better accuracy and best results. Different classifiers (Naïve Bayes, logistic regression, support vector machine (SVM), random forest, etc.) can give 'n' predictions and with the help of development of an ensemble classifier 'final prediction' can be concluded.

CONCLUSION

Sentiment analysis predicts the 'sentiments' through surveys, feedbacks, social media posts etc. Companies can use sentiment analysis tools to grow their businesses by retaining the customers. Chapter enlists and explains the initial and important steps as the basic building blocks of the sentiment analysis. There are many sectors where such systems can play a vital role in identifying the sentiments of the employees, customers. Customer-employee retention and maximizing the business are the current need of many businesses. The methodologies discussed in the chapter will surely help businesses to improve the quality of products and services. This approach helps collecting feedback about the business, services or products from employees and customers.

REFERENCES

Abd El-Jawad, M. H., Hodhod, R., & Omar, Y. M. (2018, December). Sentiment analysis of social media networks using machine learning. In *2018 14th international computer engineering conference (ICENCO)* (pp. 174-176). IEEE. 10.1109/ICENCO.2018.8636124

Abel, E., Bogatu, A., Civili, C., Fernandes, A. A., Koehler, M., Konstantinou, N., & Paton, N. W. (2017, December). Data context informed data wrangling. In *2017 IEEE International Conference on Big Data (Big Data)* (pp. 956-963). IEEE.

Agrawal, S., Das, A., Dhage, S., & Gaikwad, A. (2018, July). Customer churn prediction modelling based on behavioural patterns analysis using deep learning. In *2018 International conference on smart computing and electronic enterprise (ICSCEE)* (pp. 1-6). IEEE. 10.1109/ICSCEE.2018.8538420

Ahmad, A., Farman, H., Imran, M., Islam, I. U., Jan, B., Jeon, G., & Khan, M. (2019). Deep learning in big data analytics: A comparative study. *Computers & Electrical Engineering*, *75*, 275–287. doi:10.1016/j.compeleceng.2017.12.009

Ajayan, A. R., Al-Doghman, F., & Chaczko, Z. (2018, December). Visualizing Multimodal Big Data Anomaly Patterns in Higher-Order Feature Spaces. In *2018 26th International Conference on Systems Engineering (ICSEng)* (pp. 1-9). IEEE. 10.1109/ICSENG.2018.8638195

Annareddy, S., & Tammina, S. (2020, January). Sentiment analysis on customer reviews using convolutional neural network. In *2020 International Conference on Computer Communication and Informatics (ICCCI)* (pp. 1-6). IEEE.

Aydin, I., & Salur, M. U. (2020). A novel hybrid deep learning model for sentiment classification. *IEEE Access : Practical Innovations, Open Solutions*, *8*, 58080–58093. doi:10.1109/ACCESS.2020.2982538

Bao, F., Dai, Q., Deng, Y., Kong, Y., Ren, Z., & Suo, J. (2019). Learning deep landmarks for imbalanced classification. *IEEE Transactions on Neural Networks and Learning Systems*, *31*(8), 2691–2704. doi:10.1109/TNNLS.2019.2927647 PMID:31395564

Boyapati, S., Dutt, V., Swarna, S. R., & Vyas, N. (2020, December). Big Data Approach for Medical Data Classification: A Review Study. In *2020 3rd International Conference on Intelligent Sustainable Systems (ICISS)* (pp. 762-766). IEEE. 10.1109/ICISS49785.2020.9315870

Cao, S., Chen, Y., Liu, W., & Zhu, X. (2019, October). Deep learning based customer churn analysis. In *2019 11th International Conference on Wireless Communications and Signal Processing (WCSP)* (pp. 1-6). IEEE. 10.1109/WCSP.2019.8927877

Caraka, R. E., Chen, R. C., Dewi, C., & Huang, S. W. (2020). Selecting critical features for data classification based on machine learning methods. *Journal of Big Data*, *7*(1), 52. doi:10.118640537-020-00327-4

Goularas, D., & Kamis, S. (2019, August). Evaluation of deep learning techniques in sentiment analysis from twitter data. In *2019 International Conference on Deep Learning and Machine Learning in Emerging Applications (Deep-ML)* (pp. 12-17). IEEE. 10.1109/Deep-ML.2019.00011

Jiang, F., & Leung, C. K. S. (2014, December). A data science solution for mining interesting patterns from uncertain big data. In *2014 IEEE Fourth International Conference on Big Data and Cloud Computing* (pp. 235-242). IEEE.

Kahani, M., & Mighan, S. N. (2021). A novel scalable intrusion detection system based on deep learning. *International Journal of Information Security*, *20*(3), 387–403. doi:10.100710207-020-00508-5

Kanagasabai, R., Manai, G., Sangaralingam, K., Shangfeng, H., & Veeramani, A. (2016, December). Classification of massive mobile web log URLs for customer profiling & analytics. In *2016 IEEE International Conference on Big Data (Big Data)* (pp. 1609-1614). IEEE. 10.1109/BigData.2016.7840771

Kang, P., Kim, C., Kim, H., Mo, K., & Seo, S. (2020). Comparative study of deep learning-based sentiment classification. *IEEE Access : Practical Innovations, Open Solutions*, *8*, 6861–6875. doi:10.1109/ACCESS.2019.2963426

Nikolov, N., Roman, D., & Sukhobok, D. (2017, August). Tabular data anomaly patterns. In *2017 International Conference on Big Data Innovations and Applications (Innovate-Data)* (pp. 25-34). IEEE.

Onan, A. (2021). Sentiment analysis on massive open online course evaluations: A text mining and deep learning approach. *Computer Applications in Engineering Education*, *29*(3), 572–589. doi:10.1002/cae.22253

Park, C. H. (2018, January). Anomaly pattern detection on data streams. In *2018 IEEE International Conference on Big Data and Smart Computing (BigComp)* (pp. 689-692). IEEE. 10.1109/BigComp.2018.00127

Smart, P. S. (2021). Regression Tree Based Correlation Technique in Spatial Data Classification. *Turkish Journal of Computer and Mathematics Education*, *12*(10), 6184–6195.

KEY TERMS AND DEFINITIONS

Big Data: Data integrated from multiple sources. This could be in structured, unstructured, or semi-structured format. Its characteristics are velocity, large volume, and variety.

Classification: Categorizing the given data after successful training. In this process class labels are anticipated and model is developed based on predictive approach.

Data Wrangling: It is mainly used in data analysis where gathering the data, processing and transforming it from one form to another form takes place. Output of the data wrangling is ready to use meaningful data.

HADOOP: It is an open source software platform processes large datasets. It creates a 'cluster' of different machine where the data is stored & all the data can be made available for analysis purpose in parallel manner.

Machine Learning: It is mainly a subset of artificial intelligence (AI) where systems (computers and machines) are trained to behave / work like a human. Systems learn from the available data and past experiences. Its examples are self-automated cars, cyber fraud detection, Facial emotion recognition etc. Machine learning further classified into supervised, unsupervised and reinforcement learning.

Natural Language Processing (NLP): It can be referred to as a method of Artificial intelligence (AI) communicates with the intelligent systems (computers or other devices) with the help of languages such as English, French, Japanese etc. Once NLP is successfully implemented intelligent systems can perform the tasks in repetitive manner.

Normalization: It organizes data and has different types 1NF, 2NF, 3NF, BCNF, and 5NF. It minimizes the redundancies and helps avoiding different anomalies like – insertion, update, and deletion.

Sentiment Analysis: It helps in determining whether the given data is positive, negative or neutral. This is an emerging field in computer science and widely used in e-commerce applications. It also helps in gathering feedback from the customers and contributes in growth of the businesses.

Support Vector Machine (SVM): Support vector machine is a supervised learning algorithm widely used in classification as well as regression problems in machine learning. It transforms the given data and helps identifying the possible boundary between the outputs.

Tokenization: Splitting the words or sentences is known as tokenization. It is mainly used in natural language processing and helps converting large volume into smaller parts.

Vectorization: It is a method which helps predicting the similarities between words, phrases or 'n' objects. It is also defined as extracting the features from the given data and among those 'n' features identifying the distinct features.

Chapter 4
Consumer Decision-Making Processes in Clothing, Textile, and Fashion

Açelya Telli Danışmaz
Yildiz Technical University, Turkey

ABSTRACT

The aim of this section is to reveal how social media shapes consumer decision-making processes when purchasing textile and ready-made clothing products and to what extent it affects these processes positively or negatively. Accordingly, in this chapter, first of all, information about the consumer purchasing process and how this process works in the clothing, fashion, and textile sectors will be given, and then what kind of reflections and contributions of social media to the consumer purchasing process in these sectors will be mentioned. Finally, in the conclusion and discussion section, suggestions will be made for future research and applications for the sector.

INTRODUCTION

Since the 1970s, the textile and ready-made clothing industry has made great progress and has become one of the rapidly growing sectors today. So much so that the increase in the welfare levels of countries around the world has created an acceleration in many sectors and sub-sectors such as housing and tourism, and the need for the textile sector has increased and it has been instrumental in the growth of the sector (Sanayi ve Teknoloji Bakanlığı Kalkınma Ajansları Genel Müdürlüğü, 2021, p.1). However, the Covid-19 pandemic, which was experienced in 2020 and continued for a long time all over the world, has deeply affected the textile industry as it has affected all sectors. The main reasons for this are; supply chain disruption, cash flow problems, unemployment, changes in consumer behavior, closure of physical retail stores and disruption of fashion events (Annaldewar et al., 2021, pp.94-97). In this regard, the "The State of Fashion" report, which was prepared jointly by Business of Fashion (BOF) and McKinsey & Company in 2022, contains important data on the volume of the ready-made clothing industry. In this report, it has been stated that the ready-to-wear sector has contracted by 27-30% in 2020, in 2021 it has

DOI: 10.4018/978-1-6684-8753-2.ch004

grown by 2-4% compared to 2019, in the luxury ready-made clothing sector, there is a 35-39% shrinkage in 2020, and in 2021 there is a 1-4% growth compared to 2019. . Similarly, in the 2023 report, it was stated that supply chains were disrupted due to the Covid-19 pandemic, and therefore the need to invest in systems that could provide closer and faster production in terms of geographical location increased.

If we evaluate it from the point of view of the consumer, especially during the pandemic process, the rate of consumers who make online shopping habits instead of shopping in physical stores is quite high. Because, both for daily grocery shopping and for purchasing textile products such as clothes, consumers have now had to prefer online channels (Keenan, 2022; (McKinsey & Company, 2021, p.65). In the article written by Keenan (2022) on global trends in e-commerce, it is seen that brands create advertisements for their target audiences through social media platforms (Facebook, Instagram, Tik Tok, Snapchat, various shopping applications, etc.), especially with the acceleration of shopping made with mobile phones. is expressed. In parallel, of course, social media is of great importance for the textile and apparel industry in terms of advertising, sales and marketing channels. In the "The State of Fashion" report of BOF and McKinsey & Company (2021), it was stated that 74% of consumers were more affected when shopping on social media compared to the pre-pandemic period, and 70% of them shopped mostly from the clothing category on social media. . For this reason, it has become a matter of curiosity how social media shapes consumer purchasing processes in the textile and apparel industry.

Consumer Purchasing Process in Apparel and Textile Industry

In order for a consumer to have a purchase intention, he must first have something he needs. In the event that what is needed is available, every consumer who acts to meet this need exhibits a unique buying behavior (Firat and Azmak, 2007). If there is a difference between the current situation and the desired situation in what the consumer needs, a need arises here and the purchasing decision process begins at this stage (Erciş et al., 2007). Consumers can meet these needs in physical environments, online or virtual environments. Physical stores are examples of physical purchasing environments, and online shopping sites are examples of online (virtual) purchasing environments.

In order to understand the differences of the online purchasing process from the traditional purchasing process, the online purchasing process is expressed in five stages. These; awareness of the need, information seeking process, evaluation of alternatives, purchasing decision, post-purchase behavior (Odabaşı and Barış, 2013). First of all, the consumer realizes that he has a need, then he searches for information about the products that can meet this need, after this stage, by comparing the information he has obtained with the alternative products, he determines the most suitable product for himself and the purchase decision is made. Post-purchase behavior, on the other hand, is the stage of forming ideas about whether the product meets the needs of the individual after purchasing the product. At this stage, if a problem has arisen with the product, the consumer seeks support for the solution of the problem by contacting the seller company. If businesses cannot manage this process well, the consumer will not think of purchasing products from that company or brand in their next shopping. As a matter of fact, the common complaints of the customers who shop online are the problems such as the products coming different from the ones seen on the online shopping sites, wrong or missing products. The better the businesses can manage these post-purchase processes, the more consumers will be satisfied with that brand and business and will want to shop continuously (Akkaya, 2013, p.106; Aydın, 2019, pp.47-48). Also, according to (Papachristou et al, 2022), online shoppers can settle for longer delivery times and spend more money if the final product meets their requirements.

With the effect of today's technological developments and the diversification of consumer expectations in parallel, it is seen that consumers tend to buy goods and services over the internet from traditional purchasing behavior (Goswami and Khan, 2015, p.303). Perhaps the most basic reason for this is that online purchases offer consumers an easy way to purchase. In addition, offering the opportunity to compare prices and alternative product variety, and to evaluate the comments of previous buyers about the goods and services desired to be purchased also contributes to the preference of online purchasing behavior. (Acar and Harmankaya, 2021; Akkaya, 2013; Akel, 2015; Karaca and Gümüş, 2019; Zorlu and Uzgören, 2020). On the other hand, there are also consumers who are cold towards the online purchasing process for various reasons. In such cases, such customers may prefer to complete their purchase in a physical store after doing their research online (Özcan, 2010). Some of these reasons are; It can be listed as not being able to physically try the products, not being able to touch the fabric of the product, not being able to see the details. Also fit is considered to be one of the most important reasons for not shopping clothing products online (Ağaç et al., 2018; Algür and Cengiz, 2011; Aydın, 2019; Cheng et al., 2013; Kimmery and McCard, 2002; Peck and Childers, 2003; Yu et al., 2012).

One of the most popular product categories in online shopping is undoubtedly textile and ready-made clothing. In a study conducted by Mürütsoy (2013), textile and clothing products are in the second place after electronic products in the list of sectors where online shopping is made. In a study conducted by Olgun (2015), the most researched product category on social media was fashion and clothing. To give an example for the ready-made clothing and textile industry, an example would be the consumer's uneasiness of not being able to determine the suitable size online, and then completing the purchase process online after trying the product in the physical store. The development of the online shopping experience with augmented reality applications in recent years ensures that these concerns are gradually eliminated. As a matter of fact, according to the findings obtained from a study conducted by Yolcu et al. (2017), the rate of purchasing a clothing product from the website after researching it in a physical store was found to be 60%. Similarly, as a result of a study conducted by Genç (2014), it was determined that 76.2% of the participants purchased ready-made clothing and textile products from online shopping sites. Similar findings are supported by other studies in the literature (EY, 2016; Özgüven, 2011; Tatlı and Korkut, 2015; Toksarı and Atlı, 2018). In another study, the reasons why ready-made clothing and textile products are preferred more in online shopping are expressed as the convenience offered by payment systems and the absence of time-space restrictions (Ağaç and Solak, 2016).

From the point of view of businesses, there has been a noticeable increase in e-commerce volume worldwide since the Covid-19 pandemic in 2020 (McKinsey, 2021, p.65). In this process, while businesses operating in the e-commerce sector are trying to deliver their goods and services to their customers as much as the logistics volume of their countries allows, physical businesses that had to close their workplaces during the pandemic period have also met e-commerce and started to deliver their goods and services to their customers over the internet. Especially in this process, the role of e-commerce is very high in the supply of medical materials and equipment, daily food and other personal needs, as well as textile and clothing needs. Because, in the joint report of McKinsey & Company and Business of Fashion (2021), the following recommendations were made for businesses in the textile and ready-made clothing industry for the post-Covid-19 process: Preferring the use of multiple marketing channels due to increasing digital marketing costs, making progress with a focus on creativity in digital platforms, the ability to keep up with the adoption and processes of new digital channels. Undoubtedly, the innovative applications developed by social media platforms for their users day by day are among the important factors that especially businesses operating in the textile and ready-made clothing sector receive support in their sales and marketing efforts.

The Effect of Social Media on Consumer Purchasing Process in Apparel and Textile Industry

With the inclusion of technology in our daily lives, the purchasing process has begun to evolve from physical purchasing processes to online purchasing processes, and thus, sales channels have also diversified considerably. In this process, word of mouth communication, one of the traditional marketing channels, was integrated into digital marketing (Yıldırım and Boztepe, 2019, p.328) and started to be used by businesses (Canöz et al., 2020, p.74). In this way, consumers have started to prefer virtual shopping channels, also known as storeless retailing (Arslan, 2016, p.120). The e-commerce sector, which forms the basis of online purchasing processes, also carries out goods and service marketing processes in cooperation with these digital marketing channels. In this way, the emerging social media has become very important in terms of both its unique marketing strategies and the opportunity to establish one-to-one communication with the customer (Taştepe, 2020, p.22) and a new channel has been formed under the name of social media marketing (Akar, 2010, p.25).

Social media marketing (Social CRM) can be defined as the appearance of goods and services using social networking platforms (Odabaşı and Oyman, 2003, p.326). In other words, social media marketing refers to marketing activities that identify all kinds of missing points between consumers and businesses, offer various suggestions to eliminate these deficiencies and actively manage this process (Kim and Ko, 2012). These activities are grouped under five main headings: Entertainment, interaction, fashion, customization, word of mouth. With the active use of social media and the spread of the concept of social media marketing, the need to define a new consumer profile has arisen and this consumer profile has been named "social consumer". The social consumer draws a consumer profile that consumes information quickly, is aware of new products on the market, follows brands and businesses regularly, reads user comments and follows the responses to these comments, as well as wants to be in constant communication with brands and businesses (Marsden, 2011, p.3).

Social media is an important data source that includes demographic information and shopping behaviors of consumers in the process of creating a target audience. In this way, social media tools develop target audience-specific innovative advertising and marketing strategies for today's businesses (Arslan, 2020; Say, 2015; Tosun, 2009; Ying, 2012) and offer the opportunity to reach consumers in the most effective and fastest way (Aydın, 2019, p. 25; Black, 2012, p.57). For example, in a target audience to be created for a business operating in the men's ready-to-wear sector, a target audience consisting of not only men and individuals of a certain age range, but also a target audience that has been reduced by narrowing the criteria further and more efficient results (for example, those who have previously clicked on the advertisement of that product and added it to the cart, went to the website of a similar brand during the purchasing phase, and made similar searches on price comparison sites) have been started to be formed. For this reason, businesses actively use social media to reach customers in the target audience they have determined and to increase their sales. Social media channels such as Instagram, Twitter, Facebook, Tik Tok are among them. Here, businesses can promote their goods and services with word of mouth marketing technique through social media phenomena (influencers), so they can reach their target customers easily. According to Canoz et al. (2020), it was concluded that influencer marketing, which has become a new profession in social media, is a very effective factor in the decision-making process of consumers. To give an example for the textile industry, an Instagram phenomenon known in the field of clothing and fashion likes an outfit and shares that outfit's website link with its followers, enabling that brand to reach a large number of users at the same time and to include the target audience in the purchasing process (Aydın, 2019, pp. 27-28). In his master's thesis, Arslan (2020) analyzed the marketing strategies used by the ready-made clothing industry in the social media and as a result of the findings he obtained, he concluded that the businesses in the social media implement advertising and marketing strategies for the purchasing behaviors of their target audiences. Similarly, Çağlıyan et al. (2016), it was determined that there is a significant relationship between social media advertisements and consumers' purchasing behaviors. Social media platforms such as Youtube, where video content is published, are also suitable channels for advertising and marketing. Thanks to such social media platforms, businesses have started to achieve higher turnover and profitability by advertising, and the effect of social media on the purchasing process has become more noticeable.

In addition to the benefits it offers to businesses, social media is a factor that significantly affects the purchasing process of consumers today. Consumers now take great care to read the positive and negative comments of consumers who have purchased a product before on various internet sites (Dinç, 2018, p.5; Yıldırım and Boztepe, 2019, p.325). An example of this is when consumers can read reviews of customers who have purchased a product before, while shopping on multi-channel shopping sites (eg amazon.com, etsy.com, ebay.com, etc.). In addition, user comments with photographs and videos, which have become widespread recently, are also an important source of information for individuals who are considering purchasing that product (Altunışık et al., 2010). In this way, the customer will have a pre-purchase idea about the quality and performance of the product when comparing the price of a product he is considering to buy. In addition, complaint sites where users express their dissatisfaction and write to find solutions are also one of the important factors affecting the purchasing decision process of consumers (Enginkaya, 2006; Olgun, 2015; Söyleyici and Çetinkaya, 2017, pp.51-52). Ünver (2013) also concluded in his research that social media marketing is the most important factor that drives consumers to buy, and that consumers attach great importance to advertisements and comments before purchasing.

The factors affecting the purchasing processes of consumers in social media can be grouped under three main headings: social, psychological and personal factors. Social factors include culture/subculture, social class, reference groups, roles and family of the target audience; psychological factors are motivation, perception, learning and attitudes, personality traits; personal factors include demographic characteristics and various situational factors (Odabaşı and Barış, 2013, p.30). The opinions and experiences of other consumers (reference groups), which are among the social factors and around the target audience, are also an important factor affecting the purchasing behavior of the target audience in terms of creating social pressure (Koç, 2008: 112). In summary, the factors that lead consumers to social media marketing and purchasing behavior can be summarized as follows (Algür and Cengiz, 2011, p.3668; Kırcova, 2012, p.65; Koçak, 2012, p.86; Öztürk, 2016, p.21; Scott, 2009, p.42):

- Offering price advantage and special coupons and discounts for social media
- Saving time
- Providing 24/7 shopping opportunity
- Offering the opportunity to compare goods and services in terms of quality, price and compliance with personal needs.
- No matter where in the world, goods and services are accessible without the need for a physical store, there is no time-space constraint.

- Obtaining information by researching alternative products before deciding to purchase.
- Quickly find answers to questions about the product
- Offering returns and exchanges
- Post-purchase thoughts and experiences can be shared free of charge via social media.

In recent years, the opportunity to shop through social media platforms can be given as an example of the elements of social media that affect the consumer purchasing process. This development is a new step in the online purchasing process of consumers. For example, the "store" feature that Instagram brings to business accounts allows the company to simultaneously transfer its goods and services from the online store on Facebook or from the business's own website to the "store" section of the Instagram profile. In this way, consumers can access product types and price information more easily and quickly and complete their shopping in a shorter time. In addition, consumers who see that a product they like are tagged on Instagram can also direct to buy the product through this post. In a study conducted by Yeşildal (2017), it was determined that consumers prefer to buy textile and ready-made clothing products from boutiques with a high number of followers on Instagram and research other boutiques before purchasing. In a study conducted by Yaşa Özeltürkay et al. (2017), the reasons for preferring to shop on Instagram are the convenience of payment at the door, the opportunity to return and an easy shopping environment, the variety of products and the suitability of prices, respectively. In addition, in the same study, it was concluded that the number of followers and consumer tastes were also effective on purchasing behavior. Similarly, the Tik Tok social media platform has started to take steps that allow sales through influencers. For example, in August 2021, Shopify conducted a pilot test of payment systems to be able to sell on Tik Tok in cooperation with Tik Tok (McKinsey & Company, 2021, p.67). The emergence of such innovations makes a great contribution to both the power of social media making positive contributions to businesses in terms of turnover and profitability, and facilitating the purchasing processes of consumers. In this direction, businesses can increase their efficiency, especially by integrating in-app purchases and augmented reality applications into these processes (McKinsey & Company, 2021, p.65).

In the literature, there are various studies on the perceptions of social media marketing that lead consumers to buy. In a study conducted by Onurlubaş et al. (2016), it was seen that social media marketing creates five perceptions in the eyes of consumers. These are reliability, being useful, being able to communicate, being fun and guiding, being able to follow trends. In the research of Deveci (2019), it was concluded that the dimensions of reliability, information and usefulness, and communication dimensions, which are among these perception dimensions, are effective on consumers' social media marketing perception. In a study conducted by Kara (2012) on the Facebook social media platform, it was determined that Facebook provides awareness and customer loyalty to businesses in the short term, and that it has an increasing effect on sales in the long term. In a study conducted by Gümüş (2018), the perception dimensions of consumers for social media marketing are online word of mouth, benefit, perception and trust. Yıldırım and Boztepe (2019) concluded that as consumers' social media involvement and fashion-conscious lifestyle increase, they are more influenced by social media and exhibit purchasing behavior. Therefore, it is important for businesses to consider these dimensions when planning their social media marketing activities and build their practices accordingly (Arslan, 2020: 47-48). As a result of the findings obtained from a study conducted by Keskin and Baş (2015), it was stated that the purchasing behavior of consumers is affected by the shares made on social media. Similarly, Omarlı and Parıltı (2017) concluded in their research that consumers are affected by social media promotion activities.

When we look at the textile sector in particular, it is seen that the applications where consumers can experience the products on themselves through the cameras of their mobile phones before purchasing a product have started to become widespread recently. For example, a cosmetics brand offers the user the possibility to try lipstick, eyeshadow, lip liner, etc. on their own lips via the mobile application, or a sunglasses brand allows the consumer to choose the most suitable glasses for the face type through a similar application through the mobile application. To give another example, a ready-made clothing brand has recently developed a technology that enables the customer, who is in front of the mirror, to see the products in the store without trying them, thanks to the mirrors they have placed in the store in some of the stores it has determined around the world. In addition, the start of product sales in live broadcasts on various social media platforms (for example, Tik Tok, Instagram, etc.) that offer the opportunity to broadcast live can be given as an example of the place of social media in the marketing of goods and services. Such live broadcast sales applications are very popular especially in China, which is the leading country in textile and ready-made clothing exports. An example of this is the Tommy Hilfiger brand selling 1300 hoodies and getting 14000 views in just two minutes in a live broadcast sale in China. Similarly, on the social media platform called Snapchat, many companies such as Prada and Piaget are testing augmented reality applications to enable virtual testing of their products (Mcdowell, 2021). Twitch, Discord and Clubhouse owned by Amazon, which are among the platforms that have gained popularity recently, are among the social media channels that bring businesses together with their target audiences, with the promotions of men's clothing and street style clothing products especially for young gamer men. An example of this is the men's shoe brand StockX promoting its latest products within Discord (McKinsey, 2021, pp.66-67).

Conclusion, Discussion, and Recommendations

The rapid differentiation and change of today's technologies undoubtedly reveals the need for brands and businesses to adapt to these technological developments. In addition, the fact that the majority of the consumer profile that buys goods and services through social media is composed of Y and Z generations is among the most important factors that make it necessary for brands and businesses to easily adapt to technology with a younger and dynamic structure.

For the future, It is believed that the days when virtual experiences will become more realistic and consumers will be able to examine the product they buy as if they were in their hands, with the spread of artificial intelligence supported products that offer augmented reality all over the world. In addition, I am sure that we will see in the near future that online tailoring service will be offered to the consumers in the textile sector and that the customer's clothes will be sewn in a virtual environment and rehearsal processes will be carried out as if they were there. In addition, the production of eco-friendly (supporting recycling, minimizing carbon footprint and water consumption in production processes) products, which has come to the fore with the eco-awareness approach in recent years, is a very important factor in terms of the positive perception created by brands and businesses in consumers. Shen et al., 2017). In this context, It is believed in the importance of brands and businesses that support eco-friendly practices to announce such production processes and product features to consumers through social media.

In summary, based on the Organizational Population Ecology Theory of Hannan and Freeman (1977), It is believed that brands and businesses that are flexible enough to adapt to today's technologies and innovations, and that can take action by identifying consumer needs in the best way can survive. In this sense, It is thought that the impact of social media on consumers' purchasing processes for brands and businesses is undeniably important.

For future academic studies, it can be suggested to measure how the advertising and marketing strategies of social media platforms comparatively affect the purchasing processes in the textile and apparel sector on the basis of turnover and profitability of enterprises, to comparatively analyse which social media platforms are prominent in consumer purchasing processes on the basis of generations, to examine in which aspect (for example, being an advertising and marketing channel, offering live broadcast sales opportunities, offering purchasing opportunities for the application, etc.) social media platforms affect the purchasing processes in the textile and apparel sector. In addition to this, it is suggested for future work to add primary data analysis in a similar paper and not only selected literature review.

REFERENCES

Acar, A., & Harmankaya, H. (2021). İnternet ortamındaki tüketici yorumlarının üniversite öğrencilerinin giysi satın alma davranışlarına etkisinin incelenmesi. *Sanat ve Tasarım Araştırmaları Dergisi*, *2*(3), 10–21.

Ağaç, S., & Solak, C. Ö. (2016). Üniversite öğrencilerinin online giysi alışveriş davranışlarının incelenmesi. *Selçuk Üniversitesi Sosyal Bilimler Enstitüsü Dergisi*, *36*, 142–151.

Ağaç, S. D., Sevinir, S., & Yılmaz, T. (2018). Online giyim alışverişinde tüketicilerin karşılaştıkları sorunların cinsiyet değişkenine göre incelenmesi. *Karadeniz Teknik Üniversitesi Sosyal Bilimler Enstitüsü Dergisi*, *8*(15), 57–71.

Akar, E. (2010). *Sosyal medya pazarlaması*. Efil Yayınevi.

Akel, G. (2015). *Tüketicilerin internetten satın alma niyeti üzerine bir çalışma: Adnan Menderes Üniversitesi örneği*. Pamukkale Üniversitesi Sosyal Bilimler Enstitüsü, Yayınlanmış Yüksek Lisans Tezi.

Akkaya, D. (2013). *Sosyal medya reklamları: tüketici algılarının tutum, davranış ve satın alma niyeti üzerine etkisi*. Yayınlanmamış Doktora Tezi, Trakya Üniversitesi Sosyal Bilimler Enstitüsü.

Algür, S., & Cengiz, F. (2011). Türk tüketicilere göre online (çevrimiçi) alışverişin riskleri ve yararları. *Journal of Yasar University*, *6*(22), 3666–3680.

Altındal, M. (2013). Dijital pazarlamada marka yönetimi ve sosyal medyanın etkileri. In Akademik Bilişim, XV. Akademik Bilişim Konferansı Bildirileri (pp.1147-1151). Akdeniz Üniversitesi Antalya.

Altunışık, R., Sütütemiz, N., & Çallı, L. (2010). E-memnuniyeti etkileyen performans kriterlerinin tespiti üzerine bir araştırma (e-perakendecilik örneği). *Akademik Bakış Dergisi*, *6*, 85–105.

Annaldewar, B. N., Jadhav, N. C., & Jadhav, A. C. (2021). Impact of covıd-19 on sustainability in textile & clothing sectors. In S. S. Muthu (Ed.), *COVID-19. Environmental footprints and eco-design of products and processes*. Springer. doi:10.1007/978-981-16-3860-2_4

Arslan, B. (2016). Sanal mağaza atmosferi unsurlarının anlık satın almaya etkisi. *Bitlis Eren Üniversitesi Sosyal Bilimler Enstitüsü Dergisi*, *5*(1), 117–136.

Arslan, O. (2020). *Hazır giyim sektörünün sosyal medyada kullandığı pazarlama stratejilerinin analizi.* Yüksek Lisans Tezi, İstanbul Sabahattin Zaim Üniversitesi Sosyal Bilimler Enstitüsü.

Aydın, E. (2019). *İnternet tüketicilerinin hazır giyim satın alma davranışları üzerine bir araştırma.* Yüksek Lisans Tezi, Kastamonu Üniversitesi Sosyal Bilimler Enstitüsü, Kastamonu.

Çağlayan, V., Işıklar, Z., & Hassan, S. A. (2016). üniversite öğrencilerinin satın alma davranışlarında sosyal medya reklamlarının etkisi: Selçuk Üniversitesi'nde bir araştırma. *Selçuk Üniversitesi Sosyal ve Teknik Araştırmalar Dergisi, 11*, 43–56.

Canöz, K., Gülmez, Ö., & Eroğlu, G. (2020). Pazarlamanın yükselen yıldızı influencer marketing: Influencer takipçilerinin satın alma davranışını belirlemeye yönelik bir araştırma. *Selçuk Üniversitesi Sosyal Bilimler Meslek Yüksekokulu Dergisi, 23*(1), 73–91. doi:10.29249elcuksbmyd.606009

Cheng, F., Liu, T., & Wu, C. (2013). Perceived risks and risk reduction strategies in online group-buying. *Proceedings of 2013 International Conference on Technology Innovation and Industrial Management*, 18-25.

Deveci, M. (2019). *Sosyal medya pazarlama stratejilerinin tüketici üzerindeki olumlu ve olumsuz etkileri: Antalya ili örneği.* Yayınlanmamış Yüksek Lisans Tezi, Beykent Üniversitesi Sosyal Bilimler Enstitüsü.

Dinç, B. (2018). Dijitalleşmenin tüketici alışkanlıklarına etkisi. *Ekonomistler Platformu.* http://www.ekonomistler.org.tr/wp-content/uploads/2018/01/dijital_1.pdf

Enginkaya, E. (2006). Elektronik perakendecilik ve elektronik alışveriş. *Ege Akademik Bakış Dergisi, 6*(1), 10–16.

Erciş, A., Ünal, S., & Can, P. (2007). Yaşam tarzlarının satın alma karar süreci üzerindeki rolü. *Atatürk Üniversitesi İktisadi ve İdari Bilimler Fakültesi Dergisi, 21*(2), 281–311.

Ernst & Young. (2014). *Türk internet kullanıcıları alışverişte de sanal kanallara yöneliyor.* EY Global Tüketici Araştırması. http://www.ey.com

Fırat, A., & Azmak, E. (2007). Satın alma karar sürecinde beyaz eşya kullanıcılarının marka bağlılığı. *Karamanoğlu Mehmetbey Üniversitesi Sosyal ve Ekonomik Araştırmalar Dergisi, 2007*(2), 251–264.

Genç, M. (2014). *Geleneksel ve online mağazalardan ürün satın alımlarında tüketici tutumları.* Yüksek Lisans Tezi, Çağ Üniversitesi Sosyal Bilimler Enstitüsü.

Goswami, S., & Khan, S. (2015). Impact of consumer decision-making styles on online apparel consumption in India. *Vision (Basel), 19*(4), 303–311. doi:10.1177/0972262915610853

Gümüş, N. (2018). Sosyal medya pazarlamaya yönelik tüketici algılarının incelenmesi: Kırgızistan üzerinde bir araştırma. *MANAS Sosyal Araştırmalar Dergisi, 7*(3), 391–413.

Hannan, M. T., & Freeman, J. (1977). The population ecology of organizations. *American Journal of Sociology, 82*(5), 929–964. doi:10.1086/226424

Kara, Y. (2012). *Sosyal ağların tüketici davranışları üzerindeki etkisi: hazır giyim sektörü örneği.* Yayınlanmamış Yüksek Lisans Tezi, Fatih Üniversitesi Sosyal Bilimler Enstitüsü.

Karaca, Ş., & Gümüş, N. (2019). *Tüketicilerin online yorum ve değerlendirme puanlarına yönelik tutumlarının online satın alma davranışlarına etkisi. In 4. International EMI Entrepreneurship and Social Sciences Congress Book*. Dilkur Akademi.

Keenan, M. (2022). *Global commerce, industry insights and trends*. https://www.shopify.com/enterprise/global-ecommerce-statistics

Keskin, S., & Baş, M. (2015). Sosyal medyanın tüketici davranışları üzerine etkisinin belirlenmesi. *Gazi Üniversitesi İktisadi ve İdari Bilimler Fakültesi Dergisi, 17*(3), 51–69.

Kim, A. J., & Ko, E. (2012). Do social media marketing activities enhance customer equity? An empirical study of luxury fashion brand. *Journal of Business Research, 65*(10), 1480–1486. doi:10.1016/j.jbusres.2011.10.014

Kimery, K. M., & Mccard, M. (2002). Third-party assurances: Mapping the road to trust in e-retailing. *Journal of Information Technology Theory and Application, 4*(2), 63–82.

Kırcova, İ. (2012). *İnternette pazarlama*. Beta Basım Yayım.

Koç, E. (2008). *Tüketici davranışı ve pazarlama stratejileri*. Seçkin Yayınevi.

Koçak, N. G. (2012). *Bireylerin sosyal medya kullanım davranışlarının ve motivasyonlarının kullanımlar ve doyumlar yaklaşımı bağlamında incelenmesi: Eskişehir'de bir uygulama*. Yayımlanmamış Doktora Tezi, Anadolu Üniversitesi Sosyal Bilimler Enstitüsü.

Marsden, P. (2011). *Who is the social consumer?* https://digitalwellbeing.org/infographic-who-is-the-social-consumer/

Mcdowell, M. (2021). *Snapchat boosts AR try-on tools: Farfetch, Prada dive in*, https://www.voguebusiness.com/technology/snapchat-boosts-ar-try-on-tools-farfetch-prada-dive-in

McKinsey & Company. (2022). *The state of fashion 2023: holding onto growth as global clouds gather*. https://www.mckinsey.com/industries/retail/our-insights/state-of-fashion

McKinsey & Company & Business of Fashion. (2021). *The state of fashion 2022*. https://www.mckinsey.com/~/media/mckinsey/industries/retail/our%20insights/state%20of%20fashion/2022/the-state-of-fashion-2022.pdf

Mürütsoy, M. (2013). *İnternet tüketicisinin satın alma davranışlarının incelenmesi üzerine bir araştırma*. Yüksek Lisans Tezi. Niğde Üniversitesi Sosyal Bilimler Enstitüsü, Niğde.

Odabaşı, Y., & Barış, G. (2013). *Tüketici davranışı*. Mediacat Yayınevi.

Odabaşı, Y., & Oyman, M. (2003). *Pazarlama iletişimi yönetimi*. Mediacat Yayınevi.

Olgun, B. (2015). Sosyal medyanın tüketici satın alma davranışları üzerindeki etkisi. *Gümüşhane Üniversitesi Sosyal Bilimler Elektronik Dergisi, 12*, 484–507.

Omarlı, S., & Parıltı, N. (2017). elektronik pazarlamanın tüketicilerin satın alma davranışları üzerine etkisi, Türkiye'de üniversite öğrencileri arasında uygulama. *Anadolu Kültürel Araştırmalar Dergisi*, *1*(3), 91–109.

Onurlubaş, E., Öztürk, D., & Çetin, O. I. (2016). Sosyal medyada pazarlama algısının faktör analiziyle incelenmesi. *Dicle Üniversitesi Sosyal Bilimler Enstitüsü Dergisi*, *8*(16), 233–254.

Özcan, S. O. (2010). İnternet pazarlama faaliyetlerinde tüketici satın alma karar süreci. *İnternet Uygulamaları ve Yönetimi Dergisi, 1*(2), 29-39.

Özgüven, N. (2011). Tüketicilerin online alışverişe karşı tutumları ile demografik özellikleri arasındaki ilişkinin analizi. *KMÜ Sosyal ve Ekonomik Araştırmalar Dergisi*, *2011*(2), 47–54.

Öztürk, D. (2016). Tedarik zinciri yönetimi süreçlerini etkileyen faktörler. *Uluslararası Sosyal ve Ekonomik Bilimler Dergisi*, *6*(1), 17–24.

Papachristou, E., Dimou, Z., Grammatikopoulou, M., Mpaltadoros, L., & Stavropoulos, T. G. (2022). Personalized Fashion On-Demand and e-Fashion Business Models: A User Survey in Greece. In P. Kyratsis, N. Efkolidis, & J. P. Davim (Eds.), *Advances in Product Design Engineering. Management and Industrial Engineering*. Springer. doi:10.1007/978-3-030-98124-2_4

Peck, J., & Childers, T. L. (2003). Individual differences in haptic ınformation processing: The "need for touch" scale. *The Journal of Consumer Research*, *30*(3), 430–442. doi:10.1086/378619

Scott, D. M. (2009). *Pazarlamanın ve iletişimin yeni kuralları*. Mediacat Yayınevi.

Shen, B., Li, Q., Dong, C., & Perry, P. (2017). Sustainability issues in textile and apparel supply chains. *Sustainability (Basel)*, *9*(9), 1592. doi:10.3390u9091592

Söyleyici, G. T., & Çetinkaya, Ö. (2017). Sosyal medya ve tüketici davranışları ilişkisi: Türkiye'deki sosyal medya kullanıcıları üzerine bir araştırma. *Kesit Akademi Dergisi*, *3*(9), 36–54.

Taştepe, Ö. (2020). Dijital pazarlama ile hazır giyim sektöründe pazarlama iletişimi bağlamında tutundurma faaliyetlerine yönelik inceleme. *TJFDM*, *2*(1), 21–29.

Tatlı, H., & Korkut, F. (2015). Sanal alışverişte tüketici davranışlarını etkileyen faktörler: Bingöl Üniversitesi öğrencileri üzerinde bir uygulama. *Erzincan Üniversitesi Sosyal Bilimler Enstitüsü Dergisi*, *8*(1), 63–78.

T.C. Sanayi ve Teknoloji Bakanlığı Kalkınma Ajansları Genel Müdürlüğü. (2021). *Covid-19 krizine yanıt ve dayanıklılık projesi: Tekstil sektörü analiz raporu ve kılavuzu TR 32 bölgesi (Denizli, Aydın, Muğla)*. T.C. Sanayi ve Teknoloji Bakanlığı.

Toksarı, M., & Atlı, H. F. (2018). Giyim modası ve gençlerin hazır giyim tercihlerinin değerlendirilmesine ilişkin bir çalışma. In *18th International Bussiness Congress Book* (pp. 2184-2191). Osmaniye Korkut Ata Üniversitesi, Osmaniye.

Tosun, N. (2010). *İletişim temelli marka yönetimi*. Beta Yayınları.

Ünver, A. (2013). *Hazır giyimde geleneksel pazarlama ile internetten pazarlamanın karşılaştırılmasına yönelik alan çalışması*. Yüksek Lisans Tezi, Marmara Üniversitesi Fen Bilimleri Enstitüsü.

Yaşa Özeltürkay, E., Bozyiğit, S., & Gülmez, M. (2017). Instagram'dan alışveriş yapan tüketicilerin satın alma davranışları: Keşifsel bir çalışma. *Marmara Üniversitesi Öneri Dergisi, 12*(48), 175–198. doi:10.14783/maruoneri.vi.331668

Yeşildal, G. (2017). *Hazır giyim ürünlerinin sosyal medya üzerinden satın alınmasında tüketici algısının rolü (Instagram örneği)*. Yayınlanmamış Yüksek Lisans Tezi, İstanbul Gelişim Üniversitesi Sosyal Bilimler Enstitüsü.

Yıldırım, F., & Boztepe, A. (2019). Bireylerin moda satın alma davranışı ve sosyal medya kullanımı ilişkisi üzerine bir araştırma. *İstanbul Ticaret Üniversitesi Sosyal Bilimler Dergisi, 18*(35), 325-349.

Ying, M. (2012). *Sosyal medya platformları üzerinden pazarlama ve bu mecrayı etkin kullanan sektörler*. Yüksek Lisans Tezi, Kadir Has Üniversitesi Sosyal Bilimler Enstitüsü.

Yolcu, T., Ekici, S. G., Altunışık, R., & Özkaynar, K. (2017). Online mı? Offline mı? Tüketici tercihlerini etkileyen faktörlerin incelenmesi. *Uluslararası Yönetim İktisat ve İşletme Dergisi, 13*(13), 1027–1033.

Yu, U. J., Lee, H. H., & Damhorst, M. L. (2012). Exploring multidimensions of product performance risk in the online apparel shopping context: Visual, tactile and trial risks. *Clothing & Textiles Research Journal, 30*(4), 251–266. doi:10.1177/0887302X12462059

Zorlu, N., & Uzgören, E. (2020). Elektronik ağızdan ağıza iletişimin tüketicilerin satın alma davranışları üzerindeki etkisinin belirleyicileri: Üniversite öğrencileri üzerinde bir araştırma. *Dumlupınar Üniversitesi Sosyal Bilimler Dergisi, 63*, 107–130.

Chapter 5
Effects of Instagram Influencers on the Adoption of Secondhand Fashion Consumption:
Case Studies of Instagram Influencers in Depop

Erin Page
Independent Researcher, UK

Eunsuk Hur
https://orcid.org/0000-0002-9732-6407
Independent Researcher, UK

ABSTRACT

As the use of online marketplaces for second-hand clothing has increased, the effects of social media influencers have become more prominent. However, limited attention has been paid to various types of influencers and their approaches to interacting with their audiences. This chapter aims to identify best practices that social media influencers on Instagram could use to persuade their followers to shop for secondhand fashion on the Depop platform. To identify best practices, comments associated with Instagram posts that mentioned Depop were analysed to assess attitudes towards second-hand fashion. Ten influencers who promoted Depop in their Instagram content were identified, and their visual and textual content were analysed. This chapter provides several recommendations on how secondhand clothing platforms can best use social media influencers to market to consumers' interests. It can also contribute to research within the wider field of marketing in the circular economy.

INTRODUCTION

Alternative consumption models using peer-to-peer (P2P) marketplaces have recently gained attention for their potential to reduce the number of garments that need to be made to satisfy consumers' needs.

DOI: 10.4018/978-1-6684-8753-2.ch005

'Power relationships and the dominant lifestyle' (Garcia et al., 2021, p. 10) have been identified as factors affecting the uptake of more sustainable consumption habits. As these factors are closely related to the fashion influencer–follower relationship, research on this topic could be significant in increasing our knowledge of how influencers can harness these factors to facilitate rather than prevent sustainable consumption. The findings could establish whether P2P platforms should use influencer marketing to successfully increase consumer awareness and uptake of secondhand-fashion consumption. The results could also help determine whether influencers could use their platforms to implement and improve sustainability policies within the fashion industry by promoting support among their followers.

The specific P2P reselling platform on which this case study focused was Depop. Depop places a high emphasis on sustainability and inclusivity within its offerings and community. It has 30 million users (Ellen MacArthur Foundation, 2021) and is the tenth-most-visited fashion site for American Generation Z consumers (Theodosi, 2021). Depop was a logical choice because, like Instagram, it has a global audience and is popular among younger generations; therefore, the two platforms are connected due to the crossover of their audiences. Depop fits into the P2P resale category, as it allows users to take on the roles of both buyers and sellers. Users can buy and sell across a wide range of categories, encompassing womenswear, menswear, accessories, beauty and lifestyle. Depop describes its aim as creating a 'more inclusive [and] diverse and less wasteful' (Depop, 2023) fashion industry.

Thus far, there has been no extensive research into how Instagram influencers and Depop are intertwined. Additionally, Garcia et al. (2021) suggested that the consumption stage of the product lifecycle 'remains a largely under-researched topic' (Garcia et al., 2021, p. 2), which suggests that research into secondhand platforms is essential within the wider scope of sustainability research(Hur, 2020; Hur & Faragher- Siddall, 2022). Therefore, this research has the potential to unearth findings that are new, exciting and relevant to the issues and opportunities currently faced in the sector of fashion marketing. The findings have the potential to reveal whether a correlation exists between the exposure of consumers to the promotion of Depop by Instagram influencers and the attitudes of consumers towards Depop.

The results of the case study were obtained through an analysis of influencers on Instagram. Instagram is owned by Meta, a company focused on social connection platforms that also owns fellow social media giant Facebook (Meta, 2023). Instagram is the third-most-popular social media platform and is especially popular among millennials, with 71% of Americans within the 18–29-year-old age range using the app or web browser (Auxier & Anderson, 2021). The stated aim of Instagram is to 'bring you closer to the people and things you love' (Instagram Inc., 2021) by facilitating photo and video sharing. This makes Instagram an ideal platform to analyse for this case study because it has a wide reach and makes it simple for users to discover and interact with other content creators and topics they are intrigued by (Auxier & Anderson, 2021).

The aim of this research was to answer the following question: how do Instagram influencers impact consumers' attitudes regarding secondhand fashion consumption through their promotion of Depop? The objectives of this study were as follows: (1) to uncover, through the analysis of Instagram comments, whether there is a correlation between consumers' exposure to the promotion of Depop by Instagram influencers and their opinions of secondhand fashion; (2) to investigate whether influencer partnership marketing techniques could be useful to secondhand platforms by assessing the attitudes of the followers of influencers; (3) to explore, by observing how followers of influencers respond to content highlighting secondhand fashion, whether influencers could use their platforms to improve sustainability policies within the fashion industry by creating support among their followers. The case study allows us to understand how the opinions Instagram users have of Depop are influenced by Instagram influencers.

This allows for suggestions regarding actions that Depop and Instagram influencers could take to create positive environmental changes within the fashion industry.

THE SECONDHAND CLOTHING MARKET

Fashion is considered a crucial business because it contributes significantly to the global economy. However, the industry is currently experiencing difficult conditions. Declining rates of expansion (as recorded in 2022) are a result of hyperinflation and negatively affected consumer motivations (Imran Amed et al., 2022). There are increasing concerns regarding the disposal of used garments and its negative impacts on the environment. Each year, approximately 5.8 tonnes of clothing are discarded in Europe, of which 75% are either burned or sent to landfills (Strähle & Erhardt, 2017). This causes pollution and the degradation of ecosystems, which ultimately contribute to climate change (Velenturf et al., 2019). It is not only the end-of-life stages of the process in which sustainability needs to be considered. Activities such as rental models, swapping models and resale all aim to prevent garments ending up in landfills by increasing the number of times they are worn (Strähle & Gräff, 2016; Strähle & Philipsen, 2017).

Clothing accounts for 49% of the secondhand market; therefore, secondhand fashion is a topic that requires research so that we can harness its full potential in creating a more sustainable fashion industry (Walker & Stott, 2018). Encouraging consumers to buy secondhand reduces waste and therefore pollution, which helps curb negative environmental impacts (Hur, 2019, 2020). Only 20% of clothes that are thrown away are beyond repair; therefore, 80% of clothes that would normally be thrown away have the potential to be sold on a secondhand basis which would significantly reduce the greenhouse gases emitted as a result of clothing going into landfills – and thus reduce global warming (Strähle & Hauk, 2017). Responding to the benefits of maximising the utilisation of secondhand clothing, various brands offer takeback schemes to facilitate the repurposing of garments and, therefore, counteract their environmental impacts (Strähle & Höhn, 2017). However, there is growing concern that these initiatives are merely greenwashing, as the brands' main collections often still fall into the fast-fashion category (Rauturier, 2021; Robertson, 2022). Fast fashion products have few recycling possibilities because several secondhand businesses frequently reject them due to their poor quality and low value when resold. As a result, millions of tonnes of waste clothes have been produced (Nguyen et al., 2020). Despite several fast fashion brands such as Zara, H&M, and Primark trying to improve product durability and quality standards to maximise circular economy practices, there are still challenges involved in the inherent fast business model that is based on facilitating large quantities of production and consumption. Consumers are often skeptical about the take-back system or resale platforms from fast fashion brands and how those collected garments can be ultimately recycled or reused effectively.

Moreover, Hur (2020) identified the several significant barriers that prevented non-secondhand clothing consumers. Consumers often find a lack of accessible local stores, variety, and availability of clothing when seeking a required style, size, quality, and colour, and have concerns regarding cleanliness and value for money. This study also suggests that perceived images of secondhand clothing stores are frequently associated with disorganisation and lacking product information. In order to address the several challenges listed above, multiple circular economy strategies and necessary long-term infrastructure is needed to support secondhand clothing charities and community organizations, and those who actively redistribute secondhand clothing.

The Ellen MacArthur Foundation suggested a more holistic approach to approaching a garment's lifecycle through the 5Rs: 'recycle, reuse, reduce, re-design and reimagine' (Strähle & Müller, 2017). 'Recycling and reusing' can reduce garments' environmental impact at the end-of-life stage, whereas 'reducing, redesigning and reimagining' can be used in the design and production phases to ensure a more sustainable process. The 5Rs framework is closely related to the theory of a closed-loop supply chain, the aim of which is to let nothing go to waste. The 'recycle, reuse and reimagine' aspects of the 5Rs model are especially important to closed-loop theory because they ensure that garments are repurposed rather than going to landfills and causing environmental harm (Strähle & Philipsen, 2017). Other researchers have extended the 5R framework to promote a circular economy. For example, Kirchherr et al. (2017) conducted a systematic literature review to identify various types of circular-economy approaches, such as 9R models: R0: refuse, R1: rethink, R2: reduce, R3: reuse, R4: repair, R5: refurbish, R6: remanufacture, R7: repurpose, R8: recycle and R9: recover. Although the concept of circular economy (CE) is popular now in the fashion industry, the idea has obtained a lot of public attention. Criticism arises that the true meaning of CE is often diluted and often loses meaning as time goes on. Mainstream CE strategies would go a long way towards preventing environmental issues and more awareness pertaining to the environmental dangers of the use phase and throwaway culture is needed in achieving the best environmental outcomes possible.

SOCIAL MEDIA INFLUENCERS

Social media influencers have been growing in popularity as marketing agents because they are able to drive 'marketing through content' (Esber & Wong, 2020). Influencers allow brands to reach thousands, sometimes millions, of followers. However, brands are still learning about this form of marketing, such as what can happen if the influencer does not resonate with the intended audience and has a negative effect (Esber & Wong, 2020). One study of social media influencers suggested that an influencer is essentially a 'personal brand' (Enke & Borchers, 2019, p. 264). If brands feel like an influencer's brand aligns with their own, they may use that influencer as a marketing tool (Enke & Borchers, 2019). Similarly, Sun et al., (2022)'s research shows that consumers frequently adapt their views of influencers to the advertised or endorsed goods. Accordingly, when consumers trust the influencers, brands will become more popular.

Consumers often view influencers as opinion readers, and they are likely to trust them rather than other conventional marketing techniques that are facilitated by brands (Enke & Borchers, 2019). One way for social media users to find influencers they wish to follow is through the social media accounts of brands they follow as social media influencers often work in partnership with brands (Gibson, 2012). The relationship could also be established the other way around, whereby an influencer is discovered by following the brand. Social media influencers with vast followings can help firms reach a wider audience. Consumers are likelier to trust social media influencers rather than marketing directly from brands because their content does not have to be approved by 'traditional gatekeepers', and influencers seem authentic and relatable to consumers (Khamis et al., 2017).

Social media influencers create and share posts, engage with their followers and promote awareness in creative formats, but issues have been found with the role of social media influencers in marketing because occasionally, some followers of an influencer may not be real and could instead be bots, meaning that a brand's marketing efforts could be unlikely to convert into the number of customers they expected (Enke & Borchers, 2019). This suggests that influencer marketing is preferable to traditional marketing techniques, which might be less relatable. This trust is further intensified because, as Armstrong and Park (2020) found, followers of influencers feel like they are part of a community with the influencer and other followers. This might be because social media allows for a two-way interaction between influencers and their followers, which is unlike traditional marketing; therefore, consumers may feel as though they personally know the influencers they follow (Strähle & Gräff, 2016). They are also likely to trust other members of the communities they are part of.

Researchers have suggested different ways to classify influencers. Gullstrand Edbring et al. (2016) suggest three different types of influencers: 'the opinion leader, the micro-celebrity and the social leader' (cited in Gulamali & Persson, 2017, p. 21). Influencers defined as opinion leaders or social leaders aim to persuade their followers to adopt certain values or beliefs and identify as part of a particular social group – for example, sustainability advocates – and as such, their followers regard them as experts in that topic. A micro-celebrity is an influencer viewed as aspirational; they conform to society's stereotypical beauty ideals and portray the luxurious aspects of their lives, which make them appear successful (Gulamali & Persson, 2017).

The criterion for this categorisation is as follows: macro-influencers have over 100,000 followers, micro-influencers have between 10,000 and 100,000 followers and nano-influencers have fewer than 10,000 followers (Nizri, 2022). However, a more in depth review of the literature suggests that this categorisation may not be as unambiguous as it seems because different authors characterise the follower counts for the categories differently. For example, Ehlers (2021) defines micro-influencers as having 10,000 to 50,000 followers and macro-influencers as having over 500,000 followers. These numbers are very different in Nizri (2022), who does not include the nano-influencer category. Furthermore, the categories proposed by both authors are broad and could encompass a large range of followers. Therefore, it could be beneficial to create smaller categories.

It is commonly thought that influencers are the ones who influence their followers (Strähle & Grünewald, 2017) because they are the ones who bring products and brands to the attention of consumers (Khamis et al., 2017). However, the interaction between influencers and their followers flows both ways (Strähle & Gräff, 2016). In addition, Gullstrand Edbring et al. (2016) note that consumers use their buying power to influence the market. Therefore, could it be possible that consumers' purchase decisions also influence the influencers' choices about the topics on which they make content?

THE NEGATIVE IMPACTS OF SOCIAL MEDIA

While influencers may choose to promote sustainable fashion options, Armstrong and Park (2020) observed that they are also likely to post a large amount of fashion content, therefore encouraging consumers to buy more than they need. Even if products consumers are purchasing are made sustainably or are secondhand, if they are overconsumed, it still creates sustainability issues (Armstrong & Park, 2020). Gibson (2012) also expressed concerns that influencers may be promoting fast fashion because they can often afford more expensive clothing than their followers. Therefore, if consumers want to emulate the outfits of influencers, they often turn to unsustainable fast-fashion retailers for cheaper versions of garments.

Furthermore, influencers have been criticised for being misleading. Influencers often partner with brands and promote their products in return for payments or free products, and consumers may not always realise when a post is a paid partnership, which may lead to consumers being misled (Strähle & Gräff, 2016). Influencers are not always experts on the topics they discuss in their social media content, which can lead to 'fake news' that consumers take to be true (Khamis et al., 2017). The images influencers share can also be misleading. Photographs and videos can, unbeknownst to consumers, be edited to try and fit in with society's beauty ideals; however, if consumers do not realise that photographs are edited, they may strive to look the same, despite it being unattainable in reality (Gibson, 2012).

There are sustainability issues mentioned in the literature that cannot be rectified by secondhand consumption, such as unethical behaviour. Ethics refer to how people are treated throughout the supply chain, and secondhand fashion may make it harder than even fast fashion to trace the ethics involved in a garment's lifecycle because the garment may have been made a long time ago or the original retailer may not be apparent. This could also mean that consumers are not aware of how sustainable the fabrics, fibres and production processes used to make the garment were.

One approach in addressing the above challenges and facilitate secondhand clothing consumption is to further promote the idea that sustainability marketing could play an important role in promoting secondhand clothing to a mainstream audience (Hur, 2020; Hur & Cassidy, 2019). However, the full range of advantages of employing secondhand clothing is not widely known. By maximising offline and online visual merchandising tactics, including curated secondhand clothing window displays, focusing on certain fashion trends, and promoting nostalgic narratives, clothing fashion retailers and charities can optimise hedonic experiences to attract consumers (Claridge & Hur, 2021; Hur, 2020). Recent research on influencer marketing has discovered that the quality and attributes of an influencer's material has a substantial impact on their followers' engagement levels and purchasing inclinations. Influencers often reveal details about their private lives and share their personal preferences for particular styles, options, and products that link with their lifestyle (Zheng et al., 2023). Although several studies have recently explored the roles of influencers in social media marketing, there is limited research on how to effectively promote secondhand clothing in various emerging peer-to-peer marketplaces and how different groups of consumers will require different messages within secondhand fashion marketing.

CASE STUDY: DEPOP

Influencers were chosen as the focus of the case study because past research shows that they have been growing in popularity as marketing agents in recent years (Gullstrand Edbring et al., 2016) and marketing has the potential to correct misconceptions that provide a barrier to secondhand clothing consumption (Strähle & Kreuzhermes, 2017). Primary research was conducted in the form of a case study in which the social media content of nine Instagram fashion influencers was investigated to understand the impacts of their promotion of Depop and their followers' attitudes towards Depop. The case study focused specifically on the social media platform Instagram and the P2P resale platform Depop. To carry out this research, keyword searches were carried out in the Instagram search bar to identify social media posts in which influencers promoted P2P secondhand reselling platforms. The keywords included 'secondhand clothes', 'secondhand fashion', 'sustainable fashion', 'secondhand fashion influencer', 'sustainable fashion influencer', 'thrifting', 'secondhand outfit', 'resale' and 'circular economy'.

From the keyword search, 10 fashion influencers on the Instagram platform were identified as the focus of the case study. Their follower counts ranged from 4,440 to 367,000 followers, and they all posted consistently. These were important factors to consider because it is important to research a range of different categories of influencers to understand how the different types of influencers may exert different types or levels of influence. It was also important that they posted consistently to prove that they were active on their accounts, as otherwise, followers may lose interest and therefore be less easily influenced. The ten influencers were @acteevism, @emsladedmondson, @hannahxelliman, @izzy_manuel, @neverpayretail, @onestylishmoo, @slow_fashion_lottie, @sunsetsaraid, @theflippside and @trashisfortossers. All the influencers identified focused on secondhand fashion within their Instagram feeds. This was identified by reading the posts within the chosen timeframe and assessing whether they mentioned secondhand platforms. Influencers were chosen who posted at least five posts that included mentions of at least one secondhand platform. After the influencers were identified, the names of the secondhand platforms they mentioned and the number of times they mentioned them within the timeframe were recorded. This was achieved by reading each post and recording each secondhand platform mentioned. A tally was kept of the number of times they were mentioned. This was repeated to increase reliability.

Figure 1. Number of mentions of secondhand platforms

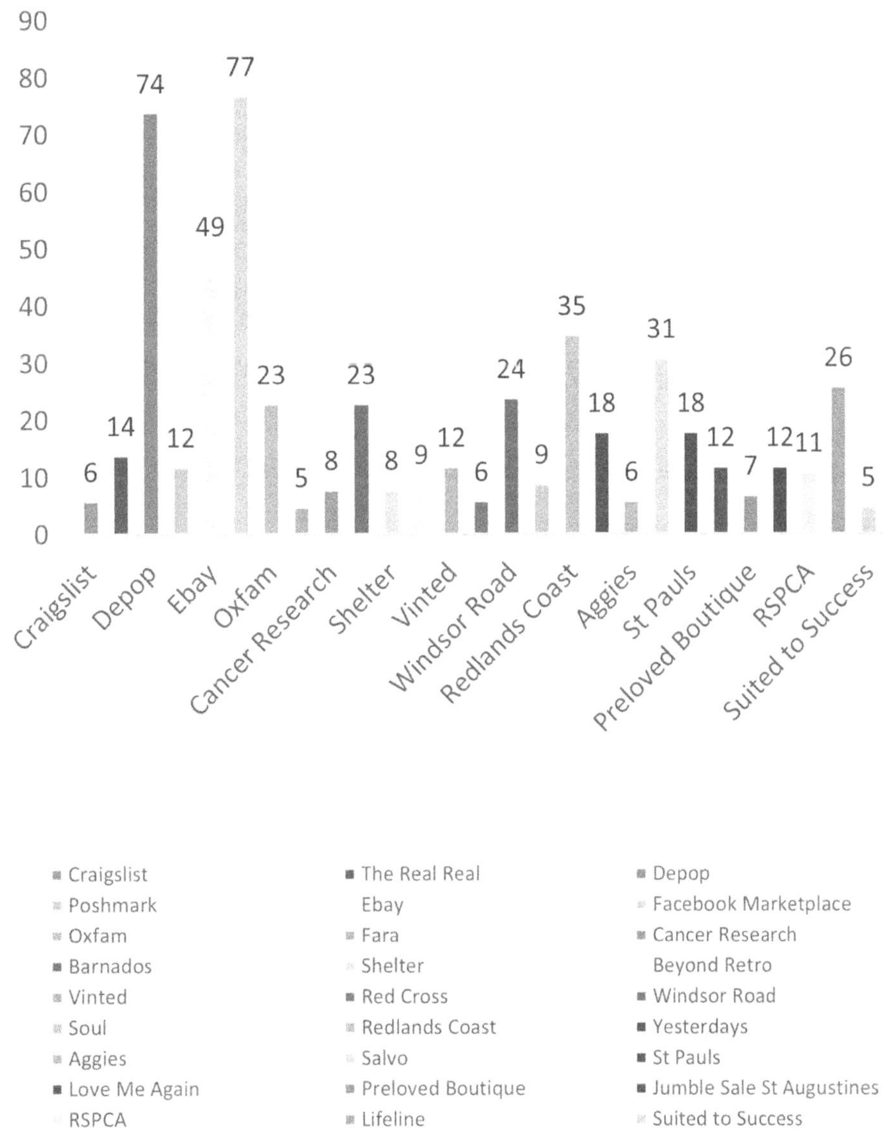

The influencers' Instagram posts from 1 January 2020 to 31 December 2021 were analysed in the case study. This timeframe was chosen because it is recent enough to represent how Instagram users are currently being influenced and how Instagram influencers currently choose to create content. It also provides a large enough timeframe to assess whether the trends and patterns discovered were flukes. The comments sections for each post that mentioned Depop were analysed to determine the effect that promoting Depop has on the followers of the influencers. To achieve this, comments referring to secondhand fashion, sustainability or the outfit the influencer was wearing were recorded. These three categories were chosen because the aim of the research was to create a more sustainable fashion industry through secondhand fashion, and the comments about the outfits may suggest whether the audience finds secondhand fashion visually appealing. During the analysis, the comments on the posts, the visuals of the posts, the captions of the posts, the differences between the content and comments in 2020 and 2021 and the number of likes on each post were studied according to the criteria identified in Table 1.

Table 1. Criteria for the analysis

Aspect being analysed	Criteria for the analysis
Commenters' response to posts	What was said? Was their reaction positive, neutral or negative? Did they ask any questions, and if so, what topics were they enquiring about? Which features/topics were mentioned most frequently? Which topics were they most positive and most negative about?
Visual content of posts	Was it a photo or a video (and what type of video, such as a reel or tiktok video)? The general aesthetic – for example, the types of fashion trends portrayed, colour palette, and what the photos and videos consisted of (including outfits and infographics)
Topics included in the captions	Subcategory of secondhand clothing Positive aspects of secondhand clothing Challenges to secondhand clothing Was secondhand clothing directly mentioned? Did the caption directly ask the audience a question about their opinions?
Differences between 2020 and 2021 posts	Type of content Focus of the caption Attitudes portrayed in the comments

CONTENT CHARACTERISTICS

The case study involved an analysis of the comment sections, content, visual appearances and numbers of likes of the influencers' posts that mentioned Depop. The analysis of this data allowed for a derivation of real-world mechanisms that could be put in place to increase the uptake of secondhand fashion consumption.

@trashisfortosser's posts about Depop and the secondhand fashion industry in general garnered a very positive response from her followers. The posts also seemed to lead her followers to think about sustainability. The comments suggested that the posts regarding Depop were educational and promoted the sustainable and environmentally friendly benefits that shopping from secondhand platforms, such as Depop, offer. In addition, one comment used the word 'pride', which suggests that the post was successful in presenting secondhand fashion websites, such as Depop, in a positive light. Such a comment may also cause others to reflect on the reasons the commenter was proud of her secondhand wardrobe and

Table 2. Content characteristics

Influencer	Visual characteristics of the account	Type of content of depop posts
@trashisfortossers (Singer, 2022)	Neutral colour palette Minimalist	Outfit photos Reels (form of short video) showcasing various secondhand outfits
@hannahxelliman (Elliman, 2022)	The backdrops of her photos are mostly outdoor locations Heavy focus on fashion content	Outfit photos (some in outdoor locations and some mirror selfies)
@onestylishmoo (onestylishmoo, 2022)	Varied poses Pops with colour 90s-inspired	Outfit photos TikTok videos
@acteevism (McSherry, 2022)	Heavily fashion-focused Captions and quotes edited onto the photos themselves Infographics	Outfit photos Reels
@sunsetsaraid (sunsetsaraid, 2022)	Use of very bright colours Fashion-focused Influenced by 60s and 70s trends and aesthetics Captions edited onto the photos themselves Attention-grabbing backdrops (using props to create a theme that matches the outfit or editing a pattern onto the background that matches the outfit)	Outfit photos Reels (showing the editing process of her posts)
@theflippside (Fabella, 2022)	Bright colours Mostly outfit photos Formal outfits (lots of tailored pieces and luxurious fabrics)	Videos Tiktok videos Outfit photos
@izzy manuel (izzy_manuel, 2022)	Bright colours Eye-catching prints Unique poses	Outfit photos
@slow_fashion_lottie (Hanson-Lowe, 2022)	Mellow colour palette Airy and feminine outfits Includes slides with written information about sustainability in fashion on some posts Uses some posts to promote items for sale on her own Depop account	Outfit photos Videos Reels Written information slides
@emsladedmondson (Edmondson, 2022)	Mix of fashion, lifestyle and interiors content Pops with colour throughout Includes written information slides about sustainability in fashion on some posts	Outfit photos Written information slides

possibly feel shame if they are not shopping secondhand. Many followers were involved in a discussion on how best to recycle old clothing, and many suggestions about methods and locations for doing so were provided by fellow followers. One of the posts promoted a Depop jumper that the influencer had upcycled, provoking a discussion among the followers in the comments section about how they could also upcycle their own clothing. This is encouraging, as the post not only promoted secondhand fashion but also encouraged followers to repair or upcycle their clothing, therefore preventing waste and providing two levels of sustainability.

When analysing the Depop posts on @acteevism's account, it was again clear that the followers were very complimentary about the outfits. However, in addition, it seemed that the followers had also been provoked to consider sustainability aspects as a result of the Depop posts, suggesting that followers would like to see more content in which influencers are transparent about where they have obtained their outfits and how the outfit choices they make impact the environment. It is evident that @acteevism's followers felt inspired by her promotion of Depop's secondhand platform because many of the comments were made by followers sharing their own positive experiences of shopping secondhand fashion and attempting to increase their awareness of sustainability while making more sustainable choices. Comments such as these built upon the information and awareness raised within @acteevism's original post and further encourage Instagram users to shop from secondhand platforms such as Depop because, as studies have shown, people are likelier to make sustainable decisions (such as shopping from secondhand platforms) if they perceive others in their peer group to also be doing so (White et al., 2019). This is because people feel more comfortable participating in a particular behaviour if they consider it to be a social norm (White et al., 2019).

Within the comments section, it was also apparent that @acteevism took the time to reply to most comments received on the posts. This could improve the awareness and adoption of secondhand shopping and more sustainable behaviours among her followers. For example, one commenter asked about how @acteevism learned to repair her clothing to make it last longer, and @acteevism's reply gave the commenter as well as other readers the information they needed to try out clothing repair and upcycling themselves, therefore lending an educational dimension to the account.

In the comments section of most of @sunsetsariad's Depop posts, there was no mention of the secondhand or sustainability aspects of the posts, with the attention instead focusing on the visual appeal of the outfits. However, in one of her posts, @sunsetsaraid posed a direct question to her followers that enquired about their own secondhand shopping habits. This post received a significantly higher number of comments than @sunsetsaraid's other Depop posts, and these comments were also much more heavily focused on the specific topic of secondhand fashion. This suggests that if Instagram fashion influencers were to make a conscious effort to directly engage their followers about secondhand fashion through the content used in their posts, more awareness could be raised about the topic, and there could be greater potential for higher uptake of secondhand shopping. The discussions also prompted followers to get involved by sharing their own online secondhand shopping experiences and tips, such as useful apps to help organise and source a secondhand shopping wishlist. These findings imply that if Instagram fashion influencers were to promote secondhand fashion through open discussions within the comments sections of their posts and in the posts themselves, the awareness and consequent uptake of secondhand shopping behaviours could be significantly increased.

In one post, @theflippside asked her followers about their tendency to rewear garments. This combines two forms of sustainable fashion consumption in one post by referring to both Depop and the habit of rewearing in the same post, resulting in a heavier focus on the importance of sustainability within fashion. The comments implied that Instagram fashion influencers can play a part in encouraging consumers to adopt more sustainable fashion consumption behaviours. This presumption suggests that secondhand fashion influencers on Instagram play an important role in making secondhand shopping less daunting for consumers and giving them the tools that they require to feel confident in making secondhand purchases. Studies have shown that consumers increasingly turn to Instagram when seeking out information (Madzunya et al., 2021). Thus, the existence of secondhand-fashion Instagram influencers is important for spreading information that could lead to a more sustainable fashion industry.

@izzy_manuel (2022) spread further awareness of Depop by replying to complimentary comments about specific garments and explaining that they were purchased from Depop. This behaviour spread awareness to followers who may not have been initially interested in the sustainability/secondhand credentials of a garment, therefore giving them a second and more direct opportunity to learn about secondhand fashion (when replying directly to a comment, the author of the original comment is directly notified). It is also interesting to note that izzy_manuel (2023) was the only one of the influencers studied that featured a comment from the official Depop account on one of their Depop posts. This comment from Depop suggests to followers that the Depop community is a close-knit one, which may encourage them to become a part of it.

The resulted in the comments sections of @slow_fashion_lottie's posts being some of the most relevant to sustainability out of all the influencers in the case study. Not only that, but the discussions also encompassed a wide range of sustainability subcategories that reflected the breadth and depth of the informative content that @slow_fashion_lottie included in her posts. Examples of such subcategories included discussions about the least environmentally harmful way to wash clothing (specifically swimwear), the arm holes in vintage clothing being smaller than those in more modern clothing (this discussion even resulted in one commenter offering to fix the problem for @slow_fashion_lottie by sewing the garment for her), wearing clothes more often rather than just saving them for certain occasions, reselling items people do not wear often, upcycling garments to make them more wearable for the owner, becoming a good seller on Depop, sustainable menstruation products, the struggle of people who require clothing in larger sizes to find these sizes in the secondhand market (which resulted in retailers with secondhand clothing in larger sizes also commenting to make people aware of their offerings) and made-to-order clothing models. The general consensus from the consumers was that it is impossible to consume fashion in a completely sustainable manner, but it is better to take at least some steps towards consuming fashion more sustainably than none at all and that every sustainable choice counts. One theme that was apparent in the content and tone of the comments on @slow_fashion_lottie's posts was that she had created a non-judgemental platform for people to share and learn about secondhand and sustainable fashion choices, whatever stage of the sustainability journey the followers might be on.

@emsladedmondson's first post to mention Depop focused in detail on the use of secondhand platforms in the advertisement breaks on television shows such as Love Island, compared to the use of fast-fashion brand advertisements in such slots. Followers then took the initiative in an attempt to promote this idea by suggesting the creation of a petition to campaign for Depop or similar secondhand platforms to replace the fast-fashion brands commonly seen in these slots. The second post by @emsladedmondson regarding Depop focused on the topic of rewearing clothing rather than constantly striving to buy new pieces. Interestingly, social media was mentioned by commenters as a forum that has discouraged the habit of rewearing. This is interesting since, while making these comments, they were simultaneously using social media to promote the opposite. The commenters making this point suggested that social media has a negative impact on rewearing due to its promotion of unrealistic expectations, yet by leaving the comments on @emsladedmondson's post about how often they are likely to rewear, they are encouraging a more realistic image.

VISUAL CONTENT ANALYSIS

The influencers each had their own unique visual identities, which increased interest in their feeds. The main form of content for the influencers was outfit photos, which suggests that the main goal of promoting Depop was to get their followers to like the clothes they purchased from that platform. Many of the influencers also made use of TikTok videos or Reels, which allowed them to feature multiple garments in a short period of time. For example, @acteevism made use of a Reel to show followers the process of mending the buttonholes of a jumpsuit she was able to get for a very good price on Depop due to the fault. This video was highly informative and could lead her followers to learn a skill that allowed them to behave more sustainably (McSherry, 2022). In addition, one video @theflippside (2022) posted was a tutorial on how to tie dye garments, which established her Instagram account as a forum for learning a new skill. Reels and TikTok videos require considerable editing and thus showcase the creativity and dedication of the influencers.

Some of the influencers also provided infographics, captions edited onto their photos or written information slides in their content. This positioned their accounts as places to go to learn more about secondhand and sustainable fashion. One such written information slide by @emsladedmondson read, "1 in 3 16-24-year olds will not wear an outfit more than once on social media" (Edmondson, 2022) This highlighted the problems with fast-fashion attitudes and helped to establish her account as focused on sustainable rather than fast fashion. This influencer enjoyed and recognised the environmental benefits of rewearing garments, which encouraged users to follow her over fast-fashion influencers.

NUMBER OF LIKES

In general, the posts that earned the most likes provided tips and advice on how to consume fashion more sustainably. However, an exception to this generalisation was one of @slow_fashion_lottie's posts, which offered advice on sustainable swimwear options and was the least liked of all her posts that mentioned Depop (Hanson-Lowe, 2022). However, this could be because, when it was posted, there were still many travel restrictions in place worldwide due to the coronavirus pandemic, and people may not have been planning holidays and needing swimwear (Charumilind & Lamb, 2020). Tutorials also received many likes, with @acteevism's post showing her followers how she mended frayed buttonholes (McSherry, 2022) and @theflippside's (2022) post showing the process she used on a tie dye project being their most liked. These findings suggest that Instagram users want more information on sustainable fashion and value the accounts of the influencers because they allow them to learn more about a topic in which they are interested. This further suggests that it would be beneficial not only for the environment for influencers to post tips on sustainable fashion consumption but also for the influencers, as it would increase their engagement levels.

RECOMMENDATIONS

The comment analysis revealed very positive comments from the followers of all the influencers studied. In fact, there were no comments that were negative towards either the influencer in question or their outfit choice. This suggests that the promotion of Depop by fashion influencers creates a positive response among consumers and is therefore beneficial to the influencer. The other type of comment that was frequently left by followers could be described as educational. This type of comment consisted of followers asking the influencer or other followers for advice on a certain aspect of secondhand shopping or sustainability or sharing their own experiences of shopping secondhand. These types of comments suggest a sense of community, where followers feel empowered to share their experiences and ask any questions, they may have in the comments section in order to increase the group's knowledge regarding secondhand fashion and shopping. This also implies that it is the influencer who facilitates the creation of this community, as the community consists of their followers.

The value-creation process involves both influencers and followers. Past studies have shown that followers can contribute knowledge by interacting with accounts in a form of cocreation. Consequently, the total number of followers could increase if followers endorse the account to others, increasing the value of the influencers, which is a crucial and dominant contemporary social media marketing mechanism (Casaló et al., 2020; Vargo & Lusch, 2008). Some of the influencers specifically asked questions in which they encouraged followers to reply in the comments, and some also replied to comments and contributed to the conversations in the comments themselves. When this was the case, the conversations often appeared to be more fruitful. If Depop or similar secondhand platforms were to use social media influencers as part of a marketing campaign, it would be beneficial for them to encourage the influencers to create questions in captions and reply to comments.

The most popular posts in terms of likes were those that had an educational element. This implies that followers are interested in finding out more about Depop and secondhand fashion. It could, therefore, be beneficial for influencers to provide information, as this appears to be what their followers are searching for. The comment analysis also revealed that commenters responded positively when the influencers acknowledged that constantly making sustainable clothing decisions can be difficult and unattainable for everyone and that it is better for everyone to try their best and do what they can rather than attempting perfection in terms of sustainable wardrobe choices. Commenters even expressed this view themselves in the comments. This suggests that influencers need to be careful that their tone does not come across as patronising or pedantic to their audience, as this may alienate followers, devalue their opinions and ultimately deter them from purchasing items from Depop. This suggests that if Depop were to make use of social media influencers as marketing partners, they need to pick which influencers they work with carefully to ensure that they have tones and mindsets that match those of their audiences.

With regard to the visuals of the influencer accounts, no single visual style garnered a more positive response than others. The visual styles ranged from very simplistic, with a neutral colour palette, to very bright and quirky. Yet all the influencers earned positive responses from followers. This suggests that consumers who shop secondhand have multiple styles. In turn, this could imply that if secondhand platforms were to employ influencers in marketing, it would be important for them to research the different style characteristics and trends possessed by large groups of their audience and find influencers to work with who represent those styles and trends, as they would then be relatable to the audience of the secondhand platforms.

Strähle and Klatt (2017) found that consumers enjoyed the social aspect that shopping secondhand provided compared to shopping for fast fashion. The findings of the case study support this, as they suggest that the followers of influencers feel like part of a community due to the discussion of secondhand platforms, such as Depop. The case study also found that Instagram users look to influencers for information and to gain knowledge, suggesting that they do not already possess that knowledge. It was found that the language used to describe the secondhand clothing of the influencers in the comments sections was highly positive. This suggests that seeing how influencers style their secondhand garments changes consumers' perceptions. In turn, this implies that it would be useful for Depop and other secondhand platforms to use social media influencers to help consumers realise the potential of secondhand fashion. The suggestions provided in this discussion section answer the research question because suggestions have been provided for use by Depop to make the most of social media influencers as marketing representatives. This research has, therefore, contributed to an understudied niche of the secondhand fashion sector. Therefore, this study not only provides suggestions for how secondhand clothing platforms can best employ social media influencers in marketing to gain consumers but also contributes to research within the wider field of secondhand fashion and provides a basis for further inquiries.

CONCLUSION

Aiming to inform influencer marketing activity, this chapter aimed to uncover the best methods social media influencers could use to increase positive attitudes towards secondhand fashion. To achieve this, the comments of Instagram posts that mentioned Depop were analysed to assess attitudes towards secondhand fashion. The main finding of the research was that, for influencers to promote a positive attitude towards Depop among their followers, they should be informative yet relatable. The study shows that resellers asking direct questions to resellers' followers in their captions encourages engagement and provokes deeper thinking about the topic among their audience. Creating posts that are informative yet relatable in terms of sustainability expectations has also been found to garner a positive response from Instagram users. The study also discovered that it is important for secondhand retailers to research which trends are most popular amongst their audiences and choose influencers who express those trends in their personalities and posts. This research focused on improving the purchase stage of the product lifecycle by researching methods of encouraging consumers to purchase secondhand garments. However, it would be beneficial for further research to focus on how Instagram influencers can encourage consumers to behave more sustainably during the use phase of the product lifecycle. Finally, while this research focused on encouraging consumers to buy from Depop, further research focusing on encouraging consumers to sell on Depop should address the end-of-life stage of the product lifecycle.

REFERENCES

Auxier, B., & Anderson, M. (2021). Social media use in 2021. Pew Research Center, 1, 1-4. https://www.pewresearch.org/internet/2021/04/07/social-media-use-in-2021/

Armstrong, C. M. J., & Park, H. (2020). Online Clothing Resale: A Practice Theory Approach to Evaluate Sustainable Consumption Gains. *Journal of Sustainability Research, 2*(2). Advance online publication. doi:10.20900/jsr20200017

Casaló, L. V., Flavián, C., & Ibáñez-Sánchez, S. (2020). Influencers on Instagram: Antecedents and consequences of opinion leadership. *Journal of Business Research, 117*, 510–519. doi:10.1016/j.jbusres.2018.07.005

Charumilind, S., & Lamb, J. (2020). When will the COVID-19 pandemic end? *McKinsey & Company*. https://www.mckinsey.com/industries/healthcare/our-insights/when-will-the-covid-19-pandemic-end

Claridge, C., & Hur, E. (2021). Revitalizing department store shopping value and in-store experiences: A case study on Debenhams and Selfridges. *Journal of Fashion Business, 25*(6), 81–101.

Depop. (2023). *How does Depop work?* Depop. https://blog.depop.com/articles/how-does-depop-work

Edmondson, E. S. (2022). *@emsladedmondson*. Instagram. https://www.instagram.com/emsladedmondson/

Ehlers, K. (2021). Micro-Influencers: When Smaller Is Better. *Forbes*, 1–6. https://www.forbes.com/sites/forbesagencycouncil/2021/06/02/micro-influencers-when-smaller-is-better/?sh=3ae55461539b

Ellen MacArthur Foundation. (2021). *Social peer-to-peer marketplace: Depop*. Ellen MacArthur Foundation. https://ellenmacarthurfoundation.org/circular-examples/depop

Elliman, H. (2022). *@hannahxelliman*. Instagram. https://www.instagram.com/hannahxelliman/

Enke, N., & Borchers, N. S. (2019). Social Media Influencers in Strategic Communication: A Conceptual Framework for Strategic Social Media Influencer Communication. *International Journal of Strategic Communication*, *13*(4), 261–277. doi:10.1080/1553118X.2019.1620234

Esber, D., & Wong, J. (2020). *Discussions in digital: Influencer marketing podcast*. McKinsey & Company. https://www.mckinsey.com/capabilities/growth-marketing-and-sales/our-insights/discussions-in-digital-influencer-marketing-is-ready-for-its-close-up

Fabella, K. (2022). *@theflippside*. Instagram. https://www.instagram.com/theflippside/

Garcia, D. G., Kipnis, E., Vasileiou, E., & Solomon, A. (2021). Consumption in the circular economy: Learning from our mistakes. In Sustainability (Switzerland) (Vol. 13, Issue 2, pp. 1–23). doi:10.3390u13020601

Gibson, P. C. (2012). Fashion and Celebrity Culture. In *Fashion and Celebrity Culture*. Berg. doi:10.2752/9781472572424/GIBSON0009

Gulamali, A., & Persson, J. (2017). *The Social Media Influencer and Brand Switching*. Lund University: School of Economics and Management. https://lup.lub.lu.se/student-papers/record/8910352/file/8910354.pdf

Gullstrand Edbring, E., Lehner, M., & Mont, O. (2016). Exploring consumer attitudes to alternative models of consumption: Motivations and barriers. *Journal of Cleaner Production*, *123*, 5–15. doi:10.1016/j.jclepro.2015.10.107

Hanson-Lowe, L. (2022). *@slow_fashion_lottie*. Instagram. https://www.instagram.com/slow_fashion_lottie/

Hur, E. (2019). Collaborative consumption for small- and medium-sized fashion enterprises in south korea. In *Global Perspectives on Sustainable Fashion* (pp. 148–159). Bloomsbury., doi:10.5040/9781350058170.ch-004.3

Hur, E. (2020). Rebirth fashion: Secondhand clothing consumption values and perceived risks. *Journal of Cleaner Production*, *273*, 122951. doi:10.1016/j.jclepro.2020.122951

Hur, E., & Cassidy, T. (2019). Perceptions and attitudes towards sustainable fashion design: Challenges and opportunities for implementing sustainability in fashion. *International Journal of Fashion Design. Technology and Education*, *12*(2), 208–217. Advance online publication. doi:10.1080/17543266.2019.1572789

Hur, E., & Faragher- Siddall, E. (2022). Young Consumer Perspectives on Government Policy Interventions for Sustainable Fashion Consumption in the UK. *Fashion Practice*, *14*(3), 405–427. doi:10.1080/17569370.2022.2125149

Amed, I., Balchandani, A., Berg, A., Hedrich, S., Jensen, J. E., Le Merle, L., & Rölkens, F. (2022). *State of Fashion 2022*. McKinsey's Retail Practice. https://www.stateoffashion.org/en/

Instagram Inc. (2021). *Instagram on the App Store*. Apple App Store. https://apps.apple.com/us/app/instagram/id389801252

izzy_manuel. (2022). *@izzy_manuel*. Instagram. https://www.instagram.com/izzy_manuel/

Khamis, S., Ang, L., & Welling, R. (2017). Self-branding, 'micro-celebrity' and the rise of Social Media Influencers. *Celebrity Studies*, *8*(2), 191–208. doi:10.1080/19392397.2016.1218292

Kirchherr, J., Reike, D., & Hekkert, M. (2017). Conceptualizing the circular economy: An analysis of 114 definitions. In *Resources* (Vol. 127, pp. 221–232). Conservation and Recycling. doi:10.1016/j.resconrec.2017.09.005

Madzunya, N., Viljoen, K., & Cilliers, L. (2021). The effect of Instagram conspicuous consumptive behaviour on the intention to purchase luxury goods: A developing country's perspective. *South African Journal of Information Management*, *23*(1). Advance online publication. doi:10.4102ajim.v23i1.1267

McSherry, M. (2022). *@acteevism*. Instagram. https://www.instagram.com/acteevism/

Meta. (2023). *Company Information, Culture, and Principles | About Meta*. Meta Platforms, Inc. https://about.meta.com/company-info/?utm_source=about.facebook.com&utm_medium=redirect

Nguyen, H. T., Le, D. M. D., Ho, T. T. M., & Nguyen, P. M. (2021). Enhancing sustainability in the contemporary model of CSR: a case of fast fashion industry in developing countries. Social responsibility journal, 17(4), 578-591. https://doi.org/ doi:10.1108/SRJ-03-2019-0108

Nizri, E. (2022). *Macro-Influencers Vs. Micro-Influencers: The Great Social Media Debate*. Forbes. https://www.forbes.com/sites/forbestechcouncil/2022/03/01/macro-influencers-vs-micro-influencers-the-great-social-media-debate/?sh=44a468c45286

onestylishmoo. (2022). *@onestylishmoo*. Instagram. https://www.instagram.com/onestylishmoo/

Rauturier, S. (2021). *How Ethical Is Aritzia?* Good on You. https://goodonyou.eco/how-ethical-is-nike/

Robertson, L. (2022). How Ethical is Nike? In *Good on You*. https://goodonyou.eco/how-ethical-is-nike/

Singer, L. (2022). *@trashisfortossers*. Instagram. https://www.instagram.com/trashisfortossers/

Strähle, J., & Erhardt, C. (2017). *Collaborative Consumption 2.0: An Alternative to Fast Fashion Consumption*. doi:10.1007/978-981-10-2440-5_8

Strähle, J., & Gräff, C. (2016). The Role of Social Media for a Sustainable Consumption. In *Green Fashion Retail* (pp. 225–247). Springer. doi:10.1007/978-981-10-2440-5_12

Strähle, J., & Grünewald, A.-K. (2017). The Prosumer Concept in Fashion Retail: Potentials and Limitations. In Green fashion retail (pp. 95–117). doi:10.1007/978-981-10-2440-5_6

Strähle, J., & Hauk, K. (2017). Impact on Sustainability: Production Versus Consumption. In Green fashion retail (pp. 49–75). doi:10.1007/978-981-10-2440-5_4

Strähle, J., & Höhn, M. (2017). Cross-Industry Learnings: What Fashion Retail Can Learn from the Used-Car Industry. In *Green Fashion Retail* (pp. 157–174). Springer. doi:10.1007/978-981-10-2440-5_9

Strähle, J., & Klatt, L. M. (2017). The Second Hand Market for Fashion Products. In Green Fashion Retail (pp. 119–134). doi:10.1007/978-981-10-2440-5_7

Strähle, J., & Kreuzhermes, S. (2017). Impact of Sustainable Manufacturing Standards for Retail Brands. In Green Fashion Retail (pp. 77–93). doi:10.1007/978-981-10-2440-5_5

Strähle, J., & Müller, V. (2017). Key Aspects of Sustainability in Fashion Retail. In Green fashion retail (pp. 7–26). doi:10.1007/978-981-10-2440-5_2

Strähle, J., & Philipsen, F. (2017). Closed-Loop Production: A Literature Review. In *Green Fashion Retail* (pp. 27–47). Springer. doi:10.1007/978-981-10-2440-5_3

sunsetsaraid. (2022). *@sunsetsaraid*. Instagram. https://www.instagram.com/sunsetsaraid/

Theodosi, N. (2021). *Depop's Sale to Etsy Highlights Secondhand Market Boom – WWD*. Women's Wear Daily. https://wwd.com/business-news/retail/depops-sale-etsy-second-hand-market-boom-1234834135/

Vargo, S. L., & Lusch, R. F. (2008). Service-dominant logic: Continuing the evolution. *Journal of the Academy of Marketing Science*, *36*(1), 1–10. doi:10.100711747-007-0069-6

Velenturf, A. P. M., Archer, S. A., Gomes, H. I., Christgen, B., Lag-Brotons, A. J., & Purnell, P. (2019). Circular economy and the matter of integrated resources. In Science of the Total Environment (Vol. 689, pp. 963–969). doi:10.1016/j.scitotenv.2019.06.449

Walker, J., & Stott, R. (2018). *LSN : Markets : Fashion Recommerce*. LSNGlobal. https://www.lsnglobal.com/markets/article/22207/fashion-recommerce

White, K., Habib, R., & Hardisty, D. J. (2019). How to SHIFT consumer behaviors to be more sustainable: A literature review and guiding framework. *Journal of Marketing*, *83*(3), 22–49. doi:10.1177/0022242919825649

Zheng, L., Huang, B., Qiu, H., & Bai, H. (2023). The role of social media followers' agency in influencer marketing: A study based on the heuristic–systematic model of information processing. *International Journal of Advertising*, •••, 1–26. doi:10.1080/02650487.2023.2229148

Chapter 6
Fashion Brands and Social Networks:
Influencers' Narratives, Sponsorship, and Consumers' Engagement

Nedka Dechkova Nikiforova
Department of Statistics, University of Florence, Italy

ABSTRACT

Social networks affect positively the consumers' brand loyalty. They represent a key tool to efficiently maintain existing consumers and/or to attract new ones. An increasingly more used strategy by several fashion brands is to engage influencers for mentions on social network platforms, also in view of brand strategies to reach certain types of consumers. In this chapter, the author proposes in a conceptual framework a novel approach to efficiently reveal the influencers' language adopted on social networks for sponsored with respect to not sponsored contents, and by also taking care of aspects related to the consumers' engagement. The core component of the approach is the structural topic model, which is a substantial improvement of the latent Dirichlet allocation method. The structural topic model can provide promising results which can be successfully employed by interested practitioners and brand managers to efficiently define marketing strategies, or to strengthen existing ones.

INTRODUCTION

Digital communication is nowadays an integral part of people's daily life, paving the way for companies to directly connect with consumers. The ongoing use of social networks ensures that consumers and/or potential consumers are actively engaged with a given company's brand, also contributing to increase the brand visibility. Such digital engagement provides marketers with the opportunity to promote intensively and efficiently their brand on the online platforms. An increasingly more used strategy adopted by brand companies is to enlist social media influencers to promote their products and/or services on the social network platforms, resulting in a marketing strategy known as influencer marketing (Kim & Kim, 2021; Phua et al., 2017). Influencers are viral content generators who have accumulated a large

DOI: 10.4018/978-1-6684-8753-2.ch006

number of followers, which ensures their high visibility on the social network platforms. They represent a fundamental source in marketing communication since they boast a considerable and loyal network of followers. Influencers embed brand products and/or services in textual and visual narratives they generate on the various social networks such as Facebook, Twitter, and Instagram. Such narratives are usually related to their personal and everyday lives, and in this way, consumers tend to consider them authentic and trustworthy (Schouten et al., 2020).

Before the advent of social media, companies advertised their products mainly through the radio and television, billboards, print advertisement and similar, and in that case, consumers were not able to directly and in real time interact with the brand. Instead, nowadays in the era of social media marketing, consumers are actively engaged, since they can now easily and in real time interact with both the brand and the influencers through comments, likes, shares and similar. The widespread use of influencer marketing leads to attempts for regulating such type of marketing strategy in order to ensure high levels of transparency in this field. For example, an increasingly more used practice by influencers is to embody a statement to unveil their paid relation with the brand (Federal Trade Commission, 2017). For instance, contents like "*advertising*," "*sponsored*", "*paid review*", "*ad*", "*sp*" and similar are all examples of expressions revealing that a given post is sponsored, and that the influencer has been paid to promote a certain brand.

The growing number of brands adopting the strategy of influencer marketing, together with an ever-increasing number of influencers involved in it, leads to a growing interest to deeply understand the user generated contents (UGCs) produced by influencers, as well as the corresponding consumers' engagement. Such UGCs are in general composed of a textual content, which can be also combined with one or more images and/or videos. In the textual contents, influencers usually embed brand related posts by sharing feelings, personal and/or working stories, some kind of experiences they go through. Such textual contents usually contain also many hashtags, captions, and emoticons which contribute to form a sort of "influencers' language" adopted to efficiently reach a certain target of consumers and/or potential consumers. When considering the consumers' engagement, in this phase it mainly relates to posting comments and likes.

In this chapter, the author proposes in a conceptual framework a novel approach to efficiently reveal the influencers' language adopted on social network platforms for sponsored versus not sponsored contents for a given fashion brand, and by also taking care of aspects related to the consumers' engagement. The core component of the approach is the Structural Topic Model (STM), developed by Roberts et al. (2014). The STM is a substantial improvement of the Latent Dirichlet Allocation (LDA) method (Blei et al., 2003). The LDA method has been increasingly applied in online marketing studies, but it has several limitations which are successfully overcome through the use of the STM. To this end, the promising use of the STM can be briefly summarized as follows. First, similarly to the LDA, the STM allows to identify a predefined number of topics from the UGCs produced by influencers for a given fashion brand. Second, differently from the LDA, the STM allows to also account for the following two main key points: topical content and topical prevalence. In the context of this chapter, the inclusion of the sponsorship statement as a topical content covariate, allows to identify for each topic the top words for both sponsored and not sponsored posts. Furthermore, the topical prevalence allows to deeply study such influencers' narratives, jointly with aspects related to the consumers' engagement. Lastly, the STM allows to also take care of the correlation between topics. The application of the STM in this framework is described in details through the following main steps composing the proposal: 1) data collection, 2) data preparation, 3) data analysis, and 4) interpretation of the results. The STM can provide promising results which can be successfully employed by interested practitioners and brand managers to efficiently define marketing strategies, or to strengthen existing ones.

The chapter is organized as follows. The next section includes a literature review related to the main qualitative and quantitative approaches for the analysis of influencers' narratives and consumers' engagement. The third section contains a detailed description of the main concepts related to influencer marketing and consumers' engagement considered in the framework of this chapter. The fourth section is devoted to the detailed description of the approach the author proposes, also including a brief discussion related to its practical implications. Conclusions and a brief outline for future research end the chapter.

BACKGROUND AND LITERATURE REVIEW ON QUALITATIVE AND QUANTITATIVE APPROACHES FOR STUDYING INFLUENCERS' NARRATIVES AND CONSUMERS' ENGAGEMENT

Several approaches, both qualitative as well as quantitative ones, have been adopted in the literature to study several and different aspects related to influencers' narratives and consumers' engagement. First, several simple and basic metrics have been largely used, mainly related to study the impact of social media influencers. For instance, Cha et al. (2012) study data on Twitter and suggest the following two metrics to this purpose: i) the mentions or name value of a given user, in degree or popularity of influencers, and ii) the number of retweets based on the content value of the tweets. Li and Gillet (2013) focus on the following two metrics: the number of followers, and the date of joining. Reilly et al. (2014) assert that influencers are more likely to create higher influence on their followers if they have a high ratio of forwarded messages with respect to the total number of messages posted. Moreover, Segev et al. (2018) study data on Instagram by considering the number of views by followers, the number of views per followers and the number of views per like, by also further considering the application of some regression models.

However, none of these studies considers the influencers' narratives generated in the form of UGCs. The UGCs from social media networks is an important source of data in online marketing studies. Outside the context of influencer marketing, several research studies found that the UGCs have a strong impact on brand image, purchase intention, and/or sales (Berni et al., 2020; Naylor et al., 2012). For instance, Lee and Bradlow (2010) and Netzer et al. (2012) employ UGCs to explore consumers' perceptions. More precisely, Lee and Bradlow (2011) pursue this objective by collecting the perceived product attributes from online discussions, while Netzer et al. (2012) study the similarity between products through their co-mention associations. Both these studies employ clustering and semantic network techniques on co-occurrences extracted from the UGCs through text-mining analysis. However, these studies do not consider the analysis of UGCs in terms of topics of narratives. To this end, several contributions in the literature have focused on topic modelling, in order to provide more information related to brand management and/or advertising practices. Among the several topic modeling approaches available in the literature, Latent Dirichlet Allocation (LDA), proposed by Blei et al. (2003), has been increasingly applied in online marketing studies. For example, Tirunillai and Tellis (2014) apply the LDA method to identify topics related to dimensions of quality and valence expressed in online reviews. Liu et al. (2017) consider LDA and sentiment analysis to study brand-related UGCs on data from Twitter. Jia (2019) apply LDA and Support Vector Machines on online reviews related to Chinese fitness clubs, while Calheiros et al. (2017) use LDA to analyse online reviews related to hotels. More recently, Francisco-Maffezzolli et al. (2021) studied video contents produced by influencers on YouTube through the LDA method, while Poushneh and Rajabi (2022) apply LDA on products rated online to better understand the customers' dynamics for such products.

When considering the context of influencer marketing, Lou et al. (2019) use LDA on two similar and comparable sets of marketing content, that is influencer-promoted branded posts and brands' reposting on influencers' branded posts. The authors found that influencer-promoted posts lead to a higher engagement in terms of consumers' likes and comments with respect to brand-promoted posts on Instagram. Feng et al. (2020) combine LDA and image analysis based on deep learning methods in order to analyse the content strategies adopted by social media influencers on Instagram. The authors also consider in their analysis the influencers' language in each post as well as the engagement performances (i.e. the number of likes, and the number of comments for the post). All these studies use the LDA, which is a generative model of word counts, based on the "bag of words" assumption according to which the order of the words in the text does not matter. Moreover, a further main drawback of LDA is the assumption that the topics are independent. To this end, the Correlated Topic Model (CTM) has been proposed (Blei & Lafferty, 2006). However, except the documents' text, neither LDA nor the CTM allow to consider any further available information, as for instance in the context of this study if influencers' posts are sponsored or not, and the number of likes, comments or shares related to consumers' engagement. To overcome this issue, in this chapter the author considers the STM, developed by Roberts et al. (2014). Like the LDA and the CTM, the STM is a generative model of word counts in which a topic is defined as a mixture over words, where each word has a given probability of belonging to a topic, while a document is a mixture over topics, meaning that a single document can be composed of multiple topics. Differently from the LDA and the CTM, the STM allows to include further available information in the topic model in the form of covariates in order to account for topical prevalence and topical content. The STM has been increasingly applied in the field of political and social sciences (Bauer et al., 2016; Chandelier et al., 2018), in the medical field to analyse prescriber-drug associations (Zafari & Ekin, 2018), and on Twitter data related to the analysis of tweets of high court judges (Curry & Fix, 2019). However, to the best of the author's knowledge, the STM has been never employed in marketing studies related to influencer marketing, a field in which it can provide very valuable information and promising results, contributing to define suitable marketing strategies for brand management and/or for advertising practises.

CONCEPTUAL FRAMEWORK

In this Section the author briefly discusses the main concepts related to influencer marketing on social media networks, influencers' narratives and sponsorship, as well as the consumers' engagement on influencers' posts.

Social Media Networks and Influencers

The evolution of Internet changed the way in which companies and consumers can interact and communicate with each other. Increasingly more persons as well as companies constantly employ the several available social networks in their working and/or personal life. Instagram, Twitter, YouTube, Tik Tok are all examples of the most popular social networks to date. Such huge digital engagement has led to the establishment of a relatively new figure in marketing known as social media influencers. Influencers appear as persons who have a substantial network of followers, and with whom they try to build high quality, dynamic and intimate relationships (De Veirman et al., 2017; Sundermann & Raabe, 2019; Zhou et al., 2021). They constantly interact with their followers through vlogging, blogging, posting short contents, stories, images and videos, and promote brand related products, also linking them to their personal life and daily routine. An example is Instagram, one of the most rapidly rising social networks, allowing to share posts escorted by images and/or short videos. The tagging (@) and hashtag (#) options available on Instagram, as well as the introduction of the "Instagram Stories" in 2016, allow influencers to tag, link and to produce narratives about brands products in a real time from all around the world. Furthermore, Instagram allows users to also actively engage with these influencers in several ways such as by following, liking, commenting, sharing and sending them direct messages.

Influencer Marketing, Narratives, and Sponsorship

Influencer marketing has rapidly become an integral part of the most widely used marketing strategies by companies (Audrezet et al., 2020; Leung et al., 2022). Leung et al. (2022) defines online influencer marketing as *a strategy in which a firm selects and incentivizes online influencers to engage their followers on social media in an attempt to leverage these influencers' unique resources to promote the firm's offerings, with the ultimate goal of enhancing firm performance.* Companies select and engage influencers to advertise their products, and give them some type of compensation, as for instance direct payments, commissions on sales via affiliate marketing programs, or gifts and products in-kind (Leung et al., 2022). To this end, influencers disseminate branded narratives in which they introduce and recommend brands' products, linking them to their personal and everyday lives. Influencers act as brand advocates, aiming to establish their personal branding, to monetize and spread their activities, fame and influential power (Campbell & Farrell, 2020; Reinikainen et al., 2020). Their strength lies in that their followers see them as trusted, authentic and credible tastemakers (De Veirman et al., 2017). In order to efficiently increase brand perception, influencers tend to constantly encourage and increase consumers' engagement, which is highlighted in posting comments, likes, and feedbacks. Through the influencers, brands build direct relationships with a targeted group of consumers, encouraging brand loyalty in them (Glucksman, 2017; Jaitly & Gautam, 2021). Furthermore, the influencers also contribute to increase brand awareness and to improve brand recognition (Sundermann & Raabe, 2019).

According to the Federal Trade Commission (2017), promotional contents published by the influencers should be clearly announced as sponsored ones, for instance through the inclusion of statements like *"#sponsored"*, *"#ad,"* *"advertisement"*, *"paid"* and similar. Different elements inside both a sponsored with respect to not sponsored narratives can be found; for example, the structure of the story, the brands used in conjunction with the sponsored one, the specific words and emoticons adopted. Therefore, it becomes essential to efficiently analyse and understand the influencers' language used in sponsored with respect to not sponsored posts, in order to also improve and strength marketing communication, and to reinforce the effectiveness of marketing strategies.

Consumers' Engagement in Influencers' Posts

In the context of influencer marketing on social networks, consumers' engagement is mainly related to liking, sharing and commenting. Several authors have focused to study these aspects by considering both qualitative and quantitative approaches (Lee et al., 2022; Lou et al., 2019). Consumers' engagement with influencers' posts can be used to reveal to what extent the followers of the influencers are loyal to potential advertiser (Chen et al., 2022; van Driel & Dumitrica, 2021). Furthermore, high consumers' engagement can ensure that social networks' algorithms prioritize such posts as "trending" ones (van Driel & Dumitrica, 2021), and consequently influencers can also require to the promoted brands higher compensations (Chen et al., 2022). Several metrics including all or only some of those including likes, comments and shares are used to calculate the consumers' engagement in social networks to analyse the performance of influencers' posts (Chen et al., 2022; Rafael, 2019). Kim and Yang (2017) conceptualize such three elements of consumers' engagement according to their intensity. More precisely, likes are considered as those requiring less effort since only a click is requested to produce them. Comments require a higher effort with respect to likes, while shares posits as having the high level of effort required. Cheng et al. (2021) and Chen et al. (2022) assert that the number of likes can be used to reveal if the user has a positive or a negative attitude towards a given influencer's post; comments are related to the users' readiness to discuss the post, while shares instead goes beyond, revealing user's availability to recommend the post content on its personal account. Influencers can heighten consumers' engagement in their followers through the contents they publish in their posts (the words, the captions, and the emoticons used). Thus, a proper analysis of influencers' narratives needs to be jointly carried out with such aspects related to consumers' engagement. For example, aspects related to the number of likes, since they reveal the popularity and the importance of a given post, and they could be seen as an expression of a positive and/or a negative affection towards a given post (Alhabash et al., 2015; Lou et al., 2019; Zhou et al., 2021).

TOPIC MODELLING TO STUDY INFLUENCERS' NARRATIVES AND CONSUMERS' ENGAGEMENT

In this Section the author describes in details two main topic models, namely the LDA and the STM. The author mainly focuses on the STM, since the LDA can be applied to find topics only, while the STM can also reveal "sub-topics" of words in sponsored versus not sponsored contents, jointly with aspects related to the consumers' engagement. Moreover, the novel approach the author conceptualizes and propose is composed of the following main steps: 1) data collection, 2) data preparation, 3) data analysis, 4) interpretation of the results. First, the main theoretical elements related to both the LDA and the STM are briefly reported and explained, by considering that the latter is an extension of the former. Following, each of the four main steps of the proposal is described and discussed in details; moreover, in the description of the final step related to the interpretation of the results, the author also briefly discusses some possible practical implications of the obtained results. Lastly, a schematic overview of these four main steps is also reported in Figure 1.

Figure 1. An overview of the proposal

LDA and STM: Main Theoretical Elements

The LDA method, proposed by Blei et al. (2003), has been increasingly applied in online marketing studies. The LDA allows to find a prespecified number of topics of words, given i) a collection of documents composed of words' indices and associated counts, and ii) a vocabulary containing the words associated with the words' indices. One of the main assumptions of the LDA method is that texts on similar topics tend to share common words. Let's define a collection of D documents, and let index each document by $d = 1,\ldots,D$, and each word in the document d by j, $j \in \{1,\ldots,J_d\}$. The observations $w_{d,j}$ are occurrences of words from a vocabulary of size $V, v \in \{1,\ldots,V\}$ In the framework of the LDA method, for a predefined number of topics K ($k = 1,\ldots K$) the data generating process of document d is defined as follows:

$$\theta_d \sim Dirichlet(\alpha) \tag{1}$$

$$\phi_k \sim Dirichlet(\beta) \tag{2}$$

$$z_{dj} \mid \theta_d \sim Multinomial\left(\theta_d\right) \tag{3}$$

$$w_{dj} \mid z_{dj} \sim Multinomial\left(\phi_{z_{dj}}\right) \tag{4}$$

where θ_d is the K-length per document topic distribution for document d, while ϕ_k is the V-length per topic word distribution for the k-th topic. The Dirichlet distribution is assumed for both the documents distribution over topic, as well as the topics distribution over words, with hyperparameters α and β respectively (equations (1) and (2)). Moreover, z_{dj} is the topic for the j-th word in the document d, which similarly to w_{dj} is assumed generated from a Multinomial distribution (formulas (3) and (4)).

Like the LDA method, the STM allows to find topics of words within a set of documents, by assuming that each topic is generated from a distribution over words, and each document is generated from a mixture of corpus-wide topics (Blei et al., 2003). The prominent improvements of STM with respect to the LDA method stem from the fact that the topics are assumed to be correlated, and a document-level structure information is introduced to account for the so-called topical prevalence and topical content. More specifically, topical prevalence refers to how much of a document is associated with a topic, while topical content accounts for the words used within a topic (Roberts et al., 2014; Roberts et al., 2016).

According to the STM, for a predefined number of topics K ($k = 1, \dots K$), the data generating process of document d is briefly defined as follows. Topical prevalence is modelled through a logistic-normal generalized linear model in which topical prevalence covariates are included:

$$\theta_d \mid \left(\boldsymbol{x}_d \Gamma, \Sigma\right) \sim LogisticNormal\left(\boldsymbol{x}_d \Gamma, \Sigma\right) \tag{5}$$

In formula (5), $\boldsymbol{x}_d$ is the vector of topical prevalence covariates for document d, dimension $1 \times p$, Γ is a $p \times \left(K-1\right)$ matrix of coefficients, and Σ is the corresponding variance-covariance matrix of dimension $\left(K-1\right) \times \left(K-1\right)$.

Following, the data generating process for the topical content is defined as follows:

$$\beta_{d,k} \propto exp\left(\boldsymbol{m} + \boldsymbol{k}_k + \boldsymbol{k}_{y_d} + \boldsymbol{k}_{y_d} k\right) \tag{6}$$

In formula (6), $\boldsymbol{y}_d$ is the vector of topical content covariates, while $\boldsymbol{m}$, $\boldsymbol{k}_k$, $\boldsymbol{k}_{y_d}$, and $\boldsymbol{k}_{y_d} k$ are vectors of length V related to the baseline word distribution, the topic specific deviation, the covariate group deviation and the interaction between $\boldsymbol{k}_k$ and $\boldsymbol{k}_{y_d}$, respectively.

Following for each word in the document d, the words topic assignment is defined as follows:

$$z_{d,j} \mid (\boldsymbol{\theta}_d) \sim Multinomial\ (\boldsymbol{\theta}_d) \tag{7}$$

Lastly, conditionally on the topic chosen, an observed word from a topic is drawn as follows:

$$w_{d,j} \mid z_{d,j} \sim Multinomial\,(\,^{2}{}_{d,k} = z_{d,j}) \quad (8)$$

In both the LDA method and the STM, the distribution of topics $z_{d,j}$ (formulas (3) and (7)), and the distribution of words (formulas (4) and (8)), are both sampled from the Multinomial one. However, both methods significantly differ when considering formulas (1), (2), (5) and (6), since STM assumes that the topics are correlated, and allows to account for the additional information related to the topical prevalence (equation (5)), and the topical content (formula (6)). To this end, in the STM the topical content covariates affect the topic-word distributions, while the topical prevalence covariates affect the document-topic proportions (Roberts et al., 2014; Roberts et al., 2016), by also accounting for the correlations among topics. The effects of covariates on the topics is estimated through a statistical model, by considering the conditional expectation of the topical prevalence given the documents' characteristics; one statistical model is estimated for each chosen topic, where the topic proportions is the corresponding response variable. Lastly, it must be also noted that the STM allows to consider topical prevalence covariates or topical content covariates only; if no covariates are included the STM reduces to the CTM (Blei & Laferty, 2007). All these improvements discussed above with respect to the LDA method make the STM extremely suitable in the context of this chapter.

Main Steps of the Proposal for the Analysis of the Influencers Language Jointly With Aspects of Consumers Engagement

Data Collection

According to the proposal, the process starts with the step of data collection. Therefore, first the data related to a given fashion brand should be collected from one or more social network platforms (for example Twitter, Instagram, Facebook). It must be noted that the data should include a sufficiently large number of documents of UGCs, which in the present framework relates to influencers' narratives in posts. In general, each document collected can be mainly composed by words, captions, hashtags, and/or emoticons. When contents like "*advertising*," "*sponsored*", "*paid review*", "*ad*", "*sp*" and similar are present in a collected document, the corresponding influencer's post can be classified as sponsored one. Moreover, information related to the consumers' engagement should be also collected for each document; for instance, number of likes, number of comments and shares received). For example, let us consider posts generated by influencers on Instagram. Each influencer's post is a document, where each post can be labelled as sponsored if contents like "*advertising*," "*sponsored*", "*paid review*", "*ad*", "*sp*" and similar are present, and as not sponsored otherwise. Furthermore, the information related to consumers' engagement for each post (i.e., document) may refer to the number of likes and/or the number of comments received (see also Step "1. Data collection", Figure 1). Lastly, it is important to note that all the data collected should be included into a single dataset in order to prepare it for the subsequent analysis.

Data Preparation

All the data collected should be stored in one file, as for example in a spreadsheet of *.csv* or *.xlsx* files. First, the textual data related to influencers' posts should be processed through the main text-mining techniques for textual analysis in order to prepare it for the subsequent analysis (Step "2. Data preparation" in Figure 1). More precisely, standard text processing procedures must be adopted, such as removal of punctuations, words lowercasing, words stemming and/or lemmatization, stop words removal (Salton, 1989). Words stemming and/or lemmatization relate to reducing the words to their root form, while stop words removal refers to the elimination of the most common words in a given language, which do not add any further information on the documents; for example, when considering documents in English language, "the", "a", "so", "on" are all examples of stop words (Salton, 1989). Furthermore, multiword should be converted into unitary strings; for example, the multiword "ice cream" should be converted in "ice-cream". If also emoticons are present in the collected documents, they can be included in the analysis by converting them in a word, or in a unitary string, depending on the emoticons. For example, the emoticon 🔥 is converted in the word "fire", while the emoticon ❣ is converted in "h*eavy heart*", and subsequently in the unitary string "h*eavy-heart*". When considering the STM, the variables related to the sponsorship and to the consumers' engagement information should be built and included in the final dataset. For example, when considering the sponsorship statement, a binary variable can be built equal to 0 if the post is not sponsored, and to 1 otherwise. Instead, a quantitative variable may be included based on the number of likes collected to evaluate the consumers' engagement.

Data Analysis: Applying Topic Modeling

Once, the data are prepared for the analysis, the STM should be estimated; to date, the STM is implemented in the R software package *stm* (Roberts et al., 2019). It must be also pointed out that for both the LDA and the STM, the number of topics should be chosen *a priori*, even though the STM encounters for model selection across numbers of topics (Roberts et al., 2019). Moreover, when considering the STM the topical content and the topical prevalence covariates to be included in the model should be also established (Step "3. Data analysis", Figure 1). In the context of this chapter, the author proposes to include the sponsorship variable as a topical content covariate, and the variable related to the number of likes (or comments and/ or shares) as topical prevalence covariates (Step "3. Data analysis", Figure 1).

STM: Interpretation of the Results and Hints on Some of Their Practical Implications

The last step of the proposal is related to the interpretation of the results obtained through the STM (Step "4. Data interpretation", Figure 1). As already noted, both the LDA and the STM allow to obtain topics of words related to the influencers' narratives. Therefore, through the topics identified, first it is possible to establish the main themes related to the posts published by the influencers. Moreover, it is also possible to find if and how many brands are present in the same topic in order to reveal which ones the influencers more associate with the fashion brand under study. All this information may be obtained through both the LDA method and the STM. But differently from the LDA, the STM allows to obtain the following additional results.

First, additional information related to the topical content which accounts for the word rates used in discussing a given topic. In the context of this chapter, the topical content covariate is the binary variable related to the sponsorship statement, equal to 0 if the post is not sponsored, and to 1 otherwise. To this end, the results obtained indicate for each topic of influencers' narratives identified, the top words used in sponsored posts, and the top words used in not sponsored posts. Therefore, the topical content covariate related to the sponsorship statement allows to further reveal the language the influencers use in sponsored versus not sponsored posts, also for purposes of comparison. Such language, which is a combination of words, hashtag words, captions, several other brands, and emoticons, provides valuable insights for better defining influencer marketing strategies.

Second, the STM allows to also account for a second important key point related to the topical prevalence, that is how much of a given document is associated with a topic. To this end, for each topic a regression model is estimated by considering the topics' proportions as the response variables and the topical prevalence covariates (Roberts et al., 2014). In the context discussed in the present chapter, the author considers the following two topical prevalence covariates: i) the sponsorship statement, that is a binary variable equal to 0 if the post is not sponsored, and equal to 1 otherwise, and ii) one or more variables related to the consumers' engagement. For instance, according to the specific aim of the analysis, it is possible to include the number of likes received on each influencer's post, and/or the number of comments received. The interpretation of the results related to the topical prevalence aspect may be summarized as follows. First for each topic it is possible to evaluate the relevance of the estimated coefficients related to the topical prevalence covariates, by considering their corresponding p-values. Furthermore, the sign of these estimated coefficients can provide an additional valuable information. For example, when the sponsorship statement and the number of likes and/or comments are included as topical prevalence covariates, it can be asserted that: i) if a given topic is more prevalent for sponsored with respect to not sponsored posts, and ii) if a given topic is more prevalent with a smaller with respect to a greater number of likes and/or comment received; this last result allows to jointly evaluate the aspects related to the consumers' engagement.

Lastly, since the STM assumes that the topics are correlated, it allows to also estimate the correlations between topics. Therefore, for instance positive correlations between topics indicate that both topics are likely to be discussed within a document (i.e., within a given influencer's post), and otherwise if negative correlations between topics is obtained. All this information combined all together can be efficiently used by practitioners and/or brand management for the purpose of defining suitable influencer marketing strategies.

CONCLUSIONS, FUTURE RESEARCH, AND DIRECTIONS

In this chapter the author proposes in a conceptual framework a novel approach for the analysis of the UGCs produced by influencers, by specifically considering the influencers' language in sponsored with respect to not sponsored posts, jointly with aspects related to the consumers' engagement. The core part of the approach consists in the proposal to apply the STM for influencer marketing studies. By specifically considering the topical content and the topical prevalence, the STM provides promising results which can be efficiently employed by interested practitioners and brand managers to efficiently define marketing strategies, and to strengthen and improve existing ones.

It must be noted that the conceptual framework discussed above is not without limitations. First, the author conceptualizes the STM by considering one brands only. Therefore, a first important improvement for a future research is related to study jointly more than one brand. Moreover, the proposed approach takes account of some main aspects only related to consumers' engagement. Thus, an important future research direction is to properly extend the proposal in order to also consider the comments the consumers' and/or the potential consumers leave on a specific influencers' posts.

REFERENCES

Alhabash, S., McAlister, A. R., Lou, C., & Hagerstrom, A. (2015). From clicks to behaviors: The mediating effect of intentions to like, share, and comment on the relationship between message evaluations and offline behavioral intentions. *Journal of Interactive Advertising*, *15*(2), 82–96. doi:10.1080/15252019.2015.1071677

Audrezet, A., De Kerviler, G., & Moulard, J. G. (2020). Authenticity under threat: When social media influencers need to go beyond self-presentation. *Journal of Business Research*, *117*, 557–569. doi:10.1016/j.jbusres.2018.07.008

Bauer, P. C., Barbera, K. A. C., & Venetz, A. (2017). Is the left-right scale a valid measure of ideology? Individual level variation in associations with 'left' and 'right' and left-right self-placement. *Political Behavior*, *39*(3), 553–583. doi:10.100711109-016-9368-2

Berni, R., Nikiforova, N. D., & Ranfagni, S. (2020). An integrated approach to estimate brand association matching and strength in virtual settings. *Journal of Global Fashion Marketing*, *11*(2), 117–136. doi:10.1080/20932685.2019.1706608

Blei, D. M., & Lafferty, J. D. (2006). Correlated Topic Models. *Advances in Neural Information Processing Systems*, *18*, 1–47.

Blei, D. M., Ng, A. Y., & Jordan, M. I. (2003). Latent Dirichlet Allocation. *Journal of Machine Learning Research*, *3*, 993–1022.

Calheiros, A. C., Moro, S., & Rita, P. (2017). Sentiment classification of consumer-generated online reviews using topic modeling. *Journal of Hospitality Marketing & Management*, *26*(7), 675–693. doi:10.1080/19368623.2017.1310075

Campbell, C., & Farrell, J. R. (2020). More than meets the eye: The functional components underlying influencer marketing. *Business Horizons*, *63*(4), 469–479. doi:10.1016/j.bushor.2020.03.003

Cha, M., Benevenuto, F., Haddadi, H., & Gummadi, K. P. (2012). The world of connections and information flow in Twitter. *IEEE Transactions on Systems, Man, and Cybernetics. Part A, Systems and Humans*, *42*(4), 991–998. doi:10.1109/TSMCA.2012.2183359

Chandelier, M., Steuckardt, A., Mathevet, R., Diwersy, S., & Gimenez, O. (2018). Content analysis of newspaper coverage of wolf recolonization in France using structural topic modeling. *Biological Conservation*, *220*, 254–261. doi:10.1016/j.biocon.2018.01.029

Chen, L., Yan, Y., & Smith, A. N. (2023). What drives digital engagement with sponsored videos? An investigation of video influencers' authenticity management strategies. *Journal of the Academy of Marketing Science*, *51*(1), 198–221. doi:10.100711747-022-00887-2

Cheng, M., Liu, J., Qi, J., & Wan, F. (2021). Differential effects of firm generated content on consumer digital engagement and firm performance: An outside-in perspective. *Industrial Marketing Management*, *98*, 41–58. doi:10.1016/j.indmarman.2021.07.001

Curry, T. A., & Fix, M. P. (2019). May it please the twitterverse: The use of twitter by state high court judges. *Journal of Information Technology & Politics*, *16*(4), 379–393. doi:10.1080/19331681.2019.1657048

De Veirman, M., Cauberghe, V., & Hudders, L. (2017). Marketing through Instagram influencers: The impact of number of followers and product divergence on brand attitude. *International Journal of Advertising*, *36*(5), 798–828. doi:10.1080/02650487.2017.1348035

Federal Trade Commission. (2017). *FTC staff reminders influencers and brands to clearly disclosure relationship: commission aims to improve disclosures in social media endorsements.* https://www.ftc.gov/news-events/news/press-releases/2017/04/ftc-staff-reminds-influencers-brands-clearly-disclose-relationship

Feng, Y., Chen, H., & Kong, Q. (2020). An expert with whom I can identify: The role of narratives in influencer marketing. *International Journal of Advertising*, *4*(7), 972–993. doi:10.1080/02650487.2020.1824751

Francisco-Maffezzolli, E., Munaro, A. C., Santos Rodrigues, J. P., Cabrera Paraiso, E., Eliane, F.-M., Ana Cristina, M., Rodrigues João Pedro, S., & Paraiso Emerson, C. (2021). Mining meaning of videos on YouTube: unravelling latent content from digital influencers and their engagement. *Proceedings of the 50th European Marketing Academy*, 93144.

Glucksman, M. (2017). The rise of social media influencer marketing on lifestyle branding: A case study of Lucie Fink. *Elon Journal of Undergraduate Research in Communications*, *8*(2), 77–87.

Jaitly, R. C., & Gautam, O. (2021). Impact of social media influencers on customer engagement and brand perception. *International Journal of Internet Marketing and Advertising*, *15*(2), 220–242. doi:10.1504/IJIMA.2021.114336

Jia, S. (2019). Toward a better fitness club: Evidence from exerciser online rating and review using Latent Dirichlet Allocation and support vector machine. *International Journal of Market Research*, *61*(1), 64–76. doi:10.1177/1470785318770571

Kim, C., & Yang, S. U. (2017). Like, comment, and share on Facebook: How each behaviour differs from the other. *Public Relations Review*, *43*(2), 441–449. doi:10.1016/j.pubrev.2017.02.006

Kim, D. Y., & Kim, H. Y. (2021). Trust me, trust me not: A nuanced view of influencer marketing on social media. *Journal of Business Research*, *134*, 223–232. doi:10.1016/j.jbusres.2021.05.024

Lee, J. A., Sudarshan, S., Sussman, K. L., Bright, L. F., & Eastin, M. S. (2022). Why are consumers following social media influencers on Instagram? Exploration of consumers' motives for following influencers and the role of materialism. *International Journal of Advertising*, *41*(1), 78–100. doi:10.1080/02650487.2021.1964226

Lee, T. Y., & Bradlow, E. T. (2011). Automated marketing research using online customer reviews. *JMR, Journal of Marketing Research*, *48*(5), 881–894. doi:10.1509/jmkr.48.5.881

Leung, F. F., Gu, F. F., & Palmatier, R. W. (2022). Online influencer marketing. *Journal of the Academy of Marketing Science*, *50*(2), 226–251. doi:10.100711747-021-00829-4

Li, N., & Gillet, D. (2013). Identifying influential scholars in academic social media platforms. *Proceedings of the 2013 IEEE/ACM International Conference on Advances in Social Networks Analysis and Mining*, 608–614. 10.1145/2492517.2492614

Liu, X., Burns, A. C., & Hou, Y. (2017). An investigation of brand-related user-generated content on Twitter. *Journal of Advertising*, *46*(2), 236–247. doi:10.1080/00913367.2017.1297273

Lou, C., Tan, S. S., & Chen, X. (2019). Investigating consumer engagement with influencer- vs. brand-promoted ads: The roles of source and disclosure. *Journal of Interactive Advertising*, *19*(3), 169–186. doi:10.1080/15252019.2019.1667928

Naylor, R. W., Lamberton, C. P., & West, P. M. (2012). Beyond the 'like' button: The impact of mere virtual presence on brand evaluations and purchase intentions in social media settings. *Journal of Marketing*, *76*(6), 105–120. doi:10.1509/jm.11.0105

Netzer, O., Feldman, R., Goldenberg, J., & Fresko, M. (2012). Mine your own business: Market-structure surveillance through text mining. *Marketing Science*, *31*(3), 521–543. doi:10.1287/mksc.1120.0713

Phua, J., Jin, S. V., & Kim, J. J. (2017). Gratifications of using Face-book, Twitter, Instagram, or Snapchat to follow brands: The moderating effect of social comparison, trust, tie strength, and network homophily on brand identification, brand engagement, brand commitment, and membership intention. *Telematics and Informatics*, *34*(1), 412–424. doi:10.1016/j.tele.2016.06.004

Poushneh, A., & Rajabi, R. (2022). Can reviews predict reviewers' numerical ratings? (e underlying mechanisms of customers' decisions to rate products using Latent Dirichlet Allocation (LDA). *Journal of Consumer Marketing*, *39*(2), 230–241. doi:10.1108/JCM-09-2020-4114

Rafael. (2019). *How to measure social media engagement + tools to track*. https://www.talkwalker.com/blog/how-to-measure-social-media-engagement

Reilly, C. F., Salinas, D., & De Leon, D. (2014). Ranking users based on influence in a directional social network. *2014 International Conference on Computational Science and Computational Intelligence, 2*, 237–240. 10.1109/CSCI.2014.127

Reinikainen, H., Munnukka, J., Maity, D., & Luoma-aho, V. (2020). 'You really are a great big sister' – parasocial relationships, credibility, and the moderating role of audience comments in influencer marketing. *Journal of Marketing Management*, *36*(3–4), 279–298. doi:10.1080/0267257X.2019.1708781

Roberts, M. E., Stewart, B. M., & Airoldi, E. M. (2016). A model of text for experimentation in the social sciences. *Journal of the American Statistical Association*, *111*(515), 988–1003. doi:10.1080/01621459.2016.1141684

Roberts, M. E., Stewart, B. M., & Tingley, D. (2019). *stm*: An R package for Structural Topic Models. *Journal of Statistical Software*, *91*(2), 1–40. doi:10.18637/jss.v091.i02

Roberts, M. E., Stewart, B. M., Tingley, D., Lucas, C., Leder-Luis, J., Gadarian, S. K., Albertson, B., & Rand, D. G. (2014). Structural topic models for open-ended survey responses. *American Journal of Political Science*, *58*(4), 1064–1082. doi:10.1111/ajps.12103

Salton, G. (1989). *Automatic text processing: The transformation, analysis, and retrieval of information by computer. Massachussetts*. Addison-Wesley.

Schouten, A. P., Janssen, L., & Verspaget, M. (2020). Celebrity vs. influencer endorsements in advertising: The role of identification, credibility, and product-endorser fit. *International Journal of Advertising, 39*(2), 258–281. doi:10.1080/02650487.2019.1634898

Segev, N., Avigdor, N., & Avigdor, E. (2018). Measuring influence on Instagram: a network-oblivious approach. *Proceedings of the 41st International ACM SIGIR Conference on Research & Development in Information Retrieval*, 1009–1012. 10.1145/3209978.3210134

Sundermann, G., & Raabe, T. (2019). Strategic communication through social media influencers: Current state of research and desiderata. *International Journal of Strategic Communication, 13*(4), 278–300. doi:10.1080/1553118X.2019.1618306

Tirunillai, S., & Tellis, G. J. (2014). Mining marketing meaning from online chatter: Strategic brand analysis of big data using Latent Dirichlet Allocation. *JMR, Journal of Marketing Research, 51*(4), 463–479. doi:10.1509/jmr.12.0106

van Driel, L., & Dumitrica, D. (2021). Selling brands while staying "Authentic": The professionalization of Instagram influencers. *Convergence (London), 27*(1), 66–84. doi:10.1177/1354856520902136

Zafari, B., & Ekin, T. (2019). Topic modeling for medical prescription fraud and abuse detection. *Applied Statistics, 68*(3), 751–769. doi:10.1111/rssc.12332

Zhou, S., Blazquez, M., McCormick, H., & Barnes, L. (2021). How social media influencers' narrative strategies benefit cultivating influencer marketing: Tackling issues of cultural barriers, commercialised content, and sponsorship disclosure. *Journal of Business Research, 134*, 122–142. doi:10.1016/j.jbusres.2021.05.011

ADDITIONAL READING

Blei, D. M. (2012). Introduction to probabilistic topic models. *Communications of the ACM, 55*(4), 77–84. doi:10.1145/2133806.2133826

KEY TERMS AND DEFINITIONS

Collection of Documents: In the context of topic modelling, a collection of D documents is composed of words' indices and associated counts, where a document is indexed by $d, d = 1, \ldots, D$.

Consumers' Engagement: In the context of influencer marketing on social networks, consumers' engagement is mainly related to liking, sharing, and commenting.

Social Media Influencer: A user on social media who have a substantial network of followers, and with whom they try to build high quality, dynamic and intimate relationships. Social media influencers constantly interact with their followers through vlogging, blogging, posting short contents, stories, images, and videos, and promoting brand related products, also linking them to their personal life and daily routine.

Topical Content: In the context of STM, it accounts for the words rates used in discussing a given topic.

Topical Prevalence: In the context of STM, it refers to how much of a document is associated with a given topic.

User-Generated Content (UGC): Any type of brand-related digital content, in the form of texts, posts, video, comments, reviews, tags, photos, likes and similar, which is created by users and hosted online.

Vocabulary: In the context of topic modelling, a vocabulary of size $V, v \in \{1,\ldots,V\}$ contains the words associated with the words' indices.

Chapter 7
How Consumption Provides a Relational Understanding of Place

Mitrajit Biswas
O.P. Jindal Global University, India

ABSTRACT

This study positions itself within the place-as-living-entity view and within the growing body of literature on the relational views of place. This study considers how consumption acts and activities provide a relational view of place. It also acknowledges that while all kinds of consumption may involve a relationship with place at some level or the other, a relational view is distinguishable in terms of ties or kinship with place that individuals perceive as of value and valuable in their lives. More essentially, a relational view involves a contribution or participation in the construction or shaping of the nature and meaning of place and its boundaries. As Coffin and Chatzidakis observe, place-making is not confined to the simple creation and manipulation of meanings; rather, it is and must be understood in terms of claiming an area in territorial acts (as those of consumption).

INTRODUCTION

Most often, studies in marketing take an 'object' view of place. This means place is approached mainly from a functional or utilitarian and commercial perspective. Questions of meaningfulness of place and relational understandings of place are not of primary concern in these studies. As Chatzidakis, McEachern & Warnaby (2017) note, place is one of the four P's that optimizes marketing outcomes. However, the idea of showcasing place in terms of fashion has been one such context that has been probably understudied. Online consumption of fashion plays an important role in showcasing place. The chapter speaks of Durga Puja as a particular context where the online fashion bloggers influence not only fashion choices but also promote a particular physical place in a social setting.

Typically, studies that take an 'object' view of place would include literature on the influence of country-of-origin of products and brands on consumers, and depending on how consumers perceive

DOI: 10.4018/978-1-6684-8753-2.ch007

products from a certain country-of-origin can be marketed as such. Studies that view cities as objects consider how the city's identity or image can be marketed to target segments such as tourists or stakeholders. This has an important implication on influencing consumption of fashion from a particular place. The role of social media comes in at this juncture which allows for the fashion influencers to showcase new fashion especially through specialized social media promotion that is based and directed on a place such as Kolkata during Durga Puja. No doubt, any value of place from a consumer perspective in place-as-object oriented studies necessarily involves some connection, advantage or benefit in a place-related consumption context and therefore affirms, establishes or is reflective of a certain nature/type of relationship with place. This could be in terms of a functional benefit, as in choice of a product from a certain country that offers product superiority as in quality, or in terms of the economical as in cheap imports from a certain country. Place-identity and place-image studies may reiterate the object-value of a place from a personal, cultural or tourism perspective.

Theoretical Frameworks

The Place-as-Living Entity View and Role of Fashion

In the last two decades or so, however, marketers have turned attention to questions and issues of how places acquire value and meaning. These studies consider place-as-a-living entity that acquires meaning and significance in and through acts, activities and experiences of various stakeholders. Visconti et al. (2010, p.512) observe *"the notion of space traditionally refers to something anonymous, whereas place distinctively accounts for the meaningful experience of a given site"*. This is where the role of the place as in social media comes in. Defining fashion on the social media in terms of the local fashion is actually kind of defining a place. The place-as-living-entity views place as fluid, as a process and as one that results in territories and boundaries. Durga Puja in Kolkata defines that place when the brands, Instagram influencers and Fashion Vloggers come up The place-as-living entity approach to the understanding and construct of place offers consumers benefits and advantages of a personal, cultural and experiential nature. The place-as-living entity is essentially a relational view and understanding of place. The same is discussed in the next sub-section.

Relational Views of Place

This study positions itself within the place-as-living-entity view and within the growing body of literature on the relational views of place. A relational view of place is one of "the process and product of relation-making, with, through and in the context of the history, materiality and sociality of space" (Pendlebury et al., 2023, p.3). This study considers how consumption acts and activities provide a relational view of place. It also acknowledges that while all kinds of consumption may involve a relationship with place at some level or the other, a relational view is distinguishable in terms of ties or kinship with place that individuals perceive as of value and valuable in their lives. More essentially, a relational view involves a contribution or participation in the construction or shaping of the nature and meaning of place and its boundaries. As Coffin & Chatzidakis (2021) observe place-making is not confined to the simple creation and manipulation of meanings, rather is and must be understood in terms of claiming an area in territorial acts (such as those of consumption), then seeking how to control, interpret and appropriate the same. Visconti et al. (2010, p.512–3) write of place as "a given site", adding that "inchoate space (such as “outer space,” “wilderness,” and “wasteland”) is rendered tractable by dwelling practices (Seamon, 1993) that can convert it into place.” In these understanding one can see that how the overall idea of the social media place holds a very important significance in the creation of place which is fluid. The idea of fashion being an important signifier of place is still underwhelming. This is what needs to be relooked at in terms of the role of fashion consumption in social media. The social media platforms are the mere instruments highlighting and promoting the place although the real objective is to influence the fashion consumption. The juxtaposition of the same bridges the two sides of the coin.

The business problem this study addresses is the lack of or insufficient knowledge and understandings of socio-culturally distinct aspects and nature of consumption that characterize place and relational understandings of place, especially at the city-level. The significance of such understanding has started to grow and build in recent times. Global brands have started to focus on developing localized marketing campaigns at city levels to recognize and connect with affiliations and bonds of a socio-cultural nature at regional and local levels. For example, H&M rolled out a localized marketing campaign to meet the desires of their local consumers in Amsterdam. These consumers were looking for more local brands in the store and for services such as altering, repairing, renting and selling clothes (Localized marketing campaigns that hit the mark). The brand used the spirit of the city as well as voices of their target audience in videos to highlight such inspiration, and by catering to and following on the interests and lifestyles of their local audiences, were able to tap into a new market opportunity that offered solutions to environmental concerns.

Similarly, the Nike New York team struck a chord with New Yorkers with the “Own the Floor” campaign (Localized marketing campaigns that hit the mark). Using the city of New York City as a backdrop, this campaign epitomized the essence of what it means to live in New York city which New York inhabitants view as one big stage. The campaign worked because it combined local talent with classic NYC locations like subway platforms, pizzerias, and laundromats. It tapped into their target audience’s connection with the city and deepened such bonds.

Such moves in marketing practice highlight the need for developing knowledge and understandings of the distinctive nature and forms of consumption at specific places.

Such understandings and insights provide opportunities for businesses to understand and cater to consumer needs and preferences in terms of developing markets, introducing new or leveraging existing brands or products, building customer relationships, and facilitating and sustaining brand loyalty in specific regions and places. Lack of such knowledge and understandings could result in lack of acceptance of products and brands, a disconnect with consumers, loss of market share, and brand equity. This is what the local fashion bloggers also tend to do and the influence of fashion in social media consumption is influenced. In the global world with local influences the role of social media consumption has to find a proper balance between the desires and the aspiration of place in the form of fashion or outfit being worn.

Studies on country-of-origin of products and brands consider how consumers perceive products depending upon the country of origin (Abraham & Patro, 2014; Bruwer & Johnson, 2010; Brand & Baier, 2022; Pappu et. al; 2006; Rezvani et. al; 2012; Suter et. al; 2018). Pappu et. al (2006) examine the impact of country of origin of a brand on its consumer brand equity. Their study showed that the consumer-based equity of a brand made in a country with stronger product category-country association was significantly higher than that of a same brand made in a country with weaker product category-country associations. Abraham and Patro (2014) examine how knowledge, experience, exposure and inclination towards a particular country create the country-of-origin effect in the minds of consumers. They note country-of-origin reduces the cognition load in consumer decision-making as it becomes a proxy for quality, reliability and acceptability of products from a specific country. Even though globalization and technological developments have resulted in considerable product and manufacturing standardization, perceptions continue to country or region bound. In India, for example, anytime silk is mentioned, places such as 'Banaras' or 'Kancheepuram' (also known as Kanchipuram or Kanchivaram) immediately come to mind. Similarly, Bruwer and Johnson (2010) observe consumers use regional branding cues, information and images in their assessment and valuation of comparative wine labels. Rezvani et. al (2012) assert that ethnocentrism negatively impacts the intention to purchase products from less developed countries, while it did not have any significant influence on the intention to purchase products from developed countries. Brand and Baier (2022) consider how extrinsic information cues affect online purchase. They find that country-of-origin effects may occur predominantly in relation to evaluation of specific attributes rather than overall evaluations. Their study reveals the need to account for a range of impact factors simultaneously. Suter et. al (2018) examine the role of country-of-origin-image (COI) as a country-specific advantage (CSA) for internationalized firms. They find that the construct is multidimensional and can be operationalized in terms of a range of dimensions such as natural resources, cultural resources, textual, visual elements, and senses.

CONCLUSION

Place-Branding, Place-Identity, Place-Image, and Evolution of Consumption

A stream of literature considers place branding, place identity or image and how such branding, identity and image is meaningful for various audiences and can be marketed to target segments such as tourists or stakeholders (Aitken & Campelo, 2011; Bruwer & Johnson, 2010; Ditoiu & Caruntu, 2015, Foroudi et.al; 2016; Foroudi et. al; 2020; Hafeez et.al; 2016, Hernandez et. al; 2016; Jiang et. al; 2016; Lee et. al; 2016)

Ditoiu and Caruntu (2015) consider the perceptual elements that tourists rely on when evaluating a destination. Bruwer and Johnson (2010) explore place-based marketing in the form of region of origin strategies used by wineries to brand themselves. They found that consumers used regional branding cues, information and images to assess and evaluate comparative wine labels. Regional information on wine labels increased consumer confidence in product quality. Now imagine this situation in a scenario where the idea is stoking emotion for online buying based behaviour. The idea is to stoke the emotion for local purchase but being influenced by the local cues and the emotions in the form of stories or rather the narratives being created by the local fashion influencers in the online sphere.

Aitken and Campelo (2011) consider how shared perceptions and community are significant to place-branding. A sense of ownership is pivotal to how a place can be positioned, represented, governed and owned. Foroudi et al (2016) investigate key indicators of place branding. These they found were national culture e.g., country attributes, social changes, geography and environment, people and culture (history, language), and infrastructure (security, economic and level of technological infrastructure, tourism, place and promotional strategy). Hafeez et al. (2016) expand on theoretical connections between place branding and image from the perspective of sectoral clusters. Sectoral clusters represent specialized industries based on certain economic activities, e.g., the IT park in Bangalore. The creation of a place brand based on specialized clusters impacts not only the economic strength but also place branding in positive ways. This brings us to the next part of the narrative which is based around heritage. It is one factor that binds all of the buying behaviour and nostalgia together.

REFERENCES

Abd Rahman, N. H., Khalifah, Z., & Ismail, H. N. (2015). Conceptual framework for experiences' quality based on senses' perception with behaviour as a mediator: In the context of cultural heritage attractions. *Advanced Science Letters*, *21*(5), 1135–1140. doi:10.1166/asl.2015.6017

Abraham, A., & Patro, S. (2014). 'Country-of-origin' effect and consumer decision-making. *Management and Labour Studies*, *39*(3), 309–318. doi:10.1177/0258042X15572408

Aitken, R., & Campelo, A. (2011). The four Rs of place branding. *Journal of Marketing Management*, *27*(9-10), 913–933. doi:10.1080/0267257X.2011.560718

Brand, B. M., & Baier, D. (2022). Measuring country of origin effects in online shopping implicitly: a discrete choice analysis approach. *International Marketing Review*.

Bruwer, J., & Johnson, R. (2010). Place-based marketing and regional branding strategy perspectives in the California wine industry. *Journal of Consumer Marketing*, *27*(1), 5–16. doi:10.1108/07363761011012903

Chatzidakis, A., McEachern, M. G., & Warnaby, G. (2018). Consumption in and of space and place: Introduction to the special issue. *Marketing Theory*, *18*(2), 149–153. doi:10.1177/1470593117732452

Coffin, J., & Chatzidakis, A. (2021). The Möbius strip of market spatiality: Mobilizing transdisciplinary dialogues between CCT and the marketing mainstream. *AMS Review*, *11*(1-2), 40–59. doi:10.100713162-020-00191-8

Foroudi, P., Cuomo, M. T., Foroudi, M. M., Katsikeas, C. S., & Gupta, S. (2020). Linking identity and heritage with image and a reputation for competition. *Journal of Business Research*, *113*, 317–325. doi:10.1016/j.jbusres.2019.09.042

Foroudi, P., Jin, Z., Gupta, S., Melewar, T. C., & Foroudi, M. M. (2016). Influence of innovation capability and customer experience on reputation and loyalty. *Journal of Business Research*, *69*(11), 4882–4889. doi:10.1016/j.jbusres.2016.04.047

Hafeez, K., Foroudi, P., Dinnie, K., Nguyen, B., & Parahoo, S. K. (2016). The role of place branding and image in the development of sectoral clusters: The case of Dubai. *Journal of Brand Management*, *23*(4), 383–402. doi:10.1057/bm.2016.18

Pappu, R., Quester, P. G., & Cooksey, R. W. (2006). Consumer-based brand equity and country-of-origin relationships: Some empirical evidence. *European Journal of Marketing*, *40*(5/6), 696–717. doi:10.1108/03090560610657903

Pendlebury, J., Veldpaus, L., & Garrow, H. (2023). Relationality, place governance and heritage: The Lower Ouseburn Valley, Newcastle upon Tyne and 'Ouseburnness'. *Planning Practice and Research*, *38*(3), 409–424. doi:10.1080/02697459.2023.2180193

Rezvani, S., Dehkordi, G. J., Rahman, M. S., Fouladivanda, F., Habibi, M., & Eghtebasi, S. (2012). A conceptual study on the country of origin effect on consumer purchase intention. *Asian Social Science*, *8*(12), 205–215. doi:10.5539/ass.v8n12p205

Seamon, D. (Ed.). (1993). *Dwelling, seeing, and designing: Toward a phenomenological ecology*. SUNY Press.

Suter, M. B., Borini, F. M., Floriani, D. E., da Silva, D., & Polo, E. (2018). Country-of-origin image (COI) as a country-specific advantage (CSA): Scale development and validation of COI as a resource within the firm perspective. *Journal of Business Research*, *84*, 46–58. doi:10.1016/j.jbusres.2017.11.006

Visconti, L. M., Sherry, J. F. Jr, Borghini, S., & Anderson, L. (2010). Street art, sweet art? Reclaiming the "public" in public place. *The Journal of Consumer Research*, *37*(3), 511–529. doi:10.1086/652731

Chapter 8
Instagram's Marketing Strategy of the Main Fast Fashion Brands:
Best Practices to Improve Customer Engagement

Naiara Martinicorena-Goñi
Universidad Pública de Navarra, Spain

Maria Elena Aramendia-Muneta
https://orcid.org/0000-0001-6167-3194
Universidad Pública de Navarra, Spain

ABSTRACT

About 1,000 million users are active on Instagram monthly, and the number of daily users is 500 million. Fifty percent of Instagrammers follow at least one business account, and 130 million Instagrammers tap on a shopping post to learn about products offered in the app every month. Moreover, more than 200 million Instagrammers visit at least one business profile every day. The objective of the study is to assess the Instagram strategy of four of the main fast fashion brands: Zara, H&M, Mango, and Forever 21. Results show videos achieve 3.88 times more engagement than pictures. The effect of the shopping bag tool, which has been recently introduced, is very promising: the pictures with the shopping bag tool achieved a 121.03% higher average. The authors also found spontaneity increases engagement, while Zara, H&M, and Mango posts experienced an increase in the average likes in the pictures that had faces in them.

DOI: 10.4018/978-1-6684-8753-2.ch008

INTRODUCTION

Fashion is an important industry globally and estimates point to an upward trend in revenues in the coming years, especially in Europe (Ananda et al., 2015). In addition, the Internet has had an impact on our lives that many would not have imagined a few years ago. It has facilitated many areas of our daily lives, one of them being online transactions where users are able to shop anytime, anywhere and from any shop, they ask themselves, wherever this shop can be set up. Instagram functions as a unifying bridge between fashion and online retail, as it functions as a huge showcase of the products available from countless brands from all over the world.

Instagram and social media are topics of much debate (Kaplan & Haenlein, 2010). On the one hand, they appeared not so long ago and have become some of the most relevant tools for social interaction in our daily lives. Although the idea behind Instagram was to share photographs and videos with friends, it has also become a marketing tool for many companies around the world (Huang & Benyoucef, 2017). One of the drivers for this research is the lack of a specific and in-depth analysis of the Instagram strategy of fashion brands, however, there is a large literature on different areas of Instagram to understand what makes Instagram posts more engaging.

Lin and Ju (2019) discuss the role of social media, particularly fashion blogging, in encouraging two-way symmetrical communication in the fashion industry. The authors argue that social media platforms like Instagram have changed the way that fashion companies communicate with consumers, and that fashion blogging in particular has created a more collaborative and interactive relationship between brands and consumers. Moreover, Thakur and Srivastava (2020) examines the relationship between Instagram usage and impulse buying behavior in the context of fashion products. The authors found that Instagram usage has a significant positive effect on impulse buying behavior, particularly for fashion products, which suggests that Instagram is an important tool for fashion companies to drive sales.

This study aims to evaluate the Instagram strategy of four major fast fashion brands: Zara, H&M, Mango and Forever 21. The idea behind the project is to understand whether Instagram is a powerful e-marketing tool and which elements make posts more attractive and generate more engagement among consumers. The selection criteria for the four fast fashion brands were based on their net sales in 2018 and the total number of Instagram users these brands have on their Instagram accounts.

Around 1 billion users are active on Instagram monthly, and the number of daily users of the app is 500 million. 32% of internet users are on Instagram, 91% of Instagrammers are contained in the highest population age group (15-64 years old), and 71% of Instagrammers are under 35 years old. All these data were considered crucial for the selection of Instagram as a social media application to understand the marketing strategy of the four brands mentioned above.

Thus, a research question is formulated: How can Instagram users be encouraged to engage in fast-fashion?

The project follows the following structure. First, some data on the fashion industry is presented. Secondly, the fashion industry is shown in figures. Next, the links between the fashion industry and the Internet, e-commerce and Instagram as key social networks are formulated. In the methodological part, the selection of fast fashion brands is justified. Finally, in the last section, the results and conclusions of the analysis of the selected brands are shown, as well as the conclusions and limitations of the research.

FASHION INDUSTRY THEORY

The original use of clothing was to protect individuals from the weather and to cover the body. Today, however, fashion functions as a social regulator, indicating social status, gender and geographical location. Consequently, fashion and society are strongly connected. Fashion is believed to be the tool for the individual's self-expression when, in reality, the person is constructed through the clothes they wear (Martínez Caballero & Vázquez Casco, 2006), which are imposed by society. Fashion also fulfils a function of social inclusion, since human beings are social beings.

However, it is true that, in general, there is a desire for distinction, but always within what is socially acceptable, to stand out just enough to be seen as an individual out of the ordinary. In fact, this desire for distinction and singularity against what society imposes as "cool" or "fashion" is a growing trend nowadays.

Furthermore, the needs covered by the garment industry are related to Maslow's hierarchy of needs pyramid. The five-stage model is divided into basic needs (physiological, safety, security, love and esteem) and growth needs (self-actualization) (Mcleod, 2007). The garment industry could be seen as satisfying the physiological need for environmental protection, however, "this has little to do with fashion" (Martínez Caballero & Vázquez Casco, 2006). In developed countries, the physiological (air, water, food, housing, clothing, etc.) and security (personal safety, employment, health, property, etc.) levels are fully covered. Therefore, fashion companies offer products to meet the need to feel part of a group (a psychological need). As already mentioned, these needs include recognition, prestige, differentiation from others, etc. At the top of Maslow's pyramid is the level of self-actualization, which would apply to the case of fashion designers.

The Fashion Cycle

The clothing cycle follows four stages: innovation, imitation, democratization and decadence. Innovation corresponds to the moment when a new product appears and represents a break from previous trends. The early adopter segment is the one that purchases this type of product. They are the channel for the introduction of new products. The break with previous trends has to be significant and daring but to a certain extent. During the second stage (imitation), consumers, called followers, start buying the new product (Jackson, 2012; Roger, 2003).

The democratization stage is the period of the greatest diffusion of new trends when the vast majority of consumers purchase the product (Jackson, 2012). The new trends spread from the early majority to the late majority of consumers, and consumers eventually acquire the good by mimicry: consumers observe other individuals wearing the new clothing lines and, in the end (at first with some hesitation), they dare to incorporate the new trend into their wardrobes. The new trends spread and, in some cases, lose their essence and become a fad.

The decadence stage consists of the total loss of meaning of a trend and the need for another new symbol, a new trend that reinforces a segment of the population. The laggards buy the product until it disappears, or is dazzled by the new product that captures our attention, closing the cycle and starting all over again.

Characteristics of Fashion as a Product

To understand the marketing of the fashion industry, first of all, it must be emphasized that it is a highly seasonal industry. Fashion is ephemeral and defies the past, even though it is nourished by it. Fashion defies tradition or reinvents it, as an act of rebellion against what is socially imposed and accepted (while keeping in mind that it is always within limits) (Bruce & Krazt, 2012). Fashion is also reactive in the sense that it works through responses to past trends, it is exhibitionist, paradoxical and global. The term paradoxical is used here because fashion tries to make individuals unique, but without going beyond what is accepted by society or the group. It is based on the idea of constant change. Furthermore, consumers must identify with the new trend in order to accept it; otherwise, it will become an eccentricity of the social elites. The last characteristic of the garment industry is that it is global. There are no significant differences between Western countries in terms of the clothes individuals wear, so it is not possible to identify the country of origin by what they wear. However, this is not the case in Asian countries such as India, which still are attached to tradition, or the Persian Gulf countries, conditioned by religious beliefs (Martínez Caballero & Vázquez Casco, 2006).

The big question is who imposes the new trends. In the past, it was the aristocracy who imposed the new fashions, however, nowadays, it is the companies or brand conglomerates who establish what is fashionable or not.

Companies such as LVMH (which includes Pucci, Dior, Louis Vuitton, Donna Karan, Loewe and Marc Jacobs), Françoise Pinault - Kering (Yves Saint Laurent, Balenciaga, Gucci, Stella McCartney, Alexander McQueen, etc.), Richemont (Chloe, Jaeger, Baume Mercier) and Prada (Prada and Miu Miu) among others, launch new trends every year based on small details that will mark the style of the new garments for that season.

There is a democratization process as explained above in the industry cycle, where trends set by luxury brands are turned into affordable products by fast fashion brands such as Zara, Mango or H&M. These brands replicate the trends created by the luxury brands and offer them at affordable prices by sacrificing quality, details, etc. In this way, fashion trends become global.

Segmentation

Heterogeneity in the fashion industry is quite common, and it is difficult to define a trend that meets the needs and tastes of all available consumers. Segmentation is a strategy that consists of dividing consumers into homogeneous subgroups according to some kind of shared characteristics. Segmentation allows companies to target each subgroup with a differentiated strategy; in this way, brands can effectively meet the needs of each of the subgroups.

Several benefits can be derived from segmentation in the fashion industry. Firstly, it allows business opportunities to come to light. Despite the enormous diversity of brands today, there is always a segment whose needs are not fully covered. The second benefit is that segmentation helps to prioritize by choosing relevant factors such as demand fit, ease of access to the segment, buying potential, etc.

The third benefit of segmenting the market is that it facilitates competitor analysis and allows you to understand which of the brands in the whole market are your direct competitors and therefore the ones to focus on. Last but not least, segmentation helps to tailor the products or services provided to the specific needs of the target customers.

Within the segmentation strategy, two different selection criteria are identified: general and specific. The general criterion is based on customer characteristics or attributes, such as age, gender, occupation, urban tribes, size, purchasing power, annual income, etc. On the other hand, the specific segmentation criterion considers dimensions that are directly related to the actual consumption of clothing: loyalty, price sensitivity, spending, perceptions, place of purchase, etc. In this case, the focus is on consumer behavior.

It is quite common to combine more than one segmentation criterion, as the more variables are considered, the more specific the target segment is and the more possibilities exist to adapt the strategy to meet the specific needs of the target segment. However, it is also true that the more variables are included, the more difficult it is to access the segment and make it profitable.

Advertising is one of the main strategic pillars for companies to achieve sales. It has three main objectives: to inform, to persuade and to educate (Mowka et al., 1980). These three objectives can be added that of reminding or remembering. Of the first three objectives, the most used is "persuade", as the fierce competition between brands makes them hesitant to convince potential customers of the benefits of buying the product.

When designing a communication plan, marketers need to consider several key points: whom they are going to target, the message they are going to send, how or what tools they are going to use to disseminate their message, when it is going to be carried out and what results they expect. But bear in mind that there are no magic formulas and that a strategic communication plan that works for one brand may not work for another.

Competitors

Fashion brands have to carefully define their target market to find out who their direct competitors are, as the fashion industry is a highly competitive market. According to Martínez Caballero & Vázquez Casco (2006), there are some basic principles of competition:

- The more similar the competitors are, the stronger the competition.
- Each surviving competitor has a unique advantage because otherwise, it would disappear.
- Co-existing competitors are in equilibrium.

As for the first principle, in the fast fashion industry, Zara, H&M and Gap, offer products based on new trends launched by top designers and watch each other closely.

Each of the three brands mentioned above has a distinct advantage in the market. Direct competitors are close to each other, but they have to distinguish themselves from the others in order to acquire the largest possible market share in a specific segment. For example, H&M reinterprets trends by targeting the younger segment of the population, Gap offers basic clothing designs without losing sight of seasonal trends, while Zara is the only brand that is fully vertically integrated from design to shop management (Martínez Caballero & Vázquez Casco, 2006). Zara tries to minimize the time lag between the appearance of new trends and the time when those specific clothing designs are available in shops.

A characteristic of fast fashion belts is the scarcity principle, which consists of a limited supply of goods, in this case, clothing and accessories, to encourage consumers to purchase them. Consumers understand that, due to the limited number of units available of an item, if they are not sure whether to buy it or not, they will buy it immediately because, otherwise, the next time the consumer visits the shop, there may not be any units of the item left. This principle also explains the constant changes in items and the constant change in their layout within the shops.

Marketing Design and Fashion

The marketing of the fashion industry has several special characteristics compared to other industries. On the one hand, the intrinsic characteristics of fashion (cyclical, fleeting, challenging the past, reactive, paradoxical, exhibitionist and global) make its marketing philosophy and activities quite particular (Le Pechoux et al., 2012). On the other hand, design plays a dual role in orienting and reflecting consumer demand. This leads to different conceptions of fashion marketing.

Fashion marketing is the way of understanding the exchange relationship of fashion companies with their market through design, the creation of new outfits, pricing, the appropriate distribution of the product with the appropriate features, and the most effective communication, to meet the unpredictable expectations of the customer, while the company makes profits and benefits society (Martínez Caballero & Vázquez Casco, 2006).

Fashion Design, Marketing, and Conflict of Interests

There are many actors in the fashion design and production chain. Two of the main actors are fashion designers, who create new pieces of clothing, and marketers, who design campaigns to sell the designed products. Fashion designers are taught to follow a creative process, where inspiration turns ideas into concepts and, in turn, into new designs and products. Designers need to be spontaneous, eclectic and willing to take risks. In contrast, marketers are taught to set quantitative targets, study markets, take into account market share and customer preferences, design campaigns with the widest possible reach, cost-effective marketing strategies, and so on. Therefore, each type of professional has different objectives. Designers consider marketing professionals as people who force freedom and imagination, while marketing professionals consider fashion designers as undisciplined and indifferent to costs and profitability (Martínez Caballero & Vázquez Casco, 2006). Still, it is important to mention that both groups share many points of view, both recognize the importance of communication and the functional aspects of the fashion industry.

Internet

Looking back fifteen years or so, no one would have imagined the impact the Internet has had on our daily lives and how it has shaped our societies and behaviors. The Internet has become one of the most important tools for brands to differentiate themselves and to express their philosophy, mission, vision, etc. The Internet allows brands to get to know their customers, build a brand community and reinforce customer loyalty to the brand. According to Faber et al. (2004), the Internet is a valuable resource for customers seeking knowledge and a powerful medium for advertising to reach consumers.

The fashion industry has always needed image as the main advertising tool. Until a few years ago, the mainstay of the industry was the specialized magazines, such as Harper's Bazaar (founded in 1867), Vanity Fair (1913) or Vogue (1892). In fact, fashion advertising is the one that launches new trends, shares them and sometimes even creates them (Martínez Caballero & Vázquez Casco, 2006). Photographs allow brands to show the product with higher quality and distribute it around the world. However, nowadays, due to the Internet, the image as an advertising tool has become more accessible to everyone, as the majority of the world's population owns a mobile phone and has access to the Internet.

Social media applications such as Instagram have replaced these fashion magazines, because most fashion brands have their own Instagram account, where they can share their new collections, easily reach their followers and create and reinforce their brand community. Consumers are now easily accessible, regardless of region or country of origin, and are closer than ever to brands.

FASHION INDUSTRY IN NUMBERS

Figure 1 shows revenues in the fashion segment in millions of US dollars for the years 2017, 2018 and 2019, and expected or forecast revenues for the years 2020 to 2024. The forecast is very promising as revenues in 2017 were USD 443.62 billion, and are expected to grow to USD 997.644 billion by 2024. This implies an expected increase in total revenues of 23.53%. The graph has a bar for each year with its actual or expected revenue. Each bar is divided into three components of the fashion industry, which are: bags and accessories (pink), footwear (blue) and apparel (purple), showing their revenues for each year. Apparel is the most significant segment, as it is the sector with the largest share for each of the years. However, the relevance of the footwear sector is expected to decline steadily and eventually become the sector with the lowest revenues of the three analyzed.

Figure 1. Actual and forecasted revenue in the fashion segment (in millions of $)
Source: Own elaboration based on data from Statista (2020)

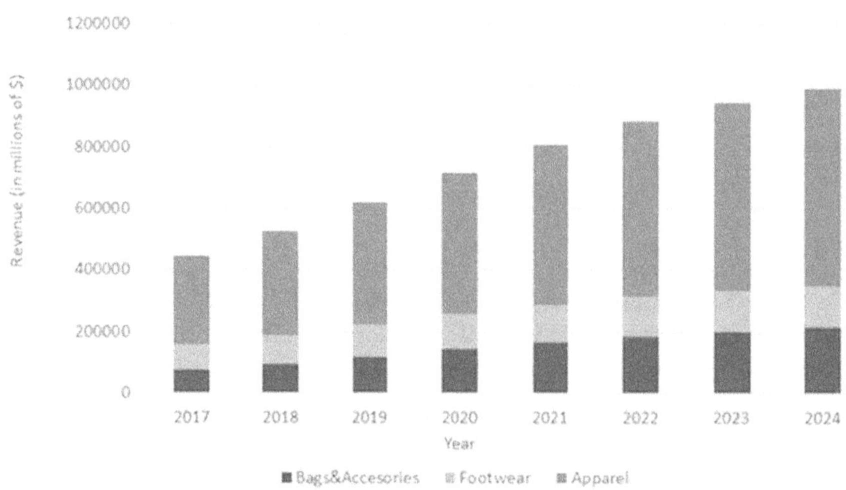

This phenomenon is easier to observe in Figure 2, which shows actual and forecast revenue growth in the fashion segment for the same period. The graph shows a trend of decreasing growth over the years, from average growth of 18.73% in 2017 to forecasted growth of 4.85% in 2024. It is worth noting that the highest percentage (and forecast) growth for each year is in the handbags and accessories sector. It is also true that it is the sector with the largest decrease in growth for the period, from 28.30% in 2017 to 6.10% in 2024 (a total decrease in growth of 78.44%). The lowest percentage growth, except in 2017, is for the footwear sector. For the fashion segment as a whole, an overall decrease in growth of 74.11% is observed. It should therefore be borne in mind that half of the data in both charts are forecasts and that the reality may turn out to be different. The expectation for revenues in the fashion segment is that they will continue to grow over time but at a slower pace.

Figure 2. Actual and forecasted revenue growth in the fashion segment
Source: Own elaboration based on data from Statista (2020)

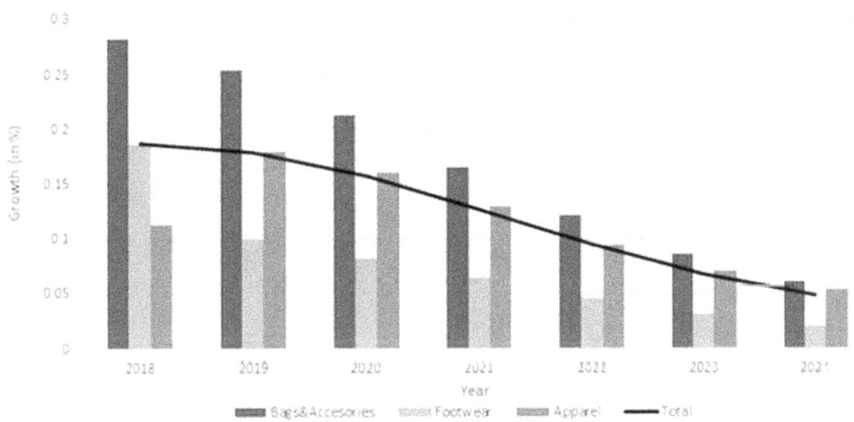

FASHION INDUSTRY, INTERNET, AND E-COMMERCE

There is confusion about the difference between e-business and e-commerce. To make a clear distinction between the concepts, e-business refers to any method of using digital information and communication technologies to conduct or support business processes. On the other hand, e-commerce refers to the actual trading of goods and services online. Thus, e-commerce is a type of e-business. E-commerce allows increasing sales volume, building brand awareness, building trust, increasing and improving services, updating information, etc. (Utz et al., 2012). Figure 3 shows how e-business comprises e-commerce.

Figure 3. E-business and e-commerce

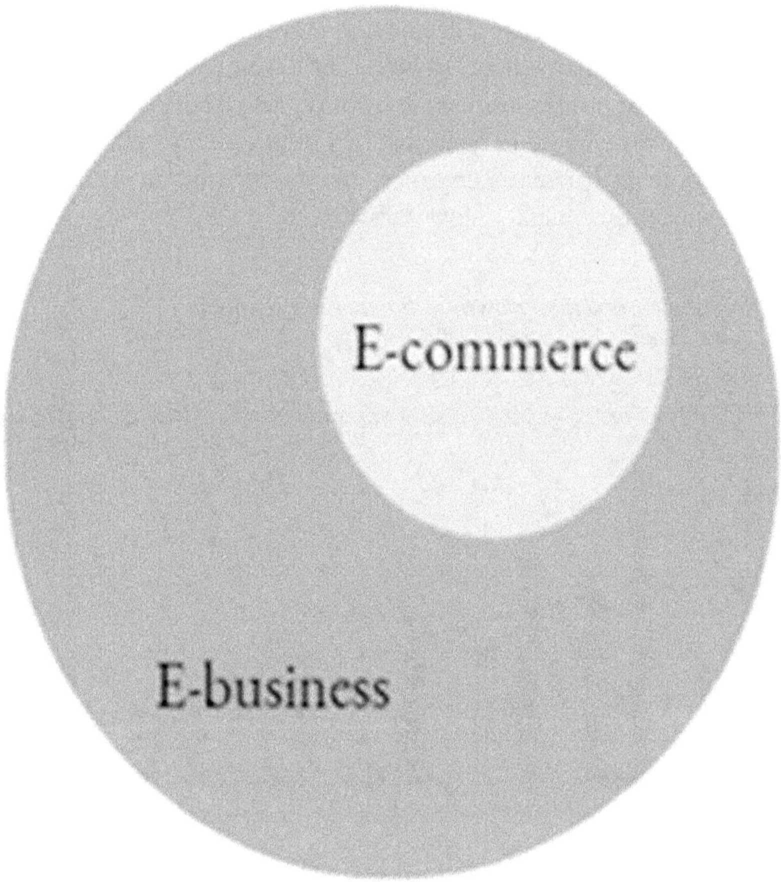

Eurostat conducted a study in 2019, obtaining responses from a total of 147,531 households in the EU-28, which had at least one person aged 16-74, and from 193,958 individuals in the same area aged 16-74, regarding their internet use, activities, etc.

According to Eurostat (2020), there was a large variation of e-shoppers across EU-28 countries in 2019, ranging from 28.75% in Romania to 90.63% in the UK, with an average of 65.71%. These data were calculated as the percentage of individuals who shopped online in the last 12 months out of the total number of internet users in each country.

Changes in the number of internet users who bought or ordered goods or services in the last 12 months by age group in the EU-28 from 2009 to 2019. There is a general upward trend, with the highest proportion for the 16-24 (78%) and 25-54 (76%) age groups. Furthermore, there has been an overall increase in online shopping of 31.94%, with the largest increase for the 16-24 age group (56.58% increase). The smallest increase has been in the 55-74 age group, with an overall increase for the aforementioned period of 20.36%.

The most purchased goods in 2019 in the EU-28 were clothing and sporting goods with a total of 65% of e-shoppers. Among this percentage, the 16-24 age group had the highest proportion of e-shoppers purchasing clothing and sporting goods. The second most purchased type of goods and services were those related to travel and holiday accommodation (54%). The 16-24 age group was the largest purchaser of clothing and sporting goods with 73%, while the 25-54 age group was the largest purchaser of travel and accommodation with 57%.

In terms of shopping frequency, 34% of e-shoppers shopped online three to five times in the three months before the survey. This proportion is the highest, followed by 32% of e-shoppers who shopped one to two times in the same period.

Finally, in terms of the amount spent, the highest proportion of e-shoppers purchased goods or services totaling between 100 and 500 euros (42%). In terms of gender differences, the proportion of male online shoppers (72%) was slightly higher than that of female online shoppers (71%).

INSTAGRAM

The fastest-growing social media platform was launched on 6 October 2010 by Kevin Systrom and Mike Krieger. It is an online social media application where users create an account where they can share photographs and videos, follow other accounts, like and comment on photographs and videos, send direct messages to Instagrammers, post stories 24 hours a day, etc. Instagram is a viral marketing tool, considered by many as a type of word-of-mouth technique used on the Internet (Nicol & Agam, 2016).

Instagram and Population

According to the World Bank, the world has 1.958 billion inhabitants in the 0-14 age group, 4.96 billion inhabitants in the 15-64 age group (World Bank, 2019c) and 673,620 thousand inhabitants in the 65 and over age group (World Bank, 2019e). The term population in this case is based on the de facto definition of population, which counts all residents regardless of citizenship or legal status. In Figure 4, the reader can see the distribution of the world's population divided into the three age groups named above. The 0-14 age group represents 25.792% of the total world population (World Bank, 2019b). The 15-64 age group accounts for 65.335% of the total population (World Bank, 2019d), while the 65 and over age group accounts for 8.873% of the total population (World Bank, 2019f).

Figure 4. Distribution of population by age groups
Source: Own elaboration based on data from World Bank (2019b, 2019d, 2019f)

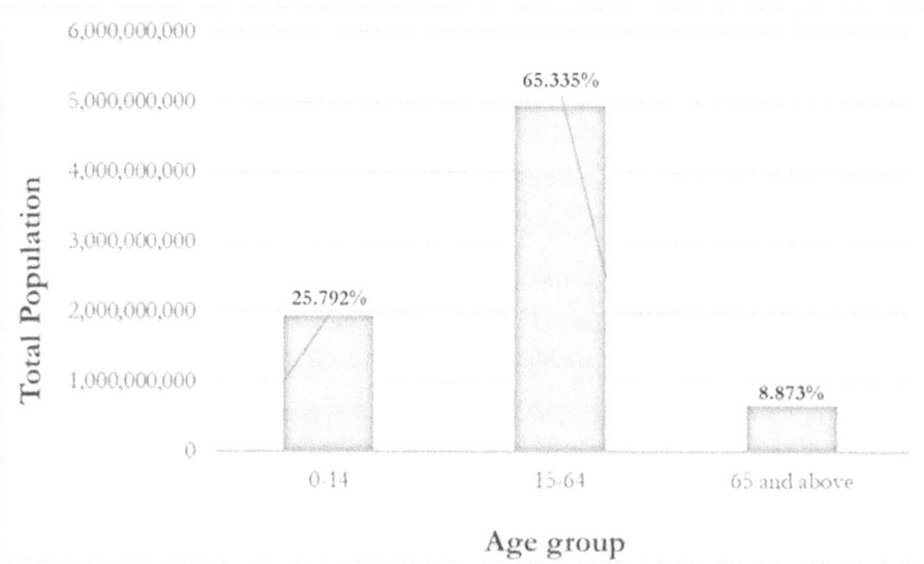

On the other hand, Figure 5 shows the percentage distribution of Instagram users in 2019 by age (Statista, 2020). The graph shows the distribution of Instagrammers among the total population. The largest group is the 25-34 age group, with 34% of all users. It is closely followed by the 18-24 age group with 31%.

The information provided is quite interesting if we take into account the distribution of the population. If we combine the different age groups to make them coincide (more or less) with the age group distribution of the population graph, we obtain that 91% of Instagrammers are contained in the age group with the highest population. It is also interesting to note that 71% of Instagrammers are under 35 years old (Statista, 2020). Therefore, Instagram is an interesting tool to reach the world's population and mainly the young population, as they are all accessible through the Internet.

Figure 5. Distribution of Instagram users in 2019 by age (in percentage)
Source: Own elaboration based on data from Statista (2020)

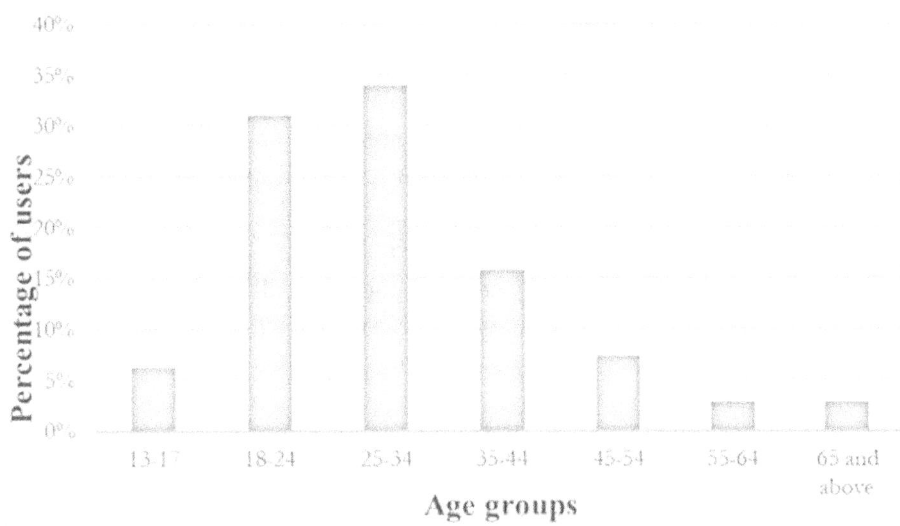

Instagram, Viral Marketing, and eWOM

Online viral marketing is a recent concept that emerged with the introduction of the Internet into our daily lives. It is a word-of-mouth marketing technique, which spreads information about brands, products or services like a virus, but on social media networks and electronic devices. Viral marketing exploits existing social networks by encouraging customers to share product information with their friends. The key difference between viral and TV advertising is that a viral ad is something that is sought after, found with pleasure and sent out for someone else to enjoy (Larson, 2009). According to Aramendia (2017), the relationship between businesses and consumers online has changed in favor of consumers with the introduction of the Internet and online marketing, making it possible for everyone to voice their opinion from anywhere and at any time.

One of the advantages of e-marketing over traditional marketing is that companies can have direct and direct contact with the customer. However, e-marketing cannot replace traditional marketing, but they complement each other. On the other hand, the impact of a negative comment on the brand is greater than with traditional marketing, as it can easily spread and it is always very difficult to undo the damage caused (Larson, 2009).

One of the main and most relevant characteristics of viral marketing is eWOM (electronic word of mouth), which consists of "interpersonal communication in which the sender spreads a message to the receivers" via the Internet (Bao & Chang, 2014, p. 21.). eWOM could be considered a type of marketing that cannot be controlled by marketers, as it is based on consumers' personal opinions about their perception of the appropriateness of the brand.

According to Aramendia-Muneta (2017), while favorable reviews increase the likelihood of purchase, unfavorable reviews have the opposite effect. As the author explains, customers choose to leave negative comments online when a serious failure occurs, and a company's trustworthiness is severely affected when companies are unable to take immediate action after receiving negative eWOM. One of the main objectives of eWOM, as the author points out, is to reduce uncertainty and search time, while anonymity incentivizes the publication of misleading information, as the reliability of the source cannot be verified.

As with traditional marketing, social media companies, which function as a means of creating consumer-to-consumer or C2C (consumer-to-consumer) communication, such as Instagram, must understand the market and the type of customer they want to target. Once a company has identified its target, it must evaluate the most appropriate platform to reach those potential buyers. It is important to pay attention to what customers want and not bury them with too much information and resources (Wert & Salovey, 2004).

Through social media, large brands can expand their reach and small businesses can increase awareness and brand awareness at almost no cost. Instagram is the social network with the highest return on investment for businesses, as they can create an account for free and directly post their products. In 2014, only 40% of major brands had an Instagram account, but in 2015 the statistic soared to 71% of the world's most recognized brands. Today, around 92% of well-known brands have an Instagram account (Statista, 2020).

Marketing on Instagram relies on the active participation of its users. Brands rely on the content and data generated by consumer engagement on social media platforms (Carah & Shaul, 2016). Through social media, companies can create brand awareness and interact with their customers, but it also allows customers to interact with other customers.

On the other hand, it is interesting to understand what makes Instagram so special that differentiates it from other social networks in terms of e-marketing. What sets Instagram apart from other social networks is that it applies a visual-based strategy (Giannoulakis & Tsapatsoulis, 2016). Everything on Instagram revolves around photography. Thus, marketing on Instagram is an effective way to advertise a product, as it is said that a picture is worth a thousand words (Silva et al., 2013).

Bakhshi et al. (2014) assessed the effect of the presence of a face, age and gender on social engagement in an Instagram photograph. The database contained one million Instagram photographs posted by different users. The authors found that "photographs with faces were 38% more likely to receive likes and 32% more likely to receive comments", elements that showed their relevance in generating engagement. However, they found no effect of the number of faces in the image, age or gender on engagement.

Face perception is perhaps one of the most highly developed human visual skills and a powerful channel of non-verbal communication (Bakhshi et al., 2014). Indeed, the presence of faces and facial expressions in a computer application affects users' performance and productivity (Walker et al., 1994). However, with millions of images, videos and stories being posted every day, the key is to figure out how to direct attention to the brand and create engagement.

The world is constantly changing and therefore marketers need to be aware of this and adapt their marketing strategies to avoid falling behind their competitors or becoming outdated. The fashion industry should create video-based strategies, as they are more effective and increase the impact on consumer behavior. The reason is that customers prefer to watch an image-based advertisement from which they can easily extract meaningful information effortlessly, rather than through tedious advertisements full of words.

METHODOLOGY

Fast Fashion Brands Sample

The term fast fashion corresponds to the clothing designs which move quickly from the catwalk to the affordable-price brands' stores. It consists of cheap clothing which follows the new trends designed by the most famous fashion designers. Together with the definition of fast fashion is Zara, acting more like a synonym rather than as an example of the concept of fast fashion. Zara has shown how to cut the time between the design, production and delivery of the products.

To be able to compare the impact of the main fast fashion brands on Instagram, the selection method of the brands followed is going to be through the net sales of the companies in 2018 (as it is the latest year from which we have information) to evaluate their global sales, and the Instagram followers and accounts to gauge the influence which they exert through the app.

According to the case of "Zara: Fast Fashion" (Ghemawat & Nueno, 2003), Zara is one of the world's leading fast fashion brands. The case also explains that Zara's main competitors, at the time the article was written, were The Gap, H&M and Benetton. The latter three have tighter vertical integration compared to Zara, which owns most of its production and shops. Both Gap and H&M outsource all their production, while Benetton invests heavily in production, but its shops are managed by licensing. Although today H&M remains one of Zara's main competitors, Gap and Benetton are brands that have lagged behind Zara and H&M.

According to Inditex's 2018 Annual Report (2019), Zara's net sales in that year were €18,021 million (the company distinguishes net sales by each of the company's integrated brands). According to H&M Group's annual report (2019), net sales for the entire group in 2018 were SEK 210.4 billion. After conversion to euros, the H&M Group's net sales for 2018 were €19,784 million. However, it should be noted that the H&M group includes H&M, COS, Weekday, Monki, H&M Home, & Other Stories, Afound, ARKET and Cheap Monday. H&M's net sales as an individual retail brand were therefore lower than those reported in the annual report. H&M as an individual brand is the backbone of the group, while the other brands are smaller in size and present in fewer markets around the world. Consequently, although the group's annual report did not distinguish between net sales data, H&M's net sales may be lower but close to those of Zara.

Gap Inc. as a group of brands (Old Navy Global, Gap Global and Banana Republic) achieved USD 16.58 billion in net sales as of 2018, or EUR 15.047 billion (Gap Inc., 2019). However, Gap Inc. also included information on its net sales by brand. In this case, the brand is well behind its competitors in terms of annual net sales.

The Benetton Group's net sales in 2018 were €1.23 billion (Benetton Group, 2019). However, the Benetton Group integrates the United Colors of Benetton and Sisley brands. The 2018 Annual Report states that 88% of the Group's net sales come from United Colors of Benetton, meaning that its net sales in 2018 were €1.08 billion.

In terms of the impact of brands on social media, the number of Instagram followers on the brand's official account will be the selection criterion for assessing its impact on actual and potential consumers. Instagram follower count establishes the reach of a user's posts (Bakhshi et al., 2014). When an Instagrammer A follows an Instagrammer B, B's photograph will appear in the feed of A. This means that the more followers an Instagrammer have, the greater his or her reach. This means that the more followers an Instagrammer has, the more Instagrammers will be able to see their posts on their user profile and the greater the chance of receiving likes and comments. If B's account is private, only his followers will be able to see his posts. However, if the account is public, B's posts will appear in his followers' feed, but anyone can access B's posts by logging into B's account.

- Zara: 37.9 million followers (Instagram, 2020f)
- H&M: 34.7 million followers (Instagram, 2020c)
- Gap: 3 million followers (Instagram, 2020b)
- United Colors of Benetton: 601,000 followers (Instagram, 2020e)

After analyzing the main fast fashion brands, and taking into account that Gap and Benetton have fallen behind Zara and H&M in both net sales and Instagram followers, two other brands will be introduced to make the comparison between brands.

The first company introduced is Forever 21, whose net sales in 2018 amounted to USD 2.7 billion or €2.438 billion (Forbes, 2019). On Instagram, Forever 21 has 16.2 million followers (Instagram, 2020a). Net sales are indeed at the same level as Gap and Benetton, however, its impact on Instagram is huge compared to them. Even so, Forever 21's total follower count is less than half that of Zara.

The second fast fashion brand introduced for comparison is Mango. Mango's net sales in 2018 were €2,233 million (Europapress, 2019) and it has 11.2 million followers on Instagram (Instagram, 2020d).

Both brands, Mango and Forever 21 have around 13% of H&M and Zara's net sales and less than half of the followers on Instagram. However, the reason for selecting these two brands is that there is no other fast fashion brand nearby in terms of Instagram followers. There are no other fast fashion brands with a such number of followers comparable to Zara and H&M. The closest brands are Forever 21 and H&M.

Method and Technical Details of the Research

We are going to analyze the Instagram strategy of each of these brands (Zara, H&M, Mango and Forever 21), as we have previously mentioned due to their relevance. The selection period for Instagram posts is from 1 December 2019 to 31 January 2020. It includes the period just after Black Friday and the beginning of the new year in which these brands used their account and posts to present their new collections. The variables analyzed are the number of likes, comments and video views.

The term post is used here as the content shared on the Instagram account and includes both images and videos. The term post refers to any type of content shared via videos or images.

A like on Instagram indicates the number of Instagrammers who have actively shown that they like the photo. The number of "likes" measures the engagement the video or photograph has created. The more likes a photograph has, the more users like it and the more engagement it generates. The number of comments on an image is also used as a measure of engagement. It is a more explicit action on the content, a Instagrammer has shared comments, which requires more effort, commitment and time (Aramendia-Muneta et al., 2021). The number of comments determines the extent to which users have discussed the photograph and can therefore be considered a measure of discussion (Bakhshi et al., 2014). Since leaving comments is effortless, the number of "likes" on posts is always higher than the number of comments. The number of posts tool is used to quantify user activity on Instagram (Bakhshi et al., 2014). This tool shows the number of photographs or videos the user has posted.

For unifying the descriptive data (likes and comments), content analysis is applied in the sample size to verify the research question. Content analysis is a research methodology that involves systematically analyzing and interpreting textual, visual, or auditory data to identify patterns, themes, and meanings within a particular context (Krippendorff, 2018). Table 1 provides technical details of the research.

Table 1. Technical details of the research

Objective	Instagram Images
Cases	@zara, @hm, @mango, @forever21
Reference period	December 1, 2019, to January 31, 2020
Sample size	413 pictures and 82 videos
Likes	23,160,627 likes
Comments	62,279 comments
Video reproductions	22,481,700
Method	Content analysis

RESULTS

The total number of posts analyzed is 495, of which 413 are images and 82 are videos. Table 2 shows the total number of posts, and distinguishes by the number of photographs and videos, by brand and by the content uploaded by the brand as a percentage of total posts. Forever 21 is the brand that during the selected period has uploaded the most content (around 50% of posts, photographs and videos). The next brand with the highest amount of content published is H&M, with 30% of the total number of posts.

Table 2. Number of posts, pictures, and videos per brand

Brand	Number of Posts	Number of Pictures	Number of Videos
Zara	55	139	57
	11.11%	9.44%	19.51%
H&M	147	130	17
	29.69%	31.48%	20.73%
Mango	46	41	5
	9.29%	9.93%	6.10%
Forever 21	247	203	44
	49.90%	4.15%	53.66%
Total	495	413	82

It is interesting to observe the content uploaded per day on average and per brand, as shown in Table 3. Forever 21, over the two months, has shared almost 4 posts per day (around 3 photographs per day). In contrast to this case, Mango has a much lower number of posts shared, over the 2 months, with the average number of posts shared per day being less than one. This means that the brand has not posted daily, but every 2 days or more.

Table 3. Number of posts, pictures, and videos shared on average per day and brand

Brand	Average Number of Posts per Day	Average Number of Pictures per Day	Average Number of Videos per Day
Zara	0.887	0.629	0.258
H&M	2.371	2.097	0.274
Mango	0.742	0.661	0.081
Forever 21	3.984	3.274	0.710

Tables 4 and 5 contain some criteria for the analysis of engagement. On the one hand, Table 4 shows the average number of likes per photograph and the average number of video views for each of the brands, as well as the maximum and minimum number of likes per photograph and video views. While Zara has achieved around 70,000 likes per photograph and H&M around 100,000 likes per photograph, Mango and Forever 21 have only recorded an average of around 25,000 likes per photograph.

In terms of video views, H&M exceeded an average of 600,000 video views, Zara achieved around 400,000, while Mango and Forever 21 again lagged behind the other two brands. In the case of Mango, the average number of video views is 132.3, and in the case of Forever 21, it is 113.7. According to the data collected, video engagement was 3.88 times higher than image engagement.

Table 4. Average, maximum, and minimum number of pictures, likes, and video reproductions per brand

Criteria	Zara	H&M	Mango	Forever 21
Average picture likes (in thousand)	71.3	106.1	23.1	27.8
Minimum picture likes (in thousand)	34.1	33.2	6.2	7.0
Maximum picture likes (in thousand)	183	303	58.9	219
Average video reproductions (in thousand)	414.4	599.1	132.3	113.7
Minimum video reproductions (in thousand)	275	350	89.5	44.8
Maximum video reproductions (in thousand)	623	1,000	153	893

Table 5 presents the average, maximum and minimum number of comments on images and videos. In this case, the number of comments turned out to be quite insignificant (compared to the number of "likes" on the posts). The maximum number of comments was 2,208 on an H&M photograph, while the maximum number of comments was 1,698 on a Forever 21 video.

However, comments were left in many different languages, so there was great difficulty in "unifying words in such a large volume of comments" (Aramendia-Muneta et al., 2020). Aramendia et al. (2020) analyzed the impact on the engagement of various criteria in tourism-related posts on an Instagram account dedicated to tourism promotion. Consequently, the lack of suitable tools and the complexity of analyzing the engagement of comments has led us to focus on analyzing the engagement of likes and video reproductions

Table 5. Average, maximum, and minimum number of comments on pictures and videos per brand

Criteria	Zara	H&M	Mango	Forever 21
Average picture comments	257	270	104	64
Minimum picture comments	90	54	31	8
Maximum picture comments	626	2208	290	1328
Average video comments	155	292	77	151
Minimum video comments	57	58	27	5
Maximum video comments	539	1574	105	1698

Despite all this data, the indicators developed to evaluate the real impact that each brand has on Instagram are the like response and the replay response. Like response has been calculated as the average number of likes on the brands' photographs, divided by the total number of followers of that brand on Instagram. Replay response follows the same criteria. It has been calculated as the division of the average number of video plays of a brand by the number of Instagram followers of the brand. What these metrics are trying to measure is the percentage of a brand's followers who like the photographs or watch the videos. It could be understood as the engagement that the brand is able to create through Instagram. Table 6 shows the indicator values for the four brands analyzed.

The results show that H&M is by far the brand with the highest response of likes and plays, with Mango being the brand closest to it. On the other hand, Forever 21 is the brand with the lowest values obtained for the indicators among the brands. Apparently, the number of posts or followers has had no impact on follower engagement, as Zara is the brand with the most followers on its Instagram account (of the brands analyzed), and Forever 21 is the brand that has shared the most content on Instagram for the selected period. In fact, these results could suggest that Forever 21's followers are a bit overwhelmed by the amount of content shared by the brand, or that the brand has not been able to adjust to the tastes of its followers, which has generated the opposite effect. Hence, why are H&M's photographs and videos so appealing that they are able to create more engagement than their direct competitors? Presumably, H&M is better able to understand what kind of content its followers enjoy and uses this information to share posts that get a higher level of engagement.

H&M has on average 62% more engagement on its photographs than its three competitors considered in this analysis, while it has been able to get on average 82% more engagement on the videos the brand has shared (in fact, it has almost 144% more engagement than Forever 21 on its videos).

Table 6. Like and reproduction response

Likes and Reproduction Response	Zara	H&M	Mango	Forever 21
Likes response	0.188%	0.305%	0.206%	0.173%
Reproductions response	1.091%	1.722%	1.181%	0.706%

Table 7 shows the number of images with or without faces and with or without shopping bags shared by the four brands. This analysis aims to understand what makes an image attractive and therefore gets more likes and engagement. The images are analyzed because, as mentioned throughout the article, images with faces are 38% more likely to receive likes (Bakhshi et al., 2014). On the other hand, the shopping bag is a new tool introduced by Instagram. It consists of a shopping bag icon that appears on some photographs indicating that the products shown in that photograph can be purchased directly. When entering the photograph and clicking on it, labels appear on the products with their respective names and prices. Figure 6 shows this shopping process.

Table 7. Number of pictures with and without faces/shopping bag

Number of Pictures	Zara	H&M	Mango	Forever 21
Pictures with faces (total)	36	82	28	154
Pictures with faces (% of total pictures)	92.308%	63.077%	68.293%	75.862%
Pictures without faces (total)	3	48	13	49
Pictures without faces (% of total pictures)	7.692%	36.923%	31.707%	24.138%
Pictures with shopping bag (total)	18	110	24	83
Pictures with shopping bag (% of total pictures)	46.154%	84.615%	58.537%	40.887%
Pictures without shopping bag (total)	21	20	17	120
Pictures without shopping bag (% of total pictures)	53.846%	15.385%	41.463%	59.113%

Figure 6. Shopping process though the shopping bag tool on H&M's posts
Source: Instagram (2020c)

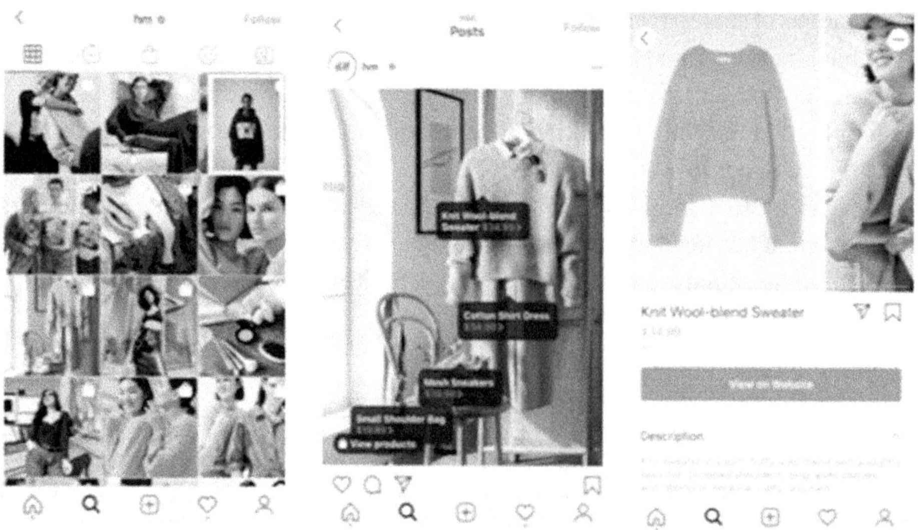

By clicking on any of the tags, the app takes the user to another screen with photographs of the product, price, description, the other products it is pictured with and other products in the shop. If the buyer wishes to purchase the product, by clicking on "website view", the link takes the Instagrammer to the specific product on the brand's official website, where it can be purchased (Figure 7).

Figure 7. Shopping process through the shopping bag tool on H&M's posts for a specific product
Source: Instagram (2020c)

This tool allows brands to facilitate the buying process for Instagrammers who view the brand's posts and products. Until a few months ago, brands could only post photographs with a description of the products, and could only post a link in the brand's bio on their Instagram account. Therefore, brands had to constantly update the link to their products in their "bio" (biography). Now, Instagrammers can buy the products they like directly from a photograph.

In general, most of the photographs posted by the brands have faces, ranging from 63% of H&M photographs to 92% of Zara photographs. On the other hand, the use of the shopping bag tool differs between the selected brands. For example, H&M has used the tool in around 84% of the posts shared in the selected period (16% of the posts without shopping bags correspond to videos and posts with multiple images). All posts with a single image of the brand during the period have the shopping tool. Mango used the shopping bag tool in almost 60%, while Zara used it in 46%. Forever 21, on the other hand, is the brand that has used the shopping bag tool the least, as only 41% of its posts have it.

Table 8 shows a more detailed analysis of the impact of the different criteria on image engagement if any. In terms of face engagement, of all the photographs analyzed, of the four brands, the pictures with faces received, on average, 21.299% fewer likes than the photographs without faces. Therefore, the brands' followers prefer content without faces and prefer posts with only products. However, interestingly, when looking at the impact of faces on image engagement per brand, this trend is only valuable for Forever 21, as the effect of faces on images is negative (-7,116%), meaning that images without faces (products only) receive on average more likes. However, the other three brands have experienced the opposite effect, Mango images with at least one face have almost 55% more likes than photographs without faces,

Zara photographs with at least one face have around 26% more likes and H&M photographs with faces get around 2% more likes.

The results of the use of the shopping bag as a sales and recruitment tool are very promising. All four brands have experienced a higher number of "likes" on posts with the shopping bag icon. The average number of "likes" on images with the shopping bag is 121.03% higher than the number of "likes" on images without the shopping bag for all four brands. Taking into account the effect of the shopping bag for each of the brands, the results are somewhat dispersed, ranging from 19.44% for Zara to 87.32% for Mango. These results show that the tool is very powerful in terms of engagement because, as explained above, the number of likes is an instrument for measuring engagement itself, and the higher the number of likes, the higher the engagement.

It is also true that the shopping bag tool implies more work when it comes to sharing content on the app, as companies have to spend more time entering product information, description and price, and inserting specific links to the products on the brand's official website.

Table 8. Average picture likes with faces, shopping bags, women, or spontaneity

Criteria	Zara	H&M	Mango	Forever 21
Average picture likes with faces (in thousand)	72.43	106.20	26.04	27.28
Average picture likes without faces (in thousand)	57.20	104.00	16.81	29.37
% variation	26.63%	2.12%	54.91%	-7.12%
Average picture likes with shopping bag (in thousand)	78.10	113.00	28.66	32.44
Average picture likes without shopping bag (in thousand)	65.39	66.50	15.30	24.56
% variation	19.44%	69.92%	87.32%	32.08%
Average picture likes with woman (in thousand)	80.47	115.00	28.23	27.11
Average picture likes with products (in thousand)	57.20	110.00	13.53	26.38
% variation	40.68%	4.55%	108.65%	2.77%
Average picture likes with spontaneity (in thousand)	98.68	128.00	28.70	29.04
Average picture likes without spontaneity (in thousand)	64.18	106.00	20.50	27.41
% variation	53.75%	20.75%	40.00%	5.95%

Another interesting element analyzed is the impact of the presence of women in the images on the engagement created. When looking at the selected images, it is noteworthy that most of them feature only women. In fact, almost 61% of the total number of images shared by the four competitors have a woman in them. Zara has the highest presence of men in its photographs (10 photographs representing 25.641%), while the rest of the brands have no or a slight presence of men in their photographs (H&M has one photograph with men, Mango has no photographs with men, and Forever 21 has only 2).

In this case, we compared the engagement generated by the presence of women in the photographs versus the presence of products. The number of posts with products is higher than the number of posts with men, so it is more representative. In addition, almost 17% of the photographs posted only show branded products.

The presence of women in the photographs seems to have an impact on the number of likes, although again, a bit scattered. The presence of women in the Mango photograph has a big impact, as pictures featuring women have registered, on average, 108.65% more likes. The same effect occurs for the other three brands, but with a moderate impact on Zara (40.68% more likes on average) and a low impact on the average number of likes for H&M and Forever 21 (4.55% and 2.777% more, respectively). If we analyze this effect for all photographs with women in them from the four brands (without focusing on any of them), we find, as with the presence of faces, the opposite effect. Of all the selected photographs of the four brands, the photographs with women have registered on average 17.01% fewer likes than the photographs without women.

Another analyzed factor was the spontaneity of the image. We wanted to assess whether spontaneous photographs generated more engagement or whether the response of the brands' followers to them was not significant. In this case, we called candid photographs with natural movement, where it was not possible to distinguish whether the person in the photograph is a model or not (although we know that they are, in fact, a model), and whether the person in the photograph is intentionally posing for the photographer or not. However, this could be a rather subjective criterion, because there are obvious photographs that the viewer can easily identify as not "natural" or "spontaneous", but there are others that could generate room for debate.

Of what we have considered as spontaneous, the results obtained follow our expectations about the impact of spontaneity on engagement. Spontaneous images have registered 33.91% more likes on average. In this case, the highest impact corresponds to Zara, with 53.747% more "likes". Thus, users are more interested in images that appear spontaneous. One of the reasons could be the fact that they feel more identified with the image if it shows a "normal" person (even if it is a model) in a natural environment, rather than a model posing intentionally in a studio.

Finally, we have analyzed the videos shared by these four competitors (Table 9). As mentioned above, the videos of the selected posts of the four brands generated 3.88 more engagement than the images. We analyzed whether the presence of faces had an impact on the average number of "likes". And it did. However, it should be noted that we were not able to analyze the H&M videos, as all of them had faces and it would not make sense to analyze them. On the other hand, the results obtained for H&M's competitors are very promising for Mango (59.78% more likes on average for videos with faces) and Forever 21 (73.13%), while there is a negative impact for Zara (-14.83%), which means that videos without faces have more likes on average and, in turn, generate more engagement.

Table 9. Average video likes with faces

Criteria	Zara	Mango	Forever 21
Average video likes with faces (in thousand)	381.25	143.00	140.76
Average video likes without faces (in thousand)	447.63	89.50	81.30
% variation	-14.83%	59.78%	73.13%

To understand what makes a post attractive, we analyzed for each of the brands the elements of the posts with the lowest and highest number of likes. As for the images with the fewest "likes", all four brands agree on one element: lack of spontaneity. This could suggest that photographs without spontaneity are more likely to receive fewer likes. Forever 21 is the brand with the lowest engagement, and in the majority of its photographs with the lowest number of likes, most of the photographs analyzed have no shopping bag (82%), no spontaneity (70%) and no faces in them (65%).

On the other hand, in the photographs with the highest number of likes of the four brands, the common element is the presence of women, while the presence of shopping bags is only relevant for H&M and Mango, as all their posts with the highest number of likes have the shopping bag tool. On the other hand, the presence of faces is only relevant for Zara and Mango, as all their posts with the highest number of likes have faces.

H&M is the brand with the highest engagement, and the elements present in most of its posts with the highest number of likes are the shopping bag tool (100%), the presence of women (77%) and the presence of faces (78%).

However, as mentioned throughout the text, there are no magic formulas, and what works for H&M may not work for the other three brands, therefore, all of them should study the common elements in their posts with the highest number of likes, in order to adapt their strategy and generate more engagement.

Result Discussion

The four fast-fashion brands selected to assess their Instagram strategy are Zara, H&M, Mango and Forever 21. The selection criterion has been based on their net sales in euros for 2018 and their number of Instagram followers. The data collected from the companies' Instagram has disclosed some interesting information. From all the posts analyzed, the engagement generated by the videos has been 3.88 times the engagement generated by the pictures; therefore, this might put forward the fact that brands should post more videos to achieve a higher engagement.

From the total number of pictures analyzed, 72.64% had faces in them. Forever 21, is the brand (from the four selected) with the largest number of posts shared over the two months (around four posts per day), while the engagement has been the lowest (0.173% like response and 0.706 reproduction response). This may signal Forever 21's Instagram strategy is quite ineffective. Forever 21's closest competitor from the four selected, according to their net sales and Instagram followers is Mango. Mango posted an average of 0.74 posts per day and achieved the second-highest engagement levels for both, the like and the reproduction response (0.21% and 1.181% respectively). The most effective Instagram strategy has been achieved by H&M, since it has the highest like and reproduction response (0.31% and 1.72% respectively) among the four brands, with an average of 2.37 posts per day.

From the pictures analyzed, the average number of total posts in which women were present is 68.48%, while the average number of pictures with brand products in them (without any model), reached 20.43%. More interesting is the fact that there is a low presence of men in the brands' posts, with an average number of posts of 6.85%. Nevertheless, for H&M, Mango and Forever 21, the number of posts with men in them does not reach 1%, whereas, in the case of Zara, men appear in 25.64% of the posts. The reason behind this may be the market segment the brands' target, and the type of followers the brands have.

When assessing Zara, H&M and Mango posts individually, these three companies have experienced an increase in the average likes in the pictures that had faces in them, while this did not hold for Forever 21, which has experienced a decrease in the average picture likes that had faces in them, as compared to the ones who did not have faces in them. The new tool introduced by Instagram to ease the shopping process through the app (the shopping bag) has helped the pictures achieve a 121.03% higher number of average likes concerning the pictures of the four brands which did not have the shopping bag. Spontaneity has also been proven, according to our data, to increase engagement. The four brands experienced an increase in average picture likes that seemed to be spontaneous. This effect holds when the brands are assessed together or individually, however, spontaneity may be a subjective criterion, and results may vary depending on what one considers a spontaneous picture.

CONCLUSION

The Internet has proven to be the new tool for reaching customers through online marketing, also called e-marketing. The customer is easily accessible, and the bond or engagement that companies create is greater than with traditional marketing because, through social media, companies can create brand awareness and interact with their customers. This engagement is greater because, through online communities, companies can interact with their customers, but even more important is the fact that these online communities allow customers to get in touch with other customers from anywhere in the world and share opinions, ideas, etc. Through these platforms, companies can collect a lot of useful information about their customers (preferences, tastes, needs, opinions, etc.) and, if properly evaluated, this information can help companies understand their customers (and their tastes) and create products or services that successfully meet customer needs.

On the other hand, it is also true that the Internet, in addition to the ease of dissemination of good opinions and comments, makes it easier for a bad opinion or comment about a brand to spread more quickly and reach a large number of customers, having a greater and "stickier" impact than positive comments. Negative online comments leave a footprint, which is not easy for companies to get rid of.

Despite the advantages of e-marketing, companies cannot forget about traditional marketing, as the two complement each other. Companies must give proper importance to each of them, balancing their efforts between the two. If a company focuses on only one of these two types of marketing, it may be neglecting part of its target segment.

FUTURE RESEARCH DIRECTIONS

Some further research could be derived from this analysis of the four fast-fashion brands' Instagram strategies. It would be very interesting to assess the percentage of Instagrammers who tap into posts from which you can buy the product or service exposed, who end up buying it. It would also be very interesting to follow the evolution of sales through Instagram and whether the shopping bag tool increases sales. One of the elements analyzed is the engagement generated by the comments on the posts. Therefore, another path of study could be the engagement comments generate and whether the posting day has any effect on engagement (as mentioned before, apparently, Instagrammers spend more time and log in on Tuesdays and Thursdays.

It would be interesting to investigate further to assess whether the engagement created by the shopping bag tool increases online sales from the application and whether the additional effort is worthwhile. As the tool is new and its feasibility and usefulness are still being tested, no information is available.

REFERENCES

Ananda, A. S., Hernandez-García, Á., & Lamberti, L. (2015). Fashion in actions on social media – Spanish SME fashion brands case studies. *Proceedings of the European Conference on e-Learning*, 488-497.

Aramendia-Muneta, M. E. (2017). Spread the word – The effect of word of mouth in e-Marketing. In G. Siegert, M. B. Von Rimscha, & S. Grubenmann (Eds.), *Commercial Communication in the Digital Age* (pp. 227–245). De Gruyter. doi:10.1515/9783110416794-013

Aramendia-Muneta, M. E., Olarte-Pascual, C., & Ollo-López, A. (2021). Key image attributes to elicit likes and comments on Instagram. *Journal of Promotion Management*, *27*(1), 50–76. doi:10.1080/10496491.2020.1809594

Bakhshi, S., Shamma, D. A., & Gilbert, E. (2014). Faces engage us: Photographs with faces attract more likes and comments on Instagram. *Proceedings of the 32nd Annual ACM Conference on Human Factors in Computing Systems - CHI '14*, 965–974. 10.1145/2556288.2557403

Bao, T., & Chang, T. L. S. (2014). Finding disseminators via electronic word of mouth message for effective marketing communications. *Decision Support Systems*, *67*, 21–29. doi:10.1016/j.dss.2014.07.006

Benetton Group. (2019). *Integrated report 2018*. Retrieved February 9, 2020 from http://assets.benettongroup.com/wp-content/uploads/2019/06/Integrated_Report_2018_.pdf

Bruce, M., & Krazt, C. (2012). Competitive marketing strategies of luxury fashion companies. In T. Hines & M. Bruce (Eds.), *Fashion Marketing: Contemporary Issues* (pp. 132–150). Taylor and Francis.

Carah, N., & Shaul, M. (2016). Brands and Instagram: Point, tap, swipe, glance. *Mobile Media & Communication*, *4*(1), 69–84. doi:10.1177/2050157915598180

Europapress. (2019). *Mango alcanzó unas ventas por 2.233 millones de euros en 2018, un 1,8% más*. Retrieved February 9, 2020 from https://www.europapress.es/economia/noticia-mango-alcanzo-ventas-2233-millones-euros-2018-18-mas-20190808120739.html

Eurostat. (2020). *E-commerce statistics for individuals - Statistics explained*. Retrieved February 11, 2020 from https://ec.europa.eu/eurostat/statistics-explained/index.php/E-commerce_statistics_for_individuals

Faber, R. J., Lee, M., & Nan, X. N. (2004). Advertising and the consumer information environment online. *The American Behavioral Scientist*, *48*(4), 447–466. doi:10.1177/0002764204270281

Ghemawat, P., & Nueno, J. L. (2003). *Zara: Fast fashion*. Retrieved February 9, 2020 from: https://www.hbs.edu/faculty/Pages/item.aspx?num=29832

Giannoulakis, S., & Tsapatsoulis, N. (2016). Evaluating the descriptive power of Instagram hashtags. *Journal of Innovation in Digital Ecosystems*, *3*(2), 114–129. doi:10.1016/j.jides.2016.10.001

H&M Group. (2019). *Annual report 2018*. Retrieved February 9, 2020 from. https://about.hm.com/content/dam/hmgroup/groupsite/documents/masterlanguage/Annual Report/Annual Report 2018.pdf

Huang, Z., & Benyoucef, M. (2017). The effects of social commerce design on consumer purchase decision-making: An empirical study. *Electronic Commerce Research and Applications*, *25*, 40–58. doi:10.1016/j.elerap.2017.08.003

Inditex. (2019). *Inditex annual report 2018*. Retrieved February 9, 2020 from https://static.inditex.com/annual_report_2018/pdfs/en/Inditex Annual Report 2018.pdf

Instagram. (2020a). *@forever21 • Fotos y videos de Instagram*. Retrieved January 28, 2020 from https://www.instagram.com/forever21/?hl=es

Instagram. (2020b). *Gap (@gap) • Fotos y videos de Instagram*. Retrieved January 28, 2020 from https://www.instagram.com/gap/?hl=es

Instagram. (2020c). *H&M (@hm) • Fotos y videos de Instagram*. Retrieved January 28, 2020 from https://www.instagram.com/hm/?hl=es

Instagram. (2020d). *MANGO (@mango) • Fotos y videos de Instagram*. Retrieved January 28, 2020 from https://www.instagram.com/mango/?hl=es

Instagram. (2020e). *United Colors of Benetton (@benetton) • Fotos y videos de Instagram*. Retrieved January 28, 2020 from https://www.instagram.com/benetton/?hl=es

Instagram. (2020f). *ZARA Official (@zara) • Fotos y videos de Instagram*. Retrieved January 28, 2020 from https://www.instagram.com/zara/?hl=es

Jackson, T. (2012). The process of trend development leading to a fashion season. In T. Hines & M. Bruce (Eds.), *Fashion Marketing: Contemporary Issues* (pp. 168–187). Taylor and Francis.

Kaplan, A. M., & Haenlein, M. (2010). Users of the world, unite! The challenges and opportunities of social media. *Business Horizons*, *53*(1), 59–68. doi:10.1016/j.bushor.2009.09.003

Krippendorff, K. (2018). Content analysis: An introduction to its methodology (4th ed). Thousand Oak: Sage Publications.

Larson, R. J. (2009). *The rise of viral marketing through the new media of social media.* Retrieved February 12, 2020 from: http://digitalcommons.liberty.edu/cgi/viewcontent.cgi?article=1009&context=busi_fac_pubs

Le Pechoux, B., Little, T. J., & Istook, C. L. (2012). Innovation management in creating new fashions. In T. Hines & M. Bruce (Eds.), *Fashion Marketing: Contemporary Issues* (pp. 188–216). Taylor and Francis.

Lin, J., & Lu, Y. (2019). The role of social media in the fashion industry: How fashion blogging encourages two-way symmetrical communication. *Journal of Global Fashion Marketing*, *10*(2), 186–200.

Martínez Caballero, E., & Vázquez Casco, A. I. (2006). *Marketing de la moda*. Pirámide.

Mcleod, S. (2007). *HCC certificate in counselling skills Maslow's hierarchy of needs*. Retrieved February 11, 2020 from https://highgatecounselling.org.uk/members/certificate/CT2%20Paper%201.pdf

Mohsin, M. (2020, February 6). *10 Instagram Statistics Everyone Should Know in 2020* [Infographic]. Retrieved February 11, 2020 from https://www.oberlo.com/blog/instagram-stats-every-marketer-should-know

Mowka, M. P., Prieve, E. A., & Dawson, W. M. (1980). *Marketing the Arts*. Praeger.

Nicol, D., & Agam, L. A. (2016). The impact of viral marketing through Instagram. *Proceedings of Bangkok annual Business and Social Sciences Research Conference.*

Rogers, E. M. (2003). *Diffusion of Innovations* (5th ed.). Simon & Schuster.

Silva, T. H., De Melo, P. O. S. V., Almeida, J. M., Salles, J., & Loureiro, A. A. F. (2013). A picture of instagram is worth more than a thousand words: Workload characterization and application. *Proceedings - IEEE International Conference on Distributed Computing in Sensor Systems, DCoSS 2013, 1*, 123–132.

Statista. (2018). *Instagram: active users 2018 | Statista*. Retrieved February 11, 2020 from https://www.statista.com/statistics/253577/number-of-monthly-active-instagram-users/

Statista. (2020). *Instagram: age distribution of global audiences 2020 | Statista*. Retrieved February 11, 2020 from https://www.statista.com/statistics/325587/instagram-global-age-group/

Thakur, R., & Srivastava, M. (2020). Instagram usage and impulse buying behavior: A study on fashion products. *Journal of Retailing and Consumer Services, 53*, 101971.

Utz, S., Kerkhof, P., & Van den Bos, J. (2012). Consumers rule: How consumer reviews influence perceived trustworthiness of online stores. *Electronic Commerce Research and Applications, 11*(1), 49–58. doi:10.1016/j.elerap.2011.07.010

Walker, J. H., Sproull, L., & Subramani, R. (1994). Using a human face in an interface. *Conference on Human Factors in Computing Systems - Proceedings*, 85–91. 10.1145/191666.191708

Wert, S. R., & Salovey, P. (2004). A social comparison account of gossip. *Review of General Psychology, 8*(2), 122–137. doi:10.1037/1089-2680.8.2.122

World Bank. (2019a). *Population ages 0-14, total | Data*. Retrieved February 4, 2020 from https://data.worldbank.org/indicator/SP.POP.0014.TO

World Bank. (2019b). *Population ages 0-14 (% of total population) | Data*. Retrieved February 4, 2020 from https://data.worldbank.org/indicator/SP.POP.0014.TO.ZS

World Bank. (2019c). *Population ages 15-64, total | Data*. Retrieved February 4, 2020 from https://data.worldbank.org/indicator/SP.POP.1564.TO

World Bank. (2019d). *Population ages 15-64 (% of total population) | Data*. Retrieved February 4, 2020 from https://data.worldbank.org/indicator/SP.POP.1564.TO.ZS

World Bank. (2019e). *Population ages 65 and above, total | Data*. Retrieved February 4, 2020 from https://data.worldbank.org/indicator/SP.POP.65UP.TO

World Bank. (2019f). *Population ages 65 and above (% of total population) | Data*. Retrieved February 4, 2020 from https://data.worldbank.org/indicator/SP.POP.65UP.TO.ZS

KEY TERMS AND DEFINITIONS

Audience: People who are interested in content, products, or services.

Community: A group of people which members relate common experiences and interests.

Engagement: The measurement of comments, likes, and shares in social networks.

H&M: Swedish fast-fashion brand born in 1968.

Forever 21: USA fast-fashion brand born in 1984.

Instagram: Online photo-and video sharing social network platform that was acquired by Facebook in 2012.

Mango: Spanish fast-fashion brand born in 1984.

Social Media: A group of internet-based application, which allow users to generate and exchange content.

Zara: Spanish fast-fashion brand born in 1974 belonging to Inditex Group.

Chapter 9
Instagramma in Fashion:
The Impact of Social Media on Purchase Decisions

Jane B. Thomas
Winthrop University, USA

Cara O. Peters
Winthrop University, USA

ABSTRACT

Although traditionally ignored by the fashion industry, senior females have purchasing power, report being interested in fashion, and are a growing portion of social media users. The literature to date has not yet unpacked the social media usage of everyday, senior females in the fashion context. Data were collected via a series of 38 interviews with women aged 50 and older. Findings showed that the majority of the senior females interviewed were following influencers online and these activities were impacting their purchase behaviors. Furthermore, the senior females in the sample had developed their own sense of style from information they gathered online and projected themselves on their social media accounts as if they too were influencers. Theoretical and managerial implications of the study are also discussed.

BACKGROUND

Women over 50 years of age are one of the fastest growing segments of the U.S. population. This demographic group, represents about $15 trillion in spending power and 27 percent of all consumer spending (McMillen, 2022). Yet despite the size and purchasing power of senior females (i.e., women over 50), the fashion industry has done a poor job of targeting this segment of the population. Historically, there has been a tendency for fashion marketers to ignore senior women and focus on the young (i.e., women under 40). The commonly held belief was that senior women were either more confident with their self-image and appearance and/or no longer cared about their appearance and the opinions of others (Reilly & Barry, 2020). Thus, fashion and apparel companies viewed this group as less important and not a

DOI: 10.4018/978-1-6684-8753-2.ch009

lucrative segment worth targeting. The truth is that senior women are still fashion conscious and care about the opinions of others (McFarlane & Samsioe, 2020).

Until recently senior women have felt ignored by the fashion industry and retailers, despite their financial viability, market size, and expected growth (Wooldridge & Kuntze, 2019). However, the ideal of youth that has dominated the fashion industry for years is beginning to change (Borland & Akram, 2007). Senior females are starting to emerge on the covers of magazines, being featured in major advertising campaigns, walking the catwalk, and signing with major modeling agencies (do Prado Lima, 2020).

Authors of the popular press are asserting that the embracing of senior females by fashion marketers is coming from an interesting source, social media. Simply put, the over 50 social media influencer is beginning to change women's and society's perceptions of age and is influencing the purchase decisions of women in this demographic group (McFarlane & Samsioe, 2020). For example, do Prado Lima (2020) stated that Maye Musk's large social media following was one factor that her current modeling agency used in deciding to sign with her. The agency recognized that Maye Musk, with her 684,000 Instagram followers, was influencing the fashion consumer behaviors of senior females. Furthermore, beyond Maye Musk, there is a growing presence of senior females who have become social media influencers with significant audiences and most of these accounts focus on fashion as a common theme to their posts (McFarlane & Samsioe, 2020; Miranda et al., 2022; Stephani, 2022).

The literature is starting to revisit the phenomenon of senior females in fashion, but studies to date have focused primarily on the perspective of influencers themselves. The literature has not yet looked at the audience for these social media sites and posts. The present study sought to examine the wider perspective of the everyday senior female, who is not a social media influencer, but is using social media and interested in fashion. Furthermore, the study also sought to unpack how the everyday senior female's social media usage is influencing her fashion decision making and consumer behaviors.

Thus, the purpose of this paper was to examine the social media usage and consumer behaviors of senior females in the context of fashion. Toward that end, the specific research questions for the study were as follows: 1) What is the social media usage behaviors of senior females and do these behaviors impact purchasing in the fashion context? 2) What is the consumer behaviors of senior females with respect to following social media influencers and being impacted by influencer marketing in fashion? 3) Do family and friends also play a role in influencing the online consumer behaviors of senior females in the fashion context? 4) And, how do senior females project themselves online with respect to their fashion-related consumer behaviors? Below is the literature review, methodology, findings and discussion.

Literature Review

Researchers began examining the fashion preferences and consumer behaviors of senior females in the 1980s. The early literature on the fashion consumption of senior females found that these women prioritize factors such as quality, comfort, fit and function when shopping for apparel (Burt & Gabbott, 1995; Littrell et al., 2005; Lumpkin et al., 1985; Nam et al., 2007; Rocha et al., 2005). The literature also found that pricing is also an important consideration in the shopping behaviors of senior females, and they are loyal to certain retailers, preferring to shop in department stores or specialty shops (Burt & Gabbott, 1995; Moore & Carpenter, 2006; Greco, 1986; Littrell et al., 2005; Lumpkin et al., 1985; Rocha et al., 2005).

And while fashion marketers tend to not focus on this older demographic segment (Wooldridge & Kuntze, 2019), research has also shown over time that senior females report having an interest in fashion and enjoy shopping for apparel (Greco, 1986; Lumpkin & Greenberg, 1982; Nam et al., 2007). Furthermore, senior females value the look or style of the clothing they choose to purchase and wear (Lumpkin et al., 1985; Nam et al., 2007; Rocha et al., 2005), and clothing is part of their self-esteem and identity that they also project to others (Joung & Miller, 2006; Thomas & Peters, 2009; Peters et al., 2011).

Since the literature on senior females and their fashion consumption first emerged, the world of fashion has changed, due to the advent of the Internet and emergence of social media. Social media first came about in the early 2000s with the popularity of websites like MySpace, and researchers began to immediately identify the impact of these sites on consumers in the fashion context (Thomas et al., 2007). Over time, social media has proliferated across a variety of platforms, including social media websites (i.e., Facebook), microblogs (i.e., Twitter), photosharing sites (i.e., Instagram), and media sharing sites (i.e., TikTok) (Tripathi, 2019). And academic research has shown that the various social media platforms have had a significant impact on both the fashion industry, as well as, consumer behaviors related to fashion (Ahmad et al., 2015; Nash, 2019; Tripathi, 2019). Chu and Seock (2020, p. 93) even go so far to assert that, "social media platforms are now the primary source of information for consumers and one of the most powerful marketing tools for fashion businesses."

As social media has grown, one particular area of marketing that has had a significant impact on the fashion industry is influencer marketing. Rodela (2022) argues that influencer marketing is one of the "most effective strategies brands can use," and that "60 percent of marketers reported that influencer marketing" was more effective than "brand-created content" (para. 2-3). Academic researchers who are interested in the fashion context are making similar assertions. For example, Chu and Seock (2020) state that "Instagram has been recognized as the most influential source for fashion insight" (p. 93). And a study by Sun et al. (2022) empirically confirmed that influencers had a greater impact on the luxury fashion consumption of Gen Z consumers, when compared to the content of advertisers. Research also shows that a host of variables, such as likability, trustworthiness, familiarity, credibility, and expertise, impact consumers attitudes toward influencers, which in turn, impacts their purchase intentions in the fashion context (Abdullah et al., 2020; Chetioui et al., 2020).

Most of the academic research on influencer marketing in the fashion context to date has been on younger generations, such as Gen X, Y, and Z (cf., Nash, 2019; Tripathi, 2019; Sun et al., 2022). This may be due to the bias toward younger consumers in fashion in general or related to the fact that younger generations are heavy users of the Internet, online shopping and social media (Wooldridge & Kuntze, 2019; Pew Research Center, 2021). However, anecdotal evidence suggests that the number of senior females using social media has been growing steadily over time. As of 2021, 45% of seniors in the U.S. were on social media, a number that has tripled since 2011 (Pew Research Center, 2021). And there is also a small, but growing, set of studies on influencer marketing related to senior females in fashion.

The first studies on senior female influencer marketing were published in 2020. McFarlane and Samisoe (2020) conducted a netnography over four months in which they collected and analyzed the pictures and posts of 32 female Instagram fashion influencers who were age 50 and older. Their analysis of the more than 300 posts provided by these women during the data collection period showed that these senior females consciously chose outfits, selected backgrounds, and posed their bodies in ways that were designed to challenge societal stereotypes of elderly females and the negative associations attributed to aging. Farinosi and Fortunati (2020) also examined the posts of senior female fashion influencers, but they did so in comparison to younger fashion influencers. Farinosi and Fortunati (2020) followed the online activities of four younger fashion influencers and 20 senior female fashion influencers, aged 70 and older. They found that the senior female fashion influencers had a more "personal and authentic" style, based on posts that displayed "perennial style, ageless active, bold beauty, and positive ageing," when compared to the younger influencers (Farinosi & Fortunati, 2020, p. 52). They also found that the senior females used humor to address ageing stereotypes, preferred text to visuals, and many of their followers were actually younger women. Finally, the results also showed that, while the fashion houses have been engaging with younger influencers for quite some time, these iconic brands are just beginning to take notice of senior female influencers and that phenomenon has yet to fully unfold.

In 2022, two more studies emerged in the literature that examined the activities of senior female fashion influencers. Miranda et al. (2022) content analyzed dozens of posts from the two most popular male and female senior influencers on Instagram over a four month period. The total sample of 286 posts consisted of the following themes: politics, fashion, birthday, art, commemorative days, memories, food and health. The posts had 10 million likes/views and 145,000 comments, demonstrating the impact of the content on the audience. One of the most common themes across the sample of posts was fashion and lifestyle. The fashion and lifestyle posts were humorous, extravagant, and exuberant as they illustrated a "discourse that clearly shows a defying stance toward age representations of the elderly" (p. 134). Stephani (2022) similarly examined the posts of three Indonesian senior female celebrities on Instagram over a seven month period. Two themes emerged from the data: sport and fashion. The posts of these senior female influencers presented an "ageing well discourse" in which the females communicated that their older bodies were capable of being active and were physically attractive (p. 174). They rejected stereotypes of older females and instead presented themselves as "active, independent and sexually influential" women (p. 175).

When looking across the literature, several conclusions can be drawn. First, senior females have long had an interest in fashion and are a potentially lucrative target market. Second, influencer marketing has grown in its impact, especially within the fashion industry. Third, senior females are starting to become social media fashion influencers in their own right, portraying themselves as authentic fashion trend setters, who are physically active and sexually attractive, rejecting senior female stereotypes of frailty, feebleness, loneliness, and unattractiveness. And finally, of the studies to date that have focused on the phenomenon of senior female influencer marketing, the literature is limited to an examination of the posts of the influencers themselves. No study to date has examined the perspectives of everyday senior females who are not influencers but are consuming social media and following these trend setters, activities that are potentially influencing their consumer behaviors.

Methodology

Because the researchers sought to study the lived experiences of senior females, phenomenology served as the ontological approach (Creswell, 1998; Moustakas, 1994; Thompson et al., 1989). Data were collected via a series of in-depth interviews and the researchers utilized criterion sampling in which each study participant had to be a female, age 50 or older and active on social media (Miles & Huberman, 1994). To recruit participants, the authors asked students who were enrolled in a consumer behavior class at a southeastern university in the U.S., to invite their friends and family members who met the above criteria to participate in a university research project on social media. The contact information was then obtained and shared with the researchers who reached out to the prospective informants, obtained informed consent, and invited the senior females to participate in an interview through Zoom. From this process, 38 interviews were completed over a five month period. The sample ranged in age from 50 to 79 years of age; the majority were employed and they represented a variety of professional occupations; 92% had children and 45% had grandchildren; and they reported using a variety of social media with Instagram and Facebook being the most popular. See Table 1 for a summary of the demographic information of the informants.

Table 1. Demographic information of the senior female sample utilized for the study

Name	Age	Occupation	Highest Degree	Offspring	Social Media Platforms Used	Frequency of Checking Social Media
Barbara	55	Radio Frequency Engineer	Bachelor's degree	4 children	Instagram, Facebook & WhatsApp	More than once a day
Julie	59	Insurance Billing Specialist	Associate degree	2 children	Instagram & Facebook	More than once a day
Harriet	55	Speech Language Pathologist	Master's degree	1 child,1 grandchild	Instagram	Daily
Monique	55	Teacher	Bachelor's Degree	3 children	Instagram, Twitter & Facebook	3-5 times a day
Lisa	64	Vice President of Business Development	Bachelor's degree	3 children, 1 grandchild	Instagram & Facebook	More than once a day
Carmella	56	Real Estate Agent	Associate degree	2 children, 1 grandchild	Instagram, Facebook, Twitter & Pinterest	More than once a day
Chloe	55	Retired Counselor	Master's	3 children, 5 grandchildren	Facebook, Instagram & Snapchat	4-5 times a day
Ruth	64	Retired	Bachelor's degree	5 children, 6 grandchildren	Facebook	More than once a day
Jade	57	Entrepreneur	High school diploma	3 children	Facebook, Instagram, LinkedIn & YouTube	More than once a day
Karen	55	Homemaker	Bachelor's Degree	2 children	Facebook, Instagram & Pinterest	2-3 times a day
Patricia	58	Director of Sales	Bachelor's Degree	1 child,1 grandchild	YouTube, Instagram & Facebook	Daily
Margaret	59	Fat Loss Coach	Bachelor's degree	3 Children	Facebook & Instagram	Daily
Cora	56	Teacher	Bachelor's Degree	3 Children	Instagram	More than once a day
Noelle	79	Retired	High school diploma	2 children, 2 grandchildren	Facebook, Twitter & Instagram	Daily
Marie	59	Program Manager	High school diploma	4 children	Instagram, TikTok, Facebook & BeReal	Daily

Continued on following page

Table 1. Continued

Name	Age	Occupation	Highest Degree	Offspring	Social Media Platforms Used	Frequency of Checking Social Media
Lucy	55	Marketing and Sales	Master's degree	3 children	Facebook, Instagram, TikTok & LinkedIn	Daily
Sarah	63	Retired Educator	Master's degree	5 children,9 grandchildren	Instagram, Facebook & YouTube	Daily
Natalie	56	Vice President of Operations	Bachelor's degree	2 children	Instagram, Facebook, Pinterest, TikTok & Snapchat	More than once a day
Rose	73	Homemaker	High school diploma	2 children,2 grandchildren	Facebook & Instagram	Daily
Kaylee	52	Practice Administrator	Bachelor's degree	2 children,1 grandchild	Facebook & Instagram	2-3 times a day
Anette	52	Non-profit Business Owner	Master's degree	2 children	Facebook & Instagram	Daily
Kayla	55	Purchasing	Associate Degree	2 children	Facebook, Instagram, Twitter & YouTube	2-3 times a day
Reese	63	Business Owner & Pharmacy Technician	Associate Degree	3 children,6 grandchildren	Facebook, Instagram & Pinterest	Daily
Hazel	56	Marketing Director	Bachelor's degree	3 children	Facebook, Instagram &WhatsApp	3-5 times a day
Scarlett	57	Pediatrician	Doctorate degree	4 children	Facebook, Instagram & Tik Tok	Once a day
Violet	61	Marketing Manager	Associate degree	1 child	Instagram, LinkedIn, Facebook & Twitter	More than once a day
Kamila	76	Retired (former Administrative Assistant)	Bachelor's degree	3 children, 6 grandchildren	Facebook & Instagram	3-5 times a day
Abigail	63	Vendor	Bachelor's Degree	3 children, 2 grandchildren	Instagram, YouTube, Pinterest, Facebook & TikTok	More than once a day
Madelyn	70	Retired (former Store Manager)	High school diploma	4 children,5 grandchildren	Instagram, YouTube & Facebook	2-3 times a week
Lillian	55	Information Technology Specialist	Bachelor's Degree	3 children	Instagram, Facebook & YouTube	2-3 times a week
Josephine	50	Paralegal	Master's degree	3 children	Instagram, Facebook & Twitter	More than once a day
Grace	55	Student Information Coordinator	Bachelor's degree	2 children, 1 grandchild	Facebook, Instagram & TikTok	Daily
Lydia	60	Retired (Former Education Administrator)	Master's degree	1 child	Instagram, Facebook & Twitter	Daily

Continued on following page

Table 1. Continued

Name	Age	Occupation	Highest Degree	Offspring	Social Media Platforms Used	Frequency of Checking Social Media
Melanie	55	Store Manager	High school Diploma	4 children, 1 grandchild	Instagram & Twitter	More than once a day
Maya	55	Tourism Director	Associate Degree	None	Instagram & Facebook	Once a week
Brianna	55	Teacher	Bachelor's degree	None	Facebook, Instagram & Twitter	Once a week
June	55	Information Technology Specialist	Bachelor's degree	None	Instagram, Facebook & TikTok	3-5 times a day
Talia	56	Occupation Health & Safety Coordinator	Master's degree	4 children,4 grandchildren	Instagram	2-3 times per week

The interviews consisted of thirteen questions presented in a semi-structured, conversational style along with the interviewer probing for additional details. Examples of interview questions included: 1.) Pick a celebrity or social media influencer who is like you. How is this person like you? 2.) Do you follow any fashion/style/beauty influencers on social media? If so, who? Why did you decide to follow them? 3.) Do your friends and family share fashion/style/beauty information on social media? Do you also share fashion/style/beauty information with them? And, 4.) do you think about what you are wearing in a picture before you post it online? The interviews ranged from approximately 40 to 75 minutes in length and were recorded via Zoom.

The recordings were converted into transcripts of text and then analyzed according to the protocols for phenomenology (Creswell, 1998; Groenewald, 2004; Moustakas, 1994). The researchers read through each transcript, coding individual lines of data, until all data were accounted. Next, the researchers listed all the codes and looked for relationships that existed among the data. The researchers then identified "units of meaning" where clusters of data appeared to coalesce (Groenewald, 2004, p. 49; citing Creswell, 1998 & Moustakas, 1994). The various meaning units were then combined into broader themes that represented the senior female perspectives on influencer marketing and their consumption behaviors (Groenewald, 2004; Creswell, 1998; Moustakas, 1994). The researchers concluded the analysis by creating a thick description of each of the themes and identifying exemplar quotes for presentation of the findings (Moustakas, 1994; Thompson et al., 1989). Finally, at the end of the whole process, the researchers invited two of the informants to review the results in order to verify the analysis and interpretation of the data before the findings were incorporated into the paper.

Findings

Based on the data analysis and interpretation, the findings were structured into the following three categories: whether the informants followed social media influencers and who they followed; where the informants sought fashion and beauty advice, and how they then used that to project themselves and their sense of style online; and how social media has influenced the senior females' purchasing behaviors. Each of these categories, along with specific sub-themes, is presented below.

Who Are They Following?

Given that previous research has examined the activities of senior female fashion influencers (Farinosi & Fortunati, 2020; McFarlane & Samisoe, 2020; Miranda et al., 2022; Stephani, 2022), a significant portion of each interview for this study focused on whether the senior females followed influencers online and who were the influencers they were following. Sixty four percent of the informants positively indicated that they followed an influencer on social media. Furthermore, when asked who they followed, the responses were divided across two general categories of influencers: national celebrities versus local connections and friends. For those who followed an influencer, 89 percent indicated that they followed a celebrity. Brianna (age 55), for example, identified several celebrities that she followed in her interview:

Yeah, there are some younger ones that I like. Um, Laurie Harvey. Mm-hmm, she gets it right every single time. Um, makeup is flawless. Her wardrobe is flawless. I mean, everything just seems to be like picture perfect. I think she gets it honest from her mom, Marjorie. You know, they both kind of have that style that I like. And then too, I also like, Tiana Taylor and Rihanna, you know, they are kind of free spirits. You never know what you're going to get from them and what they are wearing that day. And some days, you know, you wanna kind of dress down and they're like the queens of doing that, but they do it and make it look so fresh and new that it's fun and I like to do that too.

The other 11 percent of the informants that followed influencers named either a local persona or a friend they knew who they considered to be a social media influencer. Lisa (age 64), like several others in the sample, explained that she followed a local person, who is also her friend that she considered to be an influencer:

I have a friend of mine that's local here that she sells a beauty product called Lime Life and I follow her. I have it as part of my life! And she'll do videos that I like to watch, but she's not really a celebrity. She's not a celebrity, if you only consider influencers like the Kardashians, as influencers. But she's still influencing people. And she still has other people on there that contribute to the advertising on those products too. So they just had some fashion designer on for Lime Life. Rebecca Minkoff just designed a beauty bag for the brand. And so my friend posted the campaign on there with her. I thought that was so nice.

Within the interviews, the informants were also asked whether their family and friends shared fashion and beauty information with them via social media and whether the information flowed the opposite way as well. Sixty-six percent of the sample indicated that their family and friends shared fashion and beauty information with them through social media. In her interview, Lydia (age 60) explained how information flowed between she and her friend in a reciprocal fashion:

Yes, my best friend Kay shares things with me all the time. When she finds something she will post it on social media and tag me, or send it to me via a private message, and vice versa. Right now she is shopping because she wants to redo her bedroom so we are sending each other comforters, pictures of comforters and such, and you know just things like accessories that she might consider for her bedroom.

... When I was at her house sometime last year and she told me about an account that she follows called the Shabby Tree and I then started following that person. That lady is actually in Georgia, which is so interesting. But it's a lady who owns her own business, and it's called The Shabby Tree. And she sells fashion stuff, not beauty, but like clothes. And she also does a lot of crafts, arts and crafts, and she'll post that stuff very frequently.

Lydia also mentioned that she both received and shared information with her daughter, which is another key source of social media influence beyond her best friend. When the informants mentioned the influence of family members through social media, it was always related to their daughters. Thus, the reciprocal influence of the mother-daughter relationship was also a theme in the data, as illustrated by the following quote from Scarlett (age 57):

Yes, particularly with my daughter. We share both style and beauty content through social media all the time. I ask her opinion a lot because I only have one daughter and three boys, so she is the reference for fashion and style. When I see something in social media, I tag her and ask her opinion because she tells me if it's not fashionable or if it's not pretty. So it's mostly with my daughter that I share ideas with on social media. But I sometimes share with my friends too. I will share a brand that I think is good to talk about, makeup tips, good addresses or brands that I discovered.

The researchers also drilled down within the interviews, asking the informants to identify social media influencers that may be like them. The informants easily named someone they followed online that they felt shared a similarity to themselves. Three themes emerged from the data in this respect: how the influencer's "story" inspired the informant; how the informant perceived to have a similar lifestyle to the influencer; and how the influencer seemed "real" or authentic in their presentation of self. Julie (age 59), for example, followed a comedian who posted videos on social media about cooking but was also very fashion conscious:

I follow Kalen Allen. He is a stand-up comedian, and his backstory is very inspiring. He has recently started doing video blogs about food and incorporating his comedic influence into that. He's hilarious, but he's also very stylish, very bold. He just got accepted into Juilliard. So, if I have to pick a celebrity that I feel inspires me in any way. It would have to be him.

Like Julie, the other informants matched up their own similarities with the influencer they named with their overall lifestyle, rather than just their fashion focus. Kayla (age 55) chose Reese Witherspoon as the social media influencer she named because of the similarity in their lifestyles and parenting of children:

So right, Reese Weatherspoon. Love her! She does fashion stuff and she does cooking too. I love to follow her. I am always interested in what she is posting. I like to see what is posting about fashion, and then her cooking, and even just life in general. Yeah, she has kids too, that are about the same age as my kids. So it's kind of funny because she says things that, you know, I would understand more anyone else would.

The authenticity of the influencer when posting on social media also seemed to impact the choice of influencer named by the informant. Several of the senior females stated that they appreciated influencers who seemed "real" or "natural" in their presentation of self, including sharing stories about their struggles, including bodily scars and physical challenges, that other everyday women share as well. Lydia (age 60) for example explained how Martha Stewart not only shared a similar set of interests and lifestyle but also looked "real" in her appearance:

This is an easy one! I choose Martha Stewart, because she and I have common interests, such as gardening, cooking, and decorating homes. I like her style, especially her style in decor and also with her personal appearance. She seems to be a classic beauty. You know, I don't really know how to describe it. I think she's simply beautiful, and she doesn't use or appear to use a lot of finishes on her appearance. She looks real. And you prefer that from a celebrity, a more real looking person. I do for sure. I do see myself in her in terms of the interest that I mentioned earlier and her sense of style.

Self-Projection and Sense of Style

One reason that authenticity may have emerged as a theme in the data is that the senior females had a well-developed sense of self. In other words, they know who they are and are confident in their identity. When asked whether the informants ever sought fashion advice from social media, eighty-four percent indicated they had gotten advice online from influencers. But they often elaborated on their answer, explaining that they had"their own sense of style" and they drew limited pieces of information from social media in order to reinforce that sense of style. In other words, the senior females did not look online to influencers to create a new sense of style, but instead looked at social media to "borrow bits and pieces" for inspiration, to identify seasonal colors or trends, or to learn new techniques that they would incorporate into their already existing beauty and style routines. The senior females stated that they liked to consult YouTube videos for tutorials and then Pinterest and Instagram for ideas on how to put together accessories and outfits. In Sarah's (age 63) interview, she detailed how she used social media to gather information about fashion and beauty:

Sometimes, if I'm looking for something specific like "how to do my eye makeup", I'll go online and I'll find YouTube videos or tutorials that will give me ideas. Or maybe it's people that I already follow, and I'll take ideas from their page. It can give me ideas of how to assemble clothes, how to style jewelry and more. It allows me to find style ideas that corresponds to me and to find out how to assemble the clothes between their suggestions. It gives me ideas because I don't have always good ideas for putting items together to make an outfit. And for the makeup, it helps me to learn techniques, like how to highlight a part of my face or how to do eye makeup to hide flaws and imperfections. So yes, sometimes I've gone online and watch videos and am inspired by them.

Talia (age 56) also talked about how she consulted Pinterest to get ideas for putting accessories and clothes together that represented her own sense of style:

I get everything for styling off of Pinterest. If I have, just say a jacket or a pair of shoes or a pair of jeans, and I want to figure out how to put a fantastic outfit together from those pieces, I check out Pinterest posts. Or just say I want to know what to wear to a special event. I will go to Pinterest. Even if it's for hairstyles for the event, should I wear it up or down? Curled or straight? Everything is on Pinterest. So I'm just picking and choosing on the style that fits me from what I can find on there.

Even though the informants talked about preferring influencers who were "authentic" and "real" when presenting themselves online, eighty-four percent of the senior females stated that they personally prioritized presenting themselves well on their own social media posts. The informants stated that their mothers raised them to care about first impressions and to always present themselves beautifully, and these social rules apply to social media, similar to in-person occasions. Before a picture is posted by a family or friend online, the senior females stated that they wanted to see the picture to make sure their clothes, hair styles and body poses (such as avoiding a double chin or showing thinning hair in the shot) looked good.

Some of the women even stated that it's a social expectation being ingrained in young girls to present themselves as beautiful and always happy online and, like today's young women, these social expectations still exist in themselves, even though they are much older. They stated that they are very critical of themselves when posting pictures on social media and quite conscious that others would judge them from their appearance in their photos. Margaret (age 59) explained this perspective as follows:

This is sort of a negative. When it comes to posting pictures, I get very critical of myself. And I'm very careful with what is posted and how I look. I know that is not the way I should be. I know that my daughter, and my daughters-in-law would totally be horrified if they knew I said that because they wouldn't want me to feel that way. They would be like, "Mom, just put it out there. It's fine." But I do get hung up on that. I feel like I have a pretty good eye for what something should look like. Personally, I mean I'm like just talking my own style. I know what I want my personal style to look like. I always make sure they are styled the way I think they should look, so I get a little hung up on it. … I'm actually in this online group with a paid membership that provides trainings for how to best present yourself online. So I did um a couple of trainings with them, and then it's just nice, because I can go back into that group and ask questions if I have them.

Thirty-seven percent of the informants also stated that they edited their images before they posted on social media. More specifically, they talked about how they modified lighting, used filters, removed red eye, and often cropped other people or items out of the background before they posted a picture. Violet (age 61) provided an example of how the informants edited their photos before posting them on social media:

Yes, of course. I don't use any advanced software. I use only my iPhone to do editing. I use several features from that. I'm modifying the lighting. I modify red eyes also. And sometimes I crop out people so it's just me or me and my daughter.

Of those that said they did not use editing tools on their photos before posting, many of them stated that they wanted to learn how to do it, so that they could "make themselves look younger." This finding suggests that stereotypes from the fashion industry and society showing bias toward "young, tall and skinny" women still exists, despite the recognition of authenticity and recommendations for women to "be themselves" when posting online.

Influence on Purchase Decisions

Another significant component of the interviews focused on whether the senior females' purchase decisions were impacted by social media, especially influencers. The informants stated that family and friends, retail stores, and online advertisements in social media all impacted their purchase behaviors. When friends and daughters are posting and tagging the senior females, making comments and recommendations, and liking the social media posts of the senior females, all of these activities influenced the senior females' purchasing behaviors. Violet (age 61) told a story in her interview about specifically buying a purse as a result of social media influence from her daughter:

Yes, of course I have been influenced by a friend for a purchase on social media. And first of all, my daughter if she likes a product or a brand, of course I will be interested. Then I will do my own research about it. And yeah, I think my tastes are much closer to my daughter's than everybody else, so she is the person I am most influenced by. One day I saw my daughter with a Louis Vuitton bag and I wanted the same, because when I saw it on her, I thought it was very nice.

Grace (age 55) also explained how social media influencers have impacted her purchase decisions:

Oh, I definitely think so. You know, I think it's important when you see other people's opinions about the products in social media. I feel like that makes such a big difference when you see something online. You think you don't really know that much about it but when someone's using it and talking about it, or has used it and is it recommending it, or giving you some advice about why it's good because of this or that, and then showing you how to use it, all that definitely makes a big difference when I decide to buy something.

When asked about their favorite brands and whether they followed them on social media, eighty-four percent of the informants stated that they followed brands on social media. When the informants were probed about what brands they followed, they primarily talked about two types of brands: national brands (such as Ralph Lauren or Isabel Marrant) and retail stores (like Belk and J.Jill). Because of the potential role of the retailer, the informants were also asked if they preferred to shop online or in stores and whether they had ever made a purchase through social media. The informants talked about shopping both online and in stores (i.e., omni channel retailing), but stated that they preferred to shop in stores for fashion items, due to the fact that fit of the clothing is one of the most important criteria driving purchases of this age group. Chloe (age 55), for example, illustrated why many senior females preferred to shop in stores because of fit:

If it's shoes, absolutely in person, because I just prefer to have them on, feel them, and make sure they fit. I like kind of sticking to brands, like Columbia, because I know what size fits and I know which style I like. ... Shirts I have more difficult time with. I don't tend to buy those online. I will buy them in the store, because sometimes things just don't fit right on my shoulders and, um, and it gets uncomfortable. And it's just not worth the fight. Of course, it's been more difficult after Covid with not being able to try things on. But I still tend to shop more in person than online.

And when the senior females did say they preferred to shop online, it was out of convenience, such as trying to find an item that was out of a specific size in the store or shopping online due to having a busy work schedule. But even when the informant stated that she preferred to purchase online, she would also talk about the need for fit and utilizing return services when necessary.

The informants were also asked if they had ever purchased from a social media advertisement. Seventy-nine percent of the sample stated that they had in fact clicked on and purchased from a social media ad. Some of the informants talked about how social media "anticipated their needs" and their feeds presented them with tutorials and advertisements in their areas of interest which influenced them. In her interview, Barbara (age 55), for example, stated how social media advertising had influenced her:

I follow a lot of advice online. I look at a lot of advice, makeup, and clothing. I look at Instagram in particular. My news feed has a lot of handy tips and tricks. I get a lot of inspiration from that. Sometimes I also get inspired by the ads I may come across. There's a lot of advertising on Instagram and on Facebook. It helps me learn about new brands that I didn't know about too.

Like Barbara and many other senior females in the sample,Violet (age 61) also had clicked and purchased on ads from Instagram:

Yes, for example, I bought some hair product like that because I had seen it on Instagram, and there were good reviews, and so I bought it because it was not very expensive. I told myself, I will try it, and I was quite happy with my purchase. I looked at the reviews before and thought it was a good value so I bought it.

As can be seen from the findings, the senior females who participated in the study were following influencers online and these activities were impacting their purchase behaviors. The influencers they followed were not only national celebrities but also local personalities, family members, and friends. The informants seemed attracted to influencers who were authentic and shared similar lifestyles to the senior females. And, as if they were influencers themselves, the senior females then developed their own sense of style from the information they gathered online and then carefully crafted and projected their own images online in order to present themselves in the best possible fashion in social media. And finally, the social media activity of these senior females was significantly impacting their purchase behaviors, as influencer recommendations, brands, and advertisements on social media coalesced and ultimately influenced when and what they were purchasing.

Discussion and Implications

The findings of this research provide new insight into social media usage by women over 50, who utilize social media as a source of fashion advice and inspiration when making purchase decisions. Previous research on social media and senior females as it relates to the fashion and beauty context has focused on the activities of high profile senior influencers, who are often paid social media campaign campaigns (Samsioe, 2020; Miranda et al., 2022; Stephani, 2022). The present study is unique because it examines the impact of celebrity and non-celebrity (family and friends) influencers on the consumer behaviors of everyday senior females. The findings of this study provide insight into who the senior females are following on social media, how they project themselves online and construct their own sense of style from information gleaned via social media, and the impact of social media on their purchase behaviors.

Results from this study demonstrate that social media influencers are an important and trusted source of fashion information and inspiration for senior females. Most of the informants quickly named a social media influencer that they followed online, with most naming a celebrity and the remaining naming a friend or local expert. The senior females explained that people they followed exemplified a similar lifestyle with respect to fashion and personal interests. This finding suggests that even senior women are potentially heavily influenced by the images and information presented online by celebrities and non-celebrities alike.

When the researchers probed the informants for additional insight into the reasons they identified with a particular influencer online, three themes emerged: inspiring stories, perceived similarity, and perceived authenticity. Storytelling is the cornerstone of influencer marketing (Woodside, 2010; Farivar et al., 2021). Using carefully scripted stories that show pictures and videos of how to wear and use an item, and how to present a lifestyle others might want to emulate, social media wields the power to shape and influence consumer behaviors across a variety of age groups. The present study found that while senior women are drawn to inspiring stories that present confident older females living a full life, there needs to be a perceived similarity between the individual and the influencer for the story to resonate with members of the audience. For example, Reese Witherspoon and Martha Stewart were mentioned as celebrities the informants followed because they not only offered inspiring stories but also a perceived similarity between the celebrity influencer and the individual consumer. Additionally, the influencer needed to present themselves as authentic in their posts and lifestyle in order for the audience to embrace the messaging.

However, of equal importance for the fashion industry is the influence of non-celebrities on fashion information sharing and its impact on consumer behavior. A significant portion of the sample mentioned that they reciprocally shared fashion and beauty information via social media with friends and family. The power of a personal relationship (i.e., friend or family) that has long existed in face-to-face interactions appears to have migrated online and also impacts consumer behavior through social media. Among the online influence of friends and family, the mother/daughter relationship appeared to be the most influential. Perhaps because they know each other well, share similarities, and trust each other's opinions to be authentic, that they are able to identify information each would be interested in and to make influential purchase recommendations for one another. Further research into the sharing of fashion information via social media between mothers and daughters is suggested.

In addition to telling a compelling story and having a connection between the influencer and the individual, perceived authenticity was also important to the senior females when selecting a social media influencer (celebrity and non-celebrity) to follow and when posting online. Authenticity being important in marketing communication, especially for social media users, has been well established in the literature (Farinosi & Fortunati, 2020; Leigh et al., 2006; Moore et al., 2018). Whether following a well-known celebrity, a local expert, or a family member, the need for authenticity was expressed throughout the interviews. Furthermore, the senior women in this study describe authenticity of the influencer as appearing real and/or showing their personal struggles and physical challenges online.

And yet, when the senior females themselves posted online, they sought to avoid authenticity and present themselves in the best possible light, not sharing their flaws, emotional struggles, and physical challenges. The senior females themselves carefully protected their own social media persona (i.e., digital self) when sharing photos online. They often monitored images they allowed others to post, edited their own images, and cared about what they were wearing, how their hair and make-up looked, and the poses of their bodies in their own social media posts. A curious balance between desiring authenticity from influencers, and yet wanting to carefully curate their own online image, was evident in the research findings. Similar to younger demographic segments (Hogan, 2010), the senior females in this study appeared to feel pressure to look their best on social media as they perceived others were judging their appearances online.

With respect to social media and its impact on the decision making of senior females in the fashion context, the findings of the present study also showed that the posts of social media influencers were impacting senior females in the fashion context. The vast majority of the sample indicated that they had received fashion advice from online influencers. However, most of the senior females commented that they used bits and pieces of this information as inspiration to create their own style, as opposed to using the information to copy a look or create a whole a new sense of style. In other words, the senior female, while interested in looking fashionable and stylish, has a well-developed fashion identity that drives a unique sense of style, rather than simply copying what she sees online. This finding is consistent with previous research in a non-digital context on senior women and their fashion choices (Joung & Miller, 2006; Thomas & Peters, 2009; Peters et al., 2011). And yet the present study extends the literature by showing that social media provides senior women with a tool for researching fashion trends and garnering inspiration for creating a signature style that aligns with their sense of self. Future research should examine whether this finding about senior females aligns with how younger women utilize social media in fashion as well. One may wonder whether millennials or members of generation Z similarly choose bits and pieces from social media to construct their own sense of style or do they copy whole outfits and create a whole new look from online sources.

The findings of this study also suggest that all types of social media influencers, retailers, and online advertisements influence the purchase behavior of senior women. The majority of the study participants stated they had clicked on and purchased a fashion item from a social media advertisement. This finding indicates that senior women, who are a lucrative demographic segment, are motivated to purchase fashion items from social media. Additional research into advertising content and messaging that targets senior women is needed to fully understand the purchase response of senior females to social media advertising.

In conclusion, the present research provided a broader perspective into the social media usage and consumer behaviors of everyday senior females within the fashion context. Study results expanded the academic literature on influencer marketing andunpacked how social media impacts the purchase decisions of women aged 50 and over. The research findings indicated that senior women are active on social media and that their purchase decisions are impacted by social media influencer, retailer, and brand marketing. Findings from this study also present unique insights into how senior women present themselves in a digital format on social media. Finally, the commonly held assumption that influencer marketing strategies for fashion/apparel are only useful when targeting millennials and generation Z is refuted by this study.

REFERENCES

Abdullah, T., Deraman, S. N. S., Zainuddin, S. A., Azmi, N. F., Abdullah, S. S., Anuar, N. I. M., ... Hasan, H. (2020). Impact of Social Media Influencer on Instagram User Purchase Intention towards the Fashion Products: The Perspectives of UMK Pengkalan Chepa Campus Students. *European Journal of Molecular and Clinical Medicine*.

Ahmad, N., Salman, A., & Ashiq, R. (2015). The impact of social media on fashion industry: Empirical investigation from Karachiites. *Journal of Resources Development and Management, 7*.

Borland, H., & Akram, S. (2007). Age is no barrier to wanting to look good: Women on body image, age and advertising. *Qualitative Market Research, 10*(3), 310–333. doi:10.1108/13522750710754335

Burt, S., & Gabbott, M. (1995). The elderly consumer and non-food purchase behaviour. *European Journal of Marketing, 29*(2), 43–57. doi:10.1108/03090569510080941

Chetioui, Y., Benlafqih, H., & Lebdaoui, H. (2020). How fashion influencers contribute to consumers' purchase intention. *Journal of Fashion Marketing and Management, 24*(3), 361–380. doi:10.1108/JFMM-08-2019-0157

Chu, S. C., & Seock, Y. K. (2020). The power of social media in fashion advertising. *Journal of Interactive Advertising, 20*(2), 93–94. doi:10.1080/15252019.2020.1802955

Colby, S. L. (2021, June 24). *What marketers need to know about women over 50*. Muse by Clio. https://musebycl.io/musings/what-marketers-need-know-about-women-over-50

Creswell, J. W., & Poth, C. N. (2016). *Qualitative inquiry and research design: Choosing among five approaches*. Sage publications.

do Prado Lima, S. (2020, May 26). *Ageism could cost billions to the fashion industry*. Moderated. https://medium.com/moderated/ageism-could-cost-billions-to-the-fashion-industry-c2e5cfcfd837

Farinosi, M., & Fortunati, L. (2020). Young and elderly fashion influencers. In *Human Aspects of IT for the Aged Population. Technology and Society: 6th International Conference, ITAP 2020, Held as Part of the 22nd HCI International Conference, HCII 2020, Copenhagen, Denmark, July 19–24, 2020 Proceedings, 22*(3), 42–57.

Farivar, S., Wang, F., & Yuan, Y. (2021). Opinion leadership vs. para-social relationship: Key factors in influencer marketing. *Journal of Retailing and Consumer Services, 59*, 102371. doi:10.1016/j.jretconser.2020.102371

Greco, A. J. (1986). The fashion-conscious elderly: A viable, but neglected market segment. *Journal of Consumer Marketing, 3*(4), 71–75. doi:10.1108/eb008181

Groenewald, T. (2004). A Phenomenological Research Design Illustrated. *International Journal of Qualitative Methods, 3*(1), 42–55. doi:10.1177/160940690400300104

Hogan, B. (2010). The presentation of self in the age of social media: Distinguishing performances and exhibitions online. *Bulletin of Science, Technology & Society, 30*(6), 377–386. doi:10.1177/0270467610385893

Joung, H. M., & Miller, N. J. (2006). Factors of dress affecting self-esteem in older females. *Journal of Fashion Marketing and Management*, *10*(4), 466–478. doi:10.1108/13612020610701983

Leigh, T. W., Peters, C., & Shelton, J. (2006). The consumer quest for authenticity: The multiplicity of meanings within the MG subculture of consumption. *Journal of the Academy of Marketing Science*, *34*(4), 481–493. doi:10.1177/0092070306288403

Littrell, M. A., Jin Ma, Y., & Halepete, J. (2005). Generation X, baby boomers, and swing: Marketing fair trade apparel. *Journal of Fashion Marketing and Management*, *9*(4), 407–419. doi:10.1108/13612020510620786

Lumpkin, J., & Greenberg, B. (1982). Apparel-shopping patterns of the elderly consumer. *Journal of Retailing*, *58*(4), 68–89.

Lumpkin, J., Greenberg, B., & Goldstucker, J. (1985). Marketplace needs of the elderly: Determinant attributes and store choice. *Journal of Retailing*, *61*(2), 75–105.

McFarlane, A., & Samsioe, E. (2020). #50+ fashion Instagram influencers: Cognitive age and aesthetic digital labours. *Journal of Fashion Marketing and Management*, *24*(3), 399–413. doi:10.1108/JFMM-08-2019-0177

McMillen, J. (2022, October 17). *6 facts about middle-aged women retailers should know*. Forbes. https://www.forbes.com/sites/jennmcmillen/2022/10/17/6-facts-about-middle-aged-women-retailers-should-know/?sh=6a812fde4ef4

Miles, M. B., & Huberman, A. M. (1994). Qualitative data analysis: An expanded sourcebook. *Sage (Atlanta, Ga.)*.

Miranda, S., Antunes, A. C., & Gama, A. (2022, April). A different type of influencer? Examining senior Instagram influencers communication. In *Proceedings of the 9th European Conference on Social Media* (pp. 130-136). Academic Conferences International. 10.34190/ecsm.9.1.337

Moore, A., Yang, K., & Kim, H. M. (2018, January). Influencer marketing: Influentials' authenticity, likeability and authority in social media. In *International Textile and Apparel Association Annual Conference Proceedings* (*Vol. 75*, No. 1). Iowa State University Digital Press.

Moore, M., & Carpenter, J. (2006). The effect of price as a marketplace cue on retail patronage. *Journal of Product and Brand Management*, *15*(4), 265–271. doi:10.1108/10610420610679647

Moustakas, C. (1994). Phenomenological Research Methods. *Sage (Atlanta, Ga.)*.

Nam, J., Hamlin, R., Gam, H. J., Kang, J. H., Kim, J., Kumphai, P., Starr, C., & Richards, L. (2007). The fashion-conscious behaviours of mature female consumers. *International Journal of Consumer Studies*, *31*(1), 102–108. doi:10.1111/j.1470-6431.2006.00497.x

Nash, J. (2019). Exploring how social media platforms influence fashion consumer decisions in the UK retail sector. *Journal of Fashion Marketing and Management*, *23*(1), 82–103. doi:10.1108/JFMM-01-2018-0012

Peters, C., Shelton, J. A., & Thomas, J. B. (2011). Self-concept and the fashion behavior of women over 50. *Journal of Fashion Marketing and Management*, *15*(3), 291–305. doi:10.1108/13612021111151905

Pew Research Center. (2021, April 7). *Social Media Fact Sheet*. https://www.pewresearch.org/internet/fact-sheet/social-media/

Reilly, A., & Barry, B. (2020). *Crossing gender boundaries: Fashion to create, disrupt, and transcend*. Intellect Books.

Rocha, M. A. V., Hammond, L., & Hawkins, D. (2005). Age, gender and national factors in fashion consumption. *Journal of Fashion Marketing and Management*, *9*(4), 380–390. doi:10.1108/13612020510620768

Rodela, J. (2022, February 15). *Importance of influencer marketing on Instagram*. Vistasocial. https://vistasocial.com/insights/importance-of-influencer-marketing/

Stephani, N. (2022). Senior female celebrity's body and ageing well discourse on Instagram. *Jurnal Studi Komunikasi*, *6*(1), 165–178. doi:10.25139/jsk.v6i1.4312

Stephani, N. (2022). Senior female celebrity's body and ageing well discourse on Instagram. *Jurnal Studi Komunikasi*, *6*(1), 165–178. doi:10.25139/jsk.v6i1.4312

Sun, Y., Wang, R., Cao, D., & Lee, R. (2022). Who are social media influencers for luxury fashion consumption of the Chinese Gen Z? Categorisation and empirical examination. *Journal of Fashion Marketing and Management*, *26*(4), 603–621. doi:10.1108/JFMM-07-2020-0132

Thomas, J., Peters, C., & Tolson, H. (2007). An exploratory investigation of the virtual community MySpace.com. *Journal of Fashion Marketing and Management*, *11*(4), 587–603. doi:10.1108/13612020710824625

Thomas, J. B., & Peters, C. (2009). Silver seniors: Exploring the self-concept, lifestyles, and apparel consumption of women over age 65. *International Journal of Retail & Distribution Management*, *37*(12), 1018–1040. doi:10.1108/09590550911005001

Thompson, C., Locander, W., & Pollio, H. (1989). Putting consumer experience back into consumer research: The philosophy and method of existential phenomenology. *The Journal of Consumer Research*, *16*(2), 133–147. doi:10.1086/209203

Tripathi, S. (2019). Impact of social media on generation Y for buying fashion apparel. *Journal of Content. Community & Communication*, *9*(5), 105–113.

Woodside, A. G. (2010). Brand-consumer storytelling theory and research: Introduction. *Psychology and Marketing*, *27*(6), 531–540. doi:10.1002/mar.20342

Wooldridge, B. R., & Kuntze, R. (2019, November 6). Women over fifty demand 'me too' treatment from retailers: Exploring America's most ignored consumer. In *Society for Marketing Advances Proceedings* (pp. 332-333). Society for Marketing Advances Conference.

Chapter 10
Intention to Purchase Sustainable Fashion:
Influencer and Worth-of-Mouth Determinants

Cláudia Filipa Morais
School of Economics and Management, University of Porto, Portugal

Paulo Botelho Pires
CEOS, Polytechnic of Porto, Portugal

Catarina Delgado
School of Economics and Management, University of Porto, Portugal

José Duarte Santos
ISCAP, Polytechnic of Porto, Portugal

ABSTRACT

There is a recognized need to study sustainability in fashion. Several studies have documented the determinants that influence fashion purchase intention. However, the determinants that influence the purchase of sustainable fashion still need to be understood, particularly those factors associated with influencers and electronic word-of-mouth. This study aimed to examine the constructs influencer credibility, influencer expertise, influencer similarity, influencer's parasocial relationship, E-WOM homophily, E-WOM expertise, trust in the influencer, trust in social media, performance expectation, consumer knowledge, environmental beliefs, brand awareness and willingness to pay more, and their effect on purchase intention. The research methodology consisted of consumer interviews that were conducted using an online platform, and structural equation modeling was used to test the research hypotheses. The results obtained indicate that consumer knowledge and willingness to pay more are the only constructs that positively affect the purchase intention of sustainable fashion.

DOI: 10.4018/978-1-6684-8753-2.ch010

1. INTRODUCTION

The goal of this study is to determine the elements of influencers and electronic word-of-mouth in social media that impact consumers' intentions to buy sustainable apparel. Additionally, it aims to confirm the relationships between the influencers' determinants and electronic word-of-mouth (E-WOM) and how the perceptions about sustainable fashion are affected by determinants like consumer trust, performance expectations, knowledge, and environmental beliefs, as well as how consumers perceive brands and how willing they are to pay more for sustainable clothing. Thus, the central issue of the study is "How can influencers and digital social media impact the purchase intention of sustainable fashion products?"

2. LITERATURE REVIEW

2.1. Sustainable Fashion

One of the most troubling global challenges and a challenge for the fashion business has been sustainability (Kong, Ko, Chae, & Mattila, 2016). From a social, ethical, and environmental perspective, sustainable fashion is related to the creation of ethically and environmentally sound apparel (Joergens, 2006). According to the author, sustainable fashion is defined as clothing made from organic and biodegradable cotton and created under ethical working circumstances free from exploitation. Goworek et al. (2012) define sustainable clothes in terms of two broad criteria: either the garment textiles must only be of organic origin, or the production circumstances must be fair. Sustainable fashion, as opposed to fast fashion, emphasizes the high durability of conventionally trendy products while minimizing their environmental effect through the use of organic and recyclable materials (Henninger et al., 2016, Joergens, 2006; Shen et al., 2013). Additionally, one other objective is to design products with many uses so they may be used for longer periods and encourage customers to buy fewer products and consume less (Connell, 2010). The usage of secondhand fashion products, such as purchasing fashion products created under slow fashion circumstances, promotes sustainability in fashion (Connell, 2010; Harris et al., 2016). This effort seeks to reduce the unsustainable production cycle of fast fashion by concentrating on ethical production, minimizing manufacturing, valuing quality over quantity, and upcycling, in which customers use repurposed fashion products (Fletcher, 2010; Harris et al., 2016; Henninger et al., 2016; Ozdamar et al., 2015).

As a result, sustainable fashion lacks a precise definition, and the following definition will be explored in this research: sustainable fashion encourages consumers to use fashion products for an extended length of time, reducing consumption. The re-use and consumption of secondhand fashion products are two possibilities that help the consolidation of sustainable fashion. Sustainable fashion production is distinguished by using recycled and organic materials that are intended to be used for a longer time than conventional fashion, with production having a lower environmental impact and incorporating fair trade principles in safe and proper working environments.

Sustainable fashion buyers are distinguished by their concern for environmental concerns, product expertise, and anticipated positive effects from their purchase (Min Kong & Ko, 2017). The high cost, the time spent in research, the scarcity of natural materials, and, consequently, the lack of sustainable fashion products, are seen as perceived benefits by those who use them. This is because the target consumers of this market perceive these products as genuine, long-lasting, and environmentally conscious and, therefore, present psychological perceptions of value (Lundblad & Davies, 2015).

Goworek et al. (2012) noted that as customers increasingly demand openness about the production chain, there has been an increase in consumer awareness of sustainability concerns in the garment industry. Even with greater knowledge of sustainability, research shows that consumers still struggle to translate their attitudes toward ethical purchasing into actual purchases (Niinimäki, 2010; Vehmas et al., 2018). Harris et al. (2016) found that three factors – customers have various ethical concerns, sustainable clothing is difficult, and purchasing clothes is not an altruistic behavior – mean that sustainability alone does not result in major changes in consumers' purchase criteria.

According to Vehmas et al. (2018), the lack of consumer awareness of sustainability is a result of inadequate media coverage. Consumers must be educated on this issue and encouraged to do so for them to buy sustainable clothes. In their study, Kong et al. (2016) found that if fashion companies make their sustainability expertise known, Korean consumers will have a better awareness of sustainable fashion. For Cervellon & Wernerfelt (2012), forums in particular play a significant role in online communities since industry professionals exchange valuable information and instruct novices. Participants in the green forum also identified themselves as one of the key forces behind the advancement of sustainable fashion (Cervellon & Wernerfelt, 2012). An organization's perspective and the role it plays in social media about sustainability can influence whether people have a good attitude toward it and, as a result, if they choose to buy sustainable clothing (de Lenne & Vandenbosch, 2017). Consumers' attitudes about purchasing sustainable clothes are positively influenced by organizations that promote sustainability, eco-activists, and sustainable fashion businesses (de Lenne & Vandenbosch, 2017).

Given that customers' actions and behaviors are determined by the perceptions they receive from their reference group, social influence stands out as one of the factors that most influence their decision to purchase clothing from a sustainable company (Ciasullo et al., 2017). According to Salem & Alanadoly (2020), customers who are more conscious of their impact on the environment are more likely to use E-WOM on social media to educate their friends about the sustainability of companies. Additionally, customer satisfaction with sustainable fashion products encourages the sharing of E-WOM, which influences purchasing intention (Min Kong & Ko, 2017). Additionally, social media is one of the more suitable and reliable marketing strategies for sustainable fashion firms since they reach customers through E-WOM rather than the conventional advertising produced by marketing managers (Min Kong & Ko, 2017). De Lenne and Vandenbosch (2017) stated that social media is a direct and indirect predictor of the desire to purchase sustainable clothes, therefore it follows that sustainable fashion manufacturers should be aware of the potential of social media. Zhao et al. (2019) discovered that social media exposure to sustainable fashion can affect customer attitudes toward purchasing intentions.

2.2. Electronic Word-of-Mouth

Electronic word-of-mouth is defined as an opinion expressed positively or negatively about a brand or product by a prospective, existing, or past consumer that is made available to an unlimited number of people and encourages user conversation on the Internet (Hennig-Thurau et al., 2004). E-WOM differs from conventional word-of-mouth (WOM) in six ways, according to King, Racherla, & Bush (2014): volume reached, dispersion, durability and observability, anonymity and deception, the importance of valence, and community participation. E-WOM spreads through social networks because users want and need to keep up social ties with others in their network of contacts (Chu & Kim, 2011). Consumer interaction on social media encourages user-to-user (E-WOM) conversation, opinion sharing about products and companies, and social media purchase intent (Alhidari et al., 2015). The information about a brand that is obtained from the E-WOM is derived from what the consumer reads, i.e., from comments and evaluations made by other consumers, for example, in social networks and online communities, shaping the consumer's attitude toward the brand as well as the intention to purchase the specific brand (Chen et al., 2016).

Through the messages, they read and that are posted by peers on digital social media, consumers learn and adopt purchase behaviors (Wang, Yu, & Wei, 2012). Additionally, social media exerts a favorable influence on the purchase intention of the products mentioned by peers, and this influence occurs due to the indirect impact of consumer engagement with the product through peer communications (Wang et al., 2012). Identification with the peer group is essential for the diffusion of peer interaction. As a result, peer-to-peer communication through digital social media is comparable to E-WOM from only trusted sources, including friends and family.

Social media is viewed as trustworthy and safe because user interactions on these platforms are comparable to interactions between customers, which increases their value as a source of information and accelerates the spread of E-WOM (Chu & Kim, 2011). According to Chih et al. (2013), one of the most crucial sources for getting information is the E-WOM and it may spread through social media in three different ways: through seeking information, disseminating information, and transmitting information (Chu & Kim, 2011). Users that participate in E-WOM, regardless of the form they employ, are more likely to be influenced by the opinions of other users, which is reflected in their purchase behavior (López & Sicilia, 2014). Due to interaction in online reality, any user can simultaneously be an information provider, seeker, and broadcaster (Chu & Kim, 2011).

The E-WOM enables lowering the level of skepticism and risk related to the purchase and may have an impact on decision-making and purchasing intention (Jalilvand & Samiei, 2012). Additional research has revealed that it has a direct influence on consumers' trust and purchase decisions (Dellarocas, Zhang, & Awad, 2007; Duan, Gu, & Whinston, 2008). Decision-making is influenced by the user's perception of the E-WOM reliability (López & Sicilia, 2014). Besides, E-WOM encourages the development of customer loyalty to businesses by way of positive E-WOM feedback, generating a favorable brand image, and having an impact on the decision-making process, although it is still not apparent how consumers digest and use this information at each stage (King et al., 2014). E-WOM has a stronger impact on the deliberation stage than the purchase stage, according to Jang et al. (2012). Positive ratings influence the assessment and decision-making stage less than negative ones (Cheung & Thadani, 2012; Park & Lee, 2009). Positive reviews influence consumer loyalty and purchasing decisions (Pereira, Salgueiro, & Rita, 2017; Saleem, Yaseen, & Wasaya, 2018).

In their study, Saleem & Ellahi (2017) identified homophily, expertise, informational influence, trustworthiness, and high fashion engagement as the E-WOM factors that most impact fashion purchase intention and concluded that all factors affect E-WOM and fashion purchase intention in the context of Facebook use. According to this definition, homophily refers to the amount to which people communicate when they have qualities in common, such as age, gender, education level, and money. Customers are more likely to acquire a product when presented with an E-WOM from someone who shares their values, hence the higher the degree of homophily, the larger the impact of the E-WOM on purchase intention.

According to the definition of expertise, it refers to the degree to which a person is believed to possess knowledge, skills, or experience and is hence deemed to deliver correct information (Ohanian,

1990). Since it looks to be a statement of high validity and accuracy and there is a substantial correlation between it and the desire to buy, it becomes a crucial component of E-WOM (Saleem & Ellahi, 2017).

Being aware that trust is one of the most significant sources of information regarding consumers' perceptions of a particular product evaluation and is positively correlated with E-WOM and purchase intention of fashion products, trustworthiness is related to the credibility of the information source (Saleem & Ellahi, 2017). When a customer requires the advice of another person to make a choice, informational influence happens and affects the consumer's intention to make a purchase.

Consumers highly participate in fashion when they research fashion products through a variety of sites before making a purchase, fostering E-WOM, and there is a strong correlation between fashion engagement and purchase intention (Saleem & Ellahi, 2017). In their study, Wolny & Mueller (2013) found that one of the primary reasons driving engagement in E-WOM connected to fashion companies is consumers' level of fashion involvement, which makes them more inclined to engage with E-WOM related to fashion businesses.

Kim et al. (2013) discovered that respondents who had contact with E-WOM made purchases more frequently than those who did not and consumers are more influenced by negative E-WOM since it has a higher impact than positive E-WOM. Trustworthiness, attractiveness, and expertise were emphasized as sources of credibility, who discovered that these sources influenced the impacts of E-WOM. The consequences of E-WOM depend on who makes a message, and those whose writing inspires trust. Additionally, when a message is negative, the E-WOM is affected less by the author's trustworthiness than when a message is positive. Credibility affects the desire to purchase, attitude change, and intention to relay when the message is good about the product (Kim et al., 2013).

Since customers who are more concerned about environmental behavior prefer to communicate their opinions with others to promote awareness of the adoption of such behaviors, awareness of the presence of environmentally friendly products is also a driver of the usage of E-WOM to distribute information (Salem & Alanadoly, 2020).

2.3. Influencers

The main purpose of social media influencers is to play a significant role in the dissemination of businesses' marketing by pushing products to their audience, more especially to their followers. Influencers on social media are content producers and are regarded as experts in a certain field, and they also spread their books with compelling themes that had educational and entertaining value (Lou & Yuan, 2019).

An extension of WOM, influencer-driven marketing focuses on a more familiar and professional side, making it a beneficial tool for companies as it encourages stronger involvement with customers to win their trust and loyalty (Sudha & Sheena, 2017). Influencer-driven marketing is different from E-WOM even if it is seen as an extension of that strategy since marketing outcomes are simpler for marketing managers to oversee (Chetioui, Benlafqih, & Lebdaoui, 2020). An opinion leader today is referred to as a digital influencer since they have an impact on both the offline and online communities (Santiago et al., 2020). Opinion leaders have two crucial roles: they influence consumers' purchasing decisions and encourage the spread of ideas via E-WOM (Zhao et al., 2018). Casaló et al. (2020) stated that online opinion leader stands out for the perceived quality, uniqueness, and authenticity of their writings, which encourages their audience to adopt their advice. Following Zhao et al. (2018), the impact of opinion leaders tends to increase as consumer trust in them rises. Furthermore, they observed that trust is a significant factor in improving opinion leaders' power of influence, therefore they concluded that enhancing opinion leaders' credibility is essential for the success of e-commerce. Lou and Yuan (2019) claim that consumer confidence based on publications made by influencers about brands has a greater impact on purchase intention than other factors under study because the informational value of content produced by influencers positively influences consumers' trust in promoted brands as well as their purchase intention. Moreover, they found that influencer credibility is essential for building consumer trust and brand recognition and that influencers' credibility, attraction, and consumer-like qualities favorably affect the businesses they support.

According to Sokolova and Kefi's (2020) research, the credibility of the influencer and the parasocial bond that exists between them and their followers are key factors in motivating purchase intentions. This finding suggests that affective processes have an impact on consumer decision-making because consumers who are more emotionally attached to influencers are more likely to be persuaded than those who are not. Additionally, the parasocial relationship that the younger generation has with the influencer affects their decision to make a purchase more than the influencer's perceived legitimacy does.

The level of expertise of an influencer affects how customers view their content as reliable and accurate, which in turn tends to have a favorable impact on followers' perceptions of the influencers (Chetioui et al., 2020). The follower's attitude toward the advertised or suggested brand, such as their desire to purchase products featured in the influencers' publications, is considerably and favorably influenced by their perception of the influencer's knowledge (Hayes & Carr, 2015). In the study conducted by Bergkvist et al. (2016), it was also shown that the influencer's level of competence influences their audience's perception of the brand they mention favorably. Jiménez-Castillo and Sánchez-Fernández (2019) stated that the impact of an influencer increases consumer expectations of the promoted brand and increases the likelihood that consumers will buy the recommended brands (Casaló, Flavián, and Ibáez-Sánchez, 2020b; Jiménez-Castillo & Sánchez-Fernández, 2019; Lou & Yuan, 2019; Sokolova & Kefi).

The determinants that most induce consumers to follow a fashion influencer are related to the credibility, competence, and confidence that the influencer exudes in the content they share (Chetioui et al., 2020). The similarity, trust, and attractiveness of influencers positively affect trust in publications regarding brand promotions (Lou & Yuan, 2019). Also, the perceived credibility of an influencer is one of the most highlighted factors on how influencers affect purchase intention and boils down to the fact that the recipient of the message believes that the source who conveyed the information has knowledge, skill, and experience in the subject matter (Santiago et al., 2020, p.109). Chetioui et al. (2020) highlight that perceived credibility is the factor that creates the greatest impact on the attitude consumers have toward the influencer.

Considering now a narrower scope, to fashion influencers, it is still possible to gather additional information in the bibliography. An important element in developing an influencer-follower connection is consumer trust in fashion influencers since followers will be impacted by their attitudes, decisions, and purchase intents as a result of what influencers say, do, and promote (Chetioui et al., 2020; Santiago et al., 2020). The credibility of the influencer is one of the elements that most affect attitudes toward the influencer and buy intention, according to Chetioui et al. (2020). Santiago et al. (2020) also discovered that brand credibility, message credibility, and influencer similarity and credibility all increase consumer confidence in influencers. It is also relevant to know that consumers' perception of the advertised products as trustworthy and their desire to make purchases are influenced by influencer-generated content with educational and entertaining value (Lou & Yuan, 2019).

Because the influencer seems to be a highly knowledgeable individual and is thus more likely to make correct and reliable judgments, influencer expertise stands out (Chetioui et al., 2020). An influencer's perceived expertise enables them to distribute material and make highly pertinent remarks while also providing reliable assessments, which eventually have a big impact on a customer's perception of a brand and buy intent (Chetioui et al., 2020). In the Lou & Yuan (2019) study, it was discovered that influencer expertise influences trust in publications connected to brand promotion, just as it was discovered that the perceived influencer knowledge affects the brand awareness that the influencer promotes.

The parasocial interaction with influencers is presented as a partnership between online influencers and users of social media (Sokolova & Kefi, 2020). The users' perception of the influencers' attractiveness and similarity with them leads to interaction between them, and this relationship has a positive impact on the intention to buy the products that the influencer promotes. The parasocial relationship between influencers and their followers proves to be very important. The study by Farivar et al. (2021) found that the followers' perceptions of their parasocial connection with the influencer were substantially correlated with the influencer's positive recommendations, which in turn considerably increased the followers' purchase intentions.

Homophily stands out as a significant component because it affects the parasocial interaction and the credibility of the influencers when consumers identify with their traits and ideals, which makes it a persuasive factor (Sokolova & Kefi, 2020). Similarity to the content creator is the degree to which the customer feels he is similar to the content producer (van Esch et al., 2018). According to Santiago et al. (2020), users' perceived likeness to influencers impacts influencer trust and purchase intention favorably. Consumers will assess the veracity of an influencer's message based on the information's quality and correctness, which will affect their level of trust and likelihood to make a purchase (Santiago et al., 2020).

The credibility of a brand is tied to the veracity of the communication and is mostly based on the message influencers deliver and the promises they make to their followers regarding the company, as well as the influencer's reputation (Santiago et al., 2020; van Esch et al., 2018). Santiago et al. (2020) found that of all the criteria, brand credibility is the antecedent component that causes the biggest impact on confidence in influencers and provides the highest effect on purchase intention. As a result, followers see posts created by companies with influencers as trustworthy and honest.

2.4. Trust in Social Media

Social media shows us whom we can trust to share information and from whom we can accept information without further checking (Tang & Liu, 2015). A precise set of beliefs comprising competence, honesty, and consideration for the other person define trust (Gefen, 2002). Capability refers to the other party's aptitude and competency and when someone has integrity, they adhere to the standards of behavior honestly and fulfill their commitments (Mayer & Davis, 1999). The intent of the other party to achieve a justifiable profit by wishing the best for the client is what defines benevolence. Since there are more uncertainties owing to impersonal variables and distance, which are challenges that do not exist in physical selling, trust plays a significant part in online retailing's success (Featherman & Hajli, 2016; Li, Jiang, & Wu, 2014).

It has been empirically proven that the trust factor has a more personal influence on social media platforms (Wang, Min, & Han, 2016). As internet connectivity increases, users believe they need more security and trust to lower perceived transaction risks (Gefen & Straub, 2004; Hajli & Lin, 2016). Using social technologies, where users express their thoughts about products and services on social networks and online communities, as well as give ratings, suggestions, and feedback might be one approach to solving this issue (Hajli, 2015). Getting feedback from a person with a good reputation in social networks and online communities is another method that makes it possible to build trust throughout the online shopping process (Lu, Zhao, & Wang, 2010).

Consumers perceiving social media as trustworthy will drive E-WOM and product information and opinion seeking (Hennig-Thurau et al., 2004). Trustworthiness is important for those who want to evaluate product information and opinions on social media, and it has an impact on E-WOM involvement. Trust based on E-WOM drives purchase behavior, as users consult reviews made by other users on Instagram to reduce the perceived risk of buying products recommended by their idols (Djafarova & Rushworth, 2017). Then again, Hajli (2015) found that the concept of social e-commerce, which includes social networks like forums and online communities as well as assessments and suggestions made by customers online, has a significant influence on the trust factor. It was shown that social media user interactions boost consumers' trust, and that trust has the most influence on purchase intention (Hajli, 2015). Research has revealed that trust is a critical component that affects both real customer behavior and online purchasing intents and processes (Aljifri, Pons, & Collins, 2003; Buttner & Goritz, 2008; Hajli, 2014; Hong & Cho, 2011).

2.5. Trust in Influencers

Customers trust what influencers say and do define influencer-related trust (Chetioui et al., 2020). Fashion influencers have a significant impact on customers' shopping decisions and set trends that followers feel compelled to imitate because they think influencers are knowledgeable about fashion and voice their own opinions (Sudha & Sheena, 2017). Trust in an influencer and therefore influences, changing customer sentiments (Miller & Baseheart, 1969; Ohanian, 1990). Influencers' educational material boosts customers' perceptions of brands as trustworthy, which improves their propensity to make purchases (Lou & Yuan, 2019). Regarding blogging, readers' perceptions of the blogger's credibility influence their decision to buy the products discussed (Hsu, Lin, & Chiang, 2013). Santiago et al. (2020) found that trust in a fashion influencer has a statistically significant impact on consumers' intentions to buy the fashion products they are promoting. Perceived credibility toward the fashion influencer is the second element that most affect customers' views and buying intentions, according to Chetioui et al. (2020).

2.6. Consumer Knowledge

Consumer knowledge of the environment is defined as the factual knowledge that people have about the environment, the ecology of the planet, and the impact of human actions on the environment (Arcury & Johnson, 1987). Consumers who are knowledgeable about the environment typically care more about it and take it into account when making decisions (Kim & Damhorst, 1998). Additionally, the authors found that customers who are knowledgeable and conscious of environmental concerns about fashion products are more inclined to purchase used or recycled clothing. According to Lang & Wei (2019), customers who are aware of how fashion affects the environment are more likely to think about the environmental effects of their purchases before making them.

Vehmas et al. (2018) noticed that customers had a low level of understanding about how clothing is created, including the environmental effects of using synthetic fibers and intensive cotton farming. Ritch (2015) further emphasizes how customers are little aware of the environmental effect associated with the creation of fashion products and how many consumers strive to steer clear of purchasing products created under exploitative circumstances.

Consumer knowledge is made up of familiarity knowledge and product knowledge, according to Kang et al. (2013). Consumer knowledge is also examined more in connection to product familiarity and product knowledge than concerning knowledge of the environment in general. They also argue that consumers' behavioral intentions toward these products can be influenced by their familiarity with the products and their understanding of them based on prior experiences. As a result, the authors conclude that consumers develop positive perceptions and attitudes about consuming sustainable fashion products when they have a high level of information and experiences about such products, which suggests that they have higher intentions regarding purchase behavior.

Lang & Wei (2019) realized that environmental fashion awareness affects consumers' intentions to buy transformable, or reusable, clothing, and for Kang et al. (2013), the intention to purchase sustainable fashion products has a tangential link. Zheng & Chi (2015) revealed that environmental awareness among consumers has a substantial impact as a mediator between attitudes and intentions to buy sustainable fashion products.

2.7. Environmental Beliefs

Environmental beliefs are defined as judgments about behavior or product specific (about purchasing a particular product or engaging in a particular pro-environmental action) or general (about the environment and green consumerism) (Pagiaslis & Krontalis, 2014). Environmentally conscious consumers understand the value of making decisions that protect the environment, which suggests that they will engage in more sustainable behaviors (Lang & Wei, 2019). Sharma et al. (2017) observed that customers' purchase decisions are significantly influenced by their environmental attitudes. Additionally, Lang & Wei (2019) revealed that environmental beliefs have a strong impact on consumers' attitudes toward transformable fashion as well as toward subjective norms of sustainable consumption behavior. Environmental beliefs also exert a positive influence on the purchase intention of transformable or reused, fashion. Consumers that are intrinsically driven by environmental concerns are more likely to look for environmental preservation solutions, claim Davari & Strutto (2014). Therefore, even if it implies that they must pay more than they would for non-green products, people still think that by purchasing and using green products, they will help the environment.

2.8. Willingness to Pay More

Although customers care about sustainability, they are unable to translate their intentions into sustainable purchasing behaviors. As a result, price is seen as one of the major hurdles separating attitude and behavior toward sustainable fashion (Wiederhold & Martinez, 2018). They noticed that survey participants believed the high price was one of the primary reasons influencing their purchase of sustainable fashion products since the price is the primary criterion for them when making a clothes buy. Participants in Joergens' (2006) survey believed that ethical concerns were not taken into account when purchasing clothing and that price was the deciding factor since they would rather purchase more clothing at a low cost than worry about the ethical implications of clothing manufacture.

Customers who are interested in fashion are unlikely to purchase sustainable products if they believe the price is too high (T. Chang & Wong, 2012). Similarly, Roberts (1996) reported that consumers will not buy green products if they believe they are excessively pricey. Although these participants claimed they intended to be more sustainable and to be more involved with sustainable fashion, Mcneill & Moore

(2015) reported some of the participants mentioned that the high cost of sustainable fashion brands was a significant barrier to purchasing sustainable clothing.

Environmentally conscious customers are prepared to pay more for sustainable products to protect the environment (Ferraro, Uchida, & Conrad, 2005). Davari & Strutton (2014) also come to the same conclusion, finding that consumers who care about the environment and its preservation through their purchases are not concerned about paying extra for these products.

2.9. Brand Awareness

The likelihood and ease with which a brand name comes to mind are both indicators of brand awareness (Keller, 1993). Therefore, it stands out by the possibility and simplicity with which the brand name emerges in the consumer's thoughts and is defined by the consumer being able to recognize the brand in a variety of settings. According to the author, brand awareness is made up of the consumer's recognition and performance recall of the brand they have experienced. When a customer thinks about a certain product category and recalls a particular brand, brand awareness becomes crucial. In addition, brand awareness can influence the deliberation stage of the choice regarding which brands to pick. The development and strength of brand associations related to the brand image that is seen by the customer in connection to it are what drive the effect of brand awareness on the consumer's decision-making process (Keller, 1993).

Customers prefer to buy products from brands they are aware of and are familiar with while they are in the early stages of the buying process. Barreda et al. (2015)'s study showed that brand awareness is important for consumer decision-making through the E-WOM that is created by customers about the brand on social media. As social media has grown, businesses believe that these platforms may change consumer perceptions of their products and create favorable online reviews. In a similar line, Langaro et al. (2018) uncovered that customer behavior significantly and favorably affects brand awareness involvement. Influencer marketing is vital to consumers' purchase decisions since it increases brand recognition among followers who are the brand's target customers, which results in higher sales (Lou & Yuan, 2019). Similarly, the authors discovered that an influencer's credibility includes the expertise, trustworthiness, attractiveness, and similarity characteristics that consumers perceive them to possess. They also revealed that the influencer's expertise and attractiveness have a positive impact on brand awareness through publications about brands that they have created. Finally, Lou & Yuan (2019) found that customer perceptions of brand awareness have a substantial impact on purchase intention and that consumers' confidence in influencer-created material about brands is important for the growth of brand awareness and brand buy intention. Concerning E-WOM, Chakraborty & Bhat (2018) exposed that the credibility of reviews made about brands on social media exerts a significant relationship with brand awareness and, as a result, brand awareness also indicates a significant relationship with the purchase intention of the brand mentioned in E-WOM.

2.10. Intention to Purchase

The consumer's decision to buy the product at a later time after acquiring the appropriate information represents their purchasing intention (Saxena, 2011). Purchase intentions connect to the individual's awareness strategy for attempting to buy a product from a particular brand (Spears & Singh, 2004) since purchase intentions depict the likelihood that consumers are prepared to buy a specific product (Lou & Yuan, 2019). For Santiago et al. (2020), a consumer's purchasing intention is tied to a certain time or circumstance when they are willing to make the buy but the purchasing intention is related to consumer perceptions, attitudes, and behaviors, claim Mirabi et al. (2015). The intention variable serves as the most accurate predictor of a particular individual's conduct (Fishbein & Ajzen, 1975, as referred to in Dewanto & Belgiawan, 2020). For Chang and Watchravesringkan (2018), there is a significant link between consumers' behavioral intentions toward buying sustainable fashion products and their actual consumption. Pereira (2020) adds that the intention to consume environmentally sustainable textile and fashion products influences the actual purchasing behavior of these products. In agreement, Dewanto & Belgiawan (2020) determined that the intention to purchase sustainable fashion products exerts a positive, significant, and highly influential impact on the purchase of the same products.

3. RESEARCH HYPOTHESES

The literature review allowed different authors to identify the effect of the influencer and the E-WOM on purchase intention, specifically concerning fashion products. Based on this, it is anticipated that this study will confirm the relationship between the effect of the influencer's determinants and the E-WOM on the intention to buy sustainable fashion products, and it aims to establish a relationship between consumer trust, performance expectations, knowledge, and environmental beliefs, as well as the awareness of the sustainable fashion brands cited by influencers and the E-WOM. Additionally, we want to examine the connection between customers' intentions to purchase and their willingness to pay extra for sustainable fashion products.

Determining relationships between constructs that haven't been previously studied as well as validating inferences between constructs mentioned in the literature review were the goals of the hypotheses that were developed based on a heuristic process given the gap in the literature on the subject under study. Table 1 contains the definition of the constructs, research hypotheses and scales, and their authors.

Table 1. Constructs definitions, research hypotheses, and scales

Constructs	Definitions and Research Hypotheses	Scales
Influencer Credibility	The extent to which the consumer believes that the influencer conveys information that has knowledge and experience about sustainable fashion. • H1a: Influencer credibility positively affects the intention to purchase sustainable fashion products. • H1b: Influencer credibility positively affects influencer trust toward sustainable fashion products. • H1c: Influencer credibility positively affects consumers' performance expectations toward sustainable fashion products. • H1d: Influencer credibility positively affects consumer knowledge of sustainable fashion products. • H1e: Influencer credibility positively affects consumers' environmental beliefs toward sustainable fashion products. • H1f: Influencer credibility positively affects the brand awareness of the promoted sustainable fashion brand.	Chetioui et al. (2020)
Influencer Expertise	Perception of whether the influencer shares valid and accurate information on sustainable fashion. • H2a: Influencer expertise positively affects the purchase intention of sustainable fashion products. • H2b: Influencer expertise positively affects influencer trust toward sustainable fashion products. • H2c: Influencer expertise positively affects consumer performance expectations toward sustainable fashion products. • H2d: Influencer expertise positively affects consumer knowledge of sustainable fashion products. • H2e: Influencer expertise positively affects consumer environmental beliefs toward sustainable fashion products. • H2f: Influencer expertise positively affects promoted sustainable fashion brand awareness	Chetioui et al. (2020)
Influencer Similarity	The degree to which the consumer believes it is similar to the influencer by sharing the same values, characteristics, and lifestyles. • H3a: Influencer similarity positively affects the intention to purchase sustainable fashion products. • H3b: Influencer similarity positively affects influencer trust in sustainable fashion products. • H3c: Influencer similarity positively affects consumers' performance expectations toward sustainable fashion products. • H3d: Influencer similarity positively affects consumer knowledge of sustainable fashion products. • H3e: Influencer similarity positively affects consumers' environmental beliefs toward sustainable fashion products. • H3f: Influencer similarity positively affects the brand awareness of the promoted sustainable fashion brand.	Taylor, Halstead, & Haynes (2010)
Influencer's Parasocial Relationship	Perception of the relationship created between consumer and influencer. • H4a: The parasocial relationship with the influencer positively affects the purchase intention of sustainable fashion products. • H4b: The parasocial relationship with the influencer positively affects the influencer's trust in sustainable fashion products. • H4c: The parasocial relationship with the influencer positively affects the consumer's performance expectation towards sustainable fashion products. • H4d: The parasocial relationship with the influencer positively affects the consumer's knowledge about sustainable fashion products. • H4e: The parasocial relationship with the influencer positively affects the consumer's environmental beliefs toward sustainable fashion products. • H4f: The parasocial relationship with the influencer positively affects the awareness of the sustainable fashion brand promoted.	Farivar et al. (2021)
E-WOM Homophily	Perception of consumer similarity towards people who write reviews about sustainable fashion. • H5a: E-WOM homophily positively affects purchase intention for sustainable fashion products. • H5b: E-WOM homophily positively affects consumer trust in digital social media for sustainable fashion products. • H5c: E-WOM homophily positively affects consumers' performance expectations toward sustainable fashion products. • H5d: E-WOM homophily positively affects consumer knowledge of sustainable fashion products. • H5e: E-WOM homophily positively affects consumers' environmental beliefs toward sustainable fashion products. • H5f: E-WOM homophily positively affects the brand awareness of promoted sustainable fashion.	Taylor et al. (2010)
E-WOM Expertise	Perception on whether the people who write comments publish valid and accurate information about sustainable fashion. • H6a: E-WOM expertise positively affects purchase intention toward sustainable fashion products. • H6b: E-WOM expertise positively affects consumer trust in digital social media for sustainable fashion products. • H6c: E-WOM expertise positively affects consumers' performance expectations toward sustainable fashion products. • H6d: E-WOM expertise positively affects consumer knowledge of sustainable fashion products. • H6e: E-WOM expertise positively affects consumers' environmental beliefs toward sustainable fashion products. • H6f: E-WOM expertise positively affects the awareness of the promoted sustainable fashion brand.	Kim et al. (2013)
Trust in the Influencer	The degree to which the consumer believes in what the influencer talks about sustainable fashion. • H7: Trust in the influencer positively affects the purchase intention of sustainable fashion products.	Chetioui et al. (2020)
Trust in Social Media	The extent to which the consumer believes in the people who write commentaries on sustainable fashion. • H8: Trust in digital social media positively affects the intention to purchase sustainable fashion products.	Kim et al. (2013)
Performance Expectation	Consumer perception of publications on products from social media sustainable fashion products in media. • H9: Performance expectancy positively affects the purchase intention of sustainable fashion products.	Loureiro et al. (2018)
Consumer Knowledge	Factual consumer perception of sustainable fashion products. • H10: Consumer knowledge positively affects the purchase intention of sustainable fashion products.	Kang et al. (2013)
Environmental Beliefs	Convictions about the environment. • H11: Environmental beliefs positively affect the purchase of sustainable fashion products.	Lang & Wei (2019)
Brand Awareness	The likelihood that the name of a brand of sustainable fashion arises in the consumer's memory. • H12: Brand awareness positively affects the purchase intention of sustainable fashion products.	Boonghee et al. (2000); Xiaoli & Kwangjun 2007)
Willingness to Pay More	Willingness to pay a premium price for sustainable fashion products as against fast fashion products. • H13: Predisposition to pay more positively affects the purchase intention of sustainable fashion products.	Chaudhary & Bisai (2018)
Purchase Intention	Predisposition to buy products of sustainable fashion.	Kang et al. (2013)

Based on the information in Table 1, presented above, which contains the definitions, constructs, and hypotheses, the conceptual model was developed and is illustrated in Figure 1.

Figure 1. Conceptual model

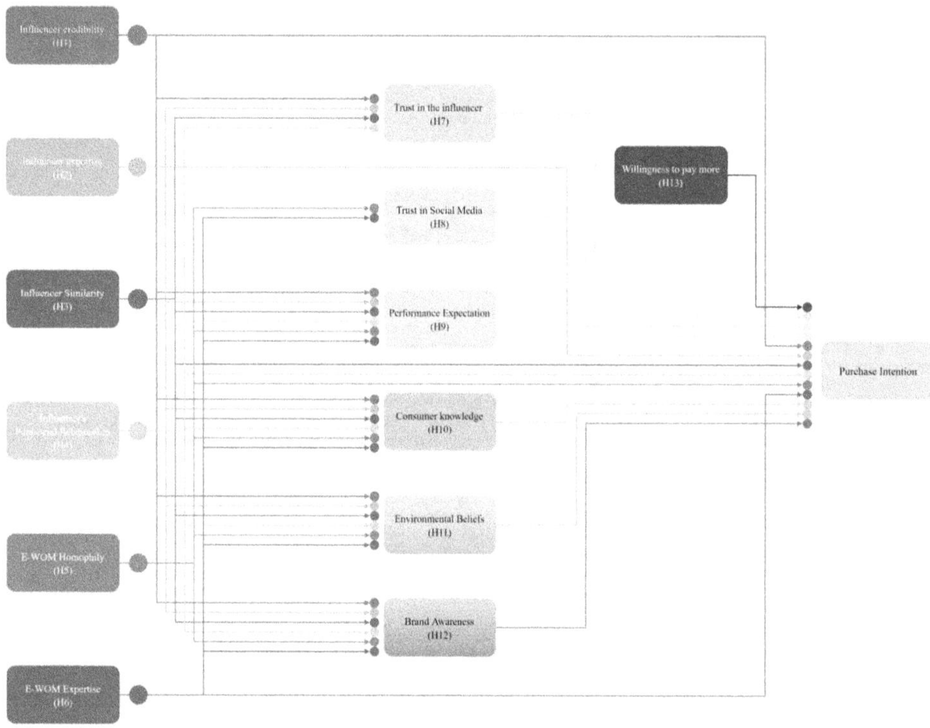

4. METHODOLOGY

To answer the research question and test the research hypotheses that were developed based on the literature evaluation, this study is quantitative. Thus, it is stated that quantitative research is based on the observation of objective facts, events, and phenomena that exist independently of the researcher and is based on the methodical process of acquiring observable and quantifiable data. Moreover, quantitative research uses statistics to undertake data analysis to quantify the data and generalize the sample results to the target population (Malhotra, 2001).

4.1. Sample and Sampling

All Portuguese adults over the age of eighteen, of both sexes, who use social media, comprise the study's target demographic, and the non-probabilistic convenience sampling method was used. Since the respondents were solicited to participate in the research using social networks like Facebook, Instagram, WhatsApp, and LinkedIn, the sample was chosen as a result of the respondents' use of social media. The foundation of the data collection was primary data using a questionnaire.

4.2. Structure of the Questionnaire

To further analyze the effect of influencers on the intention to purchase sustainable clothes, a questionnaire was created in Google Forms. A pre-test with 11 participants was conducted before the release of the questionnaire to validate it, identify any errors, and accept comments to ensure that all participants understood.

There were seventeen sections in the questionnaire. The objective is explained in the first section, along with a definition of sustainable fashion, and the confidentiality and anonymity of the responses are guaranteed. A question in the second section provides for the verification of the respondent's involvement in the sustainable fashion market. If the responder does not currently purchase sustainable clothing, the participant is instructed to answer the subsequent questions while assuming that they will do so in the future. They are then directly directed to section three. The second section deals with the habit and purchase of sustainable fashion; it questions the frequency of purchases, the values of the most recent purchase, the brands that were commonly bought, and the locations where sustainable fashion products were most frequently purchased.

The respondents rate their level of agreement or disagreement with a series of statements about each of the constructs of the conceptual model using a 7-point horizontal Likert scale between sections three and sixteen of the questionnaire. The seven-point Likert scale is a rating system that has seven response options. Point 1 denotes "strongly disagree," while point 4 denotes "neither agree nor disagree," and point 7 denotes "strongly agree."

The last section is section seventeen, in which demographic details about the sample are provided. So, in addition to asking about gender, age, education level, and location of residence, the survey also asks about the size of the household, the number of dependents, and the gross monthly income.

5. ANALYSIS AND RESULTS

Structural equation modeling makes it possible to estimate the cause-and-effect relationship of the models with the latent variables because it allows for the estimation of the coefficients that maximize the explained variance of the latent variables. The conceptual model was verified using the Partial Least Squares – Structural Equation Model (Hair Jr et al., 2014) and SmartPLS was used.

5.1. Characterization of the Habit and Purchase of Sustainable Fashion

Analyzing the answers, 220 of the 434 respondents are buyers of sustainable clothing. The fact that 47.3 percent of consumers buy sustainable fashion products once every three months, 20 percent buy them once every month, and 11.8 percent buy them more frequently than once every three months, with the remaining options being negligible, is noteworthy. Regarding the amount spent in the past year on sustainable fashion products, respondents reported that they spent an average of 175€. The average cost of the most recent purchase of sustainable fashion products is 53.71€. When given the option to choose from more than one answer to the question about where you typically purchase sustainable fashion products, nearly 50% of consumers choose to do so online. It's also interesting to note that 37.7% of respondents typically purchase from physical second-hand stores, while 38.6% prefer to shop online for used clothing. Additionally, 25.9% of customers who purchase sustainable fashion do so in the brands' physical stores.

5.2. Model Evaluation and Results

Based on the sample's (N=434) evaluation of the model, it was discovered that the model's structure had collinearity issues, which were resolved by eliminating constructs. The influencer's expertise construct was omitted as a result of multiple attempts to establish the best fit.

The outer model sometimes referred to as measurement models, shows how latent variables relate to their corresponding measures. There are two sorts of relationships between constructs and measures: formative and reflecting. Reflective methods consider that the indicators come from the underlying construct, while formative measurement models are characterized by indicators emanating from the construct (Hair Jr et al., 2014). To determine if a concept is formative or reflective when it consists of at least four signs, one turned to confirmatory tetrad analysis in SmartPLS. When all indicators' lower and upper confidence interval values have the same sign, then the constructs are formative (Wong, 2019). Additionally, a construct is considered reflective if at least one of its indicators has a positive upper confidence interval value and a negative lower confidence interval value. Influencer credibility is the only formative construct; the others are reflecting.

The evaluation of the reflective measurement model is composed by checking the reliability of the internal consistency, through Cronbach's alpha and composite reliability, through convergent validity, analyzing the external loadings and the average variance extracted, and, finally, by discriminant validity according to the Fornell-Larcker criterion (Hair Jr et al., 2014).

- All constructs show a Cronbach's alpha of at least 0.837.
- The average reliability value for each construct is at least 0.905, which is greater than the minimum permitted value. Therefore, it may be said that internal consistency reliability is attained given the values of Cronbach's alpha and composite reliability.
- All the reflective indicators' exterior loading results are higher than the minimum allowed value, thus they should all be preserved.
- In terms of convergent validity, it can be said that it has been attained because all constructs have values greater than 0.5.
- Additionally, discriminant validity has been attained.

Analyzing convergent validity, checking for potential model collinearity issues, and analyzing the significance and relevance of the external weights are the procedures necessary to evaluate a formative measurement model (Hair Jr et al., 2014). Since there is no question in the questionnaire to test the convergent validity of the formative constructs, the convergent validity stage was not carried out. The VIF of each construct indicator leads to the conclusion that no collinearity issues exist.

The significance and relevance of the external weights, which assess the relative contribution of an indicator to its corresponding construct, are the final steps in evaluating the formative mediation model. According to Hair Jr et al. (2014), non-significant indicators should retain their external weights even if their external loadings are more than 0.50. Due to the external loadings of all the influencer credibility construct indicators being more than 0.5, all external weights indicators should be maintained.

Table 2. Hypothesis test

Hypotheses	Coefficient	p-Value	Results
H1a: Influencer Credibility => Purchase Intention	0,102	0,131	Not supported
H1b: Influencer Credibility => Trust in the Influencer	0,382	0,000	Supported
H1c: Influencer Credibility => Performance Expectation	0,347	0,000	Supported
H1d: Influencer Credibility => Consumer Knowledge	0,013	0,839	Not supported
H1e: Influencer Credibility => Environmental Beliefs	0,193	0,003	Supported
H1f: Influencer Credibility => Brand awareness	0,023	0,131	Not supported
H3a: Influencer Similarity => Purchase Intention	-0,016	0,829	Not supported
H3b: Influencer Similarity => Trust in Influencer	0,249	0,000	Supported
H3c: Influencer Similarity => Performance Expectation	0,149	0,023	Supported
H3d: Influencer Similarity => Consumer Knowledge	0,162	0,019	Supported
H3e: Influencer Similarity => Environmental Beliefs	0,240	0,000	Supported
H3f: Influencer Similarity => Brand Awareness	0,171	0,025	Supported
H4a: Parasocial Relationship with Influencer => Purchase Intention	0,025	0,703	Not supported
H4b: Parasocial Relationship with Influencer => Trust in Influencer	0,265	0,000	Supported
H4c: Parasocial Relationship with the Influencer => Performance Expectation	0,049	0,409	Not supported
H4d: Parasocial Relationship with the Influencer => Consumer Knowledge	0,160	0,019	Supported
H4e: Parasocial relationship with the Influencer => Environmental Beliefs	-0,001	0,990	Not supported
H4f: Parasocial relationship with the Influencer => Brand Awareness	0,129	0,075	Not supported
H5a: E-WOM homophily => Purchase Intention	0,028	0,711	Not supported
H5b: E-WOM homophily => Trust in Digital Social Media	0,477	0,000	Supported
H5c: E-WOM homophily => Performance Expectancy	0,187	0,004	Supported
H5d: E-WOM homophily => Consumer Knowledge	0,249	0,000	Supported
H5e: E-WOM homophily => Environmental Beliefs	-0,019	0,783	Not supported
H5f: E-WOM homophily => Brand awareness	0,137	0,071	Not supported
H6a: E-WOM Expertise => Purchase Intention	0,079	0,111	Not supported
H6b: E-WOM Expertise => Trust in Digital Social Media	0,238	0,000	Supported
H6c: E-WOM expertise => Performance Expectancy	0,077	0,095	Not supported
H6d: E-WOM Expertise => Consumer Knowledge	0,052	0,335	Not supported
H6e: E-WOM expertise => Environmental Beliefs	0,035	0,488	Not supported
H6f: E-WOM expertise => Brand awareness	-0,003	0,957	Not supported
H7: Trust in Influencer => Purchase Intention	0,040	0,599	Not supported
H8: Trust in Social Media => Purchase Intention	-0,039	0,510	Not supported
H9: Performance Expectation => Purchase Intention	0,113	0,110	Not supported
H10: Consumer Knowledge => Purchase Intention	0.287	0.000	Supported
H11: Environmental Beliefs => Purchase Intention	0,046	0,296	Not supported
H12: Brand Awareness => Purchase Intention	0,124	0,105	Not supported
H13: Willingness to Pay More => Purchase Intention	0,192	0,000	Supported

The structural model known as the inner model consists of the latent variables and their respective relationships in the model. The first step, to check for collinearity, corresponds to the evaluation of a set of predictor constructs. As with the informative measurement models, if the variance inflation factor is between 0.2 and 5, there are no collinearity problems, which is the case. The analysis of the significance and relevance of the connections between the constructs, as indicated by the validation of the hypotheses, constitutes the second step. The coefficients' values, which range from -1 to +1, are determined by the PLS-SEM algorithm technique. In general, statistical significance is given to coefficients with values near these two values since they are seen to show a strong association between the two entities. It is likely that weak relationships and coefficient values near zero show that they are not statistically significant. Table 2 contains a summary of the results and allows for the verification of the research hypotheses initially formulated.

The data presented is somewhat limited, and there is a remarkable set that could be included, but for reasons of limitations the authors cannot present additional information: confirmatory tetrad analysis, internal consistency reliability measures, external loadings values of the reflective constructs, average extracted variance, discriminant validity, VIF values of the outer model, values of the external weights, external loadings values of the formative constructs, VIF values of the inner model, coefficient of determination values, effect size values, and predictive relevance values. It should also be pointed out that the analysis was performed with the moderator variable that distinguishes sustainable fashion buyers, and the results showed no differences between the two groups.

5.3. Discussion

Based on the information contained in Table 2, it is pertinent to contrast the results obtained with what was obtained in the literature reviewed. It is appropriate to remember that a significant part of the research hypotheses formulated arose from fashion literature and was transposed to this new trend which is sustainable fashion. Consequently, the discrepancy that was obtained between the results and what is prescribed in the literature is relevant. These conclusions are quite disappointing from a strict perspective of when you want to prove something, but at the same time, they are very encouraging when they show that generality cannot apply to the specific. And in this case, the generality of the prescriptions in the fashion literature that deal with the impact of influencers and social media is not fully applicable to sustainable fashion.

The most significant result is that purchase intention is only influenced by consumer knowledge and willingness to pay more constructs. For the other constructs, no statistical relationship was established. Since the willingness to pay more construct has no antecedents, it is, therefore, pertinent to evaluate which constructs influence the consumer knowledge construct.

An intriguing result is the absence of a relationship between influencer credibility and consumer knowledge, meaning that influencers may be credible but the knowledge they deliver may not be accepted by consumers. As for similarity with the influencer, this has a positive influence on consumer knowledge, meaning that the greater the similarity between them, the more likely it is that the information transmitted by the influencer will be accepted by the consumer. The same happens with the construct parasocial relationship with the influencer.

Finally, only the E-WOM homophily construct influences the consumer knowledge construct, whereas this does not occur with the E-WOM Expertise construct. This is in line with the conclusion identified above, in which similarity and the parasocial relationship with the influencer have an impact on consumer knowledge, but credibility does not. Thus, it is conceivable to hypothesize that for the consumer, proximity is more important than the credibility and expertise attributed to the influencer. To sum up, findings show that the construct purchasing intention is only influenced consumer knowledge and willingness to pay more.

6. CONCLUSION

Since this is one of the precursor studies on the topic, a void was found in the study of literature addressing the effect of influencers and E-WOM on the sustainable fashion industry. Due to the association between influencers and E-WOM and sustainable fashion purchase intention that has been established in the literature, this research sought to determine the determinants that verify this association.

The conceptual model created is centered on understanding the influence of E-WOM homophily and expertise, as well as the digital social media user's perception of the influencer's credibility, expertise, similarity, and parasocial relationship characteristics on their intention to purchase sustainable fashion. It also explores how influencers and E-WOM characteristics affect users' perceptions of trust in influencers and social media, performance expectations for sustainable fashion products, consumer knowledge and beliefs about the environment, as well as consumer awareness of sustainable fashion brands, and ultimately confirms the impact on their purchase intention. Finally, it examines the connection between purchase intention and willingness to pay more.

The results obtained indicate that consumer knowledge and willingness to pay more are the only constructs that positively affect the purchase intention of sustainable fashion. Furthermore, consumer knowledge is the construct that exerts the greatest impact on purchase intention. Regarding the influencer and E-WOM, similarity and homophily are the characteristics with the most validated hypotheses, which means that the similarity perceived towards influencers and content written by users with whom they positively identify affects trust in social media, the performance expectation of sustainable fashion products advertised and the consumer's knowledge regarding sustainable fashion. This means that consumers favor similarity over credibility and expertise.

The research findings are valuable for sustainable fashion brands by providing relevant guidance. Brands should invest in social media marketing with technical informative content about what constitutes sustainable fashion, the advantages of using it, and how the brand supports sustainability in fashion through its products. This is because the more informed social media users are the more likely they are to purchase the products of sustainable fashion brands. This research is of high relevance as there is little literature on the relationship between influencer and E-WOM characteristics and purchase intention of sustainable fashion.

REFERENCES

Alhidari, A., Iyer, P., & Paswan, A. (2015). Personal level antecedents of eWOM and purchase intention, on social networking sites. *Journal of Customer Behaviour, 14*(2), 107–125. doi:10.1362/147539215X14373846805707

Aljifri, H. A., Pons, A., & Collins, D. (2003). Global e-commerce: A framework for understanding and overcoming the trust barrier. *Information Management & Computer Security, 11*(2–3), 130–138. doi:10.1108/09685220310480417

Arcury, T. A., & Johnson, T. P. (1987). Public environmental knowledge a statewide survey. *The Journal of Environmental Education, 18*(4), 31–37. doi:10.1080/00958964.1987.9942746

Barreda, A. A., Bilgihan, A., Nusair, K., & Okumus, F. (2015). Generating brand awareness in Online Social Networks. *Computers in Human Behavior*, *50*, 600–609. doi:10.1016/j.chb.2015.03.023

Bergkvist, L., Hjalmarson, H., Mägi, A. W., & Bergkvist, L. (2016). *A new model of how celebrity endorsements work: Attitude toward the endorsement as a mediator of celebrity source and endorsement effects*. Academic Press.

Boonghee, Y., Naveen, D., & Sungho, L. (2000). An Examination of Selected Marketing Mix Elements and Brand Equity. *Journal of the Academy of Marketing Science*, *28*(2), 195–211. doi:10.1177/0092070300282002

Buttner, O. B., & Goritz, A. S. (2008). Perceived trustworthiness of online shops. *Journal of Consumer Behaviour*, *50*(October), 35–50. doi:10.1002/cb.235

Casaló, L. V., Flavián, C., & Ibáñez-Sánchez, S. (2020a). Influencers on Instagram: Antecedents and consequences of opinion leadership. *Journal of Business Research, 117*, 510–519.

Casaló, L. V., Flavián, C., & Ibáñez-Sánchez, S. (2020b). Influencers on Instagram: Antecedents and consequences of opinion leadership. *Journal of Business Research, 117*, 510–519.

Cervellon, M. C., & Wernerfelt, A. S. (2012). Knowledge sharing among green fashion communities online: Lessons for the sustainable supply chain. *Journal of Fashion Marketing and Management*, *16*(2), 176–192. doi:10.1108/13612021211222860

Chakraborty, U., & Bhat, S. (2018). The Effects of Credible Online Reviews on Brand Equity Dimensions and Its Consequence on Consumer Behavior. *Journal of Promotion Management*, *24*(1), 57–82. doi:10.1080/10496491.2017.1346541

Chang, H. J., & Watchravesringkan, K. (2018). Who are sustainably minded apparel shoppers? An investigation to the influencing factors of sustainable apparel consumption. *International Journal of Retail & Distribution Management*, *46*(2), 148–162. doi:10.1108/IJRDM-10-2016-0176

Chang, T., & Wong, C. W. Y. (2012). The consumption side of sustainable fashion supply chain. *Journal of Fashion Marketing and Management*, *16*(2), 193–215. doi:10.1108/13612021211222824

Chaudhary, R., & Bisai, S. (2018). Factors influencing green purchase behavior of millennials in India. *Management of Environmental Quality*, *29*(5), 798–812. doi:10.1108/MEQ-02-2018-0023

Chen, J., Teng, L., Yu, Y., & Yu, X. (2016). The effect of online information sources on purchase intentions between consumers with high and low susceptibility to informational influence. *Journal of Business Research*, *69*(2), 467–475. doi:10.1016/j.jbusres.2015.05.003

Chetioui, Y., Benlafqih, H., & Lebdaoui, H. (2020). How fashion influencers contribute to consumers' purchase intention. *Journal of Fashion Marketing and Management*, *24*(3), 361–380. doi:10.1108/JFMM-08-2019-0157

Cheung, C. M. K., & Thadani, D. R. (2012). The impact of electronic word-of-mouth communication: A literature analysis and integrative model. *Decision Support Systems*, *54*(1), 461–470. doi:10.1016/j.dss.2012.06.008

Chih, W. H., Wang, K. Y., Hsu, L. C., & Huang, S. C. (2013). Investigating electronic wordof-mouth effects on online discussion forums: The role of perceived positive electronic word-of-mouth review credibility. *Cyberpsychology, Behavior, and Social Networking*, *16*(9), 658–668. doi:10.1089/cyber.2012.0364 PMID:23895466

Chu, S. C., & Kim, Y. (2011). Determinants of consumer engagement in electronic Word-OfMouth (eWOM) in social networking sites. *International Journal of Advertising*, *30*(1), 47–75. doi:10.2501/IJA-30-1-047-075

Ciasullo, M. V., Maione, G., Torre, C., & Troisi, O. (2017). What about sustainability? An empirical analysis of consumers' purchasing behavior in fashion context. *Sustainability (Basel)*, *9*(9), 1–18. doi:10.3390u9091617

Connell, K. Y. H. (2010). Internal and external barriers to eco-conscious apparel acquisition. *International Journal of Consumer Studies*, *34*(3), 279–286. doi:10.1111/j.1470-6431.2010.00865.x

Davari, A., & Strutton, D. (2014). Marketing mix strategies for closing the gap between green consumers' pro-environmental beliefs and behaviors. *Journal of Strategic Marketing*, *22*(7), 563–586. doi:10.1080/0965254X.2014.914059

de Lenne, O., & Vandenbosch, L. (2017). Media and sustainable apparel buying intention. *Journal of Fashion Marketing and Management*, *21*(4), 483–498. doi:10.1108/JFMM-11-2016-0101

Dellarocas, C., Zhang, X., & Awad, N. F. (2007). Exploring the value of online product reviews in forecasting sales: The case of motion pictures. *Journal of Interactive Marketing*, *21*(4), 23–45. doi:10.1002/dir.20087

Dewanto, K. N., & Belgiawan, P. F. (2020). The Influence of Social Norms and Attitude In Sustainable Fashion Product Purchase Behaviour. *American International Journal of Business Management*, *3*(7), 64–75.

Djafarova, E., & Rushworth, C. (2017). Exploring the credibility of online celebrities' Instagram profiles in influencing the purchase decisions of young female users. *Computers in Human Behavior*, *68*, 1–7. doi:10.1016/j.chb.2016.11.009

Duan, W., Gu, B., & Whinston, A. B. (2008). Do online reviews matter? - An empirical investigation of panel data. *Decision Support Systems*, *45*(4), 1007–1016. doi:10.1016/j.dss.2008.04.001

Farivar, S., Wang, F., & Yuan, Y. (2021). Opinion leadership vs. para-social relationship: Key factors in influencer marketing. *Journal of Retailing and Consumer Services, 59*, 102371.

Featherman, M. S., & Hajli, N. (2016). Self-Service Technologies and e-Services Risks in Social Commerce Era. *Journal of Business Ethics*, *139*(2), 251–269. doi:10.100710551-015-2614-4

Ferraro, P. J., Uchida, T., & Conrad, J. M. (2005). Price premiums for eco-friendly commodities: Are "green" markets the best way to protect endangered ecosystems? *Environmental and Resource Economics*, *32*(3), 419–438. doi:10.100710640-005-7962-6

Fishbein, M., & Ajzen, I. (1975). *Belief, attitude, intention and behaviour: An introduction to theory and research.* Academic Press.

Fletcher, K. (2010). Slow Fashion: An Invitation for Systems Change. *Fashion Practice*, *2*(2), 259–265. doi:10.2752/175693810X12774625387594

Gefen, D. (2000). E-commerce: The role of familiarity and trust. *Omega*, *28*(6), 725–737. doi:10.1016/S0305-0483(00)00021-9

Gefen, D. (2002). Reflections on the Dimensions of Trust and Trustworthiness among Online Consumers. *The Data Base for Advances in Information Systems*, *33*(3), 38–53. doi:10.1145/569905.569910

Gefen, D., & Straub, D. W. (2004). Consumer trust in B2C e-Commerce and the importance of social presence: Experiments in e-Products and e-Services. *Omega*, *32*(6), 407–424. doi:10.1016/j.omega.2004.01.006

Goworek, H., Fisher, T., Cooper, T., Woodward, S., & Hiller, A. (2012). The sustainable clothing market: An evaluation of potential strategies for UK retailers. *International Journal of Retail & Distribution Management*, *40*(12), 935–955. doi:10.1108/09590551211274937

Hair, J. F. Jr, Hult, G. T. M., Ringle, C., & Sarstedt, M. (2014). *A primer on partial least squares structural equation modeling (PLS-SEM)*. Sage Publications.

Hajli, N. (2014). A study of the impact of social media on consumers. *International Journal of Market Research*, *56*(3), 387–404. doi:10.2501/IJMR-2014-025

Hajli, N. (2015). Social commerce constructs and consumer's intention to buy. *International Journal of Information Management*, *35*(2), 183–191. doi:10.1016/j.ijinfomgt.2014.12.005

Hajli, N., & Lin, X. (2016). Exploring the Security of Information Sharing on Social Networking Sites: The Role of Perceived Control of Information. *Journal of Business Ethics*, *133*(1), 111–123. doi:10.100710551-014-2346-x

Harris, F., Roby, H., & Dibb, S. (2016). Sustainable clothing: Challenges, barriers and interventions for encouraging more sustainable consumer behaviour. *International Journal of Consumer Studies*, *40*(3), 309–318. doi:10.1111/ijcs.12257

Hayes, R. A., & Carr, C. T. (2015). *Does Being Social Matter? Effects of Enabled Commenting on Credibility and Brand Attitude in Social Media*. Academic Press.

Hennig-Thurau, T., Gwinner, K. P., Walsh, G., & Gremler, D. D. (2004). Electronic word-of- mouth via consumer-opinion platforms: What motivates consumers to articulate themselves on the Internet? *Journal of Interactive Marketing*, *18*(1), 38–52. doi:10.1002/dir.10073

Henninger, C. E., Alevizou, P. J., & Oates, C. J. (2016). What is sustainable fashion? *Journal of Fashion Marketing and Management*, *20*(4), 400–416. doi:10.1108/JFMM-07-2015-0052

Hong, I. B., & Cho, H. (2011). The impact of consumer trust on attitudinal loyalty and purchase intentions in B2C e-marketplaces: Intermediary trust vs. seller trust. *International Journal of Information Management*, *31*(5), 469–479. doi:10.1016/j.ijinfomgt.2011.02.001

Hsu, C. L., Lin, J. C. C., & Sen Chiang, H. (2013). The effects of blogger recommendations on customers' online shopping intentions. *Internet Research*, *23*(1), 69–88. doi:10.1108/10662241311295782

Jalilvand, M. R., & Samiei, N. (2012). The effect of electronic word of mouth on brand image and purchase intention: An empirical study in the automobile industry in Iran. *Marketing Intelligence & Planning*, *30*(4), 460–476. doi:10.1108/02634501211231946

Jang, S., Prasad, A., & Ratchford, B. T. (2012). How consumers use product reviews in the purchase decision process. *Marketing Letters*, *23*(3), 825–838. doi:10.100711002-012-9191-4

Jiménez-Castillo, D., & Sánchez-Fernández, R. (2019). The role of digital influencers in brand recommendation: Examining their impact on engagement, expected value and purchase intention. *International Journal of Information Management*, *49*(July), 366–376. doi:10.1016/j.ijinfomgt.2019.07.009

Joergens, C. (2006). Ethical fashion: Myth or future trend? *Journal of Fashion Marketing and Management*, *10*(3), 360–371. doi:10.1108/13612020610679321

Kang, J., Liu, C., & Kim, S. H. (2013). Environmentally sustainable textile and apparel consumption: The role of consumer knowledge, perceived consumer effectiveness and perceived personal relevance. *International Journal of Consumer Studies*, *37*(4), 442–452. doi:10.1111/ijcs.12013

Keller, K. L. (1993). Conceptualizing, Measuring, and Managing Customer-Based Brand Equity. *Journal of Marketing*, *57*(1), 1–22. doi:10.1177/002224299305700101

Kim, H. S., & Damhorst, M. L. (1998). Environmental concern and apparel consumption. *Clothing & Textiles Research Journal*, *16*(3), 126–133. doi:10.1177/0887302X9801600303

Kim, S., Park, J., & Lee, Y. (2013). The E-Word-of-Mouth effect on consumers Internet shopping behaviour: Focus on apparel products. *International Journal of Fashion Design, Technology and Education*, *6*(3), 160–172.

King, R. A., Racherla, P., & Bush, V. D. (2014). What we know and don't know about online word-of-mouth: A review and synthesis of the literature. *Journal of Interactive Marketing*, *28*(3), 167–183. doi:10.1016/j.intmar.2014.02.001

Kong, H. M., Ko, E., Chae, H., & Mattila, P. (2016). Understanding fashion consumers' attitude and behavioral intention toward sustainable fashion products: Focus on sustainable knowledge sources and knowledge types. *Journal of Global Fashion Marketing*, *7*(2), 103–119. doi:10.1080/20932685.2015.1131435

Lang, C., & Wei, B. (2019). Convert one outfit to more looks: factors influencing young female college consumers' intention to purchase transformable apparel. *Fashion and Textiles, 6*(1).

Langaro, D., Rita, P., & de Fátima Salgueiro, M. (2018). Do social networking sites contribute for building brands? Evaluating the impact of users' participation on brand awareness and brand attitude. *Journal of Marketing Communications*, *24*(2), 146–168. doi:10.1080/13527266.2015.1036100

Li, H., Jiang, J., & Wu, M. (2014). The effects of trust assurances on consumers' initial online trust: A two-stage decision-making process perspective. *International Journal of Information Management*, *34*(3), 395–405. doi:10.1016/j.ijinfomgt.2014.02.004

López, M., & Sicilia, M. (2014). eWOM as Source of Influence: The Impact of Participation in eWOM and Perceived Source Trustworthiness on Decision Making. *Journal of Interactive Advertising, 14*(2), 86–97. doi:10.1080/15252019.2014.944288

Lou, C., & Yuan, S. (2019). Influencer Marketing: How Message Value and Credibility Affect Consumer Trust of Branded Content on Social Media. *Journal of Interactive Advertising, 19*(1).

Loureiro, S. M. C., Cavallero, L., & Miranda, F. J. (2018). Fashion brands on retail websites: Customer performance expectancy and e-word-of-mouth. *Journal of Retailing and Consumer Services, 41*, 131–141.

Lu, Y., Zhao, L., & Wang, B. (2010). From virtual community members to C2C e-commerce buyers: Trust in virtual communities and its effect on consumers' purchase intention. *Electronic Commerce Research and Applications, 9*(4), 346–360. doi:10.1016/j.elerap.2009.07.003

Lundblad, L., & Davies, I. A. (2015). The values and motivations behind sustainable fashion consumption. *Journal of Consumer Behaviour, 15*(2), 149–162. doi:10.1002/cb.1559

Macdonald, E. K., & Sharp, B. M. (2000). Brand Awareness Effects on Consumer Decision Making for a Common, Repeat Purchase Product: A Replication. *Journal of Business Research, 48*(1), 5–15. doi:10.1016/S0148-2963(98)00070-8

Malhotra, N. k. (2001). *Pesquisa de Marketing: Uma Orientação Aplicada*. Academic Press.

Mayer, R. C., & Davis, J. H. (1999). The effect of the performance appraisal system on trust for management: A field quasi-experiment. *The Journal of Applied Psychology, 84*(1), 123–136. doi:10.1037/0021-9010.84.1.123

Mcneill, L., & Moore, R. (2015). Sustainable fashion consumption and the fast fashion conundrum: Fashionable consumers and attitudes to sustainability in clothing choice. *International Journal of Consumer Studies, 39*(3), 212–222. doi:10.1111/ijcs.12169

Miller, G. R., & Baseheart, J. (1969). Source trustworthiness, opinionated statements, and response to persuasive communication. *Speech Monographs, 36*(1), 1–7. doi:10.1080/03637756909375602

Min Kong, H., & Ko, E. (2017). Why do consumers choose sustainable fashion? A crosscultural study of South Korean, Chinese, and Japanese consumers. *Journal of Global Fashion Marketing, 8*(3), 220–234. doi:10.1080/20932685.2017.1336458

Mirabi, V., Akbariyeh, H., & Tahmasebifard, H. (2015). A Study of Factors Affecting on Customers Purchase Intention Case Study : The Agencies of Bono Brand Tile in Tehran. *Journal of Multidisciplinary Engineering Science and Technology, 2*(1), 267–273.

Niinimäki, K. (2010). Eco-Clothing, consumer identity and ideology. *Sustainable Development (Bradford), 18*(3), 150–162. doi:10.1002d.455

Ohanian, R. (1990). Construction and validation of a scale to measure celebrity endorsers' perceived expertise, trustworthiness, and attractiveness. *Journal of Advertising, 19*(3), 39–52. doi:10.1080/00913367.1990.10673191

Ozdamar Ertekin, Z., & Atik, D. (2015). Sustainable Markets: Motivating Factors, Barriers, and Remedies for Mobilization of Slow Fashion. *Journal of Macromarketing*, *35*(1), 53–69. doi:10.1177/0276146714535932

Pagiaslis, A., & Krontalis, A. K. (2014). Green Consumption Behavior Antecedents: Environmental Concern, Knowledge, and Beliefs. *Psychology and Marketing*, *31*(5), 335–348. doi:10.1002/mar.20698

Park, C., & Lee, T. M. (2009). Information direction, website reputation and eWOM effect: A moderating role of product type. *Journal of Business Research*, *62*(1), 61–67. doi:10.1016/j.jbusres.2007.11.017

Pereira, H. G., Salgueiro, M. F., & Rita, P. (2017). Online determinants of e-customer satisfaction: Application to website purchases in tourism. *Service Business*, *11*(2), 375–403. doi:10.100711628-016-0313-6

Pereira, M. A. F. (2020). *The consuption of environmentally sustainable textiles and apparel: A generational approach*. Faculdade de Economia do Porto.

Ritch, E. L. (2015). Consumers interpreting sustainability: Moving beyond food to fashion. *International Journal of Retail & Distribution Management*, *43*(12), 1162–1181. doi:10.1108/IJRDM-04-2014-0042

Roberts, J. A. (1996). Green consumers in the 1990s: Profile and implications for advertising. *Journal of Business Research*, *36*(3), 217–231. doi:10.1016/0148-2963(95)00150-6

Saleem, A., & Ellahi, A. (2017). Influence of electronic word of mouth on purchase intention of fashion products in social networking websites. Pakistan Journal of Commerce and So. *Pakistan Journal of Commerce and Social Sciences*, *11*(2), 597–622.

Saleem, M. A., Yaseen, A., & Wasaya, A. (2018). Drivers of customer loyalty and word of mouth intentions: Moderating role of interactional justice. *Journal of Hospitality Marketing & Management*, *27*(8), 877–904. doi:10.1080/19368623.2018.1469447

Salem, S. F., & Alanadoly, A. B. (2020). Personality traits and social media as drivers of wordof-mouth towards sustainable fashion. *Journal of Fashion Marketing and Management*.

Santiago, J. K. (2020). Consumer Attitudes Towards Fashion Influencers on Instagram: Impact of Perceptions and Online Trust on Purchase Intention. *Issues in Information Systems*, *21*(1), 105–117.

Saxena, A. (2011). Blogs And Their Impact On Purchase Intention: A Structural Equation Modelling Approach. *Paradigm*, *15*(1–2), 102–110. doi:10.1177/0971890720110114

Sharma, B., Gadenne, D., & Kerr, D. (2017). Environmental beliefs, norms and behaviours: An investigation of their relationships using data from green consumers. *Journal of New Business Ideas and Trends*, *15*(1), 1–17.

Shen, D., Richards, J., & Liu, F. (2013). Consumers' Awareness of Sustainable Fashion. *Marketing Management Journal*, *23*(2), 134–147.

Sokolova, K., & Kefi, H. (2020). Instagram and YouTube bloggers promote it, why should I buy? How credibility and parasocial interaction influence purchase intentions. *Journal of Retailing and Consumer Services, 53*, 101742.

Spears, N., & Singh, S. N. (2004). Measuring attitude toward the brand and purchase intentions. *Journal of Current Issues and Research in Advertising*, *26*(2), 53–66. doi:10.1080/10641734.2004.10505164

Sudha, M., & Sheena, K. (2017). Consumer Decision Process: Impact of Influencers in the Fashion Industry. *SCMS Journal of Indian Management*, *93*(3), 14–29.

Tang, J., & Liu, H. (2015). Trust in Social Media Synthesis Lectures on Information Security, Privacy, & Trust (E. Bertino & R. Sandhu, Eds.). Academic Press.

Taylor, V. A., Halstead, D., & Haynes, P. J. (2010). Consumer responses to christian religious symbols in advertising. *Journal of Advertising*, *39*(2), 79–92. doi:10.2753/JOA0091-3367390206

van Esch, P., Arli, D., Castner, J., Talukdar, N., & Northey, G. (2018). Consumer attitudes towards bloggers and paid blog advertisements: What's new? *Marketing Intelligence & Planning*, *36*(7), 778–793. doi:10.1108/MIP-01-2018-0027

Vehmas, K., Raudaskoski, A., Heikkilä, P., Harlin, A., & Mensonen, A. (2018). Consumer attitudes and communication in circular fashion. *Journal of Fashion Marketing and Management*, *22*(3), 286–300. doi:10.1108/JFMM-08-2017-0079

Wang, X., Yu, C., & Wei, Y. (2012). Social Media Peer Communication and Impacts on Purchase Intentions: A Consumer Socialization Framework. *Journal of Interactive Marketing*, *26*(4), 198–208. doi:10.1016/j.intmar.2011.11.004

Wang, Y., Min, Q., & Han, S. (2016). Understanding the effects of trust and risk on individual behavior toward social media platforms: A meta-analysis of the empirical evidence. *Computers in Human Behavior*, *56*, 34–44. doi:10.1016/j.chb.2015.11.011

Wiederhold, M., & Martinez, L. F. (2018). Ethical consumer behaviour in Germany: The attitude-behaviour gap in the green apparel industry. *International Journal of Consumer Studies*, *42*(4), 419–429. doi:10.1111/ijcs.12435

Wolny, J., & Mueller, C. (2013). Analysis of fashion consumers' motives to engage in electronic word-of-mouth communication through social media platforms. *Journal of Marketing Management*, *29*(5–6), 562–583. doi:10.1080/0267257X.2013.778324

Wong, K. K.-K. (2019). *Mastering Partial Least Squares Structural Equation Modeling (PLS-SEM) with SmartPLS in 38 Hours*. iUniverse.

Xiaoli, N., & Kwangjun, H. (2007). Consumer responses to corporate social responsibility (CSR) initiatives: Examining the role of brand-cause fit in cause-related marketing. *Journal of Advertising*, *36*(2), 63–74. doi:10.2753/JOA0091-3367360204

Zhao, L., Lee, S. H., & Copeland, L. R. (2019). Social media and Chinese consumers' environmentally sustainable apparel purchase intentions. *Asia Pacific Journal of Marketing and Logistics*, *31*(4), 855–874. doi:10.1108/APJML-08-2017-0183

Zhao, Y., Kou, G., Peng, Y., & Chen, Y. (2018). Understanding influence power of opinion leaders in e-commerce networks: An opinion dynamics theory perspective. *Information Sciences*, *426*, 131–147. doi:10.1016/j.ins.2017.10.031

Zheng, Y., & Chi, T. (2015). Factors influencing purchase intention towards environmentally friendly apparel: An empirical study of US consumers. *International Journal of Fashion Design. Technology and Education*, *8*(2), 68–77.

ADDITIONAL READING

Brandão, A., & Costa, A. G. (2021). Extending the theory of planned behaviour to understand the effects of barriers towards sustainable fashion consumption. *European Business Review*, *33*(5), 742–774. doi:10.1108/EBR-11-2020-0306

Cabeza-Ramírez, L. J., Fuentes-García, F. J., Cano-Vicente, M. C., & González-Mohino, M. (2022). How Generation X and Millennials Perceive Influencers' Recommendations: Perceived Trustworthiness, Product Involvement, and Perceived Risk. *Journal of Theoretical and Applied Electronic Commerce Research*, *17*(4), 1431–1449. doi:10.3390/jtaer17040072

Nikolic, D., & Kostic-Stankovic, M. (2022). Improving the Economic Sustainability of the Fashion Industry: A Conceptual Model Proposal. *Sustainability (Basel)*, *14*(8), 4726. doi:10.3390u14084726

Peleg Mizrachi, M., & Tal, A. (2022). Sustainable Fashion—Rationale and Policies. *Encyclopedia*, *2*(2), 1154–1167. doi:10.3390/encyclopedia2020077

Vehmas, K., Raudaskoski, A., Heikkilä, P., Harlin, A., & Mensonen, A. (2018). Consumer attitudes and communication in circular fashion. *Journal of Fashion Marketing and Management*, *22*(3), 286–300. doi:10.1108/JFMM-08-2017-0079

KEY TERMS AND DEFINITIONS

Fast Fashion: Is the term for the relatively recent phenomena of mass production of inexpensive, stylish apparel in big numbers that closely resembles fashions seen on the runway and in popular culture. The goal is to acquire the consumer the clothing as soon as it becomes fashionable so that they can only use it a few times before tossing it.

Influencer Credibility: The degree to which the consumer believes that the influencer conveys information that has knowledge and experience about sustainable fashion. Someone having authority in their industry.

Influencer Expertise: Measure of a customer's likeliness to do repeat business with an organization or brand. Is a person or an organization who has expert product knowledge and influence.

Influencer Similarity: Perception on whether the influencer reveals legitimate and precise information about sustainable fashion.

Sustainable Fashion: A carbon-neutral fashion sector based on equity, social justice, animal welfare, and ecological integrity may be achieved by using products, processes, activities, and actors (policymakers, brands, and consumers) who are all part of what is referred to as sustainable fashion

Trust in the Influencer: The extent to which the consumer rely on in what the influencer says about sustainable fashion.

Willingness to Pay More: Motivation to pay a higher price for sustainable fashion products than for fast fashion products.

Chapter 11
Role of Information and Communication Technologies in the Sustainable Clothing and Textile Industry

Sunanda Vincent Jaiwant
CHRIST University (Deemed), India

Anusha Srinivasan Iyer
CHRIST University (Deemed), India

ABSTRACT

Information and communication technology (ICT) has an important role to play in every sector globally. These opportunities will derive from the ability of ICTs to open up parts of the supply chain (other than basic manufacturing and processing) in clothing and textile industry as well. ICT technology is used at various stages of the design process. Presently, it is rapidly changing the textile industry. Employee attendance (clocking in) to shipment dispatching are dependent on information technology. The garment industry is fully depended on IT or ERP. This chapter presents the latest trends of companies that have successfully used ICTs to move, for example, into higher-value activities such as design and logistics, or to access niche markets. The study aims to investigate the uses of information and communication technology in the clothing and textile industry and examine the recent trends of ICT usage in companies within the textile industry and identify the factors to be considered by companies in the textile industry before investing in ICT.

INTRODUCTION

The major producers in the textile and apparel sectors are interested in sustainability, and many brands have expressed their concern for safeguarding both individuals and the environment and adopted sustainable communication strategies. The circular economy offers businesses in the textile and apparel industry

DOI: 10.4018/978-1-6684-8753-2.ch011

(particularly SMEs) the chance to develop new revenue streams, improve their ability to withstand unpredictable input costs, and help their efforts to become fully sustainable and environmentally and socially conscious. Since the collapse of the Multi-Fibre Arrangement (MFA) quota system, which officially ended nearly four decades of trade restrictions, the international textile and apparel sector has been in an atmosphere of turmoil. As the worldwide apparel sector integrates within a fairly small percentage of front-runners, many developing nations today experience mounting rivalry and price reductions. Using information and communication technology (ICT), developing nations can adapt to the modern era. As an all-purpose technology, ICT may, among other things, enhance business procedures and boost the productivity and competitiveness of companies in emerging nations. Second, ICT is the primary force behind the shifting of assets across the economic chain, facilitating new companies, decomposing supply networks, and opening up new opportunities for emerging nations in the worldwide supply network.

These opportunities will derive from the ability of ICTs to open up parts of the supply chain (other than basic manufacturing and processing) to developing countries. This chapter presents current trends of companies that have successfully used ICTs to move, for example, into higher-value activities such as design and logistics, or to access niche markets The study demonstrates the variety of strategies available to producers. Many manufacturers have focused on serving major retailers through large scale production and speed-to-market through an emphasis on logistics, other examples show companies elsewhere adopting a strategy of moving into fashion design and specialized fabrics or raw materials, or alternatively identifying niche markets that do not demand large-scale production. ICTs have been crucial in each case, although the type of technology needed varies from case to case.

Yet technology alone will not provide the answers for struggling garment makers in developing countries. A suitable business environment, adequate infrastructure, and indeed a fundamental comparative advantage are also required. If an ICT-enhanced textile and garments sector is to be an effective component of a developing country's poverty-alleviation strategy, then the following broad questions must first be addressed by both policymakers and private investors considering their post-MFA strategies:

- What aspects of the wider enabling environment must be in place before investment in ICT for development makes sense?
- What are all the factors, including ICT investment, which cause value to migrate along the global supply chain?
- To what extent are the opportunities offered by ICT in the textile industry limited (or promoted) by natural and historical factors in specific countries?

The aim of the book is to provide deeper understanding of the relevant aspects of ICT impacting clothing and textile industry for better output and to generate a significant personalized experience for their customers. Readers will get reliable and comprehensive information on use of ICT in manufacturing and promotional practices. The chapter provides detailed and well-illustrated concepts of ICT and its application in clothing and textile sector in the present and the coming years.

ICT

ICT means Information Communication Technology. A good way to think about ICT is to consider all the uses of digital technologies that are already in existence to help individuals, business and organizations. ICT covers any product that will store, retrieve, manipulate, transmit or receive information electronically in a digital form for example, personal computers, digital televisions, emails, robots etc. So ICT is concerned with the storage, retrieval, manipulation or transmission of digital data. More so, it is also concerned with the way these different uses can be linked. According to Orlikowski and Iacono (2001), Information Technology (IT) is a too intended to generate value, whether productivity enhancement, cost reduction, competitive advantage and improved supplier relationships, etc. The term "information and communications technology" (ICT) refers to a broad range of communication tools and services, such as videoconferencing and distance learning, as well as hardware and software for computers, networks, satellite systems, mobile phones, and other devices. Conventional and traditional approaches to the creation, execution, and verification of information and communication technology (ICT) platforms often address one or two primary system problems at a time, such as an enterprise system's stability or operational accuracy, or a database's integrity and confidentiality. A different engineering activity is frequently used to address additional aspects. Information and communications technology (ICT) is the use of computer and communications devices, instruments, and techniques to simplify the creation, collection, processing, transmission, and storage of information. In addition to the wired and wireless communication systems which enable cell phones, the web, the Internet of Things (IoT), and the metaverse, it also comprises computing technologies like servers, laptop computers, and software applications. ICT aims to increase the availability of data and facilitate more effective human-to-human, human-to-machine, and machine-to-machine (M2M) communication.

Textile Manufacturing

This is a major industry based in the conversion of fibres into yarn then fabric, then textiles. Its primary concerned is based on the production of yarn and cloth and also subsequent design or manufacture of clothing and their distribution. Spinning and fabric forming stages coupled with finishing and colouration has variable processes which lead to the production of wide ranges of products. However, cotton remains the most important natural fibre, so it is treated in depth. The fashion sector of the international textile industry is greatly in need of the textile production procedures. More than 65% of the market for textile products was made up of the numerous textile products that the fashion industry required. Household goods and technical fabrics come after the fashion market. Large View According to research, the top three industries for the international textile market, in order of application, are fashion, technical fabrics, and home (Uddin, 2019).

Figure 1.
Source: Research (2021)

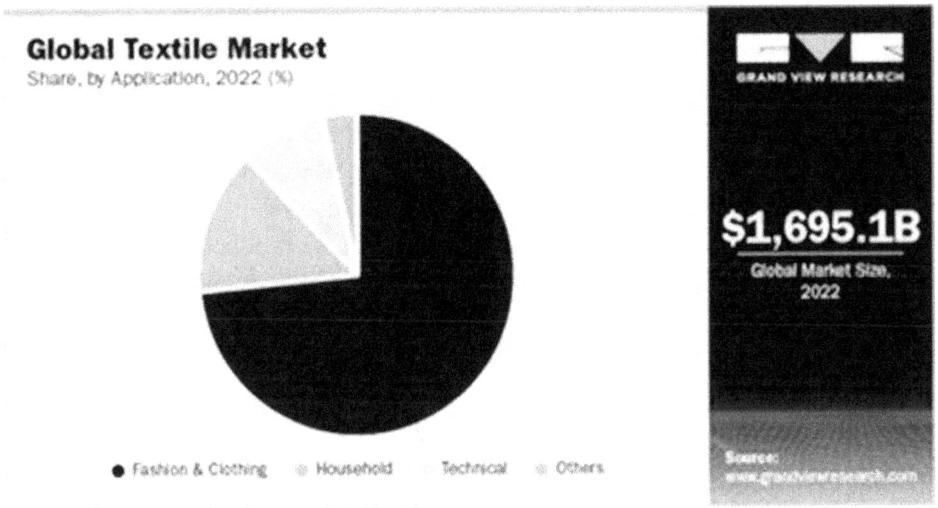

The industry has seen an increase in the use of smart textiles, which connect to the environment through optical fibres, metals, and numerous conductive polymers. These aid in identifying and responding to a wide range of external stimulation, including mechanical, thermal, chemical, and electric sources. During the anticipated period, this is anticipated to fuel the technical application segment's growth in the textiles market.

Literature Review

The Global Textile Industry has changed owing to changing international trade norms. Under the MFA system countries such as China, India and Bangladesh faced constrained growth. After phasing out of MFA and the liberalized regime under the World Trade Organization the global textile industry has changed. As a share of world exports, China was 11.1% and 18.4% in textiles and clothing respectively in 2001 during MFA system, and the exports increased as high as 35.9% and 40.3% since then (Yao& Whalley 2015) With the backdrop of phasing out of MFA system, just like other industries in textile industry too, usage of ICT slowly evolved. It started by way of introduction of computer networks during the years 1985-87 especially in textile manufacturing by companies engaged in textile and clothing manufacture found Growth in Employment and Increase in Sales (Hardill et al 1991).

Utilization of ICT in the Textile Industry: A Move to Higher Value Activities

In the textile industry, several companies have successfully utilized ICTs to move into higher-value activities such as design to access niche markets. In order to access niche markets and provide higher value functionalities, companies within the textile industry have used ICT to create smart textiles and have incorporated electronic components and devices into their products. Levis-Philips has entered into a joint venture to develop a phone jacket that integrates smart technology to incorporate Philips technology into clothing items like shirts and skirts. Similarly, Clothing+ introduced the first sports shirt with an integrated heart rate measurement device to provide enhanced functionality for athletes and sports enthusiasts. On the same line, Vicometrics developed a shirt with integrated monitoring devices that enables monitoring of vital signs through smart textiles (Fibrenamics n.d.). Zara the retail apparel giant has used ICT to streamline its supply chain and logistics processes by using advanced inventory management systems, real-time data analytics, and efficient communication networks it has become efficient in understanding and satisfying customer demands. Adidas uses 3D printing and computer-aided design (CAD) software to enable customization and tailor make products to suit customer needs. Patagonia a an apparel manufacturer of outdoor clothing has adapted traceability systems that allow customers to track the supply chain process. Customers get to know the origins of the product, where it was manufactured and how it has finally reached them. This helps customers to be more acquainted with the brand's ethical practices. These examples highlight how textile companies have successfully utilized ICTs to gain a competitive edge, improve operational efficiency, and move into higher-value activities within the industry. By adopting innovative technologies and leveraging data-driven insights, these companies have been able to meet changing consumer demands and capture new market opportunities. Such technology has become a basic requirement in order to adjust in a new business era by improving business practices and enhancing efficiency and competitiveness. In the garment sector, subcontractors in Asia involved in exports often receive orders and details for products by emails. (McNamara, 2008). There is a strong relationship between ICT usage and Logistics activities within textile manufacturing firms. The adoption of ICT tends to reduce operating costs more than improve service levels. Government should facilitate manufacturing companies' participation in global value chains through policy initiatives in specific areas by promoting technological upgrading and facilitating of compliance procedures through adoption of process and products standards (Adebambo, S., & Toyin, A.I. (2011).Talking about global value chain in the textile industry, the industry players play predominantly three types of roles- original equipment manufacturer of clothing, brand clothing manufacturer, and intermediate trader. In addition to these main roles, there are other roles played in collaborated by and with supply chain partners. Collaborations occur for reasons such as increasing production efficiency, improving negotiation skills for larger and more orders from international suppliers, grasping channel needs and management, and creating novel customer service experiences.(Chen C 2019) .While the industry tries to implement sustainable and more customer centeric practices, there is a need for flexible workforce to respond to the global demand for sustainable creative products.New training and development tool kits have to be developed to help train personnel involved in the textile and clothing industry. (Avadanei etal 2020). The use of computer networks can improve the efficiency and productivity of textile and clothing companies . For instance, the Companies which used computer networks during 1985-87, performed significantly better than those without in terms of growth in employment and return on sales. (Hardill etal 1991). Usage of ICT in the textile manufacturing organizations in Indian organizations impacts Operational Leadership and Marketing efficiency. (Tewari & Misra 2012). ICTs has changed drastically the textile design and visualization processes by using Digital Design and 3D Visualization. (Forno etal 2021). A decision support system for dyeing machine scheduling developed to empower smart manufacturing and break down information silos implemented in few companies in Taiwan showed increase in efficiency in the processes. (Chien-Chun Ku etal 2020). Companies like Gerber Technology and Lectra offer software solutions that enable digital design, pattern-making, and 3D visualization. These solutions help in visualize designs using 3D visualization, create patterns, create digital design, and help in seamlessly share data throughout the supply chain. Such enhanced processes allow companies to offer customized products to consumers (Lectra n.d)

ICT's also play an important role in Supply chain Management and in Logistics. For instance, companies use Radio frequency identification (RFID), real-time tracking systems, data analytics to improve production planning, inventory management and to optimize transportation. This helps in reducing lead times and helps in efficient delivery (InfoDev, World Bank Report 2008). E commerce platforms like Alibaba, Trade India, and Etsy enable textile manufacturers to advertise their products to a global audience and connect with niche buyers looking for specialized textiles. (Fibre2Fashion n.d) .Blockchain technology enables companies to track the origins of the product and helps in tracing production processes. It also helps in verifying the sustainability certifications. This technology is a boon for sustainability-focused companies who wish to bring more transparency in supply chain processes for their consumers (Ahmed et al. 2021) (Lenzing 2020). Companies such as Virtuality. Fashion and Zeekit provide Virtual Fitting and Augmented Reality solutions to their customers for an enhanced customer shopping experience especially for buyers of made to wear garments (Virtuality.Fashion n.d.) (Zeekit n.d.) This type of experience helps in customers in making a confident purchase decision and decreases the returns. Machine learning algorithms help in demand forecasting and trend analysis. The algorithms help in analyzing both endogenous as well as exogenous parameters. Endogenous factors are firm-specific, whereas exogenous factors are the macroeconomic indicators that significantly influence the demand forecasting of the firms involved in international trade (Yasir et al. 2022).

The customization trend is one where ICT is best put to use. For instance, companies such as Custom Ink, Printful, InkMonk, BeYoung and Printvenue help customers in get personalized tshirts, bags etc using online design tools. Not only those certain platforms such as TexIntel and CoCreateX aid in collaborative design processes, allowing designers to connect with manufacturers.

Such above trends show the powerful usage of ICT and demonstrates how textile companies are moving into high value activities and how they are providing innovating solutions to their customers. ICT helps companies in creating niche markets and catering to niche markets and thereby increasing their competitive advantage.

Factors to Be Considered by Companies in Textile Industry Before Investing in ICT

While the advantages of using ICT in Textile industry are numerous, there are few factors to be considered before a company decides to invest in ICT. Companies must consider special needs and challenges in certain aspects such as supply chain management, inventory management, production and quality control, and customer relationship management and then determine how ICT can address these needs effectively. For instance Automation and digitization is one aspect of ICT which is widely used in this industry, however it is crucial to first identify which areas can benefit the most from automation- whether it is production, inventory tracking, or order processing, Potential return on investment in ICT also needs to be determined before deciding to invest. Smart textiles and Wearables is experiencing a boom, however, a company must evaluate how ICT can support the integeration of ICT into textiles such as embedding sensors and electronics into their existing textile products. They must check on the feasibility, innovation aspect and also must consider customer acceptance level.

Access to technologies such as Internet of Things, Big data, Cloud Computing and Analytics is a very important consideration a company must make (Skills Smart 2021) Additionally, skilled and trained employees who carry necessary skills to use such technology effectively are required. Companies should invest in incorporating cybersecurity measures to protect sensitive data and implement security protocols and stay updated with cybersecurity practices (Infodev World Bank report 2020) . Before doing an investment in technology, firms business strategy needs to be finalized. The ICT implementation strategy should be aligned with the firm's long-term business plan. Investing in market research to see how the competitors or other counterparts in business have adopted ICT into their firm is a must. Firm must initiate communication with those companies within the industry, who have pioneered the use of new technologies. Buy- in from employees is a critical factor that determines the successful technology implementation. Generally, there is resistance from staff whenever a new technology is implemented. Firms have limited resources and using a resource with limited gains leads to erosion of capital. Thus, before deciding to invest in technology an investment appraisal needs to be done. A cost-benefit analysis of ICT investments while keeping in mind the opportunity cost is a must. Funding the investments is another important aspect that needs to be considered before deciding on investment in ICT. If the company is deciding on seeking funds from shareholders, Banks, or partners getting their consent on a new technology may not be that easy. Government aided funding and Co-funding routes should be explored. (IFAC, Willie and Mbaya, 2020)

These factors, along with the company's budget and long-term goals, should be carefully considered before making an investment in ICT for a textile company.

Trends of ICT Usage in Companies in the Textile Industry

A variety of usages of ICT in textile industry has emerged, giving opportunities to companies to explore rising up the value chain. Companies must consider markets, customers, stakeholders, competitors, their strengths and weaknesses prior to deciding whether they wish to go for investments in ICT or not. The following paragraphs gives a reader an overview of recent trends of ICT usage in textile industry followed by the factors to be considered while investing in ICT investment. From aiding in demand forecasting to delivering customized products, each area within the manufacturing, trading and customer service genres are being explored. Following are some ways companies are using ICT in their companies -

- **Accurate Forecasting of Demand**

The textile industry heavily relies on customers changing interests and fashion around them. Trends across the world need to be regularly assessed. Machine learning algorithms help in demand forecasting and trend analysis. Companies produce the right type of products for the right customer type in adequate quantity by using ICT.

- **Adding Functionalities**

Companies by incorporating technology into textiles such as smart watches inbuilt into textiles, or technology in built to aid health (display body statistics) etc. add more functionalities and draw more customers who are health, sports and fitness enthusiasts.

- **Aiding in Supply Chain and Logistics**

ICT helps companies to streamline its supply chain and logistics. It aids in increasing the speed of processes by using real time analytics, Radio frequency identification (RFID) and real-time tracking systems. It helps in reducing lead times and helps in efficient delivery.

- **Impetus to Ethics and Sustainability Principles**

More and more firms have begun to understand that customers look forward to learning more about the producers from the Ethical and sustainability point of view. They wish to know if any animals were harmed during production, whether the environment was harmed or if any child labour was used etc. Sustainability has become more important than any other time. Blockchain and other traceability systems help consumers trace the origins of the product and help them trace the entire processes till the product lands in their hands. Customers can also be informed about sustainability certifications.

- **Customization**

Companies make use of ICT to generate personalized designs. Products such as personalized t-shirts, bags, mugs etc are customized as per customers' requirements. Institutional customers too look forward to get custom designed t-shirts with the company's logo.

- **Improving Aesthetics**

Technologies such as 3D printing technology and computer-aided design (CAD) software is used by companies for digital design, pattern-making.

- **Enhanced Customer Shopping Experience**

In order to enhance customer shopping experience, a Virtual Fitting and Augmented Reality solutions are extended to customers. This experience helps the customer in buying confidently and decreases sales return.

- **Creative Collaboration**

Design creation as a profession is predominantly freelanced. Companies use ICT for the collaborative design processes, allowing designers from far away corners of the world to connect with manufacturers.

- **Collaborations for Better Business**

Within the textile industry, there are three roles mainly found- Th original equipment manufacturer of clothing, brand clothing manufacturer, and intermediate trader. ICT brings them all together through communication platforms for communicating their needs, negotiations and discussion on buying- selling terms.

- **Increase in Efficiency in Manufacturing Processes**

Companies use ICT to increase efficiency in manufacturing process. For instance, decision support system is used in few companies for dyeing machine scheduling which in turn empowers smart manufacturing

- **Reaching Out to Wider Audience**

Companies use ICT tools such as online ecommerce platforms to advertise their products such as specialized textiles. These platforms help sellers and buyers to come together to satisfy their needs. It helps textile companies to reach out to a wider audience and helps in showcasing niche products to customers.

Factors to Be Considered Prior to ICT Investment Decision

As seen above companies have started to explore the usage of ICT in textile industry at a fast speed. However, there are few assessments to be done and few factors to be considered before deciding on the investment in ICT. Following are few pointers for companies to consider prior to ICT investment decision.

- **Identifying Areas for ICT Implementation**

Companies must identify areas where they wish to implement ICT such as supply chain management, inventory management, production and quality control, and customer relationship management. ICT is best implemented to increase efficiency, revenue, customer satisfaction and cutting of costs and accordingly the areas must be identified.

- **Assessment of Feasibility and Customer Acceptance**

Integrating innovative technologies in textiles is a trend such as embedding Sensors and electronics and creating smart wear however, assessment of its feasibility in terms of customer traction and customer acceptance needs to be validated prior to investment decision.

- **Assessment of Workforce, Recruitment, and Training Needs**

For a company to rebuild itself using Internet of Things, Big Data and Analytics employees with technical skill sets are required. Textile companies should do skill gap analysis of their workforce and provide appropriate training to employees to transition into an ICT enabled employment. Availability of skilled employees in the Geographical area is also an important consideration and so robust recruitment strategies need to be developed.

- **Assessment of Firms Long-Term Strategy**

A firm must understand its long-term goals and plan out its long-term strategies. ICT implementation is not possible without understanding the strategies of companies. Firms plans for one year, three to five years and ten years at great length needs to be analyzed. Decision on adopting specific technologies and putting requisite investments will need to be prioritized by the firm to meet its long-term business plan phased out in between years. The impact of adopting ICT on the firm's service delivery over time needs to be projected.

- **Communication With Other Companies**

Companies must identify those firms who have already adopted new technologies and communicate with them. Learning from their mistakes and adopting best practices will help the firm save money and time in selecting the appropriate technology and service provider. Employees of these firms who have adopted ICT can give insights that can help in gathering if staff would be ready to embrace new technology and what could be the new ways of working.

- **Assessing the Resistance Level in Employees**

With implementation of new technologies, a general tendency of employees is to show resistance. Thus, proper assessment of resistance level of employees is a must. Thereafter depending on the level of resistance strategies such as appropriate discussions with employees, implementing change management techniques, designing interventions, training programs, incentives etc. will have to be applied.

- **Sources of Funding the ICT Investments**

Companies may have to go for different funding routes to fund their investments. New and innovating funding options can also be considered. However, with each route, there are advantages and disadvantages. For instance, Co-funding is an option where same technology is shared by different firms, however, it is a complicated process and may lead to conflicts during peak work cycles. Loans from Banks involve collateral and high interest rates. Certain Governments provide loans and subsidies to SMEs for technology assistance and it is ideal to explore the Government route, however, it takes a long time to get approvals. Companies cannot select the technology based on their assessments; they have to consider the opinions of the funding agency also. Thus, before deciding to invest in a technology, companies must decide, who will be funding them.

- **Investment Appraisal**

Finally, it boils down to financial decsion. Whether to invest in a new technology or not is a capital decision . For such decisions clarity on aspects of Cost of Capital, Opportunity costs, Rate of Return, Break even point and other financial aspects is a must. Thereafter a robust investment appraisal according market norms will have to be undertaken. Taking the example of considering the opportunity costs - For instance a firm may have $10,000 for investment in ICT and may produce gains worth $15,000 and on the other hand, firm may decide to invest $10,000 in another safe avenue, which may produce gains worth $5000. In this case, the gains through investment outperforms the gains through Fixed deposit and hence, it's a worthwhile decision.

- **Incorporating Cybersecurity Systems**

Companies using ICT cannot rely only on simple solutions such as anti-virus or firewall to protect themselves from cyber threats. Advanced cybersecurity solutions are required to protect against sensitive data, protected health information and personally identifiable information etc.

Information and Communication Technologies in Clothing and Textile Industry

- **RFID**

RFID is utilised in production, inventory management, storage, shipping, logistics, transportation, automated tracking of goods, and supply chain management in the textile and apparel industry (Legnani et al. 2011). In general, RFID tags are not consumer-facing. To trace products through their life cycles of production and storage, thereby all the way to the customer, and then back to the store for replacement or resale, they are instead utilised on hang tags or packages. Because RFID tags can only be read by a specific reader and cannot be scanned by customers, consumer-facing information needs to be available somewhere. As a result, RFID tags are advantageous to back-end operations and solution suppliers since they make tracking possible through the entire lifetime cycle. Since visibility over the years is crucial for cyclical garment models in the clothing sector, RFID tags generally do not exceed washing norms, which is problematic for their implementation.

Figure 2.
Source: Mokashi and Gadkari (2022)

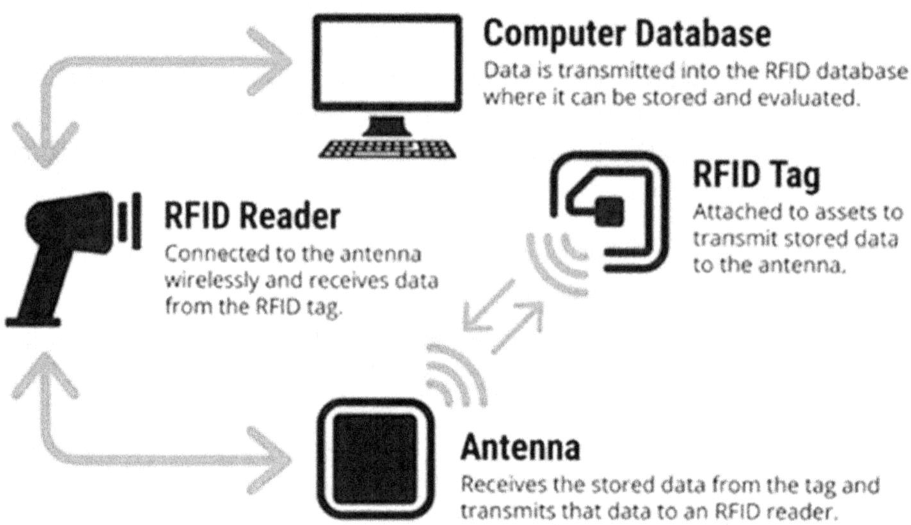

The manufacturing system's status can be tracked for final clothing, various design components, and embellishments. The textile batches can be easily tracked during manufacturing and stitching. The cotton bundles and filaments in spinning machines are easily traceable. It is possible to prevent combining of various textile sections, which is a significant issue in spinning mills. By integrating the RFID technology into various operations involved in the fashion supply chain, a variety of difficulties specific to the industry can be resolved. The fashion industry can be broken down into four different segments, including production, international shipping, distribution, and retailing. RFID may be employed in production to prevent accessory and element combining as well as product mixing. If a product is outsourced, RFID can be utilised in international transit to monitor and locate the shipment prior to and following Free on Board. According to Moon and Ngai (2008), RFID can swiftly address the problem of categorising and tracing the goods. This cuts down on the lead time during distribution. The bulk of retail stores have limited space, which must be utilised effectively. RFID is employed to keep track of inventory to rapidly and accurately recognise the product to prevent "search regret" and facilitate efforts to address the issue Reynolds et al. 2006).

- **QR Codes**

A software platform's information is accessible to consumers via a digital trigger. The type of information that a customer is able to view is determined by the brand and the supplier and may include details about a particular item of clothing, such as how to care for it and what materials are used in it, or it can enable the customer to interact with the brand in relation to their purchase, such as by leading them to an online advertisement about the garment's creation. Adding a QR code to the care tag or a distinct accompanying tag that reads "scan me" is at present the most visible and popular approach to incorporate a digital trigger in an item of clothing. The majority of people today realise that they may use their mobile phones to scan a QR code

- **NFC**

NFC is based on the radio-frequency identification (RFID) technology, which enables compatible devices to communicate and charge a normally inert and unpowered electronic tag. It is employed for monitoring, recognition, and verification. Mobile payments enable the replacement or augmentation of existing payment methods like credit cards and electronic ticket smart cards thanks to the usage of NFC chips in contactless payment networks. Sometimes, this is referred to as NFC. NFC is utilised for social networking sites and for the exchange of documents, connections, pictures, and videos. Keycards and electronic identity documents can both be used with NFC-enabled devices. A low-speed connection with easy setup is provided through NFC, which can be utilised to launch more powerful wireless connections. NFC chips are inert data storage devices that an NFC device can read from and, in certain cases, write to. They are normally read-only in everyday use but could be rewritable.

Figure 3.
Source: Seritag (2023)

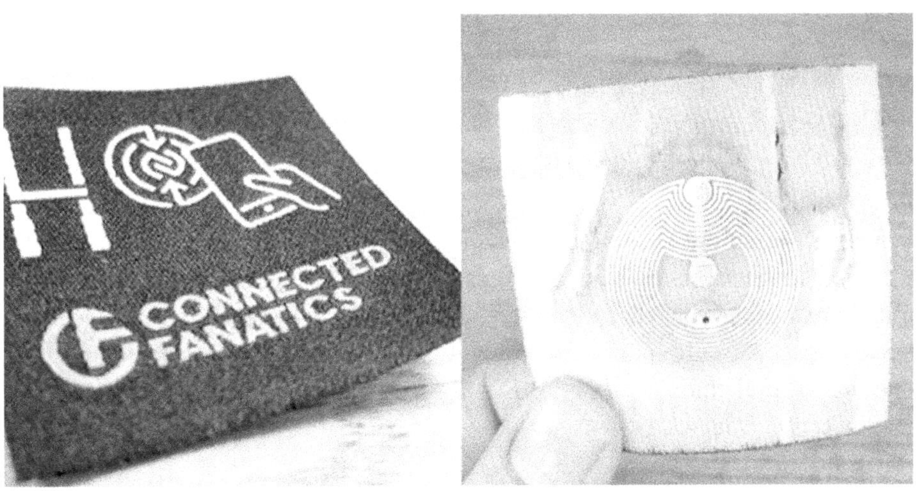

The justifications for adopting NFC technology are as diverse as the clothing itself. They include tracking, verification, promotional activities, ownership, reuse and recycling, and the circular economy. Textile producers are using a knitted tag with an integrated NFC (Near Field Communication) label that is exceedingly useful and much unlikely to be removed of destroyed by the consumers. The manufacturer of the clothing must then make it extremely clear to the consumer that it is there in the woven label and that they can download an NFC reader onto their mobile device. Many consumers must download a specialised NFC reader from the app store because not all smartphones, particularly those launched in the previous couple of years, come with NFC chips embedded into the hardware. A web link can be locked and stored in the user memory using standard NFC-based tags which remains unchangeable. The QR code, however, can be imitated from one tag to another tag using a cell phone. The tag's purpose can be to attest to the authenticity of the item or perhaps to allow for tracing. Every time they are scanned, authentication NFC tags create a special secure code that makes it impossible to copy and paste the URL; any prior codes can be recognised as "invalid." It's getting more and more common to add NFC tags to footwear, clothing, fabrics, wearables, and other apparels. A rising number of companies of all sizes are aiming to develop smart wearable clothes, whether the tags are being used for promotion, to give information about goods, or to facilitate anti-counterfeit.

- **Cloud Computing**

Figure 4.
Source: https://textilelearner.net/cloud-computing-in-textile-and-apparel-industry/

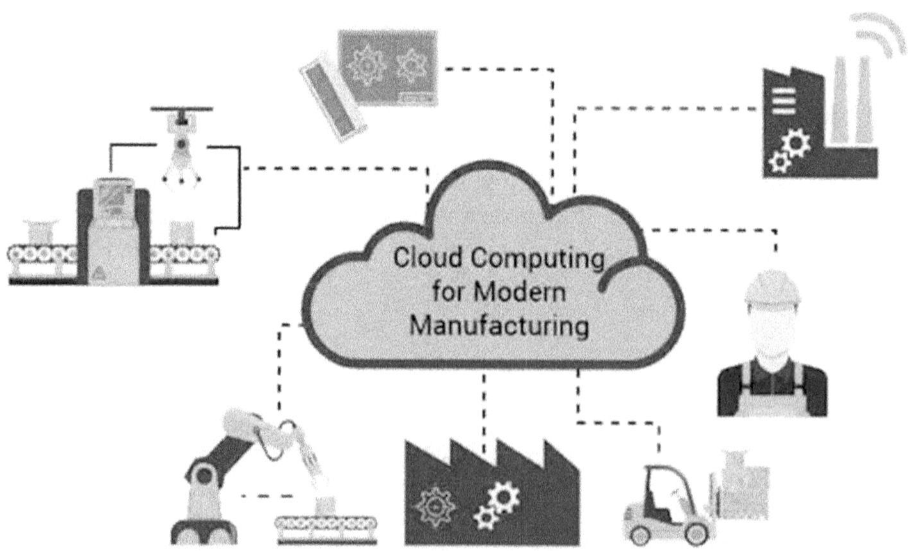

Every business is beginning to use cloud computing, and the fashion sector is no different. Through the use of technological service systems, businesses can save time and money. Additionally, it gives organisations the ability to make decisions that are better, more trustworthy, and completely recorded, leading to tracking improvements. The concept of cloud computing can be described as providing company systems or programmes as an application over the web. It is a web-based system of computation that users can utilise without the need for additional applications, servers, or equipment. To use this service, all one needs is a web connection, and it can be done from anywhere in the world. One such computing system that is frequently employed in the garment and fashion business is augmented reality (AR). Through digitally produced systems and software, it provides the customer with an augmented experience of the real world. With the use of a camera and the internet, AR applications can be obtained. Cloud computing has the potential to introduce a lot of these applications in the coming days. The clothing and garment industries can profit from cloud computing in a variety of ways. similar to how a brand continually gets notified of any process delays. There may be a delay in shipping, in the production process, or in obtaining the necessary supplies. Using cloud technology, the business is alerted straight away and has plenty of time to make the best choice to fulfil the complete order at the most convenient moment.

- **Robots**

A key step in the production of clothing is the printing of designs into fabrics. At times, the only distinction among identical products is found in the printed design. Robots are ideal for printing and sketching because, with the correct tools, complex pathways can be mechanically developed. In recent years, the transportation and packaging of goods has seen a significant increase in the number of the most innovative new uses for robotics. These duties are equally relevant to the manufacturing of fabrics as they are to other kinds of products. These applications include selecting, packing, storage, and organising, to name just a few. 3D printing is one of the most recent advancements in robotic production of textiles. Using fibres which have been embedded in a polymer for clothing like safe firemen outfits, 3D printed fabrics work similarly to regular 3D printing. The fabric is guided into the 3D structure by the robot, and then it is fixed in place by the polymer's stiffening process. Robotics is no more a niche subject; it is now a global one! As consequently, the use of robotics in both the industrial sector and the textile industry has produced notable advantages. Robotics in the clothing sector is used to reduce the need for human labour in labour-intensive procedures.

CONCLUSION

ICT technology like RFID technology is being used more and more in clothing. The RFID technology will be used by practically all textile producers, venders, and suppliers in the future. Due to their higher cost, RFID technologies can't totally eliminate barcode technology, but their precision, acceleration, and potential returns are far higher. The RFID system is an exciting innovation that, as it spreads, will help businesses overcome issues with supply chain management, safety, identity verification, and tracking of goods.

Retailers, producers, and consumer goods businesses such CVS, Tesco, Prada, Benetten, Wal-Mart, and Procter & Gamble are currently incorporating technologies and studying its effects on their operations. The advantages of RFID are accessible to others. Understanding technology and other characteristics is essential to success since it helps to reduce potential issues. It is past time for the apparel industry to begin implementing the newest RFID technology in a variety of settings, including manufacturing and storage. ICT has tremendous possibilities for use in a range of industries, including production, sales, and inventory management. Companies like GAP, a US garment company, have demonstrated the immediate advantages by increasing sales by 2% as a result of employing RFID to decrease stock-outs. J Crew, a well-known US clothing brand, used RFID to accelerate inventory keeping by five to eight times. The brief lifespan of products, the frequent fashion modifications, the variety of merchandise designs and materials used for input, fluctuating manufacturing quantities, high levels of competition, and frequently high standards for merchandise quality are characteristics of the apparel sector. The adoption of RFID adds to these difficulties and poses new ones related to cost and privacy protection. The organisations that deal with textile and clothing products should begin by monitoring costly merchandise because labour cost savings and stealing of these things can offset their cost (Nayak, et al., 2015). It is clearly apparent that RFID technology has a very promising future in the clothing and apparel sector. The technological developments will lead to the emergence of new application areas, and departments where RFID is currently underutilised will increasingly see its use. This article will serve as a helpful reference for those interested in RFID research, including researchers from academia and industry professionals, and it will provide emergence new areas of research on ICT in clothing and textile industry.

REFERENCES

Adebambo, S., & Toyin, A. I. (2011). Analysis of information and communication technologies (ICT) usage on logistics activities of manufacturing companies in southwestern Nigeria. *Journal of Emerging Trends in Economics and Management Science, 2*, 68–74.

Ahmed, W. A. H., & MacCarthy, B. L. (2021). Blockchain-Enabled Supply Chain Traceability in the Textile and Apparel Supply Chain: A Case Study of the Fiber Producer, Lenzing. *Sustainability (Basel), 13*(19), 10496. doi:10.3390u131910496

Avadanei, M., Olaru, S., Ionescu, I., Ursache, M., Ciobanu, L., Alexa, L., Luca, A. V., Olmos, M., Aslanidis, T., Beļakova, D., & Silva, C. (2020). ICT new tools for a sustainable textile and clothing industry. *Industria Textila (Bucuresti), 71*(5), 504–512. doi:10.35530/IT.071.05.1811

Brynjolfsson, E., Hitt, L., & Yang, S. (2002). Intangible Assets: Computers and Organizational Capital. *Brookings Papers on Economic Activity, 2002*(1), 137–1814. doi:10.1353/eca.2002.0003

Brynjolfsson, E., & Yang, S. (1996). Information Technology and Productivity: A Review of the Literature. *Advances in Computers*, (43), 179-214.

Chen, C. (2019). Value Creation by SMEs Participating in Global Value Chains under Industry 4.0 Trend: Case Study of Textile Industry in Taiwan. *Journal of Global Information Technology Management, 22*(2), 120–145. doi:10.1080/1097198X.2019.1603512

Dal Forno, A. J., Bataglini, W. V., Steffens, F., & Ulson de Souza, A. A. (2021). *Industry 4.0 in textile and apparel sector: a systematic literature review*. Research Journal of Textile and Apparel.

Devaraj, S., & Kohli, R. (2003). Performance Impacts of Information Technology: Is Actual Usage the Missing Link. *Management Science, 49*(3), 273-289.

Giwa, A. (2010). Information technology and the supply chain management for the textile industry. *Journals for Information Technology*, 26.

Gakunu, P. (2004). *E-Government Strategy for Kenya*. Available: https://www.apc.org/apps/img_upload/6972616672696361646f63756d656e74/egov_Presentation_for_ICT_Conven

Hardill, I., & Wynarczyk, P. (1991). A research note: Information technology and company performance in the textile industry. *New Technology, Work and Employment*, *6*(1), 65–70. doi:10.1111/j.1468-005X.1991.tb00132.x

Igyor, G. A. (1996). *The Economic and Social Benefit of Telecommunications Technology*. Paper Presented at the Animal International Conference on Information Technology Management Infotech.

Kirstein, T. (2013). The future of smart-textiles development: new enabling technologies, commercialization and market trends. In *Multidisciplinary know-how for smart-textiles developers* (pp. 1–25). Woodhead Publishing. doi:10.1533/9780857093530.1

Ku, C., Chien, C., & Ma, K. (2020). Digital transformation to empower smart production for Industry 3.5 and an empirical study for textile dyeing. *Computers & Industrial Engineering*, *142*, 106297. doi:10.1016/j.cie.2020.106297

Legnani, E., Cavalieri, S., Pinto, R., & Dotti, S. (2011). The potential of RFID technology in the textile and clothing industry: Opportunities, requirements and challenges. In *Unique radio innovation for the 21st century*. Springer. doi:10.1007/978-3-642-03462-6_14

McNamara, K. (2008). *The global textile and garments industry: the role of Information and Communication Technologies (ICTs) in exploiting the value chain*. Academic Press.

Moon, K., & Ngai, E. (2008). The adoption of RFID in fashion retailing: A business value-added framework. *Industrial Management & Data Systems*, *108*(5), 596–612. doi:10.1108/02635570810876732

Narayanan, B. G. (2008). Effects of phasing out of MFA quotas on Indian garment exports, 1992-2003. *Regional and Sectoral Economic Studies*, *8*, 71–88.

Nayak, R., Singh, A., Padhye, R., & Wang, L. (2015). RFID in textile and clothing manufacturing: Technology and challenges. *Fashion and Textiles*, *2*(1), 9. doi:10.118640691-015-0034-9

Research, G. V. (2021). *Textile Market Size, Share & Trends Analysis Report By Raw Material (Wool, Chemical, Silk), By Product (Natural Fibers, Polyester), By Application, By Region, And Segment Forecasts, 2023 - 2030*. Retrieved from https://www.grandviewresearch.com/industry-analysis/textile-market

Reynolds, K. E., Folse, J. A. G., & Jones, M. A. (2006). Search regret: Antecedents and consequences. *Journal of Retailing*, *82*(4), 339–348. doi:10.1016/j.jretai.2006.08.007

Seritag. (2023). *The Ultimate Guide to Using NFC Garment Tags for Clothing*. Retrieved from https://seritag.com/learn/using-nfc/garment-nfc-tags-in-clothing

Shweta & Gadkari. (2022). *RFID Technology Used in Apparel Industry*. Retrieved from https://textilelearner.net/rfid-technology-used-in-apparel-industry/

Tewari, S. K., & Misra, M. (2012). The Impact of ICT on Manufacturing Industry: An Empirical Analysis. *2012 International Conference on Communication Systems and Network Technologies*, 924-929. 10.1109/CSNT.2012.197

Uddin, F. (2019, August 28). *Introductory Chapter: Textile Manufacturing Processes*. doi:10.5772/intechopen.87968

Yasir, M., Ansari, Y., Latif, K., Maqsood, H., Habib, A., Moon, J., & Rho, S. (2022). Machine learning–assisted efficient demand forecasting using endogenous and exogenous indicators for the textile industry. *International Journal of Logistics Research and Applications*, 1-20.

Chapter 12
Role of Social Media Influencers in Fashion and Clothing

Anshu Agarwal
CHRIST University (Deemed), India

Sunanda Vincent Jaiwant
CHRIST University (Deemed), India

ABSTRACT

This study provides an overview of the influence of social media influencers in the fashion and clothing industry. With the increasing presence of social media in people's lives, individuals are easily influenced by what they see online, leading to the adoption of trends promoted by influencers. Influencers, who have established their personal brand and gained a substantial following, play a key role in shaping consumer preferences and driving sales. Social media platforms allow fashion brands to connect with their audience, democratizing fashion shows and enabling direct interaction. The rise of fast fashion and the influence of fashion influencers have contributed to the growth of the clothing industry. Businesses are now utilizing AI-powered analytics and dedicated platforms to enhance their influencer marketing strategies. In summary, social media influencers have a significant impact on consumer behavior, driving sales and shaping trends in the fashion and clothing industry.

INTRODUCTION

Now that the world is always on social media it directly impacts their thinking and the choices they make after using any social media app. What this means is, people are influenced easily by what they see and want to adapt to the things shown online. Without even realizing it we let social media dictate what we do, how we do it and who we do it for. Here's where influencers come in, they're people who promote various things and set up their brand, this then becomes a lifestyle. It all depends on the number of followers and how many people actually take something away from what they are saying. This leads to people copying or trying to be similar to the influencers. This not only increases the growth or demand for products that these influencers use but also, brands hire people whose ideologies align with their

DOI: 10.4018/978-1-6684-8753-2.ch012

brand image and values. Through the power of social media, these influencers are able to make a living out of it, it all comes down to how much you can make people relate to you. The more they believe in you the more the influencer grows. This process is also known as influencer marketing.

SOCIAL MEDIA

Social media makes it easier for people to communicate with one another online. Social media encompasses a wide range of applications and platforms, including Facebook, Instagram, Twitter, and YouTube, that let users share information, communicate online, and create communities. More than 4.7 billion individuals, or nearly 60% of the world's population, utilize social media.

Social media messaging platforms and applications are currently the most widely utilized websites worldwide. Early in 2023, 94.8% of users visited websites and apps for chat and messaging, closely followed by 94.6% of users who visited social media platforms. The second most popular site was a search engine, with 81.8% of visitors visiting it.

However, those who use social media have more friends and more diversified personal networks, especially in developing nations, according to a 2019 poll by the Pew Research Centre. In a poll of 13 to 17-year-old American teens conducted by the Pew Research Centre in 2022, it was discovered that social media helps 80% of teenagers feel closer to their friends. According to Pew Research Centre, one in three people said social media has a primarily beneficial impact on them, while 59% said it has neither an advantageous nor a negative impact. The article is titled "Connection, Creativity, and Drama: Teen Life on Social Media in 2022." Businesses are also utilizing social media advertising to target their customers, develop a devoted following, and develop a brand culture. More than 200 million small companies reportedly utilize Facebook's platform for marketing.

In addition, 90% of marketers claim to promote on Facebook.

Around 55% of all advertising expenditures worldwide in 2022 were spent on social media and search. Additionally, it is the advertising channel's fastest-growing sector (Dollarhide & Drury, 2023).

INFLUENCERS

An influencer is a person who: has the ability to influence other people's purchase decisions due to their authority, expertise, position, or connection to their audience a devoted audience in a certain specialty. The size of the following is determined on the size of the niche's topic.

It is crucial to keep in mind that these people are not just marketing tools, but rather social connection assets that organizations may work with to accomplish their marketing goals (Geyser, 2022).

FASHION AND CLOTHING INDUSTRY

Statistics

These statistics are given to represent the current scenario as to which we can get an idea of how many people are in the labor force and the amount of which are in the clothing and apparel industry (Fashionunited, n.d.).

Figure 1. The total population of the world and also measures the people currently in the labor force

General data

Population:	7.84 billion (in 2021)
Labor force:	3.45 billion (in 2021)
Unemployment rate:	5.9% (2022 global estimate)
GDP per capita (PPP):	16,300 US dollars 12 262.9 US$ (in 2021).

This determines the percentage of 5.9% in the unemployment rate globally.

Figure 2.

Worldwide Apparel & Footwear Market Size

*Retail Value RSP USD million

2019	2020	2021	2022 forecast	2023 forecast
1,773,406.9	1,453,277.5	1,716,952.2	1,846,222.0	1,959,592.1

The worldwide apparel market has only seen growth throughout the years as the population is growing and the demand for clothes is also increasing.

Especially with brands providing fast fashion, which promotes different styles in short spans of time.

Figure 3. Representation of the largest demand in apparel worldwide with China being the most to promote fast fashion, but that is relevant as China has the highest population in the world, which directly syncs with the demand factor

Largest Apparel and Footwear Markets Worldwide (2021)

The United States and China account for the majority of the global apparel demand. You find the five markets with the highest market size in 2021 in USD million below.

China	427,153.9
USA	364,136.6
United Kingdom	70,734.8
Germany	69,957.3
Japan	65,764.0

E-COMMERCE

For years, online buying has increased. Online shopping is becoming more and more popular income in 2020, global e-commerce sales increased to $4.2 trillion, and the trend persisted in 2021, resulting in an anticipated 2.14 billion online customers worldwide and $4.9 trillion in income from online purchases.

The entire value of international e-commerce sales is anticipated to reach $5.5 trillion in 2022. By 2025, it is anticipated that worldwide internet retail revenues would reach $7 trillion.

Online sales make up 19.6% of all retail sales.

Almost twenty percent of retail transactions globally in 2021 were made online. According to projections, that percentage will rise to 21% in 2022, and by 2025, the online sector will account for over 25% of all retail sales worldwide.

INFLUENCER MARKETING

Influencer marketing entails a company working with just an online influencer to promote one of its goods or services. Many influencer marketing partnerships are less concrete than that; for example, businesses may engage with influencers to increase brand recognition.

Influencers, unlike superstars, may be found in any location. They might be anybody. Their massive online and social media followings are what make them influential. A prominent fashion designer on Instagram, a well-read cybersecurity writer who tweets, or a recognized marketing executive at LinkedIn can all be considered influencers. There are prominent people in every industry—you simply have to look for them. Some individuals will also have tens of thousands (though not million) of followers. However, many will appear to be average folks. They may have just 10,000 followers, or even less in some situations. Nonetheless, they will have established a reputation as specialists in their industry. They are indeed the go-to persons for answering people's questions. They are the ones who create the most interesting social postings on their particular themes, depending on their field of expertise. They post the most beautiful photos, create the most amusing movies, and host the most instructive online debates (Geyser, 2022).

INFLUENCER MARKETING GROWTH

The diagram below shows the increase in influencer marketing throughout the years and it just proves how effective these influencers are and how they've taken over social media. This also means that businesses are making $5.2 ROI for every $1 spent on influencer marketing.

Figure 4.

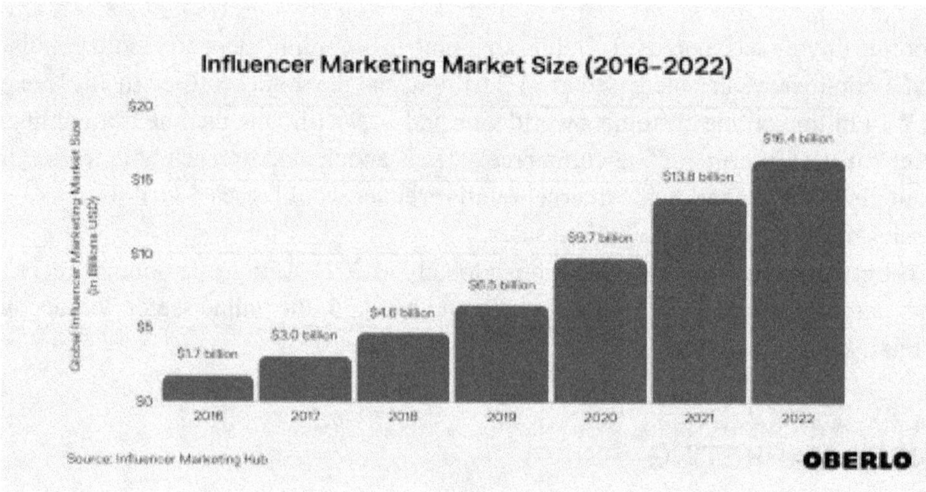

INFLUENCERS AND THE FASHION INDUSTRY

The effect of influencer marketing on boosting sales for fashion, premium, and beauty businesses rose by 18% between 2019 and 2020, with professionals naming it as one of their top aims when partnering with artists.

Even as the Fashion Market is constantly evolving, with new trends and industry patterns, there is frequently something new for everybody. With the growth of social media platforms, everybody and everyone now has accessibility to a center stage through which businesses may communicate their core marketing message. These fashion brands saw an increase of Fashion Bloggers & Fashion Influencers across Social Media Networks and realized they could engage with their target audience via Influencers to efficiently reach a larger audience and achieve a higher return on investment. Such Fashion Bloggers and Fashion Influencers have trend establishing power and can easily sway consumer purchasing behavior since they have a high confidence quotient among their following.

Fashion bloggers can have an impact on the fashion business, either directly or indirectly. A blog is a type of social media and a telecommunication network through which messages circulate internationally. Bloggers may utilize this medium to promote their preferences and affect how specific businesses or items are presented and perceived. Furthermore, blogs can start new trends in an industry or debate topics that firms may not want to discuss publicly, including such ethics or environmental issues (Launchmetrics Content Team, 2020; Irish Blogger Agency, n.d.; M&K, 2017).

Figure 5. Brand post opinion

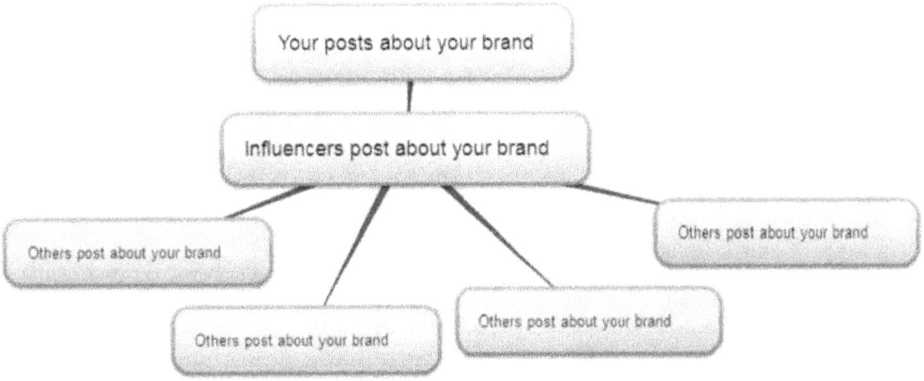

The figure above not only shows a simple representation of how the people think but also how individuals follow the crowd most of the time. The influencers hold the power to dictate the narrative for a brand and it directly affects the sales of fashion and clothing.

FACTORS THAT AFFECT THE FASHION INFLUENCERS (UPFLUENCE SOFTWARE)

- ***Number of followers***

It's common knowledge that an influencer's reach and potential effect are significantly influenced by the amount of followers they have. A larger audience that may be acquainted with the influencer's content and brand partnerships is indicated by a higher number of followers. To increase their exposure, brands frequently look for influencers that have a sizable fan base (Upfluence Software, n.d.).

Figure 6. Number of followers

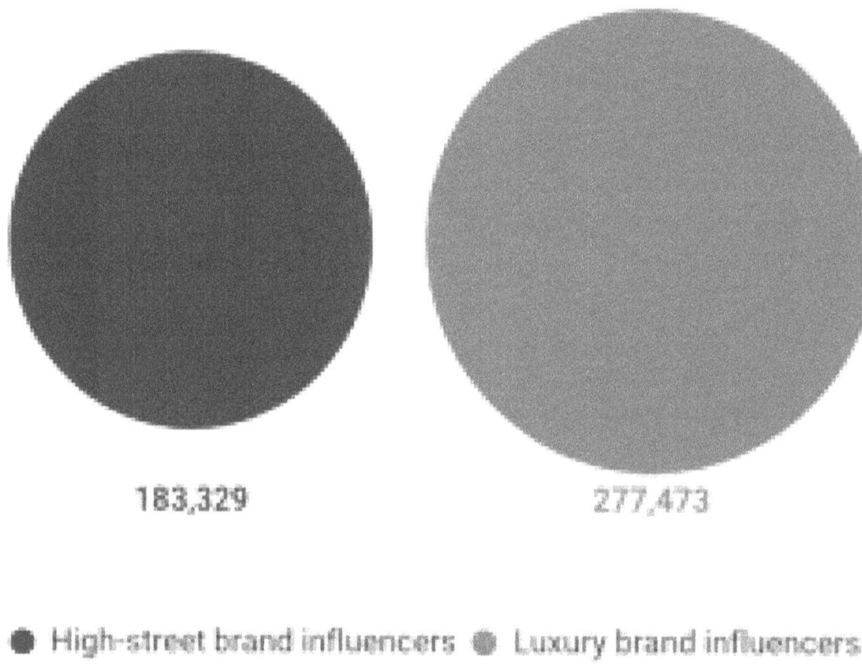

- ***Number of engagements of platforms***

Brands take into account an influencer's social media activity alongside the number of followers they have. Metrics for engagement include likes, comments, shares, and saves. An engaged and involved audience is shown by a high degree of engagement, which shows that the influencer's followers are interested in their material.

Figure 7. Number of engagements of platforms

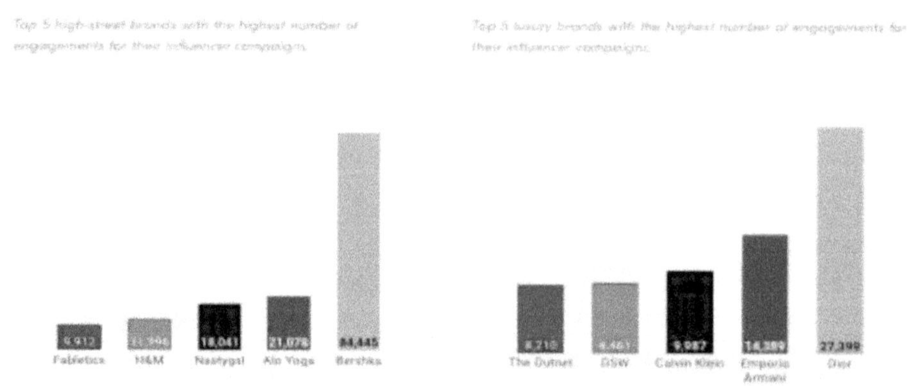

- ***Engagement rate throughout***

An important indicator, the engagement rate, gauges how many interactions an influencer gets on their material in relation to the number of followers they have. It gives information on the effectiveness and sincerity of an influencer's audience involvement. High engagement rates are sought after by brands since they suggest a more devoted and interested audience.

Figure 8. Engagement rate throughout

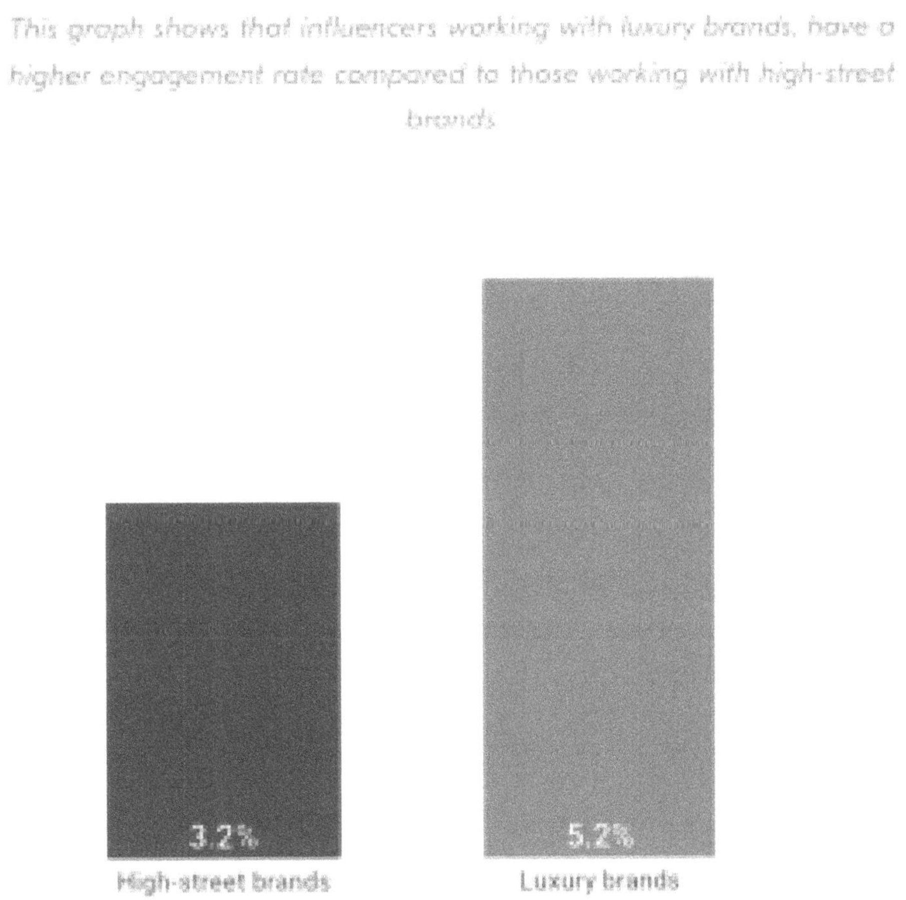

- ***Audience by country***

For companies aiming to reach certain markets, the geographic dispersion of an influencer's audience may be important. Influencers having a primarily local or regional following might be helpful for firms who want to market their apparel and fashion items to certain nations or areas.

Figure 9. Audience by country

- ***Audience by gender***

Brands that have particular gender-targeted goods or campaigns should be aware of the gender makeup of an influencer's following. It ensures that the influencer's material is in line with the marketing goals and target market for the company.

Figure 10. Audience by gender

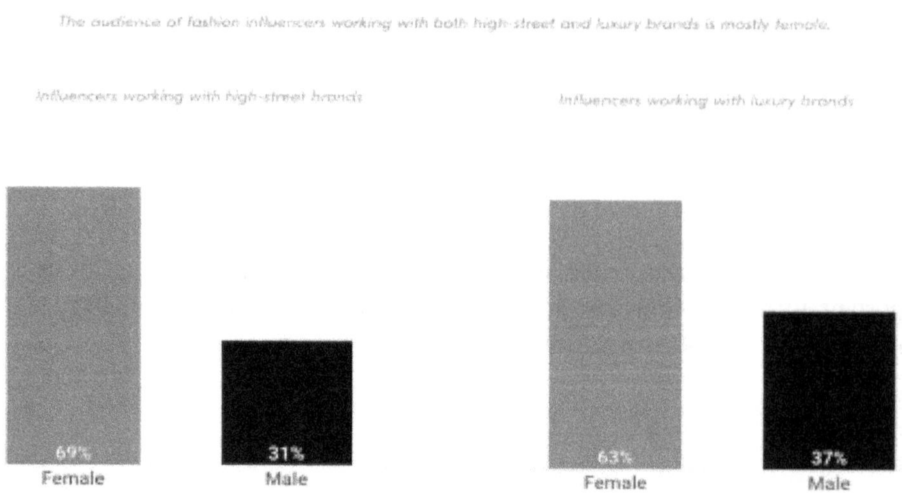

- ***Audience by age***

Another important consideration for companies is the audience's age breakdown of the influencer. Different clothes and fashion companies target particular age groups, thus it might be more successful to collaborate with influencers whose followers fit the brand's target audience to increase interest and conversions.

Figure 11. Audience by age

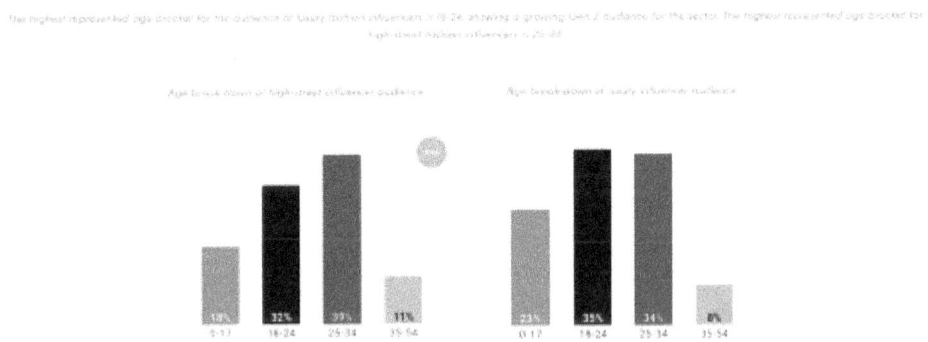

- ***Number of sponsored posts***

The quantity of sponsored content an influencer has already posted may be a good indication of their familiarity and competence working with businesses. Influencers with a healthy mix of paid and organic content are frequently taken into account by brands as it shows their sincerity and enthusiasm for the goods they promote.

Figure 12. Number of sponsored posts

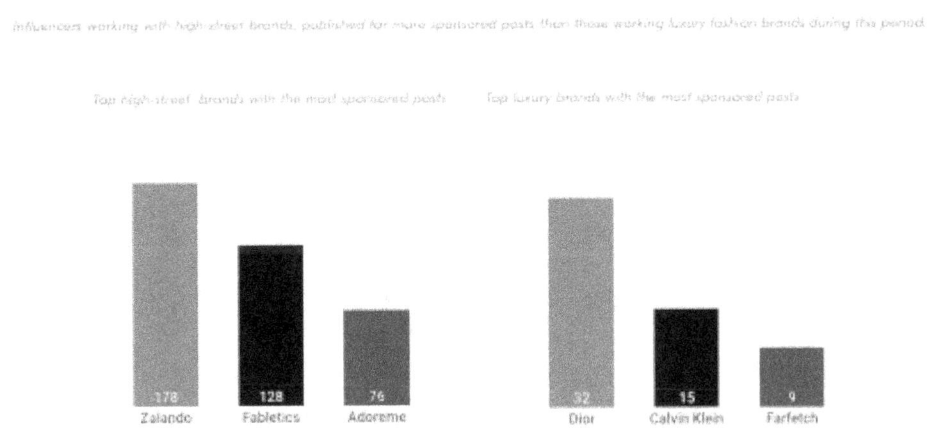

- *Hashtags*

Utilizing hashtags wisely may increase the reach and discoverability of an influencer's material. Brands evaluate an influencer's hashtag usage, their relevance for the fashion and apparel sector, and if they are well-represented in trending or specialized hashtags.

INFLUENCERS INFLUENCING THE DECISION MAKING OF PEOPLE TO BUY CLOTHING

As we know that the influencers have the upper hand in making the product marketable. They have various ways to show the appeal to the public and they do it through various apps like, Instagram, twitter, Facebook, snapchat, YouTube, etc. these apps have not only created features which help the influencers increase their reach but also altered their algorithm according to their convenience. When people think about buying the product, they see an influencer wearing it, they can find it in their bio or the post description and in case of blogs in the video itself. This makes the individual want to buy the product themselves and they end up buying products they didn't know they needed until now. That's the power of influencers over the public.

These individuals make purchase decisions based on the look of the product on the influencer, this generates more likes and comments for the influencer. If a particular influencer is famous for their style, then whatever they showcase on their platform becomes the new trend and the next thing you know, everyone is wearing those types of clothes.

REVIEW SYSTEM OF INFLUENCERS

As humans, the trust factor comes into play when we buy something be it fashion or any other goods. Influencers build this trust towards themselves over the years, this makes people who follow them, trust their judgment on products. If an influencer is reviewing a product, then the follower can assess the products and whether it's worth buying or not.

Influencers talk about their personal experience with the brands they are reviewing and you get to see the product on them and their views on it. If you end up liking the product then you end up buying it based on the influencers review.

People now depend on influencers and bloggers to make a judgment so it's easier for them to buy the product.

ENGAGEMENT OF FOLLOWERS IN THE FASHION INDUSTRY

Fashion firms utilize social media to bring their clients closer to their beliefs. Fashion shows used to be private events attended solely by the privileged. Nowadays, all well-known companies allow Instagram models to attend catwalk events in order for influencers to broadcast the event directly with their followers. All Instagrammers must do is follow a specific hashtag to have access to all of the material associated with that hashtag.

Many fashion firms struggle to foster a feeling of community, yet Instagram models include a previously established following, connect with its followers, and may legitimize a brand's products to make them more available to the general public.

The fashion business is recognized for its quick pace, and the advancement of technology has caused a shift in purchasing habits. Instagram models provide firms access to a new sort of advertising, one that might be difficult if they do not employ the proper individual and do not utilize their creativity to produce content (Fashion Gone Rogue, n.d.).

MARKET SHARE OF APPAREL

Because of the growing popularity of quick fashion among millennials, the clothing industry increased its sales share significantly in 2019. Fashion influencers frequently wear brand sponsored clothing and urge their followers to copy or develop a new style, as well as share their material on social networks using hashtags and hashtags. This enables businesses to raise awareness and measure interaction among their target consumers. To increase audience interest in influencer marketing methods, e-commerce businesses such as Myntra in India have begun hosting fashion influencer talent showcases in a digital reality format (Grand View Research, 2018).

Figure 13. Market share of apparel

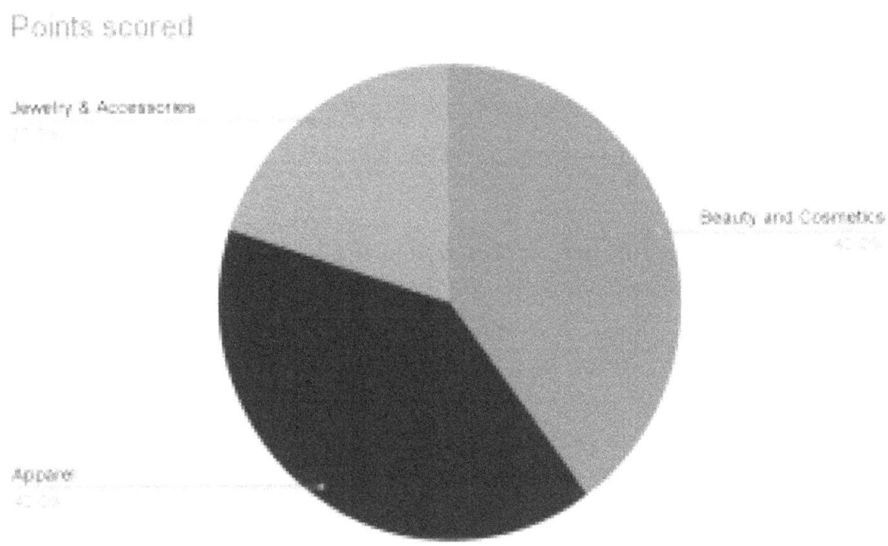

INSIGHTS

Network operators inside the fashion influencer sector have begun to offer Intelligence search engines that can provide specific data about influencers and assist clients in making their influencer selection. InfluencerDB and Upfluence Inc., for example, provide AI-enabled analytics services that allow businesses to compare campaign and influencer success more effectively. Companies have also begun to establish fashion influencer-specific platforms. During July 2019, Launchmetrics released Insights100, an interactive microsite that provides brands and agencies with competitive benchmarking versus their peers by assessing marketing campaign success and analyzing investment efficacy.

The growing customer base of social networking websites like YouTube and Facebook seems to have been critical in driving industry expansion. During September 2019, YouTube introduced '/Fashion,' a one-of-a-kind center for beauty and fashion video. Fashion firms are also attempting to interact with more diverse influencers in order to provide them with input into creative direction and filming. This has aided in the development of more authentic ties with their customers (Grand View Research, 2018).

INTENTION TO BUY AND MINDSET TOWARD THE INFLUENCER

Purchase intention (PI) (client or buyer's intent) is a measure of a consumer's proclivity to purchase a product or service. The "total of cognitive, emotional, and behavioral toward acceptance, purchase, and the use of product, service, ideas, or certain behaviors" is referred to as PI. This Theory of Buying Behavior, created by Howard and Sheth in 1969, is a theory of consumer decision-making. This theory included psychological, marketing, and societal concerns, implying that these elements influence customers' decision-making processes; the model's outputs include attention, understanding, attitude, intention, and purchase. Finally, Javed et al. introduced the multi-step flow hypothesis, which proposes the influencers have a large network that distributes material to multiple levels.

Although research has demonstrated that attitudes about purchase intention are important, attitudes toward the influencer are not a well-defined term. Followers' views of trustworthiness and attitude toward influencers are favorably influenced by perceived influencer-product congruence (Magano et al., n.d.).

CREDIBILITY AS PERCEIVED

The degree to which consumers trust the items as well as the material about them is referred to as perceived credibility. According to the Source Credibility Theory, factors of source credibility

include trustworthiness, knowledge, resemblance, and attractiveness. It was discovered that beauty, trustworthiness, knowledge, and resemblance are considered as essential factors of social media influencers' perceived legitimacy.

In uncertain scenarios, customers gather answers from many other consumers or comparable individuals, so how they view them becomes a significant problem that influences their purchase selection process. In this view, the visual display of an influencer's extroversion has a direct beneficial impact on the perceived trustworthiness of the same, which then in turn increases the possibilities of buy intention, which is the main goal of commercial businesses and campaigns.

Empirical data suggests that perceived credibility, also known as expert authority, has a favorable impact on attitudes about the influencer, attitudes toward the brand, and buying intent. Furthermore, one of the most crucial variables for membership and purchase intent on YouTube is the perceived legitimacy of any given material. Similarly, the trustworthiness of social media influencers active on Instagram and YouTube is positively related to purchase intent (Magano et al., n.d.).

TRUSTWORTHINESS

As a moral worth, trustworthiness is the ability to achieve and sustain a trustworthy, credible, quantifiable, and verifiable condition. Thus, trustworthiness is a personal characteristic that assures credibility, reliability, and honesty. "Issues with the credibility of social media are sometimes skewed and fraudulent feedback derived by purposeful manipulation of online evaluations".

The credibility of a specific influencer has a significant impact on modifying customers' perceptions of degrees of sincerity, genuineness, and truthfulness, and is a critical factor in deciding buy intention.

The reliability of social media influencers is a key predictor of buy intention, according to empirical research. Truthfulness, likeability, and familiarity impact Instagram users' purchase intention toward fashion goods. Furthermore, when moderated by the value of the digital influencers' material, trustworthiness does have an implicit effect on purchase intention. In the case of celebrities, one of the elements that positively influences buying intention was discovered as trustworthiness. Furthermore, the credibility of influencers is the most crucial prerequisite for purchase intention.

EXPERTISE ASSUMED

According to the research, digital influencers play an important role in persuasion, particularly since they impact customers' purchase intentions. Expertise is one of the predictors of purchase intentions, resulting in much of which one sees, when orthodontic doctors inevitably would seem in toothpaste commercials, as well as being an influencing factor in the intention to buy when it

arrives to celebrities, which is very apparent throughout the sale of perfume, which tries to sell a lifestyle and a willingness for status connected to the product, and also linked to certain other items as banal as body wash or, on the other hand, luxury products including such Louis Vuitton handbags. Empirical data suggests that the skill of social influencers is a significant predictor of purchase intent. Furthermore, trust and perceived knowledge have a beneficial impact on attitudes towards influencers, purchase intent, and brand attitude (Magano et al., n.d.).

LIKEABILITY

Likeability may be defined as a psychological element that determines how consumers respond to a brand, item, or service, especially in terms of physical appeal, likeability, flattery, and affiliation. In this regard, generating material that appeals to favorability in branded groups on Facebook may result in greater online engagement, which can lead to commitment, word-of-mouth, and purchase intent. People want to buy from people they like; hence, being able to develop empathy is a vital and marketable attribute evident in famous salesmen, with a growing blurring of the online and offline communities as well as what works in both.

It has been observed that Individuals with such a large number of followers (20,000 or even more) are regarded as more liked since they are regarded as more famous; this may imply that tiny concentrations of followers may have a detrimental influence on users' likeability. Likeability does have a positive predictive impact on views about influencers and companies, word-of-mouth behavior, and purchase intention in the context of digital influencers. Likewise, the likeability of a particular brand has a favorable impact on its consumers' purchase intentions (Magano et al., n.d.).

SIMILARITY

Similarity may be defined as the level to which individuals align in terms of views, values, or other factors, impacting followers' word-of-mouth when evaluating their relationship with a certain influencer. The much-desired utterance on social media may be regarded as online gossip, as customers both are entertained and looking for approval and agreement from your peers and influencers. Furthermore, similarity acts as a mediator between an influencer's endorsement connection and the inclination to acquire the promoted goods.

External (i.e., name, age, gender, birthdate, location of residence) and internal (i.e., values, activities, attitudes or views, and preferences) similarities influenced users' perceived usefulness, pleasure, and trust transfer, which in turn influenced users' social consumer behaviors. Empirical research suggests that similarity influences a specific influencer's credibility, which is a key predictor of buying intention. One is inclined to infer that reputation is everything, as previous events have demonstrated, not least at the Oscars in 2022 (Magano et al., n.d.).

FAMILIARITY

Familiarity may be defined as a consumer's collection of encounters with a certain service or product over time. Familiarity raises the receiver's degree of comfort with the writer, making the sender appear more persuasive. According to empirical research, customers' intentions are greatly impacted by familiarity with the source and the ease of the information. It has a favorable association with purchase intention if the follower is much more familiar with influencers.

Furthermore, when the audience is familiar with the endorser, influencers are more likely to be effective than celebrities.

When it comes to companies, familiarity and information quality have a big impact on social media engagement, which might influence purchase intention. On the other side, sentiments about a consumer's purchasing intent are impacted by a digital influencer's likeability and familiarity. One purchases from people they like and respect.

In this sense, recognition is among the factors of celebrity endorsement. Furthermore, familiarity with a certain brand has a moderating influence on co-appearing product identification, attitudes, and purchase intention (Magano et al., n.d.).

ATTRACTIVENESS

According to McGuire's attractiveness model, a message's success is determined by the source's "familiarity," "likeability," "similarity," and "attractiveness" to the respondent. According to the literature, beauty is one of the seven factors of purchase intention, along with trustworthiness, attitude towards the brand, influencer credibility, parasocial interaction, and competence. When materialism is strong, beauty has a significant impact on purchasing intent. In the case of celebrities, beauty is one of the factors influencing buying intent.

In terms of digital influencers, attractiveness has been found as a relevant feature that impacts components such as brand image, product satisfaction, customer loyalty, and purchase intent. Furthermore, beauty influences online interaction and purchase intention, as well as favorably predicting sentiments about the influencers, word-of-mouth, and buy intentions. It was shown that beauty is a significant element influencing customers' purchasing intentions (Magano et al., n.d.).

LUXURY BRANDS AND FASHION INFLUENCERS

Luxury businesses avoided social networking sites and influencer marketing for many years because they did not want to cheapen their brand by making it available to everyone. Instead, the luxury industry depended on high-end stores and expression marketing among rich customers to spread the news about their items.

However, in order to adapt to the new digital marketing landscape, luxury firms have gradually used social networking sites and influencer marketing. Currently, 66%+ of luxury firms use influencer marketing to advertise their brand, yet 46% believe the programme is less than a year old. Another 28% claim their influencer marketing campaign is barely two years old. Obviously, influencer marketing is getting more popular among luxury firms, but it's still a relatively new strategy.

Luxury and fashion firms may collaborate with upmarket influencers to assist in spreading the word to their target consumers. Luxury brands, more than other businesses, will need to carefully identify influencers and build campaigns for their brand in order to maintain their company's values as well as other marketing tactics.

Luxury items are seen as idealistic, something that people wish to obtain. However, for these clients to fantasize about possessing a luxury product, they must be introduced to it. A well planned influencer marketing may help introduce new audiences to premium companies and eventually turn them into devoted consumers (Voburner, 2022; Donawerth, n.d.).

LUXURY BUSINESSES ENGAGED IN INFLUENCER MARKETING

When it pertains to a luxury goods business, there is a sense of exclusivity that only the wealthiest and also most elite may be sold to. There's even been debate about influencer marketing cheapening businesses, indicating that merely by engaging a more diversified audience, luxury goods lose their 'appeal'.

However, as highlighted by Vogue Business, it is an obvious reality that customers prefer faceless brands to faceless individuals. Gen Z, in particular, would prefer buy from a known face, especially if the item is expensive. In 2020, trend predicting organization WGSN invented the term "genuinfluencers," which are defined as "passionate individuals [who] are much more interested in providing advice, expressing their hobbies, and distributing impartial knowledge than selling brands or items." Brands that utilize influencers in this category to lead their ads convey a sense of humanity for their business, with customers drawn to the charming and likable frontperson. Gucci's recent partnerships with TikTok poseur Francis Bourgeois are a perfect illustration of this. 73% of Gen Z followers on Instagram are influencers — this is a sizable market of people who understand, accept, and, to some extent, anticipate influencer marketing. For premium firms to skip out on this solely for concern of being 'cheapened' is ludicrous. After all, a "well-planned influencer campaign" may "provide the groundwork for new audiences to discover premium brands and eventually become committed consumers."

BEST METHOD TO PARTICIPATE

So, we've spoken about why, but now we'll look at how. As previously said, 'genuinfluencers' (influencers with genuine passions and hobbies who have an impartial interest in the company in question) are a terrific place to start. Customers, particularly Generation Z, want someone who appears personable and regular. According to Vogue Business, 'this type of influencer is respected since they are either or seem like a strong attachment, as opposed to aspiring celebrities and influencers that were more popular prior to the epidemic.' Brands quickly become more approachable and enticing to younger audiences that have a sincere interest in connecting with the brand by selecting an influencer who meets this criterion.

All of your requirements are addressed by picking any influencer or celebrity which helps your company to keep a premium, 'elevated' air while yet being approachable and relevant. And, like with previous brand partnerships, the influencer in consideration must have the same ideas and values as the brand with whom they are partnering. 'Brands should be screening content producers before collaborating with them, recognizing that the image of the influencer company they choose to engage with significantly influences their image,' argues The Drum. This is especially crucial given that Gen Z is typically drawn by influencers who reflect their own personal beliefs - by connecting your company to the correct influencer, you'll get a supportive audience. According to a recent Voxburner study, 77% of Gen Zers believe it is vital that renowned people share their ideals.

HIGH-END BRANDS' ALTERNATE INFLUENCER MARKETING CAMPAIGNS

Some luxury firms simply cannot afford to present their most expensive items to influencers. Giving free things with each cooperation makes no sense if you're selling diamond jewels or $10,000 handbags. Instead, marketers may devise novel methods to capitalize on the influence of influencers.

Networking events and release parties are ideal venues for collaborating with influencers. An occasion like fashion week might provide a chance to encourage influencers to come and discuss their experiences. Influencers can also become acquainted with your brand firsthand. If you want to work with stars, your luxury business may offer lending out pricey goods for celebs to wear to their own events. This enables you to disseminate the word without relying on a costly and unsustainable gifting scheme.

When a luxury business plans an influencer marketing, the authenticity of the influencer's material should be prioritized. The fashion house should seek out influencers whose material is appropriate for easy sharing so that the company can incorporate it into its native publication schedule with picture attribution. To guarantee consistency, the messaging delivered to influencers should be identical for all partners, independent of the influencer's category (food, lifestyle, luxury, etc.).

To achieve any type of success in terms of both reach amplification and cross promotion, it is critical to ensure that the relationship will fit in naturally with the influencer's typical content flow. Our staff at Socially Intuit, for example, will assess an influencer's audience to verify that they are prospective eligible consumers. We would not desire a premium client to cooperate with just an influencer who already has worked with companies that the client does not want to be connected with.

CHALLENGES AND PROBLEMS

Identifying the Right Influencer

Matching the appropriate influencer with the right brand should be self-evident. However, many brands face this problem. Marketers that are unfamiliar with the realm of influencer marketing may encounter several obstacles in locating the ideal influencer to endorse their product or business. Influencers with a rapidly growing following may persuade a company to pick them over someone with a smaller audience but a better match for the brand. Scouting for influencers may be a time-consuming and intimidating exercise, especially if the marketing is unfamiliar with the primary message. Furthermore, many casting agents are not doing an excellent job of pairing influencers with companies, resulting in more friction and volatility than required. As a result, companies frequently struggle and launch non-profitable campaigns due to poor influencer selection. Spending some time and effort to discover the perfect individual will pay dividends in the long term (EnsembleIQ, 2018; Fields, n.d.).

Dependent on Platforms

Many influencer networks have devolved into competitive marketplaces in which businesses must compete against one another to find the ideal influencer for a particular campaign. Of course, these platforms have advantages, one of which is that marketers can simply scan the group of influencers inside one spot. In most situations, the drawbacks outweigh the benefits since all these platforms are already so freely available, provide shared rather than priority access to influencers, forcing businesses to compete with one another, and ultimately increase the cost of campaigns. By shifting your attention away from influencer platforms and onto alternate routes of influencer acquisition, you will be able to negotiate better prices. These methods assist in negotiating the cost without having to compete openly with another business bidding on the same influencer. Brand ambassador agency or the conventional manual searching for influencers are two alternatives. Brands that invest more time in vetting will get greater outcomes, and no AI can screen an influencer as well as a person.

Expensive

Influencer marketing was once a lot easier to understand. An influencer would provide content, advertise a product, and be adequately rewarded for their efforts. Prices were lower since fewer brands used this type of marketing than they do now. Nowadays, macro influencers will seldom get out of bed for anything less than $30,000 - $200,000, and this is not a joke. A fashion blogger having 100,000 followers would charge $60,000 for a blog article as well as another $10,000 for just a specialized Instagram post. Brands are responding by utilizing nano and micro influencers, in addition to brand ambassadors. Micro / nano influencers may not have a large following, but they do have a loyal audience that values their advice. They also charge far less for their services while still driving sales and influencing their communities.

Brand ambassadors, on the other hand, can be large influencers, including such professional athletes, who adore the brand and have a deep and long-lasting affinity with it.

Influencer Scam

Unfortunately, being an influencer is indeed a sought vocation, many resort to deceptive methods to grow their following and interaction on articles. Influencer deception is a genuine problem in the industry, with research showing that close to 20 percent of influencers having 50k - 100k followers have a large percentage of false followers.

People Can Identify Sponsored Posts

Marketers that work in display advertising are well aware that banner blindness is one of the most difficult difficulties they confront. Audiences are accustomed to the placement and appearance of advertisements, and they typically disregard them. The same thing occurs with influencer-created sponsored content. Their viewers are not illiterate. They recognize when they are sold a product and tend to disregard everything the influencer talks about the company with whom they have worked. They prefer to read an honest product review rather than a paid one. People are annoyed by influencers always pushing items on them. This is one of the reasons why businesses are changing their investments to micro and nano influencers. Because they are not paid several hundred thousand dollars for each post, their advertisements feel more genuine because they have less to lose if they say anything unfavorable. Nowadays, the FCC and similar organizations demand influencers to reveal that the article was sponsored, which might turn off the audience when they discover that it was paid for. Even though this approach is advantageous to all, audiences are still wary about being perceived as walking wallets.

Controversies Regarding Influencers

Influencers are being closely monitored by the mainstream media. Various scandals have soiled the influencer sector and made firms leery of entering agreements with influencers, as these crises are often unanticipated.

Negative Social Media Usage

On the internet, consumers and others have an unlimited number of possibilities to critique a company's products. Unfavorable reviews, whether genuine or staged, might appear on several websites and reduce demand for a certain product. A buyer may protest to her Facebook friends about an ill-fitting clothing or publish images of broken goods on Instagram.

Some social media comments encompass a whole brand or corporation. Commenters might object to a company's commercial methods (or perceived practices), as well as a CEO's or celebrity endorser's private time or political ideas. It may be hard to prevent unfavorable reactions entirely at a time of polarized viewpoints.

The issue for businesses is to gather this data and react rapidly to it. If social media comments are based on erroneous information, customers' misconceptions must be corrected. If the negative feedback is accurate, it provides a chance to address the issue, such as changing a style to better fit or publicly vowing to modify company practices that consumers dislike.

When there's no way to counteract unfavorable views, a corporation may be compelled to participate in costly demand structuring – more marketing efforts, price cuts, even special promotions — in order to clear surplus supply. To prevent stockpiling extra inventory, knowledge concerning lower demand should be incorporated into forecasting and planning as soon as possible.

Unexpected Occurrences

The unanticipated fashion event—good or terrible—is maybe the most difficult hurdle. When visiting imprisoned immigrant children, first lady Melania Trump was spotted wearing a jacket with a provocative slogan, making it one of the year's most talked-about fashion statements. The White House presented at least three interpretations regarding what the statement meant, and independent analysts proposed several more. Another clothing manufacturer took full advantage of the outrage by producing jackets and t-shirts with the opposite slogan, making them available for buy online within an hour or two (albeit they just wouldn't ship for several months), and selling out nearly immediately. The proceeds were given to charity.

To capitalize on the close to the end social media excitement about an unexpected event, as demonstrated by this example, an exceptionally flexible distribution network is necessary.

The Social Media Tidal Wave

The social media world may appear chaotic and uncontrollable, yet technologies exist to make sense of it, respond fast to the patterns it reveals, or even (in many cases) stay ahead of it. The difficulty for garment firms is being proactive instead of reactive in handling social media. This entails understanding your consumers sufficiently to be aware of what motivates them; assisting in shaping and directing the online discourse about your organization and goods; and being agile enough to capitalize on new possibilities that appear at any time. In a 2018 episode, Nike took a proactive stance by jumping headlong into the debate surrounding NFL players' demonstrations of police misconduct and launched an ad campaign featuring player Colin Kaepernick, a protester leader. Customers who disagreed with Kaepernick responded by torching Nike merchandise and threatening boycotts. However, there were more approvals than disapprovals. Nike's bold strategy paid off; it quickly gained a massive following via Instagram, Twitter, and Facebook. In a research note, Wedbush Securities analyst Christopher Svezia stated that Nike management "knows its American customer well, and the ad starring Mr. Kaepernick is really a plus for the company and likely its sales." Shortly after, the company's stock price reached a new high.

INFLUENCER MARKETING FUELING BRANDS

- ***Influencers assist you get to know your target audience better.***

Influencer marketing efforts can help you better grasp your target audience's preferences. The way your advertisements are received by people may reveal a lot about just how your brand or product is viewed. This will also assist you in making successful product modifications to meet the wants of your target market (Social, n.d.).

- ***Make it possible for your audience to engage with your brand.***

When celebrities talk about your business on social media, the audience is able to engage with it. With the support of celebrities, you can successfully express your marketing message while also conveying your business's USP. Influencers will also emphasize why your brand is important.

- ***Influencers assist you reach an untapped audience.***

A large number of users follow influencers. Brands might also gain access to an untapped audience pool. Influencer marketing efforts may also help you target a passive audience, which can enhance brand 's reach and engagement.

- ***Influencers aid in the creation of a need for your product/brand.***

Consumers only purchase items and services when they understand why they require them. Influencers can contribute to the creation of that demand! The influencer marketing you create will explain why your product is necessary and demonstrate how it will profit them. This is critical for increasing sales.

- ***Assists you in gaining an advantage over your opponents***

Influencer marketing gives you a competitive advantage. This marketing method helps you to properly present your brand highlights and offers the audience an idea of why they should choose your brand over others.

- ***Enables you to put appropriate CTAs***

With the support of influencers, you may direct the audience's behavior toward your business. This might be done to increase sales or to raise brand recognition. Influencers will assist you in creating content that achieves the goals of your campaign.

LIFESTYLE AND FASHION BRANDS MAY BENEFIT FROM INFLUENCER MARKETING

- ***Product marketing***

Influencer marketing allows you to advertise your brand's products across various social media channels. When it pertains to doing the same, influencers are creative and may utilize multiple video forms such as Reels, YouTube Shorts, and so on to market your business (Social, n.d.).

- ***Special discounts and promotions***

When it comes to discounts and sales, brands may use influencers by providing them with unique promo codes. This can also help businesses meet their sales goals.

- ***Contests and giveaways***

To keep viewers interested, brands might sponsor prizes and contests. This may be accomplished efficiently with the assistance of influencers. Influencers can conduct giveaways on behalf of the company and assist achieve the necessary reach and engagement.

- ***Live performances***

During the epidemic, brands used the most of live events. Influencers may be a component of your brand's events via live videos, allowing the public to engage from afar. This can assist in increasing brand recognition and reach.

- ***Influencers take over social media accounts***

When companies engage mega/celebrity influencers, they frequently choose social media takeovers. In this situation, influencers take over business's social media accounts for a set amount of time in order to attract more users and promote the brand. Takeovers frequently incorporate user interactions, media interviews, and so forth.

- ***Product evaluations***

Influencers are frequently allowed to review brands' products. This helps people make better decisions and, in the long run, improves brand loyalty. Users who are persuaded by the evaluations of influencers may become frequent buyers of your brand.

SELF BRANDING

Now that social media is such a huge revolution which can make or break a person's image. We should consider that not only clothing brands but the people who went unnoticed before are getting attention for their unique fashion and designs.

So self-branding means, when a person creates their own brand and creates an entity in the market which is not already existing. When this brand goes big or makes a huge profit, it can go for trademarking their name and make it official.

How Is All This Related to Social Media?

When people are able to put their designs out there it not only promotes new talent but also generates revenue for those who are new to the industry. This gives opportunity to everyone and a chance to become something in the fashion world, where big brands like Gucci, Louis Vouitton, etc., rule the industry.

This also gives way to more demand for fast fashion or unique pieces, with the help of social media the people are able to see what's out there and explore their own style.

The new features on so many social media apps allow you to go through a person's feed and pick out the pieces you like and save them, they also sometimes provide links to buy these clothes. This process of buying and selling creates demand in the industry and for app developers to add more features which make users' experience easier.

Influencers and Their Merchandise

All influencers, after making it big in the social media game, have come up with their own merchandise which includes a lot of clothing and apparel. This is done by self-branding their name and their influence in their followers' lives.

This makes way for them to actually start their own fashion lines and promote it on social media. These can be anything ranging from ladies' wear to couture to men's clothing, etc. the price range may depend on the popularity of the influencer as the more popular ones end up charging more because the followers are in their favor. With smaller and still growing influencers it's hard to price and start their own lines, but that's where they end up partnering with various brands to collaborate and help with the mass produce, their prices are also more reasonable comparatively.

FASHION BLOGGING

A fashion blog can cover a wide range of topics, including individual clothing items and accessories, trends in various garment marketplaces (such as haute couture, prêt-à-porter, and so on), celebrity fashion choices, and street fashion trends. They cover all levels of fashion, from the greatest brands to the small indie designers. Because "much of the dialogue is buying advice, generously sprinkled with consumer suggestions," many fashion blogs may also be classified as shopping blogs. This closely resembles the contents of fashion publications. Some fashion merchants have even created their own blogs to market their wares. Blogs that only reference fashion on occasion are not classified as fashion blogs, even if the author labels them as such.

Fashion is a multibillion-dollar industry with a significant influence on how common people dress and show themselves. But fashion is made up of more than just clothes; it is composed of designers, shoppers, retailers, editors, and editorialists. While all parties collaborate to establish a reputation, all of these partners can be impacted by outside influences, particularly blogs. Fashion is trend driven, and fashion blogs give a new method to track and supervise these fast-paced movements. As the quantity of fashion-based blogs grows, it is possible that the blogosphere will have a significant long-term effect on the industry (Apparel Search Company, 2006).

INFLUENCERS' PROMOTION OF FAST FASHION IS PROBLEMATIC AND UNSUSTAINABLE

Slow vs. Fast Fashion

When manufacturers mass-produce the most fashionable items and offer them to vendors at reduced costs, they take advantage of current fashion trends to earn quick money. This practice, characterized as fast fashion, deprives people of fair wages and has a severe impact on the environment by selling unethically made and low-quality apparel. The enormous amount of these badly manufactured clothes is a significant contributor to pollution in the globe – landfills and rubbish sites are filled in shredded, ragged garments created from cheap dyes by workers who are not given a decent wage for their labor.

Brands and apparel departments must achieve sustainability in order to put an end to the pollution and abuse caused by rapid fashion. Prioritizing quality above the number of items of clothing is a cultural concept that people must adopt if the climate disaster is to be slowed. This involves wearing clothes as long as possible, caring for each piece, buying less, and being a more informed product consumer. Slow fashion is a more environmentally responsible approach to clothing that promotes the idea that style is about adaptability rather than the next social media sensation (Larson, 2021).

Clothing Customs

We don't yet understand the extent to which social influencers have influence over their massive followings. Whether it's buying clothing online and seeing a retail advertisement, when your favorite influencer promotes a product, it makes you desire it.

A viral buzz produced. TikTok can spread to millions of phones, allowing fashion trends to emerge quickly and practically instinctively. Instant satisfaction is a crucial aspect in both quick fashion and social networking. Social media connection provides influencers with feedback and money, while followers gain joy from owning what is popular.

Fast fashion's rapid pleasure is damaging to our planet and the way garments are used and treated. Not only does the development, manufacture, and transportation of fast fashion generate greenhouse gasses, but it also generates a considerable number of waste byproducts. "More than nearly half of fabric fibers are now synthetic drugs, made from petroleum, so even if our clothing ends in a landfill (about eighty percent of textile waste produced in the United States ends up going to landfills or is annihilated), it will not decay," wrote writer Tatiana Schlossberg in a newspaper article titled "How Fast Fashion Is The Destroying the Planet." It's not simply a question of manufacturing costs, since fashion boosts carbon dioxide emissions and water use, but also of how our wasteful behaviors harm ecosystems.

Human Consequences

The affirmation that influencers gain from comments and likes reflects on their audiences and causes them to behave similarly. This harms our wallets and our ideas of fashion, implying that owning more apparel corresponds to having more style. A never-ending cycle of inexpensive fashion purchasing leads to bad working conditions and a pressure on resources. The moment has arrived for sustainability & slow fashion to become the norm.

As a shopper, avoid cheap runway looks in order to get more bang for your cash. Of course, no one is flawless, and no brand that supports sustainability in its manufacturing is either. Yet, to benefit society in its entirety, individuals must adopt a new perspective in order to comprehend the significance of fashion in our lives. Whether you like or dislike the notion of fashion, everyone wears clothing and participates in an industry that is geared to generate what is in demand and what is in style. It's a domino effect: as demand for sustainable fashion production grows, it turns into the new normal. This places the onus on customers to purchase wisely. Fashion may thus be defined as more than just a set of trends.

CONCLUSION

The increasing presence of social media in people's lives has a direct impact on their thoughts and decision-making processes. Social media platforms have the power to influence individuals, shaping their behavior and preferences. This influence is particularly evident in the fashion and clothing industry, where social media influencers play a significant role. Influencers are individuals who promote various products and establish their own personal brand, which becomes a lifestyle that others aspire to emulate. The size of an influencer's following and their ability to resonate with their audience, determine their influence and impact. Influencer marketing has become a crucial strategy for brands, as they collaborate with influencers whose values align with their brand image. Social media provides a platform for influencers to make a living, and their success depends on how well they can connect with their followers. This symbiotic relationship between influencers and brands is known as influencer marketing. Social media platforms also facilitate global communication, allowing individuals to connect with others worldwide. This connectivity is particularly valuable for teenagers, who feel closer to their friends through social media interactions. Businesses leverage social media advertising to target customers, build a loyal following, and establish a brand culture. The majority of online users visit social media platforms, making them the second most popular online destinations after messaging platforms.

The fashion and clothing industry has experienced significant growth in e-commerce, with online shopping becoming increasingly popular. Global e-commerce sales have risen steadily, with projections indicating continued growth. Influencer marketing has played a crucial role in boosting sales for fashion, premium, and beauty brands. Fashion bloggers and influencers have the power to shape consumer preferences and drive purchasing decisions, as their followers trust their judgment and seek to replicate their style. Influencers hold the ability to dictate brand narratives and directly impact the sales of fashion and clothing products. Factors such as the number of followers, engagement rates, audience demographics, and the use of sponsored posts influence an influencer's effectiveness. Social media platforms like Instagram, Twitter, Facebook, and YouTube provide influencers with the tools to showcase products and create trends. Influencers' reviews and personal experiences with brands help build trust among their followers, influencing their purchasing decisions.

Fashion firms leverage social media to engage with customers, allowing Instagram models and influencers to attend fashion shows and share the experience with their followers. This creates a sense of community and accessibility, bridging the gap between fashion brands and the general public. The clothing industry has gained market share due to the popularity of fast fashion among millennials, and fashion influencers play a vital role in promoting sponsored clothing and inspiring new styles. To enhance influencer marketing strategies, businesses are utilizing AI-enabled analytics services to measure campaign success and select suitable influencers. Fashion influencer specific platforms are also emerging, providing companies with more targeted and effective influencer marketing options. Overall, social media influencers in the fashion and clothing industry have significant influence over consumer behavior and play a crucial role in driving sales and shaping trends.

REFERENCES

Apparel Search Company. (2006). Fashion Blogs Definition. *Apparel Search*. https://www.apparelsearch.com/definitions/fashion/fahion_blogs_definition.htm

Dollarhide, M., & Drury, A. (2023). Social Media: Definition, Effects, and List of Top Apps. *Investopedia*. https://www.investopedia.com/terms/s/social-media.asp

Donawerth, S. (n.d.). *Carro*. https://www.getcarro.com/blogs/influencer-marketing-for-luxury-brands

Ensemble, I. Q. (2018). Social Media and Influencers: Impact on the Fashion and Apparel Supply Chain. *RIS News*. https://risnews.com/social-media-and-influencers-impact-fashion-and-apparel-supply-chain

Fashionunited. (n.d.). Global Fashion Industry Statistics. *Fashion news and fashion jobs*. https://fashionunited.com/global-fashion-industry-statistics

Fields, M. (n.d.). Biggest Problems with Influencer Marketing. *BrandChamp*. https://brandchamp.io/blog/biggest-problems-with-influencer-marketing/

Geyser, W. (2022). What is Influencer Marketing? The Ultimate Guide for 2023. *Influencer Marketing Hub*. https://influencermarketinghub.com/influencer-marketing/#toc-0

Grand View Research. (2018). Fashion Influencer Marketing Market Size Report, 2020-2027. *Grand View Research*. https://www.grandviewresearch.com/industry-analysis/fashion-influencer-marketing-market

Irish Blogger Agency. (n.d.). Why is Influencer Marketing Important for the Fashion Industry in 2022? — Irish Blogger Agency. *Irish Blogger Agency*. https://www.irishbloggeragency.com/why-use-fashion-influencers-for-fashion-brand-marketing

Larson, C. (2021). The Promotion of Fast Fashion from Influencers Is Problematic and Unsustainable. *The Daily Utah Chronicle*. https://dailyutahchronicle.com/2021/06/18/the-promotion-of-fast-fashion-from-influencers-is-problematic-and-unsustainable/

Launchmetrics Content Team. (2021). The Impact of Influencer Marketing on Fashion, Beauty and Luxury Sales. *Launchmetrics*. https://www.launchmetrics.com/resources/blog/influencer-marketing-impact-on-sales

M & K. (2017). Impact of Influencers in Consumer Decision Process: the Fashion Industry. *SCMS Cochin School of Business*. https://pdfs.semanticscholar.org/1469/eccb29f76b24e85cba8b6b60adf5ab4932d8.pdfm

Magano, J. (n.d.). Attitudes toward Fashion Influencers as a Mediator of Purchase Intention. *MDPI*. https://www.mdpi.com/2078-2489/13/6/297

Rogue, F. G. (n.d.). How Instagram Models Are Influencing the Fashion Industry. *Fashion Gone Rogue*. https://www.fashiongonerogue.com/how-instagram-models-are-influencing-the-fashion-industry/

Social, U. (n.d.). Influencer Marketing Guide for Fashion and Lifestyle Brands. *Unbox Social*. https://www.unboxsocial.com/blog/influencer-marketing-for-fashion-and-lifestyle/

Upfluence Software. (n.d.). The State of Influencer Marketing in the Fashion Industry. *Upfluence*. https://www.upfluence.com/industry-reports/fashion

Voxburner. (2022). Influencer Marketing for Luxury Brands | Gucci, Chanel and Savage X Fenty. *Voxburner*. https://www.voxburner.com/influencer-marketing-luxury-brands-gucci-chanel-savage-x-fenty/

Chapter 13
Role of Social Media to Enhance Brand Engagement and Brand Perception in the Textile, Apparel, and Fashion Industry

Vandana Ahuja
https://orcid.org/0000-0002-4512-7203
Symbiosis Institute of Business Management, Noida & Symbiosis International University (Deemed), Pune, India

Pooja Sehgal Tabeck
https://orcid.org/0000-0001-7473-3096
Symbiosis Institute of Business Management, Noida & Symbiosis International University (Deemed), Pune, India

ABSTRACT

The growth of the apparel industry in India is taking place at a brisk pace, and significant growth in private consumption is expected to create strong domestic demand for textiles and apparel. While textile and apparel exports from India are expected to increase rapidly, it is the manmade garments that remain the most significant contributor to the total revenue generated by this sector. The era of social media has moved fashion into the hands of the mass consumer base, which has access to large volumes of information through smartphones, mobile apps, and social networking sites. Apparel and fashion brands are using social networking sites to propagate what they term their DNA. Using social networking platforms tools like Instagram, Facebook, and Twitter helps drive influencer marketing, display and document outfits, help consumers compare brands, build brand-consumer loyalty and commitment, and generate trust and credibility for the brand. These platforms enable TAF brands to monitor their social media presence through social media metrics.

DOI: 10.4018/978-1-6684-8753-2.ch013

INTRODUCTION

India allows 100% Foreign Direct Investment in the textile and clothing sector. Subsequently the growth of the apparel industry in India is taking place at a brisk pace and significant growth in private consumption is expected to create strong domestic demand for textiles and apparel. While textile and apparel exports from India are expected to increase rapidly, it is the manmade garments that remain the largest contributor to the total revenue generated by this sector. The production and transaction costs are decreasing, price stability is rising and overall, this sector is witnessing a period of growth and profitability. Research further shows that India's domestic apparel market, comprising of the *ready to wear* category and the *ready to stitch* market will grow at a compounded annual growth rate of over 10%.

Salient Features of the Apparel Industry in India

1. India has an abundance of production of raw materials i.e.. Cotton, silk, jute etc.
2. There has been an increase in the penetration of organised retail in India.
3. India has a demographic dividend in terms of number of consumers for this sector.
4. Income levels of consumers are going up.
5. Skilled manpower is available at low prices.
6. Integrated Textile parks have been set up by the Govt. to give impetus to the clothing/textile/apparel industry.
7. Technological advancements are being embraced by this industry at a fast rate. The Ministry of Textiles in India is encouraging investments through increasing focus on schemes such as Technology Up-gradation Fund Scheme (TUFS).

Clothing is one of the rudimentary human needs, and with the evolution of civilisation, and the growth of commercialisation, clothing has transformed into apparel and fashion. The progression of the Indian fashion industry has been significant over the last few years and the new attributes of this industry are-

1. Displaying and documenting outfits in the online world is in vogue.
2. Designers and trends can be popularised online.
3. Representation, accessibility, and consumer convenience are the most important elements of this industry.
4. Fashion standards are subjective and malleable, and diversity has led to a scenario where people are willing to take risks, and nothing is taboo anymore.
5. Receptivity to new ideas and experimentation is at an all-time high.
6. The e-commerce era has supported hyper consumerism because of the huge discounts being given to consumers.
7. Influencer marketing is driving consumer choices.
8. Responsible consumerism is driving the need for eco-friendly apparel(Cowan & Kinley,2014).
9. Digitisation has changed the way organisations and brands interact with consumers.
10. Mobile platforms are dominating apparel, fashion, and accessory purchases. India's economy is becoming mobile-first and mobiles can drive sales and consumer influence, with the aid of social networking sites and ecommerce platforms.

Figure 1. The textile, apparel, and fashion industry and social media

Organisations in the Textile, Apparel and Fashion (TAF) world have taken note of all the above and are making use of social networking platforms tools like Instagram, Facebook and Twitter to drive influencer marketing, display and document outfits, help consumers in comparing brands, building brand-consumer loyalty and commitment and generating trust and credibility for the brand.

Fashion bloggers are popularising designers and trends and voicing their opinions over fashion inclinations and consumer choices. They are providing a commentary on fashion benchmarks and standards and supporting innovation and miscellany.

Mobile apps are the rage of the day. They are showcasing apparel brands, building differentiation, providing distinctive competitive advantages, and bringing access and convenience to the consumer, resulting in a lot of impulsive purchases. Additional cashbacks, promotional coupons, getting peer reviews etc. is helping these apps drive a wave of hyper consumerism.

To summarise, the three major social media tools used by TAF players include Social Networking platforms, fashion blogs and mobile apps (Figure 1).

Social Networking Platforms

The era of social media has moved fashion (which was earlier the prerogative of the elite only) into the hands of the mass consumer base, who has access to large volumes of information through smartphones, mobile apps, and social networking sites. Apparel and fashion brands are making use of social networking sites to propagate what they term as their DNA. This encompasses their perspective, their offerings, their catalogues, their brand personality, their socio-cultural-political views and whatever they stand for. Social networking sites are providing vast coverage of fashion events and literally the followers of brands are gaining complete access to these events via live coverage and explicit visual content. Videos, celebrity spotting and showcases have become the order of the day and the consumer is far closer to the apparel and fashion brands, than in earlier times. Consistent usage of Instagram stories by apparel brands, for store launches, new fashion lines, ready to wear collections has broken the walls of exclusivity and has substantially increased the resonance between brands and consumers. Well shot, clear, high-quality images create showroom quality display experiences for consumers and transform social networking platforms into virtual apparel and fashion marketplaces.

CASE STUDY 1: MANISH MALHOTRA-A STYLISH SOCIAL MEDIA PRESENCE

Manish Malhotra is a top Indian fashion designer and costume stylist who works with the topmost models and film fraternity, in India. His fashion label, Manish Malhotra, is one of the most sought-after fashion brands, with a turnover of several billion rupees. His clothes are an excellent blend of heritage Indian, imbibed with contemporary fashion trends. His Instagram handle @ManishMalhotraworld, helps create a distinctive identity for his fashion brand with the topmost global models and film stars posing for pictures after adorning his fashion line. His twitter profile 'The intricacy of embellishments and attention to detail, elevates the attire making it a signature creation', denotes the very essence of his creations. His youtube channel has over 37000 subscribers and over 36 lakh views and videos tracing his creative journeys, the meticulous choices of fabrics and cuts, the intricacy of designing and finishing touches are becoming descriptive journeys describing his dreams and growth from a simple fashion brand to an international label. The apt usage of social media to showcase his glamorous ensembles has made him a popular, respected, well sought-after brand. He has won further appreciation for his corporate social responsibility endeavours and his promotional work for several NGOs.

Some popular TAF brands on social networking platforms (Instagram, Facebook, Twitter and Pinterest) include (Table1):

Table 1. Popular TAF brands on social networking platforms and their competitive positioning

Brand	Competitive Positioning Using Social media
Nike	Emphasises sportswear and uses sportspersons as models to showcase their outfits
Raymond	A sartorial choice for the modern man, uses models to promote fashion for males
Van Heusen, India	Motivates customers to shop more, wear more and wear what they want and carry it with grace
Zara	Uses video apps and background filters and maintains a very stylish presence on social media.
Biba	Uses pretty female models to showcase itself as an ethnic brand which has made wearing traditional Indian clothes fashionables
Zodiac	Carries a distinctive campaign comprising clothes based on zodiac signs
Craftsvilla	A truly ethnic fashion destination for fresh designs, latest styles and trend updates
Siyaram's	An Indian brand, primarily for men, invites people to come home to Siyaram's, come home to style

Benefits of social networking platforms for TAF brands.

- Brands can use these platforms to create a distinctive positioning about themselves by hosting content that is unique and depicts them as a superior value proposition.
- Svelte models adorning outfits from a particular brand, with vivid visually appealing content can be used to trigger purchase intent in the consumer minds.
- Brands can use social networking platforms to reach out to customers in nearby locations. For instance, Facebook's proximity marketing feature can be used to reach customers in nearby locations and target them with ads about nearby places offering great products at good prices. Proximity marketing is associated with localised wireless distribution of advertising content that is associated with a particular location. As more and more consumers carry smartphones, thereby giving

access about their location, to several apps that they are using, organisations can push location specific information onto the consumers' mobiles. TAF brands can entice consumers moving in specific locations by serving advertisements that highlight their exclusive products, superior quality and large discounts.

- Some social networking platforms host a *shop now* feature, enabling consumers to indulge in impulse purchases. Ethnic fashion brand, Craftsvilla uses its social media presence to depict its understanding of tradition and trends and allows users to click on the *shop now* link to purchase whatever they have liked on the online domain.
- Brands can make use of these platforms to build a consumer brand relationship by showcasing themselves as emotionally sensitive, socially responsible, eco-friendly brands, contributing positively to society, at large(Nyilasy et al.,2014). Additionally, brands supporting movements like *body positivity* on social media, motivating men and women to feel more confident about their physical appearances and not compare themselves with others become more relatable and likeable for consumers. Fashion retailer *PrettyLittleThing* used social media to promote campaigns picturing plus size models and won accolades for its effort on Twitter, for challenging outdated practices and thought processes and featuring curvy individuals in their campaigns.
- The TAF world can also use social networking platforms to use brand influencers, who are significant opinion leaders in the TAF world, by virtue of their expertise or social standing, to promote their products. This also includes creative influencers who are considered authoritative and trustworthy in that specific domain. By ensuring that the target markets align with the opinion of these individuals, brands can use the power of social influence for triggering purchase intent among consumers. Fashion brand Siyaram's recently engaged film celebrity Ranveer Singh as its ever stylish and trendsetting new face. Ranveer Singh is characterised by his energetic and flamboyant image and a spiralling growth chart. His effervescence and spirited appeal heralds positive times for brand Siyaram's.
- Brands can also find ways to host specific theme-based campaigns to attract customers. Brands like Adidas have been using a *#HereToCreate* campaign to host the sayings of notable personalities from the sports, athletics, music and other domains. With content taglines like *Give her visibility and she will break barriers,* Adidas started an inspirational theme-based campaign for the next generation of female athletes, creators and leaders, which resonated well with the masses.
- TAF brands can use social networking platforms to generate link ads that promote discounts and can subsequently follow up with prospective consumers who engage with the ad, and offer them directions to the nearest outlet from where they can purchase the products.
- TAF brands can use social networking platforms to host user generated trivia by organising weekly contests or participatory forums in the online world, to solicit the ideas and opinions of their consumers.
- These platforms can be used to provide live coverage of fashion shows.

These platforms enable TAF brands to monitor their social media presence through social media metrics, like total number of interactions (comments, posts, likes) and interactions per posts. Additionally, metrics like post quality and page views enable organisations to identify what type of content garners more views and engagement from consumers (Geissinger & Laurell,2016). The Click Through rate (CTR) enables organisations to understand how many users are clicking through their content and is indicative of the effectiveness of the content being generated.

Case Study 2: Lakme Fashion Week

Lakme Fashion Week is the most sought after, coveted, and glamorous fashion event in India and receives tremendous social media coverage. The event is jointly organised by Lakme and IMG Reliance Ltd. and has been responsible for launching the successful careers of several Indian designers. An infographic compiled using marketing analytics software, Prophesee by social media firm, Social Samosa, in 2016 stated that day 1 of the event garnered 3274 mentions across Twitter and Instagram and over 290500 engagements. Interestingly, while there were more mentions on Twitter, it was Instagram that was actively able to engage the audience. Manish Malhotra and Sahil Aneja were the most sought-after designers. The most popular post was that actress Shradha Kapoor had walked the ramp for Manish Malhotra. Shradha Kapoor, Sushant Singh Rajput and Arjun Kapoor were the most talked about celebrities. In 2018, Lakme Fashion week partnered with Instagram, to hold a workshop featuring a host of fashion designers and brands including Pero, Shantanu & Nikhil, Nicobar, Jaypore, IMG Reliance's fashion team and so on. The objective was to conduct a masterclass intended at helping designers and fashion entrepreneurs in creating narratives to use the symbiotic relationship between Instagram and the fashion world successfully.

In addition to fashion brands promoting products in the TAF world, brand influencers, also play a significant role. Well established people in society unconsciously become opinion leaders and social media is used to propagate their thoughts. Whenever these people buy new products or try new experiences, they share details of the same on their social media pages and their followers or friends get to see the content. By creating mild feelings of envy and appreciation, these individuals influence their friends and peers in a subtle way and trigger their purchase intentions.

Interestingly, many brands including Monte Carlo, Allen Solly and Numero Uno do not have a very active or significant social media presence.

Fashion Bloggers in India

Akanksha Redhu, Fashion Oomph, Vanity No Apologies-Beauty and Makeup Blog, Purushu, Guilty Bytes, Gia says that, Let's Expresso, Shalini Mehta, Stilettos Diary, Style Inked, Calorific, Tashiara etc. are some popular fashion blogs in India. These blogs cover a multitude range of topics spanning fashion tips, lifestyle, hairstyles, trends, garments, street fashion, reviews on fashion products, blogger expertise pertaining to illustration, draping, pattern making, creativity etc. Several others carry beauty ideas, fashion tutorials, styling methods etc. and inspire people to become more fashionable.

This virtual presence benefits the bloggers in the following ways-

(i) These blogs serve as advertising channels to market their products. Bloggers can use their blogs to promote fashion events and provide coverage about these events, including digital photos and videos. If content on the blogs is unique and consumers are able to relate to it (Esteban-Santos et al.,2018), blogs garner a significant fan following and this fan base gives them their power.

(ii) Fashion bloggers are becoming trend setters and are major opinion leaders and influencers in the fashion world, owing to a very high status of legitimacy and large number of followers.

(iii) These blogs present opportunities for interactivity and networking. As word of mouth develops, the blogs gain visibility, thereby providing visibility for their writers (fashion designers). Word of mouth is a significant product adoption medium in the TAF world, as it is an influential source of marketplace information. People tend to buy what their friends or other opinion leaders recommend, endorse, support and buy. These bloggers inadvertently serve as brand influencers, and their product endorsements lead people towards the purchase decision.

(iv) These blogs enable consumer engagement and relationship building and enhance the connection between the blog writer and the followers (Sudha & Sheena,2017).

(v) Blogging breaks geographic boundaries and provides the fashion bloggers with a global exposure and reach. By connecting with other bloggers or hosting outbound links, citing other global fashion bloggers, the fashion writers can build a community online and enhance their reach.

Additionally, third party organisations, centred around specific themes and objectives can also serve as key influencers in the TAF world. For example, *Weddingsutra.com* is India's leading bridal media brand which serves to provide potential brides and grooms with information pertaining to all apparel, accessories and other services required for a nice wedding. By becoming a leading bridal brand hosting fresh ideas, advice and connections, *Weddingsutra* is generating a lot of media content tracing the grandeur and extravagance of Indian weddings. Interestingly, the organisation allows individuals to submit information pertaining to their upcoming weddings, provides support and coverage and a complete commentary on their blog. By hosting details of the fashion designers associated with the bride and groom's attire in the event, the blog hosts opinion pieces about the outfits, thereby giving visibility to the designers in a subtle, but very influential way.

MOBILE APPS

Popular TAF brands having mobile apps that are being increasingly used are Craftsvilla, Koovs, Zaara, Mango, Voonik, Limeroad, amongst several others. Smartphone apps allow users to shop, receive fashion tips or recommendations, offers and prizes, access latest fashion tips through the news feed in the apps and chat with their friends. With the arrival of geo-location technology, brands can use apps to connect with their shoppers at the point of purchase. Several brands also allow consumers to use apps to mix and match outfits in a virtual environment, while trying them on. This successfully induces consumer engagement.

Case Study 3: Zara

Zara is a prestigious global fashion brand which has embraced digitisation in a big way. In the global arena, the brand is effectively using technology to usher in augmented reality experiences, comprising simulated versions of real fashion models. Zara launched the Zara AR app for iOS and Android.

At the international level, augmented reality activations were launched across Zara's 120 stores, showing images of international models exhibiting Zara's new studio collection in augmented reality for 10 seconds. Additionally, customers could download the app, point the camera, and shop the look that they had liked. The Zara app allows consumers to get access to contemporary trends available, both for women and men, get information pertaining to new arrivals, fashion catalogues, collections and look books.

Brands like Mango, H&M, Stradivarius, Bershka have also launched apps that are very popular.

Consumer purchase of apparel is all about their perception of the brand, level of their engagement and relationship with the apparel brand (Garbarino & Johnson,1999). The following section details how

TAF brands can use social media to improve brand perceptions, levels of consumer engagement and consumer-brand relationship.

ENHANCING BRAND PERCEPTIONS USING SOCIAL MEDIA

Simply defined, perception refers to what a consumer thinks or feels about a brand. This takes into account his sensitivities, observations, insights and discernments. Perceptions are developed over time and govern a consumer's behavior towards a brand. Consumer perception in the TAF world, depends upon a consumer's experience (D'Souza et.al,2006), beliefs, knowledge, emotions, preferences, feelings, habits and reactions, and can be shaped by advertising and marketing messages. Organizations can influence the consumer thought process through external stimuli, and social media can play a vital role in this direction.

Using Van der Walt's theory (1991) of consumer perception, experience, beliefs and knowledge can be classified as the *cognitive* factors, the mental predisposition of a consumer prior to being subjected to an advertising message. This is the information about a brand, that the consumer formerly holds. Emotions and preferences can be categorised as *affective* factors and feelings, habits and reactions can be classified as *behavioural* components.

The following table (Table 2) details how social media can be used by the TAF sector to impact consumer perceptions. This can be done by analysing the cognitive factors and influencing the affective and behavioural components.

Table 2. Influencing consumer perception towards TAF brands, using social media

Factor	Implication	Social Media Usage by TAF Brands
Cognitive	Consumers rely on their past experiences before buying apparel and their attitude and behaviour towards specific brands depends on their past purchase and usage experiences(Padel & Foster,2005). Additionally, social aspects and social recognition for a brand shape consumer beliefs. Prior knowledge about a brand helps consumers evaluate brand attributes considering their own specific requirements, leading to the development of subconscious feelings for a brand.	TAF brands can use social media campaigns to not only collect consumer feedback pertaining to their past experiences, but also posting positive consumer testimonials. This will impact other consumers favourably. Additionally, TAF brands can use consumer feedback for consumer segmentation and personalisation of their marketing messages for better consumer targeting. Informational social media content about a brand's achievements, special recognition, new additions and latest items also add to a consumer's knowledge and impact the purchase decision.
Affective	Affirmative feelings, optimistic consumer sentiments and positive emotions towards clothing brands guide consumer preferences. Confirmatory opinions about brands shape constructive consumer perceptions.	Brands can use social media to show their socially responsible and emotional side. This can be done by hosting information about their corporate social responsibility endeavours on their social media pages or hosting content pertaining to garment care methods, eco-friendly and green approaches etc(Baker& Ozaki,2008).
Behavioural	Suitable TAF brand identities elicit relevant consumer responses in terms of product purchase. As consumer appreciation of a brand's achievements and personality grows, positive feelings for the brands develop and consumers are willing to revisit their routine habits and try out new brands.	Social media can be used to generate content to garner consumer empathy and brand resonance. This can be done by TAF brands by sharing content that is relatable, attractive, likeable and makes the consumer feel that he is in sync with the brand. For instance, if a TAF brand is trying to entice the middleclass consumers, social media content should focus on displaying striking apparel at affordable prices.

Case Study 4: Craftsvilla.com

Known for its unique ethnic apparel options, Craftsvilla, is an e-commerce portal that sells fashion accessories as well as beauty and lifestyle products. Craftsvilla has successfully tied up with the Ministry of Textiles, in India for promoting handloom products and with several small players, by aggregating artisans, designers and retailers onto the platform. Craftsvilla maintains a commendable social media presence across a diverse range of platforms. In a bid to get its customers and partners to interact with the brand and share their experiences, Craftsvilla has launched two closed groups on social media. These are the Craftsvilla fashion group and the Craftsvilla style partner group. Both the groups focus on encouraging members to participate in conversations and share their experiences and ideas with brand Craftsvilla. In addition to this, explicit social media posts by the brand, pertaining to breezy tassel earrings, patiala suits, low hem kurtis, crepe sarees, floral designs, stylish jewellery, festive colors, lehenga goals, dazzling evening gowns, bright spring silhouettes, monochrome georgettes and charming classics help Craftsvilla in addressing the cognitive components in shaping consumer perceptions towards the brand. There is a significant opportunity for the brand to showcase its sensitive side to come across as an emotional brand to address the affective components in shaping consumer perceptions. The striking consumer appreciation of the content visible through the huge volume of likes, shares and retweets clearly indicate that Craftsvilla's social media presence has been successful in soliciting the appreciation of its consumers.

Hence it is important for TAF brands to focus on the cognitive, affective and behavioral components, which will subsequently enhance consumer brand perception levels. It is vital for companies to keep collecting consumer responses and identifying whether they need to improve brand performance with respect to improving the consumer experience or strengthening consumer belief in the brand. Companies need to focus on enhancing consumer brand knowledge to ensure that consumers prefer the respected green brand and have positive feelings for it. Relevant social media campaigns will help develop positive consumer disposition towards the TAF brands, by making consumers feel good about interacting with a brand at a social level. Once this happens, there will be an automatic improvement in the level of consumer perception.

Enhancing Brand Engagement and Relationship Using Social Media

Consumers become more engaged with a brand, move up the continuum to a state of involvement and subsequently, enter a loyal relationship with a brand when they are satisfied with the brand, trust the brand and formulate an attachment with it (Aldlaigan & Buttle,2005). Brand satisfaction is achieved when a customers' expectations from a brand purchase are met and when his experience with the brand is positive. Customer expectations are met when he perceives value in his purchase. Value is defined as benefits from the purchase minus the cost of the purchase. Apparel brands can make use of social media to enhance the perceived value of the customers by reducing post purchase dissonance and making the customer feel that he has done the right thing by buying the product. A continuous stream of brand specific content, showcasing the positive aspects of the brand helps in enhancing the customer value perceptions (Oh.,1999).

Customers trust a brand when they think that the brand is benevolent and reliable (Kantsperger & Kunz,2010). A benevolent brand is a caring, considerate brand which is thoughtful about the customers and society at large. Brands which engage in corporate social responsibility ventures as well as eco-friendly brands which are concerned about the deterioration of the environment and are environment friendly by virtue of their processes are considered trustworthy(Joshi & Rahman,2015). An apparel brand is considered reliable when it has been in existence for several years, is endorsed by the peer group of a consumer, enjoys a good social reputation and is internationally recognised and standardised. Social media can be used by brands to create an image of trustworthiness for themselves, by showcasing the relevant endeavours to stimulate the right emotions in the consumer minds. Companies can identify popular concerns about environment consciousness, and consumer apprehensions pertaining to product standards and use social media to host information showing their processes and accreditations (D'Souza et al.,2006). Usage of brand ambassadors and opinion leaders also helps.

Research has shown that the five antecedents of customer attachment with a brand are superior marketing characteristics, traditional customer outcomes, user derived benefits, socialisation and inter-generational influence, and sentimental and emotional memories(Grisaffe & Nguyen,2011) . Table collates the implications of these five antecedents and traces how TAF brands can use social media to address these issues.

Table 3. Usage of social media to address the antecedents of brand attachment

Antecedent	Implication	Usage of Social Media
Superior marketing characteristics	Product, price and distribution	Social media content highlighting apparel brand quality and performance, consistency of performance, durability, dependability, design, aesthetics, reasonable price, availability, innovativeness, market reputation, good image, customer focused approach can address this antecedent.
Traditional customer outcomes	Value, satisfaction and differentiation	Social media content harping on the value for money that a consumer is getting with the purchase of the TAF brand and the competitive superiority of the brand will take care of this issue. The unique differentiations, the category defining standards and the proven superiority of the brand need to be subtley brought out in the social media endeavours of the brand.
User derived benefits	Self-goals, social goals and sensory pleasure	Social media content on how usage of a particular TAF brand enhances the appearance of an individual, raises his social popularity and standing, as well as, augments his self presentation, while also being comfortable, fashionable, and providing a personalised fit will benefit brands.
Socialisation and inter-generational influence	Family and social groups	Social media posts targeting family groups and encouraging complete families to adopt particular TAF brands will be useful here.
Sentimental and emotional memories	Meaningful people, places and situations	Social media content triggering childhood memories and initiating nostalgia in the consumers mind render a certain element of positivity and meaningfulness to a particular brand purchase.

Fashion Retail and Online Shopping Using Instagram

Volatility, uncertainty and shifts in the global economy, issues pertaining to sales and profitability, competition from online and omnichannel, value chain improvements and digitisation, issues pertaining to supply chain management, decreasing foot traffic and the growth of online retail are significant aspects which have impacted the TAF world, in recent times. Changing consumer preferences and the need to enhance sustainability of their ventures, has made several apparel and fashion brands disrupt their practices to stay ahead in the competitive scenario. One such disruption has been the usage of social media platforms like Instagram, not merely for engaging in conversations with consumers, but also as an ecommerce domain. More and more fashion brands are permitting their consumers to make purchases using Instagram. A visually enamouring experience created by brands on this social media platform, triggers an immediate intent to purchase in the minds of the consumers. Consumer behavior is shifting and the need for instant gratification and newer experiences, is making consumers experiment with their brand loyalties. Impulse purchases driven by convenient shopping experiences and discounts are the order of the day. Several brands like *The Hype, WalkinWardrobe,, High on Style, Zoomberg, Sugar Box, Snobshop, FashionPolice India, The Style Hive, Missa More* and *Style Fiesta* are examples of brands making effective use of Instagram as a selling tool.

Most of these brands are using social media to establish congruence between their brand personality and consumer self-image.

As per the self-concept theory, in consumer behavior research, consumers who perceive a product's image to be consistent with their own self-concept, are more likely to buy the product. Appropriate usage of social media is being used by several brands to make sure that the brand images are in line with the target market, their expectations and self-concept.

Case Study 5: Voonik-Building Brand Attachment Using Instagram

Voonik.com is India's largest and fastest growing fashion company offering trendy clothes and providing fashionable outfits with innovative styles. An Instagram presence with 1837 posts and around 70,000 followers show Voonik's commitment towards building a significant brand with the help of customer support and participation. Voonik hosts an online marketplace, where retail brands can register and display their products, thereby offering over 15 lakh products for its customers to choose from across 6000 different brands. Voonik's organisational vision-every woman's personal stylist is reflected in the diversity offered across its social media presence and is backed by a team of trained stylists who are engaged in continuously recommending clothes to users on the basis of their physical attributes and preferences. Voonik is powered by an in-house personal shopping platform and works on a 10,000-rule algorithm to aid consumers in making appropriate product choices, by using filters like skin tone, body type and preferences. The lean marketplace model enables several fashion ecommerce players to register on Voonik and sell their products.

Voonik promotes the brand on television as well as social media. The brand is able to successfully induce consumer-brand attachment using social media by carefully addressing the antecedents of brand attachment.

Superior Marketing Characteristics and Traditional Customer Outcomes

Voonik has generated Instagram posts with pictures of models adorning fashionable clothes from high quality brands. The brand is using superior imagery in its Instagram presence to alter the way people shop by depicting its innovative styles, thereby creating a superior brand identity. A customer focussed approach shows Voonik offering its products at discounts in the range of 50-80% for several products, thereby ensuring that benefits of purchase, far exceed the cost. This enhances customer value perception pertaining to a purchase from Voonik.

This price competitiveness creates a differentiation for brand Voonik and by maintaining consistency of performance, enables the brand to form an attachment with its consumers. This brand attachment prevents consumers from switching to a competing brand whenever they must make a product choice (Aldlaigan & Buttle, 2005).

User-Derived Benefits

Voonik is making use of the benefits of artificial intelligence in the era of digitisation, and is using cloud-based platforms, with modules including object recognition, gesture recognition, emotion recognition etc., to trace and analyse the consumer journey, specifically in the virtual world. Each online click, query or comment made by a consumer can be analysed for extracting information pertaining to consumer intent and preferences. This helps Voonik identify what products will help a consumer enhance his self-presentation and add to his joy, thereby aiding consumer-brand attachment.

REFERENCES

Aldlaigan, A., & Buttle, F. (2005). Beyond satisfaction: Customer attachment to retail banks. *International Journal of Bank Marketing*, *23*(4), 349–359. doi:10.1108/02652320510603960

Cowan, K., & Kinley, T. (2014). Green spirit: Consumer empathies for green apparel. *International Journal of Consumer Studies*, *38*(5), 493–499. doi:10.1111/ijcs.12125

D'Souza, C., Taghian, M., & Lamb, P. (2006). An Empirical study on the influence of environmental labels on consumers. *Corporate Communications*, *11*(2), 162–173. doi:10.1108/13563280610661697

Esteban-Santos, L., García Medina, I., Carey, L., & Bellido-Pérez, E. (2018). Fashion bloggers: Communication tools for the fashion industry. *Journal of Fashion Marketing and Management*, *22*(3), 420–437. doi:10.1108/JFMM-10-2017-0101

Garbarino, E., & Johnson, M. S. (1999). The different roles of satisfaction, trust, and commitment in customer relationships. *Journal of Marketing*, *63*(2), 70–87. doi:10.1177/002224299906300205

Geissinger, A., & Laurell, C. (2016). User engagement in social media–an explorative study of Swedish fashion brands. *Journal of Fashion Marketing and Management*, *20*(2), 177–190. doi:10.1108/JFMM-02-2015-0010

Grisaffe, D. B., & Nguyen, H. P. (2011). Antecedents of emotional attachment to brands. *Journal of Business Research*, *64*(10), 1052–1059. doi:10.1016/j.jbusres.2010.11.002

Joshi, Y., & Rahman, Z. (2015). Factors Affecting Green Purchase Behaviour and Future Research Directions. *International Strategic Management Review*, *3*(1–2), 128–143. doi:10.1016/j.ism.2015.04.001

Kantsperger, R., & Kunz, W. H. (2010). Consumer trust in service companies: A multiple mediating analysis. *Managing Service Quality*, *20*(1), 4–25. doi:10.1108/09604521011011603

Nyilasy, G., Gangadharbatla, H., & Paladino, A. (2014). Perceived greenwashing: The interactive effects of green advertising and corporate environmental performance on consumer reactions. *Journal of Business Ethics*, *125*(4), 693–707. doi:10.100710551-013-1944-3

Oh, H. (1999). Service quality, customer satisfaction, and customer value: A holistic perspective. *International Journal of Hospitality Management*, *18*(1), 67–82. doi:10.1016/S0278-4319(98)00047-4

Padel, S., & Foster, C. (2005). Exploring the gap between attitude and behaviour: Understanding why consumers buy or do not buy organic food. *British Food Journal, 107*(8), 606-625.

Pickett-Baker, J., & Ozaki, R. (2008). Pro-environmental products: Marketing influence on consumer purchase decision. *Journal of Consumer Marketing*, *25*(5), 281–293. doi:10.1108/07363760810890516

Sudha, M., & Sheena, K. (2017). Impact of influencers in consumer decision process: The fashion industry. *SCMS Journal of Indian Management*, *14*(3), 14–30.

Van der Walt, A. (1991). Will the consumer be able to decode your advertising message correctly? *Marketing Communications Management: A South African Perspective*, 295-309.

Chapter 14
Social Media Influencers in Fashion:
Challenges and Opportunities

Albérico Travassos Rosário
GOVCOPP, IADE, Universidade Europeia, Portugal

José Morais da Silva
Universidade Europeia, Portugal

ABSTRACT

Social media influencers (SMIs) in the fashion industry become professional individuals who have a large following on social media platforms such as Instagram, Facebook, TikTok, and YouTube. Many SMIs in the fashion industry have become successful in their own right and have gained significant influence in the fashion world projecting their branded personas. Fashion industry SMIs can face several challenges including the need to constantly create new and rich content; develop engaged narratives; pressure to maintain a certain image, the rivalry from other influencers. However, there are also many opportunities for SMIs in the fashion industry. Some say it is fertile ground. They can also collaborate directly with brands and use their influence to promote products and services. Having said that, more research is needed to grant reliable data to empower SMIs with accurate knowledge. Based on a systematic bibliometric literature review at Scopus, this research aims to appraise challenges and opportunities in building a SMI landscape in fashion.

INTRODUCTION

The fashion industry is one of the fastest-growing sectors in the world, characterized by vast transformations and a dynamic business environment. According to Gazzola et al. (2020), the industry is valued at US $1.3 trillion and employs approximately 300 million people worldwide. The fashion industry is highly competitive, with global brands dominating the market. Despite the progress, the sector is experiencing changes and uncertainties due to the increasing adoption of technologies and their impact on consum-

DOI: 10.4018/978-1-6684-8753-2.ch014

ers. For instance, the emergence and popularity of social media platforms such as Facebook, Twitter, Instagram, and YouTube have significantly changed buying and selling techniques. These platforms have also increased competition as more fashion companies compete to create online content aligned with their target audience's needs and expectations (Chu & Seock, 2020). Another disruptive development that has intensified the competition has been the emergence of social media fashion influencers (SMFIs). These online personalities with established following and credibility result in high trust and connections. Companies with access to the right influencers with the power to build strong brand relationships and drive sales are winning and have better performance. Thus, it has become increasingly important for fashion brands to incorporate influencer marketing into their strategies.

With the growing popularity of influencer marketing, different scholars have published research on social media influencers and their impact on the business environment. Quelhas-Brito et al. (2020) describe social media influencers as non-traditional types of celebrities whose fame is facilitated by the active social media presence, their ability to adopt new styles, and their confidence in their tastes. Similarly, Sudha and Sheena (2017) describe an influencer as someone with an above-average number of followers in a specific niche and the capability to influence people to take a specific action. As a result, influencers can reach millions of people through their content and blogs, making them a critical component of digital marketing strategies. Social media fashion influencers influence followers' fashion consumption and decisions. Thus, most fashion companies feature them in sales campaigns and invite them to fashion events and parties to increase their reach and generate more sales (Chu & Seock, 2020). This collaboration allows fashion companies to utilize the influencer's network and credibility to market their products.

Therefore, incorporating social media fashion influencers into a company's marketing and sales strategy can increase reach and drive growth, sales, and profits. However, working with social media fashion influencers can have multiple challenges, such as measuring campaign performance and finding the right influencer. These issues undermine fashion companies' ability to leverage the rapidly growing influencer marketing. This systematic bibliometric literature review provides data on influencer marketing, identifying opportunities and challenges to aid marketers' decision-making and strategizing.

METHODOLOGICAL APPROACH

A systematic bibliometric literature review (LRSB) was conducted to identify, synthesize, analyze, and report data on the use of social media influencers in the fashion industry. Paré and Kitsiou (2017) state that review articles represent powerful information sources for practitioners looking for state-of-the-art evidence to guide their decision-making and work practices. With the growing need for social media influencers in marketing campaigns, it is crucial to present marketing practitioners and other business decision-makers with state-of-the-art evidence on influencer marketing and its potential impact on business performance and potential challenges. Based on Paré and Kitsiou (2017), a literature review can help obtain and analyze the necessary information to create a comprehensive report to be translated into practice.

The process began with identifying an appropriate database, which was settled on Scopus. This database was selected based on Baas et al. (2020) description of the Scopus database as one of the largest curated databases providing access to global and regional publications, such as scientific journals, books, and conference proceedings. In addition, the authors indicated that a rigorous content selection process is used when indexing journals on Scopus, thus ensuring that only the highest quality data is indexed.

Thus, the use of bibliometric analysis can help understand its development and adoption in businesses to identify potential challenges. The use of the LRSB review process is divided into 3 phases and 6 steps (Table 1), as proposed by Rosário and Dias (2023); Rosário (2021); Rosário and Dias (2022); Rosário, et al. (2021).

Table 1. Process of systematic LRSB.

Phase	Step	Description
Exploration	Step 1	formulating the research problem
	Step 2	searching for appropriate literature
	Step 3	critical appraisal of the selected studies
	Step 4	data synthesis of individual sources
Interpretation	Step 5	reporting findings and recommendations
Communication	Step 6	Presentation of the LRSB report

Source: Rosário and Dias (2023);Rosário (2021); Rosário and Dias (2022).

The database of indexed scientific and/or academic documents used was Scopus, the most important peer review in the scientific and academic world. However, we consider that the study has the limitation of considering only the Scopus decomposition database, excluding other scientific and academic bases. The literature search includes peer-reviewed scientific and/or academic documents published up to February 2023.

This search resulted in 141,597 document results. Adding the keyword "influencers" to the search term reduced the search results to 2,065 documents, while "fashion" reduced the results to 135. The research then limited the search to the subject area "Business, Management and Accounting", published until 2023, resulting in 64 (N=64) relevant sources (Table 2).

Table 2. Screening methodology

Database Scopus	Screening	Publications
Meta-search	keyword: social media	141,597
Inclusion Criteria	keyword: social media, influencers	2,065
	keyword: social media, influencers, fashion	135
Screening	keyword: social media, influencers, fashion Business, Management and Accounting Published until February 2023	64

Source: own elaboration

Finally, content and theme analysis techniques were used to identify, analyze and report the various documents proposed by Rosário and Dias, (2023); Rosário (2021); Rosário and Dias (2022); Rosário, et al. (2021).

The 64 scientific and/or academic documents indexed in Scopus are later analyzed in a narrative and bibliometric way to deepen the content and possible derivation of common themes that directly respond to the research question (Rosário & Dias, 2023; Rosário, 2021; Rosário & Dias, 2022; Rosário, et al., 2021).

Of the 64 selected documents, 47 Articles; 8 are Book chapters; 5 are Conference papers; 2 are Conference reviews; and 2 are reviews.

PUBLICATION DISTRIBUTION

Peer-reviewed articles on marketing management in retail customer satisfaction until February 2023. The year 2020 and 2021 had the highest number of peer-reviewed publications on the subject, reaching 19.

Figure 1 summarizes the peer-reviewed literature published in February 2023.

The publications were sorted out as follows: Journal of Fashion Marketing and Management (5); Developments in Marketing Science Proceedings of The Academy of Marketing Science (4); Springer Proceedings in Business and Economics (4); Fashion Style and Popular Culture (3); International Journal of Advertising (3); Journal of Global Fashion Marketing (3); Journal of Retailing and Consumer Services (3); Fashion and Textiles (2); International Journal of Scientific and Technology Research (2); Journal of Business Research (2); Journal of Product and Brand Management (2); Technological Forecasting and Social Change (2); the remaining publications with 1.

Interest in the subject of evolution has not been constant.

Figure 1. Documents by year
Source: own elaboration

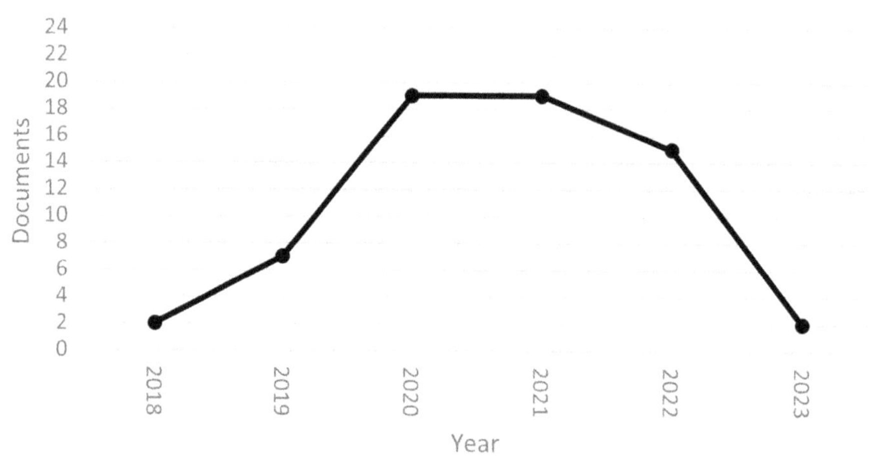

Table 3. Scimago journal and country rank impact factor

Title	SJR	Best Quartile	H Index
Journal of Fashion Marketing and Management	0.97	Q1	56
Developments in Marketing Science Proceedings of The Academy of Marketing Science	-	-	-
Springer Proceedings in Business and Economics	-	-	-
Fashion Style and Popular Culture	0.19	Q2	4
International Journal of Advertising	1.74	Q1	67
Journal of Global Fashion Marketing	1.05	Q1	22
Journal of Retailing and Consumer Services	2.26	Q1	104
Fashion and Textiles	0	-	22
International Journal of Scientific and Technology Research	2.32	Q1	217
Journal of Business Research	1	Q1	90
Journal of Product and Brand Management	2.34	Q1	90
Technological Forecasting and Social Change	2.34	Q1	134
Business Horizons	2.38	Q1	97
California Management Review	3.79	Q1	139
Communication Research and Practice	0.58	Q1	9
Communication Today	0.29	Q2	7
Creativity and Marketing the Fuel for Success	-	-	-
Global Business Review	0.45	Q2	30
Indian Journal of Marketing	0.32	Q3	11
Informacijos Mokslai	0.21	Q3	2
International Conference on Information and Knowledge Management Proceedings	1.04	-	127
International Journal of E Entrepreneurship and Innovation	0.27	Q3	26
International Journal of Information Management	4.58	Q1	132
International Journal of Internet Marketing and Advertising	0.28	Q3	21
International Journal of Recent Technology and Engineering	0	-	23
Journal of Advertising	2.7	Q1	119
Journal of Digital and Social Media Marketing	0.18	Q3	3
Journal of Interactive Advertising	1.81	Q1	11
Journal of Interactive Marketing	3.62	Q1	114
Journal of Islamic Marketing	0.55	Q2	43
Journal of Promotion Management	0.65	Q2	32
Journal of Research in Interactive Marketing	1.56	Q1	42
Journal of The Association for Consumer Research	1.46	Q1	20
Management Croatia	-	-	-
Palgrave Advances in Luxury	-	-	-
Palgrave Studies in Practice Global Fashion Brand Management	-	-	-
Proceedings of The International Conference on Industrial Engineering and Operations Management	0	-	15
Promotional Practices and Perspectives from Emerging Markets	-	-	-
Qualitative Market Research	0.56	Q2	59
Rutgers Business Review	0.22	Q3	4
Strategic Direction	0.11	Q4	14

Note: "-"data not available.
Source: own elaboration

In Table 3, we analyze the Scimago Journal & Country Rank (SJR), the best quartile, and the H index by publication. The Journal of Management Studies is the most quoted publication with a SJR of 4,640, a Q1 and an H index of 194.

There are a total of 24 publications in Q1, 9 publications in Q2, 11 publications in Q3, and 3 publications in Q4. Publications from the best quartile Q1 represent 16% of the 56 publication titles; the best quartile Q2 represents 20%; the best quartile Q3 represents 5%; and the best quartile Q4 represents 3% of each of the 56 publication titles. Finally, 9 publications still do not have data available, representing 16% of publications.

As shown in Table 3, the significant majority of publications still do not have indexed data.

The subject areas covered by the 80 scientific and/or academic documents were: Business, Management and Accounting (64); Social Sciences (22); Psychology (9); Economics, Econometrics and Finance (7); Engineering (5); Materials Science (5); Decision Sciences (3); Computer Science (2).

The most cited article was "Celebrity vs. Influencer endorsements in advertising: the role of identification, credibility, and Product-Endorser fit" by Schouten et al. (2020) with 373 citations published in the Sustainability 1,740 (SJR), the best quartile (Q1), and with an H-index (67), this article "investigated the impact of celebrity vs. influencer endorsements on advertising effectiveness".

In Figure 2 we can analyze the evolution of citations of the documents published until February 2023. The number of citations shows a positive net growth with R2 of 43% for the period ≤2013-2023, with 2022 reaching 736 citations.

Figure 2. Evolution of citations between ≤2013 and 2023
Source: own elaboration

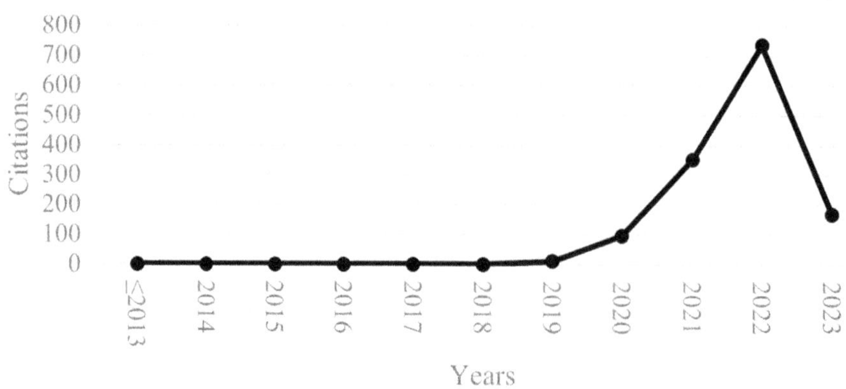

The h-index was used to determine the productivity and impact of the published work, based on the largest number of articles included that had at least the same number of citations. Of the documents considered for the h-index, 14 have been cited at least 14 times.

Citations of all scientific and/or academic documents from the published date until February 2023 totaled 1364, of which 21 were not cited. The self-citation of documents up until February 2023 was self-cited 22 times.

The bibliometric study was carried out to investigate and identify indicators of the dynamics and evolution of scientific and/or academic information in documents based on the main keywords (Figure 3). The results were extracted from the scientific software VOSviewe, which aims to identify the main search keywords "social media, influencers, and fashion".

Figure 3. Network of all keywords

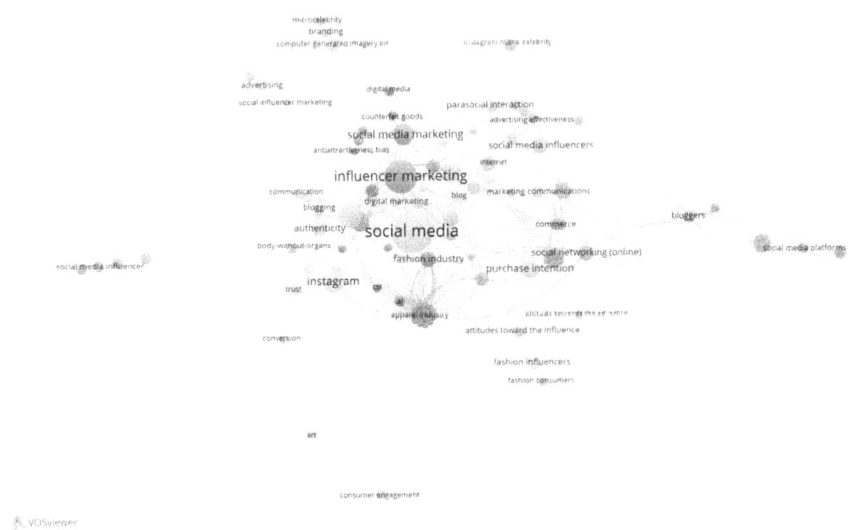

The research was based on scientific and/or academic documents concerning the challenges of social media influencers in the fashion sector. In Figure 4, we can analyze the linked keywords. It is possible to highlight the network of keywords that appear together or are linked in each scientific article. It is possible to identify the topics studied by research and research trends. Finally, in Figure 5, an abundant bibliographic union is presented with an analysis of the cited references.

Figure 4. Network of linked keywords

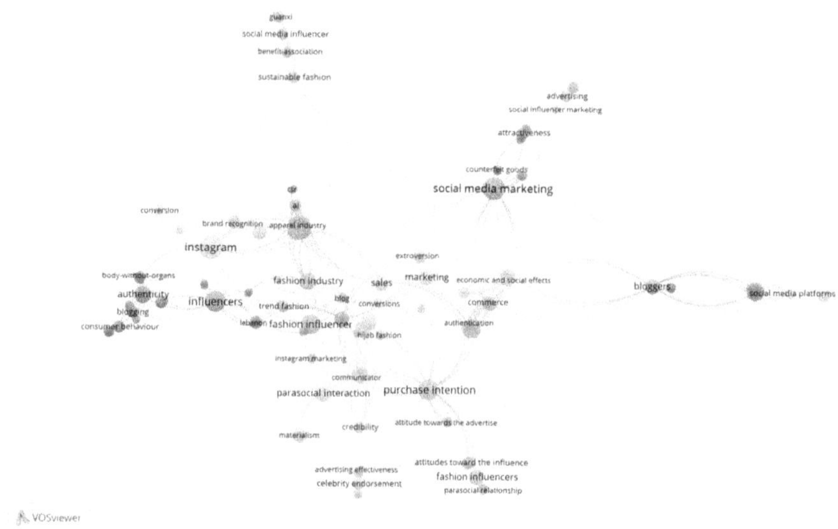

Figure 5. Network of bibliographic coupling

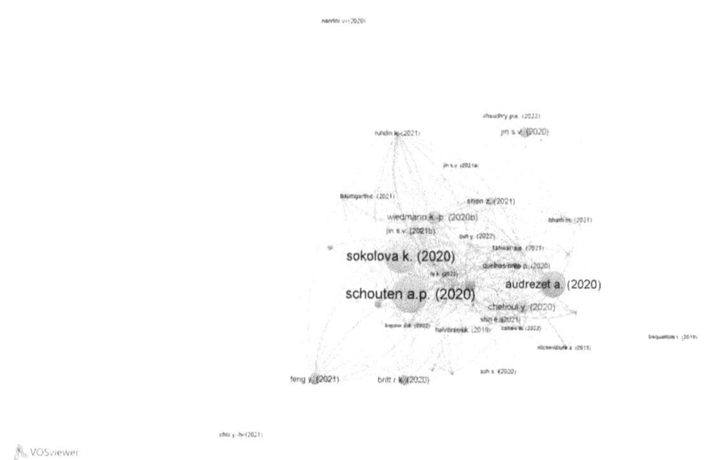

THEORETICAL PERSPECTIVES

Over the past decade, social media influencers have dominated the fashion industry. These individuals have millions of followers on platforms like Instagram, YouTube, and TikTok. These influencers build these audiences by sharing personal stories, life events, interests, and hobbies that connect them with the audience, thus building strong relationships (Feng et al., 2021). As a result, the connection with the followers enables social media influencers in the fashion niche to influence what they wear, how they style their clothes, and the brands they choose to support. Following this power in influencer marketing, fashion brands have increasingly turned to social media influencers to target audiences, especially younger consumers who are more digitally savvy (Haenlein et al., 2020). Brands work with these influencers in various ways, including fashion collaborations, sponsored posts, and brand partnerships. As a result, social media influencers have become an integral part of the fashion ecosystem.

Influencer Marketing and the Rise of Social Media Influencers

In this era of social media, influencer marketing has become an increasingly popular form of marketing. Sudha and Sheena (2017) define influencer marketing as identifying and activating individuals with an influence in a particular target audience, niche, or medium to be part of a brand's marketing campaign. Its goals can range from increasing reach, sales, or engagement, depending on the marketing team's strategies and overall objectives. The growth of influence marketing is depicted in Haenlein et al. (2020) research, which indicates that in 2020, the influencer marketing industry was worth $10 billion. In addition, the study indicates that two-thirds of firms plan to increase their spending on influence marketing, with at least 80% planning to allocate approximately 10% of their marketing budget to influencer marketing. This marketing strategy is rapidly growing due to its relevance to business-to-consumer businesses. Brands use social media influencers for advertising their products and services to a targeted audience. One significant way that differentiates influencer marketing from other forms of marketing is the social media influencers' ability to connect with their followers on a personal level (Jin & Muqaddam, 2021). The relationship between influencers and their followers enables them to influence their purchasing decisions. As a result, companies of all sizes are investing in influencer partnerships to promote their products or services. This has led to the rapid growth of influencer marketing, making it a multi-billion-dollar industry.

The rise of social media influencers can be attributed to several factors. Firstly, social media platforms have allowed individuals to publish content that enables them to build large followings and establish themselves as experts or authorities in specific niches. As a result, there has been an increase in a new breed of celebrity that is more relatable and accessible to the average person (Jin & Muqaddam, 2021). Secondly, the number of people using traditional forms of advertising, such as print and television, has significantly declined, leading to a shift in marketing strategies. For instance, Haenlein et al. (2020) indicates that 60% of people aged 34 and below in the US use Instagram, while 40% of teenagers aged 10 and 19 are on TikTok. These numbers indicate the massive use of and reliance on social media among younger generations. They use these platforms to network and communicate, access entertainment and educational materials, and find more information about products and services they are interested in (Feng et al., 2021). This shift to online platforms has reduced the use of traditional media among these consumer generations, prompting companies to look for more authentic ways to connect with their target audience. Influencer marketing provides a means to do so. Moreover, e-commerce growth has created a need for more targeted advertising, and social media influencers provide an effective strategy to reach niche audiences.

One of the most significant benefits of influencer marketing is the potential for increased brand awareness and reach. Social media influencers' large following and consistent content creation enables them to reach a large and engaged audience, which can translate into increased brand visibility and exposure (Tanwar et al., 2021). These opportunities can be valuable for companies targeting a specific demographic or niche audience. For example, fashion vloggers attract an audience that admires their fashion tastes and styling (Haenlein et al., 2020). Thus, promoting a fashion brand to this audience through the vlogger increases reach and awareness. In this case, the influencers provide a direct line of communication between a brand and its target audience, which can be challenging to achieve through traditional advertising methods. Partnering with influencers enables brands to tap into the trust and credibility that these individuals have established with their followers, which can result in brand loyalty and drive sales.

Additionally, influencer marketing can increase brand engagement and social proof. Social media influencers' content often influences their followers' perception, making them view them as experts or authorities in their respective niches. As a result, these perceptions help build trust, creating a sense of social proof since the followers may be more likely to purchase a product or service if they see it promoted by someone they admire or respect (Jin et al., 2021). When an influencer promotes a product related to their niche, followers are more likely to perceive it as better than traditional marketing. Besides, influencers often have highly engaged followers (Le & Aydin, 2022). They are more likely to like, comment, and share content that they find interesting or valuable, including a brand's promoted content. This engagement can expand a brand's reach and create a sense of community around a brand or product.

Despite the many benefits of influencer marketing, companies must understand that influencer marketing may not consistently achieve the desired results. For instance, failure to choose influencers who align with a brand's value and messaging may fail to achieve the set marketing goals ("Influential choices: How fashion....," 2020). In addition, they must ensure that all partnerships are transparent and disclosed to followers since transparency can potentially influence followers' attitudes toward the marketing campaign. Moreover, it is important to carefully track and measure the effectiveness of influencer marketing campaigns to ensure that they generate a positive return on investment (Argyris et al., 2021). Despite these issues, when used correctly, influencer marketing can be a highly effective way for companies to connect with their target audience and drive growth and success.

The Role and Importance of Social Media Influencers in the Fashion Industry

In the fashion industry, social media influencers are essential in shaping trends and driving consumer behavior. Their large, engaged following gives them the power to introduce new brands and products to their audiences and can help to create a buzz around particular items or styles (Arduini & Paoloni, 2020). For example, Gucci collaborated with 23 artists on Instagram in 2019 to support the launch of its new fragrance line, Gucci Bloom. Under this campaign, 135 pieces of content were created, reaching approximately 750000 people and significantly increasing brand awareness (Haenlein et al.,2020). Feng et al. (2021) explain this success indicating that influencers tend to integrate product reviews into their personal lives, making the audience perceive them as authentic and relatable. For example, a fashion brand can collaborate with an influencer wearing branded products like clothes or shoes. In this case, the reviews will be authentic since the influencer's audience can see them in the promoted product. The collaboration between fashion brands and influencers can occur in multiple ways, including sponsored content or gifting products, which enables them to increase their visibility and reach a wider audience.

Social media influencers are valuable to the fashion industry because they can build trust and credibility with their followers. Becoming a social media influencer involves creating valuable content that increases the individual's reputation in a specific niche (Audrezet et al., 2020). Unlike in traditional marketing, the content influencers create is highly requested and consumed since it is more relatable and authentic. Wiedmann & von Mettenheim (2020) explain this phenomenon, indicating that messages from influencers are created to appear from a "person like you or me" instead of mass targeting used in traditional marketing. As a result, their followers often view them as relatable and trustworthy, which can translate into increased sales for the brands they promote (Baumgarth et al., 2021; Bazaki & Cedrola, 2023). In addition, consumers follow influencers of their free will, meaning that they are willing to consume the content the influencer promotes. This increases influencers' ability to reach niche audiences that may be difficult for brands to reach through traditional marketing channels.

In addition to influencing consumer behavior, social media influencers provide valuable feedback to fashion brands. Social media allows the audience to publish feedback through comments (Brachtendorf, 2022). For example, followers can comment about the partnership, the products or services promoted, and their impact. By monitoring the engagement and feedback from their followers, influencers can provide brands with insights into what their target audience is looking for in terms of style, fit, and price point (Audrezet et al., 2020). These companies can use this feedback to inform product development and marketing strategies. In addition, influencers can also provide brands with insights into their competitors' strengths and weaknesses (Brewster & Sklar, 2022). Such insights provide opportunities for differentiation and improvement and can be particularly valuable for smaller brands or startups that may not have the resources to conduct extensive market research. Therefore, businesses of all sizes can leverage influencer marketing to achieve varying goals and objectives.

Finally, working with social media influencers can help fashion brands to create a sense of community around a brand or product. This benefit is achieved by featuring real people wearing and using their products, which helps fashion brands tap into the social aspect of shopping and create a sense of belonging among the influencers' followers (Britt et al., 2020). Unlike mainstream celebrities, social media influencers build their power by creating relatable content. They are more accessible and prioritize building their communities of people with shared interests (Zhou et al., 2021). Thus, brands that collaborate with them can leverage these communities to establish their communities with other people interested in their products and services (Wiedmann & von Mettenheim, 2020). These communities allow them to share the pros and cons of specific fashion products, thus providing insights that businesses can integrate into product development and marketing strategies.

Factors Influencing the Effectiveness of Influencer Marketing

Fashion brands aiming to integrate influencer marketing into their strategies must consider various factors. For instance, they must understand that not all influencers are fit for any campaign since each influencer has a different audience with varying interests (Bharti, 2021). Therefore, companies must approach influencer marketing cautiously to minimize the risks of failure. This section evaluates vital research findings on factors that can influence the effectiveness of influencer marketing.

Relevance of the Influencer to the Brand

The effectiveness of influencer marketing significantly depends on the relevance of the influencer to the brand. An influencer with a natural alignment with the brand's values, goals, and audience can significantly enhance the brand's credibility and reputation (Cabeza-Ramírez et al., 2022). Furthermore, followers are more likely to consider an endorsement genuine and trustworthy if the influencer is perceived as an expert or authority in a particular niche. For example, a fashion influencer who constantly creates and publishes content on fashion, can easily influence people to purchase fashion-related products than if the influencer selected was in another niche (Gomes et al., 2022). Sudha and Sheena (2017) explored the impact of fashion bloggers on consumer decision-making. The scholars explained that fashion bloggers often cover content ranging from industry news and trends, clothing items and collections reviews, and personal styles. They may also cover topics that fashion brands may not want to be covered, including the ethical and environmental impacts of the fashion industry (Wiedmann & von Mettenheim, 2020). The diversity of this coverage helps create a strong persona that appeals to specific audience segments interested in such content. This approach can increase engagement, conversion rates, and sales (Casais & Gomes, 2022). However, if the influencer's content or image doesn't match the brand's image or messaging, the audience may perceive the partnership as inauthentic or forced, leading to decreased trust and engagement. Therefore, selecting the right influencer relevant to the brand is critical in ensuring a successful influencer marketing campaign.

Size and Quality of the Influencer's Audience

The size and quality of an influencer's audience can influence the effectiveness of influencer marketing since it determines the reach and potential impact of the influencer's content. Larger audiences are associated with higher reach since more people are likely to see the content, which increases the potential for brand exposure and engagement (Suh, 2020).

However, brands nowadays are abandoning mega influencers for micro-influencers since they tend to have higher engagement and conversion rates. For example, Britt et al. (2020) found that micro-influencers with 5000 to 10000 followers have an engagement rate of 6.3% compared to 3.6% for influencers with more than 10000 followers. Despite their smaller followings, micro-influencers are perceived to be more credible and relatable and have better interpersonal relationships with their followers (Sinha & Fung, 2021). These arguments indicate that in addition to audience size, the quality of the audience is equally important. A high-quality audience consists of individuals who are genuinely interested in the influencer's content and have a high level of engagement with it (Pérez del Castillo et al., 2020; Choobchain et al., 2019).

Markets can use metrics such as likes, comments, shares, and click-through rates to measure engagement before collaborating with an influencer, thus ensuring they are a good fit. An influencer with an engaged and relevant audience is more likely to effectively drive conversions, brand awareness, and overall success of influencer marketing campaigns.

Type of Content and Engagement With the Audience

Brands seeking to collaborate with influencers must ensure that the content shared by the influencer aligns with the brand's values and goals. For instance, an influencer fashion marketing campaign is more likely to succeed if the influencer featured creates fashion-related content (Chaudhry, 2022). The content should be engaging, informative, and entertaining to capture the audience's attention. In addition, the influencer must engage with their audience by responding to comments and messages to build trust and authenticity (Kapoor et al., 2022; Trequattrini et al., 2019).

This two-way communication helps establish a strong bond between the influencer and their followers, which can enhance the marketing campaign's effectiveness. The followers feel valued and connected with the influencer, thus increasing their trust and the likelihood of acting upon their recommendations

(Karakavak & Özbölük, 2022). Therefore, the failure or success of influencer marketing can be determined by the type of content an influencer publishes and engagement with the audience.

Goals and Objectives of the Marketing Campaign

The goals and objectives of a marketing campaign can determine the kind of influencer to collaborate with. A well-planned marketing campaign aims to achieve specific business objectives, such as increasing brand awareness, driving sales, or promoting a new product or service (Quelhas-Brito et al., 2020). When working with influencers, aligning the campaign's goals and objectives with the influencer's audience and expertise help ensure relevance and authenticity. For instance, brands aiming to increase brand awareness among younger demographics can partner with a famous social media influencer with a large following among that age group (Chetioui et al., 2020). A fashion brand promoting sportswear can consider collaborating with athletes. These collaborations are more likely to succeed since they feature influencers with a specific audience demographic or within a particular niche (Von Mettenheim & Wiedmann, 2021). Moreover, setting measurable objectives and tracking key performance indicators (KPIs) such as reach, engagement, and conversions help evaluate the campaign's effectiveness (Rrustemi & Baca, 2021).

The information gathered from the evaluations can help adjust strategies as deemed appropriate. Overall, a clear understanding of the goals and objectives of the marketing campaign is essential for influencer marketing to be successful.

Opportunities for Using Social Media Influencers in Fashion Marketing

With social media influencers' rise, brands recognize the value of partnering with these individuals to promote their products. In addition, these influencers can influence their followers' purchasing decisions through their content (Samarage & Ratnayake, 2021). As a result, fashion brands are increasingly leveraging the power of these influencers to reach new audiences, boost brand awareness, and increase sales. This section explores the various opportunities social media influencers create and how fashion brands can benefit from featuring them in their marketing campaigns.

Niche Marketing and Targeting Specific Audiences

Social media influencers have revolutionized how fashion brands market their products, particularly by facilitating niche marketing and targeting specific audiences. For example, fashion brands can partner with influencers who have established themselves as experts in specific niches or subcultures (Copeland & Lyu, 2020). This collaboration allows these companies access to a highly targeted audience that is more likely to be interested in their products. For example, a fashion brand specializing in sustainable fashion may partner with a social media influencer passionate about environmental protection and sustainability (Jacobson & Harrison, 2022). Since the influencer creates content regarding these topics, they are more likely to have a large following of like-minded individuals interested in ethical fashion and reducing their environmental impact. Therefore, working with this influencer connects the fashion brand to a highly targeted audience, allowing it to promote its sustainable products to people who may buy them.

Additionally, social media influencers employ a more authentic and aspirational approach to product promotion, which may facilitate targeting specific audiences. Followers often view influencers as trusted sources of information and inspiration (Satria et al., 2019). When influencers showcase fashion products in an authentic way related to their style, they can inspire their followers and provide valuable insights that aid purchasing decisions. For instance, an influencer specializing in plus-size fashion may partner with a fashion brand offering inclusive sizing options (Triani & Vusparatih, 2019). Wearing such a brand and publishing related content can inspire and encourage followers looking for stylish, inclusive fashion options. Overall, social media influencers specializing in specific niches tend to have very targeted audiences (Waltenrath et al., 2022).

Therefore, marketing campaigns featuring such influencers provides brands access to niche markets, and audiences are more likely to be interested in the products or services promoted (Vardhan & Mahato, 2022). Consequently, this approach to influencer marketing can increase conversion rates and engagement and generate more sales.

Cost-Effectiveness and Efficiency

One of the key advantages of using social media influencers in fashion marketing is their ability to increase cost-effectiveness. For example, partnerships with influencers enable a brand to reach a large and highly targeted audience at a fraction of the cost of traditional advertising methods (Veresiu & Parmentier, 2021). Although different influencers have varying rate cards, the growing influencer marketing sector provides access to a vast pool of influencers. This market saturation and competition ensure that brands find influencers willing to work within a specific budget (Twumasi et al., 2022; Singh et al., 2018). In addition, influencer marketing occurs in paid and unpaid promotions, where an influencer can receive compensation in the form of money, gifts, or free access to VIP events and parties. The diversity of influencer marketing strategies provides smaller brands that may not have the budget for expensive television or print ads access to cost-effective marketing solutions.

Social media influencers also increase efficiency in fashion marketing. Traditional marketing methods often involve a lengthy process of developing a campaign, creating content, and then distributing it through various channels. However, influencer marketing simplifies this process by allowing influencers to create content customized to their followers and the brand's needs (Sokolova & Kefi, 2020). This strategy results in a more efficient and effective marketing strategy. In addition, social media influencers already have a large and engaged following interested in their content. This means that brands can quickly and easily collaborate with them to promote their products without requiring lengthy campaigns or extensive content creation (Mickevičiute & Siudikiene, 2019). Furthermore, social media influencers increase the authenticity of a brand's marketing efforts. Modern-day consumers increasingly distrust traditional advertising methods and savvier (Jin & Ryu, 2020). They prefer recommendations from people they trust, including credible and authentic influencers. Therefore, influencer marketing provides an opportunity for brands to connect with their audience in a more genuine way. This authenticity can be critical in the fashion industry, where consumers often seek unique and personalized experiences.

Access to New Markets and Audiences

Social media influencers have large followings distributed worldwide due to increased internet adoption and social media use. Therefore, brands can access new markets and audiences by leveraging influencers' large followings and influential status. (Elton & Lopez, 2018). These individuals can help brands expand their reach and connect with consumers who may not have been reached through traditional marketing channels. For instance, social media platforms such as Instagram and TikTok enable influencers to connect with people worldwide (Choi et al., 2021). In the fashion marketing context, this means that brands can tap into new markets previously inaccessible through traditional marketing methods such as television and billboards, which are limited to specific geographical locations. Fashion brands aiming to expand to new audiences can leverage influencer marketing. For example, a fashion brand primarily focuses on Gen X consumers and intends to market to millennials and Gen Zs can partner with social media influencers with followers within these demographics (Sun et al., 2022; Copeland & Lyu, 2020). By doing so, the brand can increase visibility among the new target audience and the likelihood of gaining new customers. Besides, working with influencers with a strong reputation and loyal followings can increase brand credibility and consumer visibility.

Creativity and Innovation in Content Creation

Social media influencers are skilled at creating content that resonates with their followers and has a unique understanding of their audience. By collaborating with influencers, fashion brands can tap into their creativity and innovation (Elhajjar, 2023). This can result in on-trend and engaging campaigns. Another aspect that results in higher captivity and innovation in content creation is the influencers' ability to bring fresh perspectives and introduce new concepts and ideas (Rundin & Colliander, 2021).

These insights are often integrated into marketing planning and strategizing, inspiring brands to think outside the box and explore new creative territories. In addition, most influencers have a better understanding of new technologies and platforms. From TikTok to Instagram Reels, influencers always explore new ways to connect with their followers and create exciting, engaging content (Schouten et al., 2020). Thus, collaborating with these individuals provides fashion brands access to these new technologies and platforms, enabling them to use them to create innovative campaigns that capture the attention of their target audience.

Increased Credibility and Loyalty

Social media influencers are known for their ability to create engaging content and connect with their followers. These approaches help them build loyal audiences and increase their credibility, thus providing social proof (Cabigiosu, 2020). When an influencer share a product or a brand with their followers, they are essentially vouching for the quality and value of that product or brand. This type of endorsement can be compelling, especially if the followers trust and admire the influencer. Secondly, social media influencers increase a brand's credibility and loyalty by creating a sense of community (Sokolova & Kefi, 2020).

Influencer marketing goes beyond promoting a product or a service. It involves promoting a lifestyle and a set of values, thus building a community of like-minded individuals. Followers follow specific influencers because they relate to published content or admire their lifestyles or values (Dávila-Ruiz & Vazquez, 2021).

In this case, the influencer builds a community of people with shared interests. The sense of belonging resulting from this connectedness can be compelling, leading to increased loyalty and repeat business.

Finally, social media influencers can increase a brand's credibility and loyalty by providing valuable information and insights. For instance, Sudha and Sheena (2017) explained that influencers often share their likes and dislikes when providing fashion reviews, influencing how certain brands or products are perceived or consumed. This means that when influencers provide positive information about a brand and its products, they will likely increase its credibility and build loyalty (Argyris et al., 2021).

Moreover, their deep understanding of the fashion industry empowers them to provide their followers with insider knowledge and tips on how to style different outfits, recommend brands worth investing in, and project trends likely to be popular in the coming seasons (Nannini, 2020).

This type of information is incredibly valuable to followers. It can help establish the influencer as an authority in the fashion industry, strengthening followers' willingness to trust their opinion and make a purchase.

Challenges of Using Social Media Influencers in Fashion Marketing

Despite the benefits and opportunities created by influencer marketing, this strategy comes with particular challenges. For instance, some consumers may be skeptical about promoting products by perceiving endorsements as purely motivated by financial gain (Perry et al., 2020). This issue will likely result in a negative attitude toward the brand and its products. Besides, an influencer's controversial behavior or opinion can damage a brand's reputation.

The impact of these issues on a brand's marketing initiatives and public perception indicates the need to identify and discuss the potential negative impacts of using social media influencers.

Difficulty in Measuring ROI and Effectiveness

Measuring the return on investment (ROI) and the effectiveness of influencer marketing campaigns is a major challenge hindering the adoption of this marketing strategy. The lack of standardized metrics or tools for measuring the effectiveness of influencer campaigns is the primary cause of this problem (Jain, 2021). This is because most brands find it challenging to determine their actual value. Metrics such as reach, engagement, and impressions are commonly used, but don't provide comprehensive insights into the campaign's effectiveness (Shen, 2021). For example, a campaign's impressions and reach might be high but with low conversion rates, meaning that the campaign had little impact on sales or leads.

Fake Followers and Engagement

With the rise of social media, brands have increasingly adopted strategies to tap into the vast audience that influencers command. However, some influencers have exploited this demand by purchasing fake followers and engagement, which provide deceiving numbers (Anand et al., 2022). These fake numbers may cause brands to believe they are reaching a wider audience than they are.

The pressure to maintain large following and high engagement rates has been the main driving factor causing influencing buying fake followers and engagement (Costello & Biondi, 2020). Most influencers believe that more significant followings and higher engagement rates translate to better brand deals and sponsorships. Companies are more likely to pay higher rates to mega influencers than micro-influencers due to their reach and high possibility of generating more sales.

As a result, influencers struggling to grow their following or engagement naturally may resort to purchasing fake followers and engagement to maintain the appearance of popularity (Zhou et al., 2023).

These activities can have severe impacts on the effectiveness of influencer marketing campaigns. If a brand pays an influencer to promote its product or service to a large following that is predominantly fake, the campaign will not generate the desired results. The fake audience will not engage with the brand, and the investment will be wasted.

Consumer Skepticism in Sponsored Content

Many consumers are becoming increasingly skeptical of influencers and their endorsements. Constant endorsements of different products make followers perceive the promotions as insincere or motivated purely by financial gain (Shin & Lee, 2021). The proliferation of sponsored content on social media platforms is a major cause of this problem. With so many influencers promoting products and services, consumers may feel overwhelmed and find it difficult to discern which endorsements are genuine and which are not (Yeo et al., 2022).

Moreover, failure to disclose that certain products featured in an influencer's content are paid can further erode trust in their recommendations (Zhang & Caverlee, 2019). Some followers may feel that influencers do not genuinely believe in the products they endorse, but only promote products because they are paid to do so. This can lead to a perception that influencers are "sellouts" willing to promote anything for a price, damaging both the influencer's reputation and the product being promoted.

CONCLUSION

The fashion industry is one of the fastest-growing industries worldwide. This growth can be attributed to the increased adoption of influencer marketing to reach wider global audiences. The rise of social media influencers has been a game-changer in fashion marketing.

These individuals can influence consumer purchasing decisions more efficiently than traditional marketing. For example, influencer marketing is based on influencer-follower relationships often created through content creation and high engagement. Unlike traditional marketing, where promotional messages are forced, influencer marketing is characterized by an audience that craves the influencer's content.

These followers follow the influencer out of their free will, making it easy to connect and sell to them. However, not all influencers are a good fit for a fashion company's marketing campaign. The various factors to consider before partnering with a social media influencer include determining their relevance to the brand, evaluating the size and quality of their audience, assessing the type of content they publish and engagement rates, and if they align with the marketing campaign's goals and objectives. Therefore, hiring a social media influencer should involve a comprehensive screening process to ensure the campaign's effectiveness and success.

Influencer marketing creates multiple opportunities for fashion brands to leverage social media to reach their target customers. These opportunities include increased ability to target a specific audience within a niche market, improved efficiency and cost-effectiveness, higher access to new markets and audiences, and increased credibility and loyalty. However, exploiting these challenges can be hindered by multiple challenges. For instance, the lack of standardized metrics or tools for measuring results in difficulties in measuring ROI and the campaign's effectiveness. In addition, the pressure to attract higher audiences and maintain high engagement rates prompts influencers to buy fake followers and engagement.

Moreover, the followers are becoming highly skeptical of influencers' intentions with endorsements, with some believing that the influencer is endorsing a product or brand for monetary gains.

These concerns can slow the adoption of influencer marketing and reduce consumers' trust in the influencers' recommendations. Therefore, brands intending to increase their investments in influencer marketing must find ways of maneuvering these challenges to maximize benefits and leverage the presented opportunities.

ACKNOWLEDGMENT

We would like to express gratitude to the Editor and the Arbitrators. They offered extremely valuable suggestions or improvements. The author was supported by the GOVCOPP Research Center of the University of Aveiro.

REFERENCES

Anand, A., Dutta, S., & Mukherjee, P. (2022). Influencer marketing with fake followers. *IIM Bangalore Research Paper*, (580). https://repository.iimb.ac.in/bitstream/2074/8180/1/WP_IIMB_580.pdf

Arduini, S., & Paoloni, P. (2020). The IT strategy in the luxury sector: The case of a fashion company. *Springer Proceedings in Business and Economics,* 211-226. 10.1007/978-3-030-46874-3_12

Argyris, Y. A., Muqaddam, A., & Miller, S. (2021). The effects of the visual presentation of an influencer's extroversion on perceived credibility and purchase intentions—Moderated by personality matching with the audience. *Journal of Retailing and Consumer Services*, *59*, 102347. Advance online publication. doi:10.1016/j.jretconser.2020.102347

Audrezet, A., de Kerviler, G., & Guidry Moulard, J. (2020). Authenticity under threat: When social media influencers need to go beyond self-presentation. *Journal of Business Research*, *117*, 557–569. doi:10.1016/j.jbusres.2018.07.008

Baas, J., Schotten, M., Plume, A., Côté, G., & Karimi, R. (2020). Scopus as a curated, high-quality bibliometric data source for academic research in quantitative science studies. *Quantitative Science Studies*, *1*(1), 377–386. doi:10.1162/qss_a_00019

Baumgarth, C., Kirkby, A., & Kaibel, C. (2021). When fake becomes real: The innovative case of artificial influencers. Creativity and marketing: The fuel for success, 149-167. doi:10.1108/978-1-80071-330-720211010

Bazaki, E., & Cedrola, E. (2023). *Becoming a fashion blogger entrepreneur: The case of Chiara Ferragni.* doi:10.1007/978-3-031-11185-3_6

Bharti, M. (2021). E-business through social media: An instagram page attribute-conversion model in context of fashion apparel industry. *Global Business Review*. Advance online publication. doi:10.1177/09721509211038832

Brachtendorf, C. (2022). Lil miquela in the folds of fashion: (ad-)dressing virtual influencers. *Fashion, Style & Popular Culture*, *9*(4), 483–499. doi:10.1386/fspc_00157_1

Brewster, M. L., & Sklar, M. (2022). 'Brand, community, lifestyle': Fashioning an authentic, body positive influencer brand on instagram. *Fashion, Style & Popular Culture*, *9*(4), 501–521. doi:10.1386/fspc_00158_1

Britt, R. K., Hayes, J. L., Britt, B. C., & Park, H. (2020). Too big to sell? A computational analysis of network and content characteristics among mega and micro beauty and fashion social media influencers. *Journal of Interactive Advertising*, *20*(2), 111–118. doi:10.1080/15252019.2020.1763873

Britt, R. K., Hayes, J. L., Britt, B. C., & Park, H. (2020). Too big to sell? A computational analysis of network and content characteristics among mega and micro beauty and fashion social media influencers. *Journal of Interactive Advertising*, *20*(2), 111–118. doi:10.1080/15252019.2020.1763873

Cabeza-Ramírez, L. J., Sánchez-Cañizares, S. M., Santos-Roldán, L. M., & Fuentes-García, F. J. (2022). Impact of the perceived risk in influencers' product recommendations on their followers' purchase attitudes and intention. *Technological Forecasting and Social Change*, *184*, 121997. Advance online publication. doi:10.1016/j.techfore.2022.121997

Cabigiosu, A. (2020). *The new consumers of luxury*. doi:10.1007/978-3-030-48810-9_3

Casais, B., & Gomes, L. R. (2022). Fashion bloggers' discourse on brands under corporate crisis: A netnographic research in Portugal. *Journal of Fashion Marketing and Management*, *26*(3), 420–435. doi:10.1108/JFMM-09-2020-0206

Chaudhry, P. E. (2022). Dupe influencers exploiting social media to peddle luxury fakes. *Business Horizons*, *65*(6), 719–727. doi:10.1016/j.bushor.2022.07.005

Chetioui, Y., Benlafqih, H., & Lebdaoui, H. (2020). How fashion influencers contribute to consumers' purchase intention. *Journal of Fashion Marketing and Management*, *24*(3), 361–380. doi:10.1108/JFMM-08-2019-0157

Choi, Y., Yoon, S., Xuan, B., Lee, S. T., & Lee, K. (2021). Fashion informatics of the big 4 fashion weeks using topic modeling and sentiment analysis. *Fashion and Textiles*, *8*(1), 33. Advance online publication. doi:10.118640691-021-00265-6

Choobchain, S., Momtaz, A. M., & Farhadian, H. (2019). Gender differences of farmers in conflict with climate change. *International Journal of Scientific and Technology Research*, *8*(7), 359–363.

Chu, S. C., & Seock, Y. K. (2020). The power of social media in fashion advertising. *Journal of Interactive Advertising*, *20*(2), 93–94. doi:10.1080/15252019.2020.1802955

Copeland, L., & Lyu, J. (2020). *Millennial Consumer's on instagram: Implications for luxury brands vs. celebrity influencers: An abstract*. doi:10.1007/978-3-030-42545-6_19

Costello, J., & Biondi, L. (2020). The art of deception: Will fake followers decay trust and can authenticity preserve it? In *Influencer Marketing* (pp. 215–232). Routledge. doi:10.4324/9780429322501-16

Dávila-Ruiz, D., & Vazquez, E. E. (2021). Examining effects of photography in social media and the mediation role of perceived authenticity. *Communication Today*, *12*(2), 112–127.

Elhajjar, S. (2023). Factors influencing buying behavior of Lebanese consumers towards fashion brands during economic crisis: A qualitative study. *Journal of Retailing and Consumer Services*, *71*, 103224. Advance online publication. doi:10.1016/j.jretconser.2022.103224

Elton, L., & Lopez, L. (2018). How ELLE leverages customer relationships to deepen brand engagement. *Journal of Digital and Social Media Marketing*, *6*(2), 102–109.

Feng, Y., Chen, H., & Kong, Q. (2021). An expert with whom i can identify: The role of narratives in influencer marketing. *International Journal of Advertising*, *40*(7), 972–993. doi:10.1080/02650487.2020.1824751

Feng, Y., Chen, H., & Kong, Q. (2021). An expert with whom i can identify: The role of narratives in influencer marketing. *International Journal of Advertising*, *40*(7), 972–993. doi:10.1080/02650487.2020.1824751

Gazzola, P., Pavione, E., Pezzetti, R., & Grechi, D. (2020). Trends in the fashion industry. The perception of sustainability and circular economy: A gender/generation quantitative approach. *Sustainability (Basel)*, *12*(7), 2809. doi:10.3390u12072809

Gomes, M. A., Marques, S., & Dias, Á. (2022). The impact of digital influencers' characteristics on purchase intention of fashion products. *Journal of Global Fashion Marketing*, *13*(3), 187–204. doi:10.1080/20932685.2022.2039263

Haenlein, M., Anadol, E., Farnsworth, T., Hugo, H., Hunichen, J., & Welte, D. (2020). Navigating the new era of influencer marketing: How to be successful on Instagram, TikTok, & co. *California Management Review*, *63*(1), 5–25. doi:10.1177/0008125620958166

Haenlein, M., Anadol, E., Farnsworth, T., Hugo, H., Hunichen, J., & Welte, D. (2020). Navigating the new era of influencer marketing: How to be successful on instagram, TikTok, & co. *California Management Review*, *63*(1), 5–25. doi:10.1177/0008125620958166

Influential choices: How fashion influencers can affect the purchasing intentions of consumers. (2020). *Strategic Direction, 36*(8), 11-12. doi:10.1108/SD-05-2020-0108

Jacobson, J., & Harrison, B. (2022). Sustainable fashion social media influencers and content creation calibration. *International Journal of Advertising*, *41*(1), 150–177. doi:10.1080/02650487.2021.2000125

Jain, V. (2021). An overview on social media influencer marketing. *South Asian Journal of Marketing & Management Research*, *11*(11), 76–81. doi:10.5958/2249-877X.2021.00112.0

Jin, S. V., & Muqaddam, A. (2021). 'Fame and envy 2.0' in luxury fashion influencer marketing on Instagram: Comparison between mega-celebrities and micro-celebrities. *International Journal of Internet Marketing and Advertising*, *15*(2), 176–200. doi:10.1504/IJIMA.2021.114335

Jin, S. V., & Ryu, E. (2020). Instagram fashionistas, luxury visual image strategies and vanity. *Journal of Product and Brand Management*, *29*(3), 355–368. doi:10.1108/JPBM-08-2018-1987

Jin, S. V., Ryu, E., & Muqaddam, A. (2021). I trust what she's #endorsing on Instagram: Moderating effects of parasocial interaction and social presence in fashion influencer marketing. *Journal of Fashion Marketing and Management*, *25*(4), 665–681. doi:10.1108/JFMM-04-2020-0059

Kapoor, P. S., Tagore, A., & Dua, S. (2022). Social media influencer promoted sustainable fashion: Effects of sponsorship and benefit association. *Journal of Promotion Management*. Advance online publication. doi:10.1080/10496491.2022.2163034

Karakavak, Z., & Özbölük, T. (2022). When modesty meets fashion: How social media and influencers change the meaning of hijab. *Journal of Islamic Marketing*. Advance online publication. doi:10.1108/JIMA-05-2021-0152

Le, K., & Aydin, G. (2022). Impact of the pandemic on social media influencer marketing in fashion: A qualitative study. *Qualitative Market Research*. Advance online publication. doi:10.1108/QMR-11-2021-0133

Mickevičiute, A., & Siudikiene, D. (2019). The role of fashion bloggers in fashion marketing communication [Mados tinklaraštininku isitraukimas i mados rinkodaros komunikacija]. *Informacijos Mokslai, 85*, 8–50. doi:10.15388/Im.2019.85.15

Nannini, V. (2020). Fashion consumption in digital media: Multiple practices and new identities. *Fashion, Style & Popular Culture*, *7*(4), 519–537. doi:10.1386/fspc_00041_1

Paré, G., & Kitsiou, S. (2017). *Methods for literature reviews. In Handbook of eHealth Evaluation: An Evidence-based Approach.* University of Victoria. https://www.ncbi.nlm.nih.gov/books/NBK481583/

Pérez del Castillo, T., Díaz Soloaga, P., & McColl, J. (2020). Lifestyle branding as a brand-oriented positioning strategy: Insights from Spanish fashion consultants [以品牌为导向的定位策略之生活方式品牌:西班牙时尚顾问的见解]. *Journal of Global Fashion Marketing*, *11*(4), 361–379. doi:10.1080/20932685.2020.1791727

Perry, P., Ashman, R., & Stalker, I. D. (2020). *Special session: Corporate social responsibility and AI: The case of fashion: An abstract.* doi:10.1007/978-3-030-42545-6_36

Quelhas-Brito, P., Brandão, A., Gadekar, M., & Castelo-Branco, S. (2020). Diffusing fashion information by social media fashion influencers: Understanding antecedents and consequences. *Journal of Fashion Marketing and Management*, *24*(2), 137–152. doi:10.1108/JFMM-09-2019-0214

Quelhas-Brito, P., Brandão, A., Gadekar, M., & Castelo-Branco, S. (2020). Diffusing fashion information by social media fashion influencers: Understanding antecedents and consequences. *Journal of Fashion Marketing and Management*, *24*(2), 137–152. doi:10.1108/JFMM-09-2019-0214

Rosário, A., Vilaça, F., Raimundo, R., & Cruz, R. (2021). Literature review on Health Knowledge Management in the last 10 years (2009-2019). *The Electronic Journal of Knowledge Management, 18*(3), 338-355. doi:10.34190/ejkm.18.3.2120

Rosário, A. T. (2021). The Background of artificial intelligence applied to marketing. *Academy of Strategic Management Journal*, *20*(6), 1–19.

Rosário, A. T., & Dias, J. C. (2022). Sustainability and the Digital Transition: A Literature Review. *Sustainability (Basel)*, *14*(7), 4072. doi:10.3390u14074072

Rosário, A. T., & Dias, J. C. (2023). How Industry 4.0 and Sensors Can Leverage Product Design: Opportunities and Challenges. *Sensors (Basel)*, *23*(3), 1165. doi:10.339023031165 PMID:36772206

Rrustemi, V., & Baca, G. (2021). the impact of social media activities on raising brand awareness during the covid-19 pandemic: The case of fashion industry in Kosovo [Utjecaj aktivnosti na društvenim medijima na povećanje svijesti o tržišnim markama tijekom pandemije covida-19: slučaj modne industrije na Kosovu]. *Management, 26*(2), 295–310. doi:10.30924/mjcmi.26.2.17

Rundin, K., & Colliander, J. (2021). Multifaceted influencers: Toward a new typology for influencer roles in advertising. *Journal of Advertising, 50*(5), 548–564. doi:10.1080/00913367.2021.1980471

Samarage, H. P., & Ratnayake, G. (2021). Impact of celebrity endorsement through social media on consumer purchasing intentions in sri lankan fashion industry. *Proceedings of the International Conference on Industrial Engineering and Operations Management,* 2313-2325.

Satria, A. D., Jatipuri, S., Hartanti, A. D., & Sanny, L. (2019). The impact of celebrity endorsement by social influencer celebgram on purchase intention of generation Z in fashion industry. *International Journal of Recent Technology and Engineering, 8*(2), 397-404.

Schouten, A. P., Janssen, L., & Verspaget, M. (2020). Celebrity vs. influencer endorsements in advertising: The role of identification, credibility, and product-endorser fit. *International Journal of Advertising, 39*(2), 258–281. doi:10.1080/02650487.2019.1634898

Shen, Z. (2021). A persuasive eWOM model for increasing consumer engagement on social media: Evidence from Irish fashion micro-influencers. *Journal of Research in Interactive Marketing, 15*(2), 181–199. doi:10.1108/JRIM-10-2019-0161

Shin, E., & Lee, J. E. (2021). What makes consumers purchase apparel products through social shopping services that social media fashion influencers have worn? *Journal of Business Research, 132*, 416–428. doi:10.1016/j.jbusres.2021.04.022

Singh, J., Quamina, L. T., & Xue, T. (2018). *Ten million followers and counting: How digital brand alliances between online influencers and brands impact consumer value: An abstract perceptions.* doi:10.1007/978-3-319-66023-3_239

Sinha, J. I., & Fung, T. T. (2021). How social media micro-influencers are disrupting the business of youth fashion. *Rutgers Business Review, 6*(1), 44–50.

Sokolova, K., & Kefi, H. (2020). Instagram and YouTube bloggers promote it, why should I buy? how credibility and parasocial interaction influence purchase intentions. *Journal of Retailing and Consumer Services, 53*, 101742. Advance online publication. doi:10.1016/j.jretconser.2019.01.011

Sudha, M., & Sheena, K. (2017). Impact of influencers in consumer decision process: the fashion industry. *SCMS Journal of Indian Management, 14*(3), 14-30. https://pdfs.semanticscholar.org/1469/eccb29f76b24e85cba8b6b60adf5ab4932d8.pdf

Suh, S. (2020). Non-boundaries of style represented in fashion Instagram: A social media platform as a digital space–time. *Fashion and Textiles, 7*(1), 33. Advance online publication. doi:10.118640691-020-00222-9

Sun, Y., Wang, R., Cao, D., & Lee, R. (2022). Who are social media influencers for luxury fashion consumption of the Chinese gen Z? categorisation and empirical examination. *Journal of Fashion Marketing and Management*, *26*(4), 603–621. doi:10.1108/JFMM-07-2020-0132

Tanwar, A. S., Chaudhry, H., & Srivastava, M. K. (2021). Influencer marketing as a tool of digital consumer engagement: A systematic literature review. *Indian Journal of Marketing*, *51*(10), 27–42. doi:10.17010/ijom/2021/v51/i10/166439

Trequattrini, R., Manfredi, S., Lardo, A., & Cuozzo, B. (2019). Social media as a new opportunity for female entrepreneurs: An analysis of the fashion industry. *Springer Proceedings in Business and Economics,* 287-298. 10.1007/978-3-030-00335-7_19

Triani, D., & Vusparatih, D. S. (2019). "The role of social media Instagram in creating youth trend fashion (19-22 years old)" case study of fashion influencer on Instagram towards Binus University faculty of economics and communication department students year 2014-2017). *International Journal of Scientific and Technology Research*, *8*(7), 248–250.

Twumasi, Y. A., & Dzahene-Quarshie, B. (2022). Shaping the perceptions of fashion consumers by influencers on digital platforms in the era of COVID-19. *International Journal of E-Entrepreneurship and Innovation*, *12*(2), 1–13. Advance online publication. doi:10.4018/IJEEI.314466

Vardhan, J., & Mahato, M. (2022). Prosocial behavior and impact of influencers during CrisisA study based on sentiment analysis. Promotional practices and perspectives from emerging markets, 246-260. doi:10.4324/9781003315582-13

Veresiu, E., & Parmentier, M. (2021). Advanced style influencers: Confronting gendered ageism in fashion and beauty markets. *Journal of the Association for Consumer Research*, *6*(2), 263–273. doi:10.1086/712609

Von Mettenheim, W., & Wiedmann, K. (2021). The role of fashion influencers' attractiveness: A gender-specific perspective. *Communication Research and Practice*, *7*(3), 263–290. doi:10.1080/22041451.2021.2013087

Waltenrath, A., Brenner, C., & Hinz, O. (2022). Some interactions are more equal than others: The effect of influencer endorsements in social media brand posts on engagement and online store performance. *Journal of Interactive Marketing*, *57*(4), 541–560. doi:10.1177/10949968221096591

Wiedmann, K., & von Mettenheim, W. (2020). Attractiveness, trustworthiness and expertise – social influencers' winning formula? *Journal of Product and Brand Management*, *30*(5), 707–725. doi:10.1108/JPBM-06-2019-2442

Wiedmann, K., & von Mettenheim, W. (2020). *An adaptation of the source credibility model on social influencers: An abstract.* doi:10.1007/978-3-030-42545-6_65

Yeo, S. F., Tan, C. L., Kumar, A., Tan, K. H., & Wong, J. K. (2022). Investigating the impact of AI-powered technologies on Instagrammers' purchase decisions in digitalization era–A study of the fashion and apparel industry. *Technological Forecasting and Social Change*, *177*, 121551. Advance online publication. doi:10.1016/j.techfore.2022.121551

Zhang, Y., & Caverlee, J. (2019). Instagrammers, fashionistas, and me: Recurrent fashion recommendation with implicit visual influence. *International Conference on Information and Knowledge Management, Proceedings,* 1583-1592. 10.1145/3357384.3358042

Zhou, L., Jin, F., Wu, B., Chen, Z., & Wang, C. L. (2023). Do fake followers mitigate influencers' perceived influencing power on social media platforms? The mere number effect and boundary conditions. *Journal of Business Research, 158,* 113589. doi:10.1016/j.jbusres.2022.113589

Zhou, S., Barnes, L., McCormick, H., & Blazquez Cano, M. (2021). Social media influencers' narrative strategies to create eWOM: A theoretical contribution. *International Journal of Information Management, 59,* 102293. Advance online publication. doi:10.1016/j.ijinfomgt.2020.102293

KEY TERMS AND DEFINITIONS

Brand/Digital Brand: A name to characterize a type of product or service made by a particular company and available in a marketplace environment, whether physical or digital.

Fashion Industry: An activity in which a company designs, produces, and sells new styles of clothes, shoes, bags, etc., especially expensive ones.

Gen X and Gen Z: Are groups of people of approximately the same age within a society or within a particular family. It has several points in common: experiences, values, visions of life, and an approximation of ages. These characteristics will shape this group of people, causing them to behave in the same way. Generation X identifies individuals born between 1965 and 1979, and Generation Y identifies individuals born between 1980 and 1994.

KPI: Abbreviation for key performance indicator, a way of measuring a company's progress towards the goals it is trying to achieve. Provide managers with advanced warning signals that there may be problems ahead.

Social Media: Are interactive digital platforms that facilitate the creation and sharing of information, ideas, interests, and other forms of expression through virtual groups, communities, and networks.

Social Media Influencer: Is a content creation and distribution activity that takes place through social media platforms such as YouTube, Twitter, Facebook, and Instagram.

Sponsorship and Sponsored Content: An association with a website or a person that gives an advertiser some visibility and advantage when associated with specific content, sponsorship can provide a more targeted audience. Sponsorship also implies "synergy and resonance" between the website and the advertiser. Some sponsorships are available as value-added opportunities for advertisers who buy a certain minimum amount of advertising.

Chapter 15
Social Media Marketing Applications and Fashion Brands:
A South Asian Perspective

Bikramjit Rishi
Shiv Nadar Institution of Eminence (Deemed), India

Junaid Mohammed
Duke University, USA

Akriti
The University of Pennsylvania, USA

ABSTRACT

South Asia's large size and economic diversification make it a diverse market. This diversity becomes crucial for marketers to reach consumers and share social media information about their products. Social media positively impacts branding and helps in fostering positive customer relationships. The chapter focuses on the South Asian market with detail on the social media marketing applications followed by the fashion brands in this region. The chapter sees the details from a theoretical lens and tries to comprehend the benefits and applications of social media marketing for fashion brands in South Asia. The chapter proposes an approach to designing a social media strategy and provides guidelines on how fashion brands can effectively use social media marketing. The chapter concludes by considering some obstacles the industry could face in the South Asian region and suggesting ways to overcome them by strategically using social media marketing.

DOI: 10.4018/978-1-6684-8753-2.ch015

INTRODUCTION

South Asia, a growth champion, hit a major setback since the outbreak of the COVID-19 pandemic resulting in stringent lockdowns and disrupted supply chains turning it into one of the worst-performing economic regions in the world (Un.org, 2021). With the global demand shocks, recovery, and containment measures against COVID-19, the South Asian economy is predicted to slow down to 5.5% in 2023 before growing in 2024. The largest economy in South Asia, and the fifth largest in the world, is India, which alone is estimated to drop by 6.9% in the 2022-23 fiscal year, while Bangladesh is expected to slow down by up to 5.2% due to rising inflation and tightening financial conditions (World Bank Group, 2023). Responding to the pandemic, technological changes, and widespread structural transformation, the global economy has given rise to digital technologies, enabling productivity enhancements in some sectors, such as manufacturing and creating new markets (The World Bank, 2021). The economic diversifications are low or minimal in this region; achieving resilience to external shocks is a top priority which would mean that a more integrated regional economy, along with the expedition of economic reforms and transformations, would help the countries in the South Asian region grow significantly (Un.org, 2021).

In low-income economies with rapidly developing markets like South Asia, globalization and technological advancements have resulted in a collective increase in smartphone usage and penetration of Internet services, leading to more active online communities, which marketers use to reach their customers (Otugo et al., 2015). It was also found that most people from emerging and developing economies are more likely than others to use social media platforms such as Facebook and Twitter and use these services more frequently (Poushter, 2016).

Social media is built on the ideological and technological foundations afforded by Web 2.0 in the form of internet-based applications that facilitate creating and disseminating user-generated content. Social media has overtaken traditional forms of marketing recently (Borker, 2014; Doshi et al., 2023). Social media provides a cost-effective platform for social conversation, promoting goods and services, and allowing interactive engagement regardless of customers' location (Olotewo, 2016). Users can interact with products and services positively or negatively through direct editing or generating information about an organization and sharing it with members of their networks (Gilfoil & Jobs, 2012). It, therefore, results in a multidirectional message that signals to organizations, current or potential consumers, thereby engaging the entire ecosystem, rather than a one-way message between the brand and the consumer (Parveen et al., 2015).

The rising internet usage rates and the expanding social media user base have led Asia-Pacific to become a top contributor to social media penetration. Social media sites experience a much higher volume of usage than other sites (Rahman, 2016). The South Asian region alone contributes to 18.5% of global internet users, second only to Eastern Asia (Kemp, 2023). The APAC region has positioned itself as a high-volume market in the social media space, expecting to add about 59 million more users than the rest of the world, even with just a 2.7% predicted YoY growth in 2023 (Cheung, 2023). Within APAC, India (467 million) and China (983 million) maintain a stronghold of active users (Kameke, 2023). Facebook retains its stronghold as the most widely used platform globally, with ~2.9 billion users (Dixon, 2023).

As Table 1 indicates, Facebook, alone or along with other social media sites, is the most popular and widespread social media platform in South Asia. In Bangladesh, videos and animations receive more engagement as users interact more with motion than static images. However, static graphics, which include images, infographics, short videos, and text, which have posts and status updates, are the most common types of content (Rahman, 2016). Similarly, in India, it was found that videos, images, and GIFs

Table 1. Country-wise use of social media platforms

Country	Most Used Social Media Platform(s)
Bangladesh	Facebook, Twitter, and YouTube
India	Facebook, YouTube, and Instagram
Nepal	Facebook, Twitter, and YouTube
Pakistan	Facebook, Twitter, and Instagram
Sri Lanka	Facebook, Twitter, and YouTube

(Graphics Interchange Format) receive better engagement and enhance brand awareness and reach than long articles (Chitra & Sasikala, 2016). The organized content and short videos, quizzes, questions, and personal comments tailored to specific audiences have the maximum impact in Nepal (Upadhaya, 2017). Even in Pakistan, like other South Asian countries, video posts have received maximum engagement, and images and giveaways with questions and answers are among the best strategies to use on social media platforms such as Facebook (Ahmed et al., 2019). In Sri Lanka, consistent branding through quality and visually appealing content works better than text-heavy posts or updates (De Bustis et al., 2018). Social media marketing allows businesses to increase their visibility by using online platforms and building customer relationships through virtual communities (Celine, 2012). Therefore, social media marketing is the logical next step for most marketers in emerging economies citing its low cost, effectiveness, and fast-growing reach (Rahman, 2016; Rishi & Bandyopadhyay, 2017; Rishi & Kuthuru, 2021a).

Marketing on social media has produced a strong branding effect for the fashion industry, especially in South Asian markets, where there is a tremendous opportunity to engage in social media and build identity, awareness, relationships, and revenue (Hsiao et al., 2020). Because of the rising buying power, the global fashion industry shows significant double-digit growth, mainly dependent on growing economies such as Asia (Ananda, 2019). The fashion industry is among the initial few to adopt social media. It is the ideal platform for brands and consumers to interact and reflect on their style and fashion. It also helps spread eWOM (electronic word of mouth), thus increasing the brand's online presence by building a community (Ananda, 2019). Although international brands such as Pepe Jeans London, Levi Strauss, and Lee have been in South Asian markets for a long time, luxury brands like Gucci, Chanel, and Tommy Hilfiger have also started investing in these markets profoundly due to their vast potential and rapidly upgrading consumption patterns among the masses because of the use of media (Role of Media in Fashion Industry of India, 2021).

Instagram, launched in 2010 and acquired by Facebook in 2012, is a community of over a billion users and 25 million businesses. It has emerged as the most widely used social media platform, where fashion is the third most followed category after music and entertainment (Talati-Parikh, 2021). Facebook has even started organising offline events to promote the segment. One such fashion seminar in Delhi hosted numerous fashion designers and brand owners who discussed the rising prevalence of marketing on social media for the fashion industry (Tandon, 2021). With a 13.3% annual growth rate (2023-27), fashion brands have a tremendous opportunity to invest in the South Asian market to grab online retailing opportunities (Fashion – Southern Asia: Statista Market Forecast, 2023). Further, ad spending on social media sites in South Asia continues to increase with higher click-through rates and decreasing response time to customer queries (The Drum, 2021).

A recent survey revealed that marketers plan to increase social media's marketing budget to about 18.9% from 2022 to 2023. (Social Media Advertising – Worldwide, 2023). For global fashion brands, the social media engagement rate is highest on Tiktok (2.51%), followed by Instagram (0.36%), Facebook (0.05%), and Twitter (0.07%) and continues to rise with tap-to-buy features integrated into posts and stories (Cucu, 2023). A 2023 Yahoo Entertainment report identified Influencer Marketing to grow at a CAGR of 30.81% over 2023-2031 to a US$ 118.0 billion market (Yahoo & AstuteAnalytica, 2023). As such, marketers are increasingly using and prioritizing influencer marketing. Avantika Mohan, a travel, lifestyle, and fashion influencer, said, "I've noticed an influx of briefs focusing on fashion (particularly festive wear), online shopping portals, and jewelry (Sharma, 2021). Influencer marketing is also rising on platforms like TikTok and YouTube, and brands are increasing spending accordingly, especially in India (Chaturvedi & Laghate, 2021). Experts from the fashion industry believe that increased spending on social media is necessary as lacking a social media presence devalues the brand. Social media can engage the customers and build a story around the brand and its community, which is particularly important for premium brands to re-create the experience (Golikeri, 2021).

With over a billion users only in South Asia, social media is the fastest-growing and most defining technology surpassing all forms of traditional media by allowing people to interact freely and providing marketers with a space to employ multiple strategies to engage with consumers (Siriwardana, 2020; Rishi & Kuthuru, 2021b). Thus, spending on social media by growing industries such as fashion will only increase.

BACKGROUND

As shown in Appendix 1, the review of existing literature indicates that integrating social media in marketing focuses on the purchase behavior and purchase intention in the e-commerce and consumption of luxury goods (especially in developed countries). The synthesis indicates that the literature focuses on online consumption patterns of consumers for various products and services, lacking an emphasis on the fashion industry. So it becomes paramount importance to understand the social media marketing applications in the fashion industry because the fashion industry is on the rise, as is the adoption of social media in marketing. The linchpin of current studies in this area focuses only on developed countries, discussing renowned brands, luxury fashion consumption, and customer purchase intention. A few existing studies on this domain also justify the proposed work with high relevance for South Asian markets. Furthermore, more than ever, South-Asian consumers are active on social media platforms, making it an enticing way to reach existing and potential consumers, allowing fashion brands to expand their customer base.

As businesses increasingly adapt to social media as a tool for marketing, fashion brands across the globe have to adjust to the changing marketing landscape and engage with their customers. There is a growing need to make a prominent presence on social media platforms and keep up with current trends in how businesses and customers interact. To do this, fashion brands would require understanding strategies for running effective social media campaigns and harnessing the true potential of social media marketing tools. This chapter provides a means for this by detailing highly appropriate methods and strategies for the fashion industry to augment the adoption and optimization of their social media usage to influence consumers. A specific emphasis on the fashion industry will further reinforce the approach brands across the spectrum can use to bring the proven benefits of social media to their way of engaging with their customers.

SOCIAL MEDIA MARKETING APPLICATIONS IN THE FASHION INDUSTRY

As consumers continue to use social media for networking, entertainment, and, increasingly, shopping, the potential for social media as a sales channel cannot be overlooked. Brands are leveraging this platform to convey their messages, amplify their vision and develop a connection with their customers (Rishi et al., 2023).

The crucial role of social media, specifically Instagram, is playing in the fashion industry; Jaspreet Chandok, vice-president and head of fashion at IMG Reliance, says, "In the last one-and-a-half years, for the fashion industry, the platform has been changing behaviour. Fashion brands and designers are aligning themselves with an Instagram-only strategy. They are shooting only for Instagram." (Tandon, 2021). Designer labels such as Burberry and Roberto Cavalli use social media to make critical business announcements, including the announcement of the new CEO on Instagram (Chopra, 2019). IMG Reliance also manages "The Lakme Fashion Week," India's flagship fashion event. Even the co-founder of ethnic fashion brand Jaypore, Shilpa Sharma, says that Instagram is an "indispensable" asset for their company (Tandon, 2021).

Burberry was among the first brands to embrace Instagram. It has consistently been exemplary in creating content and using social media to make its brand feel omnipresent while remaining exclusive and luxurious (Best Fashion Brands in Social Media, 2021). Luxury brands such as Gucci, Dolce & Gabbana, and Dior creatively use social storytelling on platforms like Instagram and YouTube. Fast-fashion brands such as Forever 21 use Facebook and Instagram to reach their lively young target group (Best Fashion Brands in Social Media, 2021). Dior, Burberry, and Prada were among the first to utilize Instagram's new online feature launched in 2019, where customers could directly purchase from the social media platform (Chopra, 2019).

Global fashion brands have constantly been realigning their social media marketing strategies to get maximum ROI by launching various campaigns. One such example was Superdry's creative use of social media to launch itself into new markets with the "Superdry Tweet Fuel" campaign, an online Twitter campaign that it launched when it wanted to enter the Indian market (Superdry Used Social Media Marketing To Reach More Than 1.5 Million People On Twitter, (n.d.)). Even Max Fashion's recent campaign #YouAreSoBeautiful, an initiative started on International Mother's Day, resonated very well with their target audience as they collaborated with over 300 influencers. The brand also held numerous contests across its social media platforms while using Augmented Reality (AR) filters to compliment women, which got over 60 million views (Max Fashion's new initiative creates a strong resonance with women, 2021).

Notable fashion retail brands such as Zara and H&M have pioneered the social media game and have captured the attention of the masses. With a presence in over 88 countries and about 6500 stores, the Spanish retailer brand Zara is the world's largest apparel retailer. Its Instagram serves as a catalog of the retailer's latest offerings. It has evolved into a veritable lookbook of the latest fashion trends because the brand can predict new clothing trends, design affordable pieces, and manufacture stylish products faster than any other retailer (Koivulehto, 2017). With over 30.89 million Facebook followers, Zara has also been able to establish itself as a fashion maven in this way, rising above the thousands of other fashion brands and fashion-focused Instagrammers vying for the attention of the platform's 57 million followers (Koivulehto, 2017). The brand creates visually appealing content utilizing Instagram's video capabilities to captivate audiences while highlighting the brand's new products.

The Swedish clothing giant H&M, the second-largest clothing retailer with a global footprint in about 74 countries and over 5000 stores, has a Facebook account with 41.07 million followers and engages customers and visitors. H&M's Facebook page features beautiful models dressed in H&M clothes, as well as local brand ambassadors and other styles (Nguyen, 2018). Customers who are pleased or dissatisfied can communicate with the brand via its Facebook page and express their delight or displeasure as they see fit. This way, Facebook facilitates effective communication between the brand and its customers (Nguyen, 2018).

H&M's recent collaboration with famous Indian fashion designer Sabyasachi Mukherjee to launch a collection with a boho-chic vibe, the sell-out of which declared it to be an absolute success (Dwivedi, 2021). It was the first time sarees to feature in a fast-fashion collection. It sold out immediately as Sabyasachi's 4.7 million followers on his official Instagram account saw him on Instagram reels talking about his recent H&M collection (Dwivedi, 2021). H&M's previous high-end collaborations with others like Alexander Wang, Diane von Furstenberg, Stella McCartney and even with pop stars such as Madonna and Kylie Minogue and Sabyasachi's successful partnership with New York-based luxury department store, Bergdorf Goodman and French Shoe Designer Christian Louboutin, there was bound to be massive traffic at the e-stores (Dwivedi, 2021).

Renowned Indian fashion designers such as Sabyasachi Mukherjee, Anita Dongre, Tarun Tahiliani, Shantanu Nikhil, Ritu Kumar, Masaba Gupta, and so on are bringing about a social media revolution in fashion. These fashion designers use social media, especially Instagram, to build a story around style and excite followers about their latest collections (Tandon, 2021). Because of social media's broad reach, brands have begun to pay attention to their lavish sets and fashion shows, tailoring them for the brand's Instagram feed. Instagram is helping fashion brands boost their online presence, and pages like Diet Prada and Diet Sabya acknowledge acts of plagiarism in the fashion industry. It also influences how customers consume fashion content (Chopra, 2019).

Through social media's visual storytelling ability, brands can document the entire journey of their collection from fabric to the final finished product, including various behind-the-scenes sequences that intrigue and captivate the audience. In one of his interviews, Narresh Kukreja from Shivan said, "Fashion is an imagery-driven industry. It is one of the biggest passion points on Instagram, sharing space with the other two F's, food and fitness. The platform has evolved immensely, providing innovative communication and increased effectiveness for image-driven industries. Ensuring a fine balance between permanent and transient content—post vs. stories—Instagram has been an extremely advantageous medium for us to connect personally and interact directly with the customers, as it provides them with an opportunity for immediate call to action." (Chopra, 2019). Shivan and Narresh are among the Indian fashion designers who use relevant hashtags, maintain a unique relationship with the online consumer base, and have a notable social media presence.

Pakistani designers and fashion houses have been creating creative campaigns using unique hashtags that have captured the attention of their audiences. Pakistani fashion designer Zara Shahjahan's #IMadeIt campaign on Instagram garnered a positive response from customers as the skilled labourers who made clothes for the brand were appreciated and featured on the brand's Instagram page (Raza, 2016). Generation, a Pakistani fashion house, came up with a #StepOutside campaign to support the Girls at Dhabas movement, a social movement showing women reclaiming public places, and they got women from different professions as well as a few models to be a part of the campaign (Raza, 2016). Even Sanam Chaudhri's #AntiSizeZero campaign to promote body positivity and Deepak Perwani's #FixIt campaign, where models wearing his collection posed in areas that needed fixing, such as neglected exteriors or garbage bins, received excellent responses (Raza, 2016). Pakistani designers like Hassan Sheheryar Yasin, Sania Maskatiya, Bunto Kazmi, and Asim Jofa increasingly use social media to engage with their audience and drive sales (Ghosh, 2016).

Not only are large fashion houses and famous designers using Instagram, but even smaller brands and other home-grown brands are now using social media marketing. For example, in India, where the fashion market's estimated worth is $96.47 billion (Apparel – India: Statista Market Forecast, 2023), out of which approximately $22.97 billion is through online transactions placing more importance on the presence of the internet in the region (Technavio, 2023). Instagram's market will rise by $30 million soon as more and more designers (about 40%) do their business transactions on Instagram (Instagram is Playing a Huge Role In India's Fashion Market, 2018).

Brands are promoting themselves and their products and adding value to the lives of their online customer base are receiving a better response from their audience. The companies like Zara are updating their followers about the latest trends in the fashion industry (The Best Brands On Instagram: How Zara Got 10M Followers, 2021). Brands like Steve Madden have successfully integrated social media analytics into their operations to gain valuable insights regarding the number of likes or visits. The brands try to understand the kind of content that receives maximum engagement. For example, Superdry's "Superdry Tweet Fuel" campaign reached over a million people in just five days. The brand innovatively invited its customers and potential customers to participate in its campaign, creating a link between the brand and the users. The engagement encouraged the followers to promote the brand, increasing its chances of getting more views through increased likes and shares (Superdry Used Social Media Marketing To Reach More Than 1.5 Million People On Twitter, (n.d.)). Max Fashion's recent success shows how brands can leverage advances in artificial intelligence, augmented reality, and related technology to attract people. More and more brands are also using big data analytics to profile their customers and make different strategies for different segments. Sabyasachi's approach demonstrates that social media allows for active consumer communication and engagement through content. Using relevant hashtags, a combination of social media sites including Instagram, Facebook, Twitter, and YouTube, and hopping on to the latest trends like reels, TikToks, stories, collaboration with influencers, chatbots, and so on have worked for the brands. Improved response time to customer queries and requests also presents brands in a positive light. It has resulted in better social reviews and eWOM (Electronic Word of Mouth), which has helped create brand awareness and promote these brands. Since the pandemic, there has also been a lot of discussion around fair treatment of employees and labourers, better work practices, and the need for sustainability. As people focus on these aspects, brands must also meet the set standards. Most brands that successfully build a story around their collections while adding a human touch to their stories, such as the #IMadeIt or #FixIt campaign, can attract followers and drive sales through their social media strategies.

SOLUTIONS AND RECOMMENDATIONS: DESIGNING SOCIAL MEDIA STRATEGY FOR FASHION BRANDS

Social media marketing has revolutionized how businesses interact with their customers and enable creating and sharing of content like words, audio, videos, and pictures (Brake, 2009). Social media and fashion are inextricably linked because both have become a part of daily life. Wearing fashion brands is a way to present oneself at social events, particularly if fashion has become a social passion (Loureiro et al., 2018). People want to express themselves as unique through clothing, and some people use their fashion and style to influence others socially. Social media is increasingly being used to persuade others to purchase specific products and make recommendations based on personal experiences (Morra et al., 2018).

With numerous avenues for change and the potential to leverage data existing beyond the visible horizon, companies can use social media in a way that can harness the countless benefits it bestows on companies and their customers. The demonstrated importance of social media, companies maintain an active presence on various social media platforms without any defined scope, structured processes, or monitoring mechanisms, rendering the whole exercise a waste of time, effort, and money (Baptista et al., 2017). It becomes imperative to have a tailored social media strategy that caters to a wide range of customers' varying socio-economic conditions, consumption patterns, and behaviours.

While planning and developing the social media strategy for any company, it is essential to identify the short-term and long-term goals to be addressed through objectives and tactics. Designing a social media strategy for any brand begins with thoroughly examining the business environment. Basis this, the company can formulate specific goals. Then the particular objectives address these goals. For the social media strategy to be helpful, the marketer must implement it in a specific group of people, in this case, the target audience. The marketer must have complete knowledge of their behaviours and preferences. Evaluating the consumer base provides a comprehensive picture of the expectations, how a marketer should address them, and where they will be met, enabling the selection of appropriate channels and developing content creation and engagement strategies.

1. Understanding the business

The first step to developing a successful social media strategy is understanding the business landscape, which is even more crucial in the fashion industry, given its dynamic nature. It is critical to gauge the actual state of the industry, the brand, its competitors, its offerings, market trends and preferences, and its previous marketing mix and campaigns. It helps in discerning opportunities and areas for improvement.

2. Setting the objectives

The first step facilitates the creation of an initial list of expectations that the company needs to address through its social media campaign. Considering the availability or constraint on resources such as personnel, budget, and time, marketers should set SMART (Specific, Measurable, Attainable, Realistic, and Timely) objectives.

3. Identifying the target audience and knowing them

Reaching out to the relevant audience is important for effectively materializing a brand's social media strategies. The brand and other product teams may have defined the target audience profile, which has been crucial to understanding their demographic and psychographic characteristics. Through profiling, brands can better understand their consumers' activities, patterns, perceptions, and participation on various social media platforms, which could inform different tactics required for different segments (Popli &

Rishi, 2021). Marketers should consider the primary target audience's descriptions, motivations to use and engage on social media platforms, accessibility to various devices, general social media usage, and means to reach out to them. This understanding allows the creation of a comprehensive profile of the brand's current and potential target audience to tailor the campaigns to drive engagement and interaction.

4. Choosing the relevant social media platform

Following the identification of target audiences, the next step is to determine the most appealing social media platform or a combination of social media platforms to reach out to them. Marketers can select the social media platform based on accessibility by users, suitability for the identified target audience, and the nature of the product or content. Typically, the choice is made based on the primary goal of reaching out to the target audience: fostering community relationships, entertaining, publishing, or engaging in social commerce. The content volume generated, paid, and promoted is decided on, estimated, and aligned to resonate with the customers.

5. Competitor analysis

Analysing the business landscape, as was done at the beginning of this process, is necessary to determine the competition in the market to inform the brand's marketing strategies. After identifying existing and potential competition, the next step is to perform a social media audit on social media platforms to ascertain the brand's and its competitors' presence and performance on social media. This understanding enhances a brand's SWOT (Strengths, Weaknesses, Opportunities, and Threats) analysis and provides insights regarding potential customers' expectations by analyzing user engagement.

6. Outlining strategies

Following the above steps helps a brand understand its current social media presence. The brand can use it to outline the following steps to achieve the objectives and, in turn, the company's marketing goals. The brand must create a sync within the defined actions and outlined strategies. It will help the brand to achieve its marketing objectives with the help of social media plan.

7. Content creation and engagement

The content strategy should be well-rounded and resonate with what the brand stands for so that the customers are interested. The content, which could be stories, posts, or even user-generated content, should generate curiosity or evoke emotions and be visually appealing to create a hook that keeps the user engaged.

Brands could pick a variety of themes and concepts that their content could follow over time. The brand should unify the content on all social media platforms under a specific theme or idea. The user is familiar with the brand across all marketing channels. A content calendar could also be designed to determine a posting schedule and time spent answering customer queries or interacting with them. Polls, giveaways, coupons, contests, and promotions get maximum user response, maximizing engagement and boosting brand awareness.

8. Brand-Consumer synergy

The social media content and ethos should be consistent with the brand and target audience to synchronize its personality, products, and how they are represented on the platform. Additionally, all platforms with the brand's presence should send a unified message or idea encapsulating the brand's strategy and the creative aspects of the marketing campaign. This strong coherence across all marketing channels will create a positive experience for the audience.

9. Metrics and analysis

Marketers can determine the effectiveness of a brand's social media strategy by using specific metrics to measure the achievement of goals. Insightful observations could be gathered from analysing these metrics about how the strategies could be tweaked to improve results.

Below are some metrics that could be analysed to evaluate the results of a strategy:

- Influence and engagement - Monitor the participation observed during a campaign, performance, and patterns of views, likes, comments, shares, reactions, clicks, time spent, and subscriptions.
- Popularity - Measure the popularity of a specific campaign or post by analyzing the number of views, clicks, shares, bookmarks, and CTC across all platforms
- Reach - Observe how viral the campaign has been and how many users it has reached.
- The ratio of earned media to paid media - A way to understand the actual drivers of a campaign could be to measure what percentage of total media is being paid for and what percentage of complete media is being generated by users
- Value – The marketer can measure the success or failure of a campaign in terms of its translation into business value, such as its contribution to sales, acquisition cost, retention rate, and so on.
- Volume - The total volume of content posted across all platforms should be considered to recognize patterns and methods working or others that might need to be altered.

Fashion brands increasingly use social media platforms, realising their importance in consumer communication, resulting in brand awareness, engrossment, engagement, and visibility in augmented purchase behaviour (Sharma et al., 2021). Millennials search for, collect and share fashion brand-related information on social media, specifically brand-created fan pages on Facebook, Twitter, and Instagram (Samala & Singh, 2019). As an effective marketing tool over the last decade, social media has allowed marketers to engage with consumers transparently and interactively, helping forge public relations (Ahmad et al., 2015). The effectiveness of a brand's social media strategy will determine a customer's involvement through interaction with the brand making it crucial for brands to establish the critical elements of their social media strategy (Faraoni et al., 2016). It is essential to influence consumer behaviour, awareness, and attitude to maximize the returns from social media marketing (Nash, 2018).

FUTURE RESEARCH DIRECTIONS

Undertaking a comprehensive outlook of the role of the adoption of social media in the fashion industry can be described as a tool that targets customers and is oriented according to their perspectives, respecting their sentiments for a product. Social media application varies across platforms, has been embraced by fashion brands, and have been explored across many services promoting fashion products. It becomes a pertinent decision for fashion firms to use social media wisely and effectively to achieve their marketing objectives.

Though the medium has a lot to offer, understanding the competition across companies, one cannot deny that it thoroughly relies on the small and medium-sized fashion businesses and the firm's expertise and social media evaluation to outshine and create its place amongst the humongous crowd. Social Media Marketing for fashion brands necessitates knowledge and much effort, and it comes with its own set of problems and hazards to overcome before attaining success. Social media marketing is not always simple or cost-effective. Depending on the sort of firm, its size, age, and management style, extra work may be required in various areas. To begin, fashion brands must devote human and time resources to managing their social media profiles. Employees involved in social media activities should be highly skilled and trained to effectively respond to every question and complaint that customers have daily and manage and control any potential negative comments.

To stay on consumers' radar, social media staff must be active and produce fresh content regularly, depending on the type of fashion brands. It is vital because it allows fashion brands to interact with customers constantly. One of the most significant concerns for fashion brands adopting social media marketing is reputational damage due to inefficient use of their social media platforms. Overuse of advertising, commercial presentation of products and services, and overzealous sales efforts are frequently seen negatively by audiences, who may become irritated and unfollow the business on social media.

Privacy, security, intellectual property, employment practices, and other legal risks are all possible with social media. Security risks occur when malware, viruses, or spyware is downloaded through Social Media sites; security concerns are a major negative factor because Fashion brands fear financial risks from viruses and spyware. Before engaging in social media activities, social media personnel must comprehend information technology law. Security and operational risks are high and may deter fashion brands from adopting Social Media Marketing. So it is concluded that all the issues mentioned above need the attention of the researchers. Hence researchers should undertake studies focusing on a particular brand or multiple brands using a single country or cross-country perspective.

CONCLUSION

Although social media marketing is rapidly rising in developing countries, there are obvious challenges in reaching out to diverse consumer groups through this channel because of low literacy rates, relatively underdeveloped infrastructure, and fragmented industries (Sharma & Rehman, 2016). The United Nations Development Programme (UNDP) report states that the multiplier effect on the growth of an economy is because of inequality, poverty, and unemployment, which are also the major causes of human underdevelopment (UNDP, 2019). South Asia's socio-economic outlook is markedly different from other economies worldwide, owing to the region's large share of multidimensional poverty and global income (UNDP, 2019). Economies such as Bangladesh, Nepal, and India have shown positive growth in the past few years, while Pakistan and Sri Lanka have deteriorated (United Nations, 2019). However, the COVID-19 pandemic has stunted the growth of these economies because of interruptions in business activities and supply chain disintegrations. The fashion industry saw a massive decline in sales, particularly offline retail, which experienced almost zero sales given the stringent lockdowns imposed by countries; there was a minimal conversion from idle scrolling to actual sales (Baum et al., 2020). The global fashion and apparel industry was expected to decline by 27% to 30% in 2020 (Mickensey, 2021). Consumer spending on the fashion industry is expected to decline as the pandemic has not only affected demand with cancelled orders or restricted access to online shopping, but it also led to a supply-side shock with restrained travel and unavailability of raw materials. The built-up inventory and fewer selling options have resulted in huge losses for most brands (Kumar, V & Kumar, S., 2021). The already dynamic consumer behaviour patterns have further been altered, especially with the rise in social media usage, as the constant information overload has induced changes in consumer behaviour (George, 2016). The excelled fashion brands are either concentrating on strengthening their digital outreach or focusing on the Asia-Pacific region (Mickensey, 2020). People, places, and products have become more accessible, approachable, and affordable due to globalisation and digitization (Sharma & Jhamb, 2020). Users are now quickly taking suggestions from friends and family by simply sharing pictures or videos of products through social media and even going through reviews on these platforms to make their final decisions giving consumers more access to information and power (George, 2016). In 2021, it will be critical to actively manage commercial opportunities and be astute in selecting winning segments, markets, and channel combinations (Rishi & Popli, 2021). Social media platforms are now used to exchange information about various brands and significantly influence purchase decisions, making them valuable tools for brands, businesses, and marketers (Naeem & Ozuem, 2021). Previous studies have found strong brand passion and engagement can result in a willingness to pay a high price, positive word of mouth, brand engagement, and purchasing intentions. It is true for fashion, where consumers follow numerous celebrities, influencers, and bloggers and constantly seek advice from fashion experts (Naeem & Ozuem, 2021). Brands are therefore focusing on maintaining a social presence across social media channels with fresh and frequent content that includes incentives for consumer participation (Ashley & Tuten, 2014). Social media has exhibited an ability to prompt the transition from social fashion brand engagement to actual consumer fashion brand engagement (Naeem & Ozuem, 2021). The COVID-19 pandemic has exacerbated the current situation of growth and development in the South Asian region, and the fashion industry uses social media to study trends and anticipate fashion behaviours (Ahmad et al., 2015). The upsurge of emerging economies has led to the rise of the fashion industry as a global enterprise. The South Asian consumer is switching from offline to online modes of purchase. Hence, brands must reinforce their omnichannel presence using social media platforms (Digital Marketing in 2021: 6 Trends APAC Marketers Should Prepare for | Criteo, 2021). With soaring digital adoption during the pandemic, brands embrace social media features such as social shopping, virtual customer service, and live streaming. Hence, fashion brands must optimise their online experience and channel mix while convincingly incorporating the human touch (McKinsey & Company, 2021). Fashion brands must reflect on changing consumer behaviour and align with key trends to finalise a holistic approach to thrive in the post-pandemic business landscape (McKinsey & Company, 2021). As more brands leverage social media to drive profits, it is crucial to understand that even with the right goals and ideas, there could still be challenges in learning the most useful sites and methods for interacting with customers. Curating unique out-of-the-box content so frequently could also be a struggle that brands must deal with, considering the posting frequency, the need for internal alignment with different departments, and the stiff competition. The brands must follow the original ideas, the latest social media trends, and overall brand image. Creating meaningful content that sparks an interest in audiences across multiple social platforms while using a one-of-a-kind platform-specific approach is essential to make the most of their social media marketing campaigns. Once a brand has established itself on social media, it must use a good analytics tool to track account engagement and demographics. It will assist social media managers in utilising the appropriate social platform for their clients. Moving forward, brands must create a dedicated social media team to manage the entire process, from ideas generation to planning and execution.

REFERENCES

Ahmad, N., Salman, A., & Ashiq, R. (2015). The impact of social media on fashion industry: Empirical investigation from Karachiites. *Journal of Resources Development and Management*, *7*, 1–7.

Ahmed, R. R., Streimikiene, D., Berchtold, G., Vveinhardt, J., Channar, Z. A., & Soomro, R. H. (2019). Effectiveness of online digital media advertising as a strategic tool for building brand sustainability: Evidence from FMCGs and services sectors of Pakistan. *Sustainability (Basel)*, *11*(12), 3436. doi:10.3390u11123436

Ananda, A. S. (2019). *Analysis of consumer-brand engagement with fashion brands in social media* [Doctoral dissertation]. Universidad Politécnica de Madrid.

Ashley, C., & Tuten, T. (2015). Creative strategies in social media marketing: An exploratory study of branded social content and consumer engagement. *Psychology and Marketing*, *32*(1), 15–27. doi:10.1002/mar.20761

Baptista, J., Wilson, A. D., Galliers, R. D., & Bynghall, S. (2017). Social media and the emergence of reflexiveness as a new capability for open strategy. *Long Range Planning*, *50*(3), 322–336. doi:10.1016/j.lrp.2016.07.005

Borker, D. R. (2014). Social media marketing in emerging economies: A Mongolian case study. *International Journal of Marketing Studies*, *6*(2), 31. doi:10.5539/ijms.v6n2p31

Cascone, S. (2021). *How Steve Madden Approaches eCommerce Marketing*. Retrieved March 20, 2023, from https://www.bluecore.com/blog/steve-madden-approaches-ecommerce-marketing/

Chaturvedi, A., & Laghate, G. (2021). *Festive ad spends on social media platforms expected to go up significantly this year*. Retrieved March 15, 2023, from https://economictimes.indiatimes.com/industry/services/advertising/festive-ad-spends-on-social-media-platforms-expected-to-go-up-significantly-this-year/articleshow/87164745.cms?from=mdr

Cheung, M.-C. (2023). *Asia-Pacific Social Media Outlook 2023*. Insider Intelligence. Retrieved March 15, 2023, from https://www.insiderintelligence.com/content/asia-pacific-social-media-outlook-2023

Chitra, K., & Sasikala, K. (2016). Social media marketing strategies for enhancing brand awareness: A study with reference to select startups. *Asian Journal of Research in Social Sciences and Humanities*, *6*(9), 1081–1095. doi:10.5958/2249-7315.2016.00856.X

Chopra, Y. (2019). *How Instagram is changing the game for fashion*. Retrieved March 20, 2023, from https://www.vogue.in/content/how-instagram-has-changed-the-game-for-fashion

Criteo. (2021). *Digital Marketing in 2021: 6 Trends APAC Marketers Should Prepare for* Retrieved March 15, 2023, from https://www.criteo.com/blog/digital-marketing-in-2021-6-trends-apac-marketers-should-prepare-for/

Cucu, E. (2023). *2023 social media industry benchmarks: Socialinsider. Socialinsider Blog: Social media marketing insights and industry tips*. Retrieved March 15, 2023, from https://www.socialinsider.io/blog/social-media-industry-benchmarks/#5

Dash, G., Rishi, B., Akmal, S., Paul, J., & Chakraborty, D. (2023). Digitization, Marketing 4.0, and Repurchase Intention in E-Tail: A Cross-National Study. *Journal of Global Information Management, 31*(1), 1–24. doi:10.4018/JGIM.322303

De Bustis, A., Ganesan, V., & Herath, G. (2018). *Unlocking Sri Lanka's digital opportunity*. McKinsey Digital.

Dixon, S. (2023). *Biggest social media platforms 2023*. Retrieved March 15, 2023, from https://www.statista.com/statistics/272014/global-social-networks-ranked-by-number-of-users/

Doshi, P., Nigam, P., & Rishi, B. (2023). Customer values and patronage intention in social media networks: mediating role of perceived usefulness. *VINE Journal of Information and Knowledge Management Systems*. doi:10.1108/VJIKMS-07-2022-0217

Dwivedi, V. (2021). *Sabyasachi x H&M: A classic example grand play, successful legacy and marketing masterstroke* Retrieved March 20, 2023, from https://www.businesstoday.in/opinion/columns/story/sabyasachi-x-hm-a-classic-example-grand-play-successful-legacy-and-marketing-masterstroke-305678-2021-09-01

Faraoni, M., Bandinelli, R., & Rinaldi, R. (2016). Social media strategy in the Italian fashion industry: A new model of analysis. In *Workshop on Business Models and ICT Technologies for the Fashion Supply Chain* (pp. 253-269). Springer.

Fibre2fashion.com. (2021). *Role of Media in Fashion Industry of India*. Retrieved March 20, 2023, from https://www.fibre2fashion.com/industry-article/6134/role-of-media

George, J. (2016). Growing & changing trends in consumer behavior. In *2016 International Conference on Electrical, Electronics, and Optimization Techniques (ICEEOT)* (pp. 4804-4809). IEEE. 10.1109/ICEEOT.2016.7755633

Ghosh, S. (2016). *Five Pakistani Fashion Designers You Must Follow On Instagram*. Retrieved March 20, 2023, from https://www.thequint.com/lifestyle/five-pakistani-fashion-designers-instagram-asim-jofa-deepak-perwani-bunto-kazmi-hsy-sania-maskatiya#read-more

Golikeri, P. (2021). *The luxury network: How social media lure is still compelling enough for any brand.* Retrieved March 20, 2023, from https://www.dnaindia.com/business/report-the-luxury-network-2694950

Hsiao, S. H., Wang, Y. Y., Wang, T., & Kao, T. W. (2020). How social media shapes the fashion industry: The spillover effects between private labels and national brands. *Industrial Marketing Management, 86*, 40–51. doi:10.1016/j.indmarman.2019.02.022

Ilfoil, D. M., & Jobs, C. (2012). Return on investment for social media: A proposed framework for understanding, implementing, and measuring the return. *Journal of Business & Economics Research, 10*(11), 637–650. doi:10.19030/jber.v10i11.7363

Kemp, S. (2023). *Digital 2023: Global Overview Report - DataReportal – Global Digital Insights. DataReportal.* Retrieved March 15, 2023, from https://datareportal.com/reports/digital-2023-global-overview-report

Koivulehto, E. I. (2017). *Do social media marketing activities enhance customer equity? A case study of fast fashion brand Zara.* Aalto University.

Kumar, V., & Kumar, S. (2021). Impact of covid-19 on textile and fashion industry India: An economic perspective. *Burnieshed Law Journal, 2*, 312–327.

Loureiro, S. M. C., Maximiano, M., & Panchapakesan, P. (2018). Engaging fashion consumers in social media: The case of luxury brands. *International Journal of Fashion Design, Technology and Education, 11*(3), 310–321.

McKinsey & Company. (2021). *Fashion industry during--and after--the coronavirus crisis* Retrieved March 15, 2023, from https://www.mckinsey.com/industries/retail/our-insights/perspectives-for-north-americas-fashion-industry-in-a-time-of-crisis

McKinsey & Company. (2021). *State of Fashion.* Retrieved March 15, 2023, from https://www.mckinsey.com/industries/retail/our-insights/state-of-fashion

Mediakix. (2021). *The Best Brands On Instagram: How Zara Got 10M Followers.* Retrieved March 15, 2023, from https://mediakix.com/blog/best-brands-on-instagram zara channel-followers/

Medium. (2018). *Instagram is Playing A Huge Role in India's Fashion Market.* https://medium.com/@ifashionseo/instagram-is-playing-a-huge-role-in-indias-fashion-market-2677eb1e009e

Morra, M. C., Gelosa, V., Ceruti, F., & Mazzucchelli, A. (2018). Original or counterfeit luxury fashion brands? The effect of social media on purchase intention. *Journal of Global Fashion Marketing, 9*(1), 24–39. doi:10.1080/20932685.2017.1399079

Naeem, M., & Ozuem, W. (2021). Understanding the social consumer fashion brand engagement journey: Insights about reputed fashion brands. *Journal of Brand Management, 28*(5), 1–16. doi:10.105741262-021-00239-5

Nash, J. (2019). Exploring how social media platforms influence fashion consumer decisions in the UK retail sector. *Journal of Fashion Marketing and Management, 23*(1), 82–103. doi:10.1108/JFMM-01-2018-0012

Nguyen, D. (2018). *Social media marketing strategy-Case study H&M Hennes & Mauritz* [Bachelor dissertation]. The Haaga Helia University of Applied Sciences.

Olotewo, J. (2016). Social media marketing in emerging markets. *International Journal of Online Marketing Research, 2*(2), 10–18. doi:10.5455/IJOMR.2016254411

Otugo, N. E., Uzuegbunam, C. E., & Obikeze, C. O. (2015). Social media advertising/marketing: A study of awareness, attitude and responsiveness by Nigerian youths. *International Conference on Communication, Media, Technology, and Design, 1*(2), 1-17. 10.30935/ojcmt/5679

Parveen, F., Jaafar, N. I., & Ainin, S. (2015). Social media usage and organizational performance: Reflections of Malaysian social media managers. *Telematics and Informatics, 32*(1), 67–78. doi:10.1016/j.tele.2014.03.001

Popli, S., & Rishi, B. (2021a). The What, Why and How of Customer Experience. In Crafting Customer Experience Strategy. Emerald Publishing Limited. doi:10.1108/978-1-83909-710-220211001

Popli, S., & Rishi, B. (2021b). Customer Experience Management – The Road Ahead. In Crafting Customer Experience Strategy. Emerald Publishing Limited. doi:10.1108/978-1-83909-710-220211011

Poushter, J. (2016). Smartphone ownership and internet usage continues to climb in emerging economies. *Pew Research Center, 22*(1), 1–44.

Prime One Global, L. L. C. (2021). *What has the Internet done to the Sri Lankan Marketing Industry?* Retrieved March 15, 2023, from https://www.primeone.global/sri-lankan-digital-marketing-industry/

Raza, M. (2016) *6 Pakistani fashion brands that wowed us with winning social media campaigns*. Retrieved March 15, 2023, from https://images.dawn.com/news/1175906

Rishi, B., & Agarwal, S. (2022). An Unexpected Journey: Designing a Framework to Use Social Media for Consumer Well-Being. In J. Bhattacharyya (Ed.), *Dealing with Socially Responsible Consumers*. doi:10.1007/978-981-19-4457-4_7

Rishi, B., Anand, A., & Sharma, T. (2023). An Unexpected Journey: Designing a Social Media Marketing Framework for Small and Medium Enterprises (SMEs). In *Strengthening SME Performance Through Social Media Adoption and Usage* (pp. 1–20). IGI Global. doi:10.4018/978-1-6684-5770-2.ch001

Rishi, B., & Bandyopadhyay, S. (Eds.). (2017). *Contemporary issues in social media marketing*. Routledge. doi:10.4324/9781315563312

Rishi, B., & Kuthuru, N. R. (2021a). A Review for Managerial Guidelines for Social Media Integration of IMC in Digital Era. In Digital Entertainment (pp. 187-212). Palgrave Macmillan. doi:10.1007/978-981-15-9724-4_10

Rishi, B., & Kuthuru, N. R. (2021b). Leveraging Social Media to Create Socially Responsible Consumers. In Social and Sustainability Marketing (pp. 415-432). Productivity Press. doi:10.4324/9781003188186-15

Rishi, B., & Mohammed, J. (2022). Design, execute, and manage promotions: Study on social media platforms. In *Promotional practices and perspectives from emerging markets* (pp. 226–245). Routledge India. doi:10.4324/9781003315582-12

Rishi, B., & Popli, S. (2021). Getting Into the Customers, Shoes: Customer Journey Management. In Crafting Customer Experience Strategy. Emerald Publishing Limited. doi:10.1108/978-1-83909-710-220211002

Samala, N., & Singh, S. (2018). Millennial's engagement with fashion brands: A moderated-mediation model of brand engagement with self-concept, involvement and knowledge. *Journal of Fashion Marketing and Management, 23*(1), 2–16. doi:10.1108/JFMM-04-2018-0045

Sharma, A., & Jhamb, D. (2020). Changing Consumer Behaviours Towards Online Shopping-An Impact Of Covid 19. *Academy of Marketing Studies Journal, 24*(3), 1–10.

Sharma, K. (2021). *As brands turn to influencer marketing for the festive season, experts are optimistic about seeing about a 40-50% growth in ad spends.* Retrieved March 25, 2023, from https://www.businessinsider.in/advertising/brands/article/as-brands-turn-to-influencer-marketing-for-the-festive-season-experts-are-optimistic-about-seeing-about-a-40-50-growth-in-ad-spends/articleshow/87210056.cms

Sharma, S., & Rehman, A. (2016). Social media marketing: A study of select sectors in India. *International Journal of Management, 5*(4), 1–9.

Sharma, S., Singh, S., Kujur, F., & Das, G. (2021). Social media activities and its influence on customer-brand relationship: An empirical study of apparel retailers' activity in India. *Journal of Theoretical and Applied Electronic Commerce Research, 16*(4), 602–617. doi:10.3390/jtaer16040036

Siriwardana, A. (2020, November). Social Media Marketing: A Literature Review on Consumer Products. *Proceedings of the International Conference on Business & Information (ICBI).* 10.2139srn.3862924

Sprinklr.com. (2021). *Best Fashion Brands in Social Media.* Retrieved March 25, 2023, from https://www.sprinklr.com/blog/fashion-brands-social-media-marketing/

Statista. (2023a). *Apparel - India: Statista market forecast.* Retrieved March 15, 2023, from https://www.statista.com/outlook/cmo/apparel/india#revenue

Statista. (2023b). *Fashion - southern Asia: Statista market forecast.* Retrieved March 15, 2023, from https://www.statista.com/outlook/dmo/ecommerce/fashion/southern-asia

Statista. (2023c). *Social Media Advertising - Global: Market Forecast.* Retrieved March 15, 2023, from https://www.statista.com/outlook/dmo/digital-advertising/social-media-advertising/worldwide

Talati-Parikh, S. (2021). *Instagram's big impact on fashion.* Retrieved March 15, 2023, from https://www.livemint.com/Leisure/hRFOEgmk2I0W58M0Y1lisK/Instagrams-big-impact-on-fashion.html

Tandon, S. (2021). *Instagram is changing the way fashion sells in India.* Retrieved March 15, 2023, from https://qz.com/india/1321163/from-sabyasachi-to-nicobar-instagram-is-changing-the-way-fashion-sells-in-india/

Technavio. (2023). *Online fashion retail market in India growth, size, trends, analysis report by type, application, Region, and Segment Forecast 2022-2026.* Retrieved March 25, 2023, from https://www.technavio.com/report/online-fashion-retail-market-industry-in-india-analysis

The Drum. (2021). *Social ad spend continues to accelerate in South East Asia.* Retrieved March 15, 2023, from https://www.thedrum.com/news/2021/11/10/social-ad-spend-continues-accelerate-south-east-asia

UNDP. (2019). *New data challenges traditional notions of 'rich' and 'poor'.* Retrieved March 15, 2023, from https://www. in.undp.org/content/india/en/home/presscenter/pressreleases/2019-MPI-India.html

United Nations. (2019). *World economic situation and prospects*. Retrieved March 15, 2023, from https://www.un.org/development/desa/dpad/wpcontent/uploads/sites/45/WESP2019_BOOK-CH3-5-south-asia-en.pdf

Un.org. (2021). *World Economic Situation and Prospectus 2021: South Asia* Retrieved March 15, 2023, from https://www.un.org/development/desa/dpad/wp-content/uploads/sites/45/WESP2021_CH3_SA.pdf

Upadhaya, V. (2021). *A Study on Increasing Digital Media Marketing Platforms in Nepal*. Retrieved March 15, 2023, from https://e-research.siam.edu/wp-content/uploads/2019/05/BBA-2017-coop-Marketing-Digital-marketing-platform-A-case-study-on-increasing-digital-media-marketing-platform-in-Nepal-compress.pdf

Vidya, D. (n.d.). *Superdry Used Social Media Marketing To Reach More Than 1.5 Million People On Twitter*. Retrieved March 25, 2023, from https://www.digitalvidya.com/blog/superdry-used-social-media-marketing-to-reach-more-than-1-5-million-people-on-twitter-dmblog-0503/

von Kameke, L. (2023). *APAC: Active social media users by country 2022*. Retrieved March 15, 2023, from https://www.statista.com/statistics/295606/social-media-mau-asia-pacific-countries/

World Bank Group. (2023). *Global Economic Prospects: Sharp, long-lasting slowdown to hit developing countries hard. World Bank*. Retrieved March 15, 2023, from https://www.worldbank.org/en/news/press-release/2023/01/10/global-economic-prospects

Yahoo. (2023). *Global Influencer marketing platform market to generate revenue of US$ 118.0 billion by 2031*. Retrieved March 15, 2023, from https://www.yahoo.com/entertainment/global-influencer-marketing-platform-market-113000397.html

ADDITIONAL READING

Doshi, P., Nigam, P., & Rishi, B. (2023). Customer values and patronage intention in social media networks: mediating role of perceived usefulness. *VINE Journal of Information and Knowledge Management Systems*. doi:10.1108/VJIKMS-07-2022-0217

Fetais, A. H., Algharabat, R. S., Aljafari, A., & Rana, N. P. (2023). Do social media marketing activities improve brand loyalty? An empirical study on luxury fashion brands. *Information Systems Frontiers*, *25*(2), 795–817.

Quiles-Soler, C., Martínez-Sala, A. M., & Monserrat-Gauchi, J. (2023). Fashion industry's environmental policy: Social media and corporate website as vehicles for communicating corporate social responsibility. *Corporate Social Responsibility and Environmental Management*, *30*(1), 180–191. doi:10.1002/csr.2347

Rishi, B., & Bandyopadhyay, S. (Eds.). (2017). *Contemporary issues in social media marketing*. Routledge. doi:10.4324/9781315563312

Rishi, B., & Kuthuru, N. R. (2021a). A Review for Managerial Guidelines for Social Media Integration of IMC in Digital Era. In Digital Entertainment (pp. 187-212). Palgrave Macmillan. doi:10.1007/978-981-15-9724-4_10

KEY TERMS AND DEFINITIONS

Brand Synergy: Perfect branding is based on clearly understanding what a company does, its stands for, and its customers. The concept should be reproduced throughout all sales channels, and the business should focus on building stronger brand loyalty, more trust, and, as a result, increased sales.

Industrialization: It is the gradual transition of an economic system from primitive to more complex production processes. It is a systematic reform aimed at reshaping a country's productive forces.

Microblogging: A web service that allows users to post short messages or videos primarily on the mobile web for the audience to interact with them more frequently and efficiently, like Twitter.

Social Media Integration: Involving the utility of different social media platforms as a part of the marketing strategy for a brand and, in turn, extending its reach to its target audience and customers.

Social Media Marketing: Social media marketing, often known as the use of social media to market brands, is the promotion of brands through social media platforms to interact with potential clients.

Target Audience: A target audience is a group of people who share specific characteristics and behaviors. User personas are frequently created by firms based on what they know about their target audience. These personalities govern their marketing campaign decisions.

Text Mining: To classify and segregate the unstructured text passages into literal meaning giving quality outputs such as summary or in-depth analysis with the help of software tools.

Web 2.0: Web 2.0 defines the current state of the internet, which contains more user-generated content and end-user usability than its previous form.

Website Traffic: It refers to the number of users who visit a website determining the potential, loyal, and regular customers a brand has on average.

APPENDIX

Table 2. The literature review

Sr. No.	Paper Type (Empirical / Non-Empirical)	Authors	Theoretical Underpinnings	Industry Focus	Methods (Survey/ Interviews/ Focus Group Discussion/ Observation/ Mixed Methods)	Findings	Constructs Identified
1	Empirical	Nawaz Ahmad, Atif Salman and Rubab Ashiq	Brand image, customer perception, online customer behavior, purchase intention, networking, fashion brands on social media	Fashion brands, online shopping, social media	Surveys	Social media is the most cost-effective and easiest way to promote the dynamic fashion industry in Karachi and is also a predictor of the fashion industry.	Social networking, promotion attractiveness, affinity to fashion profiles, brand awareness
2	Empirical	Rizwan Raheem Ahmed, Dalia Streimikiene, Gerhard Berchtold, Jolita Vveinhardt, Zahid Ali Channar and Riaz Hussain Soomro	Digital media advertising, brand sustainability, Effectiveness of digital media	Online media, FMCG, service sector	Surveys	Pakistan's fast-moving consumer goods (FMCG) and services industries have experienced favorable marketing impacts on digital media.	Customer attitude, previous purchase experience, brand loyalty
3	Empirical	Artha Sejati Ananda	Consumer behavior, such as purchasing behavior, relationship marketing, and brand community in social networks	Fashion brands, social media marketing	Mixed methods	In the fashion community, social media consumer-brand engagement reliably predicts brand loyalty. In some cases, it occasionally also proves reliable in predicting purchase intention.	Customer engagement, consumer interaction, purchase intention, brand affinity

Continued on following page

Table 2. Continued

Sr. No.	Paper Type (Empirical / Non-Empirical)	Authors	Theoretical Underpinnings	Industry Focus	Methods (Survey/ Interviews/ Focus Group Discussion/ Observation/ Mixed Methods)	Findings	Constructs Identified
4	Empirical	Christy Ashley and Tracy Tuten	Branding, customer relationship management, service and sales promotion, social networks as brand persona, psychological engagement	E-commerce, social media, fashion brands	Mixed methods	The most often used technologies were microblogs (e.g., Twitter), social networks (e.g., Facebook), and socialized microsites (e.g., Doritos Crash the Superbowl), followed by video sharing (e.g., YouTube postings) and discussion forums. Social bookmarking, photo sharing, mobile applications, and social games were less popular.	Consumer engagement, content creativity, brand image, consumer participation
5	Empirical	David R. Borker	Emerging economies, social media marketing, traditional and anti-globalism attitude of developing countries	Social media, various sectors (public and corporate)	Observation	For a small number of significant Mongolian listed stock businesses that make up the MSE Top 20, indirect and direct use of Twitter, Facebook, and YouTube was observed and categorized. The data show various development levels, with the strongest direct usage in the food/beverage and specific service industries, primarily in the hotel/travel and finance sectors. The indirect use of SMM was often higher than the direct use, and various corporate and public sector organizations and individuals facilitated it.	Content creativity

Continued on following page

Table 2. Continued

Sr. No.	Paper Type (Empirical / Non-Empirical)	Authors	Theoretical Underpinnings	Industry Focus	Methods (Survey/ Interviews/ Focus Group Discussion/ Observation/ Mixed Methods)	Findings	Constructs Identified
6	Empirical	Celine ARCA	Social media marketing, brand exposure, targeted traffic, lead generation, market research, customer interaction, marketing effectiveness, public relations, and human resources	Social media, various business sectors	Mixed methods	The economic benefits can differ in volume and value depending on whether a company develops its social media presence across all channels or just a few. The most prevalent benefits include enhanced brand exposure and reputation management, increased targeted traffic and Search Engine Optimization, word-of-mouth and lead generation, market insights relating to the target audience and competitors, public relations facilities, and recruiting.	Awareness, consideration, purchase, customer experience, customer loyalty, customer opinion, brand reputation, customer service
7	Empirical	Monica Faraoni, Romeo Bandinelli, Rinaldo Rinaldi	Brand life, social engagement, social media strategy, customer involvement, marketing communications	Social media, fashion brands	Mixed methods	Companies with a high level of social involvement consider resource allocation, internal policies, and content definition to be more strategic than those with a low level of social engagement.	Brand awareness, social media engagement, social media channel affinity
8	Empirical	Shih-Hui Hsiaoa, Yen-Yao Wang, Tawei Wang and Ta-WeiKao	Social media marketing, branding, SMEs	Social media, fashion	Observation	In fashion social media, large national brands have a positive spillover effect on the reputation of private labels. It affects the sale of private-label products.	The popularity of the product, the effectiveness of social media

Continued on following page

Table 2. Continued

Sr. No.	Paper Type (Empirical / Non-Empirical)	Authors	Theoretical Underpinnings	Industry Focus	Methods (Survey/ Interviews/ Focus Group Discussion/ Observation/ Mixed Methods)	Findings	Constructs Identified
9	Non-Empirical	J. George	Consumer behavior, e-commerce, consumer lifestyle, digitization	E-commerce, social media	Observation	Advances in digital technology and globalization deepen the interconnectedness of marketplaces while economics and our society evolve, as do our purchasing patterns and consumer behavior. A digital priority is to improve the consumer experience. Consumer behavior is changing at an ever-increasing rate.	Purchase intention, consumer experience, convenience
10	Empirical	Sandra Maria Correia Loureiro, Maria Maximiano and Padma Panchapakesan	Self-perception, social values, luxury fashion consumption, desire	Social media, luxury fashion	Surveys	Consumer engagement is driven by desire; subjective well-being is a byproduct of consumer engagement, and prior experience is significant in the relationship between engagement and subjective well-being.	Consumer experience, consumer engagement, self-perception

Continued on following page

Table 2. Continued

Sr. No.	Paper Type (Empirical / Non-Empirical)	Authors	Theoretical Underpinnings	Industry Focus	Methods (Survey/ Interviews/ Focus Group Discussion/ Observation/ Mixed Methods)	Findings	Constructs Identified
11	Empirical	Maria Cristina Morra, Valeria Gelosa, Francesca Ceruti and Alice Mazzucchelli	Consumer behavior, luxury fashion consumption	Social media, luxury fashion, Italian fashion market	Surveys	UGC has a favourable influence on both OBE and buy intention of counterfeit products. In contrast, OBE and FCC positively impact the purchase intention of original luxury fashion companies. Because of their moderating effect on the relationship between FCC and intention to buy original luxury fashion labels, the findings highlight the importance of UGC as a tool that businesses must manage and monitor.	Overall Brand Equity (OBE), Purchase Intention
12	Empirical	Muhammad Naeem and Wilson Ozuem	Social consumer fashion brand engagement (SCFBE), social impact theory, brand passion, brand engagement, consumer behavior	Social media communication, fashion brands	In-depth interviews	Social passion, social inclination, personal warmth, and social like all help to increase social fashion brand engagement. The study discovered proper fit, bearability, and viability as three critical elements of fashion brand relevance. Finally, purchasing decisions for fashion labels are influenced by trust and social ties, homophily, credibility, and discounts. The article proposes an SCFBE model based on the findings, backed up by the triangular theory of love and social impact theory.	Social Fashion Brand engagement, Purchase Intention, Trust, Credibility, Homophily

Continued on following page

Table 2. Continued

Sr. No.	Paper Type (Empirical / Non-Empirical)	Authors	Theoretical Underpinnings	Industry Focus	Methods (Survey/ Interviews/ Focus Group Discussion/ Observation/ Mixed Methods)	Findings	Constructs Identified
13	Empirical	Jill Nash	Consumer behavior, retail theory, digital influence, high street fashion	Social media, the retail fashion industry	Interviews and focus-group discussions	Consumers are influenced by a range of internal and external elements that affect their behaviour and opinions of high-street fashion businesses, and the usage of SM aids and facilitates these aspects. The study discovered, however, that social media is not the only source that influences consumer decision-making and that as the number of active users on social media grows, these platforms are having (and will continue to have) an ever-increasing impact on consumer decision-making.	Consumer Motivations, Purchase Intention

Continued on following page

Table 2. Continued

Sr. No.	Paper Type (Empirical / Non-Empirical)	Authors	Theoretical Underpinnings	Industry Focus	Methods (Survey/ Interviews/ Focus Group Discussion/ Observation/ Mixed Methods)	Findings	Constructs Identified
14	Non - Empirical	Dung Nguyen	Marketing, retail theory	Social media, fashion brands	Mixed methods	According to the survey, the Facebook page of the brand H&M has a higher number of followers and likes. Although Instagram has fewer followers than Facebook, it is the channel with superior user integration. Instagram postings attract more involvement in the form of likes and comments than Facebook posts. The research suggests that H&M encourages greater interactions with user-generated content when choosing a picture to promote the brand's products.	Consumer Engagement, Consumer Experience
15	Empirical		Social media marketing, traditional marketing communication	Social media, emerging markets	Surveys	There is a straight positive link between social media participation and the market success of a company's brand. It is suggested that an organisation have an effective social media marketing plan to promote brand engagement and consumer delight.	Social Media Activity, Brand Success, Customer Engagement

Continued on following page

Table 2. Continued

Sr. No.	Paper Type (Empirical / Non-Empirical)	Authors	Theoretical Underpinnings	Industry Focus	Methods (Survey/ Interviews/ Focus Group Discussion/ Observation/ Mixed Methods)	Findings	Constructs Identified
16	Empirical	Nkiru Esther Otugo, Chikezie Emmanuel Uzuegbunam and Chinedu Okey Obikeze	Uses-and-gratification theory, social cognitive theory, consumer behavior	Social media, advertising	Surveys	According to the report, young people in Nigerian universities are pretty aware of Facebook advertising. However, these teenagers' "attention problems" in detecting and observing the adverts were discovered during their vicarious encounters with Facebook. Their attitude toward Facebook Ads is also concerning: despite liking and seeing Facebook Ads as advantageous, most of them would not choose to buy the product, visit the website for additional information, or even "Like" products or services recommended by their friends.	Customer Perception of Advertisements, Customer Attitude, Customer Responsiveness, Channel Affinity, Content Creativity

Continued on following page

Table 2. Continued

Sr. No.	Paper Type (Empirical / Non-Empirical)	Authors	Theoretical Underpinnings	Industry Focus	Methods (Survey/ Interviews/ Focus Group Discussion/ Observation/ Mixed Methods)	Findings	Constructs Identified
17	Empirical	Farzana Parveen, Noor Ismawati Jaafar and Sulaiman Ainin	Social media, organizational performance, promotion and advertising, customer service	Social media, advertising, various businesses	In-depth interviews	Organizations use social media for various goals, including advertising and marketing, branding, information search, customer relationship building, and more. In terms of boosting customer interactions and customer service activities, expanding information accessibility, and lowering marketing and customer service expenses, the data imply that social media has a higher impact on organisational performance.	Promotion Attractiveness, Nature of Customer Relationship

Continued on following page

Table 2. Continued

Sr. No.	Paper Type (Empirical / Non-Empirical)	Authors	Theoretical Underpinnings	Industry Focus	Methods (Survey/ Interviews/ Focus Group Discussion/ Observation/ Mixed Methods)	Findings	Constructs Identified
18	Empirical	Jacob Poushter	Emerging economies, digitization, technology adoption	Technology, social media, emerging economies	Mixed methods	As the world becomes increasingly interconnected economically and socially, technology adoption remains one of the defining determinants of human growth. To that aim, the percentage of individuals in emerging and developing countries who say they use the internet and own a smartphone has climbed dramatically in the previous two years, according to Pew Research Center. People in affluent economies still use the Internet and own more high-tech equipment, but the rest of the developing world is catching up.	Degree in Technology Adoption, Social Interaction, Networking
19	Empirical	Nagaraj Samala and Sapna Singh	Brand engagement, self-schema, consumer behavior	Social media, fashion brands	Surveys	The study bolsters the moderating function of participation and knowledge by confirming Brand Engagement in Self-Concept (BESC), complementing mediating role. With high involvement and expertise, millennials strengthen the positive association between brand love, BESC, and brand advocacy.	Brand Engagement in Self-Concept, Brand Love, Brand Advocacy, Purchase Intention

Continued on following page

Table 2. Continued

Sr. No.	Paper Type (Empirical / Non-Empirical)	Authors	Theoretical Underpinnings	Industry Focus	Methods (Survey/ Interviews/ Focus Group Discussion/ Observation/ Mixed Methods)	Findings	Constructs Identified
20	Empirical	Smita Sharma and Asad Rehman	Marketing communications, social media, consumer behavior	Social media, various business sectors	Surveys	Most brands have begun establishing a presence on non-traditional platforms, with many including social media in their communication strategy. The major social media outlets where brands have a more substantial presence are Facebook, Twitter, and YouTube. Users are abandoning traditional advertising venues in favour of new media, giving it more time, attention, and "impressions." The main goals of using social media are to provide product information and knowledge, customer service, and sales promotions.	Brand Awareness, Brand Presence

Continued on following page

Table 2. Continued

Sr. No.	Paper Type (Empirical / Non-Empirical)	Authors	Theoretical Underpinnings	Industry Focus	Methods (Survey/ Interviews/ Focus Group Discussion/ Observation/ Mixed Methods)	Findings	Constructs Identified
21	Empirical	Anupam Sharma and Deepika Jhamb	E-commerce, social commerce, consumer behavior, digitization, COVID-19	Social media, e-commerce	Surveys	Some firms could use social commerce to market goods and services via social media. According to 46% of users, social networks are critical for exchanging information and making product decisions. While the evidence suggests that internet marketing and shopping will soon return to normal, the epidemic's losses and downshift should not be underestimated.	Purchase Intention
22	Empirical	Sukanya Sharma, Saumya Singh, Fedric Kujur and Gairik Das	Social media marketing, customer-brand relationships, consumer behavior	Social media, apparel industry	Surveys	Social Media Marketing Activities (SMMA) are powerful tools for establishing a business marketing plan. It has evolved into a crucial tool for collaborating with businesses and individuals. The "customer"-brand interaction, it is found, has a positive and statistically significant impact on customers' purchase intent via SM.	Purchase Intention, Brand Relationship, Trustworthiness, Satisfaction, Commitment, Personalization

Continued on following page

Table 2. Continued

Sr. No.	Paper Type (Empirical / Non-Empirical)	Authors	Theoretical Underpinnings	Industry Focus	Methods (Survey/ Interviews/ Focus Group Discussion/ Observation/ Mixed Methods)	Findings	Constructs Identified
23	Non-empirical	A Siriwardana	Marketing communications, consumer behavior, digitization, social media	Social media, various business sectors	Observation	Billions of people use social media worldwide, and it has swiftly become one of our generation's defining technologies. On social media, people may freely speak with one another, and marketers can reach out to customers in various ways. The success of social media as a marketing communication channel has brought several issues for marketers due to its dynamic and emergent nature. It is thought to be distinct from typical marketing channels.	Social media Platform Affinity, Customer Engagement, Customer Opinion
24	Non-empirical	David M. Gilfoil and Charles Jobs	Social media, viral marketing, return on investment (ROI), social broadcast behavior	Social media, various business sectors	Observation	The summary of the SM ROI literature includes a wide range of opinions/ models/calculations published in academic and trade periodicals. It implies that the SM ROI issue is significantly more complicated than most reports and offers a business "unit of analysis" framework for better comprehending it. It also examines SM ROI measurement in the context of business process/ performance management fundamentals, as well as guidelines and principles for how and when to do so.	Social Media Platform Affinity, Customer Opinions, Social Media Effectiveness

Continued on following page

Table 2. Continued

Sr. No.	Paper Type (Empirical / Non-Empirical)	Authors	Theoretical Underpinnings	Industry Focus	Methods (Survey/ Interviews/ Focus Group Discussion/ Observation/ Mixed Methods)	Findings	Constructs Identified
25	Non-empirical	Vikas Kumar and Sanjeev Kumar	Consumer behavior	Fashion and apparel, textile, imports, and exports	Observation	Fashion businesses, retailers, influencers, and fashion magazines have all done some introspection and pivoting in recent months in both expected and unexpected ways. Some have made minor changes, while others have been forced to make more drastic changes. The Indian fashion industry has responded wisely and imaginatively to the situation. For example, the Fashion Design Council of India (FDCI) was one of the first to create a COVID-19 Support Fund for small businesses and emerging designers.	Design Innovation, Purchase Intention

Chapter 16
The Use of Social Media in the Fashion Industry During the Post-COVID-19 Period:
Evidence From Central Greece

Nikolaos Sklavounos
International Hellenic University, Greece

Agapi Paraskevi Papadopoulou
International Hellenic University, Greece

ABSTRACT

The use of social media to promote clothing and textile businesses has revealed several changes in consumer behavior during the post-COVID-19 era. In this study, the social media tools which provide useful information in regards to consumer preferences and their decision-making processes in the fashion industry are presented. Moreover, the marketing strategy used and the strong presence of social media influencers in the fashion industry both during and after the COVID-19 pandemic period are also examined. A mixed research methodology is applied through the conduction of interviews with 20 owners of small fashion businesses and a questionnaire survey of 200 consumers who use social media for their purchases from the region of Thessaly in Central Greece. Furthermore, the results are analyzed and the research findings are discussed in detail. Finally, suggestions for further research are also included.

INTRODUCTION

During the Covid-19 pandemic period, very strict measures had been taken from the authorities worldwide to protect the health of every citizen and limit the spread of the virus. This resulted in a strict curfew for at least three months, stopping any kind of commercial transactions and any physical presence at the stores. This created a feeling of insecurity and anxiety in people, causing them to "run" to acquire items they consider necessary for survival. Then came the "freezing" of the market, which led to an

DOI: 10.4018/978-1-6684-8753-2.ch016

economic downturn in turnover. As such, the pandemic managed to accelerate the pace of change in the business world, making it difficult for businesses to adapt to the changing environment. Of course, under the current pandemic situation, the percentage of consumers who shop online has increased faster than before. In the past, many people had doubts about online shopping, how to buy the product, when it will be received, how it was paid for and other relevant factors. With the emergence of Covid-19, in order to survive, businesses generally used e-commerce and social media to sell and advertise their products. As people spend a lot of time online and on social media due to the quarantine which forced them to stay more at home, the constant interaction with the online world has led to the need for most people to buy clothing products that they love even if they don't need them.

COVID-19 PANDEMIC AND E-COMMERCE

1.1 The COVID-19 Pandemic

With the virus spreading at an alarming rate, many countries took the bold decision to limit social interaction. To do this, they implemented various measures ranging from canceling large gatherings, closing schools and universities, and even temporarily suspending business activities (European Commission, 2020). In the areas that imposed these closures, many retail stores and services also had to close. Due to rising unemployment and limited employment opportunities, consumers started to face significant financial uncertainty. As a result, meeting their shopping needs became a challenge and online retail was considered the only viable option (European Commission, 2020).

The pandemic will likely have a lasting impact on consumer behavior, which could negatively impact businesses. It is imperative for e-commerce companies to learn how consumers behaved during this time so they can maintain an edge over their competitors. While online retailing of Greek clothing has grown steadily over the last ten years, the pandemic has had some mixed effects on online retailing. First, it may have caused complications with supply chains, but on the other hand, more customers have shopped online due to the containment measures that have been put in place (Emmanouil, 2021). The unpredictability of the apparel industry means that business models rely heavily on rapid response to market changes, as large sales are crucial (Cachon and Swinney, 2011; Tokatli, 2008). Consumer demand can change quickly and apparel companies must respond quickly to remain competitive. To maintain their edge, reliable information on consumer demands is vital at all times, even in the face of the COVID-19 pandemic. The ability to predict consumer behavior is especially crucial for apparel companies right now.

1.2 E-Commerce Boom

Due to the pandemic, there has been a boom in e-commerce. As a result, many consumers can seek more exposure on social media, contributing to the growth in this area. Social media is a powerful tool today that connects brands with their target audience, as noted in Apparel Magazine (2010).

According to Olivier (2008), when customers shop online, they are more than happy to buy products from retail sites they can trust. The relationship that social media creates between brands and consumers is critical to increasing their sales in the future. According to Laura Elizabeth, as mentioned in Dorado (2011), people connect with brands using social media, which provides a platform for brands to interact with consumers and promote their products. In addition, fashion brands continue to use creative online marketing strategies as a result of the dramatic increase in media in recent years since the start of the pandemic. Due to the reduction in time spent by consumers in stores due to the COVID-19 pandemic and the increase in the use of social media by the same consumers, individuals often make purchasing decisions after receiving recommendations from trusted sources. In addition, consumers may be socially influenced by information from satisfied customers (Mason et al., 2021).

Social distancing has highlighted the importance of digital channels more than ever, while lockdowns have highlighted the priority of social media across the value chain. Consumers' demands in this space are increasing and brands must act quickly to deliver (Business of Fashion, 2020).

1.3 The Functionality of E-Commerce

According to Scarpi et al. (2014), a big question that emerges from the existing literature is whether e-commerce leads to more targeted purchases, i.e. purchases of one or more of a specific product by comparing prices and saving time, or whether it leads to more purchases through design, aesthetics and the functionality of the site is useful only for pleasure and entertainment. The impression is that e-commerce is more of a functional market and more targeted. Some possible reasons for the prevalence of this impression are the time savings offered by e-commerce and the possibility of direct and rapid market research (Wolfinbarger and Gilly, 2001). In fact, research by Wolfinbarger and Gilly (2000) shows that consumers who prefer targeted shopping often choose to shop online for the following reasons: convenience and accessibility, variety of choices, readily available information, price comparisons, an easy-to-use website based on its design, the personalization it offers and due to a lack of social skills. In particular, the availability of the website 24 hours a day, 7 days a week, greatly facilitates shopping at any time of the day (Gilly and Wolfinbarger, 2000). According to Tabatabaei (2009), consumers shop without the pressure of time, space and distance by using social media. In modern times, technology has successfully bridged the gap between the in-store shopping experience and the online shopping experience. According to Blazquez (2014), this is achieved by creating a pleasant website atmosphere and the interaction that the website provides. More specifically, an example of this interaction is the ability to enlarge images, 3D visualization and even augmented reality with a digital test chamber and the ability to personalize by saving favorites and more. (Blazquez, 2014). As a result, consumers seem to embrace online shopping and integrate it into their daily lives, not only for functional reasons but also for pleasure.

1.4 Advantages of E-Commerce

To begin with, using e-commerce is the fastest process of buying and selling products as it helps to find them easily and quickly. A consumer can find what he/she is looking for effortlessly and does not waste much time searching (Vipin and Satyendra, 2021). The online store is accessible and "open" 24 hours a day. We live in an age where people are quite stressed about the lack of time, but with e-commerce, consumers can search and buy whatever they want at any time (Vipin and Satyendra, 2021). Businesses do not need to rely on physical presence to provide quality services, which results in the selling price of products being much lower in e-commerce than in traditional commerce (IGNOU Renmin University, 2010). There are no geographical boundaries in e-commerce and the consumer market is global (Lefebvre and Lefebvre, 2002). Even the best customer service relies on the availability of 24/7 customer service and support throughout the year if they require not listed information (IGNOU University of the People, 2010). Finally, through electronic consumer transactions, companies can differentiate many elements about consumer habits, tastes and needs (Vipin and Satyendra, 2021). This is done to align these elements and create a relationship between the company and the needs of the consumer or group of consumers.

1.5 Disadvantages of E-Commerce

The lack of connection between customers and businesses is one of the things that play a very important role (IGNOU University of the People, 2010). More specifically, many customers want to see and "feel" the quality of the product and this is the reason why they don't prefer e-commerce. The creditworthiness of the seller is another reason why many customers are reluctant to use e-commerce as they cannot be sure that what they see in the company's website corresponds to reality. One of the main responsibilities and commitments of e-commerce businesses is the product delivery time. During the delivery of online purchased products, a number of problems may arise such as delays due to supply chain issues, bad weather etc. (IGNOU University of the People, 2010). Finally, another drawback is the potential breakdown of the store's website.

WEB APPLICATIONS AND SOCIAL MEDIA FOR CONSUMER RESEARCH

2.1 Digital Reality (VR): Augmented Reality (AR)

With many stores closed and quarantined during the pandemic, fashion customers have had to learn to shop online. But even online shopping became quite difficult, as the restrictions imposed delayed several packages, making it dangerous to go to the post office to return unwanted items. In order to face that arising problems, some clothing companies decided to present their products through Virtual Reality (VR) or Augmented Reality (AR), where customers could adjust their avatars to their body shape and size and see how the clothes will look on them from different angles, resulting in reduced uncertainty and fewer packet returns (Nunan, 2017). Mass media are incorporating VR and AR in general and COVID-19 acted as the right engine to accelerate the adoption of these technologies. Obsess (2020) enables brands to challenge customers to shop remotely using proprietary VR technology, creating a High Definition (HD) quality version of a virtual retail store that can be accessed and used from anywhere in the world.

2.2 Artificial Intelligence (AI) and Social Media

After the pandemic, Artificial Intelligence (AI) has been effectively implemented on e-commerce sites to enrich the shopping experience. Today, several fashion brands use a subscription model in their business, providing each customer with valuable insights into their clothing, in addition to personalized customer service through StitchFix, because they do not know what products they will receive (Luce, 2019). The company Ubisend researched the acceptance of chatbots (software that performs specific functions, imitating human written and spoken speech as best as possible) by users and found that 47% of consumers would buy from a chatbot, 35% would like to see more companies using chatbots and 57% are interested in the immediacy of chatbots. During and after the pandemic, chat has become the most popular form of communication as customers use iPhones to browse e-commerce sites, especially among younger generations (Ubisoft, 2020).

Social media are defined as Web 2.0 engines that allow Internet users to create, edit, and transmit content (Konstantinidis, 2014). Web 2.0 is based on a technical structure where members of the new generation create content, share information and collaborate online (Berthon, 2012). Much of the internet access and online shopping is due to the widespread use of mobile phones. For example, 87% of smartphone users (iPhone, Android) claim that these devices are one of the most important aspects of their overall shopping experience and behavior (Parker and Wang, 2016). According to Parker and Wang (2016), they add a key feature of the mobile phone, which is that you can always be on the move with it. Unlike the traditional brick-and-mortar commerce, online commerce can and does take place over the phone while consumers are on the move. Most mobile phone purchases are made using online applications ("apps"), which increase consumer knowledge (Rezaei et al., 2016). In addition, these online applications allow users to search for products and services, read reviews, research and compare prices and trade through them. In this way, online applications successfully create and sustain consumer interest (Rezaei et al., 2016).

2.3 The Role of Social Media in the Fashion Industry

Social media provides consumers with abundant opportunities for online collaboration because such collaboration can take place anywhere and does not involve physical contact (Lin and Kant, 2021). In addition, new digital tools provide stimuli such as simplicity, entertainment and a wealth of information, which are overall valued by users (Frąckiewicz, 2021). According to Hwang et al. (2021), Internet users embrace social media to gather information and make purchase decisions influenced by dimensions, content, and social satisfaction. Satisfaction refers to the content and information shown to users from social media to decide where they want to buy a product (Hwang et al., 2021). The emergence of social media as a communication platform that creates a purpose of serving consumers and businesses is seen as unwelcome in this environment (Fournier and Avery, 2010).

Many store owners have embraced social media as it has improved their company's sales performance (Adoeng et al., 2019; Taobangdan and Taobao, 2019). Social media presence helps entrepreneurs to "authorize" online customers to buy products. In traditional online marketing, consumers learn about goods and services through text and images, while in modern online marketing, commercial online platforms show users real-time product videos and update the overall performance and quality of products (Wongkitrungrueng and Assarut, 2020). Online shopping and e-commerce have created an innovative and profitable business model. Both consumers and sellers connect to social media and ask questions about products and monitor products and their features (Attfield et al., 2011). The COVID-19 pandemic has empowered social media users to create new partnerships that will likely lead to stronger communication over time (Almansoori and Habtoor, 2018). According to Li Edelkoort, the pandemic has changed not only people's daily lives but also the pace of consumption practices (Fairs, 2020). McCarthy, as cited in Manneh (2017), claims that fashion and social media share common characteristics and provide ways for people to express their preferences and feelings and engage with the world. Zara, Balenciaga, Gucci, Prada, Dolce Gabbana and many other designers use social media to promote their products and brands. Wang et al. (2019) argue that many fashion shoppers want to learn about the latest fashion trends in their city and reward themselves. Similarly, online social media users want to get likes from their 'friends', which is why clothing businesses need to be active on social media.

2.4 Advantages of Social Media

Most social networking sites are free to visit, create a profile and post. Social networking sites have become so ubiquitous that they are the most popular destinations on the Internet (Burmaster, 2009). It turns out that new media cannot only change how often people communicate online, but also expand the range of their communication and bring new ways to influence their behavior (Burmaster, 2009). Social media gives marketers the ability to target audiences and consumers based on website users' personal information, interests and what their friends like.

2.5 Disadvantages of Social Media

Someone should be responsible for monitoring each network, responding to comments and questions and posting product information that customers value (Barefoot & Szabo, 2010). Businesses without services to manage these social networks will find it difficult to compete. The first initial consideration, and perhaps the most important one, is that social media marketing requires a significant investment of time (Barefoot and Szabo, 2010). As a general rule, you only need to enter a few social media sources and the prospect of great returns can be realized. Firms must meet the necessary time commitment and accept or reject this commitment based on the rationale for their activities (Barefoot and Szaboo, 2010).

One aspect of social media that can be particularly detrimental to marketing campaigns is negative responses to posts. Disgruntled customers or industry competitors may post demeaning or offensive photos, posts, or videos, and marketers cannot actually do much to prevent these incidents (Cheung, Lee, and Thadani 2009). However, negative or unconstructive comments cannot be ignored. Social networks must be managed effectively enough to quickly respond and eliminate harmful posts, which takes more time (HennigThurau et al., 2004).

2.6 The Basic Applications of the Online Market

The shopping cart is nothing more than a list of products that a customer intends to buy. While browsing, shoppers can add products to their shopping carts, inspect them and put them back on the 'shelf'. This feature is important because shoppers don't feel "tied in" to an order by placing items in their cart. Also, it is very important that the buyer can at any time "look" at his/her basket to see what he/she ordered and how much his/her order costs. Many stores also apply the practice of "holding" baskets for a limited time. This enables shoppers to navigate to other websites, even shut down their computers and continue shopping at a later date without re-searching the contents of their shopping carts. Another cart-like feature is "Add to Favorites". While browsing an online store, a shopper may come across some products that he/she does not intend to buy immediately but is of interest to him/her for future purchases. To be able to keep them in "Tips" or "Notes" without any purchase obligation, he/she must link his/her code to the store and add these products to the "Favorites" category. Then, as long as he/she is connected to the store's website, he/she can "see" them and move them to the cart or delete them. This app is very useful for both buyers and online stores.

BRAND EQUITY AND CONSUMER BUYING BEHAVIOR

3.1 The Value of the Brand

According to Aaker (1991), the brand equity model consists of five characteristic elements that symbolize brand value: brand awareness, brand loyalty, perceived quality, association and other brand value. These factors help businesses attract new customers and create an emotional connection between customers and the business (Lemon et al., 2001). Keller (1993) explained the stages of brand equity management. First, business leaders must organize the direction and goals of the brand, and then decide what image they want to project in the minds of consumers. Managers should then test strategic options to create consumer value (Keller, 1993). In the process, marketers develop forward-looking strategies and assess the prospects for affordable profitability and brand image expansion (Keller, 1993). Even after the opening of physical stores, many consumers will continue to shop online (Roggeveen and Sethuraman, 2020), while another category of consumers will be forced to adapt to online shopping instead of the stores they are used to (Evans et al., 2010). Business owners will have to adopt new ways of approaching and interacting with all online shopping users in response to changing consumer behavior (Kursan, 2021). Wang et al. (2020) emphasize that business managers must make marketing decisions based on the most appropriate and profitable strategies for each business (Hulland and Houston, 2020).

3.2 The Purchasing Behavior of the Greek Public

The fact that citizens were forced to stay at home, combined with the temporary closure of dozens of businesses during COVID-19 pandemic, created a new reality in which digital marketing seems to play a leading role. So, what exactly is changing the buying behavior of the Greek public? Quite simply, the fact that more and more consumers are turning to digital commerce. The number of people using the internet today will increase significantly and even those who are online for hours will spend much more time in front of their phones, tablets and laptops. Thus, a large buying public will be created who will be online most of the time of the day and will be able to buy goods, products and services online (Tsiftsakis, 2021).

This new reality is fertile ground for any business with an online store or even a business that can quickly transition to the new digital environment and invest in creating an online store. After all, the fact that the digital market is expected to grow substantially cannot be ignored. Businesses can protect themselves by launching a comprehensive online digital marketing campaign, using new communication media to promote their products and digital stores, and of course incentivizing consumers to enter the online marketplace. In this way, they can maintain an important source of income, increase their online sales or get the first online sales of their products and services by creating an online store. Consumer support now creates the right environment for any business to invest in a strong and well-developed online store.

3.3 Factors Influencing the Purchasing Behavior of Consumers

Many social media platforms such as Facebook, Twitter, Snapchat and Instagram influence consumers' online purchasing behavior (Gupta et al., 2020). The price factor seems to influence to some extent the characteristics of online shopping and the purchasing behavior of consumers. Therefore, we conclude that when consumers shop for pleasure, they are more willing to spend more time doing online marketing, researching, and finding deals, as their goal is to find the lowest possible price for the product they want (Scarpi, Pizzi, and Visentin, 2014). As in the first case, so in the second case the preference for online shopping is due to the possibility of quick, easy and instant price comparisons offered by the Internet. Celebrities provide useful information about products to potential customers (Lee et al., 2008; Ashfag and Ali, 2017), thereby exerting a significant influence on consumer purchasing decisions (Ohanian, 1990). Through the use of advertising, consumer behavior is influenced (Meng et al., 2020) and a good advertising image can have a positive impact on consumer acceptance of a product (Ibok, 2013).

Some companies use celebrities to promote their products with the aim of getting customers to buy products based on the credibility of the celebrity (Khatri, 2006). Celebrities and influencers share their stories and opinions about the products they have used to motivate consumers to buy products (Chung and Cho, 2017; Xiang et al., 2016). For many years, the only advertising and promotion channels were television, radio, newspapers and magazines, and in the current era, online advertising is the driving force behind many advertising programs and efforts (Kotler and Armstrong, 2010). According to Keller (2001), marketing relationships are some tools with which companies can inform, encourage, empower and recall consumers about their brands directly and indirectly and through this relationship they can advertise their brand (Keller, 2001). Online advertising is a powerful weapon (even now) that any business can use to expand its brand reputation, attract new customers, and increase sales and turnover. With online visibility, with targeted and measurable results, businesses aim for the majority of citizens who stay at home in front of a digital screen and spend their day browsing social media, watching YouTube videos or reading articles and searching on the Internet. Therefore, the reason why social networks should be used by businesses as a promotional mix tool is to combine classic marketing (communication with consumers) with increased word-of-mouth communication (communication between consumers). Social media are hybrid elements of the promotional mix as they result from the combination of technology and communication media, enabling immediate and real-time communication and dissemination using various forms of information presentation and platforms. The main goal of using blogs and other social networks is to create engaged customers. When consumers have the ability to criticize a product, suggest fixes, etc., they feel closer to the business. In short, companies need to combine traditional marketing techniques to create two-way communication with them.

RESEARCH METHODOLOGY

4.1. Research Approach

In this research project a large sample of Greek consumers was collected and the mixed methodology was applied. More specifically, we used quantitative research, through a questionnaire survey distributed through social media to determine the impact of the COVID-19 pandemic on social media in the fashion industry and qualitative research through interviews conducted with various shopkeepers in the area of Thessaly in Central Greece.

4.2. Questionnaire Design

The questionnaire used consisted of two sections. In the first section, participants were asked to answer questions designed to elicit their demographics. In the second section, respondents answered questions related to the social media they used as consumers in the fashion industry and the impact of the COVID-19 pandemic. All questions were closed-ended, meaning participants could express what they think through specific answers.

4.3. Sampling Process

The poll was conducted among adults 18 to 65 years of age who participated through social media platforms. The sampling procedure lasted for ten days and yielded a satisfactory sample of 222 individuals.

4.4 Validity Assessment

The measurement of any concept in this study is performed by professional researchers who have developed previous research needs on similar issues, tested for their effectiveness. The validity control of the questionnaire consists of the check of the validity of the content (content validity) and the check of the validity of the structure of the questionnaire (construct validity). Content validation aims to correct, rephrase or even delete questions that are not clear enough and confuse participants. The aim of this process is to make sure that the questions are formulated in a simple and understandable way (Sotiroudas, 2011). Therefore, before starting to write the questionnaire, discussions were held with professors and academics in order to avoid any inappropriate question. In addition, spelling and grammatical errors were corrected, and to confirm the simplicity and clarity of the questionnaire, some difficult words were replaced with simpler ones, where possible. After the necessary redesign, the questionnaire was distributed to the research participants and in this way, assurance was given that the questions were in the appropriate format and consistent with the present study.

4.5. Statistical Analysis Tool

In order to carry out the statistical processing and analysis of the responses, the MS Excel software was used. Through this software, the statistical analysis was conducted and the opportunity to present the results graphically in the form of tables and charts was also offered, so that the analysis of the results is presented in an even more understandable and clear way.

4.6. Personal Interviews

The sample selected, as mentioned above, were 20 shopkeepers in the region of Thessaly in Central Greece. Before taking part in the personal interviews, the shopkeepers had been informed about the purpose of the interviews, they had been briefly informed about the way the interview would work and they had given their consent. An appointment was made with each of them individually either on a working day after their working hours or on a Sunday morning. All appointments took place in the area of Thessaly and specifically in the areas where the stores of each interviewee are located. Then, at the predetermined place and time, before the start of the process, the content of the interviews was presented and detailed information was given regarding the way they were conducted. The time of the interviews ranged from 40 minutes the shortest to 1 hour the longest. The interviews took place over a period of three months.

4.7. Qualitative Data Analysis

The function of data analysis is the distant goal of research since data cannot produce results. To be able to analyze the data, once collected, they should be recorded in detail. In the case of the present research, the personal interviews were transcribed. The transcription was so detailed that even the pauses or any comments of the interviewees that may not have been meaningfully related to the subject of the research were recorded. Such detailed recording had two important results. Firstly, it was much easier for the researcher to recall the data collection procedures she carried out, and secondly, all the recorded details were instrumental in understanding what was said.

4.8. Reliability of the Research

The first methodological strategy that was followed in this particular research and that attempted to ensure its accountability was the "triangulation" of data. This triangulation provided the necessary credibility to the research findings (Pyrgiotakis and Symeou, 2016). At the same time, the reader is able to comment on whether the results the research reached are a result of what the participants have presented, which, in addition to being reliable, makes the research clear and verifiable. Finally, the reliability of this research is also based on the control carried out by the participants themselves (member checks). As soon as the first conclusions were reached, all the interviewees were informed about them and the purpose of the information was to confirm the findings, but also to comment on them by anyone who wished to do so.

ANALYSIS AND RESULTS

For the statistical processing and analysis of the responses, the MS Excel program was used through which the results from all the answered questionnaires were interpreted and the results of the interviews were further analyzed throughout the duration of the research.

5.1. Questionnaire Survey Results

First, a presentation of the demographic data of the respondents is made, so that the characteristics of the sample are known. From Figure 1, we notice that of the 222 adults who participated in the survey, 165 (74.32%) are women, 56 (25.23%) are men and 1 person (0.45%) stated otherwise.

As can be seen in Figure 2, the majority of adults belong to the age group of 18 - 25 years, which amounts to 41.44%. Moreover, 83 (37.39%) belong to the age group of 26 - 35 years, 29 (13.06%) belong to the age group of 36 - 45 years, 17 (7.66%) belong to the age group of 46 - 65 years old and 1 person (0.45%) belongs to the age group of 65 years and above.

Regarding the educational level of the participants, 95 (42.79%) are University - TEI Graduates, 67 (30.18%) are High School - Technical Graduates, 40 (18.02%) are Master's Degree Holders, 18 (8.11%) are Vocational School (IEK) Graduates and 2 (0.90%) are PhD holders (See Figure 3).

Regarding the professional status of the respondents, 93 (41.89%) are Private Employees, 66 (29.73%) are Students, 26 (11.71%) are Public Employees, 22 (9.91%) are Freelancers, 11 (4.95%) are Unemployed and 4 (1.80%) declared Household duties (See Figure 4).

Figure 1. Gender

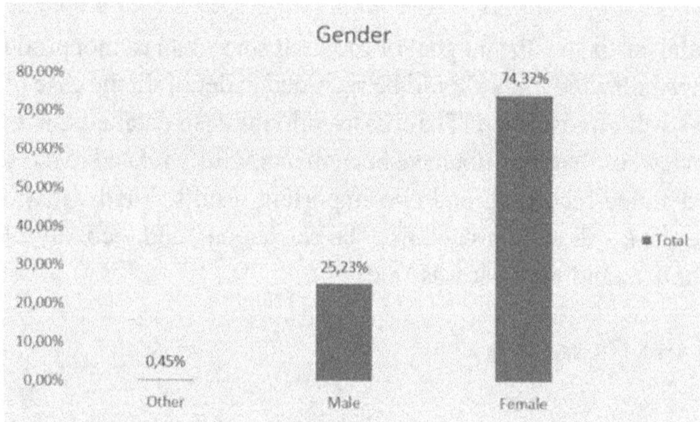

Figure 2. Age

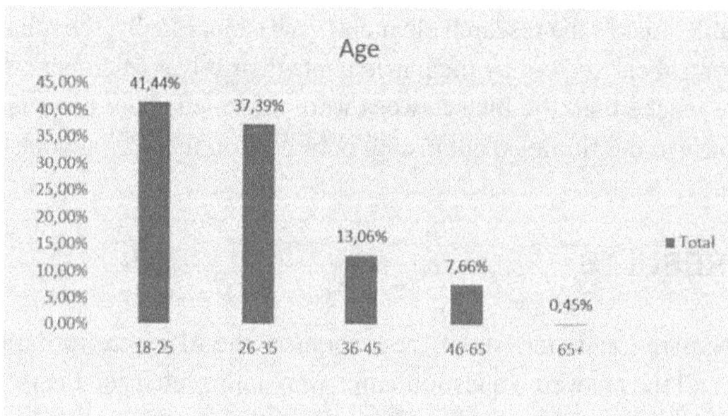

Figure 3. Education

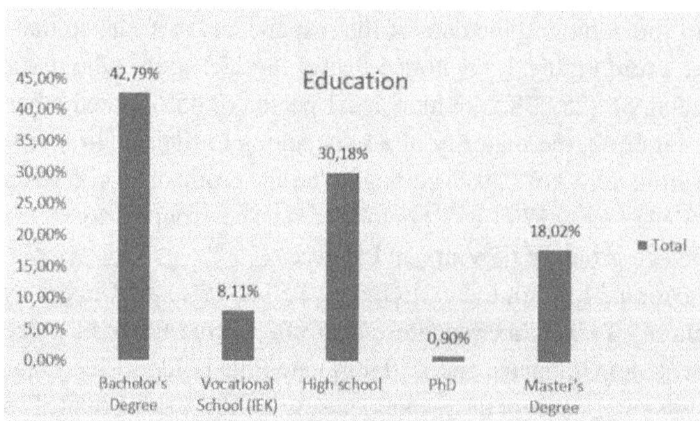

Regarding the second section of the general questions that refer to questions on the topic of social media in the fashion industry and the impact of the COVID-19 pandemic, the respondents in the first question were asked about how much importance they attach to new fashion trends and majority. The results depicted in Figure 5 show that 88 (39.64%) declare moderate importance, while the minority, i.e. 10 (4.50%) declare no importance at all.

In the second question, the participants were asked in what way they are mainly informed about new fashion trends and the majority, i.e. 149 (67.12%) answered with the use of social media, while the minority, namely 2 (0.90%) answered with the use of television (See Figure 6).

In the third question, the respondents were asked which social media do they use the most and the majority of them, i.e. 157 (70.72%) answered that the social media they use mostly is Instagram, while the minority, i.e. 3 (1.35%) answered Twitter (See Figure 7).

In the fourth question regarding how many times the consumer respondents have purchased products advertised on social media, the majority, i.e. 102 (45.95%) answered that they shopped more than three times, while those who never shopped were only 33 (14.86%). (See Figure 8).

In the fifth question, the respondents were asked if they follow influencers who promote products and promotions and the majority i.e. 140 (63.06%) answered yes while the remaining 82 (36.94%) answered no (See Figure 9).

In the sixth question, the participants were asked if they have bought products that they saw displayed by influencers and most of them, i.e. 91 (40.99%) answered that they have never bought such products, while those who bought more than three times were 52 (23,42%) (See Figure 10).

In the seventh question, the respondents were asked whether the information about clothing products from social media is reliable and most of them, i.e. 123 (55.41%) answered moderately, while 13 (5.86%) answered not at all (See Figure 11).

In the eighth question, the respondents were asked how much social media has influenced them in their buying process during the time of COVID-19 and the majority i.e. 69 (31.08%) answered a lot, while the minority i.e. 28 (12, 61%) answered a little (See Figure 12)

In the ninth question, participants were asked how often they shopped online for clothing during the COVID-19 pandemic, and the majority, i.e. 62 (27.93%) answered very often, while those who did not shop at all were 26 (11.71%) (See Figure 13).

In the tenth question, the respondents were asked how much their shopping behavior has changed regarding their preference to buy online after the end of the COVID-19 pandemic and the majority, i.e. 77 (34.68%) answered that they buy a little more often products/services they had viewed online, while those who did not shop at all were 51 (22.97%) (See Figure 14).

In the eleventh question, the participants were asked how much their purchasing behavior has changed regarding their preference for purchasing products seen through social media after the end of the COVID-19 pandemic, and the majority, i.e. 72 (32.43%) answered not at all, while the minority, i.e. 11 (4.95%) answered that they buy much more often products/services they saw through social media (See Figure 15).

In the twelfth and last question, the respondents were asked how much their purchasing behavior has changed regarding their preference for purchasing products that they saw influencers promote after the end of the COVID-19 pandemic and the majority, i.e. 122 (54.95%)) answered not at all, while the minority, i.e. 9 (4.05%) answered that they much more often buy products/services that they saw the influencers promote (See Figure 16).

Figure 4. Occupation

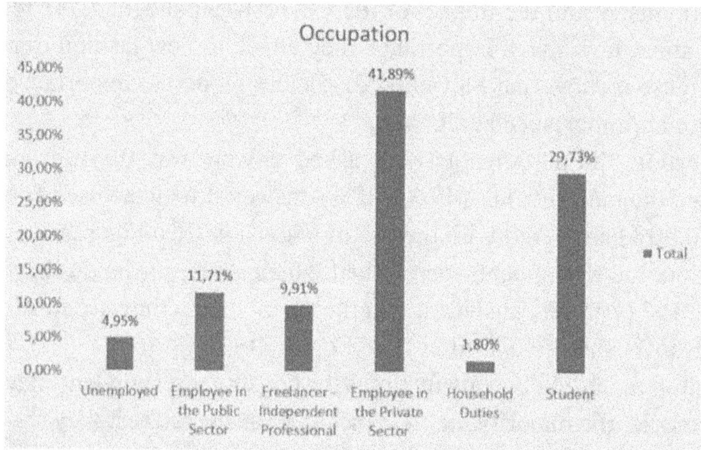

Figure 5. How much importance do you give to new fashion trends?

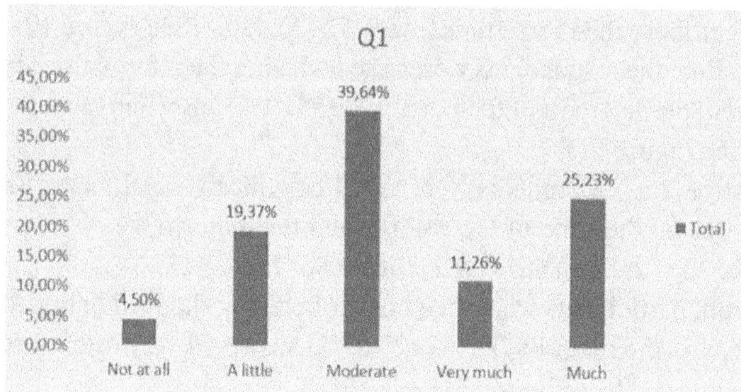

Figure 6. How do you mainly get informed about new fashion trends?

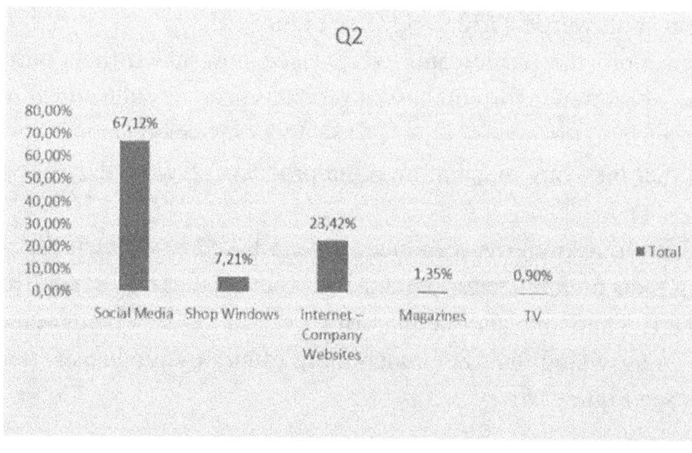

Figure 7. Which social media do you use the most?

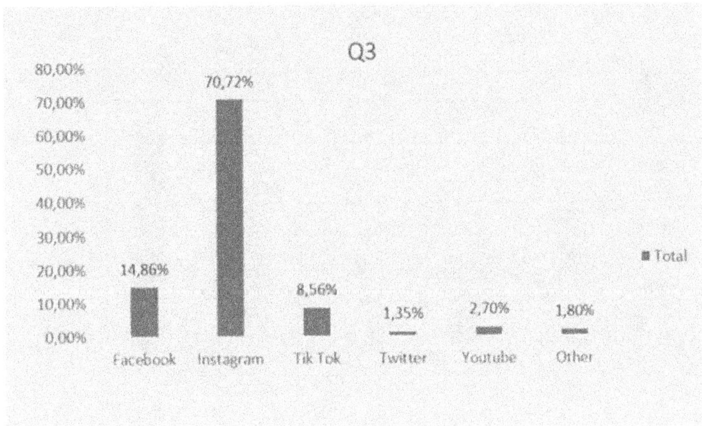

Figure 8. Have you purchased products you saw advertised on social media?

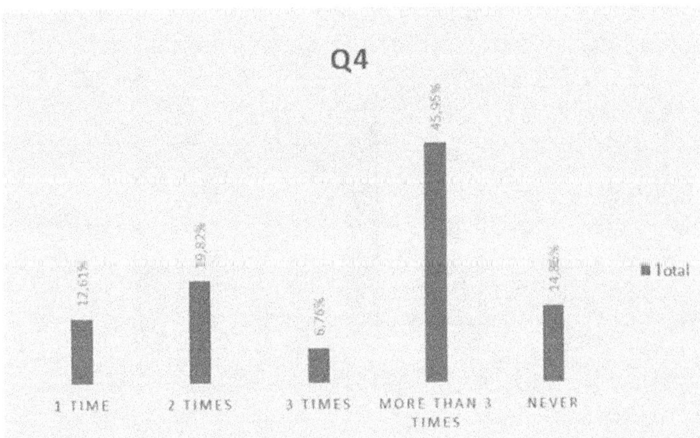

Figure 9. Do you follow influencers who promote products and promotions?

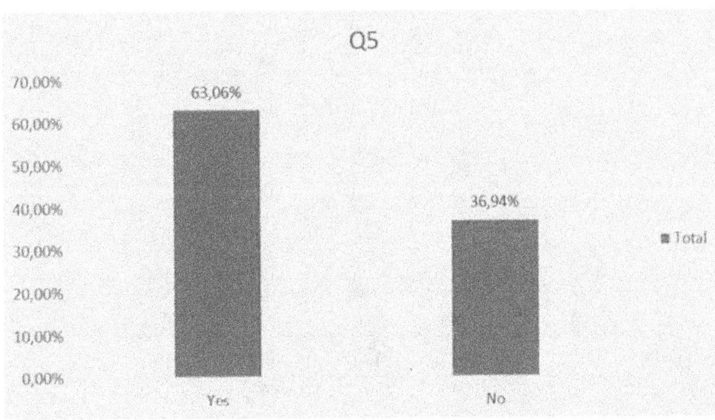

Figure 10. Have you purchased products you saw influencers promoting?

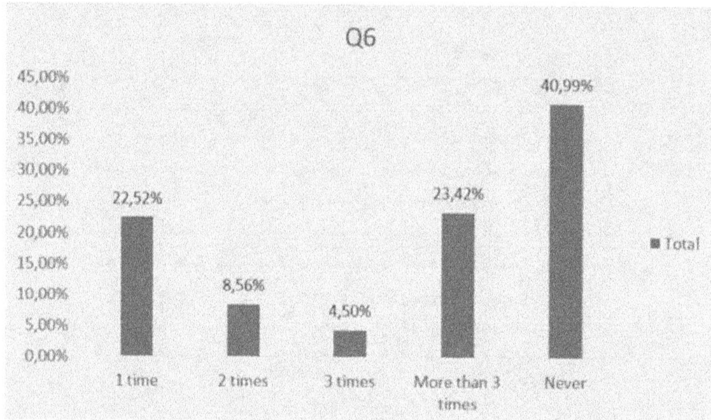

Figure 11. Is information about clothing products from social media reliable?

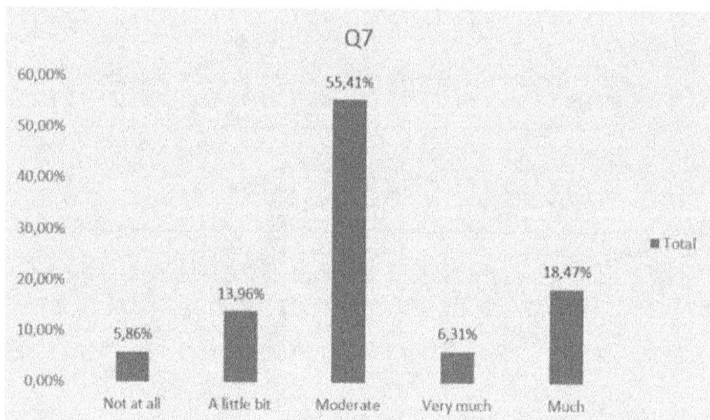

Figure 12. During the COVID-19 pandemic, how much has social media affected you in your buying process?

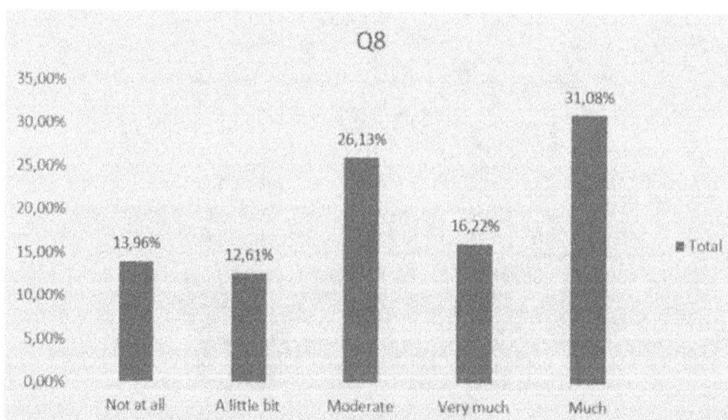

Figure 13. During the COVID-19 pandemic, how often did you shop for clothing online?

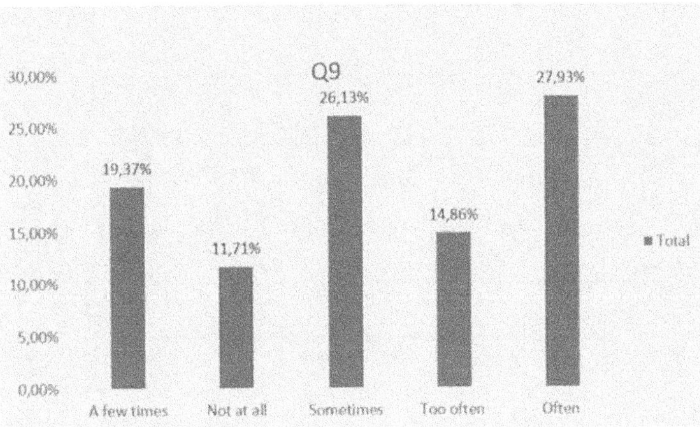

Figure 14. After the end of the COVID-19 pandemic, how much has your shopping behavior changed in terms of your preference to buy online?

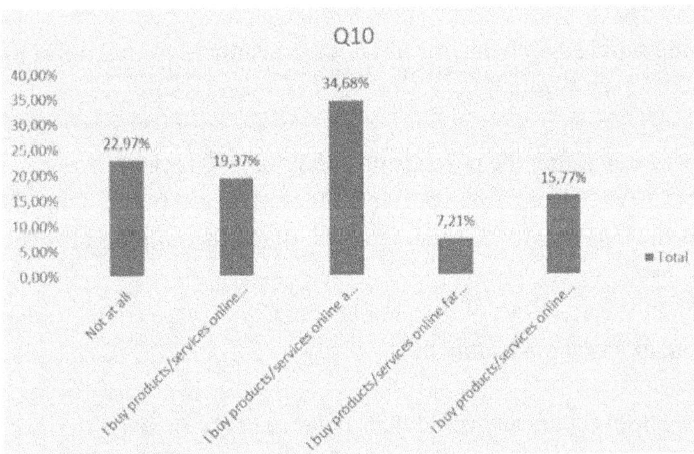

Figure 15. After the end of the COVID-19 pandemic, how much has your purchasing behavior changed in terms of your preference for purchasing products you saw through social media?

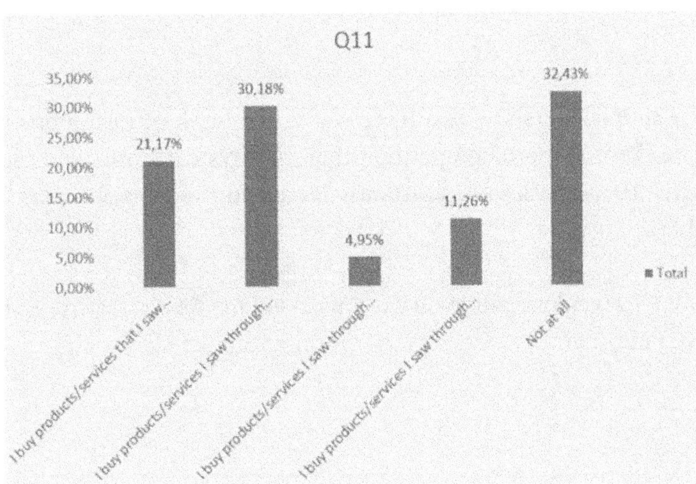

Figure 16. After the end of the COVID-19 pandemic, how much has your purchasing behavior changed in terms of preference for purchasing products that you saw an influencer promote?

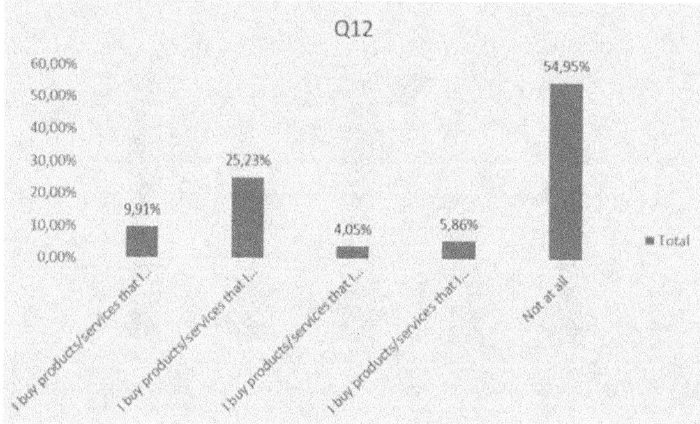

5.2. Personal Interviews Results

1. How much has the purchasing behavior of Greek consumers changed through e-commerce in the era of the COVID-19 pandemic?

Most of the shopkeepers stated that the purchasing behavior of Greek consumers changed rapidly since with the appearance of COVID-19 and the confinement of people at home. They themselves were driven to online shopping, as they spent a lot of time on social media and on the internet in general.

2. In order to maintain the activities of the shopkeepers, was there an easy adaptation to the changes in the internal and external environment?

The majority of the shopkeepers answered that it was not easy to adapt to the changes in the internal and external environment because marketing had to be readjusted and even more so because most of the shopkeepers had no experience in the social media part, it was quite difficult for them at the beginning to learn how the internet world works.

3. Was there a risk of losing profitability and competitiveness due the changes caused by the COVID-19 pandemic?

The response of the shopkeepers was that there was a great risk of losing profitability and competitiveness because online there is more competition than in physical stores and on top of that, with the consolidation of COVID-19, activities are constantly increasing and shopkeepers are trying to maintain their profile level stable.

4. During the COVID-19 pandemic did you use any social media platform (e.g. Facebook, Instagram, Tik Tok, Youtube) in order to advertise your clothing products?

Most of the shopkeepers (i.e. 13) responded that they used social media platforms to advertise their apparel products such as Instagram and Tik Tok, while the remaining 6 used Facebook and Instagram. Finally, one in 20 stated that they used all available social media.

5. What are the advantages and disadvantages of e-commerce and respectively for shopping through physical stores?

To this particular question, all 20 shopkeepers answered in the same way. Regarding the advantages of e-commerce, they stated that it has lower costs, reduced marketing costs and more effective marketing, saving time when making a purchase for the customer and that the network is global. On the other hand, regarding the disadvantages of e-commerce, they answered that there is more competition, loyalty to a customer is more difficult and sometimes the website can go down, resulting in several lost sales. Now, regarding the advantages of physical stores, the shopkeepers answered that there is greater loyalty to the customer because the service is done face-to-face, there is direct communication, the product can be bought at a better price through consultation with the shopkeeper and his/her contact, and clothing seen from inside the store is completely different than when you see it from a picture. On the contrary, in terms of the disadvantages of physical stores, the costs are higher because you have to pay for rent, for decoration, for the sign, for the equipment, for the staff and the investment in advertising is more expensive and it is not as functional as the digital one.

6. Is the use of e-commerce now a part of people's daily lives?

The majority of shopkeepers agree that the use of e-commerce is part of people's daily lives today, even in shops that operate through acquaintances, friends and not so much through the internet, and they notice that consumers are increasingly becoming internet users.

7. Do the reviews and comments of the consumers affect the image of the store and correspondingly their purchasing behavior?

The majority of shopkeepers stated that consumer reviews and comments can affect the store's image because a bad review or comment directly affects the purchasing behavior of the consumer and, accordingly, of all the others.

8. How do consumers learn about clothing companies (via social media, influencers, word of mouth)?

Ten of the 20 shopkeepers responded through social media, 7 through word of mouth and the remaining 3 through social media and influencers.

9. Have you used a marketing strategy on YouTube, Instagram, and other social media in order to enhance your brand image?

13 shopkeepers stated that they mainly used Instagram and Facebook, while the remaining 7 stated that they did not use any social media in order to increase the preference for their brand because they

did not think it was necessary, but it was also pointed out that their brand became known through acquaintances and thus its brand reputation grew faster and faster.

10. Have the way traders – shopkeepers and consumers communicate changed since the pandemic?

The majority of shopkeepers, i.e. 13, answered that the way of communication has changed. There is no such direct communication with the consumers and they have become more demanding, formal and "cold" towards the shopkeepers. On the other hand, 7 out of the 20 shopkeepers, stated that there is a balance in online and traditional communication as the specific shops operate through acquaintances, friends, etc.

DISCUSSION

From the overall findings of the questionnaire survey and the interviews, one can reach some conclusions regarding the use of social media in the fashion industry, consumer attitudes and the impact of the COVID-19 pandemic. After all, the purpose of this study was to investigate the use of social media in the fashion industry and the impact of the COVID-19 pandemic. To begin with, the period of the pandemic was not an easy time. The use of social media during the purchase process is now widespread across all age groups and across all clothing businesses. It has been established that the use of social media in the purchase process has flourished during the pandemic period, however, there is little research that compares the purchasing behavior of Greek consumers before, during and after the pandemic.

Based on our research findings, we can understand that people who were under curfew for a long time, in quarantine, adopted new technologies that facilitated their work, the way they buy products, and also their activities. In addition, through our research results, we see that the use of social media has a significant impact on the decision-making process of consumers as it motivates them to change their preferences. We also show that the pandemic has changed many things for both consumers and clothing entrepreneurs in terms of e-commerce. The main objective of this research was to determine how important role the use of social media played in the fashion industry during the consumer buying process.

For the purpose of this research, 222 answers from Greek consumers were collected, through a questionnaire survey and 20 interviews were conducted with shopkeepers in the Thessaly region. The largest sample of the research consists of women at the age group of 18-25 years. Also, based on the professional status of each respondent, most are employed in the private sector and the majority of them are Bachelor's Degree holders. In addition to the extraction of the demographic data, Graphs as well as frequency analysis for the data were extracted on whether Greek consumers increased their online shopping during the COVID-19 pandemic and which social media were used more for online shopping during this period. Looking at the results, we can understand that there was a noticeable large increase in the purchase of clothing products through e-commerce, but also that the social media that was most used for online consumer shopping was Instagram, which was also an important tool for shopkeepers in order to promote clothing products to consumers.

Finally, regarding the change in the purchasing behavior of Greek consumers in online markets, many of the respondents stated that it has changed significantly and they now shop online much more often. This is also seen in the change in behavior towards shopkeepers due to the fact that they shop online and their relationship has become more direct than before.

LIMITATIONS: OBJECTIVES FOR FUTURE RESEARCH

The main limitation of this research project in the sample size. The data set of 222 participants may not be representative of the whole Greek consumer population. Future studies should include a larger sample size to enable for the generalization of results (Comrey & Lee, 2013). Moreover, results were collected via online fixed questions. This method was selected since it was inexpensive and easy to share and distribute to the target audience. However, respondents have less possibilities to express their opinion (Babbie, 2013). Therefore, the results of the study may not be reliable to some extent. In addition, online surveys may contain inaccurate responses due to misunderstanding of the questions (Bryman, 2016). Future studies should involve larger population sample in order to allow for better generalization of the results and be even more representative of the Greek consumer perceptions regarding the use of social media in the fashion industry.

REFERENCES

Aaker, D. A. (2009). *Managing brand equity*. Simon and Schuster.

Adoeng, W., Kalangi, J.B., & Wangke, S.J. (2019). A comparative analysis of E-advertisement between jd. Id and shopee customers in Manado. *Jurnal EMBA: Jurnal Riset Ekonomi, Manajemen, Bisnis dan Akuntansi, 7*(3).

Algharabat, R., Rana, N. P., Alalwan, A. A., Baabdullah, A., & Gupta, A. (2020). Investigating the antecedents of customer brand engagement and consumer-based brand equity in social media. *Journal of Retailing and Consumer Services, 53*, 101767. doi:10.1016/j.jretconser.2019.01.016

Almansoori, M. K., & Habtoor, N. (2018). The role of social media in crisis preparedness and responses. *International Journal of Engine Research, 9*, 1347–1353.

Amed, I., Balchandani, A., Berg, A., Hedrich, S., Jensen, J. E., & Rölkens, F. (2020). *It's time to rewire the fashion system: State of Fashion coronavirus update*. McKinsey & Company.

Ashfaq, M., & Ali, M. (2017). Impact of celebrity endorsement on consumer buying behavior in FMCG sector of Pakistan. *Arabian Journal of Business and Management Review, 7*(1), 1–12. doi:10.12816/0041744

Attfield, S., Kazai, G., Lalmas, M., & Piwowarski, B. (2011, February). Towards a science of user engagement (position paper). In WSDM workshop on user modelling for Web applications (Vol. 1). Academic Press.

Barefoot, D., & Szabo, J. (2009). *Friends with benefits: A social media marketing handbook*. No Starch Press.

Berthon, P. R., Pitt, L. F., Plangger, K., & Shapiro, D. (2012). Marketing meets Web 2.0, social media, and creative consumers: Implications for international marketing strategy. *Business Horizons, 55*(3), 261–271. doi:10.1016/j.bushor.2012.01.007

Blázquez, M. (2014). Fashion shopping in multichannel retail: The role of technology in enhancing the customer experience. *International Journal of Electronic Commerce*, *18*(4), 97–116. doi:10.2753/JEC1086-4415180404

Bryman, A. (2016). *Social Research Methods* (5th ed.). Oxford University Press.

Burmaster, A. (2009). *Global faces and networked places.* Online at: http://blog. nielsen. com/nielsen-wire/wpcontent/uploads/2009/03/nielsen_globalfaces_mar09. pdf

Cachon, G. P., & Swinney, R. (2011). The value of fast fashion: Quick response, enhanced design, and strategic consumer behavior. *Management Science*, *57*(4), 778–795. doi:10.1287/mnsc.1100.1303

Cheung, C. M., Lee, M. K., & Thadani, D. R. (2009). *The impact of positive electronic word-of-mouth on consumer online purchasing decision*. Springer Berlin Heidelberg. doi:10.1007/978-3-642-04754-1_51

Chung, S., & Cho, H. (2017). Fostering parasocial relationships with celebrities on social media: Implications for celebrity endorsement. *Psychology and Marketing*, *34*(4), 481–495. doi:10.1002/mar.21001

Comrey, A. L., & Lee, H. B. (2013). *A First Course in Factor Analysis* (2nd ed.). Psychology Press. doi:10.4324/9781315827506

Constantinides, E. (2014). Foundations of social media marketing. *Procedia: Social and Behavioral Sciences*, *148*, 40–57. doi:10.1016/j.sbspro.2014.07.016

Dorado, L. E. (2011). *The Effect of Social Media on the Fashion Retail Industry*. Elon University.

Du Plessis, C. (2017). *Towards a more universal understanding of content marketing: The contribution of academic research.* Academic Press.

Emmanouil, S. (2021). *Καλπάζει το ηλεκτρονικό εμπόριο μόδας*. EURO2DAY. Available at: https://www.euro2day.gr/news/economy/article/2062409/kalpazei-to-hlektroniko-emporio-modas-.html

European Union. (2020a). *Κοινός ευρωπαϊκός οδικός χάρτης για την άρση των μέτρων περιορισμού του COVID-19.* Available at: https://ec.europa.eu/info/live-work-travel-eu/health/coronavirus-response/european-roadmap-lifting-coronavirus-containment-measures_en

European Union. (2020b). *Μέτρα περιορισμού για τον COVID-19.* Available at: https://reliefweb.int/map/italy/european-union-covid-19-restriction-measures-dg-echo-daily-map-20042020

Evans, D. (2010). *Social media marketing: the next generation of business engagement.* John Wiley & Sons.

Fairs, M. (2020). *Coronavirus offers "a blank page for a new beginning" says Li Edelkoort.* Dezeen Magazine.

Frąckiewicz, E. (2021). Information and communication technologies as a source of customer value in the context of balancing the positions of younger and older consumers. *Sustainability (Basel)*, *13*(9), 4722. doi:10.3390u13094722

Gilly, M. C., & Wolfinbarger, M. (2000). A comparison of consumer experiences with online and offline shopping. *Consumption Markets & Culture*, *4*(2), 187–205. doi:10.1080/10253866.2000.9670355

Gupta, Y., Agarwal, S., & Singh, P. B. (2020). To study the impact of instafamous celebrities on consumer buying behavior. *Academy of Marketing Studies Journal*, *24*(2), 1–13.

Hennig-Thurau, T., Gwinner, K. P., Walsh, G., & Gremler, D. D. (2004). Electronic word-of-mouth via consumer-opinion platforms: What motivates consumers to articulate themselves on the internet? *Journal of Interactive Marketing*, *18*(1), 38–52. doi:10.1002/dir.10073

Holliday, R. C., Ballinger, C., & Playford, E. D. (2007). Goal setting in neurological rehabilitation: Patients' perspectives. *Disability and Rehabilitation*, *29*(5), 389–394. doi:10.1080/09638280600841117 PMID:17364791

Hulland, J., & Houston, M. B. (2020). Why systematic review papers and meta-analyses matter: An introduction to the special issue on generalizations in marketing. *Journal of the Academy of Marketing Science*, *48*(3), 351–359. doi:10.100711747-020-00721-7

Hwang, J., Eves, A., & Stienmetz, J. L. (2021). The impact of social media use on consumers' restaurant consumption experiences: A qualitative study. *Sustainability (Basel)*, *13*(12), 6581. doi:10.3390u13126581

Ibok, N. I. (2013). Factors determining the effectiveness of celebrity endorsed advertisements: The case of Nigerian telecommunication industry. *American Journal of Business and Management*, *2*(3), 233–238. doi:10.11634/216796061302394

Jain, V., Malviya, B., & Arya, S. (2021). An overview of electronic commerce (e-Commerce). *Journal of Contemporary Issues in Business and Government*, *27*(3), 666.

Kastner, M., Tricco, A. C., Soobiah, C., Lillie, E., Perrier, L., Horsley, T., Welch, V., Cogo, E., Antony, J., & Straus, S. E. (2012). What is the most appropriate knowledge synthesis method to conduct a review? Protocol for a scoping review. *BMC Medical Research Methodology*, *12*(1), 1–10. doi:10.1186/1471-2288-12-114 PMID:22862833

Keller, K. L. (1993). Conceptualizing, measuring, and managing customer-based brand equity. *Journal of Marketing*, *57*(1), 1–22. doi:10.1177/002224299305700101

Keller, K. L. (2003). *Strategic Brand Management: Best Practice Cases in Branding: Lessons from the World's Strongest Brands*. Pearson Education.

Khan, Z., Yang, Y., Shafi, M., & Yang, R. (2019). Role of social media marketing activities (SMMAs) in apparel brands customer response: A moderated mediation analysis. *Sustainability (Basel)*, *11*(19), 5167. doi:10.3390u11195167

Khatri, P. (2006). Celebrity endorsement: A strategic promotion perspective. *Indian Media Studies Journal, 1*(1), 25-37.

Kotler, P., Armstrong, G., Ang, S. H., Leong, S. M., Tan, C. T., & Ho-Ming, O. (2012). *Principles of marketing: an Asian perspective*. Pearson/Prentice-Hall.

Kursan Milaković, I. (2021). Purchase experience during the COVID-19 pandemic and social cognitive theory: The relevance of consumer vulnerability, resilience, and adaptability for purchase satisfaction and repurchase. *International Journal of Consumer Studies*, *45*(6), 1425–1442. doi:10.1111/ijcs.12672 PMID:33821146

Lee, J., Park, D. H., & Han, I. (2008). The effect of negative online consumer reviews on product attitude: An information processing view. *Electronic Commerce Research and Applications*, *7*(3), 341–352. doi:10.1016/j.elerap.2007.05.004

Lefebvre, L. A., & Lefebvre, E. (2002). E-commerce and virtual enterprises: Issues and challenges for transition economies. *Technovation*, *22*(5), 313–323. doi:10.1016/S0166-4972(01)00010-4

Lemon, K. N., Rust, R. T., & Zeithaml, V. A. (2001). What drives customer equity? *Marketing Management, 10*(1), 20-25.

Lin, Y., & Kant, S. (2021). Using social media for citizen participation: Contexts, empowerment, and inclusion. *Sustainability (Basel)*, *13*(12), 6635. doi:10.3390u13126635

Luce, L. (2019). *Artificial Intelligence for Fashion How AI is Revolutionizing the Fashion Industry*. Apress. doi:10.1007/978-1-4842-3931-5

Magazine, A. (2010). How social media is revolutionizing the apparel industry: One message at a time. *Apparel Magazine*, *52*(4), 1–6.

Manneh, M. (2017). *The influence of social media on e-commerce: Fast fashion multinational companies*. Academic Press.

Mason, A. N., Narcum, J., & Mason, K. (2021). Social media marketing gains importance after Covid-19. *Cogent Business & Management*, *8*(1), 1870797. doi:10.1080/23311975.2020.1870797

Meng, X., Zhang, W., Li, Y., Cao, X., & Feng, X. (2020). Social media effect, investor recognition and the cross-section of stock returns. *International Review of Financial Analysis*, *67*, 101432. doi:10.1016/j.irfa.2019.101432

Niculescu, A., Dumitriu, D., Purdescu, C., & Popescu, M. A. M. (2019). Enhancing brand value of modern organizations through digital marketing tools and techniques: A study on top ten Romanian companies. *TEM Journal*, *8*(1), 171.

Ohanian, R. (1990). Construction and validation of a scale to measure celebrity endorsers' perceived expertise, trustworthiness, and attractiveness. *Journal of Advertising*, *19*(3), 39–52. doi:10.1080/00913367.1990.10673191

Oliver, C. (2008). *Social networks change the online retail game*. Academic Press.

Parker, C. J., & Wang, H. (2016). Examining hedonic and utilitarian motivations for m-commerce fashion retail app engagement. *Journal of Fashion Marketing and Management*, *20*(4), 487–506. doi:10.1108/JFMM-02-2016-0015

Pyrgiotakis, E. I., & Symeou, L. (2016). Qualitative research and the scientific value of the knowledge produced in the Social Sciences and Humanities. Research Methodology in Social Sciences and Education, 193-226.

Rezaei, S., Shahijan, M. K., Amin, M., & Ismail, W. K. W. (2016). Determinants of app stores continuance behavior: A PLS path modelling approach. *Journal of Internet Commerce*, *15*(4), 408–440. doi:10.1080/15332861.2016.1256749

Roggeveen, A. L., & Sethuraman, R. (2020). How the COVID-19 pandemic may change the world of retailing. *Journal of Retailing*, *96*(2), 169–171. doi:10.1016/j.jretai.2020.04.002

Scarpi, D., Pizzi, G., & Visentin, M. (2014). Shopping for fun or shopping to buy: Is it different online and offline? *Journal of Retailing and Consumer Services*, *21*(3), 258–267. doi:10.1016/j.jretconser.2014.02.007

Silvestri, B. (2020). The future of fashion: How the quest for digitization and the use of artificial intelligence and extended reality will reshape the fashion industry after COVID-19. *ZoneModa Journal*, *10*(2), 61–73.

Siomkos, G., & Mavros, D. (2008). *Ερεύνα Αγοράς*. Stamoulis Publishing.

Sotiroudas, B. (2011). *Research Paper Handbook*. Athens: iWrite. gr.

Stanciu, S., Radu, R. I., Sapira, V., Bratoveanu, B. D., & Florea, A. M. (2020). Consumer Behavior in Crisis Situations. Research on the Effects of COVID-19 in Romania. *Annals of the University Dunarea de Jos of Galati: Fascicle: I, Economics & Applied Informatics, 26*(1).

Tabatabaei, M. (2009). Online shopping perceptions of offline shoppers. *Issues in Information Systems*, *10*(2), 22–26.

Theofanidis, S. M. (2002). *Μεθοδολογία της επιστημονικής σκέψης και έρευνας: Πώς γίνεται η επιστημονική έρευνα και πώς γράφεται μια επιστημονική εργασία* (2nd ed.). Benou Publishing.

Tsiftsakis, N. (2021). *The impact of covid-19 on e-commerce*. Academic Press.

Wang, Y., Chowdhury Ahmed, S., Deng, S., & Wang, H. (2019). Success of social media marketing efforts in retaining sustainable online consumers: An empirical analysis on the online fashion retail market. *Sustainability (Basel)*, *11*(13), 3596. doi:10.3390u11133596

Wang, Y., Hong, A., Li, X., & Gao, J. (2020). Marketing innovations during a global crisis: A study of China firms' response to COVID-19. *Journal of Business Research*, *116*, 214–220. doi:10.1016/j.jbusres.2020.05.029 PMID:32501308

Wolfinbarger, M., & Gilly, M. C. (2001). Shopping online for freedom, control, and fun. *California Management Review*, *43*(2), 34–55. doi:10.2307/41166074

Wongkitrungrueng, A., & Assarut, N. (2020). The role of live streaming in building consumer trust and engagement with social commerce sellers. *Journal of Business Research*, *117*, 543–556. doi:10.1016/j.jbusres.2018.08.032

Xiang, L., Zheng, X., Lee, M. K., & Zhao, D. (2016). Exploring consumers' impulse buying behavior on social commerce platform: The role of parasocial interaction. *International Journal of Information Management*, *36*(3), 333–347. doi:10.1016/j.ijinfomgt.2015.11.002

Zafeiropoulos. (2005). *Πως γίνεται μια επιστημονική εργασία. Επιστημονική έρευνα και συγγραφή εργασιών*. Kritiki Publishing.

Chapter 17
How Social Media Affects Consumer Behavior in the Fashion Industry

Theodore K. Tarnanidis
University of Macedonia, Greece

Evridiki (Eurydice) Papachristou
International Hellenic University, Greece

Michail Karypidis
International Hellenic University, Greece

Vasileios Ismyrlis
Hellenic Open University, Greece

ABSTRACT

Social media is experiencing unprecedented success in terms of usage levels. They cause significant changes in the way people connect and communicate with each other, in the way they express themselves and share ideas, and even in the way they engage with products, brands, and organizations/companies. This research attempts to answer the following useful questions, all by examining the fashion industry and its presence on social media. To what extent does social media influence consumer purchasing behavior? Which social media is used the most? To what extent do so-called influencers influence purchasing decisions? How powerful and decisive is electronic word of mouth (eWOM) in influencing a consumer either positively or negatively? The conclusions will be drawn from the secondary research conducted.

1. INTRODUCTION

This chapter attempts to shed light on certain practices that are closely linked to the particularities of modern society, which is often characterized as a digital or information age. As Castells (2011a) notes, it is considered the era of contemporary capitalism in both political and cultural dimensions, character-

DOI: 10.4018/978-1-6684-8753-2.ch017

ized by globalization as a trend that relies heavily on developments in technology and networking, with consumer practices at its core (James and Szeizman, 2010). Another notable feature of modern society is networking, which is articulated through various systems of socio-technological practices that set the tone of modern life. Although networks are established forms of communication, digital networking, overcoming the traditional limitations of networked forms of organization to manage complexity beyond a certain network size" (Castells, 2011b). The pillar of such growth is the internet and its continuous expansion – almost half of the world's population (46.4%) in 2015 had access to the internet, which is an impressive increase of 832.5% since the beginning of the 21st century. At the heart of this rapid expansion are social networks, a pillar of Web 2.0. The beginning of the century saw a huge spread of social networks, which brings them to the top of the popular sectors of the Internet (World-Wide-Web). Very few people with constant or periodic access to the internet are absent or have no experience with some form of social networks (be it the "first" Facebook, Twitter, Myspace, or the more modern Snapchat, TikTok, etc.) Within a period of no more than a decade, social networks took over society and completely changed both the online, as well as the off-line world. Social networks are understood as relatively stable aggregations of relationships between social actors (be they individuals, groups, enterprises, organizations), which involve exchanges of various resources (materials, services, information, values, rules, social practices, etc.) and have a certain structure.

According to Kemp (2020), the Internet is now used by more than 4.5 billion people, while social media users have exceeded 3.8 billion, making about 85% of Internet users regular users of various social media platforms. This represents a significant increase compared to 2007 (56%) and 2008 (75%). As Kaplan and Haenlein noted in 2010, this increase "is not limited to adolescents. Members of Generation X, aged 35-44 today, are becoming increasingly active users. As such, it is reasonable to say that social media represents a new revolutionary trend that should interest companies operating in the online space – or in any space, to be precise." This finding is even more crucial when you consider that it's not just Gen Z, Gen X, and millennials who use social media.

2. LITERATURE REVIEW

According to a recent survey implemented by Pew (2021), 62% of internet users aged 65 and older use Facebook, as do 72% of 50-64 year olds. Facebook has the highest number of users at these ages. In 2017 the average social media user has 7.6 active accounts. On top of that, the average user spends about 142 minutes a day browsing various platforms – plenty of time for businesses to get in front of potential customers and spread their brand message.

The development of social media activities is the direct consequence of the rapid development of technology, which due to its affordable price and simplicity of use became popular among users. The exponential increase in CPU power, data storage and processing capacity has put significant power in the hands of users who can now communicate mutually through social media. The advent of smartphones and their ability to quickly process images on a device marked another revolutionary step in the expansion of social media. Thus, the internet and social media in particular, offer new possibilities, broaden existing perspectives and set new standards and values.

The emergence of the World Wide Web, and especially Web 2.0, has forced companies to make significant changes in their communication strategies and tactics to customers, suppliers and employees, while increasing their efficiency, effectiveness and image. Today, the World Wide Web and especially

Figure 1. Increasing the percentage of U.S. adults using at least one social media platform
Source: Pewresearch.com

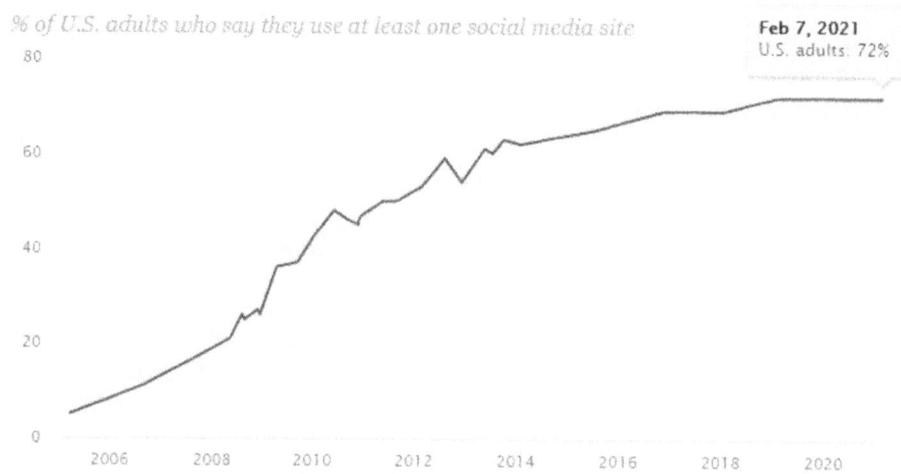

Figure 2. Increasing the percentage of U.S. adults using at least one social media platform
Source: Statista.com

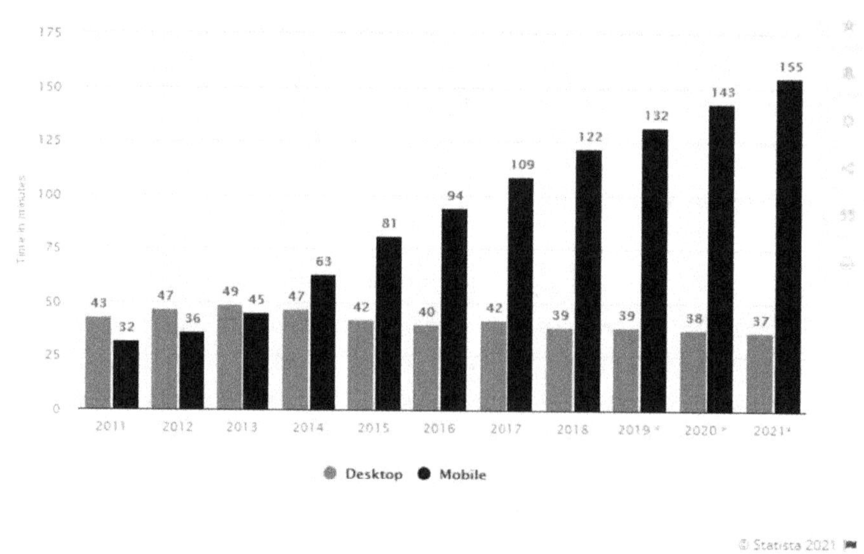

Social Media are considered a place of innovation and interaction. Using the aforementioned features of Web 2.0, the company can expect business results to progress in a variety of areas – from improving user experience to more sophisticated billing/payment methods. The new rules of on-line presence, direct communication with customers and the logic of Web 2.0 can bring positive results in strategic innovations that are the result of advanced collaboration with all members of the business circle.

The innovative use of web 2.0, especially social media, is the vehicle of growth in the field of modern businesses. The majority of business entities use the most important social media (Facebook, Instagram, Linked IN,) for internal and external purposes, from recruitment, to brand awareness and direct sales. Therefore, understanding the principles by which social media shape modern business strategies and tactics is not only beneficial, but also necessary in every sector of commerce, especially in the fashion industry, as it is one of the industries where frequent changes occur and social media is the most direct and cheapest way to communicate.

In light of all this, various authors observed changes in consumer behavior patterns, caused by the fact that "virtual communities become important consumer knowledge networks that influence their behavior" (De Valck, et al, 2009), where they observe that "consumers are more likely to participate than to watch" stating that in recent years we are witnessing a shift in consumer behavior from "consumers as spectators" to "consumers as participants". This new form of consumer behavior, participation that takes the form of "consumers as experts" is a result of the possibilities offered by social media, combined with the so-called social "ethos" of individuality (Bauman, 2000) in which one's personal opinion/experience is articulated in the public sphere (Habermas, 1989) where traditionally (historically) the views of experts were (exclusively) presented.

This is illustrated by Kaplan and Haenlein (2010) when they state that "historically, companies have been able to control available information about them through strategically placed press releases and public relations managers. Today, however, companies have increasingly been sidelined as mere observers, not having the opportunity – or, sometimes, even the right – to change publicly posted comments coming from their customers. Wikipedia, for example, explicitly prohibits companies from participating in its online community." Thus, the role of social media becomes paramount in various stages of consumer behavior and occupies a central place in modern marketing strategies.

The spread of the World Wide Web also meant an increase in the base of users who began looking for platforms that would meet their diversified needs. Although Kaplan and Haenlein (2010) argue that "there is no systematic way in which different social media applications can be categorized", many other authors cite various classifications and categorizations (Fotis, 2015; Kim et al, 2010; Fischer and Reuber, 2011; Cavazza, 2010. The number of social media formats proposed ranges from 2 (Social Networking Sites and Social Media) to 26, which includes not only social media but also tools, mechanisms and platforms that facilitate the use of social media and/or the sharing of user-generated content. Arguing that the classification of 6 types (Blogs, Social Networking Sites, Collaborative projects, Content communities, Virtual social worlds and Virtual game worlds) proposed by Kaplan and Haenlein (2010) lacks, among others, Microblogs, wikis, consumer review sites, and Internet forums. Fotis focused his research on travel-related topics, but due to the fact that his classification includes 3 types of great importance for the fashion industry (microblogs, consumer review websites and location-based services).

Social Networking Sites (SNS): Facebook, Instagram, Vkontakti, Linkedin, and Xing are considered typical examples of PCIs. In the UK, more than half of adults visit an IOF at least once a week (Ofcom, 2020), a number that has increased significantly over the past decade. This makes them the most widespread type of networking and their popularity continues to grow worldwide. .

Blogs: The term blog describes a personal website (either standalone or hosted on a hosting platform such as blogger.com or wordpress.com) that contains regularly updated entries, which consist mainly of text, but also images, videos, and links to other websites (Fotis, 2015). The importance of blogs for businesses in general and fashion businesses in particular is clear when considering the content created on blogs: users who maintain a blog usually post photos (70%), recommended websites (43%), favorite music tracks listened to (34%), videos (32%), opinions about products and brands (32%), stories from other blogs (29%), songs in the form of uploads (26%), useful widgets (18%). Another important aspect when it comes to blogs is the issue of trustworthiness, where blog content ranks high.

Microblogs: Microblogs have been defined as "web applications that allow users to exchange small pieces of content, such as short sentences, individual images, or video links" (Kaplan and Haenlein 2011). Among the variety of various microblogs, Twitter is the largest, most important and with more than 192 million daily users. Microblogging apps (e.g. Twitter) differ from the majority of social networking sites (e.g. Facebook) in that (a) the relationship with followers does not require reciprocity: User A can follow User B, but it is not necessary for User B to follow User A; b) posts are public by default and users can be followed without their approval (Kwak et al. 2010); c) compared to blogging, microblogging applications are considered a faster way to communicate and updated more frequently.

Wikis: Wikis are "a freely expandable collection of interconnected 'pages' of the World Wide Web, a hypertext system for storing and modifying information – a database where each page is easily editable by any user". The largest and most important is Wikipedia, a multilingual, free online encyclopedia written by its users (Gardner 2008). With nearly 6.3 million English-language articles and hundreds of new articles daily, Wikipedia is one of the most visited websites worldwide (Alexa, 2021). Wikipedia, as the most elaborate collaborative project, is of paramount business importance, as "from a corporate perspective, companies need to be aware that collaborative projects tend to become the primary source of information for many consumers. Therefore, although what is written on Wikipedia is not necessarily accurate, more and more Internet users believe it to be true" (Kaplan and Haenlein, 2010). The same authors, when describing how businesses have less and less control over the information available about them in cyberspace, underscore the importance of Wikipedia – "Today, if an Internet user types in the name of any leading brand in Google search, what appears among the top results usually includes not only the corporate website, but also the company's website. but also the corresponding article on Wikipedia".

Content Community Sites: Content communities are web applications that allow users to share multimedia content, such as videos, photos, documents and presentations, and music (Fotis, 2015). Among the various applications include Vimeo, Dailymotion, Instagram, Flickr. Since its launch in 2005, Youtube has become one of the most visited websites and most frequently used applications worldwide. According to its official statistics, it has more than 2 billion users (1/3 of all Internet users), reaches more people in the 18-34 age group of the American audience than any television network, with 1 billion hours watched daily. Instagram was founded in 2010 and by 2018, the platform had reached 1 billion monthly active users, making it one of the largest and most influential social media platforms worldwide. Fashion accounts for 25% of brand interactions on Instagram (Bern, 2020), while an estimated 55% of fashion consumers have made a purchase based on a user's Instagram post. For the above reasons and numbers, content community sites will be covered in a separate section.

Consumer Evaluation Websites: Consumer review websites (CRWs) are social networking applications that allow users to upload reviews and ratings about products (Fotis, 2015). Multiple studies confirm that consumers not only take online reviews into account, but are also influenced by them when making purchasing decisions (Chevalier and Mayzlin 2006, Dellarocas et al. 2007) and are even willing to pay more for higher-rated products. Chevalier and Mayzlin (2006) demonstrated that online information in the form of online book reviews has a causal impact (positive effect) on consumer purchasing behavior (sales). As a result of technological progress, these new means of communication have led to changes in consumer behavior (Cantallops and Salvi, 2014; Gómez-Suárez et al., 2017), due to the influence they allow consumers to exert on each other (Jalilvand and Samiei, 2012), allowing them to acquire or share information about companies, or products (Gómez-Suárez et al., 2017). Where consumers once trusted the word of mouth of their friends and family, today they look for information about a product or service in online comments.

Internet Forum: Online forums (IFs) can be thought of as online virtual spaces where users who share common interests can initiate or participate in discussions, post messages, questions or answers organized on user-generated topics (Poel 2009- Laughlin and MacDonald 2010- Carbonaro 2011). Even before the development of social media in its current form, forums have been identified as important sources of consumer information (Bickart and Schindler 2001).

Location-Based Social Media: Location-based social media (LBSM) are applications that allow users to articulate a list of other users with whom they share their geographic location at a specific time (referred to as "check-in"), which is usually associated with a specific place or place (Fotis, 2015). The motivations for using such applications are varied and range from discovering and visiting new places, coordinating with friends and signaling availability to them, tracking the places visited as a form of presenting themselves, as "eavesdropping" so they know where others are (Lint et al. 2019).

Consumer behaviour, consumption patterns and the importance they carry as a social practice are of paramount importance to both industry and academia. Some authors place consumption at the core of contemporary culture and consider it an integral part of the process of creating meaning in the modern world (Fiske, 1989; Featherstone, 1991). Consumer behavior is therefore both an academic field of research and a sub-branch of marketing (MacInnis and Folkes 2009). Fotis (2015) argues that there is no universal consensus on a definitive definition of consumer behavior and accordingly, he analyzed the evolution of the definition over the course of 40 years in order to give a synthesis. "Consumer behavior can be defined as the physical and mental activities undertaken by individuals either as part of processes, or as independent actions, when dreaming, seeking, evaluating, acquiring, consume or dispose of goods, services, ideas and experiences, within physical or virtual environments").

As clearly identified by Stephen (2016), patterns, spaces, and behaviors of consumption have taken an irreversible direction toward digital environments: People are exposed to more and more digital and social media – from 75 minutes per day in 2011 to 192 minutes per day in 2021 (Statista, 2021). This is done for many purposes, including in their role as consumers, as they seek information about products or services, buy and consume them, and communicate their experiences to others. Advertisers have reacted to this shift and increased their use of digital marketing channels. Future marketing for consumers will largely take place in digital environments, in particular on social media and mobile phones. In the context of this changing landscape, five themes were identified as nascent and relevant (Stephen, 2016): (a) digital consumer culture, (b) digital advertising, (c) the impact of digital environments, (d) mobile telephony, and (e) eWOM and reviews. Below we will examine each of them in detail.

Digital Consumer: Culture Research on consumer digital culture focuses on the digital environments in which consumers and businesses find themselves, with a key aspect of understanding how consumers' identities and concepts of self extend to digital worlds (Belk, 2013) and the ability of consumers to have multiple selves due to having multiple online "personalities". In addition, digital consumer culture includes, among other things, significant changes in the way we reach the public, and a phenomenon called the "megaphone effect", i.e. the ability of ordinary consumers to access large audiences through digital/social media (McQuarrie et al, 2013; McQuarrie and Phillips, 2014).Whereas previously access was given to specific people, today almost anyone can appear in the media, either institutionally (TV star) or individually/directly (bloggers). Since this fact is of great importance for consumer behavior in the fashion industry, the popular shift, bloggers, and digital culture will be examined in detail below.

Digital Advertising: The study of advertising in the digital environment has become an important field of research with an impressive amount of knowledge in the marketing literature, especially in the areas examining changing patterns of consumer behaviour and the different ways in which consumers react to digital advertising and digital advertising. Given that spending on digital advertising globally in 2021 is projected to be 56.1% of total advertising in the media, studies related to this research deal with the consequences of personalized advertising made possible by various online tracking systems (Schumann et al, 2014; Lambrecht and Tucker, 2013). In this context, Tucker (2014) concludes that personalized ads on websites are more favorably received when consumers are more aware that they have control over the personalization.

Impact of Digital Environments: As the Internet and its technologies are neither new nor revolutionary, its scope and impact have broadened to cover all spheres of human life, including professional, private, family and other sectors. In the same way, "the internet, and mobile digital technologies are more than just 'technologies'. It is a set of social relationships that integrate the use of technologies with various outcomes." (Miller, 2020). One of the most important impacts of digital environments is the creation and proliferation of social networks, which have brought about profound changes in cultures around the world, changing forms of taste, norms, products, communication styles and consumption patterns, both symbolic and material (McLean, 2016). It is reasonable to assume that digital environments influence consumer behavior in many ways, among which two main directions are identified. First, they influence social media behavior (Lamberton et al., 2013). Exposure to the opinions (e.g. reviews) or choices (e.g. offers in online auctions) of other consumers, or even simply to the lives of their friends through social media, can influence consumer behaviour. Second, digital environments influence behavior in other, unrelated environments, a fact that was evident in research done by Wilcox and Stephen (2013) which showed that when exposed to closer friends on Facebook, consumers subsequently demonstrate lower self-control over choices related to healthy behaviors.

The role of the consumer has shifted from passive observation to activated dominance. It is no longer content with simply buying fashion products. The exponential growth in the use of digital technologies has enabled them to be empowered. They want to interact, belong, influence, and be the brands they buy from. Informed, selective and responsible, they care about how they appear in public and on social media."

Mobile Devices: The introduction of mobile devices has brought with it a shift in our cultures, most notably by blurring the boundaries between activities and locations (Pinchot et al, 2011) and introducing the culture of "always connected" (Baron, 2008) and "always available". Mobile devices are key to understanding consumer behaviour and patterns, especially since consumers use them more often. Brasel and Gips (2014) show that touchscreen devices – smartphones, tablets – influence online shopping behavior by reinforcing the phenomenon of "owning". This is the case, as Stephen (2016) summarizes, because "touch (versus mouse click) increases the perception of psychological ownership of products while browsing the internet. More people are buying goods via mobile devices, either enjoying the comfort of their couch or while "on the go" than ever before, while smartphones make up 80% of social media browsing – 91.5% for Facebook, 86% for Twitter and 60% for Linkedin (Broadband, 2021). Instagram, as one of the most mobile-oriented platforms engaged in image-sharing activities, confirms the importance of social media in the fashion industry (Park et al, 2016).

eWOM: Online Word of Mouth and online reviews are one of the most representative and most important topics in linking social media and consumer behavior. A significant body of research deals with the linguistic properties of eWoWs and their impact on consumer behavior and decisions (Stephen, 2016: 3). Another important topic recently addressed is the differences between online and offline WOM.

Eisingerich et al. (2015) studied the differences between WOM transmission on social media (e.g., Facebook) versus offline (in person), showing that consumers are less willing to broadcast WOM on social media due to higher perceived social risk, as eWOM is more sensitive to self-reinforcement motivations and social risk perceptions than WOM. Tjhin and Aini (2019) turned their attention to understanding the impact of E-WOM and social media use on purchasing decision in the clothing industry in the Indonesian context. They conclude that although eWOW has limited influence on the purchase decision mediated by trust, "companies operating in the apparel industry must also have conversation-based social media accounts and use them to distribute campaigns about fashion product specifications, such as information about the size and material used". The encouragement of eWOM activities is particularly evident in fashion consumer blogs.

3. THE FASHION INDUSTRY

The Fashion Industry Fashion has become a legitimate field of academic study ever since Roland Barthes published his foundational work "The System of Fashion" (1990), in which the master of semiotics presented the life and times of clothing and its industry as a language system, and like any language, it must have its own grammar. Being a language, it is most evident in its clothing and production ("Why does fashion pronounce such abundant clothing, which he inextricably links to consumer society and its consumption patterns - "The computational, industrial society is obliged to shape consumers who do not count. Furthermore, Barther draws our attention to the fact that fashion, and particularly the garment industry, operates within the framework of the "now", which is largely in line with the cultural boundaries of modern, postmodern society and its blurred boundaries (as explained briefly in the section on social media and mobile devices) – "Every new fashion is a refusal to inherit, a reversal against the oppression of the previous fashion. Fashion experiences itself as a right, the natural right of the present over the past". Consequently, the fashion industry is naturally willing to participate in social media platforms and this has been the case since the beginning of social media.

The fashion industry, like any other industry, has its own characteristics. Customers can feel like they're part of the big brand family, and the interactive element further deepens that relationship. Social media has actually become the human voice of the brand and can be used for free advertising. Haute couture fashion houses, designers and retailers in an effort to shape their brand's personality on global online platforms in real time, tweet, blog and regularly update their profiles. The same author notes that fashion industry professionals use social media to spread videos, ads, behind-the-scenes and fashion shows. The emerging trend and influence of fashion blogging has brought a change in everything from publishing to the way brands are promoted online. "Well-known fashion brands and designers such as Dolce & Gabanna, Burberry, Alexander McQueen, along with major fashion magazines such as Vogue and Elle, recognized brilliant fashion bloggers such as Gala Darling, Tavi, Scott Schuman etc. Other important trends that will transform the ways the fashion industry operates, based on the logic of mobile devices and user-generated content, such as a) the adoption of mobile apps, b) the rise of star bloggers, and c) the impact of user-generated content. Reflecting on the latter, Wright Lee states: "User generated content is key to social media and fashion. From blogs to Facebook photos to product reviews -- user-generated content is where it stands".User-generated content-sharing platforms were the most important technological change that enabled the creation of fashion influencers, as will be discussed in detail below. Noricks (2010) foresaw the importance of social media in the fashion industry when he stated that it is another communication channel, alongside fashion magazines – "Social media platforms serve as an interactive medium to cover even fashion news and are no longer seen as an addition to print magazines. Members of social networking sites become the "new professionals" of the industry." Social media proved to be the most powerful tool for communicating all non-dress elements to the public, from values, standards, to private photos and snippets of the private lives of key industry players (Phillips (2008).

Social media helps fashion break away from the fashion industry itself – as hey help develop "social fashion", where know-how is applied to support art. Fashion bloggers and independent stylists are considered an integral part of brand marketing and promotion strategies. According to Agresta (2010), social media marketing also involves understanding consumers' online behavior. Print, radio and television advertising has now been replaced by social media advertising, which has become a major marketing channel. Today, people communicate through social networking sites, where peer ratings and opinions matter a lot.

4. DISCUSSION, CONCLUSION, AND RECOMMENDATIONS

Social media adoption levels and usage behavior are still in a state of constant change within the fashion industry there are a large number of studies trying to understand the level of impact that social media has on the fashion industry nowadays, and especially on consumer behavior. This brief literature review provided the highlights from the existing body of knowledge in order to demonstrate the enormity of the topic and the possible ways one could follow in trying to understand the multifaceted connections between consumers and industry, with the involvement of social media. Another point equally important is the introduction of mobile devices and social media. When the two are combined, they create a key new player in the fashion business environment. In the following section, this connection will be analyzed in detail.

Digital technologies allow individuals to produce a say in fashion and are a means of engaging in the fashion industry to generate financial and cultural capital, as has been widely argued in relation to fashion blogging (Rocamora, 2018). de Perthuis and Findlay (2019) present a critical analysis of the modern ideal and the specific stunning of fashion photography influenced by the activities of Instagram influencers. If anyone can open an account on Instagram, what are the forces that signal the account's popularity? What makes one account more influential than another? It's the conservative aesthetic and adherence to the ideals set by the fashion industry, not the innovative, liberating, free-willed choices sometimes portrayed by influencers "- The influencer's position in space and time, while imaginary, remains underpinned by commercial logics that reinforce hegemonic aesthetics"). However, this aesthetic shapes an ideal of people, places and products, and this is the research theme of Aljukhadar, Bériault Poirier and Senecal (2020). In their research, they show that imaginary consumption is strongly present in social media use. They define the aesthetic value of consumption (inspiration, sense of inwardness and entertainment) as a central driver of social media use and a key concept of e-commerce. This is in line with the findings of Kusumasondjaja (2020) study, which examined the strategic importance of visual aesthetics and presentation for consumer reactions to luxury fashion brand content posted on Instagram. Not surprisingly, "brand posts using images of expressive aesthetics received more likes and comments on Instagram than those with a classic aesthetic. Video content received more likes and comments than static content.

Influencers are public figures with a significant following on social media who use their profile to beautify and leverage their lifestyles in a variety of ways – through posting sponsored content, ads, and participating in brand partnerships – thereby promoting brand awareness among their followers. As Instagram has become a website that consumers use to engage in fashion, influencers have also become intermediaries between fashion producers and their target market.

This change has important implications, as the link between fashion companies and consumers is less in the hands of product/service producers and traditional promoters and more in the hands of influential professionals. This means that the process of creating meaning that strongly influences consumer behavior and the consequent purchasing decision is constructed in complex relationships between influencers themselves and the public, in the digital space and facilitated by social media platforms. In the context of the fashion industry, then, what influencers leverage is the engagement of their followers with specific brands, as their posts act as an invitation for their followers to identify with them, pursue their lifestyle and imitate them through targeted consumption? Uniquely positioned to harness social media's supposed qualities of authenticity and immediacy to like-minded people over whom they have a kind of detached effect, influencers are part of a direct-to-consumer marketing style. Their position in the fashion sector is therefore ambiguous, as their work fulfils the qualities of both professional and amateur: they produce professional-level content that mimics the look, feel and discourse of professional media about fashion, but for the most part they do so without working or having previously worked in this field. The results also show that electronic Word of mouth is quite important and certainly leads to positive consumer decisions. With this in mind, companies, either directly or through influencers, should create ample opportunities for clients to share their experiences, create eWoM, or engage directly with the brand. The implications of this study, in addition to highlighting the importance of influencers, the most important fruit of social networking sites, are the realization of how much influencers' perceived honesty shapes consumer trust and brand loyalty, leading to positive purchasing decisions.

The fashion industry is going through a transformation when it comes to advertising on social media, and the future looks bright for the fashion industry's connection to them. For brands and designers joining social networking sites, the benefits are many. In addition to a free PR tool, they also connect potential buyers with merchants. Emerging designers, as well as high-quality companies use social media as one of their marketing strategies. On the other hand, the passion with which consumers have embraced these media is remarkable and has contributed to the creation of a new and important player in the field, this influencer. The most significant changes in both the fashion industry and consumer behavior came from the involvement of influencers, who were able to take advantage of the features of Web 2.0 and become important commentators and opinion leaders in the fashion sector, influencing consumer behavior and purchasing decisions. This connection between the fashion industry and consumers, mediated by influencers, is linked to the context of digital and Web 2.0.

As a whole, we can argue that social media marketing has made a number of advances and improvements in its digital strategy, and therefore fashion companies are advised to be aware of the benefits and drawbacks of the digital tools they use in order to make the best use of them. Consumers around the world choose mobile devices as their preferred means to connect with other people, gather information, and more. As a result, many businesses are actively working on new mobile marketing strategies to reach their audience.

REFERENCES

Agresta, S. (2010). *Perspectives on Social Media Marketing*. Cengage Learning.

Al-Emadi, F. A., & Yahia, I. B. (2020). Ordinary celebrities related criteria to harvest fame and influence on social media. *Journal of Research in Interactive Marketing*, *14*(2), 195–213. doi:10.1108/JRIM-02-2018-0031

Alexa. (2021). *The top 500 sites on the web*. https://www.alexa.com/topsites

Aljukhadar, M., Bériault Poirier, A., & Senecal, S. (2020). Imagery makes social media captivating! Aesthetic value in a consumer-as-value-maximizer framework. *Journal of Research in Interactive Marketing*, *14*(3), 285–303. doi:10.1108/JRIM-10-2018-0136

Bauman, Z. (2000). *Liquid Modernity*. Polity.

Belk, R. W. (2016). The Extended Self in a Digital World. *Current Opinion in Psychology*, *10*, 50–54. doi:10.1016/j.copsyc.2015.11.003

Bern, T. (2020). *Social Media Trends Report: Key Insights From Q3 2020*. https://www.socialbakers.com/blog/social-media-trends-report-q3-2020

Bickart, B., & Schindler, R. M. (2001). Internet forums as influential sources of consumer information. *Journal of Interactive Marketing*, *15*(3), 31–40. doi:10.1002/dir.1014

Brasel, S. A., & Gibbs, J. (2013). Tablets, touchscreens, and touchpads: How varying touch interfaces trigger psychological ownership and endowment. *Journal of Consumer Psychology*, *23*(2), 226–233. doi:10.1016/j.jcps.2013.10.003

Broadband. (2021). *Mobile vs Desktop Internet Usage*. https://www.broadbandsearch.net/blog/mobile-desktop-internet-usage-statistics

Cantallops, A. S., & Salvi, F. (2014). New Consumer Behavior: A Review of Research on eWOM and Hotels. *International Journal of Hospitality Management*, *36*, 41–51. doi:10.1016/j.ijhm.2013.08.007

Castells, M. (2011a). *The power of identity: The information age: Economy, society, and culture* (Vol. 2). John Wiley & Sons.

Castells, M. (2011b). *The rise of the network society: The information age: Economy, society, and culture* (Vol. 1). John Wiley & Sons.

Cavazza, F. (2010) *Social Media Landscape 2011*. http://www.fredcavazza.net/2010/12/14/social-media-landscape-2011/

Chevalier, J. A., & Mayzlin, D. (2006). The effect of word of mouth on sales: Online book reviews. *JMR, Journal of Marketing Research*, *43*(3), 345–354. doi:10.1509/jmkr.43.3.345

Constantinides, E., & Fountain, S. (2008). Web 2.0: Conceptual foundations and marketing issues. *Journal of Direct, Data and Digital Marketing Practice*, *9*(3), 231–244. doi:10.1057/palgrave.dddmp.4350098

De Perthuis, K., & Findlay, R. (2019). How Fashion Travels: The Fashionable Ideal in the Age of Instagram. *Fashion Theory*, *23*(2), 219–242. doi:10.1080/1362704X.2019.1567062

De Valck, K., Van Bruggen, G., & Wierenga, B. (2009). Virtual communities: A marketing perspective. *Decision Support Systems*, *47*(3), 185–203. doi:10.1016/j.dss.2009.02.008

Dellarocas, C., Zhang, X. M., & Awad, N. F. (2007). Exploring the value of online product reviews in forecasting sales: The case of motion pictures. *Journal of Interactive Marketing*, *21*(4), 23–45. doi:10.1002/dir.20087

Eisingerich, A. B., Chun, H., Liu, Y., Jia, H., & Bell, S. J. (2015). Why recommend a brand face-to-face but not on Facebook? How word-of-mouth on online social sites differs from traditional word-of-mouth. *Journal of Consumer Psychology*, *25*(1), 120–128. doi:10.1016/j.jcps.2014.05.004

Featherstone, M. (1991). *Consumer Culture and Postmodernism*. Sage.

Fischer, E., & Reuber, A. R. (2011). Social interaction via new social media: (How) can interactions on Twitter affect effectual thinking and behavior? *Journal of Business Venturing*, *26*(1), 1–18. doi:10.1016/j.jbusvent.2010.09.002

Fiske, J. (1989). *Understanding Popular Culture*. Routledge.

Fotis, J. (2015) *The use of social media and its impacts on consumer behaviour: the xontext of holiday travel* [PhD dissertation]. Bournemouth University.

Gardner, J. (2008). Blogs, wikis and official statistics: New perspectives on the use of Web 2.0 by statistical offices. *Statistical Journal of the IAOS: Journal of the International Association for Official Statistics*, *25*(3), 81–92.

Gómez-Suárez, M., Pilar Martinez-Ruiz, M., & Martinez-Caraballo, N. (2017). Consumer-Brand Relationships under the Marketing 3.0 Paradigm: A Literature Review. *Frontiers in Psychology*, *8*(252), 1–4. doi:10.3389/fpsyg.2017.00252 PMID:28275360

Jalilvand, M. R., & Samiei, N. (2012). The impact of electronic word of mouth on a tourism destination choice: Testing the theory of planned behavior (TPB). *Internet Research*, *22*(5), 591–612. doi:10.1108/10662241211271563

James, P., & Szeman, I. (2010). Globalization and Culture: Vol. 3. *Global-Local Consumption*. Sage Publications.

Kaplan, A., & Haenlein, M. (2010). Users of the World, Unite! The Challenges and Opportunities of Social Media. *Business Horizons*, *53*(1), 59–68. doi:10.1016/j.bushor.2009.09.003

Kemp, S. (2020) *Digital 2020: 3.8 billion people use social media*. https://wearesocial.com/blog/2020/01/digital-2020-3-8-billion-people-use-social-media

Kim, W. G., Jeong, O. R., & Lee, S. W. (2010). On social Web sites. *Information Systems*, *35*(2), 215–236. doi:10.1016/j.is.2009.08.003

Kusumasondjaja, S. (2020). Exploring the role of visual aesthetics and presentation modality in luxury fashion brand communication on Instagram. *Journal of Fashion Marketing and Management, 24*(1), 15–31. doi:10.1108/JFMM-02-2019-0019

Kwak, H., Lee, C., Park, H., & Moon, S. (2010) What is Twitter, a social network or a news media? In *Proceedings of the 19th International Conference on World Wide Web (WWW2010)*. ACM. 10.1145/1772690.1772751

Lamberton, C. P., Naylor, R. W., & Haws, K. L. (2013). Same destination, different paths: When and how does observing others' choices and reasoning alter confidence in our own choices? *Journal of Consumer Psychology, 23*(1), 74–89. doi:10.1016/j.jcps.2012.01.002

Lambrecht, A., & Tucker, C. (2013). When does retargeting work? Information specificity in online advertising. *Journal of Marketing, 50*, 561–576.

Lin, H. C., Bruning, P. F., & Swarna, H. (2018). Using online opinion leaders to promote the hedonic and utilitarian value of products and services. *Business Horizons, 61*(3), 431–442. doi:10.1016/j.bushor.2018.01.010

MacInnis, D., & Folkes, V. (2009). The Disciplinary Status of Consumer Behavior: A Sociology of Science Perspective on Key Controversies. *The Journal of Consumer Research, 36*(6), 899–914. doi:10.1086/644610

McCarthy, S. (2013). *The Effects of Social Media on Fashion Consumption*. Honors Theses, Sally McDonnell Barksdale Honors College.

McLean, P. (2016). *Culture in Networks*. Wiley.

McQuarrie, E. F., Miller, J., & Phillips, B. J. (2013). The megaphone effect: Taste and audience in fashion blogging. *The Journal of Consumer Research, 40*(1), 136–158. doi:10.1086/669042

McQuarrie, E. F., & Phillips, B. J. (2014). The Megaphone Effect in Social Media: How Ordinary Consumers Become Style Leaders. *GfK MIR, 6*(2), 16–20. doi:10.2478/gfkmir-2014-0092

Miller, V. (2020). *Understanding Digital Culture* (2nd ed.). Sage.

Park, J., Ciampaglia, G. L., & Ferrara, E. (2016) Style in the Age of Instagram Predicting Success within the Fashion Industry using Social Media. *Proceedings of the 19th ACM Conference on Computer-Supported Cooperative Work & Social Computing*, 64-73. 10.1145/2818048.2820065

Parker, C. (2011). *301 ways to use social media to boost your marketing*. McGraw-Hill.

Pew. (2021). *Social Media Fact Sheet*. https://www.pewresearch.org/internet/fact-sheet/social-media/

Phillips, D. (2008). The psychology of social media. *Journal of New Communications Research, 3*(1), 79–85.

Pinchot, J., Paullet, K., & Rota, D. (2011). How Mobile Technology is Changing Our Culture. *Journal of Information Systems Applied Research, 4*(1), 39–48.

Poel, T. (2009). Conceptualizing forums and blogs as public spheres. In M. V. D. Boomen, S. Lammes, A. S. Lehmann, J. Raessens, & M. T. Schafer (Eds.), *Digital material: tracing new media in everyday life and technology* (pp. 239–251). Amsterdam University Press.

Rocamora, A. (2018). The Labour of Fashion Blogging. In L. Armstrong & F. McDowell (Eds.), *Fashioning Professionals: Identity and Representation at Work in the Creative Industries* (pp. 65–81). doi:10.5040/9781350001879.ch-004

Schumann, J. H., von Wangenheim, F., & Groene, N. (2014). Targeted online advertising: Using reciprocity appeals to increase acceptance among users of free web services. *Journal of Marketing*, *78*(1), 59–75. doi:10.1509/jm.11.0316

Statista. (2021) *Daily time spent with the internet per capita worldwide from 2011 to 2021*. https://www.statista.com/statistics/319732/daily-time-spent-online-device/

Stephen, T. A. (2016). The role of digital and social media marketing in consumer behavior. *Current Opinion in Psychology*, *10*, 17–21. doi:10.1016/j.copsyc.2015.10.016

Tjhin, V.U., &Aini, S.R. (2019). *Effect of E-WOM and Social Media Usage on Purchase Decision in Clothing Industry*. doi:10.1145/3332324.3332333

Tucker, C. E. (2014). Social networks, personalized advertising, and privacy controls. *JMR, Journal of Marketing Research*, *51*(5), 546–562. doi:10.1509/jmr.10.0355

Compilation of References

Aaker, D. A. (2009). *Managing brand equity*. Simon and Schuster.

Abd El-Jawad, M. H., Hodhod, R., & Omar, Y. M. (2018, December). Sentiment analysis of social media networks using machine learning. In *2018 14th international computer engineering conference (ICENCO)* (pp. 174-176). IEEE. 10.1109/ICENCO.2018.8636124

Abd Rahman, N. H., Khalifah, Z., & Ismail, H. N. (2015). Conceptual framework for experiences' quality based on senses' perception with behaviour as a mediator: In the context of cultural heritage attractions. *Advanced Science Letters*, *21*(5), 1135–1140. doi:10.1166/asl.2015.6017

Abdullah, T., Siti, N. S. D., Zainuddin, S. A., Azmi, N. F., & Siti, A. S. (2020). Impact Of Social Media Influencer On Instagram User Purchase Intention Towards The Fashion Products: The Perspectives Of Students. *European Journal of Molecular & Clinical Medicine*, *7*(8), 1–10. https://www.ejmcm.com/article_4700_1df3f69fec2f7e3402c757af9e91f3ae.pdf

Abdullah, T., Deraman, S. N. S., Zainuddin, S. A., Azmi, N. F., Abdullah, S. S., Anuar, N. I. M., ... Hasan, H. (2020). Impact of Social Media Influencer on Instagram User Purchase Intention towards the Fashion Products: The Perspectives of UMK Pengkalan Chepa Campus Students. *European Journal of Molecular and Clinical Medicine*.

Abel, E., Bogatu, A., Civili, C., Fernandes, A. A., Koehler, M., Konstantinou, N., & Paton, N. W. (2017, December). Data context informed data wrangling. In *2017 IEEE International Conference on Big Data (Big Data)* (pp. 956-963). IEEE.

Abraham, A., & Patro, S. (2014). 'Country-of-origin' effect and consumer decision-making. *Management and Labour Studies*, *39*(3), 309–318. doi:10.1177/0258042X15572408

Acar, A., & Harmankaya, H. (2021). İnternet ortamındaki tüketici yorumlarının üniversite öğrencilerinin giysi satın alma davranışlarına etkisinin incelenmesi. *Sanat ve Tasarım Araştırmaları Dergisi*, *2*(3), 10–21.

Adebambo, S., & Toyin, A. I. (2011). Analysis of information and communication technologies (ICT) usage on logistics activities of manufacturing companies in southwestern Nigeria. *Journal of Emerging Trends in Economics and Management Science*, *2*, 68–74.

Adoeng, W., Kalangi, J.B., & Wangke, S.J. (2019). A comparative analysis of E-advertisement between jd. Id and shopee customers in Manado. *Jurnal EMBA: Jurnal Riset Ekonomi, Manajemen, Bisnis dan Akuntansi, 7*(3).

Ağaç, S. D., Sevinir, S., & Yılmaz, T. (2018). Online giyim alışverişinde tüketicilerin karşılaştıkları sorunların cinsiyet değişkenine göre incelenmesi. *Karadeniz Teknik Üniversitesi Sosyal Bilimler Enstitüsü Dergisi*, *8*(15), 57–71.

Ağaç, S., & Solak, C. Ö. (2016). Üniversite öğrencilerinin online giyisi alışveriş davranışlarının incelenmesi. *Selçuk Üniversitesi Sosyal Bilimler Enstitüsü Dergisi*, *36*, 142–151.

Agrawal, S., Das, A., Dhage, S., & Gaikwad, A. (2018, July). Customer churn prediction modelling based on behavioural patterns analysis using deep learning. In *2018 International conference on smart computing and electronic enterprise (ICSCEE)* (pp. 1-6). IEEE. 10.1109/ICSCEE.2018.8538420

Agresta, S. (2010). *Perspectives on Social Media Marketing*. Cengage Learning.

Ahmad, N., Salman, A., & Ashiq, R. (2015). The impact of social media on fashion industry: Empirical investigation from Karachiites. *Journal of Resources Development and Management, 7*.

Ahmad, A., Farman, H., Imran, M., Islam, I. U., Jan, B., Jeon, G., & Khan, M. (2019). Deep learning in big data analytics: A comparative study. *Computers & Electrical Engineering, 75*, 275–287. doi:10.1016/j.compeleceng.2017.12.009

Ahmad, N., Salman, A., & Ashiq, R. (2015). The impact of social media on fashion industry: Empirical investigation from Karachiites. *Journal of Resources Development and Management, 7*, 1–7.

Ahmed, R. R., Streimikiene, D., Berchtold, G., Vveinhardt, J., Channar, Z. A., & Soomro, R. H. (2019). Effectiveness of online digital media advertising as a strategic tool for building brand sustainability: Evidence from FMCGs and services sectors of Pakistan. *Sustainability (Basel), 11*(12), 3436. doi:10.3390u11123436

Ahmed, W. A. H., & MacCarthy, B. L. (2021). Blockchain-Enabled Supply Chain Traceability in the Textile and Apparel Supply Chain: A Case Study of the Fiber Producer, Lenzing. *Sustainability (Basel), 13*(19), 10496. doi:10.3390u131910496

Aitken, R., & Campelo, A. (2011). The four Rs of place branding. *Journal of Marketing Management, 27*(9-10), 913–933. doi:10.1080/0267257X.2011.560718

Ajayan, A. R., Al-Doghman, F., & Chaczko, Z. (2018, December). Visualizing Multimodal Big Data Anomaly Patterns in Higher-Order Feature Spaces. In *2018 26th International Conference on Systems Engineering (ICSEng)* (pp. 1-9). IEEE. 10.1109/ICSENG.2018.8638195

Ajzen, I., & Fishbein, M. (1980). *Understanding Attitudes and predicting social Behavior*. Prentice- Hall.

Akar, E. (2010). *Sosyal medya pazarlaması*. Efil Yayınevi.

Akel, G. (2015). *Tüketicilerin internetten satın alma niyeti üzerine bir çalışma: Adnan Menderes Üniversitesi örneği*. Pamukkale Üniversitesi Sosyal Bilimler Enstitüsü, Yayınlanmış Yüksek Lisans Tezi.

Akkaya, D. (2013). *Sosyal medya reklamları: tüketici algılarının tutum, davranış ve satın alma niyeti üzerine etkisi*. Yayınlanmamış Doktora Tezi, Trakya Üniversitesi Sosyal Bilimler Enstitüsü.

Akram, U., Ansari, A. R., Fu, G., & Junaid, M. (2020). Feeling hungry? let's order through mobile! examining the fast food mobile commerce in China. *Journal of Retailing and Consumer Services, 56*, 102142. doi:10.1016/j.jretconser.2020.102142

Aldhmour, F., & Sarayrah, I. (2016). An investigation of factors influencing consumers? Intention to use online shopping: An empirical study in south of Jordan. *Journal of Internet Banking and Commerce*, 21.

Aldlaigan, A., & Buttle, F. (2005). Beyond satisfaction: Customer attachment to retail banks. *International Journal of Bank Marketing, 23*(4), 349–359. doi:10.1108/02652320510603960

Al-Emadi, F. A., & Yahia, I. B. (2020). Ordinary celebrities related criteria to harvest fame and influence on social media. *Journal of Research in Interactive Marketing, 14*(2), 195–213. doi:10.1108/JRIM-02-2018-0031

Alexa. (2021). *The top 500 sites on the web*. https://www.alexa.com/topsites

Algharabat, R., Rana, N. P., Alalwan, A. A., Baabdullah, A., & Gupta, A. (2020). Investigating the antecedents of customer brand engagement and consumer-based brand equity in social media. *Journal of Retailing and Consumer Services, 53*, 101767. doi:10.1016/j.jretconser.2019.01.016

Algür, S., & Cengiz, F. (2011). Türk tüketicilere göre online (çevrimiçi) alışverişin riskleri ve yararları. *Journal of Yasar University, 6*(22), 3666–3680.

Alhabash, S., McAlister, A. R., Lou, C., & Hagerstrom, A. (2015). From clicks to behaviors: The mediating effect of intentions to like, share, and comment on the relationship between message evaluations and offline behavioral intentions. *Journal of Interactive Advertising, 15*(2), 82–96. doi:10.1080/15252019.2015.1071677

Alhidari, A., Iyer, P., & Paswan, A. (2015). Personal level antecedents of eWOM and purchase intention, on social networking sites. *Journal of Customer Behaviour, 14*(2), 107–125. doi:10.1362/147539215X14373846805707

Aljifri, H. A., Pons, A., & Collins, D. (2003). Global e-commerce: A framework for understanding and overcoming the trust barrier. *Information Management & Computer Security, 11*(2–3), 130–138. doi:10.1108/09685220310480417

Aljukhadar, M., Bériault Poirier, A., & Senecal, S. (2020). Imagery makes social media captivating! Aesthetic value in a consumer-as-value-maximizer framework. *Journal of Research in Interactive Marketing, 14*(3), 285–303. doi:10.1108/JRIM-10-2018-0136

Almansoori, M. K., & Habtoor, N. (2018). The role of social media in crisis preparedness and responses. *International Journal of Engine Research, 9*, 1347–1353.

Alomoush, K. S., Yaseen, S. G., & Alma'aitah, M. A. (2012). The Impact of Arab Cultural Values on Online Social Networking: The Case of Facebook. *World Academy of Science, Engineering and Technology*, 67.

Alshibly, H. (2014). An Empirical Investigation into Factors Influencing the Intention to Use E-learning System: An Extended Technology Acceptance Model. *British Journal of Applied Science and Technology, 4*. Advance online publication. doi:10.9734/BJAST/2014/10033

Altındal, M. (2013). Dijital pazarlamada marka yönetimi ve sosyal medyanın etkileri. In Akademik Bilişim, XV. Akademik Bilişim Konferansı Bildirileri (pp.1147-1151). Akdeniz Üniversitesi Antalya.

Altunışık, R., Sütütemiz, N., & Çallı, L. (2010). E-memnuniyeti etkileyen performans kriterlerinin tespiti üzerine bir araştırma (e-perakendecilik örneği). *Akademik Bakış Dergisi, 6*, 85–105.

Amed, I., Balchandani, A., Berg, A., Hedrich, S., Jensen, J. E., Le Merle, L., & Rölkens, F. (2022). *State of Fashion 2022.* McKinsey's Retail Practice. https://www.stateoffashion.org/en/

Amed, I., Balchandani, A., Berg, A., Hedrich, S., Jensen, J. E., & Rölkens, F. (2020). *It's time to rewire the fashion system: State of Fashion coronavirus update*. McKinsey & Company.

Anand, A., Dutta, S., & Mukherjee, P. (2022). Influencer marketing with fake followers. *IIM Bangalore Research Paper*, (580). https://repository.iimb.ac.in/bitstream/2074/8180/1/WP_IIMB_580.pdf

Ananda, A. S. (2019). *Analysis of consumer-brand engagement with fashion brands in social media* [Doctoral dissertation]. Universidad Politécnica de Madrid.

Ananda, A. S., Hernandez-García, Á., & Lamberti, L. (2015). Fashion in actions on social media – Spanish SME fashion brands case studies. *Proceedings of the European Conference on e-Learning*, 488-497.

Anderson, M., & Brook, A. (2021). Social Media Use in 2021. *Pew Research Center, 1*, 1–4. https://www.pewresearch.org/internet/2021/04/07/social-media-use-in-2021/

Annaldewar, B. N., Jadhav, N. C., & Jadhav, A. C. (2021). Impact of covıd-19 on sustainability in textile & clothing sectors. In S. S. Muthu (Ed.), *COVID-19. Environmental footprints and eco-design of products and processes*. Springer. doi:10.1007/978-981-16-3860-2_4

Annareddy, S., & Tammina, S. (2020, January). Sentiment analysis on customer reviews using convolutional neural network. In *2020 International Conference on Computer Communication and Informatics (ICCCI)* (pp. 1-6). IEEE.

Apparel Search Company. (2006). Fashion Blogs Definition. *Apparel Search*. https://www.apparelsearch.com/definitions/fashion/fahion_blogs_definition.htm

Aramendia-Muneta, M. E. (2017). Spread the word – The effect of word of mouth in e-Marketing. In G. Siegert, M. B. Von Rimscha, & S. Grubenmann (Eds.), *Commercial Communication in the Digital Age* (pp. 227–245). De Gruyter. doi:10.1515/9783110416794-013

Aramendia-Muneta, M. E., Olarte-Pascual, C., & Ollo-López, A. (2021). Key image attributes to elicit likes and comments on Instagram. *Journal of Promotion Management, 27*(1), 50–76. doi:10.1080/10496491.2020.1809594

Arcury, T. A., & Johnson, T. P. (1987). Public environmental knowledge a statewide survey. *The Journal of Environmental Education, 18*(4), 31–37. doi:10.1080/00958964.1987.9942746

Arduini, S., & Paoloni, P. (2020). The IT strategy in the luxury sector: The case of a fashion company. *Springer Proceedings in Business and Economics,* 211-226. 10.1007/978-3-030-46874-3_12

Argyris, Y. A., Muqaddam, A., & Miller, S. (2021). The effects of the visual presentation of an influencer's extroversion on perceived credibility and purchase intentions—Moderated by personality matching with the audience. *Journal of Retailing and Consumer Services, 59*, 102347. Advance online publication. doi:10.1016/j.jretconser.2020.102347

Armstrong, C. M. J., & Park, H. (2020). Online Clothing Resale: A Practice Theory Approach to Evaluate Sustainable Consumption Gains. *Journal of Sustainability Research, 2*(2). Advance online publication. doi:10.20900/jsr20200017

Arslan, B. (2016). Sanal mağaza atmosferi unsurlarının anlık satın almaya etkisi. *Bitlis Eren Üniversitesi Sosyal Bilimler Enstitüsü Dergisi, 5*(1), 117–136.

Arslan, O. (2020). *Hazır giyim sektörünün sosyal medyada kullandığı pazarlama stratejilerinin analizi*. Yüksek Lisans Tezi, İstanbul Sabahattin Zaim Üniversitesi Sosyal Bilimler Enstitüsü.

Ashfaq, M., & Ali, M. (2017). Impact of celebrity endorsement on consumer buying behavior in FMCG sector of Pakistan. *Arabian Journal of Business and Management Review, 7*(1), 1–12. doi:10.12816/0041744

Ashley, C., & Tuten, T. (2015). Creative strategies in social media marketing: An exploratory study of branded social content and consumer engagement. *Psychology and Marketing, 32*(1), 15–27. doi:10.1002/mar.20761

Attfield, S., Kazai, G., Lalmas, M., & Piwowarski, B. (2011, February). Towards a science of user engagement (position paper). In WSDM workshop on user modelling for Web applications (Vol. 1). Academic Press.

Audrezet, A., De Kerviler, G., & Moulard, J. G. (2020). Authenticity under threat: When social media influencers need to go beyond self-presentation. *Journal of Business Research, 117*, 557–569. doi:10.1016/j.jbusres.2018.07.008

Avadanei, M., Olaru, S., Ionescu, I., Ursache, M., Ciobanu, L., Alexa, L., Luca, A. V., Olmos, M., Aslanidis, T., Beļakova, D., & Silva, C. (2020). ICT new tools for a sustainable textile and clothing industry. *Industria Textila (Bucuresti), 71*(5), 504–512. doi:10.35530/IT.071.05.1811

Aydın, E. (2019). *İnternet tüketicilerinin hazır giyim satın alma davranışları üzerine bir araştırma*. Yüksek Lisans Tezi, Kastamonu Üniversitesi Sosyal Bilimler Enstitüsü, Kastamonu.

Aydin, I., & Salur, M. U. (2020). A novel hybrid deep learning model for sentiment classification. *IEEE Access : Practical Innovations, Open Solutions*, *8*, 58080–58093. doi:10.1109/ACCESS.2020.2982538

Baas, J., Schotten, M., Plume, A., Côté, G., & Karimi, R. (2020). Scopus as a curated, high-quality bibliometric data source for academic research in quantitative science studies. *Quantitative Science Studies*, *1*(1), 377–386. doi:10.1162/qss_a_00019

Baek, T. H., Yoo, C. Y., & Yoon, S. (2018). Augment yourself through virtual mirror: The impact of self-viewing and narcissism on consumer responses. *International Journal of Advertising*, *37*(3), 421–439. doi:10.1080/02650487.2016.1244887

Bailey, James, & Pearson, W., Sammy. (1983). Development of a Tool for Measuring and Analyzing Computer User Satisfaction. *Management Science*, *29*, 530–545. doi:10.1287/mnsc.29.5.530

Bakhshi, S., Shamma, D. A., & Gilbert, E. (2014). Faces engage us: Photographs with faces attract more likes and comments on Instagram. *Proceedings of the 32nd Annual ACM Conference on Human Factors in Computing Systems - CHI '14*, 965–974. 10.1145/2556288.2557403

Bao, F., Dai, Q., Deng, Y., Kong, Y., Ren, Z., & Suo, J. (2019). Learning deep landmarks for imbalanced classification. *IEEE Transactions on Neural Networks and Learning Systems*, *31*(8), 2691–2704. doi:10.1109/TNNLS.2019.2927647 PMID:31395564

Bao, T., & Chang, T. L. S. (2014). Finding disseminators via electronic word of mouth message for effective marketing communications. *Decision Support Systems*, *67*, 21–29. doi:10.1016/j.dss.2014.07.006

Baptista, J., Wilson, A. D., Galliers, R. D., & Bynghall, S. (2017). Social media and the emergence of reflexiveness as a new capability for open strategy. *Long Range Planning*, *50*(3), 322–336. doi:10.1016/j.lrp.2016.07.005

Barefoot, D., & Szabo, J. (2009). *Friends with benefits: A social media marketing handbook*. No Starch Press.

Barreda, A. A., Bilgihan, A., Nusair, K., & Okumus, F. (2015). Generating brand awareness in Online Social Networks. *Computers in Human Behavior*, *50*, 600–609. doi:10.1016/j.chb.2015.03.023

Bauer, P. C., Barbera, K. A. C., & Venetz, A. (2017). Is the left-right scale a valid measure of ideology? Individual level variation in associations with 'left' and 'right' and left-right self-placement. *Political Behavior*, *39*(3), 553–583. doi:10.100711109-016-9368-2

Bauman, Z. (2000). *Liquid Modernity*. Polity.

Baumgarth, C., Kirkby, A., & Kaibel, C. (2021). When fake becomes real: The innovative case of artificial influencers. Creativity and marketing: The fuel for success, 149-167. doi:10.1108/978-1-80071-330-720211010

Baytar, F., Chung, T., & Shin, E. (2020). Evaluating garments in augmented reality when shopping online. *Journal of Fashion Marketing and Management*, *24*(4), 667–683. doi:10.1108/JFMM-05-2018-0077

Bazaki, E., & Cedrola, E. (2023). *Becoming a fashion blogger entrepreneur: The case of Chiara Ferragni*. doi:10.1007/978-3-031-11185-3_6

Belk, R. W. (2016). The Extended Self in a Digital World. *Current Opinion in Psychology*, *10*, 50–54. doi:10.1016/j.copsyc.2015.11.003

Benetton Group. (2019). *Integrated report 2018*. Retrieved February 9, 2020 from http://assets.benettongroup.com/wp-content/uploads/2019/06/Integrated_Report_2018_.pdf

Bennett, S., Maton, K., & Kervin, L. (2008). The digital natives' debate: A critical review of the evidence. *British Journal of Educational Technology, 39*(5), 775–786.

Bergkvist, L., Hjalmarson, H., Mägi, A. W., & Bergkvist, L. (2016). *A new model of how celebrity endorsements work: Attitude toward the endorsement as a mediator of celebrity source and endorsement effects.* Academic Press.

Bern, T. (2020). *Social Media Trends Report: Key Insights From Q3 2020.* https://www.socialbakers.com/blog/social-media-trends-report-q3-2020

Berni, R., Nikiforova, N. D., & Ranfagni, S. (2020). An integrated approach to estimate brand association matching and strength in virtual settings. *Journal of Global Fashion Marketing, 11*(2), 117–136. doi:10.1080/20932685.2019.1706608

Berthon, P. R., Pitt, L. F., Plangger, K., & Shapiro, D. (2012). Marketing meets Web 2.0, social media, and creative consumers: Implications for international marketing strategy. *Business Horizons, 55*(3), 261–271. doi:10.1016/j.bushor.2012.01.007

Bharti, M. (2021). E-business through social media: An instagram page attribute-conversion model in context of fashion apparel industry. *Global Business Review.* Advance online publication. doi:10.1177/09721509211038832

Bickart, B., & Schindler, R. M. (2001). Internet forums as influential sources of consumer information. *Journal of Interactive Marketing, 15*(3), 31–40. doi:10.1002/dir.1014

Biørn-Hansen, A., Rieger, C., Grønli, T.-M., Majchrzak, T. A., & Ghinea, G. (2020). An empirical investigation of performance overhead in cross-platform mobile development frameworks. *Empirical Software Engineering, 25*(4), 2997–3040. doi:10.100710664-020-09827-6

Birdsall, W. F. (2007). Web 2.0 as a social movement. *Webology, 4*(2). http://www.webology.ir/2007/v4n2/a40.html

Blázquez, M. (2014). Fashion shopping in multichannel retail: The role of technology in enhancing the customer experience. *International Journal of Electronic Commerce, 18*(4), 97–116. doi:10.2753/JEC1086-4415180404

Blei, D. M., & Lafferty, J. D. (2006). Correlated Topic Models. *Advances in Neural Information Processing Systems, 18*, 1–47.

Blei, D. M., Ng, A. Y., & Jordan, M. I. (2003). Latent Dirichlet Allocation. *Journal of Machine Learning Research, 3*, 993–1022.

Boonghee, Y., Naveen, D., & Sungho, L. (2000). An Examination of Selected Marketing Mix Elements and Brand Equity. *Journal of the Academy of Marketing Science, 28*(2), 195–211. doi:10.1177/0092070300282002

Borker, D. R. (2014). Social media marketing in emerging economies: A Mongolian case study. *International Journal of Marketing Studies, 6*(2), 31. doi:10.5539/ijms.v6n2p31

Borland, H., & Akram, S. (2007). Age is no barrier to wanting to look good: Women on body image, age and advertising. *Qualitative Market Research, 10*(3), 310–333. doi:10.1108/13522750710754335

Boyapati, S., Dutt, V., Swarna, S. R., & Vyas, N. (2020, December). Big Data Approach for Medical Data Classification: A Review Study. In *2020 3rd International Conference on Intelligent Sustainable Systems (ICISS)* (pp. 762-766). IEEE. 10.1109/ICISS49785.2020.9315870

Boyd, D. M., & Ellison, N. B. (2008). Social network sites: Definition, history and scholarship. *Journal of Computer-Mediated Communication, 13*(1), 210–230.

Brachtendorf, C. (2022). Lil miquela in the folds of fashion: (ad-)dressing virtual influencers. *Fashion, Style & Popular Culture, 9*(4), 483–499. doi:10.1386/fspc_00157_1

Brand, B. M., & Baier, D. (2022). Measuring country of origin effects in online shopping implicitly: a discrete choice analysis approach. *International Marketing Review*.

Brasel, S. A., & Gibbs, J. (2013). Tablets, touchscreens, and touchpads: How varying touch interfaces trigger psychological ownership and endowment. *Journal of Consumer Psychology*, *23*(2), 226–233. doi:10.1016/j.jcps.2013.10.003

Brewster, M. L., & Sklar, M. (2022). 'Brand, community, lifestyle': Fashioning an authentic, body positive influencer brand on instagram. *Fashion, Style & Popular Culture*, *9*(4), 501–521. doi:10.1386/fspc_00158_1

Britt, R. K., Hayes, J. L., Britt, B. C., & Park, H. (2020). Too big to sell? A computational analysis of network and content characteristics among mega and micro beauty and fashion social media influencers. *Journal of Interactive Advertising*, *20*(2), 111–118. doi:10.1080/15252019.2020.1763873

Broadband. (2021). *Mobile vs Desktop Internet Usage*. https://www.broadbandsearch.net/blog/mobile-desktop-internet-usage-statistics

Bruce, M., & Krazt, C. (2012). Competitive marketing strategies of luxury fashion companies. In T. Hines & M. Bruce (Eds.), *Fashion Marketing: Contemporary Issues* (pp. 132–150). Taylor and Francis.

Bruwer, J., & Johnson, R. (2010). Place-based marketing and regional branding strategy perspectives in the California wine industry. *Journal of Consumer Marketing*, *27*(1), 5–16. doi:10.1108/07363761011012903

Bryman, A. (2016). *Social Research Methods* (5th ed.). Oxford University Press.

Brynjolfsson, E., & Yang, S. (1996). Information Technology and Productivity: A Review of the Literature. *Advances in Computers*, (43), 179-214.

Brynjolfsson, E., Hitt, L., & Yang, S. (2002). Intangible Assets: Computers and Organizational Capital. *Brookings Papers on Economic Activity*, *2002*(1), 137–1814. doi:10.1353/eca.2002.0003

Burmaster, A. (2009). *Global faces and networked places.* Online at: http://blog. nielsen. com/nielsenwire/wpcontent/uploads/2009/03/nielsen_globalfaces_mar09. pdf

Burt, S., & Gabbott, M. (1995). The elderly consumer and non-food purchase behaviour. *European Journal of Marketing*, *29*(2), 43–57. doi:10.1108/03090569510080941

Buttner, O. B., & Goritz, A. S. (2008). Perceived trustworthiness of online shops. *Journal of Consumer Behaviour*, *50*(October), 35–50. doi:10.1002/cb.235

Cabeza-Ramírez, L. J., Sánchez-Cañizares, S. M., Santos-Roldán, L. M., & Fuentes-García, F. J. (2022). Impact of the perceived risk in influencers' product recommendations on their followers' purchase attitudes and intention. *Technological Forecasting and Social Change*, *184*, 121997. Advance online publication. doi:10.1016/j.techfore.2022.121997

Cabigiosu, A. (2020). *The new consumers of luxury*. doi:10.1007/978-3-030-48810-9_3

Cachon, G. P., & Swinney, R. (2011). The value of fast fashion: Quick response, enhanced design, and strategic consumer behavior. *Management Science*, *57*(4), 778–795. doi:10.1287/mnsc.1100.1303

Çağlayan, V., Işıklar, Z., & Hassan, S. A. (2016). üniversite öğrencilerinin satın alma davranışlarında sosyal medya reklamlarının etkisi: Selçuk Üniversitesi'nde bir araştırma. *Selçuk Üniversitesi Sosyal ve Teknik Araştırmalar Dergisi*, *11*, 43–56.

Calheiros, A. C., Moro, S., & Rita, P. (2017). Sentiment classification of consumer-generated online reviews using topic modeling. *Journal of Hospitality Marketing & Management*, *26*(7), 675–693. doi:10.1080/19368623.2017.1310075

Campbell, C., & Farrell, J. R. (2020). More than meets the eye: The functional components underlying influencer marketing. *Business Horizons*, *63*(4), 469–479. doi:10.1016/j.bushor.2020.03.003

Canöz, K., Gülmez, Ö., & Eroğlu, G. (2020). Pazarlamanın yükselen yıldızı influencer marketing: Influencer takipçilerinin satın alma davranışını belirlemeye yönelik bir araştırma. *Selçuk Üniversitesi Sosyal Bilimler Meslek Yüksekokulu Dergisi*, *23*(1), 73–91. doi:10.29249elcuksbmyd.606009

Cantallops, A. S., & Salvi, F. (2014). New Consumer Behavior: A Review of Research on eWOM and Hotels. *International Journal of Hospitality Management*, *36*, 41–51. doi:10.1016/j.ijhm.2013.08.007

Cao, S., Chen, Y., Liu, W., & Zhu, X. (2019, October). Deep learning based customer churn analysis. In *2019 11th International Conference on Wireless Communications and Signal Processing (WCSP)* (pp. 1-6). IEEE. 10.1109/WCSP.2019.8927877

Carah, N., & Shaul, M. (2016). Brands and Instagram: Point, tap, swipe, glance. *Mobile Media & Communication*, *4*(1), 69–84. doi:10.1177/2050157915598180

Caraka, R. E., Chen, R. C., Dewi, C., & Huang, S. W. (2020). Selecting critical features for data classification based on machine learning methods. *Journal of Big Data*, *7*(1), 52. doi:10.118640537-020-00327-4

Casais, B., & Gomes, L. R. (2022). Fashion bloggers' discourse on brands under corporate crisis: A netnographic research in Portugal. *Journal of Fashion Marketing and Management*, *26*(3), 420–435. doi:10.1108/JFMM-09-2020-0206

Casaló, L. V., Flavián, C., & Ibáñez-Sánchez, S. (2020a). Influencers on Instagram: Antecedents and consequences of opinion leadership. *Journal of Business Research*, *117*, 510–519.

Casaló, L. V., Flavián, C., & Ibáñez-Sánchez, S. (2020b). Influencers on Instagram: Antecedents and consequences of opinion leadership. *Journal of Business Research*, *117*, 510–519.

Casaló, L. V., Flavián, C., & Ibáñez-Sánchez, S. (2020). Influencers on Instagram: Antecedents and consequences of opinion leadership. *Journal of Business Research*, *117*, 510–519. doi:10.1016/j.jbusres.2018.07.005

Cascone, S. (2021). *How Steve Madden Approaches eCommerce Marketing*. Retrieved March 20, 2023, from https://www.bluecore.com/blog/steve-madden-approaches-ecommerce-marketing/

Castells, M. (2011a). *The power of identity: The information age: Economy, society, and culture* (Vol. 2). John Wiley & Sons.

Castells, M. (2011b). *The rise of the network society: The information age: Economy, society, and culture* (Vol. 1). John Wiley & Sons.

Cavazza, F. (2010) *Social Media Landscape 2011*. http://www.fredcavazza.net/2010/12/14/social-media-landscape-2011/

Cervellon, M. C., & Wernerfelt, A. S. (2012). Knowledge sharing among green fashion communities online: Lessons for the sustainable supply chain. *Journal of Fashion Marketing and Management*, *16*(2), 176–192. doi:10.1108/13612021211222860

Chakraborty, U., & Bhat, S. (2018). The Effects of Credible Online Reviews on Brand Equity Dimensions and Its Consequence on Consumer Behavior. *Journal of Promotion Management*, *24*(1), 57–82. doi:10.1080/10496491.2017.1346541

Cha, M., Benevenuto, F., Haddadi, H., & Gummadi, K. P. (2012). The world of connections and information flow in Twitter. *IEEE Transactions on Systems, Man, and Cybernetics. Part A, Systems and Humans*, *42*(4), 991–998. doi:10.1109/TSMCA.2012.2183359

Chandelier, M., Steuckardt, A., Mathevet, R., Diwersy, S., & Gimenez, O. (2018). Content analysis of newspaper coverage of wolf recolonization in France using structural topic modeling. *Biological Conservation, 220*, 254–261. doi:10.1016/j.biocon.2018.01.029

Chang, H. J., & Watchravesringkan, K. (2018). Who are sustainably minded apparel shoppers? An investigation to the influencing factors of sustainable apparel consumption. *International Journal of Retail & Distribution Management, 46*(2), 148–162. doi:10.1108/IJRDM-10-2016-0176

Chang, T., & Wong, C. W. Y. (2012). The consumption side of sustainable fashion supply chain. *Journal of Fashion Marketing and Management, 16*(2), 193–215. doi:10.1108/13612021211222824

Charumilind, S., & Lamb, J. (2020). When will the COVID-19 pandemic end? *McKinsey & Company*. https://www.mckinsey.com/industries/healthcare/our-insights/when-will-the-covid-19-pandemic-end

Chaturvedi, A., & Laghate, G. (2021). *Festive ad spends on social media platforms expected to go up significantly this year*. Retrieved March 15, 2023, from https://economictimes.indiatimes.com/industry/services/advertising/festive-ad-spends-on-social-media-platforms-expected-to-go-up-significantly-this-year/articleshow/87164745.cms?from=mdr

Chatzidakis, A., McEachern, M. G., & Warnaby, G. (2018). Consumption in and of space and place: Introduction to the special issue. *Marketing Theory, 18*(2), 149–153. doi:10.1177/1470593117732452

Chaudhary, R., & Bisai, S. (2018). Factors influencing green purchase behavior of millennials in India. *Management of Environmental Quality, 29*(5), 798–812. doi:10.1108/MEQ-02-2018-0023

Chaudhry, P. E. (2022). Dupe influencers exploiting social media to peddle luxury fakes. *Business Horizons, 65*(6), 719–727. doi:10.1016/j.bushor.2022.07.005

Chau, P. Y. K., & Hu, P. J. H. (2001). Information technology acceptance by individual professionals: A model comparison approach. *Decision Sciences, 32*(4), 699–719.

Chen, C. (2019). Value Creation by SMEs Participating in Global Value Chains under Industry 4.0 Trend: Case Study of Textile Industry in Taiwan. *Journal of Global Information Technology Management, 22*(2), 120–145. doi:10.1080/1097198X.2019.1603512

Cheng, F., Liu, T., & Wu, C. (2013). Perceived risks and risk reduction strategies in online group-buying. *Proceedings of 2013 International Conference on Technology Innovation and Industrial Management*, 18-25.

Cheng, M., Liu, J., Qi, J., & Wan, F. (2021). Differential effects of firm generated content on consumer digital engagement and firm performance: An outside-in perspective. *Industrial Marketing Management, 98*, 41–58. doi:10.1016/j.indmarman.2021.07.001

Cheng, T., Lam, D., & Yeung, C. (2006). Adoption of internet banking: An empirical study in Hong Kong. *Decision Support Systems, 42*, 1158–1572.

Chen, J., Teng, L., Yu, Y., & Yu, X. (2016). The effect of online information sources on purchase intentions between consumers with high and low susceptibility to informational influence. *Journal of Business Research, 69*(2), 467–475. doi:10.1016/j.jbusres.2015.05.003

Chen, L., Yan, Y., & Smith, A. N. (2023). What drives digital engagement with sponsored videos? An investigation of video influencers' authenticity management strategies. *Journal of the Academy of Marketing Science, 51*(1), 198–221. doi:10.100711747-022-00887-2

Chetioui, Y., Benlafqih, H., & Lebdaoui, H. (2020). How fashion influencers contribute to consumers' purchase intention. *Journal of Fashion Marketing and Management, 24*(3), 361–380. doi:10.1108/JFMM-08-2019-0157

Cheung, M.-C. (2023). *Asia-Pacific Social Media Outlook 2023*. Insider Intelligence. Retrieved March 15, 2023, from https://www.insiderintelligence.com/content/asia-pacific-social-media-outlook-2023

Cheung, C. M. K., & Thadani, D. R. (2012). The impact of electronic word-of-mouth communication: A literature analysis and integrative model. *Decision Support Systems*, *54*(1), 461–470. doi:10.1016/j.dss.2012.06.008

Cheung, C. M., Lee, M. K., & Thadani, D. R. (2009). *The impact of positive electronic word-of-mouth on consumer online purchasing decision*. Springer Berlin Heidelberg. doi:10.1007/978-3-642-04754-1_51

Chevalier, J. A., & Mayzlin, D. (2006). The effect of word of mouth on sales: Online book reviews. *JMR, Journal of Marketing Research*, *43*(3), 345–354. doi:10.1509/jmkr.43.3.345

Chih, W. H., Wang, K. Y., Hsu, L. C., & Huang, S. C. (2013). Investigating electronic wordof-mouth effects on online discussion forums: The role of perceived positive electronic word-of-mouth review credibility. *Cyberpsychology, Behavior, and Social Networking*, *16*(9), 658–668. doi:10.1089/cyber.2012.0364 PMID:23895466

Chitra, K., & Sasikala, K. (2016). Social media marketing strategies for enhancing brand awareness: A study with reference to select startups. *Asian Journal of Research in Social Sciences and Humanities*, *6*(9), 1081–1095. doi:10.5958/2249-7315.2016.00856.X

Choi, Y., Yoon, S., Xuan, B., Lee, S. T., & Lee, K. (2021). Fashion informatics of the big 4 fashion weeks using topic modeling and sentiment analysis. *Fashion and Textiles*, *8*(1), 33. Advance online publication. doi:10.118640691-021-00265-6

Choobchain, S., Momtaz, A. M., & Farhadian, H. (2019). Gender differences of farmers in conflict with climate change. *International Journal of Scientific and Technology Research*, *8*(7), 359–363.

Chopra, Y. (2019). *How Instagram is changing the game for fashion*. Retrieved March 20, 2023, from https://www.vogue.in/content/how-instagram has changed the game-for-fashion

Chung, S., & Cho, H. (2017). Fostering parasocial relationships with celebrities on social media: Implications for celebrity endorsement. *Psychology and Marketing*, *34*(4), 481–495. doi:10.1002/mar.21001

Chu, S. C., & Kim, Y. (2011). Determinants of consumer engagement in electronic Word-OfMouth (eWOM) in social networking sites. *International Journal of Advertising*, *30*(1), 47–75. doi:10.2501/IJA-30-1-047-075

Chu, S. C., & Seock, Y. K. (2020). The power of social media in fashion advertising. *Journal of Interactive Advertising*, *20*(2), 93–94. doi:10.1080/15252019.2020.1802955

Ciasullo, M. V., Maione, G., Torre, C., & Troisi, O. (2017). What about sustainability? An empirical analysis of consumers' purchasing behavior in fashion context. *Sustainability (Basel)*, *9*(9), 1–18. doi:10.3390u9091617

Coffin, J., & Chatzidakis, A. (2021). The Möbius strip of market spatiality: Mobilizing transdisciplinary dialogues between CCT and the marketing mainstream. *AMS Review*, *11*(1-2), 40–59. doi:10.100713162-020-00191-8

Colby, S. L. (2021, June 24). *What marketers need to know about women over 50*. Muse by Clio. https://musebycl.io/musings/what-marketers-need-know-about-women-over-50

Comrey, A. L., & Lee, H. B. (2013). *A First Course in Factor Analysis* (2nd ed.). Psychology Press. doi:10.4324/9781315827506

Connell, K. Y. H. (2010). Internal and external barriers to eco-conscious apparel acquisition. *International Journal of Consumer Studies*, *34*(3), 279–286. doi:10.1111/j.1470-6431.2010.00865.x

Constantinides, E. (2014). Foundations of social media marketing. *Procedia: Social and Behavioral Sciences, 148*, 40–57. doi:10.1016/j.sbspro.2014.07.016

Constantinides, E., & Fountain, S. (2008). Web 2.0: Conceptual foundations and marketing issues. *Journal of Direct, Data and Digital Marketing Practice*, *9*(3), 231–244. doi:10.1057/palgrave.dddmp.4350098

Copeland, L., & Lyu, J. (2020). *Millennial Consumer's on instagram: Implications for luxury brands vs. celebrity influencers: An abstract.* doi:10.1007/978-3-030-42545-6_19

Costello, J., & Biondi, L. (2020). The art of deception: Will fake followers decay trust and can authenticity preserve it? In *Influencer Marketing* (pp. 215–232). Routledge. doi:10.4324/9780429322501-16

Cowan, K., & Kinley, T. (2014). Green spirit: Consumer empathies for green apparel. *International Journal of Consumer Studies*, *38*(5), 493–499. doi:10.1111/ijcs.12125

Creswell, J. W., & Poth, C. N. (2016). *Qualitative inquiry and research design: Choosing among five approaches.* Sage publications.

Criteo. (2021). *Digital Marketing in 2021: 6 Trends APAC Marketers Should Prepare for* Retrieved March 15, 2023, from https://www.criteo.com/blog/digital-marketing-in-2021-6-trends-apac-marketers-should-prepare-for/

Cucu, E. (2023). *2023 social media industry benchmarks: Socialinsider. Socialinsider Blog: Social media marketing insights and industry tips.* Retrieved March 15, 2023, from https://www.socialinsider.io/blog/social-media-industry-benchmarks/#5

Cuong, Linh, & Ha. (2015). Factors affecting Intention to use Facebook – Banking of Generation Y in Vietnam. *International Journal of Financial Research, 6*(4).

Curran, J. (2011). Academy of Marketing Studies Journal. *Suppl. Special*, *15*(1), 21–38.

Curry, T. A., & Fix, M. P. (2019). May it please the twitterverse: The use of twitter by state high court judges. *Journal of Information Technology & Politics*, *16*(4), 379–393. doi:10.1080/19331681.2019.1657048

D'Souza, C., Taghian, M., & Lamb, P. (2006). An Empirical study on the influence of environmental labels on consumers. *Corporate Communications*, *11*(2), 162–173. doi:10.1108/13563280610661697

Dai, J.-Y., & Zhao, L. (2022). Happiness and Fashion Culture of Smart Kidswear from the perspective of Metaverse. *2022 10th International Conference on Orange Technology (ICOT)*, 1–4. 10.1109/ICOT56925.2022.10008154

Dal Forno, A. J., Bataglini, W. V., Steffens, F., & Ulson de Souza, A. A. (2021). *Industry 4.0 in textile and apparel sector: a systematic literature review.* Research Journal of Textile and Apparel.

Darban, A. (2012). *The impact of online social networks on consumers purchase decision-The study of food retailers* [Master's Thesis]. Jonkoping International Business School, Jonkoping University.

Dash, G., Rishi, B., Akmal, S., Paul, J., & Chakraborty, D. (2023). Digitization, Marketing 4.0, and Repurchase Intention in E-Tail: A Cross-National Study. *Journal of Global Information Management*, *31*(1), 1–24. doi:10.4018/JGIM.322303

Davari, A., & Strutton, D. (2014). Marketing mix strategies for closing the gap between green consumers' pro-environmental beliefs and behaviors. *Journal of Strategic Marketing*, *22*(7), 563–586. doi:10.1080/0965254X.2014.914059

Dávila-Ruiz, D., & Vazquez, E. E. (2021). Examining effects of photography in social media and the mediation role of perceived authenticity. *Communication Today*, *12*(2), 112–127.

Davis, F. (1993). Users' acceptance of information technology: System characteristics, users' perception and behavioural impacts. *International Journal of Man-Machine Studies*, *38*(3), 475–487.

Davis, F. D. (1989). Perceived usefulness, perceived ease of use, and user acceptance of information technology. *Management Information Systems Quarterly*, *13*(3), 319–340.

Davis, F. D., Bagozzi, R. P., & Warshaw, P. R. (1992). Extrinsic and Intrinsic Motivation to Use Computers in the Workplace. *Journal of Applied Social Psychology*, *22*(14), 1111–1132.

Davis, F., Bagozzi, R. P., & Warshaw, P. R. (1989). User acceptance of computer technology: A comparison of two theoretical models. *Management Science*, *35*(8), 982–1002.

De Bustis, A., Ganesan, V., & Herath, G. (2018). *Unlocking Sri Lanka's digital opportunity*. McKinsey Digital.

de Lenne, O., & Vandenbosch, L. (2017). Media and sustainable apparel buying intention. *Journal of Fashion Marketing and Management*, *21*(4), 483–498. doi:10.1108/JFMM-11-2016-0101

De Perthuis, K., & Findlay, R. (2019). How Fashion Travels: The Fashionable Ideal in the Age of Instagram. *Fashion Theory*, *23*(2), 219–242. doi:10.1080/1362704X.2019.1567062

De Valck, K., Van Bruggen, G., & Wierenga, B. (2009). Virtual communities: A marketing perspective. *Decision Support Systems*, *47*(3), 185–203. doi:10.1016/j.dss.2009.02.008

De Veirman, M., Cauberghe, V., & Hudders, L. (2017). Marketing through Instagram influencers: The impact of number of followers and product divergence on brand attitude. *International Journal of Advertising*, *36*(5), 798–828. doi:10.1080/02650487.2017.1348035

Dellarocas, C., Zhang, X., & Awad, N. F. (2007). Exploring the value of online product reviews in forecasting sales: The case of motion pictures. *Journal of Interactive Marketing*, *21*(4), 23–45. doi:10.1002/dir.20087

Depop. (2023). *How does Depop work?* Depop. https://blog.depop.com/articles/how-does-depop-work

Desai, Shukla, & Thakkar. (2012). Effect of facebook on purchasing behavior of youth. *International Journal of Research in Computer Application and Management, 2*(11).

Devaraj, S., & Kohli, R. (2003). Performance Impacts of Information Technology: Is Actual Usage the Missing Link. *Management Science, 49*(3), 273-289.

Deveci, M. (2019). *Sosyal medya pazarlama stratejilerinin tüketici üzerindeki olumlu ve olumsuz etkileri: Antalya ili örneği*. Yayınlanmamış Yüksek Lisans Tezi, Beykent Üniversitesi Sosyal Bilimler Enstitüsü.

Dewanto, K. N., & Belgiawan, P. F. (2020). The Influence of Social Norms and Attitude In Sustainable Fashion Product Purchase Behaviour. *American International Journal of Business Management*, *3*(7), 64–75.

Dinç, B. (2018). Dijitalleşmenin tüketici alışkanlıklarına etkisi. *Ekonomistler Platformu*. http://www.ekonomistler.org.tr/wp-content/uploads/2018/01/dijital_1.pdf

Dixon, S. (2023). *Biggest social media platforms 2023*. Retrieved March 15, 2023, from https://www.statista.com/statistics/272014/global-social-networks-ranked-by-number-of-users/

Djafarova, E., & Bowes, T. (2021). 'Instagram made Me buy it': Generation Z impulse purchases in fashion industry. *Journal of Retailing and Consumer Services*, *59*, 102345. doi:10.1016/j.jretconser.2020.102345

Djafarova, E., & Rushworth, C. (2017). Exploring the credibility of online celebrities' Instagram profiles in influencing the purchase decisions of young female users. *Computers in Human Behavior*, *68*, 1–7. doi:10.1016/j.chb.2016.11.009

do Prado Lima, S. (2020, May 26). *Ageism could cost billions to the fashion industry*. Moderated. https://medium.com/moderated/ageism-could-cost-billions-to-the-fashion-industry-c2e5cfcfd837

Dollarhide, M., & Drury, A. (2023). Social Media: Definition, Effects, and List of Top Apps. *Investopedia*. https://www.investopedia.com/terms/s/social-media.asp

Donawerth, S. (n.d.). *Carro*. https://www.getcarro.com/blogs/influencer-marketing-for-luxury-brands

Dorado, L. E. (2011). *The Effect of Social Media on the Fashion Retail Industry*. Elon University.

Doshi, P., Nigam, P., & Rishi, B. (2023). Customer values and patronage intention in social media networks: mediating role of perceived usefulness. *VINE Journal of Information and Knowledge Management Systems*. doi:10.1108/VJIKMS-07-2022-0217

Du Plessis, C. (2017). *Towards a more universal understanding of content marketing: The contribution of academic research*. Academic Press.

Duan, W., Gu, B., & Whinston, A. B. (2008). Do online reviews matter? - An empirical investigation of panel data. *Decision Support Systems*, *45*(4), 1007–1016. doi:10.1016/j.dss.2008.04.001

Dwivedi, V. (2021). *Sabyasachi x H&M: A classic example grand play, successful legacy and marketing masterstroke* Retrieved March 20, 2023, from https://www.businesstoday.in/opinion/columns/story/sabyasachi-x-hm-a-classic-example-grand-play-successful-legacy-and-marketing-masterstroke-305678-2021-09-01

Edmondson, E. S. (2022). *@emsladedmondson*. Instagram. https://www.instagram.com/emsladedmondson/

Ehlers, K. (2021). Micro-Influencers: When Smaller Is Better. *Forbes*, 1–6. https://www.forbes.com/sites/forbesagencycouncil/2021/06/02/micro-influencers-when-smaller-is-better/?sh=3ae55461539b

Eisingerich, A. B., Chun, H., Liu, Y., Jia, H., & Bell, S. J. (2015). Why recommend a brand face-to-face but not on Facebook? How word-of-mouth on online social sites differs from traditional word-of-mouth. *Journal of Consumer Psychology*, *25*(1), 120–128. doi:10.1016/j.jcps.2014.05.004

Elhajjar, S. (2023). Factors influencing buying behavior of Lebanese consumers towards fashion brands during economic crisis: A qualitative study. *Journal of Retailing and Consumer Services*, *71*, 103224. Advance online publication. doi:10.1016/j.jretconser.2022.103224

Ellen MacArthur Foundation. (2021). *Social peer-to-peer marketplace: Depop*. Ellen MacArthur Foundation. https://ellenmacarthurfoundation.org/circular-examples/depop

Elliman, H. (2022). *@hannahxelliman*. Instagram. https://www.instagram.com/hannahxelliman/

Elton, L., & Lopez, L. (2018). How ELLE leverages customer relationships to deepen brand engagement. *Journal of Digital and Social Media Marketing*, *6*(2), 102–109.

Emmanouil, S. (2021). *Καλπάζει το ηλεκτρονικό εμπόριο μόδας*. EURO2DAY. Available at: https://www.euro2day.gr/news/economy/article/2062409/kalpazei-to-hlektroniko-emporio-modas-.html

Enginkaya, E. (2006). Elektronik perakendecilik ve elektronik alışveriş. *Ege Akademik Bakış Dergisi*, *6*(1), 10–16.

Enke, N., & Borchers, N. S. (2019). Social Media Influencers in Strategic Communication: A Conceptual Framework for Strategic Social Media Influencer Communication. *International Journal of Strategic Communication*, *13*(4), 261–277. doi:10.1080/1553118X.2019.1620234

Ensemble, I. Q. (2018). Social Media and Influencers: Impact on the Fashion and Apparel Supply Chain. *RIS News*. https://risnews.com/social-media-and-influencers-impact-fashion-and-apparel-supply-chain

Erciş, A., Ünal, S., & Can, P. (2007). Yaşam tarzlarının satın alma karar süreci üzerindeki rolü. *Atatürk Üniversitesi İktisadi ve İdari Bilimler Fakültesi Dergisi*, *21*(2), 281–311.

Ernst & Young. (2014). *Türk internet kullanıcıları alışverişte de sanal kanallara yöneliyor*. EY Global Tüketici Araştırması. http://www.ey.com

Esber, D., & Wong, J. (2020). *Discussions in digital: Influencer marketing podcast*. McKinsey & Company. https://www.mckinsey.com/capabilities/growth-marketing-and-sales/our-insights/discussions-in-digital-influencer-marketing-is-ready-for-its-close-up

Esteban-Santos, L., García Medina, I., Carey, L., & Bellido-Pérez, E. (2018). Fashion bloggers: Communication tools for the fashion industry. *Journal of Fashion Marketing and Management*, *22*(3), 420–437. doi:10.1108/JFMM-10-2017-0101

Europapress. (2019). *Mango alcanzó unas ventas por 2.233 millones de euros en 2018, un 1,8% más*. Retrieved February 9, 2020 from https://www.europapress.es/economia/noticia-mango-alcanzo-ventas-2233-millones-euros-2018-18-mas-20190808120739.html

European Union. (2020a). *Κοινός ευρωπαϊκός οδικός χάρτης για την άρση των μέτρων περιορισμού του COVID-19*. Available at: https://ec.europa.eu/info/live-work-travel-eu/health/coronavirus-response/european-roadmap-lifting-coronavirus-containment-measures_en

European Union. (2020b). *Μέτρα περιορισμού για τον COVID-19*. Available at: https://reliefweb.int/map/italy/european-union-covid-19-restriction-measures-dg-echo-daily-map-20042020

Eurostat. (2020). *E-commerce statistics for individuals - Statistics explained*. Retrieved February 11, 2020 from https://ec.europa.eu/eurostat/statistics-explained/index.php/E-commerce_statistics_for_individuals

Evans, D. (2010). *Social media marketing: the next generation of business engagement*. John Wiley & Sons.

Fabella, K. (2022). *@theflippside*. Instagram. https://www.instagram.com/theflippside/

Faber, R. J., Lee, M., & Nan, X. N. (2004). Advertising and the consumer information environment online. *The American Behavioral Scientist*, *48*(4), 447–466. doi:10.1177/0002764204270281

Fairs, M. (2020). *Coronavirus offers "a blank page for a new beginning" says Li Edelkoort*. Dezeen Magazine.

Faraoni, M., Bandinelli, R., & Rinaldi, R. (2016). Social media strategy in the Italian fashion industry: A new model of analysis. In *Workshop on Business Models and ICT Technologies for the Fashion Supply Chain* (pp. 253-269). Springer.

Farinosi, M., & Fortunati, L. (2020). Young and elderly fashion influencers. In *Human Aspects of IT for the Aged Population. Technology and Society: 6th International Conference, ITAP 2020, Held as Part of the 22nd HCI International Conference, HCII 2020, Copenhagen, Denmark, July 19–24, 2020 Proceedings*, *22*(3), 42–57.

Farivar, S., Wang, F., & Yuan, Y. (2021). Opinion leadership vs. para-social relationship: Key factors in influencer marketing. *Journal of Retailing and Consumer Services*, *59*, 102371.

Farivar, S., Wang, F., & Yuan, Y. (2021). Opinion leadership vs. para-social relationship: Key factors in influencer marketing. *Journal of Retailing and Consumer Services*, *59*, 102371. doi:10.1016/j.jretconser.2020.102371

Fashionunited. (n.d.). Global Fashion Industry Statistics. *Fashion news and fashion jobs*. https://fashionunited.com/global-fashion-industry-statistics

Featherman, M. S., & Hajli, N. (2016). Self-Service Technologies and e-Services Risks in Social Commerce Era. *Journal of Business Ethics, 139*(2), 251–269. doi:10.100710551-015-2614-4

Featherstone, M. (1991). *Consumer Culture and Postmodernism.* Sage.

Federal Trade Commission. (2017). *FTC staff reminders influencers and brands to clearly disclosure relationship: commission aims to improve disclosures in social media endorsements.* https://www.ftc.gov/news-events/news/press-releases/2017/04/ftc-staff-reminds-influencers-brands-clearly-disclose-relationship

Feng, Y., Chen, H., & Kong, Q. (2020). An expert with whom I can identify: The role of narratives in influencer marketing. *International Journal of Advertising, 4*(7), 972–993. doi:10.1080/02650487.2020.1824751

Ferraro, P. J., Uchida, T., & Conrad, J. M. (2005). Price premiums for eco-friendly commodities: Are "green" markets the best way to protect endangered ecosystems? *Environmental and Resource Economics, 32*(3), 419–438. doi:10.100710640-005-7962-6

Fibre2fashion.com. (2021). *Role of Media in Fashion Industry of India.* Retrieved March 20, 2023, from https://www.fibre2fashion.com/industry-article/6134/role-of-media

Field, A. (2009). *Discovering Statistics using SPSS.* Sage.

Fields, M. (n.d.). Biggest Problems with Influencer Marketing. *BrandChamp.* https://brandchamp.io/blog/biggest-problems-with-influencer-marketing/

Fırat, A., & Azmak, E. (2007). Satın alma karar sürecinde beyaz eşya kullanıcılarının marka bağlılığı. *Karamanoğlu Mehmetbey Üniversitesi Sosyal ve Ekonomik Araştırmalar Dergisi, 2007*(2), 251–264.

Fischer, E., & Reuber, A. R. (2011). Social interaction via new social media: (How) can interactions on Twitter affect effectual thinking and behavior? *Journal of Business Venturing, 26*(1), 1–18. doi:10.1016/j.jbusvent.2010.09.002

Fishbein, M., & Ajzen, I. (1975). *Belief, attitude, intention and behaviour: An introduction to theory and research.* Academic Press.

Fishbein, M., & Ajzen, I. (1975). *Belief, attitude, intention and behavior: An introduction to theory and research.* Addison-Wesley.

Fiske, J. (1989). *Understanding Popular Culture.* Routledge.

Fletcher, K. (2010). Slow Fashion: An Invitation for Systems Change. *Fashion Practice, 2*(2), 259–265. doi:10.2752/175693810X12774625387594

Foltz, C., Newkirk, H., & Schwager, P. (2016). An Empirical Investigation of Factors that Influence Individual Behavior toward Changing Social Networking Security Settings. *Journal of Theoretical and Applied Electronic Commerce Research, 11*, 2–2. doi:10.4067/S0718-18762016000200002

Fornell, C., & Larcker, D. F. (1981). Evaluating Structural Equation Models with Unobservable Variables and Measurement Error. *JMR, Journal of Marketing Research, 18*, 39–50.

Foroudi, P., Cuomo, M. T., Foroudi, M. M., Katsikeas, C. S., & Gupta, S. (2020). Linking identity and heritage with image and a reputation for competition. *Journal of Business Research, 113*, 317–325. doi:10.1016/j.jbusres.2019.09.042

Foroudi, P., Jin, Z., Gupta, S., Melewar, T. C., & Foroudi, M. M. (2016). Influence of innovation capability and customer experience on reputation and loyalty. *Journal of Business Research, 69*(11), 4882–4889. doi:10.1016/j.jbusres.2016.04.047

Fotis, J. (2015) *The use of social media and its impacts on consumer behaviour: the xontext of holiday travel* [PhD dissertation]. Bournemouth University.

Frąckiewicz, E. (2021). Information and communication technologies as a source of customer value in the context of balancing the positions of younger and older consumers. *Sustainability (Basel), 13*(9), 4722. doi:10.3390u13094722

Francisco-Maffezzolli, E., Munaro, A. C., Santos Rodrigues, J. P., Cabrera Paraiso, E., Eliane, F.-M., Ana Cristina, M., Rodrigues João Pedro, S., & Paraiso Emerson, C. (2021). Mining meaning of videos on YouTube: unravelling latent content from digital influencers and their engagement. *Proceedings of the 50th European Marketing Academy*, 93144.

Gakunu, P. (2004). *E-Government Strategy for Kenya*. Available: https://www.apc.org/apps/img_upload/69726166726 96361646f63756d656e74/egov_Presentation_for_ICT_Conven

Garbarino, E., & Johnson, M. S. (1999). The different roles of satisfaction, trust, and commitment in customer relationships. *Journal of Marketing, 63*(2), 70–87. doi:10.1177/002224299906300205

Garcia, D. G., Kipnis, E., Vasileiou, E., & Solomon, A. (2021). Consumption in the circular economy: Learning from our mistakes. In Sustainability (Switzerland) (Vol. 13, Issue 2, pp. 1–23). doi:10.3390u13020601

Gardner, J. (2008). Blogs, wikis and official statistics: New perspectives on the use of Web 2.0 by statistical offices. *Statistical Journal of the IAOS. Journal of the International Association for Official Statistics, 25*(3), 81 92.

Gaziano, C. (1988). How credible is the credibility crisis? *The Journalism Quarterly, 65*, 267–278, 375.

Gazzola, P., Pavione, E., Pezzetti, R., & Grechi, D. (2020). Trends in the Fashion Industry. The Perception of Sustainability and Circular Economy: A Gender/Generation Quantitative Approach. *Sustainability (Basel), 12*(7), 2809. doi:10.3390u12072809

Gefen, D. (2000). E-commerce: The role of familiarity and trust. *Omega, 28*(6), 725–737. doi:10.1016/S0305-0483(00)00021-9

Gefen, D. (2002). Reflections on the Dimensions of Trust and Trustworthiness among Online Consumers. *The Data Base for Advances in Information Systems, 33*(3), 38–53. doi:10.1145/569905.569910

Gefen, D., & Straub, D. W. (1997). Gender differences in the perception and use of e-mail:an extension of the technology acceptance model. *Management Information Systems Quarterly, 21*(4), 389–399.

Gefen, D., & Straub, D. W. (2004). Consumer trust in B2C e-Commerce and the importance of social presence: Experiments in e-Products and e-Services. *Omega, 32*(6), 407–424. doi:10.1016/j.omega.2004.01.006

Geissinger, A., & Laurell, C. (2016). User engagement in social media–an explorative study of Swedish fashion brands. *Journal of Fashion Marketing and Management, 20*(2), 177–190. doi:10.1108/JFMM-02-2015-0010

Genç, M. (2014). *Geleneksel ve online mağazalardan ürün satın alımlarında tüketici tutumları*. Yüksek Lisans Tezi, Çağ Üniversitesi Sosyal Bilimler Enstitüsü.

George, J. (2016). Growing & changing trends in consumer behavior. In *2016 International Conference on Electrical, Electronics, and Optimization Techniques (ICEEOT)* (pp. 4804-4809). IEEE. 10.1109/ICEEOT.2016.7755633

Geyser, W. (2022). What is Influencer Marketing? The Ultimate Guide for 2023. *Influencer Marketing Hub*. https://influencermarketinghub.com/influencer-marketing/#toc-0

Ghemawat, P., & Nueno, J. L. (2003). *Zara: Fast fashion*. Retrieved February 9, 2020 from: https://www.hbs.edu/faculty/Pages/item.aspx?num=29832

Ghosh, S. (2016). *Five Pakistani Fashion Designers You Must Follow On Instagram*. Retrieved March 20, 2023, from https://www.thequint.com/lifestyle/five-pakistani-fashion-designers-instagram-asim-jofa-deepak-perwani-bunto-kazmi-hsy-sania-maskatiya#read-more

Giannoulakis, S., & Tsapatsoulis, N. (2016). Evaluating the descriptive power of Instagram hashtags. *Journal of Innovation in Digital Ecosystems*, *3*(2), 114–129. doi:10.1016/j.jides.2016.10.001

Gibson, P. C. (2012). Fashion and Celebrity Culture. In *Fashion and Celebrity Culture*. Berg. doi:10.2752/9781472572424/GIBSON0009

Gilly, M. C., & Wolfinbarger, M. (2000). A comparison of consumer experiences with online and offline shopping. *Consumption Markets & Culture*, *4*(2), 187–205. doi:10.1080/10253866.2000.9670355

Giwa, A. (2010). Information technology and the supply chain management for the textile industry. *Journals for Information Technology*, 26.

Glucksman, M. (2017). The rise of social media influencer marketing on lifestyle branding: A case study of Lucie Fink. *Elon Journal of Undergraduate Research in Communications*, *8*(2), 77–87.

Godes, D., & Mayzlin, D. (2004). Using online conversations to study word-of-mouth communication. *Marketing Science*, *23*(4), 545–560.

Golikeri, P. (2021). *The luxury network: How social media lure is still compelling enough for any brand*. Retrieved March 20, 2023, from https://www.dnaindia.com/business/report-the-luxury-network-2694950

Gomes, M. A., Marques, S., & Dias, Á. (2022). The impact of digital influencers' characteristics on purchase intention of fashion products. *Journal of Global Fashion Marketing*, *13*(3), 187–204. doi:10.1080/20932685.2022.2039263

Gómez-Suárez, M., Pilar Martinez-Ruiz, M., & Martinez-Caraballo, N. (2017). Consumer-Brand Relationships under the Marketing 3.0 Paradigm: A Literature Review. *Frontiers in Psychology*, *8*(252), 1–4. doi:10.3389/fpsyg.2017.00252 PMID:28275360

Goswami, S., & Khan, S. (2015). Impact of consumer decision-making styles on online apparel consumption in India. *Vision (Basel)*, *19*(4), 303–311. doi:10.1177/0972262915610853

Goularas, D., & Kamis, S. (2019, August). Evaluation of deep learning techniques in sentiment analysis from twitter data. In *2019 International Conference on Deep Learning and Machine Learning in Emerging Applications (Deep-ML)* (pp. 12-17). IEEE. 10.1109/Deep-ML.2019.00011

Goworek, H., Fisher, T., Cooper, T., Woodward, S., & Hiller, A. (2012). The sustainable clothing market: An evaluation of potential strategies for UK retailers. *International Journal of Retail & Distribution Management*, *40*(12), 935–955. doi:10.1108/09590551211274937

Grand View Research. (2018). Fashion Influencer Marketing Market Size Report, 2020-2027. *Grand View Research*. https://www.grandviewresearch.com/industry-analysis/fashion-influencer-marketing-market

Greco, A. J. (1986). The fashion-conscious elderly: A viable, but neglected market segment. *Journal of Consumer Marketing*, *3*(4), 71–75. doi:10.1108/eb008181

Grisaffe, D. B., & Nguyen, H. P. (2011). Antecedents of emotional attachment to brands. *Journal of Business Research*, *64*(10), 1052–1059. doi:10.1016/j.jbusres.2010.11.002

Groenewald, T. (2004). A Phenomenological Research Design Illustrated. *International Journal of Qualitative Methods*, *3*(1), 42–55. doi:10.1177/160940690400300104

Gulamali, A., & Persson, J. (2017). *The Social Media Influencer and Brand Switching*. Lund University: School of Economics and Management. https://lup.lub.lu.se/student-papers/record/8910352/file/8910354.pdf

Gullstrand Edbring, E., Lehner, M., & Mont, O. (2016). Exploring consumer attitudes to alternative models of consumption: Motivations and barriers. *Journal of Cleaner Production*, *123*, 5–15. doi:10.1016/j.jclepro.2015.10.107

Gümüş, N. (2018). Sosyal medya pazarlamaya yönelik tüketici algılarının incelenmesi: Kırgızistan üzerinde bir araştırma. *MANAS Sosyal Araştırmalar Dergisi*, *7*(3), 391–413.

Gupta, Y., Agarwal, S., & Singh, P. B. (2020). To study the impact of instafamous celebrities on consumer buying behavior. *Academy of Marketing Studies Journal*, *24*(2), 1–13.

H&M Group. (2019). *Annual report 2018*. Retrieved February 9, 2020 from. https://about.hm.com/content/dam/hmgroup/groupsite/documents/masterlanguage/Annual Report/Annual Report 2018.pdf

Haenlein, M., Anadol, E., Farnsworth, T., Hugo, H., Hunichen, J., & Welte, D. (2020). Navigating the new era of influencer marketing: How to be successful on Instagram, TikTok, & co. *California Management Review*, *63*(1), 5–25. doi:10.1177/0008125620958166

Hafeez, K., Foroudi, P., Dinnie, K., Nguyen, B., & Parahoo, S. K. (2016). The role of place branding and image in the development of sectoral clusters: The case of Dubai. *Journal of Brand Management*, *23*(4), 383–402. doi:10.1057/bm.2016.18

Hair, J. F., Hult, G. T. M., Ringle, C. M., & Sarstedt, M. (2014). *A primer on partial least squares structural equation modeling (PLS-SEM)*. Sage.

Hair, J. F., Ringle, C. M., & Sarstedt, M. (2011). PLS-SEM: Indeed a silver bullet. *Journal of Marketing Theory and Practice*, *19*(2), 139–151.

Hajli, N. (2014). A study of the impact of social media on consumers. *International Journal of Market Research*, *56*(3), 387–404. doi:10.2501/IJMR-2014-025

Hajli, N. (2015). Social commerce constructs and consumer's intention to buy. *International Journal of Information Management*, *35*(2), 183–191. doi:10.1016/j.ijinfomgt.2014.12.005

Hajli, N., & Lin, X. (2016). Exploring the Security of Information Sharing on Social Networking Sites: The Role of Perceived Control of Information. *Journal of Business Ethics*, *133*(1), 111–123. doi:10.100710551-014-2346-x

Hannan, M. T., & Freeman, J. (1977). The population ecology of organizations. *American Journal of Sociology*, *82*(5), 929–964. doi:10.1086/226424

Hanson-Lowe, L. (2022). *@slow_fashion_lottie*. Instagram. https://www.instagram.com/slow_fashion_lottie/

Hardill, I., & Wynarczyk, P. (1991). A research note: Information technology and company performance in the textile industry. *New Technology, Work and Employment*, *6*(1), 65–70. doi:10.1111/j.1468-005X.1991.tb00132.x

Harris, F., Roby, H., & Dibb, S. (2016). Sustainable clothing: Challenges, barriers and interventions for encouraging more sustainable consumer behaviour. *International Journal of Consumer Studies*, *40*(3), 309–318. doi:10.1111/ijcs.12257

Hayes, R. A., & Carr, C. T. (2015). *Does Being Social Matter? Effects of Enabled Commenting on Credibility and Brand Attitude in Social Media*. Academic Press.

Hendijani Fard, M., & Marvi, R. (2019). Viral marketing and purchase intentions of mobile applications users. *International Journal of Emerging Markets*, *15*(2), 287–301. doi:10.1108/IJOEM-06-2018-0291

Hennig-Thurau, T., Gwinner, K. P., Walsh, G., & Gremler, D. D. (2004). Electronic word-of- mouth via consumer-opinion platforms: What motivates consumers to articulate themselves on the Internet? *Journal of Interactive Marketing, 18*(1), 38–52. doi:10.1002/dir.10073

Henninger, C. E., Alevizou, P. J., & Oates, C. J. (2016). What is sustainable fashion? *Journal of Fashion Marketing and Management, 20*(4), 400–416. doi:10.1108/JFMM-07-2015-0052

Hogan, B. (2010). The presentation of self in the age of social media: Distinguishing performances and exhibitions online. *Bulletin of Science, Technology & Society, 30*(6), 377–386. doi:10.1177/0270467610385893

Holliday, R. C., Ballinger, C., & Playford, E. D. (2007). Goal setting in neurological rehabilitation: Patients' perspectives. *Disability and Rehabilitation, 29*(5), 389–394. doi:10.1080/09638280600841117 PMID:17364791

Hong, I. B., & Cho, H. (2011). The impact of consumer trust on attitudinal loyalty and purchase intentions in B2C e-marketplaces: Intermediary trust vs. seller trust. *International Journal of Information Management, 31*(5), 469–479. doi:10.1016/j.ijinfomgt.2011.02.001

Hsiao, S. H., Wang, Y. Y., Wang, T., & Kao, T. W. (2020). How social media shapes the fashion industry: The spillover effects between private labels and national brands. *Industrial Marketing Management, 86*, 40–51. doi:10.1016/j.indmarman.2019.02.022

Hsu, C. L., Lin, J. C. C., & Sen Chiang, H. (2013). The effects of blogger recommendations on customers' online shopping intentions. *Internet Research, 23*(1), 69–88. doi:10.1108/10662241311295782

Huang, Z., & Benyoucef, M. (2017). The effects of social commerce design on consumer purchase decision-making: An empirical study. *Electronic Commerce Research and Applications, 25*, 40–58. doi:10.1016/j.elerap.2017.08.003

Hu, Chau, & Sheng, & Kar. (1999). Examining the technology acceptance model using physician acceptance of telemedicine technology. *Journal of Management Information Systems, 16*(2), 91–112.

Hulland, J., & Houston, M. B. (2020). Why systematic review papers and meta-analyses matter: An introduction to the special issue on generalizations in marketing. *Journal of the Academy of Marketing Science, 48*(3), 351–359. doi:10.100711747-020-00721-7

Hur, E. (2020). Rebirth fashion: Secondhand clothing consumption values and perceived risks. *Journal of Cleaner Production, 273*, 122951. doi:10.1016/j.jclepro.2020.122951

Hur, E., & Cassidy, T. (2019). Perceptions and attitudes towards sustainable fashion design: Challenges and opportunities for implementing sustainability in fashion. *International Journal of Fashion Design. Technology and Education, 12*(2), 208–217. Advance online publication. doi:10.1080/17543266.2019.1572789

Hur, E., & Faragher- Siddall, E. (2022). Young Consumer Perspectives on Government Policy Interventions for Sustainable Fashion Consumption in the UK. *Fashion Practice, 14*(3), 405–427. doi:10.1080/17569370.2022.2125149

Hutter, K., Hautz, J., Dennhardt, S., & Fuller, J. (2013). The impact of user interactions in social media on brand awareness and purchase intention, the case of MINI on facebook. *Journal of Product and Brand Management, 22*(5/6), 342–345.

Hwang, J., Eves, A., & Stienmetz, J. L. (2021). The impact of social media use on consumers' restaurant consumption experiences: A qualitative study. *Sustainability (Basel), 13*(12), 6581. doi:10.3390u13126581

Ibok, N. I. (2013). Factors determining the effectiveness of celebrity endorsed advertisements: The case of Nigerian telecommunication industry. *American Journal of Business and Management, 2*(3), 233–238. doi:10.11634/216796061302394

Idrees, S., Vignali, G., & Gill, S. (2023). Interactive Marketing with Virtual Commerce Tools: Purchasing Right Size and Fitted Garment in Fashion Metaverse. In The Palgrave Handbook of Interactive Marketing (pp. 329–351). Springer International Publishing. doi:10.1007/978-3-031-14961-0_15

Igyor, G. A. (1996). *The Economic and Social Benefit of Telecommunications Technology*. Paper Presented at the Animal International Conference on Information Technology Management Infotech.

Ilfoil, D. M., & Jobs, C. (2012). Return on investment for social media: A proposed framework for understanding, implementing, and measuring the return. *Journal of Business & Economics Research, 10*(11), 637–650. doi:10.19030/jber.v10i11.7363

Inditex. (2019). *Inditex annual report 2018*. Retrieved February 9, 2020 from https://static.inditex.com/annual_rcport_2018/pdfs/en/Inditex Annual Report 2018.pdf

Influential choices: How fashion influencers can affect the purchasing intentions of consumers. (2020). *Strategic Direction, 36*(8), 11-12. doi:10.1108/SD-05-2020-0108

Instagram Inc. (2021). *Instagram on the App Store*. Apple App Store. https://apps.apple.com/us/app/instagram/id389801252

Instagram. (2020a). *@forever21 • Fotos y videos de Instagram*. Retrieved January 28, 2020 from https://www.instagram.com/forever21/?hl=es

Instagram. (2020b). *Gap (@gap) • Fotos y videos de Instagram*. Retrieved January 28, 2020 from https://www.instagram.com/gap/?hl=es

Instagram. (2020c). *H&M (@hm) • Fotos y videos de Instagram*. Retrieved January 28, 2020 from https://www.instagram.com/hm/?hl=es

Instagram. (2020d). *MANGO (@mango) • Fotos y videos de Instagram*. Retrieved January 28, 2020 from https://www.instagram.com/mango/?hl=es

Instagram. (2020e). *United Colors of Benetton (@benetton) • Fotos y videos de Instagram*. Retrieved January 28, 2020 from https://www.instagram.com/benetton/?hl=es

Instagram. (2020f). *ZARA Official (@zara) • Fotos y videos de Instagram*. Retrieved January 28, 2020 from https://www.instagram.com/zara/?hl=es

Irish Blogger Agency. (n.d.). Why is Influencer Marketing Important for the Fashion Industry in 2022? — Irish Blogger Agency. *Irish Blogger Agency*. https://www.irishbloggeragency.com/why-use-fashion-influencers-for-fashion-brand-marketing

izzy_manuel. (2022). *@izzy_manuel*. Instagram. https://www.instagram.com/izzy_manuel/

Jackson, T. (2012). The process of trend development leading to a fashion season. In T. Hines & M. Bruce (Eds.), *Fashion Marketing: Contemporary Issues* (pp. 168–187). Taylor and Francis.

Jacobson, J., & Harrison, B. (2022). Sustainable fashion social media influencers and content creation calibration. *International Journal of Advertising, 41*(1), 150–177. doi:10.1080/02650487.2021.2000125

Jain, V. (2021). An overview on social media influencer marketing. *South Asian Journal of Marketing & Management Research, 11*(11), 76–81. doi:10.5958/2249-877X.2021.00112.0

Jain, V., Malviya, B., & Arya, S. (2021). An overview of electronic commerce (e-Commerce). *Journal of Contemporary Issues in Business and Government, 27*(3), 666.

Jaitly, R. C., & Gautam, O. (2021). Impact of social media influencers on customer engagement and brand perception. *International Journal of Internet Marketing and Advertising, 15*(2), 220–242. doi:10.1504/IJIMA.2021.114336

Jalilvand, M. R., & Samiei, N. (2012). The effect of electronic word of mouth on brand image and purchase intention: An empirical study in the automobile industry in Iran. *Marketing Intelligence & Planning, 30*(4), 460–476. doi:10.1108/02634501211231946

Jalilvand, M. R., & Samiei, N. (2012). The impact of electronic word of mouth on a tourism destination choice: Testing the theory of planned behavior (TPB). *Internet Research, 22*(5), 591–612. doi:10.1108/10662241211271563

James, P., & Szeman, I. (2010). Globalization and Culture: Vol. 3. *Global-Local Consumption.* Sage Publications.

Jang, J., & Kim, J. (2023). Exploring the Impact of Avatar Customization in Metaverse: The Role of the Class Mode on Task Engagement and Expectancy-Value Beliefs for Fashion Education. *Mobile Information Systems, 2023*, 1–13. doi:10.1155/2023/2967579

Jang, S., Prasad, A., & Ratchford, B. T. (2012). How consumers use product reviews in the purchase decision process. *Marketing Letters, 23*(3), 825–838. doi:10.100711002-012-9191-4

Jeon, H.-J., & Kim, G.-D. (2022). Suggestion of Metaverse based Online Fashion Shopping Mall Application Service : Focused on the Virtual Fitting Service. *Journal of Digital Contents Society, 23*(4), 589–601. doi:10.9728/dcs.2022.23.4.589

Jiang, F., & Leung, C. K. S. (2014, December). A data science solution for mining interesting patterns from uncertain big data. In *2014 IEEE Fourth International Conference on Big Data and Cloud Computing* (pp. 235-242). IEEE.

Jia, S. (2019). Toward a better fitness club: Evidence from exerciser online rating and review using Latent Dirichlet Allocation and support vector machine. *International Journal of Market Research, 61*(1), 64–76. doi:10.1177/1470785318770571

Jiménez-Castillo, D., & Sánchez-Fernández, R. (2019). The role of digital influencers in brand recommendation: Examining their impact on engagement, expected value and purchase intention. *International Journal of Information Management, 49*(July), 366–376. doi:10.1016/j.ijinfomgt.2019.07.009

Jin, S. V., & Muqaddam, A. (2021). 'Fame and envy 2.0' in luxury fashion influencer marketing on Instagram: Comparison between mega-celebrities and micro-celebrities. *International Journal of Internet Marketing and Advertising, 15*(2), 176–200. doi:10.1504/IJIMA.2021.114335

Jin, S. V., & Ryu, E. (2020). Instagram fashionistas, luxury visual image strategies and vanity. *Journal of Product and Brand Management, 29*(3), 355–368. doi:10.1108/JPBM-08-2018-1987

Jin, S. V., Ryu, E., & Muqaddam, A. (2021). I trust what she's #endorsing on Instagram: Moderating effects of parasocial interaction and social presence in fashion influencer marketing. *Journal of Fashion Marketing and Management, 25*(4), 665–681. doi:10.1108/JFMM-04-2020-0059

Joergens, C. (2006). Ethical fashion: Myth or future trend? *Journal of Fashion Marketing and Management, 10*(3), 360–371. doi:10.1108/13612020610679321

Joshi, Y., & Rahman, Z. (2015). Factors Affecting Green Purchase Behaviour and Future Research Directions. *International Strategic Management Review, 3*(1–2), 128–143. doi:10.1016/j.ism.2015.04.001

Joung, H. M., & Miller, N. J. (2006). Factors of dress affecting self-esteem in older females. *Journal of Fashion Marketing and Management, 10*(4), 466–478. doi:10.1108/13612020610701983

Joy, A., Zhu, Y., Peña, C., & Brouard, M. (2022). Digital future of luxury brands: Metaverse, digital fashion, and non-fungible tokens. *Strategic Change, 31*(3), 337–343. doi:10.1002/jsc.2502

Kahani, M., & Mighan, S. N. (2021). A novel scalable intrusion detection system based on deep learning. *International Journal of Information Security*, *20*(3), 387–403. doi:10.100710207-020-00508-5

Kanagasabai, R., Manai, G., Sangaralingam, K., Shangfeng, H., & Veeramani, A. (2016, December). Classification of massive mobile web log URLs for customer profiling & analytics. In *2016 IEEE International Conference on Big Data (Big Data)* (pp. 1609-1614). IEEE. 10.1109/BigData.2016.7840771

Kang, J., Liu, C., & Kim, S. H. (2013). Environmentally sustainable textile and apparel consumption: The role of consumer knowledge, perceived consumer effectiveness and perceived personal relevance. *International Journal of Consumer Studies*, *37*(4), 442–452. doi:10.1111/ijcs.12013

Kang, J.-Y. M. (2019). What drives omnichannel shopping behaviours? *Journal of Fashion Marketing and Management*, *23*(2), 224–238. doi:10.1108/JFMM-07-2018-0088

Kang, P., Kim, C., Kim, H., Mo, K., & Seo, S. (2020). Comparative study of deep learning-based sentiment classification. *IEEE Access : Practical Innovations, Open Solutions*, *8*, 6861–6875. doi:10.1109/ACCESS.2019.2963426

Kantsperger, R., & Kunz, W. H. (2010). Consumer trust in service companies: A multiple mediating analysis. *Managing Service Quality*, *20*(1), 4–25. doi:10.1108/09604521011011603

Kaplan, A. M., & Haenlein, M. (2010). Users of the world, unite! The challenges and opportunities of social media. *Business Horizons*, *53*(1), 59–68. doi:10.1016/j.bushor.2009.09.003

Kapoor, P. S., Tagore, A., & Dua, S. (2022). Social media influencer promoted sustainable fashion: Effects of sponsorship and benefit association. *Journal of Promotion Management*. Advance online publication. doi:10.1080/10496491.2022.2163034

Karaca, Ş., & Gümüş, N. (2019). *Tüketicilerin online yorum ve değerlendirme puanlarına yönelik tutumlarının online satın alma davranışlarına etkisi. In 4. International EMI Entrepreneurship and Social Sciences Congress Book*. Dilkur Akademi.

Karakavak, Z., & Özbölük, T. (2022). When modesty meets fashion: How social media and influencers change the meaning of hijab. *Journal of Islamic Marketing*. Advance online publication. doi:10.1108/JIMA-05-2021-0152

Kara, Y. (2012). *Sosyal ağların tüketici davranışları üzerindeki etkisi: hazır giyim sektörü örneği*. Yayınlanmamış Yüksek Lisans Tezi, Fatih Üniversitesi Sosyal Bilimler Enstitüsü.

Kastner, M., Tricco, A. C., Soobiah, C., Lillie, E., Perrier, L., Horsley, T., Welch, V., Cogo, E., Antony, J., & Straus, S. E. (2012). What is the most appropriate knowledge synthesis method to conduct a review? Protocol for a scoping review. *BMC Medical Research Methodology*, *12*(1), 1–10. doi:10.1186/1471-2288-12-114 PMID:22862833

Keenan, M. (2022). *Global commerce, industry insights and trends*. https://www.shopify.com/enterprise/global-ecommerce-statistics

Keil, M. (1995). Usefulness and Ease of use: Field study evidence regarding task consideration. *Decision Support Systems*, *13*, 75–91.

Keller, K. L. (1993). Conceptualizing, Measuring, and Managing Customer-Based Brand Equity. *Journal of Marketing*, *57*(1), 1–22. doi:10.1177/002224299305700101

Keller, K. L. (2003). *Strategic Brand Management: Best Practice Cases in Branding: Lessons from the World's Strongest Brands*. Pearson Education.

Kemp, S. (2020) *Digital 2020: 3.8 billion people use social media.* https://wearesocial.com/blog/2020/01/digital-2020-3-8-billion-people-use-social-media

Kemp, S. (2023). *Digital 2023: Global Overview Report - DataReportal – Global Digital Insights. DataReportal.* Retrieved March 15, 2023, from https://datareportal.com/reports/digital-2023-global-overview-report

Keskin, S., & Baş, M. (2015). Sosyal medyanın tüketici davranışları üzerine etkisinin belirlenmesi. *Gazi Üniversitesi İktisadi ve İdari Bilimler Fakültesi Dergisi, 17*(3), 51–69.

Khamis, S., Ang, L., & Welling, R. (2017). Self-branding, 'micro-celebrity' and the rise of Social Media Influencers. *Celebrity Studies, 8*(2), 191–208. doi:10.1080/19392397.2016.1218292

Khan, Z., Yang, Y., Shafi, M., & Yang, R. (2019). Role of social media marketing activities (SMMAs) in apparel brands customer response: A moderated mediation analysis. *Sustainability (Basel), 11*(19), 5167. doi:10.3390u11195167

Khatri, P. (2006). Celebrity endorsement: A strategic promotion perspective. *Indian Media Studies Journal, 1*(1), 25-37.

Kim, A. J., & Ko, E. (2012). Do social media marketing activities enhance customer equity? An empirical study of luxury fashion brand. *Journal of Business Research, 65*(10), 1480–1486. doi:10.1016/j.jbusres.2011.10.014

Kim, C., & Yang, S. U. (2017). Like, comment, and share on Facebook: How each behaviour differs from the other. *Public Relations Review, 43*(2), 441–449. doi:10.1016/j.pubrev.2017.02.006

Kim, D. Y., & Kim, H. Y. (2021). Trust me, trust me not: A nuanced view of influencer marketing on social media. *Journal of Business Research, 134*, 223–232. doi:10.1016/j.jbusres.2021.05.024

Kimery, K. M., & Mccard, M. (2002). Third-party assurances: Mapping the road to trust in e-retailing. *Journal of Information Technology Theory and Application, 4*(2), 63–82.

Kim, H. S., & Damhorst, M. L. (1998). Environmental concern and apparel consumption. *Clothing & Textiles Research Journal, 16*(3), 126–133. doi:10.1177/0887302X9801600303

Kim, J.-H., Kim, M., Park, M., & Yoo, J. (2023). Immersive interactive technologies and virtual shopping experiences: Differences in consumer perceptions between augmented reality (AR) and virtual reality (VR). *Telematics and Informatics, 77*, 101936. doi:10.1016/j.tele.2022.101936

Kim, S., Park, J., & Lee, Y. (2013). The E-Word-of-Mouth effect on consumers Internet shopping behaviour: Focus on apparel products. *International Journal of Fashion Design, Technology and Education, 6*(3), 160–172.

Kim, W. G., Jeong, O. R., & Lee, S. W. (2010). On social Web sites. *Information Systems, 35*(2), 215–236. doi:10.1016/j.is.2009.08.003

King, R. A., Racherla, P., & Bush, V. D. (2014). What we know and don't know about online word-of-mouth: A review and synthesis of the literature. *Journal of Interactive Marketing, 28*(3), 167–183. doi:10.1016/j.intmar.2014.02.001

Kirchherr, J., Reike, D., & Hekkert, M. (2017). Conceptualizing the circular economy: An analysis of 114 definitions. In *Resources* (Vol. 127, pp. 221–232). Conservation and Recycling. doi:10.1016/j.resconrec.2017.09.005

Kırcova, İ. (2012). *İnternette pazarlama.* Beta Basım Yayım.

Kirstein, T. (2013). The future of smart-textiles development: new enabling technologies, commercialization and market trends. In *Multidisciplinary know-how for smart-textiles developers* (pp. 1–25). Woodhead Publishing. doi:10.1533/9780857093530.1

Koçak, N. G. (2012). *Bireylerin sosyal medya kullanım davranışlarının ve motivasyonlarının kullanımlar ve doyumlar yaklaşımı bağlamında incelenmesi: Eskişehir'de bir uygulama*. Yayımlanmamış Doktora Tezi, Anadolu Üniversitesi Sosyal Bilimler Enstitüsü.

Koç, E. (2008). *Tüketici davranışı ve pazarlama stratejileri*. Seçkin Yayınevi.

Koivulehto, E. I. (2017). *Do social media marketing activities enhance customer equity? A case study of fast fashion brand Zara*. Aalto University.

Kong, H. M., Ko, E., Chae, H., & Mattila, P. (2016). Understanding fashion consumers' attitude and behavioral intention toward sustainable fashion products: Focus on sustainable knowledge sources and knowledge types. *Journal of Global Fashion Marketing*, *7*(2), 103–119. doi:10.1080/20932685.2015.1131435

Kotler, P., Armstrong, G., Ang, S. H., Leong, S. M., Tan, C. T., & Ho-Ming, O. (2012). *Principles of marketing: an Asian perspective*. Pearson/Prentice-Hall.

Krippendorff, K. (2018). Content analysis: An introduction to its methodology (4th ed). Thousand Oak: Sage Publications.

Ku, C., Chien, C., & Ma, K. (2020). Digital transformation to empower smart production for Industry 3.5 and an empirical study for textile dyeing. *Computers & Industrial Engineering*, *142*, 106297. doi:10.1016/j.cie.2020.106297

Kumar, V., & Kumar, S. (2021). Impact of covid-19 on textile and fashion industry India: An economic perspective. *Burnieshed Law Journal*, *2*, 312–327.

Kursan Milaković, I. (2021). Purchase experience during the COVID-19 pandemic and social cognitive theory: The relevance of consumer vulnerability, resilience, and adaptability for purchase satisfaction and repurchase. *International Journal of Consumer Studies*, *45*(6), 1425–1442. doi:10.1111/ijcs.12672 PMID:33821146

Kusumasondjaja, S. (2020). Exploring the role of visual aesthetics and presentation modality in luxury fashion brand communication on Instagram. *Journal of Fashion Marketing and Management*, *24*(1), 15–31. doi:10.1108/JFMM-02-2019-0019

Kwak, H., Lee, C., Park, H., & Moon, S. (2010) What is Twitter, a social network or a news media? In *Proceedings of the 19th International Conference on World Wide Web (WWW2010)*. ACM. 10.1145/1772690.1772751

Lamberton, C. P., Naylor, R. W., & Haws, K. L. (2013). Same destination, different paths: When and how does observing others' choices and reasoning alter confidence in our own choices? *Journal of Consumer Psychology*, *23*(1), 74–89. doi:10.1016/j.jcps.2012.01.002

Lambrecht, A., & Tucker, C. (2013). When does retargeting work? Information specificity in online advertising. *Journal of Marketing*, *50*, 561–576.

Lang, C., & Wei, B. (2019). Convert one outfit to more looks: factors influencing young female college consumers' intention to purchase transformable apparel. *Fashion and Textiles*, *6*(1).

Langaro, D., Rita, P., & de Fátima Salgueiro, M. (2018). Do social networking sites contribute for building brands? Evaluating the impact of users' participation on brand awareness and brand attitude. *Journal of Marketing Communications*, *24*(2), 146–168. doi:10.1080/13527266.2015.1036100

Larson, C. (2021). The Promotion of Fast Fashion from Influencers Is Problematic and Unsustainable. *The Daily Utah Chronicle*. https://dailyutahchronicle.com/2021/06/18/the-promotion-of-fast-fashion-from-influencers-is-problematic-and-unsustainable/

Larson, R. J. (2009). *The rise of viral marketing through the new media of social media.* Retrieved February 12, 2020 from: http://digitalcommons.liberty.edu/cgi/viewcontent.cgi?article=1009&context=busi_fac_pubs

Launchmetrics Content Team. (2021). The Impact of Influencer Marketing on Fashion, Beauty and Luxury Sales. *Launchmetrics.* https://www.launchmetrics.com/resources/blog/influencer-marketing-impact-on-sales

Lau, O., & Ki, C.-W. (2021). Can consumers' gamified, personalized, and engaging experiences with VR fashion apps increase in-app purchase intention by fulfilling needs? *Fashion and Textiles*, *8*(1), 36. doi:10.118640691-021-00270-9

Le Pechoux, B., Little, T. J., & Istook, C. L. (2012). Innovation management in creating new fashions. In T. Hines & M. Bruce (Eds.), *Fashion Marketing: Contemporary Issues* (pp. 188–216). Taylor and Francis.

Lee, J. A., Sudarshan, S., Sussman, K. L., Bright, L. F., & Eastin, M. S. (2022). Why are consumers following social media influencers on Instagram? Exploration of consumers' motives for following influencers and the role of materialism. *International Journal of Advertising*, *41*(1), 78–100. doi:10.1080/02650487.2021.1964226

Lee, J., Cho, H., Gay, G., Davison, B., & Ingraffea, T. (2003). Technology acceptance and social networking in distance learning. *Journal of Educational Technology & Society*, *6*(2), 50–61.

Lee, J., Park, D. H., & Han, I. (2008). The effect of negative online consumer reviews on product attitude: An information processing view. *Electronic Commerce Research and Applications*, *7*(3), 341–352. doi:10.1016/j.elerap.2007.05.004

Lee, T. Y., & Bradlow, E. T. (2011). Automated marketing research using online customer reviews. *JMR, Journal of Marketing Research*, *48*(5), 881–894. doi:10.1509/jmkr.48.5.881

Lefebvre, L. A., & Lefebvre, E. (2002). E-commerce and virtual enterprises: Issues and challenges for transition economies. *Technovation*, *22*(5), 313–323. doi:10.1016/S0166-4972(01)00010-4

Legnani, E., Cavalieri, S., Pinto, R., & Dotti, S. (2011). The potential of RFID technology in the textile and clothing industry: Opportunities, requirements and challenges. In *Unique radio innovation for the 21st century*. Springer. doi:10.1007/978-3-642-03462-6_14

Leigh, T. W., Peters, C., & Shelton, J. (2006). The consumer quest for authenticity: The multiplicity of meanings within the MG subculture of consumption. *Journal of the Academy of Marketing Science*, *34*(4), 481–493. doi:10.1177/0092070306288403

Le, K., & Aydin, G. (2022). Impact of the pandemic on social media influencer marketing in fashion: A qualitative study. *Qualitative Market Research*. Advance online publication. doi:10.1108/QMR-11-2021-0133

Lelisho, M. E., Pandey, D., Alemu, B. D., Pandey, B. K., & Tareke, S. A. (2023). The negative impact of social media during COVID-19 pandemic. *Trends in Psychology*, *31*(1), 123–142.

Lemon, K. N., Rust, R. T., & Zeithaml, V. A. (2001). What drives customer equity? *Marketing Management, 10*(1), 20-25.

Leng, G. S., Lada, S., & Muhammad, M. Z. (2011, August). An Exploration of Social Networking Sites (SNS) Adoption in Malaysia using Technology Acceptance Model (TAM), Theory of Planned Behavior (TPB) and Intrusive Motivation. *Journal of Internet Banking and Commerce*, *16*(2).

Lerner, R. M., & Steinberg, L. (2009). *Individual Bases Adolescent Development*. Handbook of Adolescent Psychology. John Wiley and Sons.

Leung, F. F., Gu, F. F., & Palmatier, R. W. (2022). Online influencer marketing. *Journal of the Academy of Marketing Science*, *50*(2), 226–251. doi:10.100711747-021-00829-4

Liang, Y., Lee, S.-H., & Workman, J. E. (2020). Implementation of Artificial Intelligence in Fashion: Are Consumers Ready? *Clothing & Textiles Research Journal*, *38*(1), 3–18. doi:10.1177/0887302X19873437

Liberati, A., Altman, D. G., Tetzlaff, J., Mulrow, C., Gøtzsche, P. C., Ioannidis, J. P. A., Clarke, M., Devereaux, P. J., Kleijnen, J., & Moher, D. (2009). The PRISMA Statement for Reporting Systematic Reviews and Meta-Analyses of Studies That Evaluate Health Care Interventions: Explanation and Elaboration. *PLoS Medicine*, *6*(7), e1000100. doi:10.1371/journal.pmed.1000100 PMID:19621070

Li, H., Jiang, J., & Wu, M. (2014). The effects of trust assurances on consumers' initial online trust: A two-stage decision-making process perspective. *International Journal of Information Management*, *34*(3), 395–405. doi:10.1016/j.ijinfomgt.2014.02.004

Li, N., & Gillet, D. (2013). Identifying influential scholars in academic social media platforms. *Proceedings of the 2013 IEEE/ACM International Conference on Advances in Social Networks Analysis and Mining*, 608–614. 10.1145/2492517.2492614

Lin, H. C., Bruning, P. F., & Swarna, H. (2018). Using online opinion leaders to promote the hedonic and utilitarian value of products and services. *Business Horizons*, *61*(3), 431–442. doi:10.1016/j.bushor.2018.01.010

Lin, J., & Lu, Y. (2019). The role of social media in the fashion industry: How fashion blogging encourages two-way symmetrical communication. *Journal of Global Fashion Marketing*, *10*(2), 186–200.

Lin, K., & Lu, H. (2011). Intention to Continue Using Facebook Fan Pages from the Perspective of Social Capital Theory. *Cyberpsychology, Behavior, and Social Networking*, *14*.

Lin, Y., & Kant, S. (2021). Using social media for citizen participation: Contexts, empowerment, and inclusion. *Sustainability (Basel)*, *13*(12), 6635. doi:10.3390u13126635

Li, R., & Suh, A. (2015). Factors influencing information credibility on social media platforms: Evidence form Facebook pages. *Procedia Computer Science*, *72*, 314–328.

Lissitsa, S., & Kol, O. (2021). Four generational cohorts and hedonic m-shopping: Association between personality traits and purchase intention. *Electronic Commerce Research*, *21*(2), 545–570. doi:10.100710660-019-09381-4

Littrell, M. A., Jin Ma, Y., & Halepete, J. (2005). Generation X, baby boomers, and swing: Marketing fair trade apparel. *Journal of Fashion Marketing and Management*, *9*(4), 407–419. doi:10.1108/13612020510620786

Liu, X., Burns, A. C., & Hou, Y. (2017). An investigation of brand-related user-generated content on Twitter. *Journal of Advertising*, *46*(2), 236–247. doi:10.1080/00913367.2017.1297273

López, M., & Sicilia, M. (2014). eWOM as Source of Influence: The Impact of Participation in eWOM and Perceived Source Trustworthiness on Decision Making. *Journal of Interactive Advertising*, *14*(2), 86–97. doi:10.1080/15252019.2014.944288

Lou, C., & Yuan, S. (2019). Influencer Marketing: How Message Value and Credibility Affect Consumer Trust of Branded Content on Social Media. *Journal of Interactive Advertising*, *19*(1).

Lou, C., Tan, S. S., & Chen, X. (2019). Investigating consumer engagement with influencer- vs. brand-promoted ads: The roles of source and disclosure. *Journal of Interactive Advertising*, *19*(3), 169–186. doi:10.1080/15252019.2019.1667928

Loureiro, S. M. C., Cavallero, L., & Miranda, F. J. (2018). Fashion brands on retail websites: Customer performance expectancy and e-word-of-mouth. *Journal of Retailing and Consumer Services*, *41*, 131–141.

Loureiro, S. M. C., Maximiano, M., & Panchapakesan, P. (2018). Engaging fashion consumers in social media: The case of luxury brands. *International Journal of Fashion Design, Technology and Education*, *11*(3), 310–321.

Luce, L. (2019). *Artificial Intelligence for Fashion How AI is Revolutionizing the Fashion Industry*. Apress. doi:10.1007/978-1-4842-3931-5

Lumpkin, J., & Greenberg, B. (1982). Apparel-shopping patterns of the elderly consumer. *Journal of Retailing*, *58*(4), 68–89.

Lumpkin, J., Greenberg, B., & Goldstucker, J. (1985). Marketplace needs of the elderly: Determinant attributes and store choice. *Journal of Retailing*, *61*(2), 75–105.

Lundblad, L., & Davies, I. A. (2015). The values and motivations behind sustainable fashion consumption. *Journal of Consumer Behaviour*, *15*(2), 149–162. doi:10.1002/cb.1559

Lu, Y., Zhao, L., & Wang, B. (2010). From virtual community members to C2C e-commerce buyers: Trust in virtual communities and its effect on consumers' purchase intention. *Electronic Commerce Research and Applications*, *9*(4), 346–360. doi:10.1016/j.elerap.2009.07.003

Lynch, S., & Barnes, L. (2020). Omnichannel fashion retailing: Examining the customer decision-making journey. *Journal of Fashion Marketing and Management*, *24*(3), 471–493. doi:10.1108/JFMM-09-2019-0192

M & K. (2017). Impact of Influencers in Consumer Decision Process: the Fashion Industry. *SCMS Cochin School of Business*. https://pdfs.semanticscholar.org/1469/eccb29f76b24e85cba8b6b60adf5ab4932d8.pdfm

Macdonald, E. K., & Sharp, B. M. (2000). Brand Awareness Effects on Consumer Decision Making for a Common, Repeat Purchase Product: A Replication. *Journal of Business Research*, *48*(1), 5–15. doi:10.1016/S0148-2963(98)00070-8

MacInnis, D., & Folkes, V. (2009). The Disciplinary Status of Consumer Behavior: A Sociology of Science Perspective on Key Controversies. *The Journal of Consumer Research*, *36*(6), 899–914. doi:10.1086/644610

Mackay, J. B., & Lowrey, W. (2011). The credibility divide: Reader trust of online newspapers and blogs. *Journal of Media Sociology*, *3*(1-4), 39–57.

Madzunya, N., Viljoen, K., & Cilliers, L. (2021). The effect of Instagram conspicuous consumptive behaviour on the intention to purchase luxury goods: A developing country's perspective. *South African Journal of Information Management*, *23*(1). Advance online publication. doi:10.4102ajim.v23i1.1267

Magano, J. (n.d.). Attitudes toward Fashion Influencers as a Mediator of Purchase Intention. *MDPI*. https://www.mdpi.com/2078-2489/13/6/297

Magazine, A. (2010). How social media is revolutionizing the apparel industry: One message at a time. *Apparel Magazine*, *52*(4), 1–6.

Malhotra, N. k. (2001). *Pesquisa de Marketing: Uma Orientação Aplicada*. Academic Press.

Mann, B.J.S., & Sahni, S.K. (2012). Profiling Adopter Categories of Internet Banking in India: An Empirical Study. *Vision: The Journal of Business Perspective, 16*(4), 283-295.

Manneh, M. (2017). *The influence of social media on e-commerce: Fast fashion multinational companies*. Academic Press.

Manzoor, U., Baig, S. A., Hashim, M., & Sami, A. (2020). Impact of Social Media Marketing on Consumer's Purchase Intentions: The Mediating role of Customer Trust. *International Journal of Entrepreneurial Research*, *3*(2), 41–48. doi:10.31580/ijer.v3i2.1386

Marsden, P. (2011). *Who is the social consumer?* https://digitalwellbeing.org/infographic-who-is-the-social-consumer/

Martínez Caballero, E., & Vázquez Casco, A. I. (2006). *Marketing de la moda*. Pirámide.

Martinka, L. (2012). *How social media communities impact consumer behavior* [Dissertation]. Gonzaga University.

Mason, A. N., Narcum, J., & Mason, K. (2021). Social media marketing gains importance after Covid-19. *Cogent Business & Management*, *8*(1), 1870797. doi:10.1080/23311975.2020.1870797

Mayer, R. C., & Davis, J. H. (1999). The effect of the performance appraisal system on trust for management: A field quasi-experiment. *The Journal of Applied Psychology*, *84*(1), 123–136. doi:10.1037/0021-9010.84.1.123

McCarthy, S. (2013). *The Effects of Social Media on Fashion Consumption*. Honors Theses, Sally McDonnell Barksdale Honors College.

Mcdowell, M. (2021). *Snapchat boosts AR try-on tools: Farfetch, Prada dive in*, https://www.voguebusiness.com/technology/snapchat-boosts-ar-try-on-tools-farfetch-prada-dive-in

McFarlane, A., & Samsioe, E. (2020). #50+ fashion Instagram influencers: Cognitive age and aesthetic digital labours. *Journal of Fashion Marketing and Management*, *24*(3), 399–413. doi:10.1108/JFMM-08-2019-0177

McKinsey & Company & Business of Fashion. (2021). *The state of fashion 2022*. https://www.mckinsey.com/~/media/mckinsey/industries/retail/our%20insights/state%20of%20fashion/2022/the-state-of-fashion-2022.pdf

McKinsey & Company. (2021). *Fashion industry during--and after--the coronavirus crisis* Retrieved March 15, 2023, from https://www.mckinsey.com/industries/retail/our-insights/perspectives-for-north-americas-fashion-industry-in-a-time-of-crisis

McKinsey & Company. (2021). *State of Fashion*. Retrieved March 15, 2023, from https://www.mckinsey.com/industries/retail/our-insights/state-of-fashion

McKinsey & Company. (2022). *The state of fashion 2023: holding onto growth as global clouds gather*. https://www.mckinsey.com/industries/retail/our-insights/state-of-fashion

McLean, P. (2016). *Culture in Networks*. Wiley.

Mcleod, S. (2007). *HCC certificate in counselling skills Maslow's hierarchy of needs*. Retrieved February 11, 2020 from https://highgatecounselling.org.uk/members/certificate/CT2%20Paper%201.pdf

McMillen, J. (2022, October 17). *6 facts about middle-aged women retailers should know*. Forbes. https://www.forbes.com/sites/jennmcmillen/2022/10/17/6-facts-about-middle-aged-women-retailers-should-know/?sh=6a812fde4ef4

McNamara, K. (2008). *The global textile and garments industry: the role of Information and Communication Technologies (ICTs) in exploiting the value chain*. Academic Press.

Mcneill, L., & Moore, R. (2015). Sustainable fashion consumption and the fast fashion conundrum: Fashionable consumers and attitudes to sustainability in clothing choice. *International Journal of Consumer Studies*, *39*(3), 212–222. doi:10.1111/ijcs.12169

McQuarrie, E. F., Miller, J., & Phillips, B. J. (2013). The megaphone effect: Taste and audience in fashion blogging. *The Journal of Consumer Research*, *40*(1), 136–158. doi:10.1086/669042

McQuarrie, E. F., & Phillips, B. J. (2014). The Megaphone Effect in Social Media: How Ordinary Consumers Become Style Leaders. *GfK MIR*, *6*(2), 16–20. doi:10.2478/gfkmir-2014-0092

McSherry, M. (2022). *@acteevism*. Instagram. https://www.instagram.com/acteevism/

Mediakix. (2021). *The Best Brands On Instagram: How Zara Got 10M Followers*. Retrieved March 15, 2023, from https://mediakix.com/blog/best-brands-on-instagram-zara-channel-followers/

Medium. (2018). *Instagram is Playing A Huge Role in India's Fashion Market.* https://medium.com/@ifashionseo/instagram-is-playing-a-huge-role-in-indias-fashion-market-2677eb1e009e

Meng, X., Zhang, W., Li, Y., Cao, X., & Feng, X. (2020). Social media effect, investor recognition and the cross-section of stock returns. *International Review of Financial Analysis, 67*, 101432. doi:10.1016/j.irfa.2019.101432

Meta. (2023). *Company Information, Culture, and Principles | About Meta.* Meta Platforms, Inc. https://about.meta.com/company-info/?utm_source=about.facebook.com&utm_medium=redirect

Mickevičiute, A., & Siudikiene, D. (2019). The role of fashion bloggers in fashion marketing communication [Mados tinklaraštininku isitraukimas i mados rinkodaros komunikacija]. *Informacijos Mokslai, 85*, 8–50. doi:10.15388/Im.2019.85.15

Miles, M. B., & Huberman, A. M. (1994). Qualitative data analysis: An expanded sourcebook. *Sage (Atlanta, Ga.).*

Miller, G. R., & Baseheart, J. (1969). Source trustworthiness, opinionated statements, and response to persuasive communication. *Speech Monographs, 36*(1), 1–7. doi:10.1080/03637756909375602

Miller, V. (2020). *Understanding Digital Culture* (2nd ed.). Sage.

Min Kong, H., & Ko, E. (2017). Why do consumers choose sustainable fashion? A crosscultural study of South Korean, Chinese, and Japanese consumers. *Journal of Global Fashion Marketing, 8*(3), 220–234. doi:10.1080/20932685.2017.1336458

Mirabi, V., Akbariyeh, H., & Tahmasebifard, H. (2015). A Study of Factors Affecting on Customers Purchase Intention Case Study : The Agencies of Bono Brand Tile in Tehran. *Journal of Multidisciplinary Engineering Science and Technology, 2*(1), 267–273.

Miranda, S., Antunes, A. C., & Gama, A. (2022, April). A different type of influencer? Examining senior Instagram influencers communication. In *Proceedings of the 9th European Conference on Social Media* (pp. 130-136). Academic Conferences International. 10.34190/ecsm.9.1.337

Mohsin, M. (2020, February 6). *10 Instagram Statistics Everyone Should Know in 2020* [Infographic]. Retrieved February 11, 2020 from https://www.oberlo.com/blog/instagram-stats-every-marketer-should-know

Moisander, J., Närvänen, E., & Valtonen, A. (2020). Interpretive marketing research. In *Marketing Management* (pp. 237–253). Routledge. doi:10.4324/9780203710807-19

Moon, K., & Ngai, E. (2008). The adoption of RFID in fashion retailing: A business value-added framework. *Industrial Management & Data Systems, 108*(5), 596–612. doi:10.1108/02635570810876732

Moore, A., Yang, K., & Kim, H. M. (2018, January). Influencer marketing: Influentials' authenticity, likeability and authority in social media. In *International Textile and Apparel Association Annual Conference Proceedings* (*Vol. 75*, No. 1). Iowa State University Digital Press.

Moore, M., & Carpenter, J. (2006). The effect of price as a marketplace cue on retail patronage. *Journal of Product and Brand Management, 15*(4), 265–271. doi:10.1108/10610420610679647

Morra, M. C., Gelosa, V., Ceruti, F., & Mazzucchelli, A. (2018). Original or counterfeit luxury fashion brands? The effect of social media on purchase intention. *Journal of Global Fashion Marketing, 9*(1), 24–39. doi:10.1080/20932685.2017.1399079

Moustakas, C. (1994). Phenomenological Research Methods. *Sage (Atlanta, Ga.).*

Mowka, M. P., Prieve, E. A., & Dawson, W. M. (1980). *Marketing the Arts.* Praeger.

Muntinga, D. G., Moorman, M., & Smit, E. G. (2011). Introducing COBRAs; exploring motivations for brand-related social media use. *International Journal of Advertising*, *30*, 13–46. doi:10.2501/IJA-30-1-013-046

Mürütsoy, M. (2013). *İnternet tüketicisinin satın alma davranışlarının incelenmesi üzerine bir araştırma.* Yüksek Lisans Tezi. Niğde Üniversitesi Sosyal Bilimler Enstitüsü, Niğde.

Naeem, M., & Ozuem, W. (2021). Understanding the social consumer fashion brand engagement journey: Insights about reputed fashion brands. *Journal of Brand Management*, *28*(5), 1–16. doi:10.105741262-021-00239-5

Nam, J., Hamlin, R., Gam, H. J., Kang, J. H., Kim, J., Kumphai, P., Starr, C., & Richards, L. (2007). The fashion-conscious behaviours of mature female consumers. *International Journal of Consumer Studies*, *31*(1), 102–108. doi:10.1111/j.1470-6431.2006.00497.x

Nannini, V. (2020). Fashion consumption in digital media: Multiple practices and new identities. *Fashion, Style & Popular Culture*, *7*(4), 519–537. doi:10.1386/fspc_00041_1

Narayanan, B. G. (2008). Effects of phasing out of MFA quotas on Indian garment exports, 1992-2003. *Regional and Sectoral Economic Studies*, *8*, 71–88.

Naresh & Dash. (2013). *Marketing Research: An applied orientation*. Pearson.

Nash, J. (2019). Exploring how social media platforms influence fashion consumer decisions in the UK retail sector. *Journal of Fashion Marketing and Management*, *23*(1), 82–103. doi:10.1108/JFMM-01-2018-0012

Nasir, M. A., Yago, M., & Wu, J. (2015). Influence of psychographics and risk perception of internet banking adoption: Current State of affairs in Britain. *Marketing Intelligence and Planning*. Accessed at https://www.researchgate.net/publication/281752024

Nayak, R., Singh, A., Padhye, R., & Wang, L. (2015). RFID in textile and clothing manufacturing: Technology and challenges. *Fashion and Textiles*, *2*(1), 9. doi:10.118640691-015-0034-9

Naylor, R. W., Lamberton, C. P., & West, P. M. (2012). Beyond the 'like' button: The impact of mere virtual presence on brand evaluations and purchase intentions in social media settings. *Journal of Marketing*, *76*(6), 105–120. doi:10.1509/jm.11.0105

Netzer, O., Feldman, R., Goldenberg, J., & Fresko, M. (2012). Mine your own business: Market-structure surveillance through text mining. *Marketing Science*, *31*(3), 521–543. doi:10.1287/mksc.1120.0713

Nguyen, D. (2018). *Social media marketing strategy-Case study H&M Hennes & Mauritz* [Bachelor dissertation]. The Haaga Helia University of Applied Sciences.

Nicol, D., & Agam, L. A. (2016). The impact of viral marketing through Instagram. *Proceedings of Bangkok annual Business and Social Sciences Research Conference.*

Niculescu, A., Dumitriu, D., Purdescu, C., & Popescu, M. A. M. (2019). Enhancing brand value of modern organizations through digital marketing tools and techniques: A study on top ten Romanian companies. *TEM Journal*, *8*(1), 171.

Niinimäki, K. (2010). Eco-Clothing, consumer identity and ideology. *Sustainable Development (Bradford)*, *18*(3), 150–162. doi:10.1002d.455

Nikolov, N., Roman, D., & Sukhobok, D. (2017, August). Tabular data anomaly patterns. In *2017 International Conference on Big Data Innovations and Applications (Innovate-Data)* (pp. 25-34). IEEE.

Nizri, E. (2022). *Macro-Influencers Vs. Micro-Influencers: The Great Social Media Debate*. Forbes. https://www.forbes.com/sites/forbestechcouncil/2022/03/01/macro-influencers-vs-micro-influencers-the-great-social-media-debate/?sh=44a468c45286

Nunnally, J. C. (1978). *Psychometric theory* (2nd ed.). Mc Graw Hill.

Nyilasy, G., Gangadharbatla, H., & Paladino, A. (2014). Perceived greenwashing: The interactive effects of green advertising and corporate environmental performance on consumer reactions. *Journal of Business Ethics*, *125*(4), 693–707. doi:10.100710551-013-1944-3

Odabaşı, Y., & Barış, G. (2013). *Tüketici davranışı*. Mediacat Yayınevi.

Odabaşı, Y., & Oyman, M. (2003). *Pazarlama iletişimi yönetimi*. Mediacat Yayınevi.

Ohanian, R. (1990). Construction and validation of a scale to measure celebrity endorsers' perceived expertise, trustworthiness, and attractiveness. *Journal of Advertising*, *19*(3), 39–52. doi:10.1080/00913367.1990.10673191

Oh, H. (1999). Service quality, customer satisfaction, and customer value: A holistic perspective. *International Journal of Hospitality Management*, *18*(1), 67–82. doi:10.1016/S0278-4319(98)00047-4

Olgun, B. (2015). Sosyal medyanın tüketici satın alma davranışları üzerindeki etkisi. *Gümüşhane Üniversitesi Sosyal Bilimler Elektronik Dergisi*, *12*, 484–507.

Oliver, C. (2008). *Social networks change the online retail game*. Academic Press.

Olotewo, J. (2016). Social media marketing in emerging markets. *International Journal of Online Marketing Research*, *2*(2), 10–18. doi:10.5455/IJOMR.2016254411

Omarlı, S., & Parıltı, N. (2017). elektronik pazarlamanın tüketicilerin satın alma davranışları üzerine etkisi, Türkiye'de üniversite öğrencileri arasında uygulama. *Anadolu Kültürel Araştırmalar Dergisi*, *1*(3), 91–109.

Onan, A. (2021). Sentiment analysis on massive open online course evaluations: A text mining and deep learning approach. *Computer Applications in Engineering Education*, *29*(3), 572–589. doi:10.1002/cae.22253

onestylishmoo. (2022). *@onestylishmoo*. Instagram. https://www.instagram.com/onestylishmoo/

Onurlubaş, E., Öztürk, D., & Çetin, O. I. (2016). Sosyal medyada pazarlama algısının faktör analiziyle incelenmesi. *Dicle Üniversitesi Sosyal Bilimler Enstitüsü Dergisi*, *8*(16), 233–254.

Otugo, N. E., Uzuegbunam, C. E., & Obikeze, C. O. (2015). Social media advertising/marketing: A study of awareness, attitude and responsiveness by Nigerian youths. *International Conference on Communication, Media, Technology, and Design*, *1*(2), 1-17. 10.30935/ojcmt/5679

Özcan, S. O. (2010). İnternet pazarlama faaliyetlerinde tüketici satın alma karar süreci. *İnternet Uygulamaları ve Yönetimi Dergisi*, *1*(2), 29-39.

Ozdamar Ertekin, Z., & Atik, D. (2015). Sustainable Markets: Motivating Factors, Barriers, and Remedies for Mobilization of Slow Fashion. *Journal of Macromarketing*, *35*(1), 53–69. doi:10.1177/0276146714535932

Özgüven, N. (2011). Tüketicilerin online alışverişe karşı tutumları ile demografik özellikleri arasındaki ilişkinin analizi. *KMÜ Sosyal ve Ekonomik Araştırmalar Dergisi*, *2011*(2), 47–54.

Öztürk, D. (2016). Tedarik zinciri yönetimi süreçlerini etkileyen faktörler. *Uluslararası Sosyal ve Ekonomik Bilimler Dergisi*, *6*(1), 17–24.

Padel, S., & Foster, C. (2005). Exploring the gap between attitude and behaviour: Understanding why consumers buy or do not buy organic food. *British Food Journal, 107*(8), 606-625.

Pagiaslis, A., & Krontalis, A. K. (2014). Green Consumption Behavior Antecedents: Environmental Concern, Knowledge, and Beliefs. *Psychology and Marketing, 31*(5), 335–348. doi:10.1002/mar.20698

Pandey, B. K., Pandey, D., Wairya, S., Agarwal, G., Dadeech, P., Dogiwal, S. R., & Pramanik, S. (2022). Application of integrated steganography and image compressing techniques for confidential information transmission. *Cyber Security and Network Security*, 169-191.

Pandey, D., Aswari, A., Taufiqurakman, M., Khalim, A., & Azahrah, F. F. (2021). System Of Education Changes Due to Covid-19 Pandemic. *Asian Journal of Advances in Research*, 10-15.

Pandey, B. K., Mane, D., Nassa, V. K. K., Pandey, D., Dutta, S., Ventayen, R. J. M., & Rastogi, R. (2021). Secure text extraction from complex degraded images by applying steganography and deep learning. In *Multidisciplinary approach to modern digital steganography* (pp. 146–163). IGI Global.

Pandey, B. K., Pandey, D., Wairya, S., & Agarwal, G. (2021). An advanced morphological component analysis, steganography, and deep learning-based system to transmit secure textual data. *International Journal of Distributed Artificial Intelligence, 13*(2), 40–62.

Pandey, B. K., Pandey, D., Wariya, S., & Agarwal, G. (2021). A deep neural network-based approach for extracting textual images from deteriorate images. *EAI Endorsed Transactions on Industrial Networks and Intelligent Systems, 8*(28), e3–e3.

Pandey, B. K., Pandey, D., Wariya, S., Aggarwal, G., & Rastogi, R. (2021). Deep learning and particle swarm optimisation-based techniques for visually impaired humans' text recognition and identification. *Augmented Human Research, 6*, 1–14.

Pandey, D., Wairya, S., & Pradhan, B. (2022). Understanding COVID-19 response by twitter users: A text analysis approach. *Heliyon, 8*(8), e09994.

Papachristou, E., Dimou, Z., Grammatikopoulou, M., Mpaltadoros, L., & Stavropoulos, T. G. (2022). Personalized Fashion On-Demand and e-Fashion Business Models: A User Survey in Greece. In P. Kyratsis, N. Efkolidis, & J. P. Davim (Eds.), *Advances in Product Design Engineering. Management and Industrial Engineering*. Springer. doi:10.1007/978-3-030-98124-2_4

Pappu, R., Quester, P. G., & Cooksey, R. W. (2006). Consumer-based brand equity and country-of-origin relationships: Some empirical evidence. *European Journal of Marketing, 40*(5/6), 696–717. doi:10.1108/03090560610657903

Paré, G., & Kitsiou, S. (2017). *Methods for literature reviews. In Handbook of eHealth Evaluation: An Evidence-based Approach.* University of Victoria. https://www.ncbi.nlm.nih.gov/books/NBK481583/

Park, C. H. (2018, January). Anomaly pattern detection on data streams. In *2018 IEEE International Conference on Big Data and Smart Computing (BigComp)* (pp. 689-692). IEEE. 10.1109/BigComp.2018.00127

Park, C., & Lee, T. M. (2009). Information direction, website reputation and eWOM effect: A moderating role of product type. *Journal of Business Research, 62*(1), 61–67. doi:10.1016/j.jbusres.2007.11.017

Parker, C. (2011). *301 ways to use social media to boost your marketing*. McGraw-Hill.

Parker, C. J., & Wang, H. (2016). Examining hedonic and utilitarian motivations for m-commerce fashion retail app engagement. *Journal of Fashion Marketing and Management, 20*(4), 487–506. doi:10.1108/JFMM-02-2016-0015

Park, H., & Kim, S. (2023). Do Augmented and Virtual Reality Technologies Increase Consumers' Purchase Intentions? The Role of Cognitive Elaboration and Shopping Goals. *Clothing & Textiles Research Journal, 41*(2), 91–106. doi:10.1177/0887302X21994287

Park, J., Ciampaglia, G. L., & Ferrara, E. (2016) Style in the Age of Instagram Predicting Success within the Fashion Industry using Social Media. *Proceedings of the 19th ACM Conference on Computer-Supported Cooperative Work & Social Computing,* 64-73. 10.1145/2818048.2820065

Park, J., & Gursoy, D. (2012). Generation effects on work engagement among U.S. hotel employees. *International Journal of Hospitality Management, 31*(4), 1195–1202.

Parveen, F., Jaafar, N. I., & Ainin, S. (2015). Social media usage and organizational performance: Reflections of Malaysian social media managers. *Telematics and Informatics, 32*(1), 67–78. doi:10.1016/j.tele.2014.03.001

Peck, J., & Childers, T. L. (2003). Individual differences in haptic ınformation processing: The "need for touch" scale. *The Journal of Consumer Research, 30*(3), 430–442. doi:10.1086/378619

Pendlebury, J., Veldpaus, L., & Garrow, H. (2023). Relationality, place governance and heritage: The Lower Ouseburn Valley, Newcastle upon Tyne and 'Ouseburnness'. *Planning Practice and Research, 38*(3), 409–424. doi:10.1080/02697459.2023.2180193

Pereira, H. G., Salgueiro, M. F., & Rita, P. (2017). Online determinants of e-customer satisfaction: Application to website purchases in tourism. *Service Business, 11*(2), 375–403. doi:10.100711628-016-0313-6

Pereira, M. A. F. (2020). *The consuption of environmentally sustainable textiles and apparel: A generational approach.* Faculdade de Economia do Porto.

Pérez del Castillo, T., Díaz Soloaga, P., & McColl, J. (2020). Lifestyle branding as a brand-oriented positioning strategy: Insights from Spanish fashion consultants [以品牌为导向的定位策略之生活方式品牌:西班牙时尚顾问的见解]. *Journal of Global Fashion Marketing, 11*(4), 361–379. doi:10.1080/20932685.2020.1791727

Perry, P., Ashman, R., & Stalker, I. D. (2020). *Special session: Corporate social responsibility and AI: The case of fashion: An abstract.* doi:10.1007/978-3-030-42545-6_36

Peslak, A., Cecucci, W., & Sendall, P. (2011). *An Empirical Study of Social Networking Behavior using theory of Reasoned action.* Conference for Information Systems Applied Research.

Peters, C., Shelton, J. A., & Thomas, J. B. (2011). Self-concept and the fashion behavior of women over 50. *Journal of Fashion Marketing and Management, 15*(3), 291–305. doi:10.1108/13612021111151905

Pew Research Center. (2021, April 7). *Social Media Fact Sheet.* https://www.pewresearch.org/internet/fact-sheet/social-media/

Pew. (2021). *Social Media Fact Sheet.* https://www.pewresearch.org/internet/fact-sheet/social-media/

Phillips, D. (2008). The psychology of social media. *Journal of New Communications Research, 3*(1), 79–85.

Phua, J., Jin, S. V., & Kim, J. J. (2017). Gratifications of using Face-book, Twitter, Instagram, or Snapchat to follow brands: The moderating effect of social comparison, trust, tie strength, and network homophily on brand identification, brand engagement, brand commitment, and membership intention. *Telematics and Informatics, 34*(1), 412–424. doi:10.1016/j.tele.2016.06.004

Pickett-Baker, J., & Ozaki, R. (2008). Pro-environmental products: Marketing influence on consumer purchase decision. *Journal of Consumer Marketing, 25*(5), 281–293. doi:10.1108/07363760810890516

Pikkarainen, T., Pikkarainen, K., Karjaluoto, H., & Pahnila, S. (2004). Consumer acceptance of online banking: An extension of the technology acceptance model. *Internet Research, 14*, 224–235.

Pinchot, J., Paullet, K., & Rota, D. (2011). How Mobile Technology is Changing Our Culture. *Journal of Information Systems Applied Research, 4*(1), 39–48.

Poel, T. (2009). Conceptualizing forums and blogs as public spheres. In M. V. D. Boomen, S. Lammes, A. S. Lehmann, J. Raessens, & M. T. Schafer (Eds.), *Digital material: tracing new media in everyday life and technology* (pp. 239–251). Amsterdam University Press.

Popli, S., & Rishi, B. (2021a). The What, Why and How of Customer Experience. In Crafting Customer Experience Strategy. Emerald Publishing Limited. doi:10.1108/978-1-83909-710-220211001

Popli, S., & Rishi, B. (2021b). Customer Experience Management – The Road Ahead. In Crafting Customer Experience Strategy. Emerald Publishing Limited. doi:10.1108/978-1-83909-710-220211011

Pop, R.-A., Hlédik, E., & Dabija, D.-C. (2023). Predicting consumers' purchase intention through fast fashion mobile apps: The mediating role of attitude and the moderating role of COVID-19. *Technological Forecasting and Social Change, 186*, 122111. doi:10.1016/j.techfore.2022.122111

Pourmoneh, A., & Rajabi, R. (2022). Can reviews predict reviewers' numerical ratings? (c underlying mechanisms of customers' decisions to rate products using Latent Dirichlet Allocation (LDA). *Journal of Consumer Marketing, 39*(2), 230–241. doi:10.1108/JCM-09-2020-4114

Poushter, J. (2016). Smartphone ownership and internet usage continues to climb in emerging economies. *Pew Research Center, 22*(1), 1–44.

Prime One Global, L. L. C. (2021). *What has the Internet done to the Sri Lankan Marketing Industry?* Retrieved March 15, 2023, from https://www.primeone.global/sri-lankan-digital-marketing-industry/

Pyrgiotakis, E. I., & Symeou, L. (2016). Qualitative research and the scientific value of the knowledge produced in the Social Sciences and Humanities. Research Methodology in Social Sciences and Education, 193-226.

Quelhas-Brito, P., Brandão, A., Gadekar, M., & Castelo-Branco, S. (2020). Diffusing fashion information by social media fashion influencers: Understanding antecedents and consequences. *Journal of Fashion Marketing and Management, 24*(2), 137–152. doi:10.1108/JFMM-09-2019-0214

Rafael. (2019). *How to measure social media engagement + tools to track.* https://www.talkwalker.com/blog/how-to-measure-social-media-engagement

Rausch, T. M., & Kopplin, C. S. (2021). Bridge the gap: Consumers' purchase intention and behaviour regarding sustainable clothing. *Journal of Cleaner Production, 278*, 123882. doi:10.1016/j.jclepro.2020.123882

Rauturier, S. (2021). *How Ethical Is Aritzia?* Good on You. https://goodonyou.eco/how-ethical-is-nike/

Raza, M. (2016) *6 Pakistani fashion brands that wowed us with winning social media campaigns.* Retrieved March 15, 2023, from https://images.dawn.com/news/1175906

Reilly, A., & Barry, B. (2020). *Crossing gender boundaries: Fashion to create, disrupt, and transcend.* Intellect Books.

Reilly, C. F., Salinas, D., & De Leon, D. (2014). Ranking users based on influence in a directional social network. *2014 International Conference on Computational Science and Computational Intelligence, 2*, 237–240. 10.1109/CSCI.2014.127

Reinikainen, H., Munnukka, J., Maity, D., & Luoma-aho, V. (2020). 'You really are a great big sister' – parasocial relationships, credibility, and the moderating role of audience comments in influencer marketing. *Journal of Marketing Management, 36*(3–4), 279–298. doi:10.1080/0267257X.2019.1708781

Remco & Helms. (2014). *Analyzing social influence through social media.* IADIS International Conference on Information Systems, Madrid, Spain.

Research, G. V. (2021). *Textile Market Size, Share & Trends Analysis Report By Raw Material (Wool, Chemical, Silk), By Product (Natural Fibers, Polyester), By Application, By Region, And Segment Forecasts, 2023 - 2030.* Retrieved from https://www.grandviewresearch.com/industry-analysis/textile-market

Reynolds, K. E., Folse, J. A. G., & Jones, M. A. (2006). Search regret: Antecedents and consequences. *Journal of Retailing, 82*(4), 339–348. doi:10.1016/j.jretai.2006.08.007

Rezaei, S., Shahijan, M. K., Amin, M., & Ismail, W. K. W. (2016). Determinants of app stores continuance behavior: A PLS path modelling approach. *Journal of Internet Commerce, 15*(4), 408–440. doi:10.1080/15332861.2016.1256749

Rezvani, S., Dehkordi, G. J., Rahman, M. S., Fouladivanda, F., Habibi, M., & Eghtebasi, S. (2012). A conceptual study on the country of origin effect on consumer purchase intention. *Asian Social Science, 8*(12), 205–215. doi:10.5539/ass.v8n12p205

Rhee, H.-L., & Lee, K.-H. (2021). Enhancing the Sneakers Shopping Experience through Virtual Fitting Using Augmented Reality. *Sustainability (Basel), 13*(11), 6336. doi:10.3390u13116336

Rishi, B., & Kuthuru, N. R. (2021a). A Review for Managerial Guidelines for Social Media Integration of IMC in Digital Era. In Digital Entertainment (pp. 187-212). Palgrave Macmillan. doi:10.1007/978-981-15-9724-4_10

Rishi, B., & Kuthuru, N. R. (2021b). Leveraging Social Media to Create Socially Responsible Consumers. In Social and Sustainability Marketing (pp. 415-432). Productivity Press. doi:10.4324/9781003188186-15

Rishi, B., & Popli, S. (2021). Getting Into the Customers, Shoes: Customer Journey Management. In Crafting Customer Experience Strategy. Emerald Publishing Limited. doi:10.1108/978-1-83909-710-220211002

Rishi, B., & Agarwal, S. (2022). An Unexpected Journey: Designing a Framework to Use Social Media for Consumer Well-Being. In J. Bhattacharyya (Ed.), *Dealing with Socially Responsible Consumers.* doi:10.1007/978-981-19-4457-4_7

Rishi, B., Anand, A., & Sharma, T. (2023). An Unexpected Journey: Designing a Social Media Marketing Framework for Small and Medium Enterprises (SMEs). In *Strengthening SME Performance Through Social Media Adoption and Usage* (pp. 1–20). IGI Global. doi:10.4018/978-1-6684-5770-2.ch001

Rishi, B., & Bandyopadhyay, S. (Eds.). (2017). *Contemporary issues in social media marketing.* Routledge. doi:10.4324/9781315563312

Rishi, B., & Mohammed, J. (2022). Design, execute, and manage promotions: Study on social media platforms. In *Promotional practices and perspectives from emerging markets* (pp. 226–245). Routledge India. doi:10.4324/9781003315582-12

Ritch, E. L. (2015). Consumers interpreting sustainability: Moving beyond food to fashion. *International Journal of Retail & Distribution Management, 43*(12), 1162–1181. doi:10.1108/IJRDM-04-2014-0042

Roberts, J. A. (1996). Green consumers in the 1990s: Profile and implications for advertising. *Journal of Business Research, 36*(3), 217–231. doi:10.1016/0148-2963(95)00150-6

Roberts, M. E., Stewart, B. M., & Airoldi, E. M. (2016). A model of text for experimentation in the social sciences. *Journal of the American Statistical Association, 111*(515), 988–1003. doi:10.1080/01621459.2016.1141684

Roberts, M. E., Stewart, B. M., & Tingley, D. (2019). *stm*: An R package for Structural Topic Models. *Journal of Statistical Software, 91*(2), 1–40. doi:10.18637/jss.v091.i02

Roberts, M. E., Stewart, B. M., Tingley, D., Lucas, C., Leder-Luis, J., Gadarian, S. K., Albertson, B., & Rand, D. G. (2014). Structural topic models for open-ended survey responses. *American Journal of Political Science, 58*(4), 1064–1082. doi:10.1111/ajps.12103

Robertson, L. (2022). How Ethical is Nike? In *Good on You*. https://goodonyou.eco/how-ethical-is-nike/

Rocamora, A. (2018). The Labour of Fashion Blogging. In L. Armstrong & F. McDowell (Eds.), *Fashioning Professionals: Identity and Representation at Work in the Creative Industries* (pp. 65–81). doi:10.5040/9781350001879.ch-004

Rocha, M. A. V., Hammond, L., & Hawkins, D. (2005). Age, gender and national factors in fashion consumption. *Journal of Fashion Marketing and Management, 9*(4), 380–390. doi:10.1108/13612020510620768

Rodela, J. (2022, February 15). *Importance of influencer marketing on Instagram*. Vistasocial. https://vistasocial.com/insights/importance-of-influencer-marketing/

Rogers, E. M. (2003). *Diffusion of Innovations* (5th ed.). Simon & Schuster.

Roggeveen, A. L., & Sethuraman, R. (2020). How the COVID-19 pandemic may change the world of retailing. *Journal of Retailing, 96*(2), 169–171. doi:10.1016/j.jretai.2020.04.002

Rogue, F. G. (n.d.). How Instagram Models Are Influencing the Fashion Industry. *Fashion Gone Rogue*. https://www.fashiongonerogue.com/how-instagram-models-are-influencing-the-fashion-industry/

Rosário, A., Vilaça, F., Raimundo, R., & Cruz, R. (2021). Literature review on Health Knowledge Management in the last 10 years (2009-2019). *The Electronic Journal of Knowledge Management, 18*(3), 338-355. doi:10.34190/ejkm.18.3.2120

Rosário, A. T. (2021). The Background of artificial intelligence applied to marketing. *Academy of Strategic Management Journal, 20*(6), 1–19.

Rosário, A. T., & Dias, J. C. (2022). Sustainability and the Digital Transition: A Literature Review. *Sustainability (Basel), 14*(7), 4072. doi:10.3390u14074072

Rosário, A. T., & Dias, J. C. (2023). How Industry 4.0 and Sensors Can Leverage Product Design: Opportunities and Challenges. *Sensors (Basel), 23*(3), 1165. doi:10.339023031165 PMID:36772206

Rrustemi, V., & Baca, G. (2021). the impact of social media activities on raising brand awareness during the covid-19 pandemic: The case of fashion industry in Kosovo [Utjecaj aktivnosti na društvenim medijima na povećanje svijesti o tržišnim markama tijekom pandemije covida-19: slučaj modne industrije na Kosovu]. *Management, 26*(2), 295–310. doi:10.30924/mjcmi.26.2.17

Rundin, K., & Colliander, J. (2021). Multifaceted influencers: Toward a new typology for influencer roles in advertising. *Journal of Advertising, 50*(5), 548–564. doi:10.1080/00913367.2021.1980471

Ruth, Parasuraman, Hoefnagels, Migchels, Kabadayi, Gruber, Komarova, & Solnet. (2013). Understanding Generation Y and their use of social media: A review and research agenda. *Journal of Service Management, 24*(3), 245-267.

Saleem, A., & Ellahi, A. (2017). Influence of electronic word of mouth on purchase intention of fashion products in social networking websites. Pakistan Journal of Commerce and So. *Pakistan Journal of Commerce and Social Sciences, 11*(2), 597–622.

Saleem, M. A., Yaseen, A., & Wasaya, A. (2018). Drivers of customer loyalty and word of mouth intentions: Moderating role of interactional justice. *Journal of Hospitality Marketing & Management, 27*(8), 877–904. doi:10.1080/19368623.2018.1469447

Salem, S. F., & Alanadoly, A. B. (2020). Personality traits and social media as drivers of wordof-mouth towards sustainable fashion. *Journal of Fashion Marketing and Management.*

Salton, G. (1989). *Automatic text processing: The transformation, analysis, and retrieval of information by computer. Massachussetts*. Addison-Wesley.

Samala, N., & Singh, S. (2018). Millennial's engagement with fashion brands: A moderated-mediation model of brand engagement with self-concept, involvement and knowledge. *Journal of Fashion Marketing and Management, 23*(1), 2–16. doi:10.1108/JFMM-04-2018-0045

Samarage, H. P., & Ratnayake, G. (2021). Impact of celebrity endorsement through social media on consumer purchasing intentions in sri lankan fashion industry. *Proceedings of the International Conference on Industrial Engineering and Operations Management,* 2313-2325.

Santiago, J. K. (2020). Consumer Attitudes Towards Fashion Influencers on Instagram: Impact of Perceptions and Online Trust on Purchase Intention. *Issues in Information Systems, 21*(1), 105–117.

Sarah, Kearns, Bennett, & Kawalek. (2011). Consumer Behavior in Social Networking Sites: Implications for marketers. *Irish Journal of Management, 30*(2), 47.

Satria, A. D., Jatipuri, S., Hartanti, A. D., & Sanny, L. (2019). The impact of celebrity endorsement by social influencer celebgram on purchase intention of generation Z in fashion industry. *International Journal of Recent Technology and Engineering, 8*(2), 397-404.

Saxena, A. (2011). Blogs And Their Impact On Purchase Intention: A Structural Equation Modelling Approach. *Paradigm, 15*(1–2), 102–110. doi:10.1177/0971890720110114

Scarpi, D., Pizzi, G., & Visentin, M. (2014). Shopping for fun or shopping to buy: Is it different online and offline? *Journal of Retailing and Consumer Services, 21*(3), 258–267. doi:10.1016/j.jretconser.2014.02.007

Scholz, J., & Duffy, K. (2018). We ARe at home: How augmented reality reshapes mobile marketing and consumer-brand relationships. *Journal of Retailing and Consumer Services, 44*, 11–23. doi:10.1016/j.jretconser.2018.05.004

Schouten, A. P., Janssen, L., & Verspaget, M. (2020). Celebrity vs. influencer endorsements in advertising: The role of identification, credibility, and product-endorser fit. *International Journal of Advertising, 39*(2), 258–281. doi:10.1080/02650487.2019.1634898

Schumann, J. H., von Wangenheim, F., & Groene, N. (2014). Targeted online advertising: Using reciprocity appeals to increase acceptance among users of free web services. *Journal of Marketing, 78*(1), 59–75. doi:10.1509/jm.11.0316

Scott, D. M. (2009). *Pazarlamanın ve iletişimin yeni kuralları*. Mediacat Yayınevi.

Seamon, D. (Ed.). (1993). *Dwelling, seeing, and designing: Toward a phenomenological ecology.* SUNY Press.

Segev, N., Avigdor, N., & Avigdor, E. (2018). Measuring influence on Instagram: a network-oblivious approach. *Proceedings of the 41st International ACM SIGIR Conference on Research & Development in Information Retrieval,* 1009–1012. 10.1145/3209978.3210134

Seritag. (2023). *The Ultimate Guide to Using NFC Garment Tags for Clothing*. Retrieved from https://seritag.com/learn/using-nfc/garment-nfc-tags-in-clothing

Sharma, K. (2021). *As brands turn to influencer marketing for the festive season, experts are optimistic about seeing about a 40-50% growth in ad spends*. Retrieved March 25, 2023, from https://www.businessinsider.in/advertising/brands/article/as-brands-turn-to-influencer-marketing-for-the-festive-season-experts-are-optimistic-about-seeing-about-a-40-50-growth-in-ad-spends/articleshow/87210056.cms

Sharma, A., & Jhamb, D. (2020). Changing Consumer Behaviours Towards Online Shopping-An Impact Of Covid 19. *Academy of Marketing Studies Journal*, *24*(3), 1–10.

Sharma, B., Gadenne, D., & Kerr, D. (2017). Environmental beliefs, norms and behaviours: An investigation of their relationships using data from green consumers. *Journal of New Business Ideas and Trends*, *15*(1), 1–17.

Sharma, S., & Rehman, A. (2016). Social media marketing: A study of select sectors in India. *International Journal of Management*, *5*(4), 1–9.

Sharma, S., Singh, S., Kujur, F., & Das, G. (2021). Social media activities and its influence on customer-brand relationship: An empirical study of apparel retailers' activity in India. *Journal of Theoretical and Applied Electronic Commerce Research*, *16*(4), 602–617. doi:10.3390/jtaer16040036

Shen, B., Li, Q., Dong, C., & Perry, P. (2017). Sustainability issues in textile and apparel supply chains. *Sustainability (Basel)*, *9*(9), 1592. doi:10.3390u9091592

Shen, D., Richards, J., & Liu, F. (2013). Consumers' Awareness of Sustainable Fashion. *Marketing Management Journal*, *23*(2), 134–147.

Shen, Z. (2021). A persuasive eWOM model for increasing consumer engagement on social media: Evidence from Irish fashion micro-influencers. *Journal of Research in Interactive Marketing*, *15*(2), 181–199. doi:10.1108/JRIM-10-2019-0161

Shih, H.-P. (2004). An empirical study on predicting user acceptance of e-shopping on the web. *Information & Management*, *41*(6), 351–368.

Shin, E., & Lee, J. E. (2021). What makes consumers purchase apparel products through social shopping services that social media fashion influencers have worn? *Journal of Business Research*, *132*, 416–428. doi:10.1016/j.jbusres.2021.04.022

Shi, S., Wang, Y., Chen, X., & Zhang, Q. (2020). Conceptualization of omnichannel customer experience and its impact on shopping intention: A mixed-method approach. *International Journal of Information Management*, *50*, 325–336. doi:10.1016/j.ijinfomgt.2019.09.001

Shweta & Gadkari. (2022). *RFID Technology Used in Apparel Industry*. Retrieved from https://textilelearner.net/rfid-technology-used-in-apparel-industry/

Silva, T. H., De Melo, P. O. S. V., Almeida, J. M., Salles, J., & Loureiro, A. A. F. (2013). A picture of instagram is worth more than a thousand words: Workload characterization and application. *Proceedings - IEEE International Conference on Distributed Computing in Sensor Systems, DCoSS 2013*, *1*, 123–132.

Silva, S. C., Duarte, P., & Sundetova, A. (2020). Multichannel versus omnichannel: A price-segmented comparison from the fashion industry. *International Journal of Retail & Distribution Management*, *48*(4), 417–430. doi:10.1108/IJRDM-07-2019-0232

Silvestri, B. (2020). The future of fashion: How the quest for digitization and the use of artificial intelligence and extended reality will reshape the fashion industry after COVID-19. *ZoneModa Journal*, *10*(2), 61–73.

Singer, L. (2022). *@trashisfortossers*. Instagram. https://www.instagram.com/trashisfortossers/

Singh, J., Quamina, L. T., & Xue, T. (2018). *Ten million followers and counting: How digital brand alliances between online influencers and brands impact consumer value: An abstract perceptions.* doi:10.1007/978-3-319-66023-3_239

Sinha, J. I., & Fung, T. T. (2021). How social media micro-influencers are disrupting the business of youth fashion. *Rutgers Business Review*, *6*(1), 44–50.

Siomkos, G., & Mavros, D. (2008). *Ερεύνα Αγοράς*. Stamoulis Publishing.

Siriwardana, A. (2020, November). Social Media Marketing: A Literature Review on Consumer Products. *Proceedings of the International Conference on Business & Information (ICBI).* 10.2139srn.3862924

Smart, P. S. (2021). Regression Tree Based Correlation Technique in Spatial Data Classification. *Turkish Journal of Computer and Mathematics Education, 12*(10), 6184–6195.

Social, U. (n.d.). Influencer Marketing Guide for Fashion and Lifestyle Brands. *Unbox Social.* https://www.unboxsocial.com/blog/influencer-marketing-for-fashion-and-lifestyle/

Sokolova, K., & Kefi, H. (2020). Instagram and YouTube bloggers promote it, why should I buy? How credibility and parasocial interaction influence purchase intentions. *Journal of Retailing and Consumer Services, 53*, 101742.

Sokolova, K., & Kefi, H. (2020). Instagram and YouTube bloggers promote it, why should I buy? how credibility and parasocial interaction influence purchase intentions. *Journal of Retailing and Consumer Services, 53*, 101742. Advance online publication. doi:10.1016/j.jretconser.2019.01.011

Soni, M., Jain, K., & Kumar, B. (2019). Factors affecting the adoption of fashion mobile shopping applications. *Journal of Global Fashion Marketing, 10*(4), 358–376. doi:10.1080/20932685.2019.1649165

Sotiroudas, B. (2011). *Research Paper Handbook.* Athens: iWrite. gr.

Söyleyici, G. T., & Çetinkaya, Ö. (2017). Sosyal medya ve tüketici davranışları ilişkisi: Türkiye'deki sosyal medya kullanıcıları üzerine bir araştırma. *Kesit Akademi Dergisi, 3*(9), 36–54.

Spears, N., & Singh, S. N. (2004). Measuring attitude toward the brand and purchase intentions. *Journal of Current Issues and Research in Advertising, 26*(2), 53–66. doi:10.1080/10641734.2004.10505164

Sprinklr.com. (2021). *Best Fashion Brands in Social Media.* Retrieved March 25, 2023, from https://www.sprinklr.com/blog/fashion-brands-social-media-marketing/

Stanciu, S., Radu, R. I., Sapira, V., Bratoveanu, B. D., & Florea, A. M. (2020). Consumer Behavior in Crisis Situations. Research on the Effects of COVID-19 in Romania. *Annals of the University Dunarea de Jos of Galati: Fascicle: I, Economics & Applied Informatics, 26*(1).

Statista. (2018). *Instagram: active users 2018 | Statista.* Retrieved February 11, 2020 from https://www.statista.com/statistics/253577/number-of-monthly-active-instagram-users/

Statista. (2020). *Instagram: age distribution of global audiences 2020 | Statista.* Retrieved February 11, 2020 from https://www.statista.com/statistics/325587/instagram-global-age-group/

Statista. (2021) *Daily time spent with the internet per capita worldwide from 2011 to 2021.* https://www.statista.com/statistics/319732/daily-time-spent-online-device/

Statista. (2023a). *Apparel - India: Statista market forecast.* Retrieved March 15, 2023, from https://www.statista.com/outlook/cmo/apparel/india#revenue

Statista. (2023b). *Fashion - southern Asia: Statista market forecast*. Retrieved March 15, 2023, from https://www.statista.com/outlook/dmo/ecommerce/fashion/southern-asia

Statista. (2023c). *Social Media Advertising - Global: Market Forecast*. Retrieved March 15, 2023, from https://www.statista.com/outlook/dmo/digital-advertising/social-media-advertising/worldwide

Stephani, N. (2022). Senior female celebrity's body and ageing well discourse on Instagram. *Jurnal Studi Komunikasi*, *6*(1), 165–178. doi:10.25139/jsk.v6i1.4312

Stephen, T. A. (2016). The role of digital and social media marketing in consumer behavior. *Current Opinion in Psychology*, *10*, 17–21. doi:10.1016/j.copsyc.2015.10.016

Strähle, J., & Erhardt, C. (2017). *Collaborative Consumption 2.0: An Alternative to Fast Fashion Consumption*. doi:10.1007/978-981-10-2440-5_8

Strähle, J., & Grünewald, A.-K. (2017). The Prosumer Concept in Fashion Retail: Potentials and Limitations. In Green fashion retail (pp. 95–117). doi:10.1007/978-981-10-2440-5_6

Strähle, J., & Hauk, K. (2017). Impact on Sustainability: Production Versus Consumption. In Green fashion retail (pp. 49–75). doi:10.1007/978-981-10-2440-5_4

Strähle, J., & Klatt, L. M. (2017). The Second Hand Market for Fashion Products. In Green Fashion Retail (pp. 119–134). doi:10.1007/978-981-10-2440-5_7

Strähle, J., & Kreuzhermes, S. (2017). Impact of Sustainable Manufacturing Standards for Retail Brands. In Green Fashion Retail (pp. 77–93). doi:10.1007/978-981-10-2440-5_5

Strähle, J., & Matthaei, F. S. (2017). The Value Chain of a Branded Second Hand Store—Possible Activities to Be Integrated by a Conventional Fashion Brand. In Green Fashion Retail (pp. 175–198). doi:10.1007/978-981-10-2440-5_10

Strähle, J., & Müller, V. (2017). Key Aspects of Sustainability in Fashion Retail. In Green fashion retail (pp. 7–26). doi:10.1007/978-981-10-2440-5_2

Strähle, J., & Gräff, C. (2016). The Role of Social Media for a Sustainable Consumption. In *Green Fashion Retail* (pp. 225–247). Springer. doi:10.1007/978-981-10-2440-5_12

Strähle, J., & Höhn, M. (2017). Cross-Industry Learnings: What Fashion Retail Can Learn from the Used-Car Industry. In *Green Fashion Retail* (pp. 157–174). Springer. doi:10.1007/978-981-10-2440-5_9

Strähle, J., & Philipsen, F. (2017). Closed-Loop Production: A Literature Review. In *Green Fashion Retail* (pp. 27–47). Springer. doi:10.1007/978-981-10-2440-5_3

Sudha, M., & Sheena, K. (2017). Impact of influencers in consumer decision process: the fashion industry. *SCMS Journal of Indian Management*, *14*(3), 14-30. https://pdfs.semanticscholar.org/1469/eccb29f76b24e85cba8b6b60adf5ab4932d8.pdf

Sudha, M., & Sheena, K. (2017). Consumer Decision Process: Impact of Influencers in the Fashion Industry. *SCMS Journal of Indian Management*, *93*(3), 14–29.

Sudha, M., & Sheena, K. (2017). Impact of influencers in consumer decision process: The fashion industry. *SCMS Journal of Indian Management*, *14*(3), 14–30.

Suh, S. (2020). Non-boundaries of style represented in fashion Instagram: A social media platform as a digital space–time. *Fashion and Textiles*, *7*(1), 33. Advance online publication. doi:10.118640691-020-00222-9

Sumarliah, E., Usmanova, K., Mousa, K., & Indriya, I. (2022). E-commerce in the fashion business: The roles of the COVID-19 situational factors, hedonic and utilitarian motives on consumers' intention to purchase online. *International Journal of Fashion Design. Technology and Education, 15*(2), 167–177. doi:10.1080/17543266.2021.1958926

Sundermann, G., & Raabe, T. (2019). Strategic communication through social media influencers: Current state of research and desiderata. *International Journal of Strategic Communication, 13*(4), 278–300. doi:10.1080/1553118X.2019.1618306

sunsetsaraid. (2022). *@sunsetsaraid.* Instagram. https://www.instagram.com/sunsetsaraid/

Sun, Y., Wang, R., Cao, D., & Lee, R. (2022). Who are social media influencers for luxury fashion consumption of the Chinese Gen Z? Categorisation and empirical examination. *Journal of Fashion Marketing and Management, 26*(4), 603–621. doi:10.1108/JFMM-07-2020-0132

Suter, M. B., Borini, F. M., Floriani, D. E., da Silva, D., & Polo, E. (2018). Country-of-origin image (COI) as a country-specific advantage (CSA): Scale development and validation of COI as a resource within the firm perspective. *Journal of Business Research, 84*, 46–58. doi:10.1016/j.jbusres.2017.11.006

T.C. Sanayi ve Teknoloji Bakanlığı Kalkınma Ajansları Genel Müdürlüğü. (2021). *Covid-19 krizine yanıt ve dayanıklılık projesi: Tekstil sektörü analiz raporu ve kılavuzu TR 32 bölgesi (Denizli, Aydın, Muğla).* T.C. Sanayi ve Teknoloji Bakanlığı.

Tabatabaei, M. (2009). Online shopping perceptions of offline shoppers. *Issues in Information Systems, 10*(2), 22–26.

Talati-Parikh, S. (2021). *Instagram's big impact on fashion.* Retrieved March 15, 2023, from https://www.livemint.com/Leisure/hRFOEgmk2I0W58M0Y1lisK/Instagrams-big-impact-on-fashion.html

Tandon, S. (2021). *Instagram is changing the way fashion sells in India.* Retrieved March 15, 2023, from https://qz.com/india/1321163/from-sabyasachi-to-nicobar-instagram-is-changing-the-way-fashion-sells-in-india/

Tang, J., & Liu, H. (2015). Trust in Social Media Synthesis Lectures on Information Security, Privacy, & Trust (E. Bertino & R. Sandhu, Eds.). Academic Press.

Tanwar, A. S., Chaudhry, H., & Srivastava, M. K. (2021). Influencer marketing as a tool of digital consumer engagement: A systematic literature review. *Indian Journal of Marketing, 51*(10), 27–42. doi:10.17010/ijom/2021/v51/i10/166439

Taştepe, Ö. (2020). Dijital pazarlama ile hazır giyim sektöründe pazarlama iletişimi bağlamında tutundurma faaliyetlerine yönelik inceleme. *TJFDM, 2*(1), 21–29.

Tatlı, H., & Korkut, F. (2015). Sanal alışverişte tüketici davranışlarını etkileyen faktörler: Bingöl Üniversitesi öğrencileri üzerinde bir uygulama. *Erzincan Üniversitesi Sosyal Bilimler Enstitüsü Dergisi, 8*(1), 63–78.

Taylor, V. A., Halstead, D., & Haynes, P. J. (2010). Consumer responses to christian religious symbols in advertising. *Journal of Advertising, 39*(2), 79–92. doi:10.2753/JOA0091-3367390206

Technavio. (2023). *Online fashion retail market in India growth, size, trends, analysis report by type, application, Region, and Segment Forecast 2022-2026.* Retrieved March 25, 2023, from https://www.technavio.com/report/online-fashion-retail-market-industry-in-india-analysis

Tewari, S. K., & Misra, M. (2012). The Impact of ICT on Manufacturing Industry: An Empirical Analysis. *2012 International Conference on Communication Systems and Network Technologies*, 924-929. 10.1109/CSNT.2012.197

Thakur, R., & Srivastava, M. (2020). Instagram usage and impulse buying behavior: A study on fashion products. *Journal of Retailing and Consumer Services, 53*, 101971.

The Drum. (2021). *Social ad spend continues to accelerate in South East Asia.* Retrieved March 15, 2023, from https://www.thedrum.com/news/2021/11/10/social-ad-spend-continues-accelerate-south-east-asia

Theodosi, N. (2021). *Depop's Sale to Etsy Highlights Secondhand Market Boom – WWD*. Women's Wear Daily. https://wwd.com/business-news/retail/depops-sale-etsy-second-hand-market-boom-1234834135/

Theofanidis, S. M. (2002). *Μεθοδολογία της επιστημονικής σκέψης και έρευνας: Πώς γίνεται η επιστημονική έρευνα και πώς γράφεται μια επιστημονική εργασία* (2nd ed.). Benou Publishing.

Thomas, J. B., & Peters, C. (2009). Silver seniors: Exploring the self-concept, lifestyles, and apparel consumption of women over age 65. *International Journal of Retail & Distribution Management, 37*(12), 1018–1040. doi:10.1108/09590550911005001

Thomas, J., Peters, C., & Tolson, H. (2007). An exploratory investigation of the virtual community MySpace. com. *Journal of Fashion Marketing and Management, 11*(4), 587–603. doi:10.1108/13612020710824625

Thompson, C., Locander, W., & Pollio, H. (1989). Putting consumer experience back into consumer research: The philosophy and method of existential phenomenology. *The Journal of Consumer Research, 16*(2), 133–147. doi:10.1086/209203

Thorsten, Gwinner, Walsh, & Gremler. (2003). Electronic word of mouth via consumer opinion platform: What motivates consumers to articulate themselves on the internet? *Journal of Interactive Marketing, 18*(1), 38–52.

Tirunillai, S., & Tellis, G. J. (2014). Mining marketing meaning from online chatter: Strategic brand analysis of big data using Latent Dirichlet Allocation. *JMR, Journal of Marketing Research, 51*(4), 463–479. doi:10.1509/jmr.12.0106

Tjhin, V.U., &Aini, S.R. (2019). *Effect of E-WOM and Social Media Usage on Purchase Decision in Clothing Industry*. doi:10.1145/3332324.3332333

Toksarı, M., & Atlı, H. F. (2018). Giyim modası ve gençlerin hazır giyim tercihlerinin değerlendirilmesine ilişkin bir çalışma. In *18th International Bussiness Congress Book* (pp. 2184-2191). Osmaniye Korkut Ata Üniversitesi, Osmaniye.

Tosun, N. (2010). *İletişim temelli marka yönetimi*. Beta Yayınları.

Trequattrini, R., Manfredi, S., Lardo, A., & Cuozzo, B. (2019). Social media as a new opportunity for female entrepreneurs: An analysis of the fashion industry. *Springer Proceedings in Business and Economics*, 287-298. 10.1007/978-3-030-00335-7_19

Triani, D., & Vusparatih, D. S. (2019). "The role of social media Instagram in creating youth trend fashion (19-22 years old)" case study of fashion influencer on Instagram towards Binus University faculty of economics and communication department students year 2014-2017). *International Journal of Scientific and Technology Research, 8*(7), 248–250.

Tripathi, S. (2019). Impact of social media on generation Y for buying fashion apparel. *Journal of Content. Community & Communication, 9*(5), 105–113.

Tsiftsakis, N. (2021). *The impact of covid-19 on e-commerce*. Academic Press.

Tucker, C. E. (2014). Social networks, personalized advertising, and privacy controls. *JMR, Journal of Marketing Research, 51*(5), 546–562. doi:10.1509/jmr.10.0355

Turri, A. M., Sumith, K. H., & Kemp, E. (2013). Developing affective brand commitment through social media. *Journal of Electronic Commerce Research*, 201–214.

Twumasi, Y. A., & Dzahene-Quarshie, B. (2022). Shaping the perceptions of fashion consumers by influencers on digital platforms in the era of COVID-19. *International Journal of E-Entrepreneurship and Innovation, 12*(2), 1–13. Advance online publication. doi:10.4018/IJEEI.314466

Uddin, F. (2019, August 28). *Introductory Chapter: Textile Manufacturing Processes*. doi:10.5772/intechopen.87968

Un.org. (2021). *World Economic Situation and Prospectus 2021: South Asia* Retrieved March 15, 2023, from https://www.un.org/development/desa/dpad/wp-content/uploads/sites/45/WESP2021_CH3_SA.pdf

UNDP. (2019). *New data challenges traditional notions of 'rich' and 'poor'*. Retrieved March 15, 2023, from https://www. in.undp.org/content/india/en/home/presscenter/pressreleases/2019-MPI-India.html

United Nations. (2019). *World economic situation and prospects*. Retrieved March 15, 2023, from https://www.un.org/development/desa/dpad/wpcontent/uploads/sites/45/WESP2019_BOOK-CH3-5-south-asia-en.pdf

Ünver, A. (2013). *Hazır giyimde geleneksel pazarlama ile internetten pazarlamanın karşılaştırılmasına yönelik alan çalışması*. Yüksek Lisans Tezi, Marmara Üniversitesi Fen Bilimleri Enstitüsü.

Upadhaya, V. (2021). *A Study on Increasing Digital Media Marketing Platforms in Nepal*. Retrieved March 15, 2023, from https://e-research.siam.edu/wp-content/uploads/2019/05/BBA-2017-coop-Marketing-Digital-marketing-platform-A-case-study-on-increasing-digital-media-marketing-platform-in-Nepal-compress.pdf

Upfluence Software. (n.d.). The State of Influencer Marketing in the Fashion Industry. *Upfluence*. https://www.upfluence.com/industry-reports/fashion

Utz, S., Kerkhof, P., & Van den Bos, J. (2012). Consumers rule: How consumer reviews influence perceived trustworthiness of online stores. *Electronic Commerce Research and Applications*, *11*(1), 49–58. doi:10.1016/j.elerap.2011.07.010

Vahdat, A., Alizadeh, A., Quach, S., & Hamelin, N. (2021). Would you like to shop via mobile app technology? The technology acceptance model, social factors and purchase intention. *Australasian Marketing Journal*, *29*(2), 187–197. doi:10.1016/j.ausmj.2020.01.002

Vamsi Krishna, P. (2023). Investigating the effects of the metaverse on business models. *Journal of Advances in Management, Engineering and Science*, *1*(1), 1–13. https://brpublications.com/wp-content/uploads/2023/03/paper6.pdf

Van der Walt, A. (1991). Will the consumer be able to decode your advertising message correctly? *Marketing Communications Management: A South African Perspective*, 295-309.

van Driel, L., & Dumitrica, D. (2021). Selling brands while staying "Authentic": The professionalization of Instagram influencers. *Convergence (London)*, *27*(1), 66–84. doi:10.1177/1354856520902136

van Esch, P., Arli, D., Castner, J., Talukdar, N., & Northey, G. (2018). Consumer attitudes towards bloggers and paid blog advertisements: What's new? *Marketing Intelligence & Planning*, *36*(7), 778–793. doi:10.1108/MIP-01-2018-0027

Vardhan, J., & Mahato, M. (2022). Prosocial behavior and impact of influencers during CrisisA study based on sentiment analysis. Promotional practices and perspectives from emerging markets, 246-260. doi:10.4324/9781003315582-13

Vargo, S. L., & Lusch, R. F. (2008). Service-dominant logic: Continuing the evolution. *Journal of the Academy of Marketing Science*, *36*(1), 1–10. doi:10.100711747-007-0069-6

Vehmas, K., Raudaskoski, A., Heikkilä, P., Harlin, A., & Mensonen, A. (2018). Consumer attitudes and communication in circular fashion. *Journal of Fashion Marketing and Management*, *22*(3), 286–300. doi:10.1108/JFMM-08-2017-0079

Velenturf, A. P. M., Archer, S. A., Gomes, H. I., Christgen, B., Lag-Brotons, A. J., & Purnell, P. (2019). Circular economy and the matter of integrated resources. In Science of the Total Environment (Vol. 689, pp. 963–969). doi:10.1016/j.scitotenv.2019.06.449

Venkatesh, V., & Davis, F. D. (2000). A theoretical extension of the technology acceptance model: Four longitudinal field studies. *Management Science*, *46*, 186–204. doi:10.1287/mnsc.46.2.186.11926

Veresiu, E., & Parmentier, M. (2021). Advanced style influencers: Confronting gendered ageism in fashion and beauty markets. *Journal of the Association for Consumer Research*, *6*(2), 263–273. doi:10.1086/712609

Vidya, D. (n.d.). *Superdry Used Social Media Marketing To Reach More Than 1.5 Million People On Twitter*. Retrieved March 25, 2023, from https://www.digitalvidya.com/blog/superdry-used-social-media-marketing-to-reach-more-than-1-5-million-people-on-twitter-dmblog-0503/

Visconti, L. M., Sherry, J. F. Jr, Borghini, S., & Anderson, L. (2010). Street art, sweet art? Reclaiming the "public" in public place. *The Journal of Consumer Research*, *37*(3), 511–529. doi:10.1086/652731

von Kameke, L. (2023). *APAC: Active social media users by country 2022*. Retrieved March 15, 2023, from https://www.statista.com/statistics/295606/social-media-mau-asia-pacific-countries/

Von Mettenheim, W., & Wiedmann, K. (2021). The role of fashion influencers' attractiveness: A gender-specific perspective. *Communication Research and Practice*, *7*(3), 263–290. doi:10.1080/22041451.2021.2013087

Voxburner. (2022). Influencer Marketing for Luxury Brands | Gucci, Chanel and Savage X Fenty. *Voxburner*. https://www.voxburner.com/influencer-marketing-luxury-brands-gucci-chanel-savage-x-fenty/

Walker, J., & Stott, R. (2018). *LSN : Markets : Fashion Recommerce*. LSNGlobal. https://www.lsnglobal.com/markets/article/22207/fashion-recommerce

Walker, M., & Kent, A. (2012). The Roles of Credibility and Social Consciousness in the Corporate Philanthropy-Consumer Behavior Relationship. *Journal of Business Ethics, 116*(2), 341-353.

Walker, J. H., Sproull, L., & Subramani, R. (1994). Using a human face in an interface. *Conference on Human Factors in Computing Systems - Proceedings*, 85–91. 10.1145/191666.191708

Waltenrath, A., Brenner, C., & Hinz, O. (2022). Some interactions are more equal than others: The effect of influencer endorsements in social media brand posts on engagement and online store performance. *Journal of Interactive Marketing*, *57*(4), 541–560. doi:10.1177/10949968221096591

Wang, X., Yu, C., & Wei, Y. (2012). Social Media Peer Communication and Impacts on Purchase Intentions: A Consumer Socialization Framework. *Journal of Interactive Marketing*, *26*(4), 198–208. doi:10.1016/j.intmar.2011.11.004

Wang, Y., Chowdhury Ahmed, S., Deng, S., & Wang, H. (2019). Success of social media marketing efforts in retaining sustainable online consumers: An empirical analysis on the online fashion retail market. *Sustainability (Basel)*, *11*(13), 3596. doi:10.3390u11133596

Wang, Y., Hong, A., Li, X., & Gao, J. (2020). Marketing innovations during a global crisis: A study of China firms' response to COVID-19. *Journal of Business Research*, *116*, 214–220. doi:10.1016/j.jbusres.2020.05.029 PMID:32501308

Wang, Y., Ko, E., & Wang, H. (2022). Augmented reality (AR) app use in the beauty product industry and consumer purchase intention. *Asia Pacific Journal of Marketing and Logistics*, *34*(1), 110–131. doi:10.1108/APJML-11-2019-0684

Wang, Y., Min, Q., & Han, S. (2016). Understanding the effects of trust and risk on individual behavior toward social media platforms: A meta-analysis of the empirical evidence. *Computers in Human Behavior*, *56*, 34–44. doi:10.1016/j.chb.2015.11.011

Wathen, C. N., & Burkell, J. (2002). Believe it or not: Factors influencing credibility on the Web. *Journal of the American Society for Information Science and Technology*, *53*(2), 134–144.

Watson, A., Alexander, B., & Salavati, L. (2018). The impact of experiential augmented reality applications on fashion purchase intention. *International Journal of Retail & Distribution Management*, *48*(5), 433–451. doi:10.1108/IJRDM-06-2017-0117

Weiss, C. (2022). Fashion retailing in the metaverse. *Fashion, Style & Popular Culture*, *9*(4), 523–538. doi:10.1386/fspc_00159_1

Wert, S. R., & Salovey, P. (2004). A social comparison account of gossip. *Review of General Psychology*, *8*(2), 122–137. doi:10.1037/1089-2680.8.2.122

White, K., Habib, R., & Hardisty, D. J. (2019). How to SHIFT consumer behaviors to be more sustainable: A literature review and guiding framework. *Journal of Marketing*, *83*(3), 22–49. doi:10.1177/0022242919825649

Wiederhold, M., & Martinez, L. F. (2018). Ethical consumer behaviour in Germany: The attitude-behaviour gap in the green apparel industry. *International Journal of Consumer Studies*, *42*(4), 419–429. doi:10.1111/ijcs.12435

Wiedmann, K., & von Mettenheim, W. (2020). *An adaptation of the source credibility model on social influencers: An abstract.* doi:10.1007/978-3-030-42545-6_65

Wiedmann, K., & von Mettenheim, W. (2020). Attractiveness, trustworthiness and expertise – social influencers' winning formula? *Journal of Product and Brand Management*, *30*(5), 707–725. doi:10.1108/JPBM-06-2019-2442

Wolfinbarger, M., & Gilly, M. C. (2001). Shopping online for freedom, control, and fun. *California Management Review*, *43*(2), 34–55. doi:10.2307/41166074

Wolny, J., & Mueller, C. (2013). Analysis of fashion consumers' motives to engage in electronic word-of-mouth communication through social media platforms. *Journal of Marketing Management*, *29*(5–6), 562–583. doi:10.1080/0267257X.2013.778324

Wong, K. K.-K. (2019). *Mastering Partial Least Squares Structural Equation Modeling (PLS-SEM) with SmartPLS in 38 Hours*. iUniverse.

Wongkitrungrueng, A., & Assarut, N. (2020). The role of live streaming in building consumer trust and engagement with social commerce sellers. *Journal of Business Research*, *117*, 543–556. doi:10.1016/j.jbusres.2018.08.032

Woodside, A. G. (2010). Brand-consumer storytelling theory and research: Introduction. *Psychology and Marketing*, *27*(6), 531–540. doi:10.1002/mar.20342

Wooldridge, B. R., & Kuntze, R. (2019, November 6). Women over fifty demand 'me too' treatment from retailers: Exploring America's most ignored consumer. In *Society for Marketing Advances Proceedings* (pp. 332-333). Society for Marketing Advances Conference.

World Bank Group. (2023). *Global Economic Prospects: Sharp, long-lasting slowdown to hit developing countries hard. World Bank*. Retrieved March 15, 2023, from https://www.worldbank.org/en/news/press-release/2023/01/10/global-economic-prospects

World Bank. (2019a). *Population ages 0-14, total | Data*. Retrieved February 4, 2020 from https://data.worldbank.org/indicator/SP.POP.0014.TO

World Bank. (2019b). *Population ages 0-14 (% of total population) | Data*. Retrieved February 4, 2020 from https://data.worldbank.org/indicator/SP.POP.0014.TO.ZS

World Bank. (2019c). *Population ages 15-64, total | Data*. Retrieved February 4, 2020 from https://data.worldbank.org/indicator/SP.POP.1564.TO

World Bank. (2019d). *Population ages 15-64 (% of total population) | Data*. Retrieved February 4, 2020 from https://data.worldbank.org/indicator/SP.POP.1564.TO.ZS

World Bank. (2019e). *Population ages 65 and above, total | Data*. Retrieved February 4, 2020 from https://data.worldbank.org/indicator/SP.POP.65UP.TO

World Bank. (2019f). *Population ages 65 and above (% of total population) | Data*. Retrieved February 4, 2020 from https://data.worldbank.org/indicator/SP.POP.65UP.TO.ZS

Xiang, L., Zheng, X., Lee, M. K., & Zhao, D. (2016). Exploring consumers' impulse buying behavior on social commerce platform: The role of parasocial interaction. *International Journal of Information Management*, *36*(3), 333–347. doi:10.1016/j.ijinfomgt.2015.11.002

Xiaoli, N., & Kwangjun, H. (2007). Consumer responses to corporate social responsibility (CSR) initiatives: Examining the role of brand-cause fit in cause-related marketing. *Journal of Advertising*, *36*(2), 63–74. doi:10.2753/JOA0091-3367360204

Yahoo. (2023). *Global Influencer marketing platform market to generate revenue of US$ 118.0 billion by 2031*. Retrieved March 15, 2023, from https://www.yahoo.com/entertainment/global-influencer-marketing-platform-market-113000397.html

Yang & Lin. (2011). Factors affecting intention to use Facebook to support problem-based learning among employees in a Taiwanese manufacturing company. *African Journal of Business Management*, *5*, 9014-9022.

Yaoyuneyong, G., Foster, J. K., & Flynn, L. R. (2014). Factors impacting the efficacy of augmented reality virtual dressing room technology as a tool for online visual merchandising. *Journal of Global Fashion Marketing*, *5*(4), 283–296. doi:10.1080/20932685.2014.926129

Yaşa Özeltürkay, E., Bozyiğit, S., & Gülmez, M. (2017). Instagram'dan alışveriş yapan tüketicilerin satın alma davranışları: Keşifsel bir çalışma. *Marmara Üniversitesi Öneri Dergisi*, *12*(48), 175–198. doi:10.14783/maruoneri.vi.331668

Yasir, M., Ansari, Y., Latif, K., Maqsood, H., Habib, A., Moon, J., & Rho, S. (2022). Machine learning–assisted efficient demand forecasting using endogenous and exogenous indicators for the textile industry. *International Journal of Logistics Research and Applications*, 1-20.

Yeo, S. F., Tan, C. L., Kumar, A., Tan, K. H., & Wong, J. K. (2022). Investigating the impact of AI-powered technologies on Instagrammers' purchase decisions in digitalization era–A study of the fashion and apparel industry. *Technological Forecasting and Social Change*, *177*, 121551. Advance online publication. doi:10.1016/j.techfore.2022.121551

Yeşildal, G. (2017). *Hazır giyim ürünlerinin sosyal medya üzerinden satın alınmasında tüketici algısının rolü (Instagram örneği)*. Yayınlanmamış Yüksek Lisans Tezi, İstanbul Gelişim Üniversitesi Sosyal Bilimler Enstitüsü.

Yıldırım, F., & Boztepe, A. (2019). Bireylerin moda satın alma davranışı ve sosyal medya kullanımı ilişkisi üzerine bir araştırma. *İstanbul Ticaret Üniversitesi Sosyal Bilimler Dergisi*, *18*(35), 325-349.

Ying, M. (2012). *Sosyal medya platformları üzerinden pazarlama ve bu mecrayı etkin kullanan sektörler*. Yüksek Lisans Tezi, Kadir Has Üniversitesi Sosyal Bilimler Enstitüsü.

Yolcu, T., Ekici, S. G., Altunışık, R., & Özkaynar, K. (2017). Online mı? Offline mı? Tüketici tercihlerini etkileyen faktörlerin incelenmesi. *Uluslararası Yönetim İktisat ve İşletme Dergisi*, *13*(13), 1027–1033.

Yu, U. J., Lee, H. H., & Damhorst, M. L. (2012). Exploring multidimensions of product performance risk in the online apparel shopping context: Visual, tactile and trial risks. *Clothing & Textiles Research Journal*, *30*(4), 251–266. doi:10.1177/0887302X12462059

Zafari, B., & Ekin, T. (2019). Topic modeling for medical prescription fraud and abuse detection. *Applied Statistics, 68*(3), 751–769. doi:10.1111/rssc.12332

Zafeiropoulos. (2005). *Πως γίνεται μια επιστημονική εργασία. Επιστημονική έρευνα και συγγραφή εργασιών*. Kritiki Publishing.

Zandhersami, H., & Geranmaych, P. (2014). Determinants of user acceptance of internet banking: An empirical study. *Management Science Letters*, *4*, 1369–1374.

Zhang, J., & Daugherty, T. (2009). Third-Person Effect and Social Networking: Implications for Online Marketing and Word-Of-Mouth Communication. *American Journal of Business*, *24*(2), 53–69.

Zhang, Y., & Caverlee, J. (2019). Instagrammers, fashionistas, and me: Recurrent fashion recommendation with implicit visual influence. *International Conference on Information and Knowledge Management, Proceedings,* 1583-1592. 10.1145/3357384.3358042

Zhao, L., Lee, S. H., & Copeland, L. R. (2019). Social media and Chinese consumers' environmentally sustainable apparel purchase intentions. *Asia Pacific Journal of Marketing and Logistics*, *31*(4), 855–874. doi:10.1108/APJML-08-2017-0183

Zhao, Y., Kou, G., Peng, Y., & Chen, Y. (2018). Understanding influence power of opinion leaders in e-commerce networks: An opinion dynamics theory perspective. *Information Sciences*, *426*, 131–147. doi:10.1016/j.ins.2017.10.031

Zheng, Y., & Chi, T. (2015). Factors influencing purchase intention towards environmentally friendly apparel: An empirical study of US consumers. *International Journal of Fashion Design. Technology and Education*, *8*(2), 68–77.

Zhou, L., Jin, F., Wu, B., Chen, Z., & Wang, C. L. (2023). Do fake followers mitigate influencers' perceived influencing power on social media platforms? The mere number effect and boundary conditions. *Journal of Business Research, 158*, 113589. doi:10.1016/j.jbusres.2022.113589

Zhou, S., Barnes, L., McCormick, H., & Blazquez Cano, M. (2021). Social media influencers' narrative strategies to create eWOM: A theoretical contribution. *International Journal of Information Management*, *59*, 102293. Advance online publication. doi:10.1016/j.ijinfomgt.2020.102293

Zhou, S., Blazquez, M., McCormick, H., & Barnes, L. (2021). How social media influencers' narrative strategies benefit cultivating influencer marketing: Tackling issues of cultural barriers, commercialised content, and sponsorship disclosure. *Journal of Business Research*, *134*, 122–142. doi:10.1016/j.jbusres.2021.05.011

Zorlu, N., & Uzgören, E. (2020). Elektronik ağızdan ağıza iletişimin tüketicilerin satın alma davranışları üzerindeki etkisinin belirleyicileri: Üniversite öğrencileri üzerinde bir araştırma. *Dumlupınar Üniversitesi Sosyal Bilimler Dergisi*, *63*, 107–130.

About the Contributors

Theodore Tarnanidis is a Researcher in the Business Administration Department at the University of Macedonia. He obtained Post-doc in sustainable entrepreneurship from the University of Macedonia and a PhD in Marketing from the University of London Met. He received his M.B.A from Liverpool University. His research focuses on Marketing and Decision-Making Processes in Entrepreneurship, Conjoint Models and preference measurement techniques, modelling of purchases and consumer behavior. His work has been published in various internationally renowned scientific conferences (Academy of Marketing, European Marketing Academy, PROMETHEE Days, Hellenic Operational Research) and journals (Journal of Business Ethics, Journal of Retailing and Consumer Services, Current Issues in Tourism).

Vasileios Ismyrlis works in the Hellenic Statistical Authority as a statistician for five years. He was an administrative employee, for eleven years in the social insurance institute IKA-ETAM. He has also a two-year experience in a bank and an experience of teaching economic and management lessons in vocational post-secondary education and in tertiary education. He graduated with a degree in Statistics and Insurance sciences from the University of Piraeus. His postgraduate studies are in the field of Quality Assurance. He has obtained his Ph.D. in the field of ''Quality management and Multidimensional statistics'', at the Department of Business Administration of the University of Macedonia, Greece. He has published many articles in scientific journals and conferences' proceedings. He speaks well English and French. He is a referee in five scientific journals.

* * *

Vandana Ahuja has over 24 years of experience across the corporate sector and academia. She is presently working as Director and Professor of Marketing at Symbiosis Institute of Business Management, Noida. She is the author of the book on Digital Marketing - published by Oxford University Press and is the proud recipient of the ILDC-AMP women achiever's award for excellence in Management Teaching. She has published several manuscripts in International and National journals and also serves on the Editorial Board of several International Journals. She has organised and chaired several National and International conferences and has guided PhD. students in the domain of Management. Prior to working at Symbiosis, she has worked with Jaipuria Institute of Management as Dean-Academics, Amity Business School as Professor, IILM Graduate School of Management as Dean-Research and faculty at Jaypee Business School. Her strengths include Teaching, Research and Academic Administration.

Akriti pursues a Behavioral and Decision Sciences program at the School of Arts and Sciences, The University of Pennsylvania, Philadelphia, Pennsylvania, USA.

Maria Elena Aramendia-Muneta, PhD, is Associate professor in the Business Administration Department of Universidad Pública de Navarra, Spain. Her primary research fields are digital marketing, tourism and history of marketing. She has published in journals such as Telematics and Informatics, Journal of Promotion Management, Journal of Historical Research in Marketing and Journal of Gender Studies

Pankaj Dadheech received his Ph.D. degree in Computer Science & Engineering from Suresh Gyan Vihar University (Accredited by NAAC with 'A' Grade), Jaipur, Rajasthan, India. He received his M.Tech. degree in Computer Science & Engineering from Rajasthan Technical University, Kota and he has received his B.E. in Computer Science & Engineering from University of Rajasthan, Jaipur. He has more than 18 years of experience in teaching. He is currently working as an Associate Professor & Dy. HOD in the Department of Computer Science & Engineering (NBA Accredited), Swami Keshvanand Institute of Technology, Management & Gramothan (SKIT), Jaipur, Rajasthan, India. He has published 25 Patents at Intellectual Property India, Office of the Controller General of Patents, Design and Trade Marks, Department of Industrial Policy and Promotion, Ministry of Commerce and Industry, Government of India. He has published 8 International Patents (USA, South African, Australian, Germany) & 2 Copyrights. He has 72 publications in various International & National Journals, 62 papers in various National & International conferences. He has published 9 Books & 22 Book Chapters.

Catarina Delgado, Ph.D., is an assistant professor at the Faculty of Economics, University of Porto (FEP.UP), and a researcher at CEF.UP and LIAAD/ INESC TEC. Her research interests are primarily in the areas of responsible consumers, responsible e-commerce, sustainable and responsible supply chains, ecotourism, ESG/ CSR disclosure, quality management/ kaizen/ lean six sigma, and scientometrics. Her teaching focus is on Operations and Logistics (operations management, supply chain management, operational research), Quality Management and Continuous Improvement (Kaizen, Lean, Six Sigma), and Social Responsibility and Sustainability Reporting. Author of the book "Supply Chain Social Sustainability for Manufacturing" (Springer, 2020), her academic work has been published in several leading international scientific journals, such as Journal of Cleaner Production, International Journal of Production Economics, Sustainability, Journal of Manufacturing Technology Management, JASIST, Informetrics, Scientometrics, and Social Responsibility Journal.

Santosh Durugkar has pursued PhD in Software engineering from Amity University Rajasthan Jaipur. He has completed U.G. (B.E.) and P.G. (M.E.) from SPPU, Pune. His area of interests are software engineering, database management, data analysis, information retrieval.

Naiara Martinicorena Goñi received her MS in International Business Management, Business Administration and Economics from the Public University of Navarre in 2020. In 2017, she completed a one-year stay in the University of Göttingen. She is registered in the Comisión Nacional del Mercado de Valores and Banco de España and is certified by the EFPA (European Financial Planning Association). In 2021, she began a collaboration with Banco Mediolanum as a financial advisor. As a financial advisor, she works straight with clients and companies and prepares their financial plans. She gives talks about financial planning and how to prepare for retirement. In 2015 she received the Golden Crest Award for her work on Sustainable Mobility in Tübingen, Germany.

Junaid Mohammed pursues an analytics program at Duke University, USA. He has a sound understanding of and a profound interest in linking marketing to operational agility.

José Morais da Silva holds a degree in Marketing, Advertising and Public Relations from ISLA - Instituto Superior de Linguas e Administração de Lisboa (currently Universidade Europeia - Lisboa), a Master's in Psychology of Emotions from ISCTE - Instituto Universitário de Lisboa, with specialization in Subliminal Communication and holds a PhD in Communication Sciences from Universidade Católica Portuguesa de Lisboa, with specialization in Non-verbal Communication. He investigates in the line "Media, Technology and Contexts". His main areas of interest are the Sciences of Communication, Marketing and Advertising and the Science of Consumer Behaviour. He has developed specialization in the areas of Digital Marketing, where he teaches in the Bachelor's, Master's and Executive Education programs. He masters SEO, SEM and SEA techniques and masters online Business Models. Complementarily to teaching, he works as a consultant in the area of Business Development, Digital Transformation and Strategic Communication

Erin Page graduated from University of Leeds in Fashion Marketing. She is currently working within the jewellery industry and her research interests lie within the field of sustainability within the fashion industry.

Agapi Paraskevi Papadopoulou is an undergraduate student at the Department of Creative Design and Clothing - School of Design Sciences of the International Hellenic University.

Cara Peters is a Professor of Marketing at Winthrop University. She teaches global and services marketing and has published number articles in fashion marketing and management.

Paulo Botelho Pires received his PhD in Management and has a master's degree in marketing.

Bikramjit Rishi is a Professor in Marketing at the School of Management & Entrepreneurship (SME) at Shiv Nadar Institution of Eminence (SNIoE) (Deemed to be University) – Delhi (NCR). He has spent nearly two decades making significant contributions to the success and growth of the marketing discipline. His research has been published in several A & B league journals such as the Journal of Global Information Management, Marketing Intelligence and Planning, Journal of Brand Management, Australasian Marketing Journal, Journal of Financial Services Marketing, Social Responsibility Journal, and VINE Journal of Information and Knowledge Management System. His cases are published and listed in Harvard Business School Publishing (HBSP), Ivey Publishing, Emerald Emerging Markets Case Studies (EEMCS), Asian Case Research Journal, and Emerging Economies Case Journal. He has also published several edited books on social media marketing, marketing research, and consumer behaviour and a textbook in the domain of social media marketing. He has been a faculty fellow at the doctoral consortiums supported by the American Marketing Association (AMA) and the Academy of Indian Marketing (AIM). He has designed and delivered many training programs on marketing for Hindustan Coca-Cola Beverages Limited (HCCBPL), Maruti Suzuki India Limited (MSIL), Apollo Tyres Limited, APL Apollo Tubes Limited, Jubilant Foods, and RITES Limited.

Albérico Travassos Rosário is a Ph.D. Marketing and Strategy of the Universities of Aveiro (UA), Minho (UM) and Beira Interior (UBI). With affiliation to the GOVCOPP research center of the University of Aveiro. Master in Marketing and Degree in Marketing, Advertising and Public Relations, degree from ISLA Campus Lisbon-European University | Laureate International Universities. Has the title of Marketing Specialist and teaches with the category of Assistant Professor at IADE-Faculty of Design, Technology and Communication of the European University and as a visiting Associate Professor at the Santarém Higher School of Management and Technology (ESGTS) of the Polytechnic Institute of Santarém. He taught at IPAM-School of Marketing | Laureate International Universities, ISLA- Higher Institute of Management and Administration of Santarém (ISLA-Santarém), was Director of the Commercial Management Course, Director of the Professional Technical Course (TeSP) of Sales and Commercial Management, Chairman of the Pedagogical Council and Member of the Technical Council and ISLA-Santarém Scientific Researcher. He is also a marketing and strategy consultant for SMEs.

José Duarte da Rocha Santos received his PhD in Management from Vigo University. He also holds MSc in Marketing and a bachelor's degree in Business Sciences. Between 1987 and 2002, he played various roles in sales, marketing, and management of companies in the information technology sector. From 2003 to 2018, he performed the functions of a management and marketing consultant. Since 1999, he has been a professor in higher education in Portugal in the fields of management and marketing. He is currently a marketing professor at the Accounting and Business School of the Polytechnic of Porto (ISCAP/P.PORTO). He is also a senior researcher at the CEOS.PP - Centre for Organizational and Social Studies of the Polytechnic of Porto, Portugal. His main research areas are Strategic Marketing and Digital Marketing Strategies.

Nikolaos Sklavounos is an Adjunct Lecturer at the International Hellenic University, at Perrotis College of the American Farm School and at Mediterranean College in Thessaloniki, Greece. He holds a PhD in International Business from the University of Macedonia, Thessaloniki, Greece. His research appears in the European Journal of International Management, Transnational Corporations Review, Journal of Strategy and Management, International Journal of Productivity and Performance Management, Eastern Journal of European Studies, Journal of Business Paradigms, Elsevier Procedia Economics and Finance, Springer Procedia in Business and Economics, East-West Journal of Economics and Business, Scientific Bulletin – Economic Sciences and in the proceedings of several international conferences. His academic interests include international business, international strategic alliances, strategic management, global marketing, exports, new technologies and human capital.

Pooja Sehgal Tabeck is an academician with 18 years of experience in teaching. She was a gold medallist during her MBA at CSJM University, Kanpur. She is NET qualified in management. She has published many papers in indexed International and National journals. Her area of interest is Bottom of pyramid markets, consumer behaviour, and retail.

Açelya Telli Danışmaz She received her bachelor's degree from international trade and her double major degree from banking departments in 2012, then she started master's degree in the field of banking and finance in Baskent University. After taking master's degree in 2013, she worked as a lecturer at Halic University, Istanbul Kultur University and Istanbul Arel University. In 2021, she graduated Phd programme in the field of business administration at Yildiz Technical University. Her main topics of study are organizational citizenship behavior, compulsory citizenship behavior and other related organizational behavior issues.

Jane Thomas is a Professor of Marketing at Winthrop University. She teaches consumer behavior and marketing strategy and has published numerous articles on fashion marketing and management.

Index

E

F

G

H

I

K

L

M

N

O

P

R

S

T

U

V

W

Z

www.ingramcontent.com/pod-product-compliance
Lightning Source LLC
LaVergne TN
LVHW060404300926
849162LV00006B/1342
* 9 7 8 1 6 6 8 4 8 7 5 3 2 *